THE GARDENER'S PRACTICAL GUIDE TO
ANNUALS, BULBS & PERENNIALS

THE GARDENER'S PRACTICAL GUIDE TO
ANNUALS, BULBS & PERENNIALS

AN ILLUSTRATED ENCYCLOPEDIA OF FLOWERING PLANTS
CONTAINING MORE THAN 1800 BEAUTIFUL PHOTOGRAPHS

RICHARD BIRD AND KATHY BROWN

LORENZ BOOKS

This edition is published by Lorenz Books

Lorenz Books is an imprint of
Anness Publishing Ltd, Hermes House,
88–89 Blackfriars Road, London SE1 8HA
tel. 020 7401 2077; fax 020 7633 9499
www.lorenzbooks.com; info@anness.com

UK agent: The Manning Partnership Ltd,
6 The Old Dairy, Melcombe Road, Bath
BA2 3LR; tel. 01225 478444;
fax 01225 478440;
sales@manning-partnership.co.uk

UK distributor: Grantham Book Services Ltd,
Isaac Newton Way, Alma Park Industrial Estate,
Grantham, Lincs NG31 9SD;
tel. 01476 541080; fax 01476 541061;
orders@gbs.tbs-ltd.co.uk

North American agent/distributor: National Book
Network, 4501 Forbes Boulevard, Suite 200,
Lanham, MD 20706; tel. 301 459 3366;
fax 301 429 5746; www.nbnbooks.com

Australian agent/distributor: Pan Macmillan
Australia, Level 18, St Martins Tower,
31 Market St, Sydney, NSW 2000;
tel. 1300 135 113; fax 1300 135 103;
customer.service@macmillan.com.au

New Zealand agent/distributor: David Bateman
Ltd, 30 Tarndale Grove, Off Bush Road, Albany,
Auckland; tel. (09) 415 7664; fax (09) 415 8892

Publisher: Joanna Lorenz
Editorial Directors: Judith Simons & Helen Sudell
Executive Editors: Caroline Davison & Ann Kay
Project Editors: Molly Perham & Sarah Uttridge
Compendium Editor: Lucy Doncaster
Designers: Michael Morey & Nigel Partridge
Production Controller: Lee Sargent
Editorial Readers: Rosie Fairhead &
   Jay Thundercliffe

Previously published in two separate volumes,
The Gardener's Guide to Bulbs and *The Gardener's
Guide to Annuals and Perennials*

10 9 8 7 6 5 4 3 2 1

Note: Bracketed terms are for American readers

Contents

INTRODUCTION

In spite of a modern tendency for television personalities to create gardens with few or no plants, there is no doubt in most people's minds that without plants a garden is simply not a garden. There is something about the presence of plants – their colour, shape and fragrance – that lifts the spirits in a very special way. Annuals, perennials and bulbs are the most popular types of flowering plants, offering a vast selection of ways to add that vital colour and stimulus to every kind of garden.

Enjoying plants

Plants give pleasure to people in many different ways. The majority of gardeners enjoy filling space with colour, shape and texture as well as planning a garden to make the most of their chosen plants' strong points. There are others for whom it is the plant itself that is of principal interest. They are less interested in how the plant fits into the overall picture of the garden, or indeed how the garden

Anyone can produce this magnificent array of dahlias, verbenas and salvias. It remains colourful for a long period – from midsummer well into autumn.

looks as a whole, and are more absorbed by growing a particular type of plant to absolute perfection. These gardeners may only grow plants in order to show them, or simply because they enjoy the challenge of growing rare and difficult types.

There are others still who garden simply because they enjoy working in the open air and get a real joy from cultivation. For them it is the process as well as the results that matter. The huge variety of annuals, perennials and bulbs that is available, and the many ways in which they can be grown, can easily cater to all these different approaches.

Starting out

Tackling a large bare patch may seem a rather daunting task to somebody who has not done any gardening before, but it is nothing like as difficult as some experts would have you believe.

Gardening is rather like decorating a room: naturally a certain amount of time and effort is involved, but if you are not satisfied with the result you can always change it. This is particularly true

Oenothera biennis and *Tanacetum parthenium* produce a fine yellow and white scheme.

This border mixes annuals, bulbs, hardy perennials and tender perennials.

This selection of perennials, growing beside water, shows the vast range of shapes and textures that can be used as well as the value of foliage.

right next year, or even the year after. Having said that, there are, of course, basic sensible and effective practices that have developed over many generations, and all of these are clearly described in this book.

Choosing your plants

Plants form the basis of all good gardens and we have produced detailed directories which will introduce you to the very best annuals, perennials and bulbs.

There are far more available than we could hope to include in this book, but the directories have been specially devised to act as a comprehensive basis. As you develop your garden you will become more interested in certain plants than others. You will then be able to create your own database of information from nursery catalogues, magazines, books and the internet. Soon you may even find that you have turned into one of those gardeners for whom studying plants is as fascinating as actually growing them.

with annual plants as they give you the opportunity to start from scratch each year.

Working with colour

Many beginners are worried about combining colours, but the key is simply to go for plants and effects that you like without worrying about what other people do.

Remember that we all have some ability where colour is concerned: we choose what goes with what when we get dressed each day and we choose colours for decorating and furnishing our homes. Planning a garden is really no different. In the same way that there are fashion magazines to help you choose your style, so there is no shortage of different kinds of gardening magazine to browse through for inspiration, and there is nothing more enjoyable than wandering around other people's gardens in search of good ideas.

Learning the ropes

There is also no need to worry about gardening techniques. Most gardening is common sense and if you do make a mistake, just remember that you can always put it

An informal container – featuring annual sweet peas, tender verbenas and perennial violas – demonstrates just how effectively annuals and perennials can be mixed.

How plants are named

All living things are classified according to a system based on principles that were devised by the 18th-century Swedish botanist, Carl Linnaeus. This system states that a particular plant genus (plural: genera) is a group of plants containing similar species. Beyond that there may be plants that are simply a slight variation of a species, or are a hybrid (cross) of different species or variations.

Scientific names

Under this system, plants have botanical names – often Latin but also derived from other languages – that consist of the genus name (for example, *Verbena*), followed by the name that denotes the particular species (for example, *hastata*). Some genera contain a huge number of species that may include annuals, perennials, shrubs and trees, while others contain just one species. Although all members of a genus are assumed to be related to each other, this is not always visually obvious. It is useful to keep in mind that a species is defined scientifically as individuals that are alike and tend naturally to breed with each other.

Despite this system, botanists and taxonomists (the experts who classify living things) often disagree about the basis on which a plant has been named. This is why it is useful for a plant to retain its synonym (abbreviated to syn. in the text), or alternative name. Incorrect names often gain widespread usage, and in some cases, two plants thought to have separate identities, and with two different names, are found to be the same plant.

A well-known example of naming confusion is the genus *Pelargonium*. Until the 19th century, pelargonium plants were included in the genus *Geranium*, and despite being classified separately for over a century, they are still popularly known as geraniums.

Variations on a theme

Genetically, many plants are able to change over time to adapt to a changing environment. In the wild, individuals within a species that are not well adapted will not survive, so all survivors will look the same. The average garden is a more controlled environment, so gardeners can choose to encourage and grow on variations within a species that have small but

This is *Centaurea hypoleuca* 'John Coutts'. John Coutts is the name that has been given to a dark pink form of the pink knapweed species, *Centaurea hypoleuca*.

pleasing differences such as variegated leaves and double flowers. The terms for these variations are subspecies (abbreviated to subsp.), variety (var.), form (f., similar to variety and often used interchangeably) and cultivar (cv.). A cultivar is a variation that would not occur in the wild but has been produced and maintained solely by cultivation. Variations are given names in single quotes, for example *Papaver orientale* 'Allegro'.

Hybrids

When plant species breed with each other, the result is a hybrid. Rare in the wild, crossing is very common among plant-breeders, and is done specially in order to produce plants with desirable qualities such as larger or double blooms, variegated foliage and greater frost resistance. A multiplication sign (x) is used to indicate a hybrid, and the name often gives a clear idea of the hybrid's origins.

Plant Groups

A Group of plants is a group of very similar variations. Their names do not have quotation marks around them – for example *Tradescantia* Andersoniana Group.

The geranium is a well-known case of naming confusion, as many plants that actually belong to the genus *Pelargonium* are very commonly referred to as geraniums.

How to use the directories

There are three directory sections: one features annual plants, one perennials and the other bulbs. Within each directory, plants are arranged alphabetically, by genus. Each main entry features a general introduction to that genus, plus specific information such as tips on propagation and which hardiness zone the genus belongs to. This is followed by a selection of plants from that genus, also arranged alphabetically according to their most widely accepted names. One of these entries might be a species, a hybrid (or group of hybrids), a variety, form or cultivar. Each is given a description that may include height and spread.

Caption
The full botanical name of the plant in question is given with each photograph.

Genus name
This is the internationally accepted botanical name for a group of related plant species.

Common name
This popular, non-scientific name applies to the whole of the plant genus.

Cultivation
This section gives the level of sun or shade that the plants described in the selection either require or tolerate, advice on the best type of soil in which they should be grown, and any other helpful tips that might be appropriate.

Propagation
This section gives essential information on how and when to increase the plant – from seed, by dividing plants or by taking various types of cutting. Many annuals entries also give the best temperature at which to propagate a plant, often with specific centigrade (and Fahrenheit) figures given.

Individual plant entry
This starts with the current botanical name of the plant in bold, and this can refer to a species, subspecies, hybrid, variant or cultivar. If a synonym (syn.) is given, this provides the synonym, or synonyms (alternative names) for a plant. A common name may be given after the botanical name.

Plant description
This gives a description of the plant, along with any other information that may be helpful and relevant.

Paeonia lactiflora 'Bowl of Beauty'

PAEONIA
Peony

One of the most popular of all perennial species, these beautiful plants suit almost any type of garden, from old-fashioned cottage gardens to modern formal ones. There are only about 30 species of peony, most of which are in cultivation, but hundreds of cultivars have been bred from them. The typical peony has a bowl-shaped flower in varying shades of red, pink or white. There are also some rather fine yellows. The foliage of peonies is also very attractive.
Cultivation Peonies need a deep rich soil, so add plenty of well-rotted organic material. They will grow in either sun or a light shade. They often take a while to settle down after being disturbed so try not to move them once established. Z3–5.
Propagation They can be divided in spring but this is not easy and they will take a while to settle down. Root cuttings taken in early winter is the easiest method.

Paeonia lactiflora 'Bowl of Beauty'
Deep rose-red petals and a large central boss of yellow make this a superb peony. H 75cm (30in) S 1m (3ft).

Photograph
Each entry features a full-colour photograph that makes identification easy.

Genus introduction
This provides a general introduction to the genus and may state the number of species within that genus. Other information featured here may include general advice on usage, preferred conditions, and plant-care, as well as subspecies, hybrids (indicated by an x symbol in the name), varieties and cultivars (featuring names in single quotes) that are available.

Additional information

This page shows a basic entry from the perennials directory. Other information supplied in the directories includes:

How to obtain (Annuals directory): this gives advice on getting hold of plants as seeds, plants or trays of plants.
Uses (Annuals directory): if given, this section advises on how to get the best from a plant – using in borders or containers or to brighten up dark corners, for example.
Other plants (Annuals and Perennials directories): if given, these sections provide information about common types that are available and other recommended plants to look out for.

Plant hardiness zone
A plant hardiness zone is given at the end of this section. Zones give a general indication of the average annual minimum temperature for a particular geographical area. The smaller number indicates the northernmost zone it can survive in and the higher number the southernmost zone that the plant will tolerate. In most cases, only one zone is given. (See page 512 for details of zones and a zone map.)

Size information
The average expected height and spread of a genus or individual plant is frequently given, although growth rates may vary depending on location and conditions. Metric measurements always precede imperial ones. Average heights and spreads are given (as H and S) wherever possible and appropriate, and more consistently for perennials and bulbs, although it must be noted that dimensions can vary a great deal.

ANNUALS &
PERENNIALS

Styling with annuals and perennials

Theoretically, there is no need to differentiate between annuals and perennials as they are both flowering or foliage plants. However, gardeners do tend to use them in slightly different ways. This is partly because of the annual's brief life and partly because annuals tend to be more brightly coloured than perennials, lending themselves to vivid displays. Perennials are more permanent and, although some do have bright colours, they are usually more muted.

In this section we look at the differing roles that the two types of plants can play. We also look at the different ways in which they can be combined to create a range of gardening styles, varying from the informality of the traditional cottage garden to the more clinical lines of a formal garden, where symmetry is all.

Generally, the style of a garden reflects its owner's lifestyle and personality. Gardens should always have a positive and uplifting atmosphere, so there is no point in creating a place where you feel uncomfortable. Use the following advice as guidance, but never be afraid to follow your own instinct.

A lovely cottage garden effect is created along this informal path using both annuals and perennials. The lush foliage helps to provide bulk.

Annuals and their role

Annuals are ephemeral plants: they flower for one season only and then they are gone. This may seem to be a disadvantage in a garden context, but in fact it can be a great benefit, especially for those gardeners who like to have something different in their flowerbeds each year.

What is an annual?

There are basically four different types of plant that are considered annuals from the garden point of view. The most common are the true annuals, which grow from seed, flower and produce their own seed within a year. There are many examples of these, but poppies and nasturtiums are popular ones. Closely allied to these are the biennials. These grow from seed one year and then flower during the next. Foxgloves and evening primroses are familiar examples.

Then there are those perennials that are tender, and so are treated as annuals and started afresh each year. Pelargoniums and busy Lizzies are good examples. Finally, there is another group of perennials that are used as annuals. These are simply

Limnanthes douglasii, the poached egg plant, creates a perfect border to this wildflower garden, which is dominated by annuals.

short-lived perennials that are better grown from scratch each year. Frequently planted examples of these are wallflowers and sweet Williams.

Great diversity

One of the great advantages of using annuals is that the design of a garden need not be fixed: you can change the colour, texture and shape of the plantings each year if you wish. At the end of the flowering season you simply rip out the plants, then decide which annuals you want to plant for the next season. They come in all shapes, sizes and colours, so the gardener has a virtually limitless palette from which to create planting schemes. This versatility means that annuals can be used as massed bedding or mixed with other

plants, such as perennials, or they can be used in containers such as hanging baskets, large pots or window boxes. They also provide a wide range of flowers that can be cut for the house.

Annuals can be ideal for the smallest of spaces. Here, bright red pelargoniums are used very effectively in simple pots on a wall.

Hardiness

Since most annuals grow and flower within the year, hardiness may not seem to be an important factor to take into consideration, but it can be if you plan to grow your own annuals from seed. Hardy annuals can be sown outside and will withstand late frosts, but half-hardy or tender annuals must be raised under glass and not planted out until after the risk of frost has passed. Alternatively, half-hardy or tender annuals can be sown directly where they are to flower, but again only after the threat of frost is over.

Long-flowering annuals

Ageratum
Antirrhinum majus
Argyranthemum
Begonia x *semperflorens*
Brachycome iberidifolia
Calendula officinalis
Impatiens
Lobelia erinus
Nicotiana
Pelargonium
Petunia
Salvia
Tagetes
Tropaeolum majus
Verbena x *hybrida*
Viola x *wittrockiana*
Zinnia elegans

Using annual plants is not all about making the most of showcasing the flowers. In this container, for example, silver foliage has been used to great effect.

Mixing it

Annuals can be used to great advantage mixed with perennials and shrubs. One big advantage that annuals have over perennials is that they tend to flower over long periods, often throughout the whole summer. So, in a mixed border, annuals can provide a permanent thread of colour.

Their temporary nature can also be put to good use. Often it will take several years before shrubs or perennials reach their final spread, and during this time there will be areas of bare earth around these plants. Annuals can readily be used here as attractive temporary fillers until the other plants eventually use up all of the space.

Annuals can also add a touch of lightness and almost frivolity to an otherwise staid border. For example, a border predominantly full of shrubs, perhaps planted for their interesting leaves, can be enlivened by massed plantings of bold summer annuals in front of and in between the shrubs. Each type of plant will complement the other.

Hanging displays

Annuals make wonderful container plants, whether in tubs, window boxes or hanging baskets. They usually last the whole season, providing constant attractive colour, though regular watering is a must for continuous flowering. Once the season is over, you can completely change your scheme for the following year simply by changing the plants. You might perhaps try hot oranges and reds one year, followed by softer, cooler blues and whites the next.

Pathways can provide a wonderful opportunity to display annuals to their full advantage. Change the colour and pattern each year to create a slightly different mood as you approach your front door.

Planning a bedding scheme and then watching it come to life can be a great deal of fun. Although not as popular currently as they once were, these schemes provide a stimulating challenge for the inventive mind.

Perennials and their role

When a dream garden springs into our minds, the linchpins of the borders will usually be the perennials, with their great wealth of colours, textures and forms. They provide an enormous selection of plants that will fit in with any style of gardening and will satisfy both the keen and lazy gardener.

What is a perennial?

Perennials are just what they say – perennial – though the description must be modified slightly, as it could apply to any plant that lasts more than a year. In fact, it generally applies to herbaceous material that is grown in general borders. In other words, it excludes trees, shrubs and plants that are grown in rock gardens or in greenhouses, even though these all might be long-lived. Most perennials die back in winter and then regenerate the following year, though some remain green right through the winter. From the gardening point of view, perennials are generally considered hardy – that is, they are able to withstand at least a certain amount of frost.

Changing scene

Most perennials have a relatively short flowering season. This may be seen as a disadvantage, but in fact it can be a great asset because it means that the garden is never static, it never becomes boring. It allows the borders to be planned in such a way that they present an ever-changing scene. It is possible, for example, to have a spring border of blue and yellow that transforms itself over the months into a pink and mauve border in the summer and then perhaps to hot colours for the autumn. Such coordination needs careful planning, of course, but that is half the fun of gardening.

Use vivid, exciting colours to create a "hot" border. Just like beds of annual plants, herbaceous borders of perennials can be colour themed in all kinds of creative ways.

Foliage effect

Perennials are not only about flower colour. Many have interesting foliage in a wide range of colours, from greens, silvers and purples to yellows and creams. All these help to create a backdrop against which the flowers can be seen to advantage. Longer lasting than flowers, foliage forms the main structure of the borders throughout the growing season.

Herbaceous borders

Perennials can be used in many ways. One of the most effective is creating a herbaceous border entirely from perennials. These are usually planted in drifts, creating a sumptuous tapestry of colours through summer and autumn. Traditionally, herbaceous borders were found in large gardens, but smaller versions can easily be created to great effect.

This mixed border of perennials, annuals and shrubs shows the effects that can be achieved by combining a variety of different shapes, colours and textures.

Mixed borders

Many gardeners prefer to use a mixture of plants, perhaps using shrubs as the backbone and main structure of the garden and mixing in other plants to give differing colours throughout the year. Perennials are perfect for this role, particularly as there are a large number that like to grow in the light shade that is provided by being planted under or close to shrubs. Although shrubs form the structure, the perennials usually provide the majority of the plants. In some cases these may be a single large clump, but drifts of the bigger plants and carpets of the lower growing ones look better than scattering the plants around at random.

Potted perennials

It is often thought that the only place for perennials is in a large garden, but perennials are suited to all sizes of garden. They can be grown in a patio garden or even on a balcony or roof garden. As long as you are prepared to water them, they may be grown in containers, which can then be placed anywhere, including in gardens that are paved over and have no native soil at all.

Many perennials, such as this lily, are ideal for tubs. Just move into position when in flower.

Plant-lovers

There are more varieties of perennial plants than any other type of plant available to the gardener. Some gardeners make a virtue of this and indulge their love of plants by creating special collections. Others collect a particular species, pinks (*Dianthus*) or hostas, for example, or favour broader groups – variegated plants are a very popular subject. There are also gardeners who seek out rare and difficult-to-grow plants, just to test their skills, and others who might make a collection of plants mentioned in, for example, the works of Shakespeare. The possibilities are almost endless.

Perennials are not dependent on their flowers for their attraction. Many earn their keep as foliage plants, with the shapes and colour providing plenty of interest, as seen here.

Hardy perennials

Hardy perennials, as their name implies, are those that will tolerate frost and will reappear every year. Some tender perennials may be killed by frosts, although sometimes the frost will just kill off the exposed foliage, and the plant will regenerate from the roots. Although it is mainly temperature related, hardiness can be affected by soil conditions, and often a borderline plant will be more hardy in a free-draining soil than in a heavy damp one.

Different styles of flower garden

There are various styles of garden to choose from, although there are no definitive rules and there is no reason why gardeners should not choose a mixture of designs. Having said that, there are a number of styles that have a proven track record, and it is perhaps worthwhile considering the pursuit of just one of them until you are confident enough to mix different styles.

Lifestyle considerations

The basic advice is simple: choose a style of garden that you like. There are, however, various other factors that may be worth taking into consideration. Your lifestyle is one of the most important of these. However much you may like formal gardens, there is no point in designing a neat garden that needs to be kept in pristine condition in order to look its best if you are not naturally a tidy person or never have the time to keep it neat.

Likewise, a precise garden will be an uphill struggle if you have young children playing football or riding bicycles around and over the borders.

In this cottage garden, the planting has seemingly been done at random and a wonderful mix of different types of plants creates a lively, natural atmosphere.

The family dog is also likely to have a say in this matter. A more informal style, which would be in keeping with your life, would be a more sensible and realistic choice. At a later stage in your life, a family garden may no longer be required, at which point, with possibly considerably more time on your hands, you could perhaps reconsider and think of other options.

Looking at the options

If you are new to gardening, you may have a vague idea of what you want but no firm idea about the reality. In this case, it will pay to spend a summer wandering around other gardens. Try to look at the best. The big gardens that are open to the public will have teams of gardeners at their beck and call, but there are still lessons and ideas to be learnt from them. A bit more realistic are the private gardens that open just once or twice a year. Most of these are designed and tended by their owners with little or no help. Look, make notes and, if you get the chance, talk to the owner and find out the problems and benefits of such a garden.

Another simple idea is to peer over fences (without being a nuisance) as you walk the dog and make critical appraisals of neighbouring gardens. What is right and what is wrong with them? What would you do to improve them? You can also watch television for inspiration, and look through gardening magazines and books.

A family garden needs to take into account the interests and activities of all family members (including pets) and the gardener may have to make certain compromises.

This predominantly herbaceous border also features a few roses. A keen gardener who loves to design with colour has been at work here.

Making notes

Some gardeners are able to keep detailed notes of what they see and ideas that they may adopt. Others are hopeless at this, and while they start out with good intentions, they soon run out of steam. One way around this is to take photographs as reminders. Another effective and low-effort method is to tear out pages from magazines that inspire you or leave markers tucked into books. Books and magazines can provide a really broad wealth of information, especially during the winter months when there is relatively little to look at in the gardens themselves.

Look for simple but effective ideas such as this creative use of an old window frame.

Keep it simple

One of the biggest problems that new gardeners have is that they get carried away with their plans. They have grand ideas and can visualize just how their dream garden will look when finished, but they fail to consider the reality of the situation and to ask themselves some key questions. Is the garden big enough for all these ideas? Have they got enough money to pay for all the plants or hard landscaping that is required? And, above all, will they have the time not only to do the original work but also to maintain the garden once the initial enthusiasm has worn off?

Cottage gardens

Many people dream of a cottage in the country, with roses growing around the door and a feast of colour in the garden in front. Well, the good news is that you don't need to move to the country or even have a cottage to create such an attractive garden.

What is a cottage garden?

It is very difficult to define a cottage garden. We all know one when we see one, but describing them is not the easiest thing to do. Generally, they have an old-fashioned look. The real skill in creating a successful cottage garden is to design the borders to look as if they have not been designed at all. There is not much in the way of hard landscaping, just flowerbeds, and these are full to the brim with colourful plants.

Traditionally, the plants would be tough, hardy ones that needed little care. Most would be plants that had been grown for generations, such as primulas, hollyhocks, foxgloves and aquilegias. Today many new hybrids are considered suitable, especially if they are bright and brash.

Even containers can be given a cottage garden feel, simply by keeping them informal.

Cottage plants

Plants for a cottage garden tend, as has already been noted, to be old-fashioned plants that have been around for years. Many are annuals and biennials that self-sow, so the gardener does not have to think about new plants: they just appear.

One reason for using these old favourites, apart from their appearance, is that they are usually less prone to pests and diseases and hardier than many modern cultivars (which is why they have been around for a long time). In other words, they need little looking after. Unfortunately, some of these traditional plants, such as lupins and

Plants for a cottage garden

Alcea rosea
Anemone x hybrida
Aquilegia vulgaris
Aster novae-angliae
Aster novi-belgii
Astrantia major
Bellis perennis
Campanula portenschlagiana
Campanula persicifolia
Chrysanthemum
Dianthus (pinks)
Dicentra spectabilis
Doronicum
Geranium ibericum
Geum rivale
Lathyrus odoratus
Lilium candidum
Lupinus
Lysimachia nummularia
Meconopsis cambrica
Myrrhis odorata
Paeonia officinalis
Polemonium caeruleum
Primula
Pulmonaria
Saponaria officinalis
Sedum spectabile
Sempervivum
Stachys byzantina
Viola

Old-fashioned plants such as these polyanthus, forget-me-nots and aquilegias are perfect for spring in the cottage garden.

Some old-fashioned annuals, such as this *Collomia grandiflora* (the white flowers), have almost disappeared but are well worth searching out.

hollyhocks, have now developed diseases and pests, which makes them less reliable than they once were, though they can still be grown to great effect as short-lived plants.

The layout

If there is any characteristic to a cottage garden it is the hazy effect that all the intermingled colours create. The traditional image is one of a garden in which the plants seem to have been planted at random without any thought of planning. Gaps would be filled as they became available, and self-sowing plants would dot themselves around at will. Whether cottage gardens of the past really were this accidental or were just designed to look so, we may never actually know, but these days there is a tendency to exert at least a little control over the design in order to create the most pleasing picture that you can.

Getting it right

The backdrop to a cottage-garden style is important. For example, it will look better against an older

A path leading up to a cottage's front door is definitely at its most welcoming when it is lined with an abundance of interesting colours.

house than a modern one. This certainly doesn't mean that you have to live in a cottage in order to have a cottage garden. It just means that you must modify the situation somehow: for example, perhaps soften a modern house with roses, or create a cottage garden in the rear garden away from the house, dividing it off by using shrubs or trellising covered with climbers.

Although often claimed to be low-maintenance, cottage gardens do need a great deal of work. In summer, plenty of deadheading and tidying is required to prevent the garden looking a mess. Tight planting helps to reduce the amount of weeding and staking that is needed, but this can make access difficult when deadheading plants towards the back of the border.

A selection of vegetables

Most cottage gardens had a vegetable garden that had to supply produce for the family all year round. This often ran straight into the flower garden, with flowers and vegetables mixing where they met. Many vegetables have ornamental qualities and can happily be grown among flowers. A wigwam of runner beans, for example, is wonderful visually. Many vegetable gardens were also arranged in a decorative manner known as the potager. One big disadvantage of growing vegetables among the flowers or in a decorative manner is that gaps are left when you pick the produce.

This wonderful haze of colour typifies a cottage garden. It may look totally random and unplanned but a certain degree of clever control has been exercised.

Formal gardens

Gardens usually reflect their owners in one way or another. An untidy, relaxed person will often have an untidy and relaxed garden, whereas an elegant person who likes everything to be in its place may well opt for a formal garden. Such a garden is usually a positive feature of the home rather than just an outdoor space.

What is a formal garden?

Generally, a formal garden is one that has some formal qualities about it. This usually means that the shapes within the garden are geometric. Thus lines tend to be straight or in precise curves, such as a circle, rather than sinuous and informal. Beds are frequently square, rectangular or circular. Sometimes they might even be triangular, but

this is an awkward shape in the garden because the corners are difficult to plant as well as being tricky to mow around.

Another aspect of formality is that there is often regular repetition, in other words certain plants or even whole beds may be repeated at regular intervals. This creates symmetry, which is an important part of such gardens. Calmness and tranquillity are the qualities that usually sum up the formal garden.

Sparseness

Formal gardens can contain as much planting as you like, but many rely on relatively few plants set in key positions. Often a round pond set in a gravelled area with just a couple of clumps of marginal plants – irises, perhaps, and a few water lilies – can

look quite stunning in its simplicity. Long vistas down paths also create a feeling of calmness.

Formal plants

Any plants may be used in formal gardens, but there are many that are preferred because they have a formality about them either in their natural overall shape or the quality of the leaves. Others, mainly shrubs but also some ground-cover plants, lend themselves to being trimmed into formal shapes. Clumps of hostas and irises are valuable because of their regular leaf shapes, while grasses such as miscanthus or plants such as yucca or cordyline all have their fountains of leaves. Many ferns also produce this graceful fountain shape. Other plants that work very well in formal gardens are the

Straight lines and geometric patterns make this garden look very formal. Even the container has a symmetrical appearance.

Bedding laid out in lines with a regular repeat of certain plants or colours is one way to add formality to a bed or a whole garden.

Plants for a formal garden

Good leaves or shape	Good in-fill plants
Agapanthus	Ageratum
Asplenium	Alchemilla
Athyrium	Antirrhinum
Bergenia	Bellis perennis
Cardiocrinum	Callistephus
Cortaderia	chinensis
Crambe	Diascia
Dierama	Lobelia erinus
Digitalis	Myosotis sylvatica
Euphorbia	Nicotiana alata
Foeniculum	(N. affinis)
Hosta	Petunia
Lilium	Tagetes erecta
Matteuccia struthiopteris	Tagetes patula
Miscanthus	
Pennisetum	
Sisyrinchium	
Stipa	
Veratrum	
Verbascum	
Yucca	
Zantedeschia	

Sculpture and dramatic containers, even if they do not contain plants, help to give the garden an air of formality.

statuesque ones, such as verbascum. Annuals all of the same height, such as salvias, or in rounded clumps, such as busy Lizzies in a large container, can also contribute to a very formal look.

The role of containers

Containers can often play an extremely important part in a formal garden scheme, especially large ones filled with a single plant. A classic example is agapanthus placed at the entrance to a patio or at the bottom of some steps. Again, plants with a fountain shape, such as yucca or grasses, are ideal subjects for positions such as these. A series of pots set at regular intervals down a path is also a useful device. The pots can contain perennials, annuals or shrubs, but they should have a neat overall appearance.

Maintenance

Compared with many other types of garden, formal gardens are relatively easy to maintain, although at times it is more like housework than gardening. The general design rarely needs changing, so there is little planting unless you are using areas of bedding plants. With good mulching there should be little weeding, so it is mainly down to trimming and keeping the hard surfaces in good order.

Boxed in

Many formal gardens use box hedges to line paths or even to surround beds completely. In really extravagant gardens a series of box hedges are used to create a knot garden. The beds within these hedges may be restricted to one or two plant types, with annual bedding plants often used to paint blocks of colour within the green outlines of the box. This type of formal garden is often constructed on a grand scale, but it can be successfully emulated in smaller gardens.

Straight lines – whether they consist of low hedging or bedding plants (the latter is seen here) – and geometric shapes can create great clarity of design in a formal scheme.

Informal gardens

Most of us do not have the time to commit ourselves regularly to our garden, however much we wish we could. We also have conflicting demands on the garden: it is not just something beautiful or something to contemplate but also a place to live in and enjoy. So we end up creating an informal garden that suits our lifestyle. It is none the worse for that.

What is an informal garden?

An informal garden is everything a formal garden isn't. It is a garden designed around our tastes and lifestyle. The borders are full of plants that we like but not necessarily planted with military precision. The lines are not regular but comfortable and enjoyable, a bit like a favourite chair. There are lots of different things to see, but they are not necessarily connected in such a rigid way as in a formal garden. There is plenty of room for children to play, and no one gets too hysterical if a ball gets into the beds or the shape of a shrub is spoilt by being turned into a camp. The gardener still takes a lot of trouble over how it is planted and how it looks, but the garden carries with it an air of comfortable informality.

This spot in the garden is a wonderful place to relax, as it is surrounded by a comfortable, unstructured mixture of different types of plants.

Informal plants

Virtually any plant is suitable for an informal garden – that is the joy of this garden type (this is why no box containing a listing of recommended plants has been given here). It is the way in which plants are used, not the plants themselves, that is key.

What you could do if you wish is to create different areas for different plants. For example, if you are particularly fond of plants that favour damp conditions, you could make one area into a bog garden. Similarly, a rock garden or a gravel bed could be introduced for plants that tend to favour drier conditions. You can also create a more mixed garden, with annuals, perennials, climbers, shrubs and even trees, combined and arranged as you please. You could also experiment with using colours and textures in various creative ways.

There is certainly no formality here, and the gardener is free to remove or add plants without upsetting the balance of the scheme.

Here, the delightful edging to the path has all the colour but none of the rigid formality of a bedding scheme.

The importance of grass

Grass and hard surfaces have an important role to play in informal gardens. In many cases, such a garden will be a family one and grass has the obvious importance as a play area. But grass and surfaces also have a visual importance. If the whole garden is filled with flowering plants, the eye becomes restless: there is too much to see. An expanse of grass gives the eye a chance to rest and acts as a foil to the liveliness of the borders.

The edge of the grass, paving or path also acts as a defining limit to the border by creating an edge, which, again, is very important visually. Such an area of grass does not have to be kept pristine, mown with perfect stripes. It can be a hard-wearing, everyday sort of lawn, which copes with bicycles and ball games, and still has just the same visual effect.

Maintenance

Informal gardens can become rather high in maintenance, particularly if irregular attention is given to them. It is an inescapable fact that garden jobs don't just go away if they are ignored, they just get bigger. So if you leave the weeding for a few weeks, the effort to rid the borders of weeds can become a daunting task that takes a long time to do. Similarly, if herbaceous perennials and shrubs are left growing, with no attention paid to them, they will merrily go on growing until the garden becomes almost over-run and a major operation is needed to get everything back to the original plan. It is therefore important to do a little bit of work often rather than a lot in sudden bursts. With a little bit of attention, informal gardens are easy to maintain.

The seemingly random but not untidy nature of this garden is really charming. It has a delightfully informal, but still cared for, appearance.

Containers can be used just as much in informal arrangements as they are in formal gardens. They are especially useful for providing temporary fills.

Wildflower gardens

With the increasing reduction of wild habits for many plants, many people have begun to look afresh at what they are losing and have gained an appreciation of their native flora. This has encouraged them to create areas within their own garden in which wild flowers can flourish, partly to help to preserve these flowers and partly because they simply enjoy them.

What is a wildflower garden?

A wildflower garden is one in which native flowers are grown in as near wild conditions as possible. The idea of wild conditions is not so much to create a picturesque landscape but more to create conditions in which the flowers will grow.

There are several types of garden all based on habitats in the wild. The most common is a wildflower meadow. Next are those based on plants of the cornfield and arable land, which like the disturbed soil of the open border. Then there are the woodland plants that need a shady garden. Finally, there are the wetland plants, which need a pond, stream or boggy area. Once established, wildflower gardens or borders are

The pretty *Anemone nemorosa* is an easy, non-invasive plant to grow. Plant it under shrubs or under a hedgerow.

wonderful for attracting native birds and insects. They are, after all, their natural food.

When planning a wildflower garden, do not source your plants from those growing in the wild. Although they seem to be there for the gathering, always resist the temptation and buy seed from a respectable seed merchant instead. Leave the plants in the wild for others to enjoy.

Wildflower meadows

These are best created by first sowing grass or using an existing lawn. Once the "meadow" has become established, mow it regularly to eliminate the coarser grasses. Now is the time to plant the wildflowers. They are more likely to become established if you grow the plants from seed in pots and then transplant them into the grass than if you simply scatter the seed. Prevent rank grass from taking over by mowing in high summer after the plants have seeded and then at least a couple more times before winter sets in. Do not leave the grass lying after cutting.

Cornfield plants

Many wildflowers will not grow in grass, needing disturbed soil to flourish. Poppies, cornflowers and corn marigolds are examples of these. They are mainly annuals and can be grown from seed in pots and then transplanted or sown directly from seed. Once established, they will self-sow and then reappear every year. A border can be devoted to them or they can be mixed into a general border.

Here it is early spring in the meadow garden, with *Fritillaria meleagris*, the snake's head fritillary, making a welcome appearance.

Non-invasive grasses are ideal for wildflower gardens. This is the annual *Hordeum jubatum*, sparkling in the sun.

Chrysanthemum segetum is one of many cornfield flowers that are ideal for wildflower beds.

in deciduous woods and put in an appearance in the early spring before the trees come into leaf. This is so that they get enough sun and rain to grow and develop. Primroses, wood anemones and bluebells are good examples of these. It is not necessary to have a wood in order to grow them – they will be quite happy growing under deciduous shrubs and a good use of space.

Water plants

These can be a bit more problematic in that many native water or bog plants can be rather rampant and tend to take over. They need good management to keep them under control. The conditions that these plants enjoy are also very conducive to weeds, so be prepared for regular weeding. They can be grown in the same way as any other water- or bog-loving plants.

Plants for a wildflower garden

Wildflower meadows
Achillea millefolium
Campanula rotundifolia
Cardamine pratensis
Centaurea scabiosa
Geranium pratense
Hypericum perforatum
Leontodon hispidus
Malva moschata
Narcissus pseudonarcissus
Primula veris
Ranunculus acris
Succisa pratensis

Cornfield plants
Centaurea cyanus
Chrysanthemum segetum
Papaver rhoeas

Woodland plants
Anemone nemorosa
Convallaria majalis
Digitalis purpurea
Hyacinthoides non-scripta
Primula vulgaris

Water gardens
Butomus umbellatus
Caltha palustris
Eupatorium cannabinum
Filipendula ulmaria
Iris pseudacorus
Mentha aquatica

Woodland plants

There are a number of woodland species that make very attractive planting in shady areas, perhaps under shrubs or trees or perhaps on the sunless side of a house or fence. Most woodland flowers tend to grow

Although normally considered a border plant, *Camassia* makes an excellent plant for the wild meadow garden.

Ferns make good plants for shady areas of wildflower gardens. In wetter areas the royal fern, *Osmunda regalis*, is ideal.

Coping with different conditions

Sometimes we are lucky enough when buying a house to get one with a garden that offers us pretty much what we wanted, or at least offering excellent growing conditions. If we are very lucky, we may even be able to choose the house specifically for the garden. However, for most of us, we select the house and then simply have to accept the garden along with it. This can present the keen gardener with a variety of situations, both in terms of weather and soil conditions. Although the weather cannot be altered, quite a bit can be done to improve the soil and make it suitable for our chosen plants. Alternatively, we can just decide to accept what the garden offers, and select those plants that like a wide range of conditions. Similarly, the size of the garden is usually predetermined, with little chance of increasing it. Again, it is perfectly possible to create a delightful garden within the constraints that this puts upon you.

Over the next few pages we look at the most important conditions under which you may have to create a garden. Very few gardeners start from scratch, as there is usually some form of garden already in existence, giving some indication of the conditions you might expect there.

Making the most of the slope, this gravel garden is ideal for growing dry-loving and sun-loving plants.

Dry gardens

Once upon a time there was only one type of dry garden – one that was naturally so. Nowadays, with the increasing desire to create a number of habitats in which to grow the widest range of plants, many gardeners set out actually to create these conditions. In either case, there are a large number of varied annuals and perennials that suit a dry environment.

Dry conditions

Just because a garden is dry does not necessarily mean that it receives very little rain. There are many gardens that receive a lot of rain and yet are still dry under foot. The reason for this is that the soil is very free-draining and any moisture that falls, either from clouds or from a watering can, passes quickly through it. These are mainly sandy or gravelly soil, but chalky soils can also be very free-draining. As well as losing water quickly, many dry soils are also poor

A surprisingly large number of plants like dry conditions and a very attractive garden can be built around them.

in terms of nutrients. The water passing through leeches out the nutrients, taking the food that plants require well below the level of their roots. Many seaside gardens are of this nature.

Plants for dry gardens

Allium	Glaucium flavum
hollandicum	Lavatera
Argemone	Onopordon
Artemisia	acanthium
Atriplex hortensis	Ophiopogon
Bergenia	planiscapus
Canna	'Nigrescens'
Centranthus	Papaver
Cerinthe major	somniferum
Cortaderia	Pennisetum
Crambe	Salvia
Elymus	Sedum
Eryngium	Stachys
Eschscholzia	byzantinus
Euphorbia	Verbascum
Foeniculum	Yucca

Altering the conditions

It is possible to increase the water-retentiveness of dry soil so that you can grow a much wider range of plants in it. This is done by adding well-rotted organic material to the soil when you dig it. Garden compost or farmyard manure are

Grasses are excellent for dry gardens. The larger ones create imposing clumps against which the other plants are set.

Annuals, such as this marigold (*Calendula*) and vipers bugloss (*Echium vulgare*), will self-sow to provide next year's plants.

This is the ultimate dry garden: houseleeks (*Sempervivum*) growing on a house porch. Stonecrops (*Sedum*) also like such a position.

This mixed border features plants from regions with a Mediterranean climate. Dry gardens increase the number of plants we can grow.

good additives and will improve soil conditions appreciably, especially as they are rich in nutrients. Mulching with organic materials also helps a great deal. A covering of composted bark, for example, will considerably cut down water loss into the atmosphere. It will also gradually become incorporated into the soil, improving the condition. Unfortunately, most dry soils are "hungry", and gardeners need to add material both into the soil and on to its surface on a regular basis.

Living with dry soils

While it is in general terms a good thing to try to improve soil conditions, it is possible to live with existing conditions by choosing your plants carefully. Many plants have adapted their demands so that they

are able to live with drought or partial drought, particularly plants that come originally from Mediterranean climates. It is very important to choose plants that will tolerate such dry soils. If you try to get ordinary plants to grow in them, you will be disappointed because they will not be able get enough moisture or food from the soil and will not grow very well. If, however, you choose plants that have adapted to these conditions, you should have few problems in creating an interesting garden.

Plants for dry conditions

Few gardens have desert conditions, so you don't have to go to extremes and grow only succulents, such as cacti, that tolerate such places. However, there are a lot of plants

that come from parts of the world where, for example, dry summers are followed by wet autumns and winters. Many annuals come from these areas, as do bulbs and many silver-leaved plants – try combining these to create an unusual but beautiful garden where their subtle colours are well set off by a gravel background. Weed these areas well, or the effect will be ruined.

Creating a gravel garden

Many gardeners specifically set out to create dry conditions by adding great quantities of gravel to the ordinary soil. This increases its drainage ability and makes it suitable for plants that you may not have been able to grow before.

Damp gardens

The idea of damp gardens conjures up a rather unpleasant image of a garden in which no one would want to linger, but, depending on how the situation is handled, they can be rather beautiful. Apart from anything else, many colours, especially the yellows, stand out so well in gloomy conditions.

What is a damp garden?

A garden can be considered damp in two ways. The first is where the soil is heavy and constantly damp, even though the weather is sunny and bright. The second way can occur near certain coasts. The coastal climate in question is one where the weather is frequently overcast, with rain, drizzle or mist being common, and where, even when it is sunny, the air is still "buoyant" (moving and life-sustaining as opposed to stagnant) and slightly moist, especially under trees. Both are conditions that most gardeners dread, but both can be turned to advantage. Visits to other gardens with similar conditions will soon stimulate you, showing what can be achieved with a bit of determination and a good waterproof jacket.

Aruncus dioicus does best in a moist situation, either in a bed that is moisture-retentive or on the edge of a bog garden.

Many plants like a situation where the air never dries out and the soil remains slightly damp, such as along the banks of a stream.

Wet soil

There are two solutions to the problem of wet soils: one is to deal with it and the other is to live with it. In the first case, improving the condition of the soil, especially by adding grit and organic material to it, will help greatly by improving the soil's ability to let the water pass through. Allied to this should be improved drainage. If you simply dig and improve the soil, the bed will fill up with water, held in place by the surrounding poor soil like a sump. You must make certain that the water can drain out of the bed by laying drains either to a soakaway or a nearby ditch. Another possibility is to lead the water to a lower part of the garden, where you can create a pond. Any garden that stays persistently damp should have a proper drainage system installed to get the water away.

This colourful damp meadow and ditch is full of moisture-loving plants such as candelabra primulas, astilbes and water irises.

A mass of colourful primulas – plants for which a damp position is absolutely ideal. They will self-sow to make this an even better display.

Bog gardens

Living with damp soils is another interesting prospect. The gardener simply has to accept the fact that the soil is always wet and create a bed that is based on plants that like boggy conditions. Fortunately, there are a large number of colourful plants that do like such conditions. If the soil is too heavy, it will help if plenty of well-rotted organic matter is incorporated into it. If there is water actually lying on or just below the surface, this should be removed by laying drains.

Here a small, damp garden has been built into the edge of a pond. This type of situation really broadens out the range of plants that can be grown.

Creating boggy conditions

While some gardeners go to great expense to get rid of boggy areas, others do the reverse and deliberately create such conditions. One way to do this would be to dig a pond-shaped hole about 45cm/18in deep, and line it with an old pond liner. Puncturing a few holes in the lowest places will allow excess water to drain away. The hole can then be filled with good soil laced with plenty of well-rotted organic material. The soil should not be allowed to dry out.

Grasses that grow on the damp banks of streams or ponds, hanging their leaves over the water, can look extremely effective.

Damp climate

A damp climate can be a boon if you want to grow plants such as the blue meconopsis, which likes the moist air that reminds it of its Himalayan home. Many other plants do best in a moist, buoyant atmosphere. Primulas and hostas, for example, relish it. In Britain, the maritime climate of Scotland produces some wonderful gardens, growing plants such as primulas, hostas and meconopsis. In many such areas, the soil is surprisingly free-draining. In mountain and hilly areas, for example, the underlying rocks often allow the frequent rain to filter away remarkably quickly, leaving the soil dry. So if there is a prolonged hot spell it is important to water.

Plants for a bog garden

Aconitum napellus	Gunnera manicata	Parnassia palustris
Ajuga reptans	Hemerocallis fulva	Persicaria bistorta
Aruncus dioicus	Hosta	Petasites japonicus var.
Astilbe x arendsii	Iris ensata	giganteus
Astilboides tabularis	Iris orientalis	Primula bulleyana
Astrantia major	Iris sibirica	Primula denticulata
Caltha palustris	Ligularia	Primula florindae
Cardamine pratensis	Lobelia cardinalis	Primula japonica
Cimifuga simplex	Lobelia 'Queen Victoria'	Primula pulverulenta
Darmera peltata	Lobelia siphilitica	Primula vialii
Dierama pulcherimum	Lychnis flos-cuculi	Ranunculus aconitifolius
Dodecatheon meadia	Lysichiton	Rheum palmatum
Eupatorium	Lysimachia nummularia	Rodgersia
Euphorbia griffithii	Lysimachia punctata	Sarracenia purpurea
Euphorbia palustris	Lythrum virgatum	Schizostylis coccinea
Filipendula ulmaria	Meconopsis betonicifolia	Symphytum ibericum
Gentiana asclepiadea	Mimulus cardinalis	Telekia speciosum
Geum rivale	Mimulus lewisii	Trollius

Shady gardens

Like so many other problems in gardening, this one will go away if you make a slight adjustment of attitude and decide to embrace the shade rather than be daunted by it. A visit to any of the big gardens will show shady areas that have been successfully planted, and there is no reason why you should not do the same on a smaller scale.

Coping with shade

For some reason, many people simply ignore the fact that an area is shady and attempt to grow annuals and other sun-loving plants in it. These inevitably languish and frequently die, and the gardeners get very despondent.

There is really no excuse for this problem as a large number of plants are available that actually like shady conditions. Perhaps the colours of these plants might not be so dazzling as the sun-lovers – there are not many bright reds, for example – but they are still colourful enough to put on a good display. Many plants that like shade are yellow, and so stand out well in the gloomy light.

As well as plants with bright flowers, there are many foliage plants that can be used very effectively in such areas. Some have light, variegated or silver-splashed foliage, such as yellow archangel (*Lamium galeobdolon*), which tend to illuminate the darker corners. Others, such as

hostas, have shiny leaves, and these catch and reflect the light, once again helping to brighten up the relative darkness.

Miniature woodlands

Many shade-loving plants grow in woodlands, and they appear, flower, seed and die back all before the trees come into leaf. The absence of leaves above them means that the plants have access to both the sun and the rain. Once the leaves on the trees emerge, the plants die back and remain dormant until the following winter or spring.

These plants, including wood anemones and bluebells, can be planted in a garden in odd pockets

Anemones, here the double *Anemone ranunculoides*, are perfect woodland plants to grow under the shade of shrubs.

A shady border has been carved out of this mature wood. Here there is sufficient light to grow a wide range of plants.

Even a single tree, such as this quince, is sufficient to create a small woodland garden with a range of plants.

Spring-flowering bulbs, such as these blue scillas, make natural carpets for shady areas. Hellebores are also a very good subject.

of shade, such as under deciduous shrubs. Here, the plants can be seen in spring, but later in the year nothing will grow here because the soil will be covered by the shrub's leaves. This makes good use of space. Several such shrubs, perhaps of varying height and with this type of under-planting, can be used to create a miniature woodland, even in the heart of a town.

Lack of sunlight

The north side of a house (south in the southern hemisphere) is often considered a problem area because of its lack of direct sunlight. Again, it is quite possible to create an

Reducing shade

You can increase the amount of light reaching the plants under trees by removing some of the branches, especially the lower ones. Alternatively, you can thin the branches so that more dappled light reaches the ground. If the trees are listed, then you may have to seek permission before removing any limbs. In basement and other dark patios, the amount of light can be increased by painting walls white to reflect what light there is.

Eranthis hyemalis thrives in shade. Give it a moist woodland-type soil with plenty of leaf mould and it will colonize.

effective border there simply by choosing plants that like the shade. Most woodland plants, for example, will grow there.

Dry shade

An area that is both dry and shady is one of the worst problems to cope with because most shade-loving plants are woodland plants, which thrive in a moist, fibre-rich soil. Soils can be improved by adding plenty of well-rotted organic material to them – leaf mould is a natural material to use.

Creating shade

Sometimes it can be a problem if you have no shade in the garden when you want to grow plants such as hellebores, which do not like too much sun. Try building a wooden or metal framework over which you stretch shade-netting, creating nice dappled shade. These structures may not look elegant but they are ideal for their intended purpose. They are also useful for temporarily housing shade-loving plants while bushes or trees become large enough to provide natural shade.

Anemone blanda and hellebores are two good choices to brighten up a patch of light shade.

Some plants for the shade

Alchemilla mollis	Epimedium	Persicaria affinis
Anemone nemorosa	Eranthis hyemalis	Phlox divaricata
Arum italicum	Euphorbia amygdaloides	Phlox stolonifera
Aruncus dioicus	robbiae	Podophyllum peltatum
Bergenia	Geranium	Polygonatum
Brunnera macrophylla	Helleborus	Polystichum setiferum
Caltha palustris	Hosta	Primula
Campanula latifolia	Houttuynia cordata	Pulmonaria
Cardamine	Iris foetidissima	Sanguinaria canadensis
Cardiocrinum giganteum	Kirengshoma	Smilacina
Carex pendula	Lamium galeobdolon	Smyrnium perfoliatum
Clintonia	Lathyrus vernus	Stylophorum
Convallaria majalis	Lilium martagon	Symphytum grandiflorum
Corydalis flexuosa	Liriope muscari	Tellima grandiflora
Dicentra	Meconopsis	Trillium
Digitalis purpurea	Milium effusum 'Aureum'	Uvularia
Dryopteris filix-mas	Myosotis sylvatica	Vancouveria

Small gardens

More and more people are living in houses or apartments that only have small gardens; some, indeed are minute. The keen gardener's heart may sink at such limitations, but it is surprising what you can pack into a small space. As always, it just needs some imagination and determination to create a garden to be proud of.

Packing them in

If you more interested in growing plants than having space in which to sit around or have barbecues, then the amount of hard surfaces or lawn should be reduced to a minimum and as much space as possible devoted to borders. Avoid grass unless you have somewhere to store a lawnmower, because mowers need sheds and sheds take up valuable space.

Although there are recommended planting distances for plants, these, like many rules in gardening, can be ignored and the plants set close together for maximum impact. Some will object and crowd other plants out, but these can be culled totally and replaced by something not so vigorous or kept in place by trimming. Tightly packed plants need to be watered and fed regularly because they are taking a lot of water and nutrients out of the soil.

A curved path gives the impression that more garden exists just around the corner. Such illusions make a garden seem much bigger.

One of a kind

Rather than having a drift of one particular plant, as you might in a bigger garden, you should restrict yourself to one plant of each species, otherwise the whole garden could end up with just one or two different types of plant in it. This can make the borders look rather spotty, so drifts can be created using different plants of a similar colour.

The best single plants are those that produce several stems, creating a small clump. Those that produce

just a single stem can look rather lost, although there are many such plants, verbascums for example, that make a wonderful accent as they emerge from the surrounding plants. Similarly, a single red poppy can look stunning and will definitely draw the eye.

Foliage plants

A small garden benefits from foliage plants in the same way that large gardens do from grasses. Foliage plants will help to calm down the liveliness of the border and produce somewhere for the eye to rest. This is important in a small garden packed with plants, as the overall appearance can become overly busy. Another use of foliage in any garden, but particularly in a small garden, is to surround a single flowering plant with green or silver leaves so that it makes the flowers stand out, accenting them with a posy effect.

Vertical space

Every bit of space in a small garden is at a premium to a plant-lover, so it is important to remember that a garden is three-dimensional. Climbing plants can be used against walls or fences. It may also be possible to use one or two posts or tripods, if there is space, to add to

Every inch of space needs to be used to maximum effect in a small garden, including, as here, window sills.

Use containers planted up with annuals and perennials, such as this hosta, to fill out any odd corners.

Plants to cut back

Achillea	Eupatorium
Aconitum	Foeniculum
Aruncus	Helenium
Aster	Rudbeckia
Campanula	Sanguisorba

this vertical accent. As well as climbers, annuals can be used in hanging baskets and window boxes to add colour at or above eye level.

Easy ways to cheat

It is possible to use a few optical tricks to make the garden look bigger. Cover the fences with plants so that the margins of the garden cannot be seen. This trick works particularly well if there is a neighbouring garden with shrubs and other plants peering over the fence, as it will look as if your garden continues. Use a winding path that

Miniaturizing plants

Many taller perennial plants can be made to grow shorter simply by cutting them back to the ground when they have made about 45cm/18in of growth. The plants re-grow but will usually flower when they have obtained only about half their normal height and size.

With imagination and determination, an amazing number of plants can be crammed into a small space.

Well-planned use of plenty of foliage – so that you cannot see the boundary edges of the garden – is a simple way to make the space feel a great deal larger.

disappears around a corner at the bottom of the garden so that it seems as if your garden continues out of sight. Paler-coloured plants set towards the end of a short garden will deceive the eye and appear farther away than they are.

Large mirrors covering a wall can give the impression that the wall does not exist and the garden carries on, though the mirrors must be angled so that anyone approaching cannot see their own reflection. Another idea is to erect an arch, which can be covered with climbing plants, just in front of a wall, and then back the arch with a mirror to give the impression that the garden continues under the arch. Similarly, using a *trompe l'oeil* painting on a wall, perhaps a picture of a gate opening into another garden, will deceive viewers into believing that more lies beyond.

Even a modest water feature has been fitted into this extremely small garden. Annual and perennial foliage plants help to fill space without making the garden feel cramped.

Large gardens

Most gardeners with large gardens manage to fill them in one way or another, even if involves putting much of the space down to lawns. Large lawns can be elegant, but without children to play on them they can seem a bit excessive, and there are many more interesting things you could do with the space.

Large-scale plantings

Plenty of space means that you can create large-scale plantings, including sweeping herbaceous borders. These are large borders that were traditionally filled only with perennial plants, although these days a number of annuals and even shrubs are often included. The plants are planted in drifts, often with five or more plants in each area, so that the border is "painted" with broad strokes of colour.

It is important that any such borders should be deep as well as long; tall plants in a narrow border rarely work. Try and make the depth of the border twice that of the tallest plants. Two borders often work better than one, and two parallel ones with a grass path between them is ideal. The path should preferably be as wide as the

Having a large garden not only allows you to create lavish bedding displays but also gives plenty of scope for walkways and features such as arches.

borders are deep. Such borders are displayed best if they are grown against a green hedge. Yew is ideal and it is not as slow growing as many people think. A fairly respectable hedge can be achieved in about five years and it will begin to mature at eight.

It is equally possible to use large areas of bedding material, especially if you like to create intricate patterns in colour and texture. There are a number of plants that can be used

for these, some growing to a very even height, while others can be used to vary this or to create accents or focal points. These beds can be laid out directly on the ground, surrounded by lawns, or they can form part of a more complicated plan in which a knot garden of box hedges is created, with the bedding plants used as in-fills. Great fun can be had by creating a low-level maze in this kind of way, using a mixture of paths and beds.

Plenty of space to play with means that passionate gardeners can be creative on a grand scale, as these enormous herbaceous borders show.

As well as straight borders, spacious gardens allow huge, swirling areas of plants that show off their colour and shape to maximum effect.

Large plants

Aruncus	Helianthus
Cephalaria	Heliopsis
Cimifuga	Inula magnifica
Cortaderia	Lavatera
Cosmos	cachemiriana
Cynara	Ligularia
cardunculus	Macleaya
Delphinium	Miscanthus
Eremurus	Rheum
Eupatorium	Rudbeckia
purpureum	laciniata
Gunnera	Sanguisorba
manicata	Verbascum

If you have a large space, you can indulge in some of the most impressive plants available. This *Gunnera manicata* is one of the largest perennials used in gardens.

Gardens within gardens

Another good idea for a large garden is to divide it up into a series of smaller gardens. Dividing in this way creates spaces that are more intimate – more like individual rooms than one vast space. This can be effective in country gardens, where the landscape is already expansive and open. Each "room" should be given its own individual character, some formal, some informal, with varied planting. Perhaps one could be a white garden while another could contain only fragrant flowers (a seat would be invaluable in this one).

Large plants

It sounds obvious, but many people forget that a large garden needs large plants, especially if you keep it fairly open. If you have a large pond, then a huge clump of *Gunnera manicata* will look impressive. Great fountains of leaves erupting from large clumps of grasses, such as pampas (*Cortaderia*) or miscanthus, can create focal points at the end of paths or at the bottom of long lawns. They look even better if planted where the evening light shines through them.

Working with a large space

Large gardens that are intensively cultivated can use up a lot of time and a great deal of money, so a large-scale development should be embarked on only if you feel confident that you will have sufficient time. Fortunately, time can often offset costs, because you can propagate all your own material rather than buying it, but a large garden almost always needs a lot of plants to work really successfully.

Finally, the wind is a factor that cannot be forgotten in large gardens, especially where tall plants are likely to be grown in clumps, with nothing behind or in front to protect them from being blown over. A windbreak could be created around the garden, and plants staked if necessary.

Although shrubs are another topic altogether, it is worth saying here that they can be very useful in large gardens, as providers of valuable wind protection.

Family gardens

Keen gardeners who start a family quickly discover that neat gardens and active children do not often mix. Since there is no point trying to stop the children using the garden, or constantly telling them to get off this area and not touch that plant, a compromise is needed whereby everyone can live happily. Remember that a garden should be a fun place for everyone.

Children in the garden

Whatever you do, children will always be children, and quite rightly so. They will want to play ball and racket games in the garden, and will want to career around on bikes and in go-karts. These things present problems for the gardener – balls will crash through the borders, bringing down plants; cyclists or go-karters will veer off the lawn or path and end up lying in a nest of tangled plants.

In the ideal family garden there should be plenty of space and a range of provisions, so everybody is able to relax and play in their own way.

Play space

To some extent, trouble can be avoided by creating a family garden where there is room for all activities. Plenty of lawn or hard surface should be provided on which children can play. There could also be special areas for them, perhaps with swings, sandpits, "camps" or "houses". The very best gardens are those with a variety of nooks and crannies in which children can hide, so, if possible, you could try creating some of these.

If you can, provide as much lawn area as possible – for children to play without falling on hard surfaces or wreaking havoc in the borders.

Some features can be built with the future in mind. This sand pit, for example, can eventually be turned into a water feature.

Easy plants for children to grow

Antirrhinum	Lobelia
Calendula	Tagetes
Helianthus	Thunbergia alata
annuus	Tropaeolum
Lathyrus odoratus	majus

Separate rooms

Your garden may be large enough for you to divide it up into a number of areas, each for a particular activity. This may, for example, include an area for playthings as well as a place for growing precious plants.

Children's gardens

Many young children are very keen on gardening – they love to see things growing. Although eager to help you with your gardening, most children are happiest of all with a small plot of their own. Encourage them to grow annuals, which are quick to germinate and produce colourful results of which they can be justifiably proud. A small selection of quick-growing vegetables will also delight. Children's interests can wane as rapidly as they began, so be prepared to absorb the plot back into the garden. Alternatively, provide them with long-flowering plants, such as *Tagetes*, which will fill the space over a long period.

Tough lawns

The family lawn can take quite a beating and it will be impossible to keep it perfectly pristine. Instead of using the soft grasses that would be needed for a high-quality lawn, use some of the tougher species, which will stand the considerable wear and tear of family life. These can be used singly or as mixtures of one or more species. Once the family has grown up, you can then switch to a better-quality grass.

Tough grass seed for lawns
Axonopus (carpet grass)
Eremochloa ophiuroides (centipede grass)
Lolium perenne (perennial ryegrass)
Paspalum notatum (bahia grass)
Poa pratensis (Kentucky blue grass)

Pets

Cats, dogs and other pets are also part of the family, and friction can often erupt when they flatten plants or dig up borders. Low fences can deter them from running into borders, but with some dogs it will be necessary to fence off your flower garden completely. Wild birds that you feed in winter also need to be taken into account, as they will often strip plants of flowers or berries that you want to keep. There is little you can do about this except grow plants that they do not touch (skimmia berries, for example, are rarely eaten) or cover plants with a network of dark cotton.

Dining out

It is not only children who indulge in non-gardening pursuits. Most of the family want to do other things at some time or other, and space for relaxing is very important. This may just involve a spot for sitting or for lounging in the sun, or more likely will also include some provision for eating, possibly with a barbecue area.

It is a good idea to surround places where you relax with fragrant plants. These will be most welcome if you sit outside in the evening once the sun has gone down. Remember that certain blues and whites show up especially well in the fading light, so try to use plants with flowers of these colours. In a barbecue area, grow a few herbs so that they can be easily picked and used.

Always provide plenty of space and facilities for relaxation. After all, that is one of the prime functions of a garden.

Special ways with annuals and perennials

If you have a big garden, and plenty of free time at your disposal, then you can indulge in just about every aspect of gardening. However, if you do not have these luxuries, you may well find that you have the space to do only one thing properly, and so you specialize. Alternatively, you may want to garden for just one particular purpose, such as providing cut flowers for your home or local community centre.

There are many ways in which you can specialize, and a few are suggested here. It is possible, for example, to have a border or even a whole small garden devoted to plants that include your name. There are over 100 plants that contain the name Helen, for example, including *Aster novi-belgii* 'Helen' and *Dianthus* 'Helen'. You could create a garden filled with plants mentioned in the works of Shakespeare, or in books by your favourite novelist. Research is involved here, of course, but this kind is usually very enjoyable. In any case, rather than devote a whole garden to any of these themes, you could restrict yourself to just a single border or an area within the main garden. The possibilities are endless and the result is likely to be a unique garden that no one else will have.

Borders can be restricted to one colour or a group of colours. In this scheme, yellows are predominant, but a sprinkling of hot reds has been added to provide some interest.

Fragrant gardens

When thinking of flowers, one's first thoughts normally concern their colour. One of their most important qualities as far as many gardeners are concerned, however, is their smell. Most people have evocative childhood memories of particular flower fragrances, usually associated with a specific garden – often a grandparent's.

Scents

There is nothing quite like the scent of a garden on a summer's day, particularly if associated with the drowsy hum of bees and the fluttering of butterflies. Generally, a warm, sunny day brings out the scents, but there are some that are much more noticeable during or after rain. Scent in a flower is a bonus as far as we are concerned, but nature imbued flowers with it for a reason: to attract pollinators. For this reason, many winter flowers are sweet-smelling. There are not many pollinators around at that time of year and so the flowers have to work particularly hard to attract them.

Some plants throw out their scent with gay abandon and can be smelt at large distances. Others are much more discreet, and you have to put your nose almost into them before the fragrance is detectable. Many of the latter are more apparent once they have been picked and placed in a warm room. Some are only noticeable during the evening as the light fades. Presumably these attract night-flying moths.

The fragrant garden

Not all the plants should be fragrant, or they will become too overpowering and you will be unable to differentiate between the conflicting scents. Place scented plants at key points around the

Sweet Williams, *Dianthus barbatus*, have a very distinctive smell – the kind of smell that often triggers memories such as a garden from your childhood.

Placing fragrant flowers near to a window will often flood the rooms beyond with a wonderful scent, especially on warm, balmy summer evenings.

Many pelargoniums have scented foliage, with the fragrances offered by different varieties ranging from citrus fruits and rose to nutmeg.

garden so that there is the impression that the whole garden is perfumed. Also, try if possible to get a spread of plants so that there are scents throughout the seasons, including winter.

Scent-testing

Try to smell your plants before you acquire them, as some may not be as scented as you wish. Breeders of flowers went through a long period when smell was low down on their list of priorities when creating new plants. Thus many modern sweet peas are not sweet at all: they are scentless. Similarly, many modern pinks are without scent.

Another reason for trying out scents, either in other gardens or at the point of sale, is that you may not like the fragrance of some plants: they may be too sweet and sickly or they may bring back certain unpleasant memories.

Siting fragrant flowers

Fragrant flowers can be placed anywhere you like in the garden, but there are some situations where they are a must. One of the best positions is near places where you sit and relax, as soothing scents will help to recharge your batteries.

Another good place is near windows or doors, so that the scent wafts into the house when the flowers open during a warm day or evening.

Placing fragrant plants next to the driveway, so that you notice them as you get out of the car, is a wonderful way of indicating to the senses that you have arrived home after work, and certainly helps you to relax.

Fragrant foliage

It is not only flowers that can be scented: a lot of plant foliage is too. In some cases, as with flowers, warmth brings out the fragrance, but in most cases the leaves or stems have to be crushed in order to release it. In extreme cases, such as lawn chamomile, *Chamaemelum nobile* 'Treneague', or thyme, the plants are best placed under foot, so that as you walk on them you send up clouds of scent. With most fragrantly foliaged plants, however, it is best to site them near to a path, so that you can run your fingers through them as you walk by.

Pinks (*Dianthus*), both the annual and perennial types, provide a distinctively old-fashioned fragrance to borders. Here, the plant used is *D.* 'Doris'.

Colour gardens

All plants are coloured, so what is a "colour" garden? Well, some gardeners like to use particular colour schemes, choosing either all pastel or all bright colours, for example, rather than just dotting colour around the garden at random. A favourite idea is to create a border or even a whole garden of a single colour – a particularly popular choice being white.

Here an exciting, vibrant border has been created, composed entirely of a well-selected range of hot colours such as golds, oranges and reds. These sorts of colours make us feel energetic and dynamic, so they may not be the best choice for a corner where you go to unwind.

Choosing colours

We all know what colours are, although we may see them slightly differently. What we don't all agree on is which colours are pleasing and which are not. Inevitably, because we are all different, our feelings about certain colours or combinations vary dramatically. Therefore, although there may seem to be codes or formulas for colour use, it is important to do what pleases you; after all, the garden is for you. For a long time, mixing oranges and purples would have been deemed one of the worst sins in gardening, but now influential gardeners are much more adventurous and many will readily combine these colours.

Arranging colours

Using colours in drifts can make a big impact in a garden, and if the drifts are planted so that they merge

harmoniously rather than jump suddenly from one extreme to another, then so much the better. In this way mauves might merge into blues, and yellows into oranges, creating a soft, fluid design that leads the eye around the garden.

If you want to create something more eye-catching, then try planting contrasting colours such as orange and mauve together. If you are not brave enough to put them right next to each other, use a foliage plant between them to soften the impact. As with so many other aspects of designing gardens, it is best to see how other people use colour and then follow those ideas that you like.

Creating different moods

Colours can have a significant effect on our mood. Hot colours such as oranges and flame reds are lively and exciting, whereas the lighter pastel colours are cool and soothing. Dark purples are sombre and heavy and, if overdone in a garden, can produce a leaden appearance.

Single-colour gardens

Experimental gardeners can have great fun by devoting a border or even a whole garden to a single bloom colour – white is an especially popular choice. Such gardens are not truly just one colour anyway, because you have to take the foliage into account. So, a "white" garden is usually made up of white, green and perhaps silver and grey. Even the white may vary from a creamy or a yellowish white to bluish-white, and it takes a fair amount of skill to balance these different variations.

Contrasting colours can make a bold visual statement. These pinkish-orange dahlias stand out vividly against the deep blue salvias.

Soft, pastel colours can create a tranquil, peaceful feeling. Here, pink alliums mix with white geraniums and blue salvias.

A border devoted to white flowers creates a very peaceful atmosphere. Surprisingly, using just one colour need never be boring.

Two-colour gardens

This variation on the single-colour planting idea involves a border, or whole garden, being planted with two different colours. White and gold or yellow and blue are two popular and pleasing combinations. The two colours can be equal in quantity or mainly one with a touch of the other as a contrast.

White flowers

Achillea ptarmica	Digitalis purpurea 'Alba'	Nicotiana sylvestris
Anaphalis margaritacea	Epilobium angustifolium	Omphalodes linifolia
Anemone x hybrida	'Album'	Osteospermum 'Whirligig'
'Honorine Jobert'	Geranium sanguineum	Paeonia
Anemone nemorosa	'Album'	Penstemon 'White Bedder'
Antirrhinum majus	Gypsophila paniculata	Petunia
Argyranthemum frutescens	Iberis sempervirens	Phlox paniculata 'Fujiama'
Bellis	Lamium maculatum 'White	Polygonatum x hybridum
Campanula latiloba alba	Nancy'	Ranunculus aconitifolius
Convallaria majalis	Lathyrus	Romneya coulteri
Crambe cordifolia	Leucanthemum 'Everest'	Smilacina
Dianthus	Lilium	Viola
Dicentra spectabile 'Alba'	Lysimachia clethroides	Zantedeschia aethiopica

Hot colours

Vibrant and exciting bright orange, flame red and orange-yellow can be great fun to play with. They attract the eye and can create a focal point in the garden. But, like parties, they are great fun once in a while but can lose their appeal if done to excess. Certainly, a whole garden planted in these colours would become tiring after a short while, so it is better to create just one border or a part of a border, placing them in key positions. They can also look effective on the far side of a pond.

Contrasting colours

Using colours that contrast particularly boldly with each other can add drama to a border and will draw the eye. Many people find that some contrasting colours are more acceptable than others. Most would agree that bright red looks fabulous with green, for example, but they may be more reserved about other combinations, such as orange with purple. As with hot colours, gardeners should always bear in mind that dramatic contrasts can begin to jar if used too much.

You can create a white garden in spring, as seen here, and then change the plants to have a "hot" red garden in the summer.

The hotter colours may be dramatic and thrilling, but remember that even excitement can become boring if it is overdone, and you certainly don't want to produce something that amounts to a visual assault. Restricting bold colours to one border is often much more pleasing.

Water gardens

Water has been one of the basic building blocks of decorative gardens since gardens first began. Whether it is still or moving, it has a calming tranquillity about it that sums up the essence of a garden. Water can be used in a wide variety of ways, including features that are suitable for the smaller garden.

What are water features?

There is a wide range of possibilities for using water in the garden, ranging from lakes in big ones to just a dustbin lid full of water in a small one. Water can be used in the form of a static pond or pool, or it can be used as a stream, with all the movement that implies. Streams can involve cascades, waterfalls and pools, and can become a striking feature of the garden. It is also possible to use water in such a way that there is no standing water at all, just water seeping between fixed pebbles.

All these possibilities can involve plants in one way or another, allowing you to use plants and to create effects that a garden without water cannot achieve.

Water features do not need to contain any standing water. Here, bubble fountains give sound and image without the dangers.

Areas of contrast

Water complements the plants in a garden beautifully. It can create tranquil, reflective areas as a contrast to some lively planting, or it can bustle along in a stream, in contrast to the static plants, creating a sparkling streak of silver. Water can also produce noise, such as the tinkling of a fountain or the more regular pouring of a waterspout. The movement of water in a stream can also be very soothing to watch.

Wildlife

One of the many reasons why gardeners like ponds and other water features in their gardens is that they attract wildlife. They produce a source of drinking and bathing water for a large number of birds and insects, and ponds can also attract toads. Other animals, especially nocturnal ones, may drink from a pond at night. Such wildlife is attracted not only to the water but also to the plants that surround it, which furnish them with valuable cover and food.

Plants and water

One of the advantages of having a water feature is that it lets you extend the range of plants featured in your garden to include those that enjoy growing in or around water.

Some plants, such as water lilies, thrive in the deep water itself, while others prefer the shallow water margins, where they can get their roots down into the mud. Other plants like the muddy edges of a pond, where they are generally out of

Different types of garden can always be combined. This is a water garden where colour effects have also been created – using flowers in gold and white.

You can create water gardens on a modest scale, as this stream and pool demonstrate.

Water allows the gardener to use plants that cannot be grown in any other way. These water lilies are a prime example.

the water but where their roots are occasionally submerged. Another group, such as hostas and rodgersias, like the area next to the pond, which is out of water but still damp, while mimulus and many primulas relish being planted beside a stream, where they are occasionally splashed and where the air is nice and buoyant. The range of plants within all these different groups is enormous.

Waterside plants

Aruncus	Lysichiton
Astilbe	Lysimachia
Caltha	Lythrum
Cardamine	Mimulus
Cimifuga	Onoclea sensibilis
Darmera peltata	Osmunda regalis
Eupatorum	Peltiphyllum
Filipendula	peltatum
Gunnera	Persicaria
Hosta	bistorta
Iris ensata	Phragmites
Iris sibirica	Primula
Ligularia	Rheum
Lobelia	Rodgersia
cardinallis	Trollius

Bog gardens

Many of the plants that like growing on the margins of ponds can be grown to really great effect in a bog garden. This is commonly defined as an area that has a great deal of moisture-retaining humus in the soil, so that it never dries out, though this does not mean that it has to be squelchy. If, for any reason, you want to get rid of a pond, rather than filling it in you can simply puncture the lining so that the water drains away, and then fill it up with some fibrous material to make your perfect bog garden.

Safety

Water can be dangerous, especially to young children, so very careful thought must be given before you start to dig deep holes in your garden for ponds of any kind. There are various attractive compromises. It is possible to create relatively safe features in which water bubbles out of, say, a rock and then disappears between fixed stones into a safe underground reservoir. This idea leaves no surface water, which can prove to be dangerous.

A pond can be especially appealing if it is designed so that it blends in with the rest of the garden, adding to the overall scene rather than being a totally separate feature. Placing water features where they are "discovered" as something of a surprise also adds a delightful touch.

Specialist flower gardens

The majority of people grow plants in order to create an attractive garden in which they can relax and enjoy themselves. Others, however, do so because they simply enjoy the process of growing plants or even need to grow plants. In the latter cases, the actual appearance of the garden will be of less importance than the plants it produces.

Cut flowers

These are an important part of many people's lives. Most gardeners cut a few flowers for the house, but some grow plants especially for that very purpose, devoting part or even all of the garden to producing them. Rows of flowering sweet peas or plants with attractive foliage such as hostas are their common fare. Most people don't need to have their whole garden turned over to the production of flowers for cutting, but some gardeners enjoy providing displays for churches or hospitals or even selling them at local markets.

For them it is important to know which plants can be used as cut stems and which last longest in water. There are many old favourites, but it is often exciting to discover new ones from the vast range of plants that gardeners have at their beck and call, so it is always worth experimenting. Buy one plant of something that might be suitable. Try it and, if it works, propagate it so that you have a row of unusual material.

The average gardener does not want to devote the whole garden to cut flowers and probably doesn't have room for even a border of such things. It is, however, easy to incorporate a number of plants for cutting among the other plants in the borders. Wigwams of sweet peas, for example, look good as well as providing cut material.

Sweet peas are typically grown for exhibition and cut flower purposes and need not be grown in the main decorative beds.

Phlox makes an excellent cut flower. As well as being grown in special beds for cutting, phlox is a good choice for borders.

Flower shows

There is a long tradition, especially among cottage gardeners, of growing plants for exhibition. Most tend these days to be local affairs, where there are mixed shows, but there are still a number of local and national shows that are devoted in whole or in part to one type of flower. Thus sweet peas, chrysanthemums and dahlias are still popular with exhibitors. Pinks (*Dianthus*), auriculas, and irises are also still shown fairly extensively.

These plants can be grown in the general borders, but growing them in separate beds, albeit more practical than attractive, means that the gardener can tend them easily and bring them on to their very best.

Specialist growers

Some gardeners are interested in particular plants, often to the exclusion of others. They may grow them as part of a decorative garden or they may grow them in special beds designed to suit their particular plants. Examples of some of the more popular groups of plants for growing in general beds are hellebores, geraniums and hostas.

Some collectors with large collections, however, grow them in beds devoted to their specialization. These plants will often need special growing conditions, and so lovers of alpine plants will construct special raised beds where the soil is very free-draining, while those interested in hellebores may well construct shade beds made with wooden frames covered with shade netting. These may not be the most elegant of gardens, but they serve the purpose for which the gardener requires them and certainly suit the needs of the plants, as the conditions are tailor made for them.

There are many flowers in the garden that can be cut for drying. This perennial, *Anaphalis nepalensis*, is just one good example.

Small nurseries

There are certain gardeners who get so passionate about plants that they are not content with the confines of their own garden and may want to start growing them for everybody else as well. What might have started out as a conventional garden soon turns into a small nursery. Frequently, such a garden will contain plants planted randomly in stock beds, so that they are readily available for propagation. It will also contain lots of plants grown in pots, ready for sale.

Other ways of gardening

None of these types of gardens may be conventional but they are certainly all perfectly worthwhile ways of gardening. There are undoubtedly many people who gain a great deal of enjoyment from these kinds of specialist approaches.

Most specialist gardeners are likely to have started out simply by devoting a relatively small plot to their purpose until enthusiasm has really taken over. Such specialization can be exciting and if you succumb you will come to know a great deal about plants.

Growing rare plants

As mentioned before, there are other gardeners who are not especially interested in gardens as such; they are really only interested in growing plants. While they may not specialize in any particular genus or family, they get their enjoyment from growing unusual and rare plants.

One of the reasons that some plants are rare in gardens is straightforward – they are very difficult to grow. This presents a challenge to certain gardeners, who will spend a lot of time making certain that the conditions are just right and giving nurturing attention to individual plants, much more than would be given to normal ones. Many people find this a particularly exciting form of gardening.

Flowers for cutting

Acanthus	Delphiniums
Achillea	Eryngium
Alstroemeria	Gypsophila
Aster	Heliopsis
Callistephus	Lathyrus odoratus
chinensis	Liatris
Chrysanthemum	Molucella
Convallaria majalis	Physalis
Dahlia	Rudbeckia
Dianthus	Solidago

Bear in mind that if you want to produce larger flowers, such as the delphiniums shown here, primarily for cutting purposes, then it may be best to grow them in separate beds, as cutting from a decorative bed will leave big gaps.

Container gardens

While most traditional gardens consist of beds, with possibly areas of lawn or hard surface, it is possible to have a garden without these. It is even possible to have a garden on a balcony or rooftop without any access to a conventional garden. The secret? Containers.

What are containers?

Plants can be grown in any form of container, from a small yogurt carton to a large terracotta pot. Pots made of plastic or ceramic, as well as wooden barrels and tubs, are frequently used, and there has been an increase in the popularity of metal containers. Although virtually any container can be used to contain plants, it is important to remember the dignity of the plant and avoid planting it in something completely unsuitable. A plastic tub with the name of the product it once contained still on the side, for example, does the plant no favours.

Containers come in a number of forms. The obvious one is a round pot, varying in size from a small terracotta pot to a large ceramic one.

An unusual container of perennial plants. These cowslips (*Primula veris*) and violas provide the perfect colourful and informal combination for this basket.

Wood is frequently used to construct boxes of various types, including large square Versailles tubs and rectangular window boxes. Containers can also come in the form of baskets. Ordinary willow baskets can be stood on the ground, hiding a lesser container within them, but more usually they are made of metal or plastic and are used as hanging containers.

Where to use containers

Containers can be used anywhere in the garden and are particularly useful for people who have no proper beds or borders. They can be placed on the ground, stood on plinths or walls, hung from poles or walls or stood on balconies and roof gardens.

Pots can be used singly as focal points placed at the end of paths or on the top of steps. A large,

Containers can be seasonal, such as this lovely spring bouquet of primroses and violets. Plants from these containers can be planted out in the garden after flowering.

Perennials can even be used in hanging baskets. Violas, cowslips, and feverfew feature here.

Containers need not be filled with flowering colour, as these foliage plants show. Grasses are particularly successful container choices.

A collection of pots can be used as a substitute for a border in a small garden. To change the design, all you need do is move the pots around.

stunning pot containing a plant with good architectural qualities will certainly draw the eye.

Used in pairs, pots make good punctuation points when placed on either side of gateways, archways or other entrances. A pair of terracotta pots containing standard box trees on either side of a front door can transform the entrance into something very stylish. Similarly, a pair of pots on either side of the bottom or top of a flight of stairs is very effective.

When arranged in groups, pots tend to look best if they are different sizes, especially if the plants at the back are taller than those at the front. In formal gardens, a series of containers with similar content can be placed at intervals down a path or around a pool.

Mobility
Pots can be moved around the garden, giving you the opportunity to change the scene throughout the seasons. Plants that are out of flower can be tucked away and brought out when the blooms break open. They can also be moved into areas of a border or bed that happen to be rather dull at the time. Large pots are very heavy once full of soil, so it is important to get help when moving them.

Container plants
A wide range of plants can be used in containers. In fact, virtually any plant is suitable, although those with long taproots tend to be unhappy unless the pot is really deep.

Some plants are used almost exclusively in containers. Trailing plants, for example, have been bred especially for hanging baskets and window boxes. Although annuals are the most popular for temporary baskets, which last for only one season, perennials can be useful for

more permanent settings. Many, such as agapanthus, are flowering, but some, such as hostas and ferns, are used as foliage plants to add substance to any grouping of pots.

Colour in a pot
Containers can be used to add gaiety to a scene, and these are usually bursting with bright colours. There is no reason, however, why the colours should not be more subdued and subtle. A container with a single colour can frequently be more effective than one with many colours, and the colours can be combined by grouping the pots.

Containers do not have to be complicated creations. Here, a couple of pelargoniums give plenty of foliage and flower interest.

Plants for containers

Agapanthus	Hosta
Ageratum	Impatiens
Alonsoa	Lobelia
Argyranthemum	Nemisia
Begonia	Pelargonium
Bellis	Petunia
Bidens ferulifolia	Phormium
Brachycome	Primula
iberidifolia	Senecio cinerea
Cordyline	Tagetes
australis	Tropaeolum
Diascia	Verbena x
Felicia amelloides	hybrida
Helichrysum	Viola x
petiolare	wittrockiana

Plants with a purpose

Many people come to gardening with the sole intention of keeping the space around the house tidy. Gradually they begin to realize that there can be more to it than that, and that great enjoyment can be had from creating an attractive space in which the plants play an important part.

Initial gardening attempts often tend to be lacking in unity, with donations from friends and neighbours and the occasional plant from a garden centre dotted around. Eventually, however, you realize that the best effect is created by thinking of the garden as a whole and planning it as a complete picture.

The backbone to this picture is the plants. At first, plants seem to be no more than a series of flower colours and shapes – but gradually, as you get deeper into gardening, you will become more aware of the different groups of plants and how they can be used most effectively in different circumstances. In this section we look at four of these groups. The differences are fairly obvious when you think about them, but they can be overlooked when you are planning a garden, particularly if colour has a dominant place in your mind. But, as you will discover, there is a lot more to plants than just colour.

This combination of foliage and flowering plants creates an interest that is far greater than if the two types were used separately.

Foliage plants

From a gardener's point of view, the foliage should have an equal importance to the flowers. After all, if you take away the leaves, the flowers would be lost – their colours would not have anywhere near the impact they do when surrounded by foliage.

Colour

Few people would disagree with the statement that leaves are green. But is it that simple? The first impression when looking at a garden is that most leaves certainly are green, but a closer look reveals an incredible range of greens, from pale to very dark green and often with touches of yellow or blue in them. Further variety is added by whether the leaves are shiny or dull. Dull leaves tend not to stand out, while shiny leaves add sparkle to the border, especially in shady places, where they shine out as they catch odd shafts of light.

Further examination of the borders will show that many leaves are not, in fact, green at all. A quick

This curious, little-grown annual, *Medicago echinus*, has a distinctive colour pattern that makes it perfect for borders.

survey will reveal quite a number of plants that have silver, grey, purple and yellow foliage. There are even small quantities of red-, black- and blue-leaved plants as well. This wide spectrum of leaf colour means that a great deal of variety can be created in a garden without even taking account of any flowers.

Variegation

Many plants have leaves that are more than one colour. The most common variegations are based on green and yellow – some yellows so pale as to be almost white, with others tending towards orange, and

all the variations between. Some plants have more than two colours. *Houttuynia cordata* 'Chameleon', for example, has foliage in green, brownish-red and yellow.

Variegated foliage is in itself very attractive, but can be too busy to the eye if overused and does not always make a good background for flower colour. However, it is wonderful for lightening a dark corner, where the yellows really stand out.

Other leaf qualities

The texture and shape of leaves are also important aspects to take into account when creating a picture.

Plants with variegated foliage

Acorus calamus 'Variegatus'
Aquilegia vulgaris 'Woodside'
Arum italicum 'Pictum'
Astrantia major 'Sunningdale Variegated'
Brunnera macrophylla 'Hadspen Cream'
Convallaria majalis 'Variegata'
Cortaderia selloana 'Gold Band'
Eryngium bourgatii
Euphorbia marginata (a)
Fragaria x ananassa 'Variegata'
Hakononechloa macra 'Aureola'
Hosta
Iris pallida 'Variegata'
Lamium maculatum
Miscanthus sinensis 'Zebrinus'
Myosotis scorpioides 'Maytime'
Osteospermum 'Jewel'
Phalaris arunindinacea 'Picta'
Phlox paniculata 'Harlequin'
Phlox paniculata 'Nora Leigh'
Phlox paniculata 'Pink Posie'
Phormium tenax 'Sundowner'
Pleioblastus auricomus
Pulmonaria saccharata
Silybum marianum
Sisyrinchium striatum 'Aunt May'
Symphytum x uplandicum 'Variegatum'
Tanacetum vulgare 'Silver Lace'

The texture, shape and colour of grasses well repay their use in the garden, especially when combined in this kind of way.

The play of light on plants is very important in a well-designed garden. Here, evening light rakes across *Crocosmia masoniorum* leaves.

Pulmonarias are grown as flowering plants for spring, but if they are cut back after flowering, the new foliage will remain fresh throughout the summer.

Prickly foliage may make a plant difficult to weed around, but it does provide a contrast to the surrounding leaves.

The texture can be velvety, rough or smooth. A velvety texture gives the plant interest, and the tiny hairs that give the feeling of velvet can add a greyish-white bloom to the leaves. Rough leaves may often be dull, whereas smooth leaves are frequently shiny and bright.

The shape is very important. Some plants have long, spiky leaves, while others can be almost round, with or without lobes and/or serrations, with lots of variations in between these two extremes. A mixture of shapes makes a border more interesting, especially when contrasting shapes are used. On the other hand, using plants with leaves of the same shape can make the border more calming and tranquil, though there is inevitably an inherent danger of also making it more boring.

Foliage as a background

While an eye-catching garden can be created entirely out of interesting foliage, it is more common to use a combination of foliage and flowers to create your composition. Most borders consist of a mixture of plants grown specifically for their foliage and other foliage plants that provide an especially effective backdrop for the flowers.

Green will act as the perfect background to most colours, but works particularly well with its complementary colour, red. Silver works well with softer colours, although a bright red or magenta will stand out beautifully against it. Purple is a difficult colour as a background, as it can become very leaden if used in excess, but it works well with contrasting orange and flame colours.

Foliage as foliage

Leaves are quite capable of being a feature on their own. There may not be such a wide variety of foliage colours as there are for flowers, but there are still enough to paint a picture solely made up of leaves, especially when taking shape and texture into account too.

One advantage of a purely foliage garden is that it has a much longer season than one devoted to flowers. In fact, if you take evergreen plants into account, the foliage garden is always in season. However, most plants flower at some point, so few gardens are devoted entirely to foliage, though some foliage purists cut off flower stems as they appear.

Foliage works particularly well in shady or woodland-type areas, and the addition of some variegated foliage here and there will add welcome touches of lightness.

A border devoted to silver foliage works well, but most silver-leaved plants grow only in sunny situations, so you will need to plan your borders accordingly.

Ferns are superb foliage plants to use in shady positions. They act as a brilliant foil for flowering plants.

Dramatic effects can often be created if interesting or bold shapes are used, as in these sword-like leaves.

Differently shaped plants

Some plants have such a dominant shape that they are always bound to catch the eye. A great fountain of pampas grass (*Cortaderia*) is a good example, or the jagged candelabra of the giant biennial Scotch thistle (*Onopordum*), which towers above the viewer. These spectacular plants are invaluable in the garden as focal points, since they catch the eye.

Architectural plants – those with usefully sculptural shapes – can be placed in a border to heighten its interest or in places such as at the end of a path or the end of the garden, often in splendid isolation. They can be planted in the ground or in pots. Either way, they act as living sculptures and provide features that immediately attract the eye.

Such plants work well in a formal garden, used singly as centrepieces or planted at intervals along either a path or border to give a sense of rhythm. Sometimes large plants are necessary to complete the scene. For example, the giant leaves of *Gunnera*

The ever-popular pampas grass, *Cortaderia*, is a particularly stately plant and is extremely eye-catching, whether grown by itself or as part of a border.

Salvia sclarea's upright nature makes it, quite literally, stand out in the crowd, creating a focal point in this border.

manicata look perfect beside a large pond, while not many garden sights can better a stand of *Stipa gigantea* set by itself where the evening sun can shine through its leaves.

A vast choice of shapes

Next time you visit a large garden, take a look at the wide variety of shapes there are among the plants. Some are tall and thin, others are flat and mat-like. In some the leaves

erupt like a fountain, while in others the foliage forms a tight clump, frequently in rounded hummocks, perhaps even a ball. All these different shapes can be used to great advantage to give variation within the bed or border.

Close-up shots of flowers on packets of seeds or on pot labels usually show the flower in detail but rarely the whole plant. You need to check the plant out, either in a book

The tall stems and rounded flower heads of this angelica create a distinctive, cloud-like image in the border that sets it apart.

or by looking at it in another garden, to see what shape it will have. The shape of the flowers, and their colour, can also add to a plant's architectural quality. *Liatris*, for example, erupts like fireworks, while *Limnanthes* forms a carpet.

Working with plant height

The general rule of thumb with regard to heights is perfectly sensible – plant the shorter plants at the front and the taller ones at the back.

Plants with useful sculptural shapes

Acanthus	Inula magnifica
spinosus	Ligularia
Alcea rosea	Macleaya
Angelica	cordata
archangelica	Miscanthus
Cortaderia	sinensis
selloana	Onopordum
Crambe cordifolia	Phormium tenax
Cynara	Rheum
cardunculus	Ricinus
Delphinium	Stipa gigantea
Gunnera	Telekia speciosa
manicata	Verbascum

This can, however, produce a very regimented picture, rather like a school choir, so try to vary this slightly by bringing some taller plants forwards. This will break the formality and also obscure some plants, so that they are revealed only as you walk along the length of the border, making it more interesting.

There are some plants, such as *Verbena bonariensis*, that, while tall, are also very sparse and wiry. Such plants can be planted towards the front of the border, where they will create a misty effect as you look through them to the plants behind.

Working with different shapes

Finding good ways to work with plant shapes is more complex than working with height. Learn by looking at other gardens and deciding what you think works well. Contrasting shapes certainly make a border more interesting. So, the sword-like leaves of an iris contrast well when planted in front of the giant leaves of a *Rheum* (ornamental rhubarb) or the filigree foliage of *Myrrhis* (sweet cicely). Likewise, frothy grasses or the sword-like spikes of an iris work well with the more substantially leaved hostas.

Here, sword-like, spiky leaves draw the eye up and away, and in doing so create a sudden burst of energy in the middle of the border.

Ground-cover plants

Very few gardeners have as much time to spend in their gardens as they would wish, and so anything that helps to save them some time in the garden is well worth considering. Ground cover is one such valuable aid: it cuts down the amount of weeding needed, and covers large areas with just one plant, so saving on planting.

What are ground-cover plants?
They are exactly what the name suggests: plants that cover the ground. Some are creeping plants that spread out to form a dense mat, others are a large planting of individual plants, each one merging into the next to provide a close mass. Most tend to be low-growing, though this is not essential, and any

dense-growing plant will suffice. Some gardeners consider any plants grown closely together as ground cover, but the term is usually reserved for those plants that have a proven record for dense growth.

Most ground-cover plants flower at some point, but they are mainly used as foliage plants, which ensures that they cover the ground for the maximum length of time. Many can simply be left until they die back naturally, but others, such as pulmonarias, are best sheared over at the end of flowering so that they acquire a set of fresh and more attractive leaves.

Purposes of ground cover
There are several reasons for using ground cover. The first and most obvious one is that a dense covering of plants inhibits the germination and growth of weeds from beneath them. In other words, it cuts down the amount of weeding that is required for the area they cover.

Another use is to cover large areas with attractive plants. This is particularly important in large gardens, where there are often areas that need planting but are not suitable for borders, such as under trees, where a carpet of plants can be very attractive.

A third use of ground cover is to deal with areas that are difficult to cultivate. Banks, for example, may be awkward to cope with, as are those barren strips of earth in the middle of some driveways, which are the perfect place for thymes or similar low-growing plants.

Limitations of ground cover
Ground cover is not all good news, however. There are some downsides, particularly if you have only a small garden, where space is a premium

A perfect bank of *Geranium macrorrhizum*, one of the most useful of ground cover plants for creating an effectively impenetrable layer.

Geranium macrorrhizum will grow in dry conditions in fairly dark shade, and yet it not only gives good leaf cover, but also provides attractive flowers.

Use plants such as *Pratia* to carpet and soften paving that is not walked on.

(though for larger gardens the advantages certainly outweigh the disadvantages).

The first is that a large spread of the same plant can be rather boring. This may not trouble you if you are not over-interested in plants as such but just want to keep your garden tidy. However, many gardeners feel that they would rather use their space for different plants, creating a more interesting scene.

The second disadvantage is that ground cover is not quite as efficient as it is often portrayed to be. Any perennial weeds left in the ground when it was prepared will certainly penetrate the cover, and any thinning of the cover will allow in light and aid the germination of weed seed. So it is essential to prepare the soil thoroughly in the first place, removing all traces of weeds, and then to make certain that the plants

are in the best of health and maintain their tight cover. Shearing them over from time to time helps to keep them dense.

The third problem is rubbish. So often ground-cover areas are left to themselves, and they have a habit of catching any pieces of paper or other bits of rubbish that blow past. You just need to remember to check the plants every so often and remove any rubbish that has accumulated.

Ground-cover plants

Acaena	Geranium
Alchemilla mollis	nodosum
Anemone x	Geranium x
hybrida	oxonianum
Bergenia	Gunnera
Brunnera	Hosta
macrophylla	Houtuynia
Convallaria	cordata
majalis	Lysimachia
Crambe cordifolia	nummularia
Epimedium	Maianthemum
Euphorbia	Persicaria affinis
amygdaloides	Petasites
robbiae	Pulmonaria
Geranium x	Rheum
cantabrigiense	Rodgersia
Geranium	Symphytum
endressii	Tiarella cordifolia
Geranium	Tolmiea menziesii
macrorrhizum	Vancouveria

Hostas always provide good ground cover, as long as the soil is not too dry. Use a mix of the different varieties to inject more visual interest.

Climbing plants

Most climbing plants are shrubby, but there are a number of herbaceous perennials and annuals that can be used to great effect as climbers in the garden. They have the advantage over shrubby climbers in that there is no complicated pruning regime: they are simply cut back or removed at the end of the season.

Climbing and scrambling

Most of the herbaceous and annual climbers are really scramblers rather than true climbers. Ivy, for example, will stick to any surface, and honeysuckle will twine its way up anything. In other words, they can scramble up through other plants, using them for support, rather than twining their way up a pole. Nasturtiums, for example, will not climb up a simple tripod or post but will happily scramble up through a bush, to a surprising height.

The few true climbers include the golden hop (*Humulus lupulus* 'Aureus'), which will climb up poles or even a thin string or wire. Sweet peas are another good example: they have tendrils and can cling to their support, but are often helped by being tied in at regular intervals.

Vertical planting

A three-dimensional garden is much more interesting than one on a single level: by adding height you break the monotony of a flat appearance. Height can be achieved by tall plants but further height can be obtained by using climbers held on a variety of poles, trellises or other supports.

Supports

A wide variety of supports can be used. Being mainly scramblers, most herbaceous and annual climbers are best grown through some form of twiggy framework. This could be pea sticks (branches of trees or shrubs such as hazel cut in winter) stuck in the ground. Alternatively, the climbers can be allowed to scramble up through a low-growing shrub, often providing colour after the shrub has finished flowering. Another option is a tripod of poles with string or netting wrapped round it to give the plant support.

For true climbers, such as hops or *Cobaea*, poles, strings, trellises or frameworks can be used. These can also be used by scrambling plants, as long as they are tied to the supports.

Sweet peas are probably the most widely grown of all annual climbers. They work in so many different types and styles of gardening.

Ipomoea lobata is a valuable annual climber and is one of the few that works well in colourful or exotic bedding schemes.

Lablab purpureus has become a very popular annual climber, partly because of its pea-like flowers and seed pods and partly due to its attractive purple foliage.

Marginal planting

While height can be used anywhere you like in the garden, one of the more favoured areas is around the margins. This is partly because this will form a backdrop to the rest of the garden and partly because it can be used to screen out neighbouring gardens or buildings. Trellising provides a good support for this kind of position.

Another way of using climbers around the margins is to use them on walls. Here they may cover an ugly wall or simply be used to break up its expanse. The most likely reason for keen gardeners, however, is that it is simply an available space on which yet another plant can be grown.

Different heights

With the exception of hops, the annual *Caiophera* and one or two others, herbaceous and annual climbers are not very vigorous and will not climb to great heights.

Those that can reach greater heights, however, can be used to climb over a frame to form an arbour or a pergola. Hops, for example, create a wonderfully dappled shade that is perfect for sitting under.

Less energetic climbers can also be used in conjunction with more vigorous shrubby climbers. For example, *Eccremocarpus* will grow to advantage through the bare base of clematis, which often shed their lower leaves.

Extending the season

Growing climbers through shrubs or other plants can add to the length of the flowering season. Most annual and perennial climbers flower from midsummer onwards, as the plants have to put on quite a large amount of growth before they bloom. Many shrubs flower in spring, after which they can be considered a foliage plant, but growing a late-flowering climber through them gives them another lease of life. Virtually all perennial and annual climbers can be used in this way.

Ipomoea tricolor has long been a popular favourite and is widely grown for its beautiful flowers.

The golden hop, *Humulus lupulus* 'Aureus', is a fast-growing perennial climber that will densely cover a pergola, arbour or framework.

Gardening techniques

Gardening is one of those imprecise sciences in which there are often several ways of achieving the same results – and equally enthusiastic proponents for each different method. For example, one of the most successful commercial propagators achieves incredible results simply by pushing cuttings straight into the compost, leaves and all, yet most other gardeners would throw up their hands in horror at this.

Having said that, there are many basic routines and techniques that are universally accepted as working well and which have been proved by constant use over many centuries. Many of these are included in this section. The best approach is to start by following the advice given here, but if you find that certain things work better for you when you use another method, then by all means stick with that. All our garden environments – soils, climates and plantings – are different, as is the temperament of each gardener, so it is not surprising that techniques will vary from garden to garden.

What follows are reliable, widely accepted routines recommended to achieve and maintain an attractive garden – in particular, one filled with annuals and perennials. However, since the techniques are basic ones that apply generally to all kinds of gardening, any beginner following them will get a thorough grounding that will be useful in any garden.

The excellent supports for these delphiniums will soon become invisible, hidden by the plants' foliage.

Soil preparation

Preparing the soil properly is one of the most important tasks that a gardener performs. No matter how well you design your garden, you will not get any decent results unless you have taken some trouble in preparation. This is particularly important where perennial plants are concerned, as these will remain in situ for many years without any chance of having their soil revitalized, except at surface level.

Ideal soils

Short of excavating the whole site and replacing it with perfect soil, you will have to manage with the soil that exists in your garden. However, it is possible, and usually desirable, to modify the soil to make it as near perfect as possible.

The perfect soil is a loamy one, which is open to allow free drainage of excess moisture but contains sufficient organic material to retain enough moisture for the plants. But even this ideal soil may need modifying in certain circumstances.

If you grow woodland plants, for example, then more organic material should be added to keep the soil moist, like the leaf mould that naturally forms under the trees. In addition to improving the condition of the soil, this organic material will also provide a great deal of nutrition for the plants. If, on the other hand, you grow Mediterranean-type plants, then they are likely to need sharper drainage, so more grit should be added to the soil.

Improving the soil

The best way to improve soil is to add well-rotted organic material as you dig it over. Make sure that you maintain the soil's levels of nutrition by top-dressing it with more material over the years.

Well-rotted farmyard manure is still one of the best soil conditioners.

Nowadays there is a really wide range of organic material readily available. Some of this will be available at your local garden centre, but the very best kind is homemade garden compost.

Farmyard manure is another excellent organic choice, but this needs to be well rotted before it can be put on the soil, and you may not always have the space – in a place where you don't mind strong smells lingering – to leave it to rot. Stables are a good source of manure, and it can often be had for free as long as you collect it yourself.

As much garden material as possible, such as these spent annuals, should be composted and returned to the soil.

Leaf mould can be made by collecting fallen leaves and allowing them to rot down. The leaves should be collected from your own garden or road, then either placed in a mesh enclosure or put in bags, punctured at intervals to allow air in. Do not go down to the woods and remove leaves from under the trees, as this will upset the natural balance. Bags of composted bark or other material mixed with farmyard manure are sold by garden centres and nurseries.

Avoid using peat, as this breaks down rapidly in the soil, has little nutritive value and is unsound environmentally, as the peat bogs are fast becoming depleted.

Heavy soils also benefit from having grit added to them. The best size is horticultural grit, which is about 4mm/⅛in in diameter.

Composting

Buy or make a compost bin and fill it with any material you cut from the garden: spent plant stems, leaves and flowers, grass cuttings, shredded hedge and shrub trimmings. Also add any non-cooked vegetable waste from the kitchen, such as peelings, pods and leaves.

Avoid adding thick layers of just one material, such as grass cuttings, which can go very slimy. It is better to add thinner layers of different materials in order to keep the compost well balanced, and to fork the heap over now and then. Adding more material is a constant process – continue until the box is full.

Ideally, you should have three boxes: one that you are adding to, one that is rotting down and almost ready to use, and one from which you are using the ready compost. Water the material if it is too dry, and keep each box covered. Leave until it has rotted down into a crumbly, sweet-smelling compost.

MAKING A NEW BED

1 Mark out the bed with a garden line or, as here, with canes. It is very important to remove all perennial weeds. Try to do this by hand if possible. If you do use weedkiller, always apply it according to the maker's instructions on the packet, and make sure you leave the bed until all the weeds have died.

2 Start digging a new bed by making a trench one spade's depth deep across one end. Place the excavated soil into a wheelbarrow and take it to the other end of the plot, where it will be used to fill in the final trench.

3 Now place a layer of well-rotted organic material – such as garden compost or farmyard manure – along the bottom of the trench, breaking it up and spreading it over the soil. Be generous and use as much material as possible.

4 Dig the next row, tipping the soil on top of the compost, filling in the first trench and creating a new one. Add compost to the bottom of this and repeat until the whole plot is dug, leaving the final trench empty.

5 Add a layer of compost to the final trench and then fill it in using the soil excavated from the first trench. The digging is now complete and if time allows, you can leave the bed over the winter so the weather will break the soil down.

6 If prepared in the autumn, by the spring the weather will have broken down the soil to a fine tilth (consistency). Remove any weeds that have reappeared and then rake over the bed, using the back of the rake to break up any larger lumps if necessary.

Clearing the weeds

It is vital to remove any perennial weeds from the planned borders or beds before you start any planting, as you will never be able to clear them once the plants are growing. With lighter soils, this can be done by digging the beds over and removing the weeds by hand. With heavier soils, it may be necessary to use herbicides. If this is done properly, it should be a one-off operation and there will be no need to reapply chemicals, so no damage will be done to the environment.

You can cover the area to be cleared with black plastic or an old carpet to stop weed growth, but this must be left in place for up to two years to be certain that the tougher

Organic materials

Garden compost
Farmyard manure
Leaf mould
Spent mushroom compost
Seaweed
Spent hops
Composted bark

weeds have died off. Unless the bed is out of sight, you may not want to have this unattractive covering on view for such a long time.

Digging the soil

Always aim to dig soil over several months before the bed is to be planted, adding in organic material as you go and removing any weeds. Leave it for three or four months and then remove any weeds that have returned or resprouted. Fork or rake the soil over, and then the bed should be ready for planting.

Acquiring plants

There are various different ways of obtaining plants to stock your garden. The most obvious one is to buy them from some source or another, although this can turn out to be an expensive option. If you are lucky, friends and family may give them to you. You could also grow some plants yourself – from seed, cuttings or divisions.

Plant quality

If you buy your plants, you must always try to obtain the very best. Poor-quality plants may be cheaper, but they will rarely develop in the way you hope they might and so can be a disappointment. The best plants are not necessarily the largest ones, as they often take a while to settle down, allowing more modest plants to overtake them. Those of a medium size are usually best.

The plant should be in character (in other words, growing in the way that nature intended, whether bushy, slender or hummock-forming), and not be drawn or stunted. The new growth should be strong and bushy. Below the soil, the roots should not be pot-bound (wound around and around the pot in a tight mass). This can be checked by simply removing the plant carefully from its pot and having a look.

An interesting garden has a large number of different plants, which can be acquired from a variety of sources.

Another very important thing to check for when obtaining plants is whether the plant is diseased or harbouring any pests. If it looks sick or is covered in greenfly (aphids), you should reject it out of hand. Finally, don't choose a plant in full flower unless you want to be certain of the flower colour; it is better to choose one that is still in bud.

Buying plants

A large number of different outlets sell plants these days, from nurseries and garden centres to your local grocery store or neighbour's yard sale. There are no fixed rules about which is best but there are some useful points to bear in mind.

Many specialist nurseries are extremely good places to stock up, as the owners will grow their own plants, which are frequently of high quality. As well as being knowledgeable, the owners are often sole operators with small overheads, so the plants may be cheaper than those in larger garden centres.

Plants in your local grocery store are often left over from other sales points and may be pot-bound. They are less likely to be looked after properly and may be unlabelled or labelled incorrectly (as can be the case with plants sold at local fairs).

Plants as gifts

This is one of the best ways of obtaining plants. Not only are they free, but, if you have admired a plant, and a cutting is then taken for you or the plant divided, you know exactly what you are getting. It is wise to make a note of a plant's name straightaway, especially if you have been given several different cuttings or divisions.

If you think that a dug-up plant may be infected with root pests, wash off all the soil and pot it up in fresh compost (soil mix). Put any cuttings you are offered straight into a plastic bag and seal it. Pot them up as soon as possible.

Plants can be obtained as "plugs", which contain only a small amount of compost and need transplanting as soon as possible.

Bigger plants can be obtained in modules or in pots. These also need to be potted on to larger containers or planted out.

Do not buy pot-bound plants (left). The roots should be evenly spread through the compost (soil mix) and not tightly wound (right).

Whole trays of modules can be purchased from garden centres, saving the trouble of raising your own plants.

It is quite easy (and cheaper) to obtain plants by increasing your own stock. Here, cuttings are being taken from home-grown dahlias.

Growing your own

In many ways, growing your own plants is the most satisfying way of stocking your garden, as you have the satisfaction of feeling that you have created something from nothing. Seed is still fairly cheap and is widely available in a wonderful range of perennials and annuals. You do not need much equipment to germinate them and grow them on; most can be grown in open soil.

Seeds can be bought from seed companies, garden centres and some general-purpose stores. There are also specialist societies that run seed exchanges, where you can get unusual seeds not carried by other sources. Certain botanical gardens also offer seed that can be difficult to obtain elsewhere, so giving you the chance to grow some unusual and unique plants. You can, of course, collect your own seed and propagate from this. This is not difficult and can be very rewarding, as you are actively involved with every stage of the plant's life.

There are other methods of propagating plants – dividing and taking cutting from your own plants, for example. This does mean that you won't be introducing new plants to your garden, but it is the perfect way of increasing your stock of favourite plants and ideal if you need large numbers of the same plants for creating drifts of colour.

Choosing plants for a low-maintenance garden

The ideal low-maintenance garden uses hard surfaces rather than grass, to reduce or eliminate the need for mowing. If you take this route, choose plants that you think will look good in this kind of situation – you might want more colourful or luxuriant plants to make up for the lack of green lawn, for example. Remember that using ground cover reduces the need for weeding.

Concentrate on plants that are self-supporting, so that you do not need to do any staking. Also, try to use plants that do not need deadheading and only require cutting back once a year. Foliage plants such as hostas are ideal in these kinds of situations. Long-flowering annuals are also a boon, as they will perform for the whole summer with only the occasional bit of attention – just some deadheading and the cutting back of straggling stems.

Containers and hanging baskets need daily watering and deadheading to look at their best, so you may want to stick to plants in beds, which need far less watering. Reduce the need for watering further by using plenty of mulches, which help to prevent water evaporation from the soil and cut down on weeding.

Low-maintenance plants

Acaena
Alchemilla mollis
Antirrhinum
Bergenia
Epimedium
Geranium macrorrhizum
Hosta
Impatiens
Pelargonium
Penstemon
Persicaria affinis
Pulmonaria
Tagetes
Vancouveria

Border plants can be lifted and divided in spring to provide more plants. *Sisyrinchium striatum* (seen here) is easy to divide.

Planting

Take your time when planting new acquisitions. The more attention they are given, the better they will establish themselves and the better they will continue growing. After all, there is no point in buying or raising plants from seed only to kill them later on. The techniques are simple and mainly common sense, but they are worth emphasizing.

Vital preliminaries

The importance of good soil preparation has already been explained, but it is worth restating that soil must be properly prepared prior to any planting. Even if you are just filling a gap in a bed or border, it is still worth digging over the spot, removing any weeds and adding well-rotted garden compost to rejuvenate it. An hour or so before planting, give the plants, still in their pots, a thorough watering.

If the weather is wet or the soil very wet, avoid planting until it has dried out or you will compact the soil. If it is necessary to get on with the planting, use a plank of wood to walk on to spread your weight.

This attractive border, featuring yellow and gold perennials, has benefited greatly from thorough soil preparation before any planting was done.

Finding the right place

There are two considerations to make when deciding where to plant: one visual and the other physical. Whether you are planting up a whole border or just filling a small gap, it is important to try to visualize what the small plant you have in your hand will look like when it is fully grown.

You will have to consider how big your plant will eventually become and how it will relate to its neighbours. Is it far enough away from them to avoid swamping them? Is it short enough not to hide the plants behind it or tall enough to be seen over the plants in front? Is it the right colour and shape for this spot? All these things must be considered before you start to plant. It is especially important to get it right the first time with perennials, if you can, as you may not want to move them for several years.

Plenty of space has been left around the various plants in this gravel bed. This allows them to develop healthily without swamping each other.

Limnanthes douglasii is an excellent annual for filling in temporary gaps in a perennial border.

PLANTING A BED

1 If the bed was dug in the autumn, winter weather should have broken down the soil. In spring, rake over the soil and remove weeds. Sprinkle bonemeal over the top of the soil to give plants a good start (wear rubber or latex gloves when handling bonemeal preparations).

2 Draw a grid on a planting plan and then mark out a scaled-up version on the bed, using sand or compost. Alternatively, you can use string stretched between canes to mark out the planting plan.

3 Using your planting plan and grid as a guide, lay out the plants, still in their pots, on the ground. Now stand back, and try to envisage the border as it will be, and make any necessary adjustments.

4 Dig a hole with a trowel or spade and, with the plant still in its pot, check that the depth and width is right. Adjust if necessary.

5 Remove the plant from the pot and place in the planting hole. Fill in the hole with soil and then firm the plant in.

6 When the bed is completely planted, water in all the plants. They should be kept watered until they have become established.

Temporary fillings

Perennial plants will usually take a while, sometimes up to several years, to fill out their allotted space properly. Rather than have bare earth showing while you are waiting, it is an excellent idea to fill the space with annuals. Temporary gaps in a border can also be filled with annuals. It's not a good idea to choose young annuals for this job, as they will take time to develop. Instead, keep back a few annuals growing in pots, so that they can be used as mature plants, ready to fill any space immediately.

7 Cover the soil between the plants with a layer of mulch, such as composted bark, to keep weeds down and preserve moisture.

8 If you are concerned that you will not remember what the plants are, mark each one with a plastic label. If you always put these labels in the same place – say, to the right of the plant – you can hide them from view and yet still locate them if necessary at any time.

Staking

Supporting plants is one of those tasks that many of us never seem to get around to until it is too late and the plants have collapsed in a messy heap. At this stage, trying to give them some form of support always spells disaster, as the plants look as though they have been forced into a straitjacket. The answer is to get the stakes into place before they are actually needed.

Why stake?

Some plants are used to growing in isolation and have strong stems that need no support, while others are more used to growing closely with other plants, giving each other mutual support. In the garden, an artificial situation is created and plants are often grown in discrete clumps, often with bare earth between them, which leaves them vulnerable to winds.

Plants with especially large or double flower heads are good candidates for staking. The heavy heads often make the plant droop over, particularly after rain, when the sheer number of petals means that the flower holds a lot of rainwater.

One way to avoid staking is to choose short cultivars such as this dahlia, 'Bishop of Llandaff', which needs no support.

To keep your garden looking at its best, always support the heavier and taller plants. Even low-growers may flop and need support, especially those next to a path or lawn.

Alternatives to staking

One way to keep everything upright without stakes is to emulate nature and place your plants close together, so that they support one another. This does, however, inevitably affect the appearance of the border, and so is perhaps best suited to informal and cottage-style gardens. Another natural way of offering support is to

Proprietary stakes can be used to form a linked hoop around and through the plant. They are available in different heights.

allow sprawling plants, such as geraniums, to clamber up through the lower branches of shrubs.

Timing

The most important thing about staking is not to wait until the plant is fully grown but to apply supports when the plant is about a third to half grown. In this way the stems of the plant will grow up through the support, and a few will emerge outside the framework, therefore hiding it in a very natural way. The hidden stakes will then make a good job of supporting the plant.

Hoops with cross wires make excellent supports but are rather inflexible as their width cannot be adjusted.

A hoop on a single pole can have its height adjusted as an individual plant grows, so giving it continual support.

A tall, single-stemmed plant can be supported with a cane (stake). Place it at the back of the plant, where it cannot be seen.

A network of pea sticks (branches or twigs from a shrub) can be erected over or around a plant clump to support plants as they grow.

Individual stems

Some plants, such as foxgloves, have one main flowering stem, and if these are weak or in a particularly exposed position, then they may need support. In this type of situation, a single cane (stake) – preferably painted green – can be inserted into the soil immediately behind the plant, so that it is hidden from view as much as possible. Tie the plant stem to the cane with soft string. Another alternative here is to use the widely available proprietary supports that feature an upright rod and a holding ring.

A sheet of stock fencing held horizontally on posts will give secure support to a plant covering a large area.

STAKING LILIES

1 First position the metal stake, about 15cm (6in) away from the emerging stem. Now release one side of the ring and carefully trap the lily stem within.

Home-made supports

Pea sticks (usually branches of shrubs such as hazel, cut in the winter) make good supports. Push them into the ground around the clump, then bend the tops over and intertwine them to form a horizontal mesh just above the growing plant. Tie the twigs together for extra support. If twigs are not available, stick in a number of canes around the plant and weave a web of strings between them, again forming a mesh through which the plant will grow.

For a large clump of plants, place several stout sticks around and in the clump, and tie a piece of large-mesh wire netting to them so that it is supported horizontally just above the growing plant. The stems will then pass through this as they grow.

Proprietary supports

All kinds of ready-made supports are currently available, from a range of outlets. Some of these are hoops

2 Clip the second end of the ring into the hole that is provided on the metal support. The lily now has freedom to move but is not able to stray too far.

supported horizontally above the plant, while others consist of individual stakes linked together around and across the plant. Although these are relatively expensive, they do a good job, are easily assembled and taken down, and will last for a very long time.

Staking should give plants the support they need, but must be well hidden so that the plants' beauty is not spoiled.

Watering and feeding

Plants, like animals, will not grow without water and food. To a certain extent, these are naturally provided for by way of rainfall and nutrients available from the atmosphere and from decaying vegetation. The competition for water and nutrients in a crowded border, however, frequently means that there is not enough natural supply in a full garden. These supplies can also partially or completely fail. This is why it is important keep a garden well watered and fed.

A well-watered and fed border will keep the plants looking fresh and lasting longer.

A good soaking

The principal thing about watering is that you should always make certain that adequate water is applied. Watering so that only the surface of the soil is damp will make the plant's roots grow towards the surface rather than deep down, which leaves the plant vulnerable during hot periods or times when you do not water. As a rule of thumb, try to give the equivalent of 2.5cm/1in of rain each time, which should ensure that the ground around the plant or the compost in the container is soaked.

Methods of watering

Watering cans are easy and versatile to use, and enable you to put the water exactly where you want it.

However, they do make the job quite arduous if you have a lot to do. Special pump-action watering cans can be used to water containers that are above head height, such as hanging baskets.

You can fill your watering cans from water butts placed under any drainpipes from roofs to collect rainwater. This means that not only are you "recycling" rainwater in the same way that nature would do, but also that you are watering your garden with water that is not full of chemicals and is also, for those on water meters, free.

For larger areas, garden hoses are useful. These can be connected to sprinklers, which deliver water in droplet form, like rain. To give you a rough idea of how long it takes to deliver the necessary 2.5cm/1in, place a jam jar or similar container somewhere under the sprinkler. Hand-held sprays can also be attached to hoses, but again you must be sure to apply enough water before moving on to the next plant.

Another way is to use a dribble system, whereby a special hose with small holes in it is laid throughout the border, so that water slowly

Plants can be watered individually by using a lance spray attached to a hose. This is time-consuming but worth the effort.

A large area can be covered with a sprinkler. Place jam jars or other containers around the area to judge the amount of water delivered.

A dribble hose (a hose with holes in it) can be hidden among plants in a border to allow gentle, controlled watering.

Mulching will help to preserve the moisture in a border by cutting down the amount of water that evaporates.

It is possible to feed as you water, using special attachments that add a controlled amount of fertilizer to the water.

Granular or pelleted fertilizer can be scattered around the plant, ensuring that it is only used where it is needed.

dribbles out over a long period of time. These pipes can be buried below the mulch, thus reducing wastage through evaporation.

Watering with hoses or sprinklers may be subject to local water authority controls, especially during drought conditions, when you will need them most. There may also be regulations regarding connections to the water mains. Check that you are not infringing any regulations.

Preserving moisture

In addition to watering, it is important to preserve as much of the moisture in the soil as you can for plant use. The best way to do this is to cover the soil with a mulch, such as leaf mould, grass cuttings or composted or chipped bark. A layer of about 10cm/4in is ideal. Apply the mulch either after rain or after watering the bed thoroughly.

Feeding

In the garden, we tend to clear the beds of all dying and dead vegetation, so there is little chance of it rotting down where it lies and returning to the soil as nutrients, as would happen in the wild. However, the prudent gardener does not throw away all these leftovers but composts them and then returns them to the soil, which considerably increases the nutritional value of the soil.

Preparing the soil thoroughly with garden compost will pay great dividends, but the added nutrients will not last forever. In the case of annuals, the soil can be prepared afresh each year, but for perennials, which are left in situ for several years, it is impossible to do this. It is, however, possible to top-dress the soil each autumn or spring by covering the soil with a mulch of well-rotted garden compost, farmyard manure or composted bark. This can be worked into the top

layer of the soil with a fork, while being careful not to disturb the plants' roots. Alternatively, it can be left on the top as a mulch, which the worms will gradually take down below the surface. The nutrients it contains will in any event be washed down towards the roots by the rain.

If a mulch is not available, a balanced fertilizer can be used instead to add nutrients, spread at the manufacturer's recommended levels, but this is second-best to organic material.

Collecting your own water

Place a water butt underneath the gutter of a greenhouse, shed or garage to catch the water as it runs off the roof. Rainwater is slightly acidic and so is ideal for watering acid-loving plants, especially if you live in a hard-water area. It will also save water and money spent on metered water.

You can easily collect sufficient water in a water butt to keep a collection of acid-loving plants perfectly happy right through the summer. If you are more ambitious, you can now obtain kits that link water butts together, so creating a really effective water storage system for your garden.

The butt should be easy to use, so make sure there is room to get a water can under the tap. Keep the butt covered at all times so that the water remains sweet and clean.

You can also recycle water that has been used for washing or bathing in the house. Known as "grey-water", it is suitable for applying to established plants in borders and on lawns, but is best used immediately and not stored.

Weeding

This is the aspect of gardening that the majority of people dislike the most. However, this is usually because they leave it much too late and by the time they do make the time for it, the beds are infested with weeds and it becomes an uphill battle to clear them. When weeding is done on a regular basis, it can be very quick and even pleasurable, and the resulting weed-free beds are always a joy to see.

Timing

As a general rule, the best time to weed is as soon as you see one. If you keep on top of the weeds, weeding rarely becomes a problem and certainly never a chore.

Ideally, you should go over all the beds during the winter or early spring to clear out any weeds. Once cleared of weeds, they should be mulched. If these two processes are done at the beginning of the growing season, then there is a very good chance that you will have little to do later on except pull out the odd rogue that appears. If, however, you wait until the weather warms up before tackling the weeds, you will find that they are ahead of you.

Closely packed planting in a garden border acts as a kind of natural ground cover, usefully suppressing the growth of any weed seedlings.

The safest way of controlling weeds in a border is to remove them by hand, rather than with chemicals.

Weed killers

Using chemicals in a planted border is not a good idea. They can be used to make an initial clearance, but once the plants are in place it can be a disastrous procedure. However careful you are, there is bound to be some drift, with odd drops falling on actual plants. Chemicals can also translocate from roots to roots. If a border is prepared properly in the first place and then weeded regularly by hand, there should be no need to use chemicals anyway.

Hand-weeding

The best way to tackle weeds in a border is to hand-weed. If the soil is loose or there is a good depth of mulch on it, this may simply mean pulling the weed gently out. If, however, there is a possibility of the weed breaking off and leaving its roots in the soil, use a hand fork or trowel to loosen the soil first.

In the late winter, as the plants are just appearing through the soil, it is a good idea to fork the soil over lightly, working in well-rotted organic material as you go. As you do this, you can easily pull out any weeds that are present.

If a plant becomes infested with a persistent perennial weed, such as couch grass, then it is best to dig the whole plant out, wash the soil off the roots, remove the weed and replant the plant. If you try to remove the couch grass while the plant is still in the ground, then the pieces of weed that grow through it will only regenerate and you will have to start again.

Hoeing

Some gardeners like to use a hoe to weed their beds, but this can be as dangerous as chemicals. So often, fragile new shoots or even whole plants get hoed off a fraction of a second before you realize that they are not a weed, leading to many lost plants and a considerable amount of bad temper. The other problem is that, although hoeing can be effective for annual weeds, it is no

A composted bark mulch will suppress weed growth, but clean the ground well beforehand.

good just cutting off the top of perennial weeds – you need to get the roots out as well.

Mulching

One of the greatest aids to weeding is mulching, since it prevents the weeds from forming in the first place. A layer of some material that will keep the light from the soil will inhibit the germination of weed seeds, so keeping the border free of weeds. If, however, there are already perennial weeds in the border, then the mulch will not help. This is because the weeds will simply grow through the material in the same way as the plants.

Organic mulches, such as leaf mould and composted or chipped bark, are best, as they will eventually rot down and improve the soil. Most will also look more sympathetic in the borders, creating a good background against which to see the plants, though this is not the case with straw or grass cuttings.

Black plastic mulches are efficient but ugly. Some gardeners try to avoid the plastic showing by covering it with a shallow layer of earth or another mulch, such as bark, but this inevitably washes off in places or is revealed by birds pecking among the covering layer, and the ugly plastic makes a reappearance.

Mulches

Cardboard: effective but ugly
Chipped/composted bark: very good
Farmyard manure: good if weed-free
Garden compost: good
Geotextiles and black plastic: good but very ugly
Grass cuttings: good but ugly
Gravel: good in certain areas
Leaf mould: very good
Newspaper: good but very ugly
Peat: poor
Sawdust: good but ugly
Shredded prunings: very good
Spent hops: good
Spent mushroom compost: good
Straw: good but ugly
Woodchips: good but some people find them ugly

EFFECTIVE WEEDING

1 Where plants are growing close together, the best way of removing weeds is to either pull them out by hand or dig them out using a hand fork. Perennial weeds must be dug out whole and not simply chopped off, or they will soon return.

2 Where there is more room, hoes can be used in a border, but take care not to damage your precious plants in the process. In hot weather, hoed-up weeds can be left to shrivel, but it looks much less messy if they are all removed to the compost heap.

3 After weeding, rake through the border with a fork, or if the plants are far enough apart, with a rake. This will tidy up the bed and level off the surface, removing any footprints and any weed remnants.

4 It is a good idea to apply or renew a mulch after weeding. As well as helping to prevent weeds from reappearing, this will also preserve moisture. Composted or chipped bark will set the plants off well.

Routine plant maintenance

One of the easiest ways of making a garden unattractive is to leave old flower heads and dying stalks on the plants. Trimming them off not only makes the garden look tidier and more appealing but also allows the remaining flowers to shine out and be seen, as well as encouraging new blooms. The three main techniques that will keep your plants both beautiful and healthy are pinching out, deadheading and cutting back.

Getting into the routine

The difference between a garden that is regularly attended and one that is only occasionally looked after is quite amazing, especially towards the end of summer or in the autumn. The dead or dying material not only looks untidy but also obscures those plants that are still fresh. At the start of the season, some judicious pinching out will benefit some annuals from the very beginning.

As with weeding, if you leave deadheading and cutting back for too long, they can become onerous tasks. If you do a little each week, then they become much easier as well as benefiting the appearance of the garden. This applies not only to beds and borders but also to hanging baskets and containers.

A second flush of delphinium flowers can often be obtained by removing the initial flower spikes as they fade.

Pinching out

If left to their own devices, many plants will grow only one main stem. In a bedding scheme, for example, this would result in a forest of tall spindly spikes with large gaps in between them rather than a desirable carpet of flowers and foliage. To avoid this effect, pinch out the growing tip of each main spike. This will cause the stem to produce side shoots. These will make the plants much more bushy, and further pinching out will increase the effect.

Deadheading

Once a flower starts to fade, you should cut it off. The actual point of the cut varies depending on the plant. If the flower is the only one on the stem, then the whole stem should be cut back to its base. If it is a multi-flowered stem, then the cut should be where the individual flower's stem joins the other stems. If it is a flower spike, then the whole spike should be removed. Try not to leave odd bits of stem sticking up, which looks untidy.

If the foliage is still attractive and the stem is covered with leaves, remove the flower head at some point towards the top of the stem, making the cut close to or behind a leaf so that it does not show. If this is done with, for example, spikes of lupins or delphiniums, you are likely to encourage side shoots, which will produce new spikes of flowers.

Some plants, particularly those with smaller blooms, have masses of flowers, making it almost impossible to deadhead the flowers singly. Geraniums are a good example of this, and the finished flowers are best dealt with as a whole. This means waiting until the majority of the flowers are finished, then cutting over the whole plant or cutting it down completely.

Advantages of deadheading

The improved appearance of plants after deadheading has already been stressed, but there is another benefit to this task too.

If you remove a dying flower, then instead of putting an extraordinary amount of its energy into producing a seed-head, the plant will divert its energy into producing more flowers. So the more you deadhead, the more flowers you are likely to get and the longer the plant will go on flowering.

Removing fading flowers and seed pods from annuals will preserve energy and help to keep them flowering for longer.

Pinching out the main stems from certain annuals and perennials will help them to bush out and develop into a fuller plant.

Pinching out the subsidiary shoots of plants such as these dahlias concentrates the growth in the main blooms.

DEADHEADING

1 Using scissors, a sharp knife or secateurs (pruners), snip off the flowers neatly and cleanly where they join the stem. Sometimes the whole head of flowers needs to be removed – cut these back to the first set of leaves. Dead flower heads and other clippings can be added to the compost heap.

2 Regular – and carefully executed – deadheading produces a considerably cleaner and healthier looking arrangement. Dead flowers ruin the best of plants, as well as using up vital energy in seed production. It takes only a short time and the effort is always worthwhile.

Cutting back

Once early-flowering plants are cut down to the ground, they will re-shoot. In most cases, this means that they will produce a fresh set of leaves, giving the plant a second life as a foliage plant for the rest of the season. Pulmonaria, for example, finish flowering in spring and, if left to their own devices, the leaves will soon become rather tatty and tired-looking. If, however, they are sheared over immediately after flowering, they produce new foliage that remains fresh-looking throughout the rest of the summer. A similar thing happens with *Alchemilla mollis* and many other plants. Some cut-back plants will also have a second flowering.

Once plants are dead or obviously dying, they should be cut back right down to the ground. If plants are cut back so that stumps are left, it becomes difficult to cut next year's stems close to the ground, and so with each year that passes, the plant becomes increasingly surrounded by more, and higher, stumps.

On some plants, it is only the taller flowering stems that wilt, while the base of the plant remains green. In such cases, cut off the wilting stems only, as low as possible.

Sometimes, as mentioned above, a plant may still be green but will look rather bedraggled. Here the benefit of being cut down is that it will grow afresh. Such plants should be cut close to the ground, removing all the old growth but leaving any new foliage that might already be appearing among the old stems. In this scenario, cutting back is mainly considered worth the effort for the new growth that appears, as this rejuvenates the plant. Sometimes, however, such new growth is required for propagation purposes. For example, there is not much suitable cutting growth when violas are in full flower or once they have finished flowering, but if they are cut to the ground the new shoots are just perfect for such a purpose.

CUTTING BACK GREEN PLANTS

1 Some herbaceous plants remain green throughout winter. Cut back to sound growth, removing dead and leggy material.

2 Here, the old stems have been cut off so that they are level with the emerging growth, so as not to damage it.

Autumn and winter tasks

Many non-gardeners think of the cooler months as the dead season, when little is happening. In fact, there is plenty to do: lifting certain plants, removing any remaining dead material, forking over beds to weed them and open the soil, and then top-dressing them. Your garden machinery should also be thoroughly checked over and oiled. Finally, there is the excitement of sitting down with seed catalogues and planning how your garden will look in the coming seasons.

Borders and beds

One thing to make sure you get done before the frosts set in is to lift more vulnerable plants. Tender plants such as pelargoniums should be potted up and overwintered in a greenhouse (or take cuttings if you don't have much storage space). Tender bulbs such as gladioli should be lifted if you live in a cold area, especially if your soil is heavy. Dry them, then store them somewhere frost-free and check every few weeks.

Another major job is to remove all the dead stems and foliage from the previous year. Some gardeners like to leave these as long as possible to provide the birds with a source of food in the form of seeds and any

Winter is a good time for catching up on tool and machinery maintenance. It will save a lot of time when you are busy in spring.

insects that hide in the dead foliage. Others leave it because it gives structure and something to look at during the winter months.

Other gardeners are eager to clear the ground as soon as possible. In addition to giving you a much tidier-looking garden, the main benefit of this is that you avoid leaving the clearing up to the last minute in early spring, when there are suddenly lots of other jobs to do. If work is then delayed due to bad weather, it can have a knock-on effect for the rest of the year.

You can have the best of both worlds if you cut the dead material and then hang it up so that the birds can still get at it. All the material removed from the beds should eventually be composted so that its

goodness can be returned to the soil. Hardened stems are best shredded first, if possible.

Once the borders have been cleared, lightly fork them over to open up the soil and to remove all weeds, before top-dressing them with well-rotted organic material up to 10cm/4in thick. The beds are now well prepared for the next season. Any new planting should be done in either the early autumn or spring.

Avoid working on the beds if the soil is too wet. If it becomes a necessity, then use a wooden plank to stand on, as this will spread your weight and limit damage to the soil.

Winter plant care

Remember that not all plants die back in winter and that there are a surprising number that still produce flowers and foliage. There is generally not much to do to these except enjoy them.

One thing that is generally not required is watering. If, however, you have containers that are in the lee of the house or a wall, so that they get little rain, they should be watered occasionally if the soil gets dry. This should be sparingly done so that the soil is left just moist and not wringing wet.

Here is a decorative way of giving slightly tender plants winter protection. Remove the container during warmer, damp weather.

Tender plants such as these pelargoniums need protection in a frost-free glass house during the winter months.

Winter-flowering perennials

Anemone nemorosa
Eranthis hyemalis
Euphorbia rigida
Helleborus:
   H. niger
   H. orientalis
   H. purpurascens
Iris unguicularis
Primula vulgaris
Pulmonaria rubra
Viola odorata

Garden machinery

Once autumn draws in and winter begins, the lawnmowers, strimmers and hedge cutters tend to be put away and forgotten about until they are next needed. This is, however, the ideal time to have them checked over properly and maintained, ready to use next season. Even if you are not doing this straight away, all your machines should be thoroughly cleaned and oiled.

Catalogue joys

One of the most enjoyable aspects of gardening is the planning. The weather may be unsuitable for gardening itself, but there is nothing more pleasurable than sitting down with a pile of catalogues, dreaming of what you could do if only your garden was twenty times larger.

On a more practical note, this is the time to look seriously at the catalogues to choose the seeds and plants you will be using next year in your hanging baskets and borders. The perennial plants may be constant factors, but you have much greater freedom with annuals, and if you are bold enough you can try something completely different. You might be seduced by the novelties in the catalogue or you might decide to change the colour scheme from, say, reds and yellows to blues and yellows, or even to all white.

LIFTING AND REPLANTING DAHLIAS

1 The time to lift the dahlias for winter storage is just as the first frosts blacken the foliage or when it naturally begins to die back. Remove the foliage and cut back the stems, leaving about 20cm (8in) of each one attached to the tuber.

2 Fork gently around the plant, leaving a radius of 25–40cm (10–16in) from the main stem, depending on the amount of growth it has made. Gently lift the tubers. Now carefully remove the soil from around the tubers. Heavy soils may need to be washed off with water from a hose or tap.

3 Place the plant upside down in a box so that any moisture can drain from the hollow stems. Store in a dry, frost-free place and remove the soil from the tubers once it has dried off. Dust any damaged tubers with a fungicide such as yellow or green sulphate of ammonia and then place in boxes of barely moist peat. Overwinter in a dry, well-ventilated, cool, frost-free place.

4 When green shoots emerge in spring, water sparingly to keep the compost moist. In late spring or early summer, after all risk of frost has passed, choose a sunny, sheltered spot and prepare a deep planting hole. Add a generous quantity of well-rotted manure or a long-term granular feed, and mix well into the soil at the bottom of the hole.

5 Carefully lower the dahlia into the prepared hole. Add more soil or compost around the plant as necessary to bring up to soil level. The hole should be bigger than the dahlia so that there is room to spread out the tubers. Adjust the hole depth if necessary so that the soil level is the same as the previous year (this level can be seen on the plant).

6 Gently firm the soil surrounding the plant, making sure as you do so that there are no gaps or air-pockets – either around the plant or between the tubers. Firm the soil down first with your hands, gently and carefully, and then more decisively with your foot. Water the plant and the area around it and then add a layer of mulch.

Sowing seeds in pots

There is something immensely satisfying about putting a seed, which is often no larger than a speck of dust, in the ground, knowing that it will eventually grow into a gorgeous plant. This is the basic miracle of nature, and yet although you may plant hundreds of seeds each year, every tiny seedling still seems just as wonderful as the last.

Getting the quantity right

One of the main mistakes made by beginners is to sow too much seed. Unless you are creating a large bedding scheme, you rarely need more than a dozen plants and often,

in the case of perennials, only three or five (odd numbers always look better than even ones in the garden).

Of course, you should grow a few more than you need in case some die, and you may want extras for giving away. If you grow many more than you need, however, you will waste a lot of time pricking the plants out as well as the expense of extra pots and potting compost (soil mix), most of which will end up on the compost heap. For most purposes, you need sow no more than what a 9cm (3½in) pot will contain, and very rarely indeed will you need a half tray, let alone a whole tray.

Sowing your own seed gives you plenty of plants with which you can plan magnificent container or border displays.

SOWING IN POTS

1 Fill the pot to the rim with compost (soil mix) and then gently firm it down. (Don't ram it down, or it will compact.)

2 Sow the seeds thinly across the surface. In the case of large seeds, such as sunflowers, each seed can be placed individually so that they are equidistantly spaced.

3 Cover the seeds, preferably with a layer of horticultural grit, but alternatively with a thin layer of fine compost if grit isn't available. At this stage, remember to label the pot, as one pot of seeds looks very much like another, and you will soon forget which is which.

4 Water the pot either from below, by standing it in a tray of water until the surface of the compost changes colour, or from above, by using a fine-rosed watering can. Place the pot in a propagator or in a shady place in a greenhouse.

A good start

Apart from ending up with too many plants, there are other good reasons for sowing a few seeds at a time in small pots and then pricking out to other pots or trays – and avoiding the temptation to simply sow in trays and then weed the seedlings out. Starting a few seeds at a time gives them the best conditions at the fragile start of their life. You do not want hundreds of germinating seeds vying for goodness from the growing medium, nor do you want intertwined roots. A few good seedlings is preferable to lots of sickly ones, so it is best to transfer to other pots or trays when selecting your strongest seedlings. Also, if space is at a premium, large trays can be a problem.

Composts

For sowing, use a proprietary seed compost (growing medium). This has only a limited amount of fertilizer in it because, at this stage, most of the nutrients will come from the seeds themselves. Once you prick the seedlings out, they will need extra food, and so a potting compost should be used.

There are arguments for and against using either a soil-based compost or a soilless compost as a growing medium, but in the end it comes down to personal preference and what is available locally.

Pricking out

When your seedlings do start to grow, they should be pricked out as soon as their first true leaves make an appearance (this is the second pair of leaves; the first pair are the seed leaves). To prick out your seedlings, place each one very carefully in its own individual pot. Bedding plants, which are often needed in much larger numbers than other plants, are often pricked into trays or cellular trays. The tray is filled with compost and a hole is made for each seedling. Remember that you should never leave plants in trays for too long as they are shallow and the roots will soon become terribly intertwined.

Hardening off

This is a vital part of the process. It is important that you not take plants directly from the greenhouse or cold frame and put them in the garden. The shock of sudden exposure to colder, dryer air could set back their growth significantly or even kill them off completely. Instead, harden the plants off gradually.

A couple of weeks before the plants are needed, place the pots outside for an hour or so each day and then return them to the greenhouse or cold frame. Repeat this process every day, leaving them outside for longer and longer periods of time on each occasion, until eventually they are left out over night. They are now safe to plant out in your garden. If they are tender plants, do not start hardening them off until the threat of frost has passed.

PRICKING OUT INTO POTS

1 If the seedlings have been in a heated propagator, harden them off to the greenhouse temperature before pricking out, by gradually opening the propagator vents over a couple of days. Gently knock out the pot of seedlings on to the bench.

2 Now, proceeding very gently and carefully so that you don't damage the fragile seedlings, break open the ball of compost so that individual seedlings can be removed. The compost should be relatively soft and so this should be fairly easy.

3 Separate the seedlings one at a time as each is required. Always lift and carry a seedling by its leaves, and never by its roots or stem. Use a label or pencil to ease the seedling from the compost without risk of tearing the roots.

4 Hold the seedling over the centre of the pot, keeping your hand steady by resting it against the side of the pot, and pour good quality potting compost around it until the pot is full to the brim.

5 Tap the pot on the bench to settle the compost and then gently firm down with your thumbs or fingers so that the final level is below the rim of the pot.

6 Water the pots with a watering can fitted with a fine rose. Keep the seedlings in the greenhouse or somewhere warm until they have started growing away, then harden them off over a week or more by allowing them increasing amounts of time in the open air, or with a cold frame, by gradually opening it.

Sowing seeds in open ground

Many new gardeners think that all flowers start as seeds grown in pots, but in fact a large number of flowering plants can be sown directly into the soil. This is, of course, what happens in nature anyway. The advantage of pots is that they reduce the competition for food and water, giving the seedlings a flying start. However, if weeds are kept at bay, then the same is true of seeds sown in open ground.

Which seeds to sow outside

You can try sowing virtually any seeds directly into the soil, but there are normally some types that will grow better if they are sown in pots. For example, many annuals, particularly the tender ones, are better started off in pots or trays. This is because you can steal a march on nature by getting them into growth in a greenhouse ready to be planted out as mature plants once the frosts have definitely finished. If you choose to sow them in open ground instead, you would have to wait until the end of the harsh weather, which would then mean that the resulting plants would flower four to six weeks later. In other words, they would not be coming into flower until the summer is almost over.

By contrast, hardy annuals, which will withstand the frosts, can be sown outside in either the autumn or spring, so that the plants are already mature by the beginning of summer. Sowing these plants outside in the first place saves a great deal of time and trouble.

Most perennials can be sown outside, either where they are to flower ultimately or in special beds, but because small numbers are usually involved it is often easier to sow them in pots.

The corncockle, *Agrostemma*, is a plant of disturbed ground that flourishes naturally in cornfields, so it is perfect for sowing in the flower border.

Where to sow

Most directly sown annuals are sown where they are to flower. The exception to this are the biennials, such as wallflowers or sweet Williams, which are usually grown in rows in a seedbed or the vegetable garden and then transplanted into their flowering place in the autumn.

Perennials are normally sown in rows. They can be sown where they are to grow, but because only one, three or five plants are needed at the most, the seedlings can easily get swamped and lost in the hurly-burly of the border. Draw out some shallow drills in the fine soil and sow the seeds thinly along them. Draw some of the soil back over the seeds, then water them. Label each row as you sow it so that you don't forget which is which.

Aftercare

Once your sowing is done, the soil should be kept moist, which may mean watering if the weather is dry. As the seedlings appear, thin them out, making sure that you remove any that are too close together; each plant should have enough room to develop properly. The best rule of thumb here is simple: the larger the final plant, the more space it will

The seeds of different kinds of plants can be scattered over the bare earth to create colourful mixed displays.

SOWING IN OPEN GROUND

1 Thoroughly prepare the ground by digging the soil and breaking it down into a fine tilth (consistency) using a rake. You should not work the soil when it is too wet or it will become compacted.

2 If you plan to use several different blocks of plants, mark out the design on the soil using contrasting coloured sand or compost. Broadcast the seed by hand so that it is thinly spread right across the appropriate area. It will probably be necessary to thin out the seedlings when they appear.

3 Gently rake the seed in so that it is covered by a thin layer of soil. Some gardeners prefer to sow their seed in short rows rather than by broadcasting. This makes it easier to weed when the seed first comes up. To sow in rows, first draw out shallow drills with a hoe.

4 Now sow the seed thinly along each row and rake the soil back over them. By carefully thinning the seedlings, the resulting overall pattern of the plants will appear to be random and not in rows.

5 Finally, gently water the whole bed, using a watering can fitted with a fine rose.

6 *(right)* A bed planted with annuals begins to fill out soon after sowing and planting.

require around it. This is not quite so important in row-sown plants as these will be planted into their final positions later. Keep the young plants weeded and healthy.

Transplanting

Plants that are grown in rows elsewhere can be transplanted into their final flowering position as soon as they are large enough to be handled without risk of damaging them. With biennials such as wallflowers, there is no need to do this until the ground has been cleared in the autumn.

With "broadcast" seed (handfuls of seed thrown out over the soil's surface, as opposed to being put into rows of channels), too many plants often develop. Some of these can be dug up carefully and transplanted elsewhere. Water the plants before moving them, and then dig them up, retaining as much soil as you possibly can around the roots. Dig a larger hole than the roots, place the plant in it and then refill with soil, gently but firmly pressing it down, then water again.

Dividing plants

One of the quickest ways of obtaining a new plant is to divide an existing plant into two (or more) pieces and replant both bits. This is not only a method of obtaining new plants but also a way of ensuring that old plants stay young and productive. It is not a difficult technique to learn and soon becomes second nature.

Advantages of dividing plants

Growing new plants from seed is fun and often essential if you want to grow plants to which you would otherwise have no ready access. However, seed can be a bit of a hit and miss method, because you cannot guarantee exactly what you are going to get. A plant is likely to differ from its parent: it may be shorter or taller, the foliage may be slightly different and the colour of the flower can vary considerably.

With annuals, this may not matter or there may be a sufficient degree of conformity, but with perennials it can be more of a problem. It is no good, for example, sowing seed from many of the cultivars of geraniums, as they will not come true. The plants are likely to be inferior (although there is always a chance than one might be better).

Division (and cuttings, which are dealt with elsewhere), by contrast, involves taking a bit of the original plant and reproducing it exactly. This is very important for most named perennial cultivars.

Brute force

There are several ways of dividing a plant. One popular and very easy method is by brute force: simply dig up the plant, cut a chunk off it with a sharp spade and then replant both pieces separately. This is very effective for some of the larger

Many hardy geraniums are typical of the type of plant that can be divided to increase their numbers and to keep them healthy.

clump-forming plants. It does leave a lot of severed material, which can rot and, in theory, cause problems, but which rarely seems to.

A refinement of this is to insert two forks into the dug-up clump, back to back, and then lever them apart, forcing the plant into two pieces, continuing until the pieces are small enough. With the exception of the older, centre pieces of the plant, which should be discarded, the pieces of plant can be replanted immediately. It is, however, always a good idea to use the opportunity to rejuvenate the soil by digging it and adding some well-rotted organic material. The best time to divide plants in this way is the spring.

Using two forks back-to-back is a crude but effective method of division. It is best used with fibrous-rooted plants.

Double hellebores will only come true if they are increased by division, as seed will often produce inferior plants.

Manipulation

A more sophisticated approach is to use your hands. Many plants, if shaken so the soil falls off and gently manipulated with the fingers, will fall apart into separate crowns, each of which can be either replanted in the soil or put into pots until they are needed. This is only possible with plants grown in lighter soils, although it is still possible on heavier soils if the plant is manipulated in a bucket of water. More stubborn plants, such as hellebores, can have the water washed off first with a garden hose.

It is difficult to visualize what actually happens until you try it, and then you will be surprised how easily

Dividing plants by manipulating them with your hands in a bucket of water produces divisions whose roots are not torn or broken.

the plant comes apart in your hands. Some plants, such as hostas for example, may need a sharp knife to separate the crowns, but generally they just fall apart.

Normally, divisions are made in spring, but if the plants are transferred to pots they can be divided at any point during the growing season.

Replanting

Larger divisions can be treated as normal plants and replanted immediately into the soil. Make certain that the plants are kept moist until they have re-established themselves, and protect them from strong winds. Smaller divisions recover more quickly if they are first grown on in pots and then planted out the following spring. Pot-grown divisions may need hardening off.

Splitting for health

Many perennials get old and woody after a few years. They die off towards the centre of the plant and the flowering becomes less profuse. If these plants are dug up, the old centres thrown away and some of the younger, outside growth replanted, the plant will be totally rejuvenated.

Larger divisions can be planted directly back into the soil – as long as you make sure that they are well watered and mulched.

DIVIDING BY HAND

1 Dig up a section of the plant, making sure that it is large enough to provide the quantity of material that you require.

2 Hold the plant firmly at the base and shake it vigorously so that the soil falls off and the roots are exposed.

3 Gently pull the plant into individual pieces, simply by manipulating it with your hands. Many plants, such as this sisyrinchium, will come apart very easily.

4 The pieces should now be potted up individually using a good compost (soil mix). Place in a shaded cold frame for a few days and then harden off.

Plants suitable for division

Acanthus	Epimedium	Lysimachia	Rudbeckia
Achillea	Euphorbia (some)	Lythrum	Salvia (some)
Aconitum	Galega	Meconopsis	Scabiosa
Agapanthus	Geranium (some)	Mentha	Schizostlis
Anaphalis	Helenium	Monarda	Sedum
Anemone	Helianthus	Nepeta	Sidalcea
Anthemis	Helleborus	Ophiopogon	Sisyrinchium
Artemisia	Hemerocallis	Persicaria	Smilacina
Aster	Heuchera	Phlomis	Solidago
Astilbe	Hosta	Phormium	Stachys
Astrantia	Inula	Physostegia	Symphytum
Bergenia	Iris	Polemonium	Tanacetum
Campanula (some)	Kniphofia	Polygonatum	Thalictrum
Convallaria	Lamium	Potentilla	Tradescantia
Coreopsis	Liatris	Primula	Trollius
Crambe	Ligularia	Pulmonaria	Uvularia
Delphinium	Lobelia	Ranunculus	Vancouveria
Epilobium	Lychnis	Rheum	Veronica

Cuttings

Taking cuttings requires slightly more dexterity than dividing plants, but is still surprisingly easy. This is certainly an important technique for a gardener to master, as some plants cannot be reproduced any other way. It is also the ideal method to use when the owner of an admired plant may not want to dig it up and divide it, but is more than willing to snip a little bit off for you.

Why take cuttings?

Like making divisions, taking cuttings is a vegetative way of propagation. In other words, it is taking part of the original plant and reproducing it, and

therefore it will have all the same qualities as its parent. It takes a bit more time and trouble than making divisions but is an essential technique as not all plants are easily divided. This is particularly true for those plants that do not spread, but are restricted to a central rosette, as well as many taprooted plants (which have just one long, main root).

Useful equipment

Unlike other propagation methods, you can grow cuttings with various levels of sophistication: equipment varies from costly mist propagators (for the serious gardener who wants

Plants for basal cuttings

Achillea	Lythrum
Anthemis	Macleaya
Artemisia	Mentha
Aster	Monarda
Campanula	Nepeta
Chrysanthemum	Perovskia
Crambe	Phlox
Dahlia	Physostegia
Delphinium	Platycodon
Diascia	Salvia
Epilobium	Scabiosa
Gaillardia	Sedum
Helenium	Senecio (some)
Knautia	Solidago
Lupinus	Verbena
Lychnis	Viola

STRIKING CUTTINGS

1 Take short cuttings from the new growth at the base of the plant. These cuttings are usually to be found naturally in the spring, but they can be created by cutting the plant hard back so that new growth is formed. Place your cuttings in a plastic bag and then seal the bag.

2 To pot up your cuttings, first trim their base. Cut through the stem just below a leaf joint and then remove all the leaves, except for a few at the top. Make certain that all the cuts are clean and not jagged. A scalpel or sharp scissors are the best tools to use for this purpose, although some gardeners simply use sharp fingernails.

3 Place the cuttings in a pot of cutting compost (planting mix) made up of 50:50 sharp sand and peat or peat substitute. You can grow up to 12 in a pot. If you prefer, dip the bottom 1cm/½in of the cutting in a rooting powder before putting it in the hole. This helps some of the more difficult species to root and also prevents rotting. However, many gardeners find this quite unnecessary for most perennials.

4 Label and date the pot. Thoroughly water and place the pot in a propagator. You can use a plastic bag, but do make sure that no leaves are touching the plastic. Seal with an elastic band.

5 When the roots of the cuttings start to appear at the drainage holes of the pot, gently remove the contents.

6 Pot up the rooted cuttings once again, this time in individual pots, using a good quality potting compost (soil mix). Keep covered for a few days and then harden off.

TAKING ROOT CUTTINGS

1 Very carefully dig the plant out from the ground. You must try to make sure that the thicker roots are not damaged in the process.

2 Now wash away any soil that is clinging to the roots and then remove one or more of the thicker roots.

3 Cut the roots into lengths of about 5–8cm (2–3in). Now make a horizontal cut at the top of the cutting and a slanting cut at the bottom.

4 Fill the pot with a cutting compost (planting mix) and insert the cuttings vertically with the horizontal cut at the top, so that the latter cuts are just level with the soil surface.

5 Cover with fine grit, water and put in a frame. In spring, shoots should emerge and new roots should form. Once you are sure that there are roots, pot them up individually. Treat as any young plant.

quantity or those dealing with plants that are tricky to propagate) through medium-priced propagators to simple plastic bags (fine for the average gardener). The purpose of any type of apparatus is the same: to create a close, moist atmosphere around the cuttings so that they do not dry out.

Composts

A special compost (soil mix) called cutting compost is usually used. This will vary in composition, but is basically 50 per cent sand (for drainage) and 50 per cent a moisture-retaining medium (traditionally peat but now more likely to be a peat substitute).

Taking cuttings

Cuttings should be fresh growth that is not too soft and not too old. The shoot chosen should not have flower buds, or be in flower or seed. The best cuttings for most plants are basal ones – the young growth found at the base of a plant either in spring or after the plant has been cut to the ground later in the season. With a few plants, such as penstemons, you can take cuttings from any part of a shoot, but normally you would just take them from the tip. Cuttings vary in length depending on the plant, but try to make them at least several pairs of leaves long – say, 3–7cm (1¼–3in) – or longer than this and then trim them off when potting them up. As soon as you have taken a cutting, put it in a plastic bag and seal it.

Striking cuttings

Now "strike" (pot up) your cuttings, as shown on the opposite page. Place cuttings in a hole made by a dibber or pencil, and firm the compost down, making sure that your cuttings' bottom leaves are above the level of the compost and that the leaves of different cuttings do not touch.

Aftercare

If your potted-on cuttings are in plastic bags, turn the bag inside out once a day to remove condensation. Keep the compost moist and make sure that the pot or propagator is in a light place, but out of the sun. Once roots have formed on the cuttings, pot them up in other pots.

Root cuttings

Some plants can be grown from a small piece of root. There aren't vast numbers of plants that suit this, but for some, such as pulsatilla or oriental poppies, it is the only effective reproductive method. The best time to take root cuttings is when a plant is dormant – usually winter. Because new growth often starts below ground well before the end of winter, the usual time for taking such cuttings is early winter.

Plants for root cuttings

Acanthus	Morisia
Anchusa	monanthos
Anemone x	Ostrowski
hybrida	magnifica
Campanula	Papaver orientale
Catananche	Phlox
Echinops	Primula
Eryngium	denticulata
Gaillardia	Pulsatilla
Geranium	Romneya
Gypsophila	Stokesia laevis
Limonium	Symphytum
Macleaya	Trollius
Mertensia	Verbascum

Container gardening

All kinds of garden can benefit from the use of containers. In small patios or balconies, this may be the only form of gardening possible. In larger gardens, containers are used to add another dimension to the overall design – one of their great virtues is that they add a three-dimensional quality.

Types of container

A wide variety of containers are suitable for gardens and they are generally chosen for their visual suitability. The most crucial factor is that they must have a drainage hole, so that excess water can find its way out – waterlogged plants soon die.

Another issue is that they must be frost-proof if they are to stand outside in winter without the risk of cracking or shattering. Containers should also be secure. Those that are on windowsills or are hanging must obviously be very tightly attached so that they do not fall on anyone. Perhaps less obvious, but still very important, is that pots standing on the ground must be firmly planted so that they do not topple over if

knocked. A large pot filled with damp compost (soil mix) can be extremely heavy and could potentially cause a severe injury.

Which compost?

There are various composts on the market suitable for containers. Some are just called potting composts, while others claim to be specially formulated for containers. There is not much difference between them, and the final choice is personal and depends on what works best for you.

Some of the "container composts" differ from potting compost in that they contain special water-retaining granules. These hold an amazing amount of water and release it slowly for the plants' use without the compost becoming waterlogged. These granules are readily available to buy, in several forms, and can be added to any compost, so you are not restricted to composts that already contain them. The other thing that all composts contain is a slow-release fertilizer. This comes in the form of granules, which release their nutrients over a long period.

Suitable perennials for containers

Acanthus	Hosta
Agapanthus	Iris
Bergenia	Nepeta
Cordyline	Oenothera
Dianthus	fruiticosa glauca
Diascia	Phormium tenax
Euphorbia	Primula
Geranium	Sedum
Geum	Stachys
Hemerocallis	byzantina
Heuchera	Verbena

Getting the best results

As mentioned, all containers must have good drainage in the form of one or more holes at their lowest part. Cover these with broken bits of pot, tiles or irregularly shaped stones, so that water can pass out but the compost is retained.

If you are using plain compost, pour it straight from the bag into the container. If you want to add water-retaining granules, pour some compost into a bucket, mix in the granules at the suggested rate, and pour the mixture into the container.

PLANTING UP A CONTAINER

1 Cover the bottom of the container with small stones or some pieces of tile or pottery, so that water can drain freely from the pot.

2 Partly fill the pot with a good quality potting compost (soil mix). Loose slow-release fertilizer and water-retaining granules can also be mixed with the compost before the pot is filled.

3 Scoop a hole in the compost and insert the plant, positioning it so that the top of the root-ball (roots) will be level with the surface of the compost.

4 Place any extra plants you wish to include around the edge of the main plant. Add more compost to fill any gaps, and firm down.

5 Insert a fertilizer pellet if you have decided to use one, rather than the loose fertilizer granules. Water thoroughly.

PLANTING UP A HANGING BASKET

1 Stand the basket on a large pot or bucket, in order to make it easier to work with. Carefully place the basket liner in position so that it fills the basket. Half-fill the liner with compost, then mix in some water-retaining crystals, following the manufacturer's instructions, to help prevent the basket from drying out. Also add some slow-release fertilizer; this will remove the necessity to feed throughout the summer.

2 Cut holes about 4cm (1½in) across in the side of the liner. Shake some of the earth off the root-ball (roots) of one of the side plants and wrap it in a strip of plastic. Poke it through the hole, remove the plastic and spread the roots out. When all the side plants are in place, fill up your basket with compost, adding more water-retaining crystals and slow-release fertilizer.

3 Plant up the rest of the basket, packing the plants much more tightly together than you would in the open ground. Smooth out the surface of the compost, removing any excess or adding a little more as necessary. Water, then hang the basket indoors until all danger of frost has passed.

Firm down the compost and top up with more so that the surface is about 2–5cm (1–2in) below the container's rim (depending on its size).

A container full of compost can be very heavy, so place it in its final position before planting it up, or you may not be able to move it there. You could put it on a wheeled trolley sold especially for containers, ready to move into position.

Hanging baskets

Ever increasing in popularity, hanging baskets can provide a riot of colour all summer long. Most hanging baskets include tender annuals so they cannot be placed outside until after the last frosts, but they can be made up in advance and left indoors until the danger of frosts has passed, by which time the basket will have filled out and with luck be in full flower.

The most successful baskets are those in which the framework cannot be seen, as it is entirely masked by plants. In many cases, the hanging basket will look like a ball of plants.

Any combination of plants can be used to create different schemes. A wonderful pot-pourri of colours can be achieved with a mixed planting, although a more sophisticated effect can be created if you use plants in the same colour or even plants of just one variety.

Watering

Containers need watering every day, sometimes more in hot, sunny conditions. Water-retaining granules help to provide some moisture, but you will still have to water on most days when it doesn't rain. Smaller containers dry out quicker than large ones because of their higher ratio of surface area to volume.

Containers sheltered from the rain, and those that contain large plants whose leaves may prevent the rain reaching the compost, may need watering even after rain.

In winter it is important not to overwater; the compost should be just moist. Automatic watering systems can be installed if you have a lot of pots or if you are often away.

Feeding

Most composts use a slow-release fertilizer, which will often last long enough to see you through the season – check the manufacturer's instructions. If necessary, top-dress with more fertilizer, which is readily available. If you make your own garden compost, you can add a slow-release fertilizer either in granules or in the tablets, which are just pressed into the soil.

Popular annuals for hanging baskets

Anagallis	Lathyrus
Antirrhinum	Lurential
Asarina	Lobelia
Begonia	Myosotis
Bidens	Nicotiana
Brachycome	Pelargonium
Camissonia	Petunia
Cerinthe	Sanvitalia
Chrysanthemum	Schizanthus
Diascia	Senecio
Echium	Tagetes
Felicia	Tropaeolum
Fuchsia	Viola ×
Helichrysum	wittrockiana

Pests and diseases

Most gardeners fear pests and diseases more than anything else, and these fears are only exacerbated by the vast array of bottles, packets and sprays now found in garden centres and nurseries. In fact, serious garden problems are fairly rare and there is little reason for most gardeners to worry. The good news is that common sense is often preferable to a chemical armoury.

What causes trouble?

It is surprising how few pests and diseases actually affect perennials and annuals. Those pests that are a nuisance, such as slugs and rabbits, are big enough to be dealt with manually without recourse to chemicals. The other major pest is greenfly (aphids), but even they attack only a few plants and should not present a real threat.

Viral diseases can suddenly appear, with leaves and plants becoming distorted or discoloured, and you may need to resort to chemicals to halt their spread.

Mixed planting

Many of these problems can be overcome by having a mixed community of plants. Pests and diseases are less likely to catch hold in a mixed cottage garden than in one that specializes in just one type of plant. In the latter case, a disease is likely to affect all the plants, while in the former it will affect just a few plants, and therefore not become a serious threat. Any holes that are caused by losses from pest or disease damage will also not be so visible.

A mixed garden contains a large number of beneficial insects, which prey on the pest insects, and this results in a balanced community in which the pests will rarely get the upper hand.

Rabbits can cause a lot of damage to plants, as they have done here. Placing netting round the garden is the only solution.

Good hygiene

Another way of ensuring that diseases rarely get a hold is to practise good hygiene. Remove all dead and dying material from the beds and borders, and be alert for any signs of diseased material so that you can deal with the problem promptly. If viruses attack, remove and burn the affected plants.

Attacking the problem by hand

With the best will in the world, problems do occur. There can be few gardens, for example, where slugs are not a nuisance, especially in early spring when the succulent shoots are first appearing. You can, of course, try to use only "slug-proof" plants,

Cleaning pots by washing and scrubbing them is a good basic hygiene practice that will help prevent problems with young plants.

Slugs and snails are two of the gardener's worst enemies. A night-time patrol with a torch will capture a lot of them at work.

but when slugs are hungry they will eat most plants, so if you remove their favourite food, their tastes are likely to change. You can use slug bait if you are careful to ensure that pets and other animals cannot get at either the bait or the slugs once they have eaten it.

One of the best methods for getting rid of slugs is to go out in the evening as it gets dark with a torch and collect the emerging slugs in a bucket and dispose of them at some distance. (Don't throw them over your neighbour's fence: they will just crawl back and your neighbour will not be best pleased.) After a few nights, you will have reduced the population sufficiently

With some severe outbreaks of pests or diseases it may be necessary to resort, with great care, to the use of chemicals.

Damage by the caterpillars of moths and butterflies can ruin flowers. Picking them off by hand is the most effective treatment.

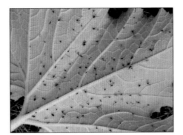

Greenfly and blackfly (aphids) are common pests. A mixed garden will usually provide sufficient predator insects to combat them.

Fungal diseases, such as this case of mildew, are a constant problem. Good hygiene and avoidance of overcrowding help.

so that they are no longer a problem, at least for a while. Caterpillars can also be removed by hand.

Rabbits are another big problem in some gardens. Here the only real solution is to place a rabbit-proof fence around the whole garden. You could just fence off individual borders, but the fencing does look ugly and is less obtrusive if placed around the whole boundary.

Natural predators

Introducing or encouraging beneficial insects can have a surprisingly dramatic impact on the number of pests in your garden. Check out which pests your plants are likely to fall prey to, and then simply encourage their natural predators into your garden.
Ladybirds (ladybugs) and larvae: eat aphids, scale insects, mealy bugs and caterpillars
Hoverflies and larvae: eat up to 50 aphids a day
Lacewings: eat aphids, woolly aphids, spider mites, scale insects and caterpillars
Ground beetles: eat slugs, flat worms, cabbage and carrot rootfly (eggs and larvae), vine weevils and spider mites
Anthocorid bugs: eat vine weevil larvae, caterpillars, midge larvae and spider mites
Centipedes: eat slugs and snails

Small outbreaks of aphids can be left to other predators to deal with, but if they begin to accumulate you can remove them either by running your fingers up the stems and squashing them or by simply removing the stem.

Chemical means

There are chemicals available for dealing for most pests and diseases, and if your garden suffers a serious outbreak then you may need to resort to them. Do not, however, spray widely as a precautionary measure, and spray only the parts of the plant that are affected. It is very

important to follow the instructions on the bottle, packet or spray. At all costs avoid spraying the whole garden "just in case".

Regulations with regard to horticultural chemicals are in a state of flux and many traditional ones have been banned. Even some new ones leave the market only a few years after going on the shelves. Similarly, some chemicals are banned in some countries and not in others. So, if you need to treat a particular problem, consult your garden centre and make certain that you obtain something that is appropriate for your problem.

Thorough soil preparation and good general hygiene routines will help to keep plants, such as this lovely wallflower, looking fresh and healthy.

Organic gardening

In recent years, organic gardening has moved to the forefront. Like so many other aspects of gardening, however, organic practice often involves little more than plain common sense: in this case, using only natural organic materials and not using inorganic (synthetically manufactured) substances unless absolutely essential. In other words, generally working with nature rather than against it. If you follow these rules in your garden, then you are pretty well organic already.

The chemicals issue

So, in essence, organic gardening amounts simply to gardening without the use of chemicals (although some naturally occurring chemicals are allowed).

Chemicals are often used by gardeners as a form of shortcut: it is so much easier to spray a border full of weeds than it is remove all of the weeds by hand. A slight change of

Sticky traps such as this use pheromones to attract insects, which then get trapped by the sticky substance inside.

mindset is all that is needed here. Gardeners need to try and accept that gardening is inherently a time-consuming occupation, and that it is far better to spend a bit more time on a chore rather than waste your money on all kinds of unnecessary chemicals.

Advantages of organic gardening

In terms of flower gardening specifically with annuals and perennials, the visual results of following organic principles are pretty minimal, but over time there are great advantages to the garden as a whole. If, for example, you treat the soil with well-rotted organic materials, such as garden compost or farmyard manure, then the structure of the soil will be improved and the plants fed at the same time. If, on the other hand, you just add chemical feeds to the soil, you will have well-grown plants, but, over the years, the structure of the soil will break down and in the long term plants will suffer.

A build-up of residues within the soil and run-off into watercourses is another problem that can develop if you use chemical fertilizers. They do not break down in the same way that organic fertilizers, such as bonemeal, do. The same is true of using

Try to provide places for lacewings and other beneficial insects to overwinter. This raised box, which has been stuffed with straw, is an ideal winter home for them.

Pests may be confused and so deterred from attacking certain plants if the latter are surrounded by another very different type of plant, such as the marigolds seen here.

Surrounding prized plants with slug traps, such as this piece of guttering filled with water, may deter attacks.

Larval and adult ladybirds eat incredible quantities of aphids, and so are worth encouraging into the garden.

You will find that this will improve the structure of the soil as well as providing nutrients.

If you need to feed plants, then choose organic fertilizers, such as bonemeal, made from naturally occurring materials. (Note that you will need to wear rubber/latex gloves when you are handling bonemeal preparations.) You can also make your own very effective foliar feeds for a quick pick-up by steeping nettles or comfrey in water and then watering or spraying the plants with the resulting liquid.

Always remove any weeds by hand, when you are digging over a bed, rather than resorting to chemicals. When you are preparing a new bed or border, rather than spray the whole thing with weedkiller, simply cover it with some black plastic sheeting or an old carpet – to deprive weeds of the light that they need to grow. When weeding existing borders, once again work by hand for the very best results.

Rid your borders of any slugs and caterpillars by manually removing them rather than killing them by bait, and keep a well-balanced border of mixed plantings, so that severe bouts of particular infestations are less likely to occur.

chemicals to kill weeds or attack pests and diseases. Also, these chemicals often have unwanted side-effects. Pesticides aimed at killing greenfly (aphids) often also destroy beneficial insects such as bees, which are essential to gardening.

How can you be organic?
Starting with the soil, always try to use well-rotted organic material when preparing or top-dressing beds.

Friendly insects

Anthocorid bugs
Bees
Centipedes
Earwigs*
Ground beetles
Harvestmen
Lacewings
Ladybirds (ladybugs)
Parasitic wasps and flies
Rove beetles (commonly known as devil's coach and horses)
Spiders

*Often considered a nuisance because they eat the petals of some plants, such as dahlias. However, they also eat many pests.

Encourage wildlife
Wildlife, such as birds and other animals, are fun to have in the garden. They are also beneficial. Although birds can be a nuisance in the fruit and vegetable garden (spreading some netting over vulnerable plants and trees should stop this), they are very useful in the flower garden as they eat a lot of pests, such as aphids and caterpillars.

Animals such as hedgehogs eat the worst enemy of most gardeners – the slug – while many garden birds make short work of snails. Flowers that attract ladybirds and lacewings are worth growing, as the larvae of these eat large quantities of greenfly.

Chemicals can be harmful to all these forms of wildlife, so this is another reason why they should be avoided if at all possible.

Birds love seed beds, so try to deter them by hanging shining kitchen foil above the bed to frighten them off.

BULBS

Introduction to bulbs

This section is bursting with ideas on how to use bulbs in your garden, whether you want to grow them in beds or borders or more naturally in open grass or shady orchard or woodland situations. It describes not only how to plant bulbs, but in which situation they will thrive best, with regard to soil moisture, drainage, acidity and alkalinity, sun or shade. It also includes details on how to look after flowering bulbs, with advice on pests and diseases, feeding, staking, and, in the case of exotic varieties, how to cope with winter protection. Propagation is another major consideration, with helpful information on which varieties can be easily grown from seed, and which may be more readily propagated from cuttings.

An entire chapter is devoted to outdoor containers showing how it is possible to enjoy inspirational arrangements throughout the year whether they are small, medium or large, with ideas for long-term planting as well.

Another major chapter deals with bulbs as houseplants with ideas for growing and displaying many different varieties for mid-winter pleasure as well as spring and summer bringing scent and colour right into your home.

Cannas provide some of the most dramatic foliage of all, with their wide tapering leaves, sometimes bronze and occasionally variegated, often with distinctive veining.

What is a bulb?

The word bulb is used in this section as an umbrella term for all those plants that have a root system that has been adapted to withstand long periods of drought by storing food reserves beneath ground. It includes not only true bulbs but also corms, tubers and rhizomes, as well as plants with fleshy roots.

Countries of origin

The bulbs we grow in our gardens today originated from around the world. Countries such as Spain, France, Italy, Greece and Turkey, which border the Mediterranean Sea, are home to a host of species daffodils, blue and white anemones, tiny scillas and chionodoxas, dainty *Galanthus* (snowdrop) and *Leucojum* (snowflake). California is the source of yellow calochortus, while South Africa is the home of colourful gladioli, stately agapanthus, shapely *Zantedeschia* (arum lily), scented freesias, pretty watsonias and gorgeous gloriosa, to name but a few. Central Asia provides brilliantly coloured tulips, tall eremurus

Crocosmias, dahlias and lilies join forces to add splendour to the summer border, where earlier narcissus and tulips took centre stage.

(foxtail lily) and scented lilies. Other, more tender plants, such as dahlias and *Tigridia* (tiger flower), are native to Mexico and Central America, while many of the begonias come from the Andes of Peru and Bolivia. Hippeastrums, sometimes known as indoor amaryllis, are native to Central and South America.

Bulbs for all seasons

Wonderful flowers for every season of the year can be grown from bulbs. As soon as midwinter has passed *Eranthis hyemalis* (winter aconite) thrusts up its shoots, together with snowdrops, early crocuses, anemones and *Iris danfordiae*. Spring welcomes daffodils, hyacinths and tulips, fritillaries and *Hyacinthoides* (bluebell). More irises follow in early summer, along with all the alliums. Then it is time for gladioli, begonias, lilies, agapanthus, eremurus and dahlias. As summer turns to autumn, dahlias are still in flower, and they are joined by a beautiful array of nerines, crinums, colchicums and cyclamen.

Choosing a site

There are bulbs for everywhere in the garden. Most prefer a sunny position and well-drained soil, with tulips and gladioli being notable examples. Others, such as bluebells and trilliums, will enjoy a shadier home. But some genera, such as alliums, are more diverse. Certain members of the family, including *A. karataviense*,

Species tulips such as *Tulipa tarda* and *T. urumiensis* will give great pleasure in a hanging basket for more than one season.

Freesias make wonderful plants for a conservatory, where they may continue to thrive for many years.

love sun, while *A. triquetrum* prefers the shade. They also vary widely in height. Short species, such as anemones and crocuses, are best near the front of a border or in a rock garden, while tall eremurus and stately lilies are usually better in the middle or back of the border. However, these rules can all be broken, for most bulbs will grow successfully in different garden settings. Lilies are an excellent example: some are so wonderfully flamboyant and beautifully scented that they deserve several homes in the border or to be planted next to a path or in a pot near a door.

In Europe in the 16th century some bulbs were so valuable that they were displayed far apart from each other in the garden so that they

Blue grape hyacinths and Double Early tulips combine to provide a sumptuous display and even the container is colour-co-ordinated.

were easy to cultivate and could be appreciated individually. Sometimes a single tulip was the only occupant of an entire bed. Today, commercial propagation allows us to buy most bulbs relatively cheaply, so that ten might be planted in one group or perhaps in a single container. Sometimes double that number may be planted in a large container, especially if small bulbs, such as crocuses, *Muscari* spp. (grape hyacinth) or anemones, are used to underplant taller ones such as hyacinths, early tulips or daffodils. There are so many possibilities that you should experiment and enjoy the results, but, whatever you do, be sure only to buy commercially cultivated bulbs. Never plant any bulbs that have been taken from the wild.

Dahlias are a brilliant choice for a sunny summer border where they will be valued for their long period of flowering and their colours.

The botany of bulbs

The word "bulb" is often used to describe true bulbs, corms, tubers, rhizomes and plants with fleshy root systems that can cope with long periods of drought by storing food reserves beneath ground. There are, however, clear differences between these five types of plant.

True bulbs

The inside of a true bulb consists of stems and fleshy leaves that have been modified for storage. In tulip, hyacinth and daffodil bulbs the modified leaves are layered closely around each other, with the outer leaves, which are often dry and brown, forming a tunic around the bulb. In other bulbs the leaves are not wrapped around each other but overlap, producing a far more succulent bulb. These bulbs are known as scaly bulbs, and the lily is one of the best-known examples.

Individual bulbs usually survive for many years in the ground, during which time the old ones will produce offsets or "daughter" bulbs and thus create small groups. Some tulip bulbs are unlikely to produce flowers for a second year, but the bulb will form replacement bulbs, which then flower the following year.

Corms

Inside all corms there is a stem that is swollen and adapted to store food. This forms the base of the new shoots. Unlike true bulbs, corms appear solid throughout. After flowering, a new corm, formed at the base of the new stem, will grow on top of the old one and the old corm will die. Each corm, therefore, has only one season in which to produce a flower. Small young corms will also form on the basal plate, which is slightly concave. Crocosmias, gladioli and crocuses are all cormous plants.

Rhizomes

A rhizome is a swollen underground stem, from the ends of which shoots, then foliage and flowers emerge, while roots grow on the underside of the rhizome. Side branches will form each year, typically after flowering has occurred, enabling the plant to spread. Cannas and zantedeschias are typical rhizomatous plants.

Chasmanthe (top left and right) has a wide corm, while freesias (bottom left) are smaller and, for their size, relatively elongated. Those of gladioli (bottom right) are more rounded.

Cannas (top) produce many fairly large, elongated rhizomes each season, and these can be severed to produce new plants. Zantedeschia rhizomes (bottom) can be treated in the same way, although the rhizomes are squatter and more rounded.

Tubers

A tuber is a swollen underground root or stem, but it is not the base of the stem, as in the corm. It is usually fleshy and rounded and may be covered with scaly leaves or with fibrous roots. Buds usually develop on top of the tuber and produce stems. Tubers get larger with age and can live for years. Dahlias, cyclamen and some types of begonia and anemone are tuberous plants.

Fleshy root systems

This last group is of plants that make leaf and root growth when the soil and atmosphere around them is moist, come into bloom and then undergo a period of dormancy during the summer drought. Such

In this group of summer- and autumn-flowering true bulbs, the crinum (top) has a long, tapering neck, while the lilies (middle) and smaller tulips (bottom) are more compact.

Begonia tubers (top left) are compact, with a hairy, round base and a concave top from which tiny pink shoots appear. Dahlias (top right) have a clutch of large, fat tuberous "legs", while ranunculus (bottom left) have thin, claw-like legs. If the legs break off they will not produce new plants. Anemones (bottom right) are hard and knobbly, and it is from these protuberances that the new growth appears.

plants come mainly from regions of the world where winters are cool and moist and summers are hot and dry.

Families, genera, species and cultivars

True bulbs, corms, tubers and rhizomes belong to a relatively small number of plant "families" based on similarities in the reproductive organs within the flower rather than on the appearance of the flower or the storage organ itself. Most true bulbs and corms belong to only a few families. The family Amaryllidaceae includes well-known genera such as *Narcissus* (daffodil), *Nerine*, *Sternbergia* and *Galanthus* (snowdrop). Iridaceae embraces the genera *Freesia*, *Schizostylis*, *Tigridia*, *Gladiolus* and *Iris*, and Liliaceae includes *Lilium* (lily), *Fritillaria* and *Tulipa* (tulip).

Tuberous and rhizomatous plants have more widespread family connections. Cyclamen are part of the family Primulaceae, *Begonia* of Begoniaceae, *Sinningia* of Gesneriaceae and *Dahlia* of Compositae.

Genera are distinct plant groups within the larger family, yet some have a strong family resemblance. For example, some bulbs of the Hyacinthaceae family, as well as the flowers, show marked similarities. The genera *Muscari*, *Chionodoxa*, *Scilla*, *Hyacinthus* and *Hyacinthoides* from Europe and the Middle East have a similar appearance to *Camassia* bulbs, which come from North America.

Each genus usually contains more than one species. These might be regarded as extremely close relatives with many common characteristics. Within the genus *Narcissus*, for example, there are about 50 species. Sometimes species vary naturally, and the resulting plants are known as varieties. A well-known example is *Narcissus poeticus* var. *recurvus*, which has been grown for centuries and is known as pheasant's eye.

Nurserymen often breed from a species, and the results are referred to as cultivars. Hence, the species *Narcissus cyclamineus*, with its distinctive swept-back petals, has been used to produce popular cultivars such as *N.* 'February Gold', 'Jetfire' and 'Peeping Tom'. As a result, we now have thousands of cultivars from around 50 species of *Narcissus*. They flower at different times, vary in height and colour and have different flower structures.

The Hyacinthaceae family is represented here by five genera: *Camassia* and *Hyacinthus* are the larger bulbs at the back, with *Muscari* (grape hyacinth), *Hyacinthoides* (bluebell) and *Scilla* (squill) from left to right at the front.

This cross-section shows that corms, such as that of the gladiolus (bottom), have a more solid appearance, while true bulbs, such as those of lilies (top), are made up of stems and fleshy, scaly leaves.

Of all these narcissus bulbs only *Narcissus poeticus* var. *recurvus*, the one with the long tapering noses, is a species growing wild in the mountains of central and southern Europe. The others are cultivars bred for the trade.

The history of bulbs

Plant hunters risked their lives to bring the bulbs that we know today from their native habitats, and sometimes it has taken several attempts to introduce them successfully to the gardens of the West. Fashion has also played a major role in their history. Tulips, for example, became almost beyond price in the heady days of the 1630s, but now they are available in their thousands and are used in spring bedding schemes right around the world.

Tulips

Of all bulbs, the tulip has one of the most colourful histories. Its principal homelands were Persia (now Iran) and Turkey, where even in the 12th and 13th centuries poets sang its praises. When Süleyman I, the Magnificent, became sultan in 1520, the Ottoman Empire stretched from the Crimea in the east to Egypt and beyond in the west, and it covered large parts of the Balkans. City gardens were well established, and tulips were one of the most popular flowers. The

The beauty of tulips and other flowers that were being discovered was captured by artists in detailed drawings and prints.

period even became known as the Tulip Age. Regular tulip festivals were held, and the flower was used to decorate tiles and pottery as well as clothes.

These tulips were introduced to Europe in the middle of the 16th century. Conrad Gesner (1516–65), the Swiss scholar and humanist, recorded how he saw a red tulip growing in a garden in Augsburg, Bavaria, in 1557. The garden belonged to Johannis Heinrich Herwart. Also important in tulip history was the part played by the Flemish ambassador Ghislain de Busbecq (1522–91), who was the representative in Constantinople of the Habsburg emperor, Ferdinand I. In 1529 the city of Vienna had withstood a siege by Ottoman forces, but the emperor was keen to maintain trading links with the Ottoman Empire and so continued to send ambassadors to the sultan. Busbecq, who was sent as Ferdinand's emissary in 1554, greatly admired the tulips he saw growing in the gardens of Constantinople. He was able to obtain seeds and bulbs at a great price, and he eventually sent them back to the imperial gardens in Vienna, where they were grown under the care of Carolus Clusius (Charles de L'Écluse; 1526–1609).

Clusius was curious to know how the bulbs tasted and asked an apothecary to preserve them in sugar in the same manner as orchids. He ate them as sweetmeats and said he preferred them to orchids. Fortunately he survived, but eating bulbs is not recommended.

The bulbs travelled with Clusius from Vienna to Frankfurt and eventually to the Netherlands, where he was appointed Professor of Botany at Leiden University in

Conrad Gesner, Swiss scholar and humanist, recorded the first tulip growing in Europe in Augsburg in 1557.

1593. There he was given the opportunity of laying out a new botanical garden. As the tulips came into flower, interest in the unusual bulbs escalated, and people wanted to buy them. Clusius was continually obtaining bulbs from new suppliers, and through his extensive network of contacts throughout Europe he was responsible for tulips reaching many new areas. He demanded high prices for his stocks, and such a precious commodity was clearly vulnerable. On many occasions bulbs were stolen and then grown on and traded, becoming the original stock of the Dutch bulb industry.

Soon, absurdly high prices were being demanded for a single bulb. To begin with the tulip was a status symbol among the aristocracy. The length and strength of the stalk, the size and shape of the flower and even the colour of the stamens were remarked upon. Each tulip was regularly afforded a lot of growing space, and sometimes a single specimen was given an entire bed in which to be shown off. Tulips came to be desired by the growing

Nico Jungman (1872–1935) painted these Dutch tulip fields near Haarlem in 1909. Born in the Netherlands, he later moved to London where he was a landscape and figure painter as well as an illustrator and painter of travel books.

merchant classes in the Netherlands. Prices rose from hundreds of florins (a florin was worth two shillings) for a specific cultivated variety to 3,000 florins in the 1620s. Such was the interest in the trade – as distinct from interest in the actual plant – that a "futures" market developed, by which bulbs were paid for in instalments between the time of lifting in early summer and the time of planting in mid-autumn. During that time the same bulb might be bought and sold several times, as each merchant tried to make a profit on the deal. A dry bulb could not show the colour or quality of the flower it was going to produce, so the whole business depended on trust.

As demand increased, the trade grew and all levels of society became involved, including landowners, farmers, sailors, artists, weavers and servants. In 1636 tulips were traded on the London Exchange. They were also traded in Scotland, but there was little interest.

Not all the bulbs were expensive. White- and red-flowered tulips, for example, could be bought for only 12 florins a pound weight, but a single bulb of the 'Viceroy' tulip fetched 4,600 florins when it was sold at auction in 1637. The 'Viceroy' was a Violette, which had flowers with wonderful, streaked purple markings on a white background. There is a story that one 'Viceroy' changed hands for 12 fat sheep, 4 fat oxen, 8 fat pigs, 2 loads of wheat, 4 loads of rye, 2 hogsheads of wine, 4 tons of beer, 2 tons of butter, 1,000 pounds of cheese, a silver drinking horn, a suit of clothes and a complete bed! The total value of this single bulb, which was probably recorded by one of the pamphleteers campaigning against the evil and misery caused by gambling, was 3,500 guilders, a fortune at a time when the average annual income was only 150 florins and a first-class house was worth 5,000 florins.

In February 1637 the bubble burst, and when the crash came many people in the Netherlands suffered. Local authorities and growers tried to stabilize the market, but it was many years before people could pay off their debts. Nevertheless, Dutch soil was ideal for growing tulips, and, because the flowers were appreciated across Europe, trade continued. In the 1630s and 1640s at least 650 varieties were still being grown. A list of those cultivated in the gardens of the Margrave of Baden-Durlach in Karlsruhe in 1730 contained almost 2,400 names; three years later he grew nearly 4,000. At the beginning of World War II, just before the German invasion, the Netherlands was exporting 100 million tulip bulbs to the United States annually. Today, there are about 5,000 cultivars in the trade.

The word "tulip" is thought to have derived from Busbecq's original description of the plant, which he wrote after first seeing it in the gardens near Constantinople around 1554. He recalled that Turkish people called them *tulipam* because of the similarity of the shape of the open flowers to a turban. In fact, the Turkish word for turban is *tulbend*, but, whatever its origin, the name tulip has stuck ever since.

Tulips still form one of the largest groups of bulbs sold each year, and they are still centred on the Dutch bulb fields.

This picture of the lesser daffodil was painted in 1786 and appeared in William Curtis's *Botanical Magazine*, volume 1, in 1793.

Narcissi

Most species of *Narcissus* are found in the countries bordering the Mediterranean, and they have long been appreciated as garden plants. There are many references to them in classical and more recent literature.

There has long been confusion about the difference between daffodils and narcissi. Today all daffodils fall into the genus *Narcissus*. The popular old names of daffodil, daffodilly and daffadowndilly are thought to be corruptions of the word asphodel or asphodelus, while the old name Lent lily refers to the season in which they flower – that is, the 40 days leading up to Easter.

Both names – narcissus and daffodil – have been used in popular poetry and literature. In the early 1800s the poet William Wordsworth and his sister Dorothy were captivated by them. She poignantly described the scene in her diary as they walked in the woods beside Ullswater in the English Lake District:

April 15th 1802
We fancied that the lake had floated seeds ashore, and that the little colony had so sprung up. But as we went along there were more and yet more; and at last, under the boughs of the trees, we saw that there was a long belt of them along the shore, about the breadth of a country turnpike road. I never saw daffodils so beautiful. They grew among the mossy stones about and about them; some rested their heads upon these stones, as on a pillow, for weariness; and the rest tossed and reeled and danced, and seemed as if they verily laughed with the wind that blew upon them over the lake; they looked so gay, ever glancing, ever changing.

Dahlias

Originating from the mountain ranges of Mexico and south to Colombia, the dahlia was probably used in medicine and as fodder by the Aztecs before the Spanish conquest. In 1789 a handful of seeds was sent by Vincente Cervantes of the Botanical Gardens in Mexico City to his friend Abbé Cavanilles, who was in charge of the Botanical Gardens at Madrid. The Abbé later named this Mexican flower after the Swedish botanist, Dr Anders Dahl (1751–89). The plant was known not so much for its single flowers and rather poor stems but for its edible root, which was introduced to Europe as an alternative to the potato. Dahlia roots came to be eaten in France and parts of the Mediterranean coast, but their peculiar, sharp flavour prevented their adoption as a staple food.

One of the keys to its success as a garden plant was the interest taken in it by the Empress Josephine (1763–1814), wife of Napoleon Bonaparte, who kept the garden at Malmaison near Paris, France. She grew dahlias and guarded the roots jealously, refusing to give any away. One of her ladies-in-waiting, Countess de Bougainville, wanted to grow some for herself. She hatched a plan with her lover, a Polish prince, who went to the gardener at Malmaison and offered money to obtain the tubers. The gardener

The popular old English names of the daffodil were daffodilly and daffadowndilly, and it is still known as Lent lily. Socrates called it "Chaplet of the infernal Gods" because of its narcotic effects.

This miniature of Empress Josephine, the wife of Napoleon Bonaparte, was painted by J.B. Isabey. The Empress grew some of the first dahlias in Europe in her garden at Malmaison near Paris.

deceived his mistress and apparently sold a hundred plants for one gold louis each. When the empress found out what had happened she was furious. She sacked her gardener, banished both the lady-in-waiting and the prince and thereafter refused to show any more interest in dahlias.

Several attempts were made to introduce the dahlia tubers to Britain. In 1789 the Marchioness of Bute visited Spain and sent one of the tubers home, but it died. A few years later Lady Holland, who scandalized polite society by divorcing Sir Godfrey Webster and eloping with Lord Holland, who was ambassador to King Philip of Spain, went to Spain and saw a dahlia in bloom. Captivated by the flower, she too sent plants home. This time they thrived, and so Lady Holland can be credited with introducing the dahlia to Britain. Nurserymen began experimenting with its form, and within a short time the single-flowered variety had been dropped in favour of a double "globular" form, which became all the rage and was known as the globe dahlia. These were the precursors of the double "show" and "fancy" types, valued respectively for their single colours and mixed hues. At one time it was recorded that as many as 10,000 varieties were available.

Nerine

Flamboyant nerines also travelled a long way to reach Europe, for these bulbs are native to South Africa. In 1652 the first 500 colonists arrived at Table Bay to join the new settlement that the Dutch East India Company had established there. Among them were two gardeners, whose task was to grow fruit and vegetables for the community and, no doubt, for all the ships that sailed to destinations in the Pacific and those returning to Europe. They were also commissioned to collect any wildflowers that might be valuable to the Dutch at home. They were successful in their work, and seven years later crates of nerines were among a cargo to be shipped to the Netherlands in one of the Dutch East India Company's vessels.

Sadly, the ship was wrecked in the English Channel, off the island of Guernsey. The nerine bulbs were washed ashore and some took root in the sand. Over the years they spread inland and they eventually produced brilliant pink flowers, which local gardeners sent to the London flower market. They became commonly known as the Guernsey lily, a name that has been used for nerines ever since.

The islanders assumed that the bulbs were native to Japan, and it was more than 100 years before the error was realized, when in 1774 Francis Masson, the first ever official to be sent out as a plant hunter by Kew Gardens, England, saw the same flower, *Nerine sarniensis*, growing on the slopes of Table Mountain in South Africa.

Nerines first found their way to Europe on a boat that was shipwrecked near the island of Guernsey, where the bulbs have since naturalized.

Easter lily and regal lily

Like other plants, bulbs were sometimes unsuccessful when they were first introduced to the gardens of western Europe. This may have been because the season was inclement, the winter was particularly harsh or the cultural conditions were unsuitable. The lily is one such plant. A German doctor, Philipp von Siebold (1796–1866), first sent the lily we now know as the Easter lily from Japan to the Botanical Garden in Ghent in 1830, and it was reintroduced in 1840.

It was, however, a storm in the Atlantic that really changed the course of its history. Sometime in the 1860s a missionary was returning home to Europe from the coast of China. Among his possessions were a few bulbs of the same lily that von Siebold had previously tried to introduce. The stormy weather caused his vessel to take refuge in the shelter of St George's harbour on the island of Bermuda. The missionary was looked after there by the Reverend Roberts, and, as thanks for his hospitality, he gave the rector

some of his special bulbs, which were planted in the rectory garden. The lilies enjoyed the mild climate and shallow limestone soil and soon became well established on their new island home. By the end of the 19th century more than three million bulbs were exported from Bermuda each year, but disease ravaged the stock and ruined it.

The plant hunter E. H. Wilson records that it was Mr Harris, an American nurseryman from Philadelphia, who first brought the bulbs to the trade. Captivated by their elegant, pure white blooms and heavenly scent, which is just like orange blossom, Harris realized that if they could be forced into flower for Easter, he would have a valuable flowering commodity to fill the church vases. He launched his find under the name *Lilium harrisii*, a name by which it is still sometimes known today, although the correct name is now *Lilium longiflorum* var. *eximium*, commonly known as the Easter lily.

Wilson was an expert in lilies from eastern Asia, and he thought he had found one that would surpass the Easter lily. His great quest was the *Lilium regale*, which grew in the remote Min valley, where western China borders on Tibet. He had first discovered it in 1903 and the following year had dispatched 300 bulbs to Veitch & Sons, the sponsors of his expedition. He tried again in 1908, but on neither occasion did he succeed in getting them established.

In 1910 Wilson set out yet again, this time working for the Arnold Arboretum in Boston, Massachusetts. His driving ambition was to introduce the lily to the gardens of the West. He recognized its great potential, for it could withstand very cold winters and extremely hot summers and thrived despite high

E. H. Wilson's epic journey to the Min valley in western China in 1910 resulted in the successful introduction of *Lilium regale* to Western gardens.

Lilium longiflorum, or Easter lily, is still used to decorate churches on Easter Day.

winds. His journal describing the expedition reveals a story of great courage and determination. He left Boston, Massachusetts, at the end of March 1910 for Europe and from there travelled on the Trans-Siberian Railway, reaching Peking in early May. He had to navigate 2,900km (1,800 miles) up the Yangtze river, and northwards up its tributary, the Min, for another 400km (250 miles) until he at last reached the remote region between China and Tibet which he described as a "no man's land".

He gathered supplies at the town of Sungpang Ting (Songpan) and travelled for seven consecutive days down the endless gorge of the Min river. The path was winding and difficult, with few passing places. Wilson walked for most of the day, although he also had a light sedan chair made of rattan which was an outward sign of importance and respectability, crucial in those far-off places where Western travellers were rare and treated with great suspicion. His dog always went with him. On the eighth day, Wilson decided to make a base camp from which to explore the area and arrange for the autumn collection of bulbs.

Wilson was in the heart of the Min valley and, although the district was barren and desolate, it was here that he found the lilies growing, clinging to the windswept hillsides. The first flowers began to open in late spring, along the banks of the river some 760m (2,500ft) above sea level. As summer advanced, the band of white trumpets rose up the mountain, so that by midsummer lilies were blooming at 1,830m (6,000ft). From his camp Wilson arranged for between 6,000 and 7,000 lily bulbs to be lifted in autumn. The bulbs were to be encased in clay, before being packed in charcoal and sent to America.

Although tired after many months travelling, it was, he recorded, with a "light heart" and "satisfied mind" that he began his long homeward journey. As before, the road was tortuous, and he was travelling in his sedan chair when disaster struck: a rock fall started down the hillside. One of the stones hit his chair; another struck his right leg and broke it in two places. He eventually managed to get up and rode in his boy's chair with his leg lashed to the right pole. It was an agonizing three days before they reached the missionary post at Chengdu. In spite of the threat of amputation, three months later Wilson was able to get about on crutches. He hired a boat to take him eastwards to Shanghai and on to America. He was able to walk again, although with a limp.

Just a few days after his return, the huge shipment of bulbs arrived. He found them in excellent condition and they were planted the following spring. Since then millions of them have been raised and planted, and they have become one of the most popular lilies in cultivation today.

E. H. Wilson recorded in his diary that he found lilies growing "not in two or threes but in hundreds, in thousands, aye, in tens of thousands".

Gardening techniques

Work in the bulb garden changes as the seasons unfold. From the initial excitement of choosing and buying a selection of bulbs in the autumn comes the pleasure of planning where to plant them, whether this is in grassland, woodland, borders or in containers. As soon as they sprout into growth, the process of caring for the bulbs begins in earnest. Sometimes taller bulbs such as dahlias need staking, while many will need protection from pests and diseases. Some require a scant diet, while others are gross feeders. Some bulbs, such as snowdrops, hyacinths, daffodils and lilies, may be left in the ground year after year, while others, such as dahlias, cannas and begonias, require an annual lifting to avoid freezing winter temperatures. This may seem like an onerous task, but these are among the most flamboyant of all garden plants and so certainly well worth the extra effort.

Most spring-flowering bulbs, tubers, corms and rhizomes should be planted as dry bulbs in autumn. There is a wonderful choice, including these *Hyacinthus* (hyacinth) and *Muscari* (grape hyacinth).

Buying and planting bulbs

Obtain bulbs from mail-order suppliers or buy them as soon as they become available in the garden centres, when the range on offer will be at its maximum. Keep the bulbs in cool, dry conditions and plant them in the garden when weather conditions are favourable.

For summer colour, tuberous begonias, fuchsias and aeoniums replace tulips and wallflowers.

Choosing bulbs

Only plant bulbs that are firm to the touch and show no sign of damage. Storage of *Eranthis hyemalis* (winter aconite), *Iris reticulata*, little *Anemone blanda* and *Galanthus nivalis* (snowdrop) can cause drying, which in turn will impair their flower production. Buy bulbs as soon as they are available in the garden centre and plant as soon as possible. Alternatively, purchase them as growing plants "in the green".

Other storage problems can arise when the bulbs have been lifted too early, which typically happens when tulip bulbs are lifted before the leaves have died down. The result will be a chalkiness and hardness of the bulb, which will look dull and feel solid to the touch. It is not worth planting bulbs like this. Mail-order companies normally take great care, and these problems are less likely to arise. In garden centres you can often select bulbs from an open display unit. Choose the plumpest and biggest, and those that show no signs of damage.

Storing bulbs

You will be able to plant some bulbs immediately after you have purchased them. However, you may have to keep others until weather conditions are more suitable or until a new bed is ready. While you are waiting, it is important to keep bulbs in cool, dry, well-ventilated conditions, away from predators, such as mice or squirrels. If the air is damp and they are kept in enclosed bags, even paper bags, bacterial infections can set in, leading to a blue mould on the outer parts. Avoid planting any bulb that shows signs of this disfigurement.

Here are two plump and two dried-out *Iris reticulata* corms. Plant with care, discarding any that are shrivelled or damaged.

Blue mould on lily bulbs has been caused by poor storage. Do not plant.

Planting times

There are two main seasons for buying bulbs: autumn and late winter. Spring-flowering bulbs and corms, such as daffodils, tulips, hyacinths and crocuses, should be planted in autumn. These are all hardy plants and can withstand winter frosts. In late winter summer-flowering bulbs, corms, tubers and rhizomes of plants such as crinum, gladioli and begonias are available. These are not necessarily hardy and are best planted outside in spring. Indeed, begonias are half-hardy and thrive only in warm summer conditions. The tubers are brought into growth indoors and moved outside only after all risk of frost has passed. Dahlia tubers are usually treated in a similar way, although in

Some narcissus bulbs are particularly large, but must still be planted at three times their depth.

The correct planting tool

The size of the bulb also usually determines the tool used for planting. A dibber or trowel may be used for small bulbs, such as crocuses and anemones, but larger ones, such as *Lilium* (lilies), *Narcissus* (daffodils), or tulips need a sharp-edged spade to make a deep hole.

less frost-prone areas they can be planted deeper than normal, with the eye bud 10–15cm (4–6in) deep, then left as a permanent planting with a thick mulch in winter.

How to plant

Most bulbs, corms, tubers and rhizomes have a rounded bottom or base from which the old roots grow, and these are sometimes still attached to the bulb. They may also have a pointed or tapering nose at the top, from which the first shoots emerge. The general rule for planting is that the rounded base sits on the soil while the nose points upwards.

The planting depth is normally determined by the size of the bulb, and the general rule is that a bulb should be planted at a depth of three times its own size. Thus, if a bulb measures 5cm (2in) from nose to base, there should be 15cm (6in) of soil on top of it. This means that the hole required for planting is actually 20cm (8in) deep. There are a few exceptions to this rule –

nerines and crinums, for example, should be planted close to the surface of the soil, as should *Lilium candidum* (Madonna lily), which should be planted at a depth of about 2.5cm (1in).

Snowdrops "in the green"

Some bulbs, such as *Galanthus* (snowdrop), do not like being out of the ground too long in late summer before autumn planting. They are among the first to flower in the new year and like to make their root growth early. Many do not adapt well to the drying-out process to which most bulbs are subjected. An alternative method, therefore, is to buy snowdrops "in the green", which are available in late winter in pots or as a loose clump of plants with the leaves still attached to the bulbs. Plant them in border soil, where they will spread quickly, or in turf, where they will spread more slowly but will still naturalize well. Plant in groups of between eight and ten, spacing the individual plants about 7.5cm (3in) apart.

Planting in borders

Techniques for planting bulbs vary according to the season, to the style of garden, and to the effect you want to create in the borders.

Informal groups

Planting informal groups of the same bulb can be highly effective and, depending on the size of the border, the groups may be repeated a number of times, with bedding plants or other herbaceous perennials between them. Groups of tulips may be surrounded by *Myosotis* (forget-me-not) or *Viola* (pansy). Groups of alliums may be grown through nearby *Erysimum cheiri* (wallflower), while groups of gladioli might appear behind penstemons or earlier flowering poppies.

Extra drainage

Lilies are extremely hardy bulbs and can be planted in autumn or in late winter, whenever they become available to buy. However, they strongly dislike sitting in wet ground, much preferring well-

Allium hollandicum 'Purple Sensation' and *Lilium regale* grow side by side and in both cases the seedheads can be left intact to encourage self-seeding, but also to be enjoyed in their own right.

drained soil. If your soil is naturally heavy add a generous layer of grit in the bottom of the hole as you plant lily bulbs. This will improve the growing conditions, so they can remain in the soil for many years.

Fritillaria imperialis (crown imperial) is another large bulb that dislikes too much moisture at its

base. Use extra grit here, too, and plant the bulbs slightly tilted to ensure that moisture does not drain into the open, funnelled tops from where the shoots emerge.

Pre-planting in pots

It is possible to lift spring-flowering bulbs in summer, after flowering is over, and replace them with other seasonal bulbs or bedding. Simply dig them up with a spade (take care not to slice them in half) and move them elsewhere while their life-cycle is completed. Alternatively, plant them in a perforated plastic pot that can be buried in the border. This makes lifting much easier and allows the bulbs to complete their growth cycle without any root disturbance. Special wide bulb-savers can be used, which control the planting area and make lifting straightforward. Simply dig a hole that is wide enough to bury the bulb-saver in the ground, at the required depth, using a layer of gravel if necessary to make a level base. Position the bulbs and fill in with soil. If bulbs are not required for the following year, lift after

USING A BULB-SAVER

1 A bulb-saver allows bulbs to be located easily at lifting time. Dig down to the required depth, level off the hole and place the bulb-saver within it.

2 Arrange bulbs in the bulb-saver and cover with soil. Lift bulbs after flowering if they are not wanted for another year or wait until the leaves have died back before lifting.

PLANTING IN A BURIED POT

1 Dig a hole deep enough to contain a large, black, plastic pot. Fill the pot with a 2.5cm (1in) layer of drainage material.

2 Add loamy compost (soil mix), and sit the bulbs 15cm (6in) below the rim of the pot. Cover with more compost.

3 Bury the pot in the hole and cover the top with a thin mulch of cocoa shells or compost to keep weeds at bay.

4 Enjoy the flowers, then remove the pot. Dry off the bulbs and fill the space with summer plants.

flowering. If they are required, allow them to complete their life-cycle and only then lift and store.

Pre-planting in pots is also a useful technique for dealing with summer-flowering bulbs that cannot survive frosty, damp conditions and are best planted in the garden only after all risk of frost has passed. Bulbs planted in containers the previous autumn, such as *Ornithogalum dubium*, or earlier in spring, such as freesias, can be transferred to the garden in early summer when they are already well into growth. Similarly, they can be lifted in autumn before the onset of wintry weather.

Planting for a succession of spring colour

Although an individual group of bulbs will enhance any border, it is possible to plant several types together at the same time in the autumn. This will create an enormous impact and give colour for many weeks. Choose from any of the dwarf early daffodils, such as *Narcissus* 'February Gold', 'Tête-à-tête', 'Topolino', 'Jumblie' or 'Jetfire', for example, and any of the early tulips, including *Tulipa* 'Shakespeare', 'Heart's Delight' or 'Stresa'. You can then interplant with crocuses, chionodoxas or *Muscari* spp. (grape

hyacinth). These can be followed by another grouping nearby of mid-season daffodils, such as *N*. 'Pipit' or 'Thalia', and tulips, such as *T*. 'White Dream' and 'Attila'. For late-spring blooms choose tulips such as *T*. 'Queen of Night' and 'Blue Heron' and late daffodils, such as *N. poeticus* var. *recurvus* (pheasant's eye). Choosing bulbs from within these three seasonal groups will give great pleasure throughout early, mid- and late spring. Plant pansies, violas, polyanthus, primroses, forget-me-nots or wallflowers on top to add extra colour.

Planting for spring and summer

A bulb border can have summer as well as spring interest, and a single planting session in autumn can give six months of delightful colour. In a formal box-hedged border, for example, a spring planting of tulips, anemones and fritillaries might give way in summer to groups of *Allium hollandicum* 'Purple Sensation' and white *Lilium regale* (regal lily). All these bulbs can be left in the ground year after year, but it would be possible to lift the tulips and plant summer bedding (annuals) to enhance the alliums and lilies.

Bulbs for borders

Late autumn to late spring	Early summer to mid-autumn
Anemone blanda	Amaryllis
Camassia	belladonna
Crocus	Begonia
Eranthis hyemalis	Crinum x powellii
Eremurus	Crocosmia
Erythronium	Eremus
Fritallaria	Galtonia
Galanthus nivalis	Hedychium
Hyacinthus	Lilium
Narcissus	Nerine
Tulipa	Tigridia

Planting in grass

Many of the bulbs that flower in late winter, early spring and mid-spring, such as *Galanthus* (snowdrop), *Eranthis hyemalis* (winter aconite), crocuses, anemones, most daffodils and some *Erythronium* (dog's tooth violet), thrive in grass, coming up year after year and self-seeding themselves. These robust bulbs can withstand competition from grass roots and are much more suitable for this type of planting. Early in the year, when the grass is short and competition for light is not a problem, the pointed shoots cut through the turf quite easily.

Late spring and summer flowering bulbs

Some of the late-flowering spring bulbs can also be grown successfully in this way. *Hyacinthoides non-scripta* (English bluebell) and *H. hispanica* (Spanish bluebell), as well as *Ornithogalum nutans*, *Narcissus poeticus* var. *recurvus* (pheasant's eye) and the camassias, such as *Camassia leichtlinii*, make attractive additions to grassy areas in meadow gardens or between orchard trees. Tall blue camassia flowers look particularly pretty with the fallen petals of apple blossom. A number of late-flowering tulips can also be used in these situations, but

Bulbs for planting in grass

Anemone blanda	*Eranthis hyemalis*
Camassia (many)	*Erythronium*
Chionodoxa	(several)
(several)	*Fritillaria*
Colchicum spec.	*meleagris*
'Album'	*Galanthus nivalis*
Crocus (many)	*Narcissus*
Cyclamen coum	(many)
Cyclamen	*Ornithogalum*
hederifolium	*nutans*

most species will need to be replanted every second or third year, and it will be difficult to know where previous bulbs have been planted.

By mid- to late summer the choice is more restricted because by this time the grass presents too much competition for most bulbs, and most gardeners are, in any case, anxious to cut the grass regularly and keep it neatly mown. It is better to rely on the earlier periods of the year for the extra colour that naturalized bulbs bring.

To ensure successful displays of flowers in future years, bulbs that are planted in grass need to complete their growing cycle before the grass can be mown and the bulbs' leaves cut off. This usually takes about six weeks after flowering. Camassias

Crocus vernus naturalized in grass.

and late daffodils should not be mown until midsummer is past or even later.

Protecting bulbs

Sometimes newly planted bulbs are discovered by squirrels and mice. Be sure to replace the turf firmly to make it more difficult for the bulbs to be found. Crocus corms will be especially at risk. Later in the year sparrows might peck out the flowers. Crisscross the area with black thread to deter them, but make sure that the supporting pegs are clearly visible or it might prove a hazard to humans as well as the birds.

PLANTING BULBS INDIVIDUALLY

1 Throw the bulbs on to the turf in a random fashion and plant accordingly, but try to allow a distance of about 7.5–20cm (3–8in) between each one.

2 Dig a deep, square hole, of about a spade's width and about 25cm (10in) deep, depending on the size of the bulb. You may need to go deeper than one spade's depth.

3 Plant the bulb, base down and the neck or nose pointing upwards. Cover the bulb with loose soil and replace the top divot. Firm down gently.

PLANTING BULBS IN LARGE GROUPS

1 Dig a trench a spade's width and fold the turf backwards on itself. Use a trowel or dig down to a depth of about 25cm (10in).

2 Plant *Narcissus poeticus* var. *recurvus* with *Camassia leichtlinii*, placing them alternately about 20cm (8in) apart.

3 Fill in with loose soil so that the tops of the bulbs are covered. Replace the turf and firm down well with the heel of your boot.

Planting individually

When you are planting small bulbs a special metal bulb dibber is ideal. Because you should be planting the bulbs to a depth three times their own height, check to see if there are any markings up the side of the dibber to indicate how far down to press. Choose the spot, push the dibber into the turf, twist slightly and pull it out. This action will remove a small clod of earth. Drop the little bulb or corm into the hole, nose upwards, and break off a little of the base soil from the clod so that it gently covers the bulb or corm before you replace the divot of earth.

Larger bulbs, such as daffodils, are better planted with a spade. Throw the bulbs down at random and plant them where they fall, although you should try to allow a distance of at least 15–20cm (6–8in) between each one. The space allows the bulbs to multiply below ground and over the years to create a much greater display. Some daffodil bulbs are large, more than 6cm (2¹/₂in) high, and so need more than one spade's depth. In fact, the hole may need to

be nearly 25cm (10in) deep. Plant a group of 10 to 20 bulbs or even more in this way so that you create a good show for spring.

Planting larger groups

Where larger planting areas are planned, it can be easier to remove a whole section of turf with a spade and plant several bulbs in one hole. The step-by-step sequence shows the planting of late-flowering *Narcissus poeticus* var. *recurvus* (pheasant's eye) with *Camassia leichtlinii* in a trench. They were planted to create an outer row of bulbs that would flower in

late spring, flanking an area of two lots of earlier flowering daffodils, which were planted formally in rows between cherry trees. In this way, there is a succession of flowering from early to mid-spring through to late spring.

Leaving the grass

Although it will look untidy, allow six weeks to pass after flowering before cutting the grass where bulbs have been growing. This will ensure good results for the following year. The grass will soon recover.

Drifts of daffodils look wonderful in spring grassland where they will multiply over the years.

Planting in the eye of a tree

Some trees and situations will be more suitable than others. The soil around the trunks of most evergreen trees is too dry for the planting of bulbs to be successful, while many conifers have comparatively shallow roots. Deciduous trees, such as apples, pears, ornamental crab apples or cherry trees and magnolias, on the other hand, are ideal. The borders can be any shape you choose, but an area about 90cm (36in) long and 60cm (24in) from the centre of the tree trunk is easiest for a lawn mower to get around.

Muscari armeniacum (grape hyacinth) will start into flower in late winter or very early spring. Here it is planted beneath *Magnolia stellata*, producing a gorgeous blue haze.

Plant a large group of blue *Muscari armeniacum* (grape hyacinth) about 5cm (2in) apart. Cover with soil so that their tips are about 5cm (2in) below soil level.

Selecting suitable bulbs

Choose bulbs that will flower before the trees come into leaf and block out all the sunlight. All the early spring-flowering dwarf daffodils are perfect, and if you combine them with *Anemone blanda*, *Muscari armeniacum* (grape hyacinth), scillas and tulips, as well as earlier flowering *Galanthus* (snowdrop), cyclamen and *Eranthis hyemalis* (winter aconite), you can have a succession of flowering that will be a delight

year after year. Herbaceous plants can be used as well. Hellebores, *Tanacetum parthenium* 'Aureum' (golden feverfew), *Lunaria annua* (honesty), *Myosotis* (forget-me-not) and *Galium odoratum* (sweet woodruff) make excellent bedfellows.

The choice of bulb will depend to some extent on the shape of the tree and its position in the garden. Where an ornamental tree with low branches such as *Magnolia stellata* or one of the soulangeana hybrids

features as a centrepiece of a formal lawn in a front or back garden, for example, low-growing bulbs are appropriate. *Muscari armeniacum* (grape hyacinth) would be perfect, massed up on their own or mixed rather more formally with short pink Double Early tulips, such as *Tulipa* 'Peach Blossom'. In this type of situation either informal or formal would be appropriate and effective. You might have to replant the tulips every two years, and eventually you would have to extend the size of the eye as the tree expanded its branches with age, but there would be no need to buy more grape hyacinths. You could simply divide the ones already established closer to the trunk.

A gnarled old apple tree on the fringes of the garden or in the orchard suggests a natural look, using species bulbs or cultivars that are close to the species. A sheet of blue or white *Anemone blanda* would look exquisite; so would a single planting of *Narcissus* 'Topolino' or *N.* 'February Gold'. But whatever you do, avoid the split corona narcissi, such as *N.* 'Cassata' or garish *N.* 'Professor Einstein', which are much less likely to do well in future years in these circumstances and

Narcissus 'February Gold' is one of the best of all the early dwarf daffodils. Lustrous in colour, it is early to flower, sturdy, long lasting and elegant in shape. Planted en masse, it creates a generous splash of yellow beneath an old cherry tree.

would not be in keeping with the spirit of the planting. If you want a display that will reliably flower for many years to come *N.* 'February Gold' is a great stalwart and easy to find. It is sturdy, long lasting and makes a wonderful show for several weeks in early spring, lasting for much longer than many of the mid-spring varieties.

Another excellent choice for a long-lasting and long-term display is *Anemone blanda*. The tubers are relatively inexpensive to buy and can be planted liberally and allowed to self-seed. Available in many shades of blue and mauve, and also in white, the anemones will eventually form a sea of colour beneath the tree, completely covering the eye border and even expanding into the grass beyond if allowed to do so. The lumpy tubers should be soaked in water overnight to rehydrate them before they are planted, about 5cm (2in) deep and 5cm (2in) apart. It is sometimes difficult to tell which is the top and which is the bottom of the tubers, but if you can detect any hairy roots you will know they are growing from the bottom. Plant them on their own or mix in the

Anemone blanda makes a wonderful display beneath an apple tree, starting its display in late winter and lasting until mid-spring.

An eye-shaped border, 90cm (36in) long and 60cm (24in) in width from the centre of a deciduous tree, is ideal for a lawnmower to get around. It can look splendid planted with early, mid- or even late spring bulbs.

company of wild primroses, golden feverfew and clumps of dwarf daffodils such as *Narcissus* 'February Gold' or 'Tête-à-tête'.

Late summer- and early autumn-flowering bulbs

Allow bulbs and corms to complete their cycle of growth before clearing away the old leaves in midsummer. By then these borders will be in heavy shade and little else will grow successfully, except perhaps a few *Digitalis* (foxglove) and a rambling rose. Just as the fruit is turning ripe a range of late summer- to early autumn-flowering bulbs will come into flower. One lovely example is *Colchicum speciosum* 'Album' (autumn crocus), whose white, goblet-shaped flowers open before the foliage appears, giving rise to the common name, naked ladies. The leaves may, in fact, dwarf any spring-flowering

bulbs planted close by. *Cyclamen hederifolium* is another autumn and winter subject for this position. It, too, often flowers before producing leaves, welcome for their distinctive shape and intricate markings.

Bulbs for planting in the eye of a tree

Anemone blanda	Hyacinthus
Anemone	orientalis
nemerosa	Muscari
Arum italicum	Narcissus
Chionodoxa	'February Gold'
Colchicum	Narcissus
speciosum	'Hawera'
Crocus	Narcissus
Cyclamen coum	'Jumblie'
Cyclamen	Narcissus
hederifolium	'Segovia'
Eranthis hyemalis	Narcissus 'Tête-
Galanthus nivalis	à-tête'
Hyacinthoides	Narcissus
non-scripta	'Topolino'

Planting in large containers

If you are planting a large container in autumn to give a spring display, you have a wide choice of medium to tall daffodils, hyacinths and tulips, which can be underplanted with polyanthus, violas, pansies, forget-me-nots or wallflowers. Combine any of these with bronze or bright golden foliage and you will have a masterpiece.

Planning

It is important to plan before you plant. Think of the overall shape you want to achieve and consider the height and spread of the plants in relation to the depth of the container. Dwarf daffodils or tulips are best for a hanging basket, but a large half-barrel will accommodate taller plants, including the mid-season tulips and daffodils, which grow to 30–40cm (12–16in). If there is room, include a shrub or conifer in the centre to give added structure, or use *Hedera* (ivy) or *Vinca* (periwinkle) to soften the edges of the container and make a pleasing shape as they trail.

Consider also when you would like the container to look its best. If you want an explosion of colour in mid-spring, use daffodils or tulips with pansies. For a later splash of colour, use late-flowering tulips with pansies, forget-me-nots or wallflowers,

Bulbs for large containers

Late autumn to late spring	Early summer to mid-autumn
Anemone blanda	Begonia
Crocus	Canna
Hyacinthus	Dahlia (small to
Iris reticulata	medium)
Muscari	Eucomis
Narcissus 'Actea'	Hedychium
Narcissus 'Pipit'	Lilium
Narcissus	Nerine
'Salome'	Tigridia
Tulipa (many)	Tulbaghia

A DAFFODIL HALF-BARREL

1 Drill six drainage holes in the base of the half-barrel. Line the base and sides with a bin liner (trash bag) or black plastic. Cut slits in the liner to match the drainage holes. Add a 7.5cm (3in) layer of drainage material, such as pieces of polystyrene (styrofoam). Fill to about two-thirds full with potting compost (soil mix).

3 Add more compost, then plant the skimmias and heucheras on opposite sides of the barrel.

which are available in a wide range of colours that complement almost any choice of tulip. Although they will not start flowering until mid-spring, they will provide greenery, and once they start to flower the show will last for many weeks.

Summer containers

Wonderful summer containers can be achieved by using lilies, begonias, eucomis, cannas and dahlias. Begonias combine well with many bedding plants and look spectacular with some fuchsias, while lilies and

2 Position the central shrub (the cornus) so that it sits just below the rim. Plant the daffodil bulbs, base down, nose up, close to the edge of the barrel, so that the tips of the bulbs will be at an eventual depth below soil level of three times their own height, allowing for a 5cm (2in) gap at the top of the container.

4 Fill in the gaps with more compost to within 2.5cm (1in) of the rim. Plant the pansies around the edge. Water well.

triteleias make simple and effective partnerships. Dahlias might team up with a fringe of lobelia, but cannas and eucomis are usually best kept as a single-species planting.

A long-lasting display

If you want colour and interest from the time of autumn planting through to mid- or late spring, you will have to choose a range of plant material. Winter-flowering pansies and violas will flower on and off from the time of planting right through to early summer, depending on the temperature and how much sun the container receives. The sunnier the spot, the better the display will be.

Coloured bark on shrubs adds drama and interest, particularly as the winter progresses and the colours deepen. *Cornus alba* 'Sibirica' (red-stemmed dogwood), with its glistening rich red stems, is an excellent choice. Evergreen shrubs can be selected to provide foliage, coloured berries, buds or flowers. *Viburnum tinus* (laurustinus) is a great favourite, or choose *Skimmia japonica* 'Rubella', which has dark red flower buds throughout the winter months, opening to white flowers in spring. It makes a dramatic association with red-stemmed dogwoods. Add a purple-leaved heuchera and mahogany-red pansies as a wonderful backdrop for the spring bulbs.

Crocuses would extend the display in spring, together with various irises or *Anemone blanda*, which could be followed by later-flowering daffodils or tulips. Any bulb with a coppery or pink colour variation will look stunning with red and bronze foliage. *Narcissus* 'Rose Caprice', with rosy salmon-pink cups, 'Salome', with pinkish-orange cups, or 'Rainbow', with coppery pink cups, would all make lovely combinations. The coppery pink hues of lilies, such as *Lilium* 'Pink Tiger', would tone well in midsummer.

Drainage

All containers need to be given adequate drainage, but you must take extra care with winter containers to avoid damaging the bulbs. Choose a soil-based potting compost (soil mix) or use a peat-based compost and add extra grit, in the ratio of approximately three parts compost to one part grit. Before planting place a layer of broken pots or polystyrene

A TULIP AND WALLFLOWER TERRACOTTA POT

1 Cover the drainage hole with broken pots or pieces of polystyrene (styrofoam) and add a layer of compost, with extra grit mixed in if using peat-based compost (soil mix).

2 Add sufficient compost so that when the tulip bulbs are planted, base down, nose up, they will be at a depth below soil level of three times their own height.

3 Wallflowers are often sold in bunches of ten. Separate them, choosing those with the best root systems.

4 Plant seven or eight of the wallflowers around the top of the container. Firm them down into the compost. Water well.

(styrofoam) at the base of the container, which will help to give extra drainage in periods of continued wet weather. The drainage layer will also help to prevent the roots of the plants from blocking the drainage holes, which are sometimes too small in relation to the size of the pot.

Wooden containers will eventually rot. To slow down the process, add a lining of plastic sheeting, which will retain the moisture in the compost and keep the wood dry on the inside. Make holes in the base of the plastic to match the holes in the container base. The lining also helps minimize

moisture loss through evaporation in late spring when the container may be in danger of drying out.

Tulipa 'Blue Heron' and orange wallflowers make a vibrant combination.

Planting in small containers and window boxes

Shorter flowering bulbs, tubers and corms are more suitable for small containers and window boxes than for medium to large containers.

Choosing suitable bulbs

There are many bulbs to choose from, including all the dwarf daffodils, such as *Narcissus* 'February Gold', 'Jack Snipe', 'Jetfire', 'Jumblie', 'Topolino', 'Tête-à-tête' and 'Peeping Tom', and the later-flowering 'Hawera'. Dwarf tulips also look wonderful in pots. All the early-flowering singles, such as *Tulipa* 'Heart's Delight', 'Shakespeare' and 'Stresa', and the doubles, such as 'Peach Blossom' and 'Willemsoord', can be used. Hyacinths also make excellent container bulbs and are available in a wide range of colours including blue (*Hyacinthus orientalis* 'Delft Blue' and 'Blue Magic'), white ('L'Innocence'), yellow ('City of Haarlem'), pink ('Lady Derby') and salmon-pink ('Gipsy Queen'). This is just a small selection: there are many others.

Four planting schemes

These main three types of spring bulb – daffodils, tulips and hyacinths – can be treated in four ways. First, plant them on their own, in generous numbers, and wait for them to flower. Second, add some bedding plants – pansies, violas, primroses or polyanthus, for example – to extend the season of colour so that there is interest before the main bulb display.

Third, adopt a two-tier planting scheme and add another type of lower-growing corm, bulb or tuber, which will flower at the same time. The white or blue star-shaped flowers of *Anemone blanda* make a lovely carpet of colour, as do late Dutch crocuses (forms of *Crocus vernus*), *Muscari armeniacum*, *M. neglectum*, *M. latifolium* or *M. botryoides* 'Album' (grape hyacinths in various shades and combinations of blue, almost black and white), *Chionodoxa* (blue or pink) and, to a lesser extent, scillas. These all have the advantage of being relatively inexpensive and are often sold in packets of ten or twenty. Try, for example, combining *Narcissus* 'February Gold' and large Dutch crocus; hyacinths with white *Anemone blanda*; Double Early tulips with *Muscari armeniacum*; or *Narcissus* 'Segovia' with pale blue *Muscari armeniacum* 'Valerie Finnis'.

The fourth approach is to adopt the two-tier planting scheme and then add a few violas or primroses. Avoid planting the bedding plants directly above the bulbs because the shoots of the bulbs are sharp and will force their way between the roots of the bedding plants, lifting them out of the compost (soil mix).

PLANTING A SMALL CONTAINER

1 Cover the base of the pot with a 2.5cm (1in) layer of drainage material. Add 5cm (2in) of a soil-based compost (soil mix).

2 Add four handfuls of grit to give extra drainage. This is important because hyacinths do not like to be too wet in winter.

3 Plant the bulbs so that their bases sit firmly on the grit, spacing them so that they do not touch each other or the sides of the container. Cover with more compost until their tips are just showing.

4 Plant the primroses in a circle between the outer bulbs. Top up with more compost, bringing the level to within 2.5cm (1in) of the rim of the container. Water well and add more compost if necessary.

Planting depths in winter containers are sometimes less than in the ground, especially when small pots or shallow containers are used. This is usually acceptable as long as the bulbs are not expected to remain as a long-term planting scheme and the pots are put in a sheltered spot during the winter.

Drainage

One of the major problems for bulbs that are overwintered outdoors is inadequate drainage. If possible, use a soil-based compost (soil mix) with plenty of grit mixed in. If you prefer to use a peat-based compost (soil mix), add extra grit in the ratio of three parts compost to one part grit. When you are planting sensitive bulbs, such as hyacinths, add an extra layer of grit beneath the bulbs. This will improve the drainage still further and avoid their roots sitting in cold, waterlogged soil.

Colour combinations

For late spring and summer colour try *Anemone coronaria*, using the single flowers in the De Caen Group or the double flowers of the St Bridgid Group. Both types are available in a range of vibrant colours. An all-white colour scheme using *A. coronaria* De Caen Group 'The Bride' would look stunning, or you might prefer a mix of red and rich blue.

If you prefer a mid- to late-summer display that lasts into autumn, Non-Stop and trailing begonias are hard to beat for length of flowering and range of colours. Start the tubers into growth in a greenhouse, placing them hollow side up on the top of the compost. You could combine Non-Stop and trailing begonias in the same display or use the Non-Stops with bedding plants such as dark blue lobelia to soften the edge.

PLANTING A WINDOW BOX

1 Cover the base of the window box with a 2.5cm (1in) layer of drainage material, such as small pieces of polystyrene (styrofoam) or broken pots.

2 Add about 5cm (2in) of soil-based compost (soil mix), or a peat-based compost with extra grit (in the ratio of three parts compost to one part grit).

3 Plant the daffodil bulbs in two rows, spacing them so that they do not touch each other or the sides of the container. Cover with more soil so that just the tips show.

4 Bring the soil to within 2.5cm (1in) of the rim and add the bedding plants. Here, two cinerarias are planted in the middle with three yellow and three white violas on either side.

The window box looks stunning with the yellow and white spring flowers set off by the silver-grey foliage of *Senecio cineraria*.

Planting in hanging baskets

Whether you choose a sophisticated white and gold colour scheme or opt for a daring riot of bright colours, you will find that spring and summer hanging baskets make a delightful addition to a house wall or patio.

Spring hanging baskets

For spring colour, hanging baskets can be planted with a wide range of bulbs, including all the dwarf daffodils, dwarf tulips and hyacinths, together with an underplanting of crocus, *Anemone blanda, Muscari armeniacum* (grape hyacinth), chionodoxa, scillas and so on. Scale is the important factor here, so avoid

any that grow more than 30cm (12in) high. *Hedera* (ivy) is a simple but effective edging plant to clothe the sides of a spring hanging basket. The main problem comes in mid- to late winter, when cold winds dry out the leaves, turning them brown and ragged. If you are using a wire basket, take a tip from Victorian gardeners and use small wires to fix the ivy trails in to the moss lining. The effect is to create a ball of ivy, where the trails stay close to the sides of the basket and do not get spoiled by the wind. By the time spring arrives, dwarf daffodils and grape hyacinths, for example, will be

in full flower. Meanwhile, the ivy will have started to root in the moss and within a season you will have an ivy ball, which will make summer and next winter's planting easy. It will dry out quickly in summer so hang the basket in a shady place where evaporation will be less of a problem. Add some shade-tolerant bedding plants in the top so that you remember to water the basket. Keep pegging in the ivy trails as they grow. After the second season, the ivy will need pruning both at its growing tips and roots or it will take over completely. Empty the basket, save some ivy trails and replant along with the bulbs in fresh soil.

Severe winter weather can spoil autumn-planted, spring-flowering baskets because neither moss nor wicker lining provides much insulation. In extremely cold or windy conditions, put the basket in a porch or garage. Never water in frosty conditions. It is better to keep all containers on the dry side in freezing weather as long as you keep the compost (soil mix) just moist. More moisture will be required in spring, when growth is taking place. If you have used bedding plants, such as pansies, apply a liquid feed in early spring to encourage a good display to coincide with the bulbs.

Summer hanging baskets

Sumptuous summer baskets can be filled with Non-Stop or trailing begonias. Start the begonias into growth in a greenhouse, planting the tubers on top of the compost, hollow side up. Three or four trailing begonias with a Non-Stop bushy begonia for the centre will make a wonderful display in a 35–40cm (14–16in) diameter basket. For something different try *Begonia* 'Picotee', a cultivar with an upright

The tulips and muscari are long lasting and make a wonderful contrast among the violas and pansies in this colourful hanging basket (see steps on page 33).

habit but large, heavy flowers, which create a natural fountain effect providing colour all round the margins of the basket as well as in the centre. Like all the tuberous begonias it will provide colour from midsummer through to late autumn. But be sure to take the basket down off its hook before the first autumn frosts and take it to the shelter of a frost-free greenhouse. Remove the topgrowth as the compost dries out and the stems break off from the tubers, and leave dormant tubers until growth buds appear in spring when watering can begin again.

Autumn and winter baskets

You can give structure to autumn and winter schemes by adding *Hedera* (ivy) or the low-growing *Euphorbia myrsinites* around the edges. Include a central herbaceous plant, such as the purple form of wood spurge, *Euphorbia amygdaloides* 'Purpurea'. Alternatively, a young shrub, such as the tree heath, *Erica arborea* 'Albert's Gold', or a rosemary with its flush of pale blue spring flowers. The variegated Japanese spindle, *Euonymus japonicus* 'Aureus', is excellent for its golden touch, or use bushy *E. fortunei* 'Emerald 'n' Gold'. If you prefer a silver and white display, include *E. fortunei* 'Silver Queen' with its white-edged leaves or *Viburnum tinus*, which is not only evergreen but has white flowers as well. Even the buds are colourful, being tinged with pink. The viburnum is a good evergreen choice, offering colour and interest through the winter months. White or pink winter-flowering heathers can be planted at the sides to soften the edges. Devise your own colour scheme by introducing pansies, violas, primroses and daisies. When the display is over, plant the shrubs in the garden and allow them to grow on.

A COLOURFUL HANGING BASKET

1 Cover the base of the basket with a generous amount of moss and line with a piece of plastic sheeting. Cut some 2.5cm (1in) slits in the bottom. Add a layer of compost (soil mix) to a depth of 5cm (2in).

2 Plant three violas, spacing them widely, on top of the moss wall with their roots firmly in the compost. Plant three of the pansies between them.

3 Tuck a large handful of moss around the shoulders of each plant so that no gaps remain. Bring the moss wall two-thirds up the sides of the basket.

4 Plant the top tier so that a viola sits above a pansy and vice versa. Add more moss around each plant, bringing the wall 2.5cm (1in) above the rim.

5 Plant the tulip bulbs in outer and inner circles. Cover with soil until just the tips of the bulbs show. Add the *Muscari armeniacum* and add more soil to completely cover all the bulbs.

6 Plant the remaining violas and pansies, making sure they do not cover any of the bulbs. Water well, and hang the basket in a sunny sheltered spot.

A long-term hanging basket

Euphorbia amygdaloides (wood spurge), a hardy herbaceous perennial, might seem an unusual choice for a hanging basket, but it has many qualities, the chief of which is that it provides interest all year round. The cultivar 'Purpurea' has dark reddish-purple stems, which deepen as the weather gets colder in late autumn, then from mid-spring to early summer it comes to life with lime-green flowers. The stems need cutting right back after flowering to encourage new growth from the base to produce the following season's flowers. Apart from this, it needs little extra attention. A simple planting of ivy around the edge of the basket provides an evergreen frill. There are many ivies to choose from, but *Hedera helix* 'Glacier' has the added attraction of its variegation, and planted with the purple spurge it, too, takes on russet, purple tones in cold winter weather. Planted alongside are a few violas. These are from the Princess Series, chosen for their compact habit and pretty colours. But there are many others to choose from, so you can replace them each autumn. The crowning glory is the dwarf daffodil, *Narcissus* 'Hawera', which flowers for many weeks spanning the season between mid- and late spring. Each stem bears up to five dainty canary yellow blooms, an effective partner for the flowering spurge. Hardy and reliable, it is a good choice for a long-lasting display both in its first season and in following years.

Winter hanging baskets

The ivy ball is just one idea for a winter hanging basket that lasts for more than one season. There are many other possibilities for using bulbs mixed with young shrubs and heathers or herbaceous perennials. If you are using a dense planting scheme, choose a lined wicker basket, rather than a wire-framed one, because this will give more planting room and will retain moisture better, both in winter and, more importantly, throughout the following summer. As with the ivy ball, plant a summer bedding plant in a gap where a pansy or viola has been flowering in winter and spring. This will add freshness to the arrangement as well as reminding you to keep the container moist through the summer.

Bulbs for hanging baskets

Late autumn to late spring	Early summer to mid-autumn
Anemone blanda	Begonia (cascade
Crocus	pendulous, or
Hyacinthus	Non-Stop)
Iris reticulata	Begonia 'Picotee'
Muscari	Tigridia
Narcissus 'Bellsong'	Tulipa clusiana 'Lady Jane'
Narcissus 'Hawera'	Tulipa 'Honky Tonk'
Tulipa 'Shakespeare'	Tulipa 'Tinka' Tulipa urumiensis

PLANTING A LONG-TERM HANGING BASKET

1 Plant *Euphorbia amygdaloides* 'Purpurea' in the centre surrounded by ten *Narcissus* 'Hawera' bulbs.

2 Alternate three *Viola x wittrockiana* (pansy) from the Princess series and three *Hedera helix* 'Glacier' ivies around the edge.

3 Deadhead the narcissi and remember to apply a liquid feed to strengthen the bulbs for next year's display.

4 Trim the euphorbia in midsummer, cutting right back to the base so that new growth will emerge for next season's flowers. Replace the violas with summer bedding. In autumn replace with new violas.

PLANTING A LINED WICKER BASKET

1 Cut slits, 2.5cm (1in) long, in the plastic lining of a 40cm (16in) lined wicker basket.

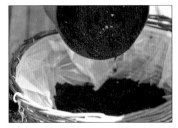

2 Add 5–7.5cm (2–3in) soil-based potting compost (soil mix).

3 Plant *Euonymus fortunei* 'Emerald 'n' Gold' towards the back, teasing out the roots.

4 Plant two *Erica carnea* 'Springwood White' on either side of the euonymus, close to the edge of the basket.

5 Plant ten *Narcissus* 'Hawera' bulbs around the central shrub and cover with soil so that just the tips of the planted bulbs show.

6 Plant small groups of *Tulipa* 'Tinka' and *Muscari* 'Valerie Finnis' in the next layer between the heathers and the central shrub.

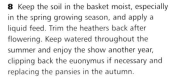

7 Add more soil, particularly around the edge of the basket so that the heathers are well surrounded. Plant four *Viola* x *wittrockiana* (pansy), making sure they do not cover any of the bulbs, and fill in any gaps with soil. Firm in the plants, water well and hang up in a sheltered spot in sun or partial shade.

8 Keep the soil in the basket moist, especially in the spring growing season, and apply a liquid feed. Trim the heathers back after flowering. Keep watered throughout the summer and enjoy the show another year, clipping back the euonymus if necessary and replacing the pansies in the autumn.

Care and maintenance

The most widely grown spring-flowering bulbs, including daffodils, tulips and hyacinths, are fully hardy and will cope with frosty weather, but some summer- and autumn-flowering plants, such as crinums and nerines, are only borderline hardy. In extreme winter weather they will benefit from a protective layer of dry peat, bracken or sacking.

Some sites may be too windy for certain bulbs, and if you cannot find a sheltered corner, it would be better to choose plants that can cope with the conditions in your garden. For example, large-flowering, mid-season daffodils are often planted in grassland. Some will be fine planted in this way, but those with weak stems are best avoided. Instead, select shorter, earlier flowering daffodils with small flowers that will stand up to the buffeting of spring winds.

Staking
Some plants – cannas, large dahlias, most lilies and some gladioli, for example – grow tall in summer and should be grown in sheltered positions where gusts of wind will not cause damage. Dahlias in particular, which put on bushy as well as high growth, must be staked. Use metal plant supports or wooden stakes with string to contain the growth in early to midsummer. This might look unsightly at first, but the supports will soon be hidden by foliage. Smaller patio dahlias do not need staking, nor do the single-flowered forms with wiry stems, such as *Dahlia* 'Dark Desire'.

Lilies with large trumpet-shaped flowers might also need support. The stems are often strong and wiry and will not break, but the weight of the flowers can pull the head down and the display is less impressive. A single metal stake with a ring support positioned behind the plant is ideal because it allows some movement and is not intrusive. A bamboo cane and string are good alternatives. Tall gladioli should be supported in the same way. *Crocosmia* 'Lucifer' is a tall plant producing large flowerheads and providing support early in the growing season will enhance the flowering display.

Drainage
Some plants, notably lilies, hate having their roots constantly in wet soil, so it is a good idea to plant lily bulbs on a layer of extra grit to aid drainage. This is true whether they are grown in pots or in garden soil. If you have clay soil in your garden, treat hyacinths in the same way.

Watering
Newly planted bulbs need adequate moisture to allow their roots to grow in autumn. Watering is important throughout the year, not just in summer. Bulbs planted in garden soil do not normally need extra watering, but it is important that the compost (soil mix) in containers is kept moist. This is most important in spring, when rainfall may miss hanging baskets and window boxes that are in the rain shadow cast by the house. In summer additional and regular watering is vital, particularly in dry spells. Some plants, notably begonias, are easily spoiled if water is allowed to splash on to leaves and petals and left when the sun is shining. The scorch marks that

Metal ring supports should be placed around dahlias as soon as growth begins to get above about 30cm (12in).

Early staking is important, especially for plants that bear large flowers, to protect them in windy weather.

It is important to add a layer of grit to aid drainage when planting lilies in a container or in the garden.

result are not only unattractive but may harm the plant itself. Always direct water to the soil, rather than watering from above the plant.

Feeding

Providing additional nutrients will help most bulbs, especially those with long-flowering displays, such as cannas and dahlias, which may be described as gross feeders. They respond well to a liberal dressing of well-rotted manure or a granular fertilizer when they are planted out in spring. A spring feed for tulips, daffodils and hyacinths, applied when the leaves are still green, will help next year's show, but it is even more important to allow the foliage to remain intact until it has died down naturally, thus allowing all the goodness from the foliage to be used in forming the basis of the following year's display. Resist the temptation to pull the leaves off tulips in the herbaceous border until they have really withered and come away easily in your hand. Allium leaves look untidy when the flowers begin to appear, but do not be tempted to tidy up at this stage. Instead, hide them by putting a herbaceous plant in front of the bulbs.

Deadheading and seedheads

Many bulbs, including fritillaries, *Eranthis hyemalis* (winter aconite), *Hyacinthoides* spp. (bluebell), lilies, *Anemone blanda* and alliums, can be propagated by seed if it is gathered before nature disperses it. Some of these bulbs have attractive seedheads – the rosette that appears on the winter aconite is especially appealing.

Much larger seedheads appear after the alliums have flowered, and those of *Allium hollandicum* 'Purple Sensation' are often used in dried-flower arrangements. Gather the

Remove foliage from daffodils only after it has died back naturally and pulls away easily.

Dry allium seedheads upside down and use them later in an indoor flower arrangement.

seedheads while they still have some purple colouring and hang them upside down in a well-ventilated spot. Those left in the border can be enjoyed for many weeks.

Some flowers are best deadheaded long before seed production is allowed to take place, especially if you want to encourage more flowers. Dahlias, cannas and begonias all benefit from thorough, regular deadheading, which will ensure an

abundance of flowers until autumn. You should also deadhead daffodils, tulips and lilies, where removing the flowers prevents the plant from wasting energy in seed production.

Deadhead *Hyacinthoides hispanica* (Spanish bluebell) rigorously to prevent self-seeding and cross-fertilization with the native *H. non-scripta* (English bluebell). Spanish bluebells are more vigorous than the native plant and difficult to control.

Dahlia 'Dark Desire' produces a wealth of small flowers. Deadhead regularly to keep the display looking good.

Remove the flowerheads of daffodils before the seed has time to develop, to preserve the energy needed for rebuilding the bulb.

Dormancy and winter treatment

Where they are grown in border setting tender summer-flowering plants, such as dahlias, begonias, cannas and gladioli should be lifted in autumn and brought into growth again in spring if they are to flower once more in the summer.

The tubers and corms of these plants should be lifted, dried and stored in dry, cool, frost-free conditions. Begonias, gladioli and watsonia are stored dry; dahlias and cannas should be stored in barely moist peat or coarse vermiculite. Most bulbs and tubers should be lifted before the first frosts. Dahlias, however, will benefit if the foliage is actually killed by frost. When this happens, the leaves become blackened. If your dahlias have stopped flowering but there have still been no autumn frosts, lift them anyway.

In some mild areas it is possible to cut off the dahlia foliage and leave the tubers in the ground, protecting them with a mulch of grit with a layer of leaf mould or bark chipping, in the same way that nerines, crinums and the hardier types of agapanthus are left in the ground. Dahlias treated in this way are always at risk,

Dust damaged bulbs with a fungicide, such as yellow or green sulphate of ammonia.

LIFTING AND REPLANTING DAHLIAS

1 When the dahlia has finished flowering, use secateurs (pruners) to remove the foliage and trim back the stems, leaving about 20cm (8in) of each stem.

2 Fork gently around the plant, leaving a radius of 25–40cm (10–16in) from the main stem, depending on the amount of growth it has made. Gently lift the root, taking care not to damage the tubers.

3 Place the plant upside down in a box so that any moisture can drain down the hollow stems. Remove the soil from the tubers once it has dried off. Store in a dry, frost-free place in boxes of barely moist peat.

4 In late spring or early summer prepare a planting hole, approximately a spade's depth. Add some well-rotted manure or a long-term granular feed, and mix well into the soil.

5 Carefully lower the dahlia into the prepared hole and add more compost (soil mix) as necessary to bring to soil level.

6 Gently firm in the plant with your hands or feet. Water well.

especially if the winter happens to be severe. When green shoots begin to emerge on lifted dahlias in spring, water sparingly to keep the compost moist. Then in late spring or early summer, after all risk of frost has passed, choose a sunny, sheltered spot and prepare a planting hole.

Cannas should be treated in the same way as dahlias, except that the stalks of cannas are not hollow and it is not necessary to hang them upside down to drain. Moreover, cannas produce rhizomes, not tubers, and these are easily separated in spring when the new shoots start to

emerge to produce new plants. Each rhizome will make a substantial show of colour in one summer, so it is a great opportunity to propagate.

Lift begonia plants in autumn and remove all foliage, leaving about 7.5cm (3in) of stem. When the soil has dried, clean the tubers and remove the stems. Store in a dry, frost-free place at a minimum temperature of 7°C (45°F). In early spring plant the begonia tubers and keep them in a warm place until the little pink buds start to expand. Water more frequently as the leaves emerge. Plant out when all risk of frost has passed.

In early spring, plant begonia tubers, hollow side up, on barely moist compost (soil mix).

LIFTING AND REPLANTING CANNAS

1 Lift cannas when they have finished flowering in the autumn, before any hard frosts. Dig round their roots with a fork and lift the entire clump. Place the clump in a large wooden box.

2 Using secateurs (pruners), carefully remove all the foliage and cut back the stems to about 7.5cm (3in).

3 Allow the soil to dry off around the rhizomes before cleaning them and storing in barely moist peat or vermiculite. Treat any damaged rhizomes with a fungicide, such as yellow or green sulphate of ammonia.

4 In spring, the clumps can be divided. Where the rhizome is severed, dust with the same fungicide as before. Pot up into moist compost (soil mix).

5 In late spring or early summer, after all risk of frost has passed, choose a sunny spot and prepare a large planting hole. Mix in a long-term granular feed or well-rotted manure.

6 Plant the canna in the prepared hole and firm in gently. Water in well.

Container-grown plants

If they are grown in containers, all bulbs that might be described as 'summer exotics' – begonias, dahlias, cannas, tulbaghias and eucomis – will need frost-free conditions at a minimum temperature of 7°C (45°F) to survive the winter. Take action before the first frosts are threatened in the autumn, or as soon after as practicable.

You must allow the plants to dry off naturally. Then carefully clean away the soil from corms, tubers, rhizomes and bulbs before storing them in cool, dry conditions. If you do not have a frost-free greenhouse, a frost-free garage or shed will be appropriate or even somewhere indoors, as long as it is not too warm. It is important that the bulbs do not start into growth too early. Replant the bulbs in fresh compost in spring.

Alternatively, the plants can be left in their container and the whole pot or basket moved into a frost-free greenhouse. Here, they will remain dormant through the darker, cold days of winter and burst into life

Use electric or paraffin heaters to maintain minimum frost-free conditions inside the greenhouse, but open the door in milder weather to allow air to circulate.

TIDYING UP BEGONIAS

Remove hanging baskets containing begonias from their brackets before the first frost.

If the basket is relatively dry you might find that whole stems come away easily, in which case simply remove them for composting. Otherwise, cut back stems to within 8cm (3in) of the base. Allow the soil to dry out and soon the base of the previously cut stems will fall away from the top of the tuber.

Move pots containing begonias into the greenhouse. This one is also planted with Fuchsia 'Thalia'. Leave the arrangement intact and only tidy away dead leaves. Later, when it has dried off, the begonia stems will come away easily. Early next spring both fuchsia and begonia will start into growth once more.

when the longer, warmer days return in spring. When temperatures fall close to or below freezing, heat the greenhouse with a thermostatically controlled electric heater, which will turn on automatically at a pre-set temperature. If you do not have electricity in your greenhouse, use a paraffin heater, relit every day as necessary. When temperatures rise above freezing in the daytime, open the greenhouse door to allow air to circulate and remove any build-up of moisture.

Although pots can be moved outside in late spring, during the daytime, cold evening temperatures mean that they are best brought back into the shelter of the greenhouse. Only leave containers outside all day and all night once all risk of frost has gone.

Watering in the greenhouse

In winter the watering of pots and baskets can be tricky. Sunny weather encourages us into the greenhouse to inspect the plants and maybe then we think of watering. For most of the plants regular watering will not be needed during the winter months; the soil needs just to be kept barely moist. Occasional light watering might be necessary as the compost will inevitably dry out where the greenhouse catches lots of sunshine. But clear skies in the daytime are often followed by frosty nights, so it is better not to water on bright sunny days. Wait for cloudy conditions when temperatures will remain slightly higher during the night.

By early to mid-spring signs of new growth will be evident, with tiny pink buds on the begonias, spiky new shoots on the cannas and leafy green tufts on the eucomis. At this stage, it is a good idea to increase the watering programme gradually.

TIDYING UP TULBAGHIAS

1 Tulbaghias will survive in the greenhouse or a potting shed. Tidy away flowering stalks and dead foliage for simple good husbandry.

2 The leaves are evergreen, so remember to water occasionally during the winter and more frequently once spring has arrived.

POTTING ON EUCOMIS

1 Eucomis will survive in the greenhouse or a potting shed. Only remove the dry leaves as they die back naturally.

2 Now the top of the pot is clean it reveals small seedlings. These can be removed and potted up.

OVERWINTERING CANNAS

1 Cannas in pots should be moved into the greenhouse for protection. Do not water the compost at this stage.

2 Cut down the canna's stems and remove the foliage, along with any snails or slugs that are lurking there. Keep the compost barely moist throughout the winter.

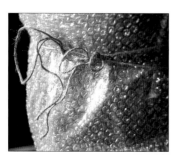

If possible, move containers close to a south-facing house or garage wall where they will have extra protection from extreme temperatures. In severely cold weather it may be better to move them inside the garage or porch.

Use a soil-based compost or a peat-based compost, both with added grit. A well-drained soil will provide better protection than over-wet compost, which may freeze around delicate roots.

Choosing hardy winter- and spring-flowering bulbs

Winter- and spring-flowering bulbs are hardy, but they will be more sensitive to the cold if they are planted in exposed containers, where they lack the insulation that is provided by the garden soil in borders or grasslands. The smaller the container, the less protection the bulbs will have against the cold.

Normal frosty weather should not be a problem, especially if sensible precautions are taken. Only plant bulbs that you know to be fully hardy in a container.

If you choose to plant daffodils, avoid the indoor-flowering types, such as 'Paper White Grandiflorus', which owe their parentage to *Narcissus papyraceus*. This species is native to the warmer climates of south-eastern France, south-western Spain and Portugal, where it flowers outdoors in winter. All other species of spring-flowering daffodils should be safe, however.

Siting containers

The siting of pots and baskets is crucial. Avoid placing pots in exposed sites, such as a windy corner of the house. A passageway would be even worse, because it will act as a wind tunnel. A position near a house or garage or a wall will be warmer than one in an exposed site in the middle of the garden. Remember that you can always move the containers away from the house and into a border once spring arrives. If you have a choice, a sunny, south-facing wall where the pots will have a chance to warm up during the day is preferable to a cold, north-facing, sunless wall.

Drainage

Make sure that all containers have adequate drainage holes in the base. After a deluge of rain you want to be certain that all excess water can run quickly out of the bottom. Half-barrels are often sold without drainage holes. Always check before planting and, if necessary, drill several holes in the base.

Always add plenty of drainage material, such as broken pots, small stones or pieces of polystyrene (styrofoam), to the bottom of a container and plant into a freely draining compost (soil mix) for all autumn and winter planting schemes.

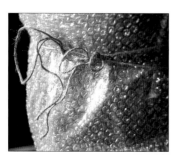

If pots are too heavy to move, use bubble wrap as a protective coat. Tie it securely in place with string.

This container has good holes at the base, which will allow adequate drainage. Always add plenty of drainage material.

Pieces of polystyrene (styrofoam), broken pots, stones or grit can be used as drainage material, depending on the container's size.

Move hanging baskets to temporary shelter in freezing weather.

Tulipa 'Tinka' has happily survived the winter outdoors and is partnered by violas, heuchera and *Millium effusum* 'Aureum'.

Weather warning

Although the compost needs to be kept moist, never water when frost is forecast, and be careful about watering on a sunny winter's day – clear night skies cause temperatures to plummet. Water on damp, dank days when cloud cover will mean less extreme temperatures. It is better to allow the compost to stay on the dry side in cold weather. In freezing conditions containers will benefit from some protection. Remove hanging baskets from their brackets to a garage, porch, greenhouse or outbuilding. Small and medium-sized pots could be placed on a level windowsill or next to the house wall. Larger containers may be wrapped in hessian (burlap) or bubble wrap. If possible, take these measures before extreme conditions have begun so that the bulbs will not be so badly affected by dropping temperatures.

A sunny windowsill affords good protection for small pots of bulbs, especially in severe winter weather.

Propagating bulbs

If you empty out a container of daffodils in summer you will find that the old bulbs are still intact but have now formed offsets, each one capable of growing on to produce flowering stems and offsets of its own.

Self-propagation

Look at the old bulbs of a *Muscari armeniacum* (grape hyacinth). They will have increased in size and produced several tiny ones, each clinging to the parent. In years to come, these will each grow on and become flowering bulbs in their own right. If left undisturbed, they will form clumps of bulbs and in time produce a beautiful carpet of bright blue flowers. Meanwhile, the flowers will have produced a generous crop of viable seeds. No wonder they naturalize so well. The same is true of alliums, which produce copious quantities of seed. The leaves spring up, looking like chives around the parent plant in spring, each little leaf with a miniature bulb at the base. Grow them on and they will produce flowers within three or four years.

Hyacinthoides spp. (bluebell) are prolific self-seeders. If you wanted to plant a new bluebell wood, you would no doubt be impatient for the

This daffodil has produced three excellent offsets in just one season's growth. It is this facility that makes daffodils such good naturalizers in grass or borders.

results, but if you had them growing in your garden borders, you would probably be waging war on the new patches of bulbs before too long. Avoid planting *Hyacinthoides non-scripta* (English bluebell) near *H. hispanica* (Spanish bluebell), because cross-fertilization will occur with a dilution of the natural stock of English bluebells, which are less vigorous than the Spanish plant.

Lifting and storing

Because bulbs multiply underground by producing daughter bulbs around the parent, sooner or later clumps become congested. Some species,

Muscari spp. (grape hyacinths) multiply surprisingly quickly. Separate the bigger bulbs and replant 7.5cm (3in) apart. The smaller ones can be grown on for another year.

Lilium regale seeds

Lilium regale will produce lots of seeds. If uncollected, these may self-seed beneath the parent plant. Alternatively, gather the seedpods, empty the contents and sow the seeds thinly in pots or trays filled with a moist, sieved, gritty compost, ready to grow on.

SELF-SEEDING ALLIUM

1 *Allium hollandicum* 'Purple Sensation' produces generous quantities of seed and will self-seed beneath the parent plant.

2 Within a short time, small bulbs have grown that can be carefully harvested in the autumn.

3 Replant the small bulbs in a pot or directly into border soil where you would like a display in the future.

such as nerines, flower better when they are congested, and these are best left alone for many years until flowering dwindles. When this happens, it is time to lift and divide the bulbs. Clumps of other bulbs, such as alliums, *Muscari* spp., narcissi, tulips and tulbaghia, are best divided every three years or so. Where they have become well established you will be amazed by the proliferation that has occurred. Lift the bulbs during the summer dormancy and tease them apart carefully, replanting the largest bulbs as needed.

All seedlings, whether they are *Galanthus* (snowdrop), *Eranthis hyemalis* (winter aconite), *Muscari* spp. (grape hyacinth) or bluebells, do better in border soil than in turf, where there is too much competition from dense, coarse grasses for the young plants to establish themselves, but these species will still multiply in grass, albeit more slowly. For best results, choose an area with fine grass, where competition will be less intense.

1 *Eucomis bicolor* produces many small black seeds. These may be sown into pots ready to be grown on for a year before being potted on the following year. They should flower within two years of sowing.

2 Alternatively, eucomis may self-seed in the pots in which they are growing. Remove the tiny new plants and grow them on in a pot in gritty compost for a year. Then repot into individual pots to flower the following summer.

Bulbils

Lilies have another way of propagating themselves. As well as forming offsets and seeds, some lilies will produce bulbils at leaf axils up their stems. These fall off in time and form new plants when they root into the soil at the foot of the parent plant, where they will soon develop. These miniature bulbs can be lifted in autumn and potted on ready for

planting out 18 months later. This type of propagation occurs most commonly on *Lilium lancifolium* (syn. *L. tigrinum*; tiger lily) and many of the Asiatic hybrids.

Another method of propagation is to collect the bulbils themselves, detaching them carefully from the stem, and plant them into small pots. Grow on for two years before planting out in the garden.

Seeds from tulbaghia may be collected and sown in small pots. After a year they may be potted on into new permanent containers.

Allium cristophii produces lots of seeds which can be sown in pots. It also multiplies quickly by offsets, which can be dug up in the autumn and moved to another spot in the garden. To make the most of their metallic sheen, try to place some where they will catch the warm evening light.

Propagating rhizomes, corms and tubers

One of the wonderful attributes of rhizomes, corms and tubers is that they are successful self-propagators, by creating both new growth below ground and seeds above.

Rhizomes

Anyone who has planted a canna from what seems like a small rhizome in late winter will be amazed at the sheer quantity of root material that can be dug up the following autumn after just one summer's growth – a mass of rhizomes all waiting to be divided and propagated. If that was not enough, some cannas are also generous producers of seed.

Corms

With corms the story is different. After flowering the old corm dies, and a new one forms on top of the old one, with clusters of cormlets around the sides. In this way some cormous plants, such as crocosmia, are able to form quite large clumps, which need to be divided every three years or so to prevent overcrowding and congestion. Cormous plants can also propagate themselves by seed – *Crocus tommasinianus*, for example, naturalizes well in late winter grassland where the grass is fine.

Begonias can be started from cuttings taken from over-wintered tubers in early- to mid-spring. They make excellent bedding plants for containers and borders, offering a wide range of colours.

Tubers

Plants grown from tubers are also great survivors. Individual tubers grow to quite large proportions – surprisingly large compared with the tiny tubers on offer in the shops – and also produce generous quantities of seeds and shoots, which can be propagated. Leave a few *Anemone blanda* tubers planted in the eye of an old apple tree and within a few years it will be a mass of blue flowers as the seeds form new plants and the tubers plump up and grow. Cyclamen and *Eranthis hyemalis* are also generous seeders, both enjoying a position beneath deciduous shrubs or trees, where they will get plenty of

PROPAGATING TUBERS

1 Take a sharp knife and cut the tuber (in this case a begonia tuber) through the middle so that each part has a shoot.

2 Dust the open cuts with a fungicide such as yellow sulphur powder. Prepare two small pots with moist potting compost (soil mix).

3 Plant both halves so that they sit firmly on top of the compost. Keep the compost moist and plant on when new growth is apparent.

TAKING BEGONIA AND DAHLIA CUTTINGS

1 Gently pull a young begonia stem away from the tuber. A small piece of rooting material may well have come away at the base of the shoot.

2 Plant the new cutting into a pot of moist compost (soil mix) and grow on in warm conditions, out of direct sunlight, until the new plant can be planted out.

3 For dahlias, slice through the bottom of a stem and plant the cutting in moist compost. Place on a windowsill, out of direct sunlight, covered with a clear plastic bag until rooted.

moisture in winter. *Eranthis hyemalis* is usually quick to establish. Scatter seed in mid-spring and within just a few years you will have sheets of golden flowers in midwinter. For best results, soak cyclamen seeds for up to ten hours before sowing.

Begonia tubers can be divided in late winter or early spring if two shoots are seen on one tuber. They can also be propagated from cuttings taken from small shoots that have grown from the tuber in late winter or early spring. Dahlias can also be propagated from cuttings taken from new growth during the same periods.

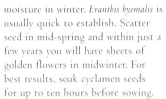

Canna rhyzomes can be propagated in early spring by cutting into short sections, leaving an eye from which new growth will be made.

Started from cuttings, dahlias will make very large plants even in just one summer's growth. Here Dahlia 'Bishop of Llandaff' makes a great show with its brilliant red flowers.

Pests, diseases and other problems

Earwigs may spoil dahlia flowers, vine weevil might damage begonia tubers, snails might attack lily shoots, and pollen beetles will seek out narcissus. Help is at hand in all these cases.

PESTS
Aphids
How to identify Clusters of tiny greenfly will infest emerging bulb buds and foliage, especially tulips and hyacinths. Blackfly are also an occasional problem. Tulip bulb aphids mainly attack stored bulbs.
Damage Unsightly and, in the extreme, deforming.
Control Encourage garden-friendly wildlife, such as ladybirds and the larval stages of both hoverfly and lacewing, which are all voracious eaters of aphids. You might choose to apply a soapy water spray as soon as the aphids appear, or an appropriate insecticide. Stored tulip bulbs should be dusted with an insecticidal powder.

Earwigs
How to identify Slender, dark, glossy creatures with pincers, which feed mainly at night on both leaves and flowers. During the daytime they hide in dark places.
Damage Particularly noticeable on dahlias. Both leaves and flowers will show rounded indentations where the earwigs have been at work. On a small scale they can be ignored, but if an infestation builds up the holes can be disfiguring.
Control Stuff small plant pots with straw or newspaper and spike them on to canes pushed into the ground close to the dahlias. They will act as a dark daytime retreat. Empty out each morning and kill the trapped earwigs. On the same principle, apply an insecticide dust on to the newspaper, thereby destroying any earwigs automatically, or simply use the dust directly on the plant.

Gladiolus thrips
How to identify From mid- to late summer, in hot dry conditions, the sap-feeding insects (*Thrips simplex*) live in the flower buds and at the base of the leaves.
Damage. The foliage develops a fine, pale mottling with tiny black excrement spots. Flowers have a pale flecking and in some cases will fail to open.

Lily beetles have become far more prevalent in recent years with devastating effects on lilies and fritillaries in particular.

Control Spray with bifenthrin, but avoid treating plants in sunny weather. Store corms in a cool, frost-free place.

Lily beetle
How to identify The adult beetle is bright red; the humpbacked, maggot-like larvae are covered with black excrement. The adults feed on the foliage of lilies and fritillaries from early spring onwards, then in midsummer they will be joined by the larvae.
Damage Severe destruction of emerging shoots and flower buds.
Control Pick off adults by hand and wash off larvae with a water spray, but where infestations are heavy, use an appropriate insecticide. This will be more effective on the grubs than the adult beetles.

Mice, squirrels and voles
How to identify These animals will eat dry-stored bulbs and those planted in the ground, especially in winter when food is scarce.
Damage Part-eaten bulbs may remain in the ground as evidence, otherwise gaps in the planting displays are an eventual sign. Crocuses are particularly susceptible.

Blackfly on dahlias can quickly multiply and spoil the appearance, especially on new growth tips below flowering buds.

Greenfly on tulips can look very unsightly where large infestations occur. Soapy water or an insecticide spray will solve the problem.

Saxifraga × urbium (London pride) will create a dense mat on top of bulbs, and this will inhibit squirrels and mice finding bulbs planted below. Cover with fine mesh in the first year, while the saxifrage is getting established, or transfer mature plants from elsewhere in the garden.

Pollen beetles are especially attracted to yellow flowers in mid- to late spring and may be found on yellow-flowered narcissi.

Control Keep stored bulbs in rodent-proof containers. Use bait or traps where pets and other wild animals will not be affected. For bulbs or corms in containers, add a top layer of bedding or foliage plants, thus avoiding bare soil. Press the soil down firmly around newly planted bulbs in the garden to make it more difficult for the bulbs or corms to be found and dug up. Bulbs that are already established will be less likely to be affected.

Narcissus bulb fly

How to identify The adult flies resemble bees, but you are more likely to find the larvae, which resemble white maggots and feed on narcissus or hyacinth bulbs.
Damage Total destruction by the larvae at the centre of the bulb.
Control Destroy all affected bulbs to limit the future spread of the fly. Individual narcissus and hyacinth bulbs can be dusted with insecticide before planting.

Narcissus eelworm

How to identify Above ground this eelworm causes stunted and distorted foliage and flower stems.
Damage Visible brown rings or arcs through a transverse section of the bulb.
Control Destroy all affected bulbs and do not replant with fresh bulbs for at least three years as the infestation will continue.

Pollen beetles

How to identify Small, shiny, black insects, which are also known as rape beetles because they are associated with oil seed rape crops. They are strongly attracted to yellow flowers, especially those of yellow narcissi.
Damage In extreme infestations the flowers will be eaten and disfigured.
Control Difficult, but spraying with water should help. If flowers are picked for display indoors, shake and leave them in a darkened place outside, where the beetles will fly off in search of the light.

Slugs and snails

How to identify Slugs will mainly attack underground, while snails will do most damage above ground, devouring allium leaves and lily shoots as well as attacking fritillaries, tulips and many other bulbs.
Damage Disfigurement or total destruction.
Control Garden-friendly wildlife should be encouraged. Song thrushes will eat snails, while devil's coach horse beetles and hedgehogs will eat slugs. Biological controls, such as nematodes, are available or simple traps, such as upturned grapefruit.

Mainly night-time feeders, slugs will severely damage young foliage on dahlias, as seen here, as well as many other plants.

Slugs can do great damage to tulip buds. Even a small nibble will be disfiguring, but often the effects are much greater.

Guard against vine weevil damage to begonia tubers by watering the container in autumn and again in spring to give six months' treatment. Use nematodes *(Steinernema kraussei)* or imidacloprid, which acts as a systemic insecticide.

Rabbits

How to identify The tops of the plants are eaten.

Damage Stalks of flowering bulbs will remain but the flowers will have been eaten. Tulips and *Fritillaria meleagris* are especially favoured.

Control Rabbit-proof netting has to be 1.2–1.5m (4–5ft) high and with an extra 30cm (12in) below ground level to be effective. Narcissi are not palatable to rabbits, so are safe.

Sparrows

How to identify House sparrows will attack crocus blooms, destroying the flowers and scattering them on the ground around the plants. Yellow crocus seem to be a favourite choice, but other colours are sometimes eaten as well.

Damage The flowers will be shredded.

Control The old-fashioned method was to crisscross the vulnerable area with black cotton thread to create a barrier to stop them feeding. Otherwise there is little to be done, except to plant early flowering narcissus nearby or among them so that the sparrows have less of a monoculture attraction.

Vine weevils

How to identify Cream-coloured vine weevil larvae live below soil level and eat roots and tubers. Begonias are a favourite. The adults are dull black with a hard, defensive back. Each female lays up to 1,000 eggs in the soil, which hatch into larvae in two to three weeks. Larvae are destroyed in temperatures below -6°C (21°F), which means that they are far more widespread in areas with milder winters. They are primarily a problem for the container gardener but, in some regions, they will overwinter in garden soil.

Damage The adults feed mainly at night on foliage, making small notches on the edges of leaves. The larvae are more destructive, particularly in spring and autumn, although they may attack at any time in a conservatory or greenhouse. They eat root systems, wreaking havoc with cyclamen, sinningia and begonia tubers to the point that the whole plant will collapse, almost overnight.

Control Be constantly vigilant and destroy any adults on sight. They are mainly night-time movers (they cannot fly, but will climb). During the day they take refuge in dark places, so check under pots and leaf debris. Special traps can be laid, such as a roll of dark corrugated paper. Apply a liquid drench of beneficial nematodes *(Steinernema kraussei)* in spring and late summer to control the larvae. They will not be effective on clay or dry soils, or where the soil temperature is less than 5°C (41°F) Alternatively, apply a soil drench of imidacloprid, which acts as a systemic insecticide. Apply barrier glue around the tops of containers to deter adult vine weevils from getting into the pots to lay eggs. Burn any tubers that have been eaten by them.

Vine weevil larvae look like cream-coloured, C-shaped maggots.

Botrytis appears as grey mould on the leaves or stems of affected plants. The foliage may be disfigured.

Lily disease has produced distorted growth on this *Lilium regale*. However, the bulb may remain healthy and grow well next year.

DISEASES

Basal rot
How to identify Bulbs are soft and there may be mould around the base.
Damage The leaves are usually yellow and tend to wilt. Narcissus bulbs are most likely to be affected.
Control Lift and destroy affected plants. Avoid replanting in contaminated soil.

Botrytis (grey mould)
How to identify Fluffy grey mould on the leaves and dying flowers. It can also cause spots on the leaves and flowers, as in the case of miniature cyclamen from the F1 Miracle Series.

A narcissus with stunted growth displays the symptoms of basal rot.

Damage Disfigurement of the foliage and bulb rot.
Control Lift and destroy if the bulb is affected, otherwise remove affected parts and spray with systemic fungicide. Prevention is possible through dry storage conditions. Take care to remove the soil and decayed outer bulb parts, and dust with a fungicidal powder before storing.

Snowdrop grey mould
How to identify The fungus *Botrytis galanthina* produces numerous spores, which cause fuzzy grey mould on the leaves and stems. It may be seen on the leaves when they first appear.
Damage Disfigurement of the foliage and bulb rot.
Control Lift and destroy affected bulbs. Do not replant *Galanthus* in the same place for at least five years.

Storage rots
How to identify Stored dahlia tubers may start to rot, with fungal growth on the surfaces. It may be caused by a range of fungi and bacteria, either as primary pathogens entering on sound tissue or as a secondary infection on previously damaged parts.

Damage Softening of the tissue.
Control Remove and destroy affected tubers. Dust any injured parts of flowers with sulphur before storing.

Dry rot of bulbs and corms
How to identify Foliage will turn brown and then die, often with a specific dark discoloration just above soil level. Narcissi, crocuses, gladioli and crocosmias may be affected.
Damage The bulbs and corms will show tiny black dots or fungal fruiting bodies.
Control Remove and destroy affected bulbs and corms. Do not replant in contaminated soil.

Lily disease
How to identify The fungus *Botrytis elliptica* produces numerous spores, which cause dark green spots to develop on the foliage. The leaves then turn brown and wither from the base of the stem upwards.
Damage Flower buds become distorted. The plant may topple over, but the bulb may remain healthy.
Control Remove debris to avoid the fungus persisting from year to year. Bulbs may be kept if they show no signs of rotting.

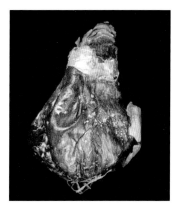

Dry rot storage disease may be evident on newly purchased bulbs. Discard diseased bulbs.

Leaf scorch, caused by a fungus, has damaged this narcissus foliage. The problem begins at the tips and spreads down the leaves.

Distorted leaves are a sign of tulip fire, which is a serious fungal problem. Affected plants must be dug up and then destroyed.

Narcissus leaf scorch

How to identify The fungus *Stagonospora curtisii* causes the leaf tips to become brown and scorched as they emerge. The problem spreads down the length of the leaves. Flowers may occasionally be attacked.
Damage Affects narcissi, crinums, hippeastrums, nerines and snowdrops.
Control Remove and destroy affected leaf tips or other affected parts.

Tulip fire

How to identify The leaves are distorted and the shoots and flowers show stunted growth. In moist conditions the leaves are covered with a grey mould with black fruiting bodies. Small, black scales develop on the outer scales of the bulbs, which may rot.
Damage Flower buds may fail to open and, if they do, they may show small bleached spots on the petals. The flower stems may topple over, and in wet weather the whole plant may rot.
Control Dig up and burn affected plants. Do not plant tulips in the same soil again for at least three years. Late planting may decrease the chance of this disease causing significant problems.

Tulip grey bulb rot

How to identify In some cases no growth appears above ground at all. Any shoots that do appear are distorted and will soon die. Alliums, amaryllis, chionodoxas, colchicums, crocuses, eranthis, fritillarias, gladioli, hyacinths, irises, lilies, narcissi, scillas and snowdrops may be affected in addition to tulips.
Damage Infected bulbs turn dry and grey as they rot. The basal plate and roots may be all that remain.
Control Dig up and burn affected plants. Do not replant in contaminated soil for five years.

Tulip viruses

How to identify Although viruses themselves are invisible, the symptoms include streaked flowers, streaked or mottled foliage, stunted growth and distorted leaves. Sap-sucking aphids transfer viruses from one plant to another. Bought bulbs might already be infected. Tulip-breaking virus also causes problems on lilies, so avoid planting lilies and tulips close to each other.
Damage Not necessarily serious, although it can be. The virus leads to a weakening of the stock.

Control Dig up and destroy any seriously affected plants. Spray against aphids to limit new infections and therefore possible damage.

OTHER PROBLEMS
Drought
How to identify The leaves will start to emerge, then turn yellow and stunted. Flowering will be impaired.
Damage Container-grown plants are susceptible, particularly those with spring bulbs that have been kept too dry in autumn when the roots are being formed.
Control Check that the soil is kept moist at all times (and water if necessary except in frosty weather). Window boxes and hanging baskets may be particularly at risk if they are in the rain shadow of a building. An easy way to recognize the symptoms is to plant some bedding plants, such as violas or primroses, on top of the bulbs. If these show signs of wilting and drought, it indicates that the bulbs might be suffering too.

Frost damage
How to identify The foliage will collapse or blacken.
Damage This could occur in the autumn when tender plants such as

Tulip virus will cause streaking on flowers and mottled foliage, weakening the plants and causing potential spread elsewhere.

dahlias are grown outside and are affected by frosty weather. The foliage will turn black. But it could also occur in late spring when the tubers have been brought into growth under glass and planted out in their summer bedding positions. It might also be seen when borderline hardy bulbs are left outside for the winter, and despite mulches protecting the bulb itself, newly emerging leaves can be affected by late frosts.

Control The autumn frost is not a problem: simply remove the topgrowth and bring tubers inside or cover with a mulch. The late-spring frost will not kill the tubers but it will damage the foliage and delay flowering. Avoid the problem by planting out only after all risk of frost has gone or be prepared to cover with horticultural fleece if frost threatens.

Leaf scorch

How to identify The foliage will show scorch marks and become desiccated.
Damage This is most likely to occur under glass on a sunny day in late spring when tender plants, such as begonias, are in strong early growth and water has been splashed on their

Cyclamen are susceptible to overwatering and dislike being watered from above. It is best to allow them to soak up moisture from below, but never leave them standing in water for long.

A late spring frost has caused the newly emerging leaves of this *Crinum x powellii* to blacken.

leaves. It could also happen if the begonias are grown outside in a sunny spot and watered from above in the middle of the day. The scorch marks will impair growth, although they will not cause the plant to die.
Control Best to avoid watering when the sun is directly on the plants.

Overwatering

How to identify The leaves will turn yellow, then flop and the whole plant will collapse.
Damage Cyclamen are particularly susceptible if grown indoors.
Control Plant in a container with adequate drainage holes, omit the drainage material and use a specially formulated indoor bulb compost.

Water only when the leaves begin to flag and then only from the base by standing the pot in a saucer of water for a short time until the moisture has been absorbed from the bottom.

Poor drainage

How to identify The leaves will turn yellow and flowering will be impaired.
Damage Particularly affects plants that prefer drier conditions, such as hyacinths, nerines and tulips.
Control Make sure that containers have good drainage holes at the base. Add a layer of drainage material so that holes do not get blocked and to provide a free-draining base to the soil area. Use a freely draining soil-based compost mixed with extra grit.

The bulb garden

The bulb garden changes constantly with the seasons. *Galanthus* (snowdrop) and *Eranthis hyemalis* (winter aconite) are the first signs of life in the winter garden, and the first daffodils are also just beginning to show themselves like daggers through the ground. Soon the garden will be filled with their golden heads waving in spring sunshine. Colourful tulips and stately *Fritillaria imperialis* (crown imperial) will take centre stage, while in woodland areas the little *Anemone nemorosa* (wood anemone) and swaths of *Hyacinthoides* spp. (bluebell) will have their moments of glory. Grasslands will be filled with camassias, and in the borders the elegant Dutch irises and rounded alliums add an air of exuberance. Summer borders are filled with lilies, begonias and gladioli, with dahlias and cannas joining the summer ranks and following on into autumn, when nerines, colchicums and cyclamen are at their best. There is so much to choose from and to enjoy.

Various alliums, including dark purple *Allium* 'Purple Sensation', and slightly later Dutch iris create a wonderful display beneath wisteria arches following on from earlier tulips.

Mid- to late winter gallery

This is always a quiet period in the garden, with short, cold days and long, frosty nights. However, some plants have adapted well to the conditions and produce exquisite flowers, even in the bleakest of environments. Given the low light levels, cold temperatures and often windy conditions, it is not surprising that most winter-flowering bulbs and corms are short in height.

Several winter bulbs, such as *Eranthis hyemalis* (winter aconite) and *Galanthus* (snowdrop) show their flower buds at ground level, lengthening their stems only gradually as the daylight increases. Even so the stems will remain relatively short, but planted en masse the displays will be marvellous.

Crocus flowers vary considerably from the palest blue to soft lavender blue to rich deep purple, often revealing a delicate veining.

About 15 different species of snowdrop are found in Europe, from Spain to western Russia, the Crimea and Turkey, their flowering times ranging from early to late winter, and many having slightly different markings or variations in flower size. From these species many, many cultivars, each with their own distinctive characteristics, have been developed.

The winter gallery also includes early crocuses, dwarf irises, tiny cyclamen and low-growing *Anemone blanda*. Only the earliest daffodils, such as *Narcissus* 'January Gold', are significantly taller than the low-growing snowdrops and aconites, and even they still reach only 25–30cm (10–12in) in height.

Most snowdrops begin to flower from midwinter onwards, becoming more and more impressive as the days begin to lengthen.

Galanthus nivalis (common snowdrop) is the most familiar of all the snowdrop species grown in gardens. It is found widely throughout Europe, from Spain to western Russia, and also in Britain. It occurs naturally, both with single and double white flowers, all with a sweet honey scent.

Narcissus 'Rijnvelds Early Sensation' (syn. N. 'January Gold') is one of only a few daffodils that flower at this time of year. It grows to 30cm (12in) high, with the large, golden flowers borne on relatively short stems, which stand up well to buffeting winds. The blooms should last three, four or even five weeks.

Eranthis hyemalis (winter aconite), which grows to 5–7.5cm (2–3in) high, produces a tightly formed yellow cup. Each cup struggles against the cold earth to meet the winter air and unfurl its golden petals. As the stems lengthen, a frill of green leafy bracts acts as a ruff beneath each flower.

Galanthus 'Atkinsii', one of several clones of G. nivalis (common snowdrop), grows to 20cm (8in) high. This comparatively tall, early flowerer is highly scented and elegant in its poise and makes an attractive addition to the winter garden. Enjoy the flowers as they open wide in the sunshine.

Iris danfordiae, which grows to 10cm (4in) high, is one of several dwarf irises that flower in late winter. A beautiful shade of yellow, it is often sweetly perfumed and intricately marked. The slightly taller Iris reticulata, 10–15cm (4–6in) high, is violet in colour with a yellow ridge to the falls.

Crocus tommasinianus is a hardy and reliable plant from Hungary, the Balkans and Bulgaria. It grows to 7.5–10cm (3–4in) high and is tolerant of sun or partial shade. It is a prolific self-seeder, and, in time, the narrow, pale silver-lilac flowers will create a delicate carpet of colour.

Cyclamen coum emerges with broad, heart-shaped leaves displaying a variety of attractive grey or silver markings. These are followed by tiny but enchanting white, pale pink or rose-pink flowers, which bring a welcome splash of warmer colour to the winter garden.

Crocus chrysanthus 'Blue Pearl' is one of the best of all the early crocuses. It grows to 7.5cm (3in) high, and its exquisite pale blue outer colouring, silvery inside and bronze base makes it the perfect choice for many displays, both in borders and in containers.

Anemone blanda grows to a height of 10–15cm (4–6in) and is a rewarding flower for both the winter and early spring garden, as it blooms for six weeks or more. The blue flowers are shy to begin with, but they gather strength as the sun begins to warm the earth.

Mid- to late winter borders

The bulbs that flower in late winter, such as *Galanthus* (snowdrop), cyclamen and early daffodils, can be used alone or in combinations of two or three different types to produce welcome colour in the winter border. Remember to plant them close to a path or within view of your window – it is more comfortable to admire the brave little flowers from indoors than outside in the cold winter garden.

Key plants for the border

Snowdrops look stunning in small individual groups. The most widely grown plant is *Galanthus nivalis*, in either the single or double form. The single flower is more poised and elegant, particularly in the cultivar *G.* 'S. Arnott', which has long stems and beautifully rounded, drop-like flowers. On warmer days the petals open wide, revealing a labyrinth of green veins. It is worth bending down and looking right into each flower to enjoy its intricacies to the full. As a bonus, you will also find that it is wonderfully scented.

The various shades of pink *Cyclamen coum* make an exquisite combination with pure white snowdrops, the whole enhanced by the silver marking on the cyclamen foliage.

Blue-flowering *Anemone blanda* self-seeds with alacrity over a period of just a few years, so that soon the area beneath a tree, for example, would be completely filled with them. The foliage provides an attractive green carpet above which the pretty daisy-like flowers are poised ready to open in the winter sunshine.

Snowdrops associate happily with many other bulbs. They make a remarkably warm and welcome grouping with the tiny pink flowers of *Cyclamen coum*, which is further enhanced by the often intricate silver veining on the cyclamen leaves. The fly-away petals of the cyclamen flower are easily recognizable, and there is a darker stain around the nose of each flower. After flowering the seedhead is pulled down to the ground by the coiled stem so that it comes to rest on the surface of the soil. In early summer the pods burst open, and the sticky seed is ready to be propagated.

In their turn, cyclamen make a pretty partnership with the purple and violet shades of the dwarf Reticulata irises, such as *Iris* 'Pauline', 'Hercules' and 'J.S. Dijt'. Although small, they are packed with colour and vibrancy. *I.* 'George' is a fine example of a Reticulata: the gorgeous purple with yellow on its falls is just enough to lift the eye and bring out the lovely pink background of the cyclamen.

Another favourite at this time of year is the bright yellow *Eranthis hyemalis* (winter aconite), which will form generous groups once it has established itself. It is an excellent choice for a damp border beneath deciduous shrubs, where it will have shade in summer but receive more light in winter when it flowers. It associates well with white snowdrops or the little irises, and looks lovely with other herbaceous plants, such as the dark bronze-leaved bugle *Ajuga reptans* 'Atropurpurea' or the lime green *Helleborus foetidus* (stinking hellebore).

The powerful colouring of *Iris* 'George', a Reticulata iris, looks striking against a background of *Cyclamen coum*.

Planting in the eye of a tree

The area beneath deciduous trees and shrubs – the eye – will usually look bare in midwinter, but then the colour will begin to appear. When moisture and light reach the soil a whole array of plant associations is possible. Late winter- and spring-flowering bulbs, corms and tubers can take advantage of the sparse canopy above to flower and complete their lifecycles before the leaves that exclude moisture and sunlight.

Similar to the snowdrop, *Leucojum vernum* (spring snowflake) has rounder flowers with six equal petals (snowdrops have three long and three short petals). They are native to France, central and eastern Europe and have become naturalized in parts of Britain, where they are easy to grow in shade or semi-shade in moist soil. *L. vernum* var. *carpathicum*, a handsome variant with yellow tips at the ends of the petals, is native to Romania and Poland. The greener, broader leaves are larger than those of snowdrops and make a happy association with winter aconites.

Daffodils and anemones

The first daffodils are in flower at this time of year. *Narcissus* 'Rijnvelds Early Sensation' (syn. *N.* 'January Gold') is one of the earliest, and the golden cupped flowers last for several

Eranthis hyemalis (winter aconite) can be planted to great advantage in front of *Helleborus foetidus* (stinking hellebore).

Leucojum vernum var. *carpathicum* makes an admirable association with the golden flowers of *Eranthis hyemalis* (winter aconite).

weeks. It is an excellent choice for planting in borders generally or in the eye beneath a deciduous tree, where later-flowering daffodils can continue the spring display. 'February Gold' will soon follow, spanning the period between late winter and early spring. By this time the first flowers of *Anemone blanda* are beginning to open in the sunshine to reveal the bluest of daisy-like flowers, the dainty petals fluttering in the winter breeze. White varieties are more expensive, but by far the cheapest are mixtures of mauve, pink, blue and white. Anemones make a glorious display on their own, but when they are planted with a few primroses and dainty early daffodils the momentum of the display can be carried forward in the most delightful way.

Mid- to late winter naturalized bulbs

Galanthus (snowdrop), *Leucojum* (snowflake), *Eranthis hyemalis* (winter aconite), *Anemone blanda* and the earliest daffodils, as well as a wide range of crocuses, create a sparkling display when they are naturalized in borders, grassland and woodland. Do not be surprised, however, if the bulbs, corms and tubers in the borders, which do not have to compete with grass and tree roots, multiply more quickly. Some genera adapt well to both meadow and woodland conditions, although be prepared for the naturalization process to take longer.

Grassland

Both *Galanthus nivalis* (common snowdrop) and *Leucojum vernum* (spring snowflake) will grow well in grassed areas, where winter and spring moisture are paramount and summer drought is avoided. Ideal conditions are the grassy swards between deciduous shrubs and around fruit trees, where other, later-flowering bulbs are grown so that the grass is not cut short until after

Positions in open grassland or light shade will suit early-flowering crocus species such as *Crocus tommasinianus*, *C. chrysanthus* and *C. vernus*, which are all good for naturalizing.

This group of mixed crocuses, which includes *Crocus tommasinianus*, *C. chrysanthus* and *C. vernus*, forms a carpet of colour.

midsummer. The same is true for *Eranthis hyemalis* (winter aconite) and *Anemone blanda*. To make the most of the display cut the grass in late autumn or early winter so that it is short enough for the mid- to late winter flowers to be appreciated.

Of the many crocus species, *Crocus tommasinianus* and its cultivars are among the most successful in grass, whether grown in sun or semi-shade. This crocus will self-seed extensively, and although each flower is narrow and delicate, a well-established group will create a broad sheet of blue when the sun shines and the petals open. *C. flavus* subsp. *flavus*, with its golden petals, will enjoy similar conditions. It will not self-seed, but will mass up in clumps as the corms multiply below ground. *C. chrysanthus*, which is native to the Balkans and Turkey, has scented, creamy yellow flowers and will compete well in winter grassland. *C. c.* 'Cream Beauty', with creamy yellow flowers, 'Ladykiller', with blue, white-edged flowers, and 'Zwanenburg Bronze', with pale yellow and bronze flowers, are popular, widely available cultivars.

Deciduous shrubs and woodland

The ground beneath deciduous shrubs and areas of woodland offers a convivial home to early snowdrops, cyclamen, daffodils and *Eranthis hyemalis* (winter aconite). The winter tracery of bare branches allows maximum light and moisture to reach early-flowering bulbs, corms and tubers, enabling them to

Aconites and mixed single and double snowdrops look glorious together, providing a tapestry of colour for several weeks.

complete most of their lifecycle before the canopy of leaves appears later in spring. For best results with snowdrops and – if possible – with aconites and cyclamen too, buy growing bulbs "in the green" so that they get off to a good start.

Galanthus nivalis (common snowdrop) will naturalize large areas of deciduous woodland, where they will revel in the cool, damp conditions if they are given a bed of moist leaf mould. Over many years, in these conditions they will create spectacular displays, providing a wonderful sight from mid- to late winter, especially with the added drama of the winter sun penetrating the naked canopy of the trees to highlight the tracery of the branches and the virginal sheet below. Plant single and double varieties in neighbouring groups. Although

majestic on a large scale, even 20 clumps will give huge pleasure on the edge of a woodland area or small copse in a domestic setting.

Eranthis hyemalis (winter aconite) colonize with the same effect, and if they are planted with snowdrops wonderful swirls of yellow and white will form on the woodland floor. For the greatest impact, plant in groups distinct from the snowdrops and then allow a few clumps to intermingle. The aconites produce lots of seed. When they are ripe give nature a helping hand and spread them around the woodland floor. Before long you will be richly rewarded.

Elsewhere *Cyclamen coum*, enjoying the damp leaf mould of late winter, will naturalize generously, creating a broad pink carpet, softened by the silver veining of the rounded leaves. Choose a selection from the Pewter

The leaves of *Cyclamen coum* are variably patterned with intricate silver veining or blotches. These create the perfect background for the tiny flowers, which appear in many appealing shades of light and dark pink.

Group, which has plants with leaves predominantly silver-grey above with a dark green margin, and from the Silver Group, with their predominantly grey-marked leaves. Mix them with earlier flowering *Cyclamen hederifolium*, the leaves of which will persist through winter.

Galanthus 'Magnet' has taller, larger flowers than *Galanthus nivalis* (common snowdrop). Here, it forms a marvellous carpet beneath the witch hazel *Hamamelis* x *intermedia* 'Pallida'.

Early spring gallery

As the days begin to lengthen, the garden starts to come alive and suddenly an array of different bulbs is in flower. This is the main season for all the many types of dwarf daffodil, including old favourites such as *Narcissus* 'February Gold' and 'Tête-à-tête', whose short, sturdy stems enable them to withstand blustery spring winds.

The little *Anemone blanda* flowers have now opened their starry faces to greet the spring sunshine. They are one of the most valuable plants in the garden, lasting for six weeks or more and spreading easily to create a dense carpet of colour. This is also the time for *Crocus* 'Large Dutch Purple', *Scilla siberica* (Siberian squill), *Chionodoxa* (glory of

Double Early tulips flower at the same time as *Muscari armeniacum* (grape hyacinth), providing ideal partners for borders or pots.

the snow) and early single, Kaufmanniana-type tulips, such as *Tulipa* 'Shakespeare', 'Stresa' and 'Heart's Delight'. All of these will happily mix and match to provide endless associations with each other.

As the weeks progress, the first gorgeous blue flowers of *Muscari armeniacum* (grape hyacinth) begin to emerge. These look superb with any of the Double Early tulips or with ordinary bedding hyacinths. The exotic blue of grape hyacinths is stunning with yellow *Tulipa* 'Mr Van der Hoef' and with 'Peach Blossom'. Violas, pansies, primroses and polyanthus act as fine bedfellows with any of these bulbs, producing wonderful planting combinations which can be changed each year to provide different colour effects.

Once established, *Anemone blanda* will soon naturalize to form large carpets.

Narcissus 'February Gold' grows to a height of 25cm (10in). It is short, sturdy and one of the longest flowering of all the dwarf daffodils. It has a long, golden trumpet with swept-back petals, so reminiscent of its parent *N. cyclamineus*. It looks lovely underplanted with white or purple large Dutch crocus.

Crocus 'Large Dutch Purple' reaches a height of 10cm (4in) and is a pivotal player in the spring garden, providing a carpet of bright colour for the early dwarf daffodils. Night-time frosts are to be expected and endured, but as the flowers open in the morning sun, they reveal their gorgeous orange stamens.

Narcissus 'Jetfire', with a height of 25cm (10in), is similar in shape to 'February Gold', having the same fly-away petals. But the trumpet is more orange (rather than yellow), making it a perfect partner for any late purple crocus as well as all the streaked orange Kaufmanniana tulips.

Double Early *Tulipa* 'Orange Nassau' reaches a height of 20cm (8in) and has a mass of vibrant orange-red petals, a bold combination wherever it grows, whether in borders or containers. This tulip is excellent with blue or yellow hyacinths, red, orange, yellow or blue primroses or with polyanthus.

Double Early *Tulipa* 'Peach Blossom' reaches a height of 20cm (8in) and is one of the most popular of all the early dwarf tulips. It has such a delicate combination of colours in its myriad of petals and looks stunning with blue grape hyacinths, a combination which will last for many happy weeks.

Double Early *Tulipa* 'Kareol' grows to a height of 20cm (8in) and is one of several early double tulips, all of which are lovely in garden borders and containers. Early to flower, sturdy and long lasting, they have wide flowering heads which make them a valuable ingredient where planting space is limited.

Scilla siberica (Siberian squill) grows to 15cm (6in) in height and can be used in pots, but it looks best where it has been planted in garden borders and allowed to colonize. Its nodding, rich blue flowers look much stronger en masse than as individuals or small groups.

Muscari armeniacum (grape hyacinth) will flower for many weeks from early to mid-spring. It grows to 20cm (8in) high and provides a memorable underplanting to many tulips, hyacinths and daffodils, both in containers and in the border.

Chionodoxa forbesii 'Pink Giant' grows to a height of 15cm (6in) and provides racemes of four or more star-shaped flowers, pale pink around the edge, white within. They make a pretty association with early spring bulbs, such as dwarf daffodils and hyacinths.

Early spring borders

Plant groups of single types of bulb beside each other or plant more densely, allowing the taller subjects to be underplanted with shorter ones. In this way, early dwarf daffodils and Kaufmanniana tulips can be associated with or underplanted by purple or white late-flowering Dutch crocuses, starry blue, mauve and (slightly later) white *Anemone blanda*, blue or pink chionodoxas, rich blue scillas and bright blue *Muscari armeniacum* (grape hyacinth). The strong yellow and blue makes a vibrant contrast.

Planting partnerships

Seasons vary, and some flowers will last longer than others, depending on the temperature and moisture, but there is usually quite an overlap between all these plants, with the exception only of the late-flowering Dutch crocuses. These flower with the early dwarf daffodils and Kaufmanniana tulips but will not usually last long enough to partner hyacinths and Double Early tulips, which will be in bloom slightly later

'Heart's Delight' is a Kaufmanniana tulip that looks lovely with blue *Chionodoxa luciliae*, *Anemone blanda* or *Muscari armeniacum*.

and flower on into mid-spring as well. It is safer to plant these with chionodoxas, grape hyacinths, scillas and *Anemone blanda*. A favourite partnership is pink hyacinth with the simple starry flowers of blue *Anemone blanda*, a combination that should flower well year after year.

Violets, violas, pansies, double daisies, primroses and polyanthus play their supportive roles in the

Narcissus 'February Gold' and the elegant *Tulipa* 'Stresa', a Kaufmanniana tulip, make a striking combination.

early spring border. Among the prettiest sights now are groups of primroses and violets with clumps of early dwarf daffodils among them. There is little to match the sheer delicacy of *Narcissus* 'Topolino', with its white petals and pale yellow cup, seen above a fragrant bed of tiny white violets. A similar effect can be achieved with the other yellow and white bicoloured daffodils, such as dainty *Narcissus* 'Minnow' underplanted with the little white grape hyacinth, *Muscari botryoides* 'Album'. You might also like to try 'Jack Snipe', or the even smaller 'Canaliculatus' or 'Little Beauty', planted with creamy white violas or *Primula vulgaris* (wild primrose).

For strength and warmth of colour, plant the brighter, more richly coloured tulips and grape hyacinths among vibrant red, orange or blue polyanthus and primroses or amid the blues and purples of violas and pansies. Plan the borders in autumn and reap the rewards next spring. You can build on your successes, adapting them if needed each season by including, for example, a selection of different

Narcissus 'Tête-à-tête' with its tiny golden heads has become deservedly popular. Like many of the early dwarf daffodils, it associates beautifully with vibrant blue *Muscari armeniacum* (grape hyacinth).

violas or primroses. New forms and colours come on the market each year, offering slightly different shades, markings, sizes and shapes. The results will be well worth the care taken over planning.

Planting in the eye of a tree

The early spring season is perfect for the border "eye" around the base of a deciduous tree. Here, the canopy of leaves will not yet have emerged, which means that sunlight and moisture will still be able to reach the ground beneath the crown. The area could be filled with just one sort of bulb – Narcissus 'February Gold', for example – or a massed planting of, say, scillas, chionodoxas and *Anemone blanda*.

If you have more than one suitable tree you can create a variety of effects. In just a few years, all these bulbs will multiply, providing colour and interest. Add a few primroses or *Tanacetum parthenium* 'Aureum' (golden feverfew), and you will have a miniature garden that is at its best in spring but that can lie dormant

Tulipa 'Oranje Nassau' is a fiery mixture of orange and red, which looks extremely vibrant with red polyanthus (primrose). Plant close to *Tanacetum parthenium* 'Aureum' (golden feverfew) or other bright green herbaceous plants.

for the rest of the year, except for the odd *Digitalis* (foxglove) or rambling rose. In the dry, shady summer months, the bulbs will lie dormant, waiting for the cooler autumn rains to bring them back into growth.

Anemone blanda are wonderful for this type of situation where they can be left to colonize undisturbed. Not only will they spread by seed, but their tubers will increase in size and provide a wealth of flowers. Plant them beneath an old apple or pear tree and enjoy the sea of blue in the spring sunshine. *Anemone blanda* is sold in autumn as small, hard, knobbly tubers. They can be difficult to establish in the first year, because the tubers can become too dry in the storing process between lifting and autumn sales. It is a good idea to soak them overnight before planting. They will expand noticeably and will be ready to plant the next day. From small beginnings in the garden centres in autumn, the tubers will increase in size over the years to 2.5cm (1in) across and may grow to as much as 7.5–10cm (3–4in) in size. Once established, they can be transferred to another part of the garden in autumn or winter.

Hyacinthus orientalis 'Pink Pearl' is splendid with blue *Scilla siberica* (Siberian squill). All other hyacinths would work well here.

The little white grape hyacinth, *Muscari botryoides* 'Album', bridges the season between early and mid-spring.

Early spring naturalized bulbs

Spring grasslands are transformed by early-flowering daffodils, which are generally quite short by nature, while scillas will create a wonderful woodland display.

Grassland

Generous clumps of daffodils can be planted in grass, but make sure that you allow a distance of 7.5–20cm (3–8in) between each one so that the bulbs have space to multiply around the original planting as well as by self-seeding.

Some species narcissi will spread extremely well if the conditions are favourable. *Narcissus bulbocodium* (hoop-petticoat daffodil), for instance, with its wide-spread cup, which is native to western France, Spain, Portugal and North Africa, seems to prefer peaty, acidic or sandy soils. The sandy conditions of the Alpine Meadow at the Royal Horticultural Society Gardens at Wisley, England, seem to be ideal – perhaps it is the slope that is vital or the natural spring water that seeps through or perhaps it is a combination of both factors.

N. pseudonarcissus, sometimes known as the Lent lily, looks delicate with its soft primrose petals and yellow cup, but it is a tolerant plant, thriving in a range of habitats, including meadows, woodland or rocky hillsides. *N. obvallaris*, formerly known as *N. pseudonarcissus* subsp. *obvallaris* and commonly known as the Tenby daffodil, is similar in size but has deep yellow petals and cup. Both naturalize well in grass, and the Tenby daffodil will cope particularly well with shady conditions. Of all the miniature trumpet daffodil cultivars, 'Topolino' must rank as one of the best for naturalizing in grass. It looks so delicate, with its white petals and pale yellow cup. A clump of primroses or violets close by would be perfect.

N. cyclamineus, which is native to north-western Spain and Portugal, enjoys damp river banks and valley bottoms rather than the higher mountain slopes, as do the many modern cultivars that have been developed from it. With its swept-back petals and long, narrow cup, this is one of the easiest of the

A bank of *Scilla bithynica* looks marvellous in the dappled sunlight beneath a broad deciduous tree.

species narcissi to identify. Although the species itself is quite difficult to purchase, its progeny is vast, and widely available garden cultivars include 'February Gold', 'Peeping Tom' and 'Jack Snipe'. Like the parent, these appreciate damp conditions but are tolerant of any well-drained soil.

The little *Narcissus bulbocodium* (hoop-petticoat daffodil) has been allowed to naturalize in the Alpine Meadow at Wisley, in England. It may not prove as prolific in all conditions.

Scilla siberica, often known as the Siberian squill, is at home in sun or shade but prefers well-drained soils. Here it makes a charming picture in short grass with wild primroses.

Narcissus cyclamineus has distinctive reflexed petals and a long, narrow cup. Here it is growing with *Iris unguicularis* 'Mary Barnard'.

Chionodoxa sardensis from Turkey has deep clear blue flowers and naturalizes well beneath deciduous shrubs or in grassland.

daffodils or other bulbs have finished flowering. Only then will they have had the chance to complete their lifecycles. By this stage the leaves will have died down and all the nutrients will have gone back into the bulbs ready for new growth in autumn. If the leaves are removed inadvertently the bulbs may well be blind – that is, without flowers – the following year.

Woodland

Some daffodils, such as *Narcissus obvallaris* (Tenby daffodil), and nearly all scillas thrive in the light shade found in deciduous woodland, and they will adapt well to shady places in the garden, where they may be grown under deciduous trees or shrubs. When you plant, leave a generous space between each bulb so they can multiply readily. Primroses and hellebores are their natural companions, with *Hyacinthoides non-scripta* spp. (English bluebells) following in mid- to late spring.

All dwarf daffodils associate well with chionodoxas, which thrive in a sunny position but will also cope with partial shade, as long as the soil is free draining. Golden daffodils look splendid with groups of vibrant blue chionodoxas nearby, while the pastel bicolour daffodils, such as 'Jack Snipe', associate well with the pinker forms. The blues and pinks of *Anemone blanda* also make good partners for daffodils, while the taller and slightly later *A. blanda* 'White Splendour' looks superb with those dwarf daffodils that bridged the gap between early and mid-spring. So much depends on the season!

Low-growing *Anemone blanda* and *Scilla siberica* (Siberian squill) will do better if they are planted where finer grasses are growing, such as between shrubs or beneath deciduous trees. *S. siberica* will cope with sun or shade, and it prefers a light, sandy soil. *A. blanda*, on the other hand, is at home in full sun or light shade, but it must have well-drained soil. Either

looks pretty in a small group beside violets or wild primroses.

As with all spring bulbs grown in grassy areas it is vital to remember that the grass should not be cut until at least six weeks after the

Chionodoxa forbesii 'Pink Giant' is another member of the chionodoxa family that is native to western Turkey and that will cope well with spring grassland.

Mid-spring gallery

The spring bulb garden reaches its zenith with mid-season tulips and daffodils flowering together, creating one of the most colourful tapestries imaginable.

The late-winter and early-spring bulbs are nearly all dwarf forms, but many of the mid-season varieties, including *Leucojum aestivum* (summer snowflake), most of the daffodils and almost all tulips, are much taller, growing to 35–60cm (14–24in). Meanwhile *Fritillaria imperialis* (crown imperial) rises to a stately 1.2m (4ft) or more, making it one of the most statuesque of all bulbs. The grape hyacinths, including *Muscari armeniacum*, *M. botryoides* 'Album' and *M. latifolium*, *Anemone nemorosa* (wood

Fritillaria meleagris is one of the most beautiful spring bulbs with flowers gracefully poised and petals intricately marked.

anemone), *Hyacinthoides* spp. (bluebell) and *Erythronium dens-canis* (dog's tooth violet) are shorter, at 15–30cm (6–12in). There are also some shorter daffodils, such as *Narcissus* 'Thalia', 'Silver Chimes', 'Segovia' and 'Hawera', and some small species tulips, such as the lilac *Tulipa saxatilis* and diminutive *T. tarda*.

While tulips and grape hyacinths prefer to bask in spring sunshine, several of the fritillaries, including *Fritillaria meleagris* (snake's head fritillary), and nearly all daffodils are happy in sun or partial shade. Others, such as wood anemones, dog's tooth violets and summer snowflakes, enjoy light shade, in damp grass or woodland. Here, the first bluebells will be starting to flower.

Tulipa 'Apricot Beauty' looks beautiful in the mid-spring border, beside scented *Viburnum* 'Anne Russell'.

Leucojum aestivum grows to 45–60cm (18–24in) high and likes damp conditions, where it soon multiplies to create a large clump of tall, graceful, white flowers, each petal tipped with a distinctive green blotch. It is called summer snowflake to distinguish it from its earlier-flowering relative *L. vernum*.

Typical of mid-season daffodils, *Narcissus* 'Romance' grows to about 50cm (20in) high. It is a beautifully proportioned white daffodil with a rich pink trumpet, and it looks stunning backlit with spring sunshine. It is excellent for borders near the lime-green foliage of newly emerging herbaceous plants.

The Lily-flowered *Tulipa* 'West Point', which grows to 50cm (20in), bridges the seasons between mid- and late spring. The vivid yellow petals are exquisitely pointed, and the flowers look dramatic with strong yellows, red or blues but also look wonderful with soft grey foliage plants, such as *Senecio cineraria*.

Erythronium dens-canis (dog's tooth violet) is native to woodlands throughout Europe. It grows from an elongated bulb that looks rather like a dog's tooth. It adapts well to conditions in a partially shady border. The flowers have attractive, fly-away petals, while the leaves are sometimes densely mottled.

Fritillaria meleagris (snake's head fritillary) is a wildflower of European meadowlands, and it adapts well to damp, grassy spots in the garden as well as to borders. It is a plant with many common names, including snake's head fritillary and ginny-hen floure, because the petals are patterned like guinea hen feathers.

Muscari latifolium is an unusual later-flowering species of grape hyacinth. It has urn-shaped flowers in shades of blue, violet and black, and its leaves are wider than those of the widely grown *M. armeniacum*. Growing to 20cm (8in) tall, the species is native to the open pine forests of north-western Turkey.

With a flowering height of about 30cm (12in), *Narcissus* 'Pipit' is one of the loveliest daffodils to flower in mid-spring. It produces two or three flowers on each stem, each flower being a strong lemon yellow suffused with white streaks.

Tulipa 'New Design' is a beautiful pink tulip growing to 50cm (20in). It is particularly pretty with the light behind it, when the petals have a translucent quality. Its leaves are edged with white, making it a favourite with garden designers.

The tall *Fritillaria imperialis* (crown imperial), which can achieve a height of 1.2m (4ft) or more, has been a favourite bulb for more than 400 years. Inside the giant cups large drops of nectar collect above the long stamens, which glisten in the sunlight.

Mid-spring borders

This is one of the most exciting times of year in the bulb garden, and it is rewarding to admire what has been planted the previous autumn, especially if some new designs have been introduced.

For example, one or more strongly coloured tulips, such as deep purple 'Attila', beetroot 'Negrita', burgundy and yellow 'Gavota', red 'Cassini', or orange and purple 'Princes Irene', will allow you to develop eye-catching schemes with *Myosotis* (forget-me-not), *Bellis perennis* (double daisy), pansies and *Erysimum cheiri* (wallflower) in rich shades of deep blue, orange, gold, red, black and purple. You will have wonderfully showy borders, no matter what the weather.

Meanwhile, the pastel-toned tulips, including salmon-pink *Tulipa* 'Apricot Beauty', shell pink 'Esther', double satin pink 'Angélique', 'White Dream' and the lovely cool, creamy white and green 'Spring Green',

Muscari latifolium bears a mixture of dark blue and lighter blue flowers on each stem.

The flowers of *Tulipa* 'Apricot Beauty' are an exquisite mixture of shades of apricot, peach and tangerine. It looks especially striking next to the biennial *Silybum marianum*, which has prominent white-veined leaves.

call for a softer colour scheme, incorporating the paler tones of polyanthus, double *Bellis* (daisy), pansies and violas, forget-me-nots and wallflowers with combinations of primrose yellows, pale pinks, creams and pale blues. Foliage plants can be used to great advantage too. The cheery golden foliage of *Tanacetum parthenium* 'Aureum' (golden feverfew), the silver variegations of *Silybum marianum* (blessed Mary's thistle) and the soft seedlings of *Nigella damascena* (love-in-a-mist) are all valuable spring-time partners: the effect is subtle but beautiful.

Formal and informal styles

So many different styles, both formal and informal, can be adopted. Where there is a strong design with clipped box hedging, the formal lines of tulips are most appropriate. The bright green of the new growth on *Buxus* (box) looks good with scarlet tulips, but a different type of

Tall *Fritillaria imperialis* make striking displays with their large bell-shaped flowers associating well with shorter daffodils. Sometimes the leaves are variegated and edged in gold, as in *F. imperialis* 'Aureomarginata', or white, as in *F. imperialis* 'Argenteovariegata'.

formality can be achieved if tulips are interplanted with co-ordinated bedding plants, whether you choose a vivid or a subtle approach.

A more informal scheme might use different types of bulb within a large herbaceous border. A few clumps of daffodils, some *Muscari latifolium* (grape hyacinth), two or three *Fritillaria imperialis* (crown imperial) and three or four groups of tulips will create a wonderful effect, informal but full and colourful. It might look haphazard, but in reality it will have been carefully thought out. You might want to use the height of the *Fritillaria imperialis* to form a bold grouping at the back of the border, placing shorter tulips or daffodils in front. These tall fritillaries come from southern Turkey to Kashmir and may be various shades of orange, red or yellow. They can grow to 1–1.5m (3–5ft) in height and have as many as six or even eight bell-

shaped flowers, often displaying an enticing drop of nectar at the end of the stamens. The distinctive cluster of green, leaf-like bracts gives the plant its common name. Plant the large bulbs on their sides so that moisture does not collect in the central gully, which will cause the bulbs to rot, and add a layer of grit or sharp sand beneath them to improve drainage. These plants like deep, well-drained, fertile soil and a position in full sun. Both the bulbs and flowers have a foxy smell, so are best planted away from paths.

If you have a sunny, well-drained site, try other dramatic fritillaries, including *F. persica*, which comes from southern Turkey and has a flowering spike to 1m (3ft) tall with bloomed, green to purple bell-shaped flowers, and the even taller *F. persica* 'Adiyaman', which has brown-purple flowers. These can be more tricky to establish, but when conditions are just right they will look stunning.

A minimalist garden

In recent years a minimalist style has become fashionable where bulbs are planted in gravel or among different coloured stones or bark, with few other plants around.

This mid-spring garden is just awakening, with the white-barked birch *Betula utilis* var. *jacquemontii* 'Jermyns' underplanted with *Narcissus* 'Salome', ornamental grasses and perovskia, and the broad, grey-green leaves of *Allium karataviense* beginning to emerge.

Fritillaria imperialis has a tuft of distinctive bract-like leaves emerging from the crown. The orange form has a dark bronze stem.

A longer-term planting scheme

For gardeners who want to experiment and are willing to change their spring borders regularly, the choice of colour and the range of bulbs is vast. If you prefer a simpler approach with a longer-term planting scheme, you also have an enormous choice

but bear in mind that some bulbs are more reliable than others, and there is little doubt that some bulbs naturalize in borders better than others. Remember, too, that your success with bulbs will depend on soil conditions and factors such as proximity to tree roots or hedges, and the aspect and rainfall in your garden. Sometimes it is difficult to determine why crown imperials grow exuberantly in some gardens for many years, but in others they will hardly flower at all after the first year. The same is sometimes true of the highly bred split corona daffodils, such as *Narcissus* 'Cassata' and 'Mondragon'.

Most daffodils will establish themselves well. They form good clumps and have a more natural appearance than bold, highly coloured tulips. So, if you like informality, grow daffodils. *Narcissus* 'Pipit' is a favourite choice, long in flower, a good naturalizer and with beautiful lemon yellow flowers streaked with white. At 30cm (12in) or just a little taller, it is a real winner.

Tulips will naturalize best in well-drained soil rather than in heavy clay. For best results be sure to plant bulbs at a depth of at least three times the size of the bulb. Among the best tulips to naturalize on loam or clay is 'Apeldoorn' and its close relatives. 'Apeldoorn' itself was introduced after World War II and is still one of the bestselling cultivars because of its vigour, boldness and reliability. Look out for bright yellow 'Golden Apeldoorn', orange-flushed 'Blushing Apeldoorn', the original scarlet red 'Apeldoorn' and 'Apeldoorn's Elite', which has red flowers edged with yellow. Any one of these – or a combination of several – will add vibrancy to your borders for many years. They associate well with self-seeding blue forget-me-nots, golden feverfew, purple-leaved heuchera and colourful primulas, all of which will naturalize.

A cottage-garden border

For a mixture of tulips and daffodils that will last for many years, try a combination of *Tulipa* 'Orange

Narcissus 'Romance' offers an attractive pink and white theme, with white petals and a warm pink cup. It naturalizes well.

Narcissus 'Pipit' is one of the best daffodils for naturalizing, combining elegance with reliability.

Mid-spring border case study

This vibrant mid-spring border combines *Tulipa* 'Orange Emperor' and 'Golden Apeldoorn' with the bicolour daffodil *Narcissus* 'Tahiti'. Meanwhile white *N.* 'Thalia' echoes the bridal wreath *Spiraea* 'Arguta' in the background. With peonies, irises and herbaceous delphiniums, and then lilies, crocosmias and dahlias to follow, this makes an excellent cottage border for spring and summer colour using bulbs, corms and tubers to great effect. Only the dahlia will need winter protection (either by lifting and storing or adding a mulch).

Earlier in the year winter-flowering aconites *Eranthis hyemalis* and snowdrops *Galanthus nivalis* had both made a welcome appearance.

Tulipa 'Orange Emperor'

Tulipa 'Golden Apeldoorn'

Narcissus 'Thalia'

Narcissus 'Tahiti'

Emperor', which is an excellent and reliable plant, flowering just before, and overlapping with, *T.* 'Golden Apeldoorn'. Clumps of yellow and orange-red *Narcissus* 'Tahiti' make a valuable addition in linking the two colours of tulips. As an alternative arrangement, try a single yellow narcissus such as *N.* 'Pipit', along with an orange tulip, *T.* 'Beauty of Apeldoorn', which is particularly beautiful and very reliable.

Flowering spring viburnums such as 'Anne Russell' or 'Park Farm Hybrid' and *Spiraea* 'Arguta' (bridal wreath) would add height and substance to the spring border. Both have white flowers, providing a

lightness of touch and an excellent background to any spring bulbs.

For a more vibrant colour theme, try the vivid red *Tulipa* 'Apeldoorn' planted alongside yellow, red or orange wallflowers, which will start to flower by mid-spring and continue blooming for several weeks, bridging the gap between spring and early summer. The tulips may be planted in straight lines or grouped in clumps to give a more cottage garden feel. The wallflowers will provide delicious fragrance, especially after a shower of rain. They will have to be replaced each year, but the tulips can be left in the soil where they will multiply well.

Otherwise, to keep the straight lines in future years, the tulips will have to be thinned. Lift them about six weeks after flowering, when all the foliage has died back.

The original *Tulipa* 'Apeldoorn' is vibrant red with dark, almost black interior.

Mid-spring naturalized bulbs

The fledgling canopy of deciduous trees, as yet immature, still allows shafts of sunlight to reach the ground at this time of year, allowing many grassland or woodland bulbs to flourish, including *Anemone blanda*, *Erythronium dens-canis* (dog's tooth violet), *Leucojum aestivum* (summer snowflake), *Anemone nemorosa* (wood anemone) and trilliums.

Grassland

One of the real stars of mid-spring is the delicate *Fritillaria meleagris* (snake's head fritillary). Their white or lilac heads hang demurely among the short grass, each flower an exquisite chessboard pattern of intricate veining. Their season overlaps with the early dwarf daffodils and primroses, but the fritillaries will continue to flower with the later bulbs and cowslips. They associate beautifully with pure white *Narcissus* 'Thalia' and starry *Anemone blanda* 'White Splendour'. They like sunny, damp conditions,

Narcissus 'Thalia' grows about 35cm (14in) tall and produces two or three flowers on each stem, each one pure white with a characteristic twist to the petals.

Anemone blanda 'White Splendour' seems to be bigger and slightly later flowering than the blue form, and it always looks wonderful with *Fritillaria meleagris* (snake's head fritillary).

and if they are really happy they will multiply quite naturally. Even a handful in a small patch of turf is well worth trying. Unfortunately, rabbits rather like them, so only plant them if your garden is a rabbit-free zone.

Many daffodils will naturalize in grass, such as the yellow Large-cupped *Narcissus* 'Carlton', and the Trumpet daffodil 'King Alfred'. Others have white petals, including the well-known Large-cupped 'Ice

Follies', with its white petals and broad, creamy white cup, or the simple white 'Mount Hood', with its well-proportioned trumpet. Another favourite is 'Actaea', again with white petals but this time with a distinctive, small, red-tipped cup, rather similar to *N. poeticus* var. *recurvus* (pheasant's eye), which will flower a few weeks later. Some daffodils have so-called pink cups, which are really a soft salmon-pink that darkens with age. 'Salome' and 'Rainbow' will grow successfully in grass. Another bicolour to look out for is golden 'Pipe Major', which has an orange-red corona. Some of the multiheaded types are excellent in borders, particularly white 'Thalia' and 'Sir Winston Churchill' and the primrose yellow 'Yellow Cheerfulness'.

Several other types of bulb will grow in grassy places. *Ornithogalum nutans*, with its nodding green and white flowers, will survive well if the soil is well drained; it will also grow among shrubs.

Woodland

Hyacinthoides spp. (bluebell), which can be white or pink as well as blue, prefers the cool, damp shade near a hedgerow or the leafy soil in a deciduous wood, especially among beech trees. It starts to flower in mid-spring, but its main season is late spring.

Erythronium dens-canis (dog's tooth violet) prefers sparse grass, although it, too, will grow in the shade of shrubs or deciduous trees. It is one

Narcissus 'Yellow Cheerfulness' naturalizes well in grass or borders. It looks especially lovely near the fresh foliage of the mock orange Philadelphus coronarius 'Aureus'.

Tolerant of sun or shade, Ornithogalum nutans will produce many pendent green and white flowers on each stem. It is worth seeking out for its quiet presence.

of the prettiest of the spring flowers, with its delicate, swept-back petals in white, pink or lilac. *Leucojum aestivum* (summer snowflake) likes damp soil where it has a good moist root run and will form a lovely graceful clump in grass or woodland.

Another wonderful naturalizer is *Anemone nemorosa* (wood anemone), which is at its best in a deciduous wood or beneath shrubs. It will soon spread to form a dainty white carpet, looking perfect with a clump of dog's tooth violets or a group or two of bluebells. Try it beneath a spring-flowering tree or in the light shade of summer-flowering shrubs, where it will thrive with a good mulch of leaf mould. *A. nemorosa* 'Allenii' is one of several blue forms, and 'Robinsoniana' is a lighter blue.

Trilliums also like the shade. They are found in the woodlands of the Appalachian Mountains in eastern North America where they revel in the damp humus, especially near mountain streams. They prefer either neutral or acid soil. The best-known species is *Trillium grandiflorum* (wake robin, wood lily), which has white flowers that turn pink as they age. Black fruits are formed, which ants take away to their nests, eating the pulp but leaving the seed and so helping to propagate the plants.

Narcissus 'Pipe Major', which reaches 45cm (18in) in height, is a distinctive bicolour with its yellow petals and orange-red cup. It is a colour combination that works well in grass.

Late spring to early summer gallery

Although most of the daffodils and many of the tulips are now over, there is still a wealth of other bulbs to enjoy at this time of year.

Late-flowering tulips are among the most exciting, both in colour and shape. Parrot tulips produce superb buds, with the petals tightly wrapped around each other, before opening to reveal sumptuous, full-bodied flowers, with streaks of secondary colours. One of the best of all the late tulips is the Fringed *Tulipa* 'Blue Heron', which is not blue at all but more a warm lilac. The Single Late 'Queen of Night', a mysterious shade of dark purple verging on black, is a great performer, whether it is grown in a formal bedding scheme, a cottage border or a container.

Dutch iris 'Sapphire Beauty' combines a sumptuous mix of deep blue and gold and looks splendid beside the dusky poppy, *Papaver orientale* 'Patty's Plum'.

The tall *Camassia* (quamash) from North America, also known as Indian lily or American bluebell, is useful for sunny borders or grassland. The flowers may be blue or white, and both forms associate well with the last of the daffodils, *Narcissus poeticus* var. *recurvus* (pheasant's eye).

At the front of a sunny border *Anemone coronaria* hybrids will make a real splash of colour with their brilliant red, white or blue flowers. Cheap and cheerful, they are also suitable for containers. For best results, just remember to soak the tubers overnight before planting. Meanwhile, alliums provide rich colours, from white to lilac and purple, and they will be joined by shapely Dutch irises, in beautiful shades of purple to gold and yellow.

Tall *Allium giganteum* and shorter *Allium hollandicum* are just poised, waiting to bloom.

Tulipa 'Blue Parrot' grows to 55cm (22in) and is a full-bodied, lilac-blue tulip, which flowers at the same time as blue forget-me-nots, red or purple aubrieta and purple- or rose-coloured wallflowers. In maturity, its large blooms are sumptuous, and make perfect cut flowers for a table decoration.

Tulipa 'Queen of Night', a tall tulip at 60cm (24in), is described as satin black but is really a deep, dark purple. It looks lovely with pale blue forget-me-nots or with tall, purple alliums, with which it overlaps for a fleeting moment. Perhaps the best of all partners, however, are orange wallflowers.

Allium cristophii grows to 60cm (24in) high and has round, open heads, about 20cm (8in) across, with large, star-shaped, amethyst-blue flowers. The leaves are long and strappy and appear early, before beginning to dry off as the flowers open. The huge seedheads are useful in dried-flower arrangements.

Anemone coronaria De Caen Group 'Die Braut' ('The Bride') is a beautiful, pure white, single-flowered anemone, with a contrasting apple-green centre. Best planted near the front of a sunny border, it grows to 25cm (10in) and associates well with almost any other plant. It does well in containers, too.

Allium karataviense grows to 20cm (8in) high and has rounded umbels, 5–8cm (2–3in) across, of small, pink, star-shaped flowers. Its broad, grey, almost elliptical leaves are a special feature. The flowerheads dry well and look attractive throughout the summer. Left in place, self-seeding will soon occur.

Iris 'Purple Sensation' grows to 45cm (18in) and is one of the many bulbous Dutch irises that are useful for bridging the gap in sunny borders between the late tulips and taller alliums. They look lovely in small groups beneath wisterias or laburnums and are pretty with pale yellow wallflowers.

Camassia leichtlinii subsp. *suksdorfii* Caerulea Group is a good subject for borders or damp grassland, where it will multiply and create large groups of tall blue flower spikes up to 75cm (30in) high. The flowering period is all too short, but the impact is magnificent.

Tall *Tulipa* 'Blue Heron' grows to 60cm (24in) and is a strong, elegant tulip, with fringing around its lilac petals. Grow it in the border or in large pots underplanted with orange or primrose yellow wallflowers or 'Ivory and Rose Blotch' winter-flowering pansies.

Allium schubertii grows to 40cm (16in) and has flowerheads about 30cm (12in) across, with an inner compact ball of flowers and an outer sphere shooting off like fireworks. It is certainly a talking point, both when in flower and when seen as a dried specimen.

Late spring to early summer borders

Late-flowering tulips bridge the seasons between mid- and late spring, enjoying the longer days and warmer temperatures.

This group includes some of the most sensational tulips of all, particularly the Parrot types, with their full-bodied, curvy petals. *Tulipa* 'Fantasy' is a mixture of salmon-pink and reds, with flushes of yellow and green, and it looks wonderful when it is grown with lime-green or deep bronze foliage plants. 'Blue Parrot' is more lilac than blue, and it looks marvellous with many spring bedding plants, including rose-pink or purple wallflowers, rose-pink or pale blue pansies and various shades of aubrieta.

Of the so-called black (actually dark purple) tulips, look out for shapely 'Black Parrot', with its dark, twisted petals, or the tall double 'Black Hero', which has a wonderful glossy sheen, as does the double, rather more purple than black, 'Blue Diamond'. Among the singles, 'Queen of Night', 'Paul Scherer' or 'Black Swan' will still be in flower, as will 'Recreado', which is another

Tulipa 'Black Parrot' is a sensational Parrot tulip with sculptured, almost black petals.

Tulipa 'Paul Scherer', one the darkest of all tulips, has velvety maroon flowers.

choice deep purple tulip. Planted in nearby groups or used as dot plants, they will certainly make a strong statement and add drama to the late spring garden. Blue forget-me-nots make a simple but glorious partnership with any of these dark coloured tulips.

If you want a black and white theme a good white double tulip is 'Mount Tacoma'. 'New Dawn' is tall, single, white with purple feathering at the sides of the petals. 'White Triumphator' is definitely one to look out for, with its tall, sturdy

stem and elegant, lily-shaped flower. Over the years it has become a firm favourite. For a more subtle effect, add to the black, purple and white theme by planting a touch of dreamy lilac with 'Lilac Perfection', which has broad, peony-type flowers, or add a group of pastel lilac Fringed tulips, such as 'Blue Heron'. Growing to 60cm (24in), this is a tall but sturdy and shapely tulip, which is one of the last to flower.

You might want to forget subtlety altogether and throw some vibrant reds into the borders. Orange-red

Tulipa 'Blue Parrot' can be used in a massed bedding display with *Aubrieta* 'Royal Red", which provides a profusion of carmine red flowers beneath the lilac pink tulips.

Tulipa 'Lilac Perfection' is a peony-flowered tulip with broad double flowers.

Camassia leichtlinii subsp. suksdorfii Caerulea Group is another candidate for mass bedding.

A group of the Dutch iris 'Symphony' creates a lively and refreshing picture. Fine and shapely in figure, no wonder they make such a popular cut flower.

'Ballerina' and 'Pieter de Leur' are both lily-flowered tulips with attitude. They can make a border come alive even on a dull day.

Architectural camassias

The tall and slender camassias, with their tapering flower spikes, are white, rich blue or pale blue. These are versatile bulbs and adapt well to the border and to unmown grassy areas as long as the soil is damp and the site is sunny. A spot beside a garden pond would be ideal, but they look just as attractive in a clump in a herbaceous border or in formal bedding patterns partnered by wallflowers. If you want to leave them in the ground for a number of years, add blue forget-me-nots, which are sure to self-seed and will avoid the need for replanting. The all-blue scheme will be enchanting.

Colourful Dutch irises

Dutch irises provide colour year after year, spanning the seasons between late spring and early summer. They vary in colour from white through to yellow, blue and purple, and sometimes a mixture of more than one colour. Each of the flowers has intricate veining. Grown from small bulbs, for a short period they will be in flower at the same time as alliums, and together they make an exciting partnership. Indeed, alliums and Dutch irises have a host of suitable homes, including the mixed herbaceous border, the cottage-style garden or beneath arches of wisteria, laburnum or Robinia hispida (bristly locust, rose acacia). Wherever they are planted they will provide a brilliant display for years.

Tulipa 'Pieter de Leur' is a dramatic lily-flowered tulip with elegant pointed petals.

Dutch iris 'Oriental Beauty' is a superb combination of lilac blues, silvers and gold, adding a touch of majesty to any border.

Medium to tall alliums with large drumstick flowerheads

Among the tallest of all alliums, reaching 1.2m (4ft) or more, is *Allium* 'Mount Everest' with its large grapefruit-sized flower heads. Its ivory white florets show up well against the darker foliage of a yew hedge or among other brighter colours. Kicking at its heels is lilac-purple *Allium giganteum*, with deep purple *A. hollandicum* 'Purple Sensation', and 'Globe Master', at 90cm (36in), close behind. All are strong and sturdy and together they make a popular choice for garden borders. *A. nigrum*, with its ivory white flowers and bold black ovaries, normally reaches 70cm (28in) high and is slightly later to flower than the purple and lilac forms. It looks lovely with silver *Cynara cardunculus* (cardoon) and *Hesperis matronalis* var. *albiflora* (the white form of sweet rocket). The pale lilac *A. hollandicum* (syn. *A. aflatunense*) has a flowering height of 60cm (24in). Rather than just choosing one or another, plant a mixture that will associate very well together, provide a long period of

The densely rounded heads of *Allium hollandicum* 'Purple Sensation' contrast beautifully with the tall spires of foxgloves.

flowering and a wonderful pattern of tiered planting. All white alliums mix happily with purple and lilac forms and together look stunning beneath all shades of wisteria whether pink, white or blue. They also associate well with yellow laburnum and white or pink *Clematis montana*.

The only drawback to most alliums is the leaves, which apppear well before the flower buds emerge,

and by the time the flowers open they look very untidy. It is best to grow some other leafy plant nearby to conceal the mess. Biennial or perennial wallflowers are a perfect foil providing both foliage and contrasting or complementary flower colour. Japanese anemones are also excellent bedfellows. Their leaves soon grow up to hide the allium leaves and in turn their flowers will provide colour in the border from late summer to autumn. Large grey-leaved hostas also make good companions, giving the alliums a strong visual base and at the same time hiding their foliage. Foxgloves make another great partner, their large basal leaves easily hiding the bulb foliage while their spires of flowers, either pink or white, offer an architectural contrast to the rounded heads of the alliums.

Later-flowering species

Allium cristophii, at around 60cm (24in) high, has a very large open flower which makes it one of the most popular of all garden alliums. Its flowers have a metallic quality

Deep purple *Allium hollandicum* 'Purple Sensation' lives up to its name as the buds open and the flowers emerge.

Allium hollandicum 'Purple Sensation' flowers well beneath an arch of honeysuckle and combines beautifully with Dutch iris.

The white *Allium nigrum* is slightly later to flower and is 70cm (28in) tall. The term *nigrum* refers to the dark green ovaries.

Allium cristophii has large heads, which take on a vibrant metallic sheen in the evening sunlight. They contrast well with hostas, hesperis and Iceland poppies, and go on to make a lasting contribution with their round dramatic seedheads.

which makes them look stunning in the evening when the warmer light seems to bring them even more to life. Many of the Dutch irises make good companions offering a contrast in shape of flower and often in colour. Meanwhile all the early roses, whether pink, purple, white or yellow, make super partners as well. *A. schubertii*, at 40cm (16in), is slightly shorter but its flower heads are even wider. Two circles of flowers appear creating an inner and outer ring which creates the effect of a firework in mid-explosion. They can reach 30–45cm (12–18in) across in a sunny warm spot. Their leaves are early to grow. Both these alliums are a little later to flower than the taller drumsticks mentioned opposite, and so they help to bridge the gap between late spring and early summer. Their untidy leaves are less noticeable for they will flower with poppies, herbaceous geraniums and hesperis, whose foliage by then is well grown, providing a valuable foil for the long strappy leaves.

Alliums look marvellous as a mass planting beneath arches dripping with wisteria, early honeysuckle, early-flowering clematis, laburnum or *Robinia hispida*. Here they are just beginning to flower, with buds ready to burst open.

All these allium flowers are notable additions to the garden, and their seedheads will last for many weeks to be enjoyed either in the garden or in the house in a dried flower arrangement. Where they have multiplied, either by natural massing of the bulb below ground or by self-seeding, the seedheads will create a noteworthy mass display. Few other bulbs can claim such a long period of interest.

Slender and shorter

Though undoubtedly tall, *Nectaroscordum siculum* is also both slender and graceful and is very happy in sun or partial shade so long as the soil is neither dry nor waterlogged. Though strictly no longer called an allium, *Nectaroscordum siculum* is of the same family and grows from a similar rounded bulb and in most bulb catalogues will be found in this section. The name is derived from Greek *nektar*, which refers to its large ovaries, and *skorodon*, which reflects the fact that the whole plant smells of garlic when crushed. It comes from France and Italy where it is known as the Sicilian honey garlic. Its flower stems reach up to 1.2m (4ft), producing bell-shaped flowers suitable for an informal cottage style of border. They are creamy white, flushed with pink and dark red, with green at the base, creating a charming combination of subtle colours. Like many alliums, it is much favoured by bees. After their visit, the seedpods become erect making this a most distinctive plant both before and after flowering.

Allium unifolium has delightful pretty pink flowers which show up well here against the blue-green slate mulch. Self-seeding is common in a sunny spot.

By contrast, many alliums are much shorter and are either suitable for growing in containers where their scale is matched, or at the front of a herbaceous border where they are not dwarfed by taller more vigorous plants. They are also a bonus in the modern garden, mulched by gravel, granite chippings or slate. Here they can live close to the path, either alone or in partnership with others.

Allium unifolium bears pretty pink flowers about 30cm (12in) high (although can be taller); its leaves are erect and though not particularly attractive, are not untidy either. Good planting partners are later-flowering herbaceous plants such as pink echinaceas, which will then fill the gap after the allium has finished its main display. These in turn associate well with ornamental grasses. All these plants look striking against a blue-green slate mulch. An alternative bulb for the gravel garden could be *A. flavum*, again only 30cm (12in) high. It has attractively coloured blue-green leaves and contrasting yellow flowers with up to 60 tiny bells on each stem. It too loves a sunny spot and will self-seed easily. Another choice could be *A. caeruleum* with its rich blue drumstick-type flower heads, only 2.5cm (1in) across, borne on slender stems in early summer. The leaves die back completely before flowers appear. All three alliums could be planted in close alliance for a late spring and early summer display

The buds of *Nectaroscordum siculum* (syn. *Allium siculum*) are about to burst into flower.

The flowers are creamy white flushed with pink and dark red, and are loved by bees.

Unlike many alliums, foliage is a positive asset in the case of *A. karataviense*, which grows around 20cm (8in) high. Each bulb produces a pair of broad grey leaves, held almost horizontal, which have a metallic sheen. This allium is suitable for a minimalist style of gardening, and looks most effective against a carpet of gravel or red granite chippings, either of which provides a sharp, clean background. It needs a sunny spot to do well and will enjoy the additional warmth of the surrounding gravel or stone which will encourage it to self-seed with ease. The individual flowers are small but numerous, star-shaped, white to pale pink, borne in umbels 5–7.5cm (2–3in) across.

Shade lovers

There are just a handful of alliums that actually prefer shade and, like many plants which grow in these conditions, they are both white in bloom. They include *Allium triquetrum* with its loose flower heads and unusual triangular stems. It is often called the three-cornered leek. Growing to around 38cm (15in), it thrives in damp shade but, being a native of southern Europe, is only borderline hardy although it has now naturalized in several parts of the British Isles. Meanwhile, its slightly shorter relation, *A. ursinum*, is native to wide regions of northern Europe into Russia and is fully hardy. It revels in damp woodland conditions where it can become invasive. It is

Here *Allium karataviense* looks very snug with the newly emerging foliage of another sun lover *Eryngium bourgatii,* whose intricate leaf shape provides a foil as the foliage of the allium dies back.

colloquially known as wild garlic on account of its smell, and like the domesticated garlic, *A. sativum,* it has many medicinal properties. Its leaves and flowers are used to flavour salads and soups.

Allium karataviense thrives in a sunny position and combines well with other sun-loving plants such as *Eryngium bourgatii* and *Perovskia*.

Late spring to early summer naturalized bulbs

Both *Hyacinthoides non-scripta* spp. (English bluebells) and camassias will naturalize where the conditions suit them, but bluebells prefer a cooler, shadier site, whereas camassias prefer a sunnier location.

Both plants, however, like moisture-retentive soil. Camassias are ideal partners for *Narcissus poeticus* var. *recurvus* (pheasant's eye), which is the last of the daffodils. Both plants flower in late spring and provide colour long after many of the spring bulbs have finished. This daffodil originates from the deep mountain valleys of Switzerland, where it flowers after snowmelt. Its delicacy of flower and lateness make it one of the most popular of the genus. However, the principal drawback of

The white form of *Hyacinthoides non-scripta* spp. (English bluebell) offers an alternative to the more commonly known bluebell. Pink forms are also known in the wild. Clumps of all three colours would look attractive in a woodland setting. The native English bluebell has flowers on one side only of a tall raceme.

naturalizing these late-flowering bulbs is that you have to delay the time when you can cut the grass. Resist the temptation to get out the lawnmower. Wait for at least six weeks after the bulbs have finished flowering before you cut the grass. By then, the bulbs will have completed their lifecycles and will be resting until root growth starts again in autumn.

A carpet of bluebells

Not many gardeners are lucky enough to have an entire woodland to plant with beautiful bluebells, but the blue carpet can still look extremely pretty on even a relatively modest scale, such as when it is confined to an orchard or beneath a mixed deciduous hedge. Both the larger *Hyacinthoides hispanica* (Spanish bluebell) and the more delicate *H. non-scripta* (English bluebell) are available in white and shades of blue

Narcissus poeticus var. *recurvus* (pheasant's eye) and camassias are a major feature of the spring garden. They will naturalize in grass and give years of pleasure. Buttercups add further colour to the picture.

The Spanish bluebell, *Hyacinthoides hispanica*, produces flowers all the way round its flower spike, which remains upright. Shades of blue, pink and white flowers are all available.

The woodland is a wonderful picture now that the *Hyacinthoides non-scripta* spp. (English bluebells) are in full flower, a vast sheet of blue beneath a canopy of emerging oak leaves. They have a sweet, heady perfume, which can be overpowering on a large scale. They self-seed freely.

and pink, and both species will settle down with ease and multiply – and this may cause a problem, for if they are planted close together they will interbreed, and the seedlings will show characteristics of both parents. While this may not be an issue in your garden, it does have wider ramifications. If bees have taken nectar from Spanish bluebells and the next generation of mixed bluebells in your garden and then fly off and take nectar from native English bluebells growing in the hedgerows or woods, the result will be a diminution of the precious and dwindling native stock. If possible, avoid the thuggish (though attractive) *H. hispanica* and remove any that are growing in your garden, including any mixed Spanish and English seedlings. Choosing the more delicate *H. non-scripta* will help to sustain numbers of one of the most evocative and beautiful of all British wildflowers. Plant bulbs of English bluebells in groups in the autumn (cut and allow them to self-seed), or buy them as growing plants in the green in late spring. Plant immediately on purchase and allow them to self-seed.

Camassia cusickii bears long racemes of cup-shaped, pale blue flowers. It will cope with quite shady positions in grass or borders.

Mid- to late summer gallery

The summer gallery contains many glorious lilies, including familiar border species, like *Lilium regale* (regal lily), as well as a host of cultivated forms, in white and all shades of pink, orange, yellow and salmon-pink. Some lilies are now bred without stamens to help people who are allergic to pollen, and these are generally sold as "Kiss" lilies.

Many summer bulbs and corms produce tall plants, but exceptional among them are the cardiocrinums, which can grow to 2–4m (6–12ft) in height. With their long, scented, trumpet-shaped flowers, they are a spectacular choice for a shrubbery or woodland area. Shorter, but still tall, are the creamy white *Galtonia candicans*

The luscious white blooms of this tall gladiolus are quite at home among the softer shapes of *Cosmos* 'Sonata Pink' and *Astrantia major* 'Ruby Wedding'.

(Cape hyacinth) and *Crocosmia* 'Lucifer', whose flowering stems, bearing rich red flowers, might need support. Gladioli are another feature of the summer border, the colourful flowers borne on long, thrusting stems. Both exuberant and elegant, white, pink or yellow zantedeschias make a bold statement at this time of year as well with their exotic, funnel-shaped, perpendicular flowers.

Begonias also flower throughout summer and well into autumn; they may be upright in habit or trailing, with single or double red, yellow, orange, white or pink flowers, which are sometimes two-toned. Always sumptuous in appearance, they are a mainstay of summer containers, and look lovely in borders, too.

Agapanthus are available in many shades of pale and rich blue and provide a fabulous display where they are well established.

Gladiolus 'Seraphin', which is a tender, early-flowering, butterfly-type cultivar, grows to 70cm (28in). It bears ruffled, pink flowers, each with a creamy white throat, and it looks especially good near lime green or yellow. Plant in spring in the herbaceous border to provide colour from mid- to late summer.

Crocosmia 'Lucifer' is a graceful plant, originally from South Africa, growing to 90cm (36in) with exotic sprays of deep orange flowers on tall, arching stems, which may need support in a windy spot. Plant the corms in spring, in sun or partial shade, and soon they will become established in large clumps.

Gladiolus 'Charming Beauty' is a hardy cultivar, growing to 60cm (24in). The small, rose-coloured, funnel-shaped flowers have delicate pointed petals. Plant the corms when they are available in autumn or spring. An ideal site would be a south-facing border beneath a sunny wall.

Agapanthus praecox subsp. *maximus* 'Albus' grows to 60–90cm (24–36in) tall. It forms bold clumps, bearing rounded umbels of large, white, trumpet-shaped flowers. Grow in a sunny border beneath a south-facing wall. If your garden is exposed, grow in containers in a potting compost (soil mix).

Zantedeschia aethiopica 'Crowborough', the hardiest of the arum lilies, grows to 90cm (36in) and is suitable for a damp border or near a pond. The rhizomes can be treated as an aquatic plant and grown in a planting basket in heavy loam. The distinctive funnel-shaped flowers appear in summer.

Galtonia candicans (Cape hyacinth) grows to 1.1m (3ft 6in) and bears tall spikes of creamy white, pendent flowers. Plant bulbs in early spring in bold groups towards the back of the herbaceous border, where the flowers will add height and grace. They show off particularly well against a dark background.

Growing to 60–90cm (24–36in), *Lilium lancifolium* (syn. *L. tigrinum*; tiger lily) has vibrant orange flowers, marked with maroon spots, the same colour as the anthers. Plant the bulbs in autumn or in late winter to early spring as soon as they are available.

Lilium regale (regal lily), which grows to 60–180cm (2–6ft), does well in containers. It bears large, white, scented, trumpet-shaped flowers that are streaked with maroon on the outside. Plant bulbs in autumn or late winter to early spring as soon as they are available.

Begonia 'Picotee' is a vigorous plant, growing to 20cm (8in) and producing large double flowers, which are suitable for centre stage in a summer bedding border, in hanging baskets or in window boxes. The tubers should be planted indoors in late winter or early spring.

Mid- to late summer borders

The mid- to late-summer border is rich in both colour and variety, with the choice of great swaths of red, orange or yellow crocosmias and brilliant blue agapanthus punctuated by tall spires of eremurus, lilies and gladioli. Large clumps of ornamental grasses offer a strong contrast.

Agapanthus and eremurus

A sunny border is perfect for rich blue or white agapanthus, which look best crowding together near the front of the border, basking in the heat, alongside the bold, tapering spikes of kniphofias and elegant watsonias. Meanwhile sand-coloured eremurus could dominate the back of the border, along with the spires of gladioli and galtonias. Groups of yellow, pink, white or orange lilies could create more focal points along the way, all planted to provide the magical highlights of this time of year. Apart from tender gladioli and watsonias, and borderline galtonias, all can be left to mature and multiply for another year. Agapanthus and eremurus do not fall into any of the

The strappy leaves of agapanthus look good with tall grasses. Blue *Agapanthus* 'Ben Hope' forms a wonderful large grouping in front of the frothy masses of *Chionochloa conspicua* (plumed tussock grass).

four main categories of bulbs, corms, tubers and rhizomes, but they have developed thick, fleshy roots to combat the annual droughts they experience in their native habitats. For this reason, they are generally considered under the wider umbrella of bulbs.

There are many agapanthus to choose from, including tall *Agapanthus* 'Bressingham White', which grows to 90cm (36in), and dark blue *A.* 'Ben Hope', flowering at 1.2m (4ft), both blooming from mid- to late summer and slightly later. Taller still, to 1.5m (5ft), is

Agapanthus 'Loch Hope' produces dense heads of broadly trumpet-shaped flowers, which are an impelling deep blue. This is a great favourite if space is not at a premium.

Agapanthus 'Loch Hope' is one of the more robust cultivars, making a strong statement on the corner of this border where it relishes its sunny position.

A. 'Loch Hope', which is also deep blue but flowers from late summer to early autumn, making a huge display. *A.* 'Lilliput' is much smaller, its deep blue flowers growing to only 40cm (16in), and it is an ideal choice for a sunny gravelled area near steps or a path. These varieties are all deciduous plants and classed as hardy, although it is safer to mulch well in winter.

There is also a good choice of eremurus, although you will succeed with these plants only if you can provide lots of space around their roots, which spread out a long way like black tentacles and do not respond well to being disturbed. Their untidy leaves might be regarded as another drawback, but the flowers more than make up for either of these factors. Known as the foxtail lily, the spectacular flower spikes can reach between 1.2 and 2.4m (4–8ft), each spike consisting of several hundred individual flowers. Plant them in rich, well-drained soil, in a sunny but sheltered spot where wind will not do damage, otherwise they will need support. Mulch in winter with coarse material, such as grit or ashes, to deter slugs and help protect them from frost and damp. Several fine cultivars are available, including pinkish-brown 'Oase', salmon 'Romance', coppery rose 'Cleopatra' and towering white 'Joanne'.

Red-hot poker

Another tall, bold plant is *Kniphofia* (red-hot poker), which produces tapering spikes of red, yellow, orange and sometimes green. They grow from rhizomes. Like agapanthus, flowering extends from midsummer to autumn, depending on the species. 'Buttercup', 'Bees' Sunset' and 'Fiery Fred' are all early flowerers.

Eremurus 'Oase' forms a dense mass of flower spikes, about 1–1.2m (3–4ft) high, which are perfect at the back of a sunny herbaceous border, where a dark green background can show them off to full advantage.

Galtonia candicans

Yet another tall, tapering plant is *Galtonia candicans*, which bears tubular white flowers on leafless stems that can reach to 1–1.2m (3–4ft) high. This is best treated as a back-of-the-border plant, where its flowers can

Gladiolus 'Seraphin' is a tender butterfly gladioli with ruffled pink flowers and a creamy white throat. It associates well with lime green or yellow, including the pubescent tall spires of *Solidago* (golden rod).

Kniphofia rooperi syn. *K.* 'C. M. Prichard' exhibits the typical fiery colours that give this plant its common name of red-hot poker. However, this species has unusually broad elliptical racemes.

be seen but its strappy leaves are well hidden. Beware slugs, which love to feast on them. The bulbs may be left in the ground with a winter mulch or lifted and stored in a frost-free place.

Gladioli

The corms of gladioli are generally sold dry in late winter for planting in spring on a bed of sand. Choose a sunny border and grow them in rows or clumps. The colours range from shades of lilac and pink to cream, yellow and white. Some of the taller types grow to more than 1m (3ft) high, but there are also shorter ones, growing to about 70cm (28in), and even smaller gladioli, known as the Nanus Group, grow to 60cm (24in). Depending on their height, they can be mixed with other summer annuals, such as crimson, pink or white cosmos, or planted in front of bronze *Atriplex hortensis* (orache). Meanwhile, many herbaceous plants, such as sidalcea, golden rod and aconitum, would make excellent companions.

Watsonia 'Tresco Dwarf Pink' grows about 35cm (14in) high and is best planted in a large group or dotted among ornamental grasses. It associates well with low-growing, silver-leaved plants.

Watsonia

Like gladioli, watsonias also have sword-like leaves, grow from corms and, in frost-prone areas, need to be planted each spring and lifted in autumn. But they are a more delicate plant, with spires of dainty, trumpet-shaped flowers symmetrically grown and pleasing to the eye. They like a sunny spot in well-drained soil and can be classed as hardy in only the warmest maritime areas of Britain, where *Watsonia* 'Best Red' is regarded as one of the most robust cultivars. However, there are many pretty colours to choose from, including sugar pink *W.* 'Tresco Dwarf Pink', which grows to about 35cm (14in). Plant them in a drift at the front of a sunny border or among ornamental grasses in a gravel garden. In either case, they will make a lovely display.

Borders in sun or partial shade

Grown from a rhizome, *Zantedeschia aethiopica* produces a succession of white spathes from early summer through to midsummer. It thrives best in moist soil in full sun or

Zantedeschia aethiopica 'Crowborough' provides an outstanding display where it has been allowed to mature in moist soil. The tall spathes look wonderful beside a reflecting pool.

partial shade. It can be grown as an aquatic plant on the margins of a pond, but it is a robust grower and may reach up to 1m (3ft). The cultivar 'Crowborough' is perhaps the most reliable, while 'Little Gem' is only half its height. It is usually treated as hardy, but mature, established plants will survive cold winters much better than younger specimens.

Crocosmia

Crocosmias also like moist soil, but it must be well drained. They grow from corms and flower from mid- to late summer and sometimes on into early autumn. *Crocosmia* 'Lucifer' is one of the best-known cultivars, with its magnificent long stems and joyous red flowers, and even the early pointed leaves and later seedheads are attractive. But, growing to 1–1.2m (3–4ft) or more, its size does mean that it is rather unruly. In sunny spots it will associate well with yellow achilleas and with bold canna leaves, dahlias and yellow lilies. Smaller cultivars,

such as *Crocosmia* 'Emberglow', C. 'Jackanapes' and C. 'Emily McKenzie', grow to 40–60cm (16–24in) high, flower in mid- or late summer and may be better suited to a smaller garden. They are regarded as borderline hardy, surviving best where the soil is well drained. Again, older clumps seem to winter best, so mulch well in early years.

Dahlias

While they love the sun and thrive in a sunny spot, dahlias will cope with shade for part of the day. They have a long season of flowering, from midsummer right through to the first frosts of autumn. Heights range from over 1.2m (4ft) to 30cm (12in) for the newer patio types.

Lilies

Most lilies enjoy sunshine on their flowers, but many like to have roots in the shade and are happy to have half the day in sun and half in shade. For midsummer flowers those from the Golden Splendour Group are hard to beat for their strong stems and scented, trumpet-shaped flowers. Growing to 1.2–1.8m (4–6ft) high, they add lightness to the summer borders and contrast well with tall

Dahlia 'Bishop of Llandaff' is prized for its single red petals surrounding an open centre with yellow anthers, and its dark foliage.

Crocosmia 'Lucifer', which flowers at the same time. Alternatively, place them beside the golden-variegated foliage of *Hedera* (ivy), *Euonymus* or *Elaeagnus*, for example, or match the maroon staining on the reverse of the flower with the dark purple leaves of *Cotinus*.

Another attractive choice is *Lilium superbum* (American 'Turk's Cap' lily), which originates in the eastern United Sates, where it grows best in moist, acid soil. It grows to 1.5–3m (5–10ft) so is best suited to the back of a border, preferably where it will be sheltered by taller shrubs or trees, against which it will show up well. Its orange flowers are unscented but attractive, with their deeply recurved, orange petals with maroon spots. They appear in late summer and last until early autumn.

Lilium regale will cope with full sun or partial shade. It will also tolerate a wide range of soils, making it not only one of the most beautiful lilies but also one of the easiest to grow.

Dead-heading lilies

After flowering, unless you want seed for propagation, remove the fading flower head. This will help to prevent viral infections striking as the flower withers, and will also channel the bulb's energy into building up next year's display.

Lilium martagon (martagon lily) grows 1–1.8m (3–6ft) tall and has attractive, but unscented, glossy, pinkish-purple, pendent flowers with darker spots.

The flowers have a strong, heady perfume that hangs on the evening air. Grow it in formal borders, behind box hedges, next to the path where the scent can be fully appreciated or try it beside deep red roses, picking up the colour of the outside petals. It can reach to 1–1.2m (3–4ft) and may need staking when its flowerheads are fully open and weighing it down. *Lilium regale* 'Album' is pure white, without the subtle extra flush of maroon on the species.

Martagon lilies will also tolerate almost any well-drained soil, in sun or partial shade, and will even cope with quite deep shade if necessary, although flowering might not be as effusive as when they receive some sunlight. From early to midsummer these lilies will produce tall stems, 1–1.5m (3–5ft) high, with up to 50, though usually fewer, turkscap-shaped flowers in shades of pink to purplish-red with darker spotting. They have a rather unpleasant smell, but this is nevertheless a choice

Lilium Bellingham Group thrive in dappled shade beneath deciduous trees or between shrubs. They have great poise and an exquisite palette of colour.

plant for a refined colour scheme.

Although many lilies will cope with light shade, hybrids in the Bellingham Group positively thrive in these conditions, but they do like acid soil. They flower from early to midsummer producing racemes of beautifully poised turkscap flowers, ranging from red to orange and yellow with darker spots.

The large, trumpet-shaped flowers of *Lilium regale* associate beautifully with *Rosa* 'Sander's White Rambler'.

Plants for dappled shade

Not all garden borders are in a sunny location. Most will be in some shade for at least a few hours of the day, and many plants will flourish in these conditions, including some lilies, veratrum and begonias.

The giant lily *Cardiocrinum giganteum* will thrive in dappled shade all day long but dislikes dry or waterlogged conditions. It originates in the forest and scrub of the Himalayas and enjoys a sheltered, shady spot among shrubs and trees. Though hardy, it will benefit from a deep winter mulch and plenty of leaf mould mixed in the soil at the time of planting. The bulbs need to be planted just beneath the surface. They take several years to reach

Veratrum album grows from a rhizome and has large, bold, pleated leaves and unusual starry green flowers, which are borne on freely branched panicles.

maturity, and after flowering die, but by then several offsets will have been produced to continue the species. The flower spikes reach a massive 1.5–4m (5–12ft) in height and produce many trumpet-shaped, white flowers, which are well scented. The basal leaves are large and glossy but unfortunately they are very attractive to slugs.

Veratrum album (false hellebore) is a spectacular plant, which grows from black, poisonous rhizomes. It likes a rich, deep soil that does not dry out and, in these conditions, will cope with a sunny site or one in partial shade. A shrubbery would be ideal, as long as you can keep the slugs away, for its bold, pleated leaves are one of the great

The flower spikes of *Cardiocrinum giganteum* can reach a massive 1.5–4m (5–12ft) and produce many well-scented, trumpet-shaped white flowers. The resulting display is a real show-stopper.

White begonias offer a simple solution to a shady or partially shaded spot in the garden, where they show up so well, especially in the evening when they appear almost luminescent.

Mid- to late summer border case study

This is a border where the house casts deeper afternoon shadow as the summer lengthens. Earlier in the year tulips and daffodils flowered against a backdrop of white bridal wreath *Spirea* 'Arguta'. Now fiery red crocosmias take centre stage with their long pleated strappy leaves and stunning red flowers held on strong slightly arching stems. They have multiplied quickly, producing a striking display for several weeks from mid- to late summer. One of the loveliest of the summer lilies from the Golden Splendour Group is blooming just behind them, producing a beautiful contrast to the red crocosmias, while to one side *Dahlia* 'Lemon Cane' has survived the winter in situ with a covering of mulch.

Lilium Golden Splendour Group

Dahlia 'Lemon Cane'

Crocosmia 'Lucifer'

characteristics of this plant. In early and midsummer it produces tall panicles of pale green flowers, reaching up to 1.8m (6ft). The black form, *Veratrum nigrum*, produces dark reddish-brown flowers, though the pleated leaves are still green.

Begonias will cope with sun, partial sun or shade, but thrive best when not baked by sun all day long. Water splashed on their broad leaves will cause scorch in sunny weather, so water them at ground level, beneath the leaves, or before or after sunset when it is cooler. In many

gardens tuberous begonias are planted out in early summer to create brilliant splashes of colour through summer and early autumn, a show that will last for months, not weeks, as is the case with most of the plants described so far. Available in self-colours of white, yellow, red, pink and orange, as well as bicolours (as trailing plants, compact bush and taller doubles), begonias can be used for formal patterns of contrasting or matching shades with other summer bedding plants, such as nasturtiums, fuchsias and lobelias, depending on

aspect. They will not tolerate frost, so be sure to lift them before sub-zero temperatures damage them.

Begonia 'Picotee' produces outstanding golden-yellow flowers, edged with deep orange.

Autumn gallery

Autumn borders are an absolute delight, with exotic dahlias and cannas vying for attention with strident colours and bold foliage.

Cannas need to be lifted before winter, and so do dahlias, unless a protective mulch is given in late autumn. Other autumn-flowering bulbs, such as eucomis, nerines, sternbergias, crinums and schizostylis, are all borderline hardy and will survive the winter best in very well-drained soil beneath the protection of a wall where they can remain undisturbed for many years.

Eucomis have stout spikes of starry pink or green flowers, with a tuft of leaves at the top that gives rise to the common name, pineapple flower. This is also the time when

Growing to a height of only 15cm (6in) *Sternbergia lutea* is also known as autumn daffodil, autumn crocus or Mount Etna lily.

nerines bear their large heads of frilly, bright pink, trumpet-shaped flowers, which bloom on naked stems, with the leaves appearing later. Other highlights include the diminutive sternbergias, with their bright yellow, crocus-like flowers, giant crinums, which produce an array of large, pink, funnel-shaped flowers, and schizostylis, available in pink or red.

Some autumn-flowering bulbs can be left in the open ground and are regarded as fully hardy. Colchicums are found in shades of lilac and pink as well as white and will grow in sun or partial shade. They are often referred to as autumn crocuses because of the shape of their flowers. In fact, several true crocuses flower in autumn. *Crocus sativus* (saffron crocus) is probably the best known.

Drama is easily achieved in the autumn border using bold *Canna* 'Striata' with their broad variegated leaves and brightly coloured flowers.

Eucomis bicolor has a flowering height of up to 60cm (24in). The flower spike is dense, with small, starry, waxy flowers, each tinged with pink. It can be grown singly in a small pot or as a group in a large container. Alternatively, try a clump of three or five at the front of a sheltered, sunny border.

Crinum x *powellii* 'Album' grows to about 1m (3ft) and produces a rosette of broad, bright green, fleshy leaves. These are followed by a stout stem with pretty, funnel-shaped, white flowers. It is a focal point of the autumn garden but requires thoughtful lower planting companions to hide the untidy leaves.

Nerine bowdenii produces its flowers before the leaves. Growing to 45cm (18in), it likes a sunny, sheltered spot – beneath a south-facing wall is ideal. Make sure that it is at or near the front of the border so that other larger plants do not cast shade on it, as it will only thrive in a sunny position.

Canna 'Rosemond Coles' is a robust plant with large green leaves that produce long racemes of brightly coloured flowers with yellow-spotted throats. The petals themselves are red edged with yellow, producing a vibrant and distinctive colour scheme. Expect it to grow to around 1.5m (5ft) tall.

Dahlia 'Clair de Lune' grows to about 1.1m (3ft 6in) high. A Collerette dahlia, the flowers have an open centre, surrounded by a collar of short, flat petals or florets, as they are known, and a single outer row of florets. The light yellow colouring shows up well in the border, particularly in the evening light.

Canna 'Wyoming' is a tall-growing rhizome with broad bronze leaves and large, flamboyant, orange flowers. It must be lifted before any severe autumnal frosts. Plant near other orange flowers, such as dahlias, or in front of silver-leaved plants such as *Eucalyptus gunnii* (cider gum).

Colchicum 'The Giant' sounds tall but actually grows to only 20cm (8in) rather than the 10–15cm (4–6in) stature of its many close relatives. Each corm produces a succession of up to five purplish-violet goblet-shaped flowers. The leaves follow after flowering.

Schizostylis coccinea 'Major' loves a sunny moist position where it is best left undisturbed. In time it will multiply to create a large clump producing 6–10 flowers per stem to a height of 60cm (24in), thus making a very welcome contribution to the autumn border.

Cyclamen hederifolium is a carpeting plant, growing to only 10cm (4in) tall, which produces its tiny blooms either before or at the same time as the leaves. It prefers well-drained soil in light shade beneath a group of trees or shrubs or in the eye of a fruit tree.

Autumn borders

Some late-flowering bulbs need the warmth of a wall to help them produce their best flowers and give them protection through the autumn and the winter cold.

Many eucomis are grown in pots so that they can be given winter protection. However, planted at the foot of a wall, they should survive the winter if they are well mulched. *Eucomis pallidiflora* has long flower spikes, to 75cm (30in), topped with a large tuft of leaf-like bracts which give it its common name, giant pineapple flower.

A warm south-facing wall will favour *Crinum x powellii*, which produces many tall stems up to 1.5m (5ft), bearing widely flared, pink flowers, creating a sumptuous display in late summer and early autumn. The flowers of *C. x powellii* 'Album' are white. At half the height, *Amaryllis belladonna* produces bright pink flowers in autumn without any foliage to set it off; the strappy, fleshy leaves follow after flowering.

Amaryllis belladonna, which is native to South Africa, produces stout stems with trumpet-shaped flowers about 60cm (24in) high. The foliage emerges after the flowers.

Like the crinum, it is an exceptionally beautiful bulb.

Nerines are another example of a pink-flowering autumn bulb, and they, too, bloom before the leaves have developed. The frilly flowers are funnel shaped and vary mainly in their shade of pink, their crinkly

Nerine bowdenii 'Blush Beauty' is an excellent specimen plant for the autumn border with its fine deep pink flowers.

margins and overall width. They are slightly shorter, usually reaching only 45cm (18in). Mulch all these bulbs to help guard against frost damage.

Dahlias

Grown from tubers, dahlias put on their main growth in summer, so by early autumn they are fully grown and at their best. They are available in a wide range of colours from

Eucomis pallidiflora produces its tall flowers in late summer. The leaf-like bracts give it its common name, giant pineapple flower.

Nerine bowdenii 'Silver Smith' is an arresting sight in the autumn border but it needs to be allowed to settle in for a few years before massing up. Like other nerines, it will flower much better when the bulbs are congested.

Dahlia 'Yellow Hammer' makes an exciting association with lime-green grasses or other golden foliage plants. It would also look dramatic mixed with purple Verbena bonariensis.

Dahlia 'Dark Desire' is a recently introduced cultivar that has been immediately admired for the delicacy of its foliage, stems and flowers. Its deep dark chocolate blooms are also a particularly winning feature.

yellow, orange, red, through to white, pink, mauve and purple, with some displaying two tones of colour or even more. And if that was not enough to choose from, you have all the different shapes of flowers, from spiky cactus, to giant decorative, to neat pompon and small patio dahlias, to name but a few.

The taller cultivars will need staking, and it is better to do this when the dahlias are first planted out so that they grow into well-shaped plants. By late summer it will be too late and at the first hint of stormy weather the stems will have been bent or broken.

An additional distinction between dahlias is the foliage colour. Usually it is an unexciting mid-green, and if you are lucky it has not been eaten by slugs! But the recent fashion has been to enjoy dark bronze foliage, as exhibited by bright red 'Bishop of Llandaff' and others, such as gold 'Elise', dark pink 'Giselle', salmon-orange 'Poeme', 'Rosamunde', which has deep rose-pink flowers, and white 'Swanlake'. These dahlias are all about 1m (3ft) high and would be suitable for the middle or back of a border, though exceptions can always be made for one of these

exciting specimens by placing it in the forefront to catch the attention. 'Poeme' is only 50cm (20in) tall, so would be ideal beside a path or next to a patio. Golden 'Yellow Hammer' is even shorter, at 45cm (18in).

Another range of dahlias offers a move away from heavy flowers and overpowering foliage. It concentrates instead on rather more open, irregularly shaped flowers, slender but sturdy wiry stems, which are often dark red, and foliage that is sometimes described as filigree. Dahlia 'Dark Desire' is a stunning

dark chocolate-purple with contrasting golden stamens, which help to lift the brooding effect of both flower and dark green foliage. It will reach around 1m (3ft) high and suits a raised bed where the foliage and stems can be admired as much as the flowers. Planting it next to a bronze aeonium augments the drama. It looks just as good in a traditional ground-level border too. 'Ragged Robin' and 'Royal Blood' are similar. Prolific in flower, there is no need to stake these dahlias, which are an exciting development.

Dahlia 'Bishop of Llandaff' was named in 1924 after Bishop Hughes, whose ecclesiastical chair was in Llandaff Cathedral, Cardiff, Wales. Within four years it had won the prestigious RHS Award of Garden Merit. It has recently enjoyed a revival and is now a popular cultivar in designer gardens as well as the garden centre stores.

Canna 'Black Knight' associates well with yellow abutilons and orange kniphofias, both acting in their supporting role to the star performer.

Winter protection

The autumn garden is full of contrasting shapes and colours. The tall, slender flower spikes of cannas rise above the large, oval leaves, sometimes with brilliant colouring, which spiral around the stem. Tall

Canna 'Black Knight' is dramatic in both bloom and foliage. The leaves are striped, dark bronze and the large, deep red flowers are stunning. Excellent as a specimen canna or for mass plantings, it grows to a height of up to 1.2m (4ft).

flower spikes are also seen from late plantings of gladioli, but here the foliage is shaped like swords. In contrast, begonias and dahlia have round flowers, varying in size and colour but always making a strong contribution until the first frosts, both fully mature now after the long growing season throughout the summer months. All these plants are from hot climates and need to be given protection before winter, but with proper care many will live for years and can be easily propagated.

Cannas seek great heights in autumn, as they reach up to the skies after a full summer's growth, loving the sunshine and creating a magnificent spectacle in the borders with flowering grasses, abutilons, colourful dahlias and towering kniphofias for company. There are many varieties to choose from, including dark red Canna 'Black Knight', which is sumptuous in flower and has dark-striped foliage. It would look awesome beside Dahlia

'Bishop of Llandaff'. Another favourite is C. 'Tropicanna', which is admired for its deep bronze, pink-striped foliage and orange flowers. C. 'Striata' has green-striped yellow leaves and orange flowers. Either would look marvellous besides Dahlia 'Nargold'. Canna 'Rosemond Coles' is attractive too with its bright red flowers edged in gold. All these cannas thrive in sunny conditions, but they will also grow well in boggy soils, and associate well with waterside planting. They will need to be lifted before the first frosts and stored in a frost-free place before starting into growth again the following spring. One small tuber will put on tremendous growth in just one season.

Bold planting schemes

Kniphofias, commonly called red-hot pokers or torch lilies, are native to grasslands or by streams in southern Africa, and, like cannas, they grow from rhizomes. They like a sunny spot with moist but well-drained soil. Kniphofia 'Percy's Pride' grows

Canna 'Tropicanna' is a recent sport of Canna 'Wyoming', which has bronze leaves and tangerine orange flowers. 'Tropicanna' has similar orange flowers, but the foliage is electrifying: vibrant pink veins run through the leaves. It is an outstanding cultivar.

The autumn border becomes architectural with sculptural *Cortaderia* (pampas grass), warmed by hot cannas.

about 1.2m (4ft) tall and produces racemes with green to canary-yellow flowers in late summer and early autumn. The species *K. rooperi* (syn. *K.* 'C. M. Prichard') flowers from early to late autumn with orange-red flowers, eventually changing to orange yellow. It is unusual among the family in that its flowers are more oval than torch shaped: definitely one to look out for. All of these cannas and kniphofias can be placed with great effect in close proximity, either right next to each other or separated by some neutral plant such as an ornamental grass.

Any *Miscanthus* and *Cortaderia* (pampas grass) will make useful partners to the autumn border, adding further textural contrast and softening the otherwise strong colours of the exotics. This is a time when bold planting schemes can work even on a modest scale.

Kniphofia rooperi (syn. *K.* 'C. M. Prichard') flowers from early to late autumn, producing blooms that are a mixture of autumnal shades of orange and yellow. This hardy, evergreen perennial has dark green, strappy leaves.

Dahlia 'Nargold' was introduced in 1994. It is a cactus dahlia with fimbriated petals and gorgeous tangerine yellow colouring. It makes an excellent colour association with any of the orange or yellow cannas and kniphofias.

Autumn naturalized bulbs

Both autumn grasslands and woodlands can be rich with flowers. Colchicums, for example, which are happy in sun or partial shade, will grow in grass or lightly shaded woodland areas.

Where a new display is required, buy the corms in late summer or early autumn just prior to flowering and be sure to plant immediately. The flowers will then be produced followed by root growth that is made as the leaves are produced in late winter and the spring. By then they will have settled in ready to create a good display for years to come.

Grassland

Colchicum autumnale is a native of western and central Europe and can tolerate temperatures down to −20°C/−4°F. It has a rather weak tube to support the flower, and sometimes flops over after a shower. Grow it in grass, where the heads may be supported by the grass itself. *C. a.* 'Alboplenum' is double white, while *C. a.* 'Plenum' is double lilac-pink. *C. bivonae* is a sturdier plant

Colchicum 'Violet Queen' is a beautiful shade of violet-pink, and it associates well with low-growing incised foliage plants, which create a foil for its naked stems.

and again easily grown, although it is susceptible to frost in severe winters, so choose a sheltered site. *C. speciosum* is a good strong-growing plant, from north-east Turkey and Iran. Here it has to cope with very cold winter temperatures and is

almost as hardy as *C. autumnale*. It can be grown in grass in the shade of a shrub or even in a sunny border so long as the soil is moist. Its goblet-shaped flowers are pinkish purple and show up well at around 18cm (7in) high. *C. speciosum* 'Album' has thick white flowers which stand up well to autumn weather.

One of the characteristics of colchicums is that the tall strappy leaves appear after the flowers. In severe winter conditions this may be as late as spring, while in milder climates they may surface in late winter. They will grow about 18–25cm (7–10in) long and must not be prematurely removed.

Many cultivars exist which offer slightly different shades of rose pink, lilac and white, some tessellated, some double. *C.* 'Violet Queen' is another beautiful choice colchicum producing fragrant pinkish violet flowers, similar to *C.* 'The Giant', while 'Lilac Wonder' is slightly pinker.

Colchicum 'Lilac Wonder' is caught by autumn sunshine as it peeps out beneath *Heuchera micrantha* var. *diversifolia* 'Palace Purple'.

Colchicum speciosum 'The Giant' has purplish-violet blooms. Together with white-flowered 'Album', it is one of the most popular cultivars.

Cyclamen hederifolium has variable leaf shape and colouring. Some forms, notably the Silver Leaved Group, are remarkable for their silver foliage, which makes such a valuable contribution to autumn and winter borders.

Woodland

Cyclamen also enjoy the partial shade of a shrubbery or woodland and will spread with ease to create an attractive autumnal carpet. *Cyclamen hederifolium* has wonderful marbled foliage which just emerges as the flowers are fully out. The flowers vary in shades of pale and deeper pink, some are white, but they have conspicuous maroon rimmed mouths. They are sweetly scented. This cyclamen grows from small dark brown tubers which are rounded below and flattened above. The roots are produced both from the apex and sides. It is a humble little plant growing only 10cm (4in) high but it is easy, reliable, stands up well to autumn weather and as winter advances produces handsome leaf formations echoing the shape of ivy leaves from which its species name is derived. Plant a group alongside *C. coum* which will flower in the following months and together will provide many months of interest.

For milder climates, there is an autumn-flowering snowdrop called *Galanthus reginae-olgae*, which is very similar to the common snowdrop *G. nivalis* but flowers three months earlier. It comes from Sicily, Greece and south-west Turkey and is best planted in a dry spot where it will flourish and naturalize well. Milder winters are changing the boundaries of some of these borderline hardy plants and in recent years this snowdrop has established well at the National Trust Gardens at Anglesey Abbey in Cambridgeshire, UK.

Cyclamen hederifolium is a diminutive plant, but it will spread to become a wonderful carpet of colour, both when it flowers in mid- to late autumn and when it is in leaf throughout late autumn and winter.

The container garden

Many bulbs make excellent container plants and even in inexperienced hands there is a very good chance of great results as all the new bulbs have, at the time of purchase, the flower bud already formed within them like a wrapped parcel waiting to be opened. Plant daffodils, tulips and hyacinths in autumn and you will reap rewards in spring with a host of pretty flowers. Plant begonias, cannas and dahlias in early spring and you will have flowers all summer long.

Looking after the bulbs year after year is slightly more of a problem. With hardy hyacinths, daffodils and grape hyacinths the show will go on for many years, especially if you divide and replant on a three-year cycle. Tulips will rarely give such long-term rewards, although the smaller, later-flowering species are more reliable than the larger cultivars.

Meanwhile the summer bulbs will last for many years if they are correctly looked after through the winter period. Lilies need little extra attention, but exotic begonias, cannas and dahlias all require frost-free conditions either still planted in their containers or dried off and kept in cool, dry conditions indoors. Nerines, tulbaghia and *Pelargonium* 'Schottii' all need winter protection as well.

This shallow stone trough of spring bulbs includes *Narcissus* 'Hawera' and 'Bell Song', *Fritillaria meleagris* and several types of *Muscari*.

Mid- to late winter containers

The weather in mid- to late winter is often cold and inhospitable for both gardeners and plants, but if you choose carefully you will find several gems to bring welcome colour, even on the dullest days.

Galanthus (snowdrop), *Leucojum vernum* (spring snowflake), dwarf irises, *Eranthis hyemalis* (winter aconite), *Anemone blanda* and the early daffodils in containers will all flower at this time. Position them in a sheltered spot outside the house and enjoy them as you enter or leave. Or simply hang them in a basket close to a window so that you can admire and appreciate them from indoors.

If you want an instant container, buy two or three pots of *Cyclamen coum*, transfer them to a little wicker basket or shallow pot with a few trails of ivy and enjoy immediately.

Snowdrop bulbs and the lumpy tubers of winter aconites are sold as small, dry specimens in autumn, and it is a sad fact that, because they are over-dried and kept out of the ground for too long, only a small number will produce leaves and flowers. Once established, however, they will flower and multiply well, massing up underground as well as by self-seeding. Instead of trying to have a container display from new bulbs and tubers bought in autumn, buy them as growing plants at flowering time in late winter, pot them on into a larger container and keep them in an out-of-the-way corner for the following year, by which time they should be nicely established. Alternatively, if you already know that you have some growing in the garden but would like to try them nearer the house in small pots, dig them up out of the ground in late autumn and plant them immediately into a well-drained, soil-based compost (soil mix). This advice also holds true for *Leucojum vernum* (spring snowflake). Treat them as single specimens in containers, and they will look simple but charming.

Mixed plantings

Instead of planting individual pots of bulbs, corms and tubers, try mixing them with winter-flowering

This winter-flowering hanging basket contains lots of different evergreen plants, including variegated ivies and *Euphorbia myrsinites*. The blooms of the winter-flowering heathers and *Viburnum tinus* add extra interest, but the highlight of the basket is the little *Iris* 'Pauline', which combines beautifully with all its bedfellows.

shrubs and herbaceous plants. Winter-flowering *Viburnum tinus* (laurustinus) makes an excellent centrepiece for a winter container or,

FROM THE BORDER TO A POT

1 *Eranthis hyemalis* (winter aconite) may be quite hard to find in border soil because at first they just look like lumps of earth. By late autumn the buds will be showing, and where tubers have grown on and matured they can be 3–4cm (1¼–1½in) across.

2 Prepare a small pot with some drainage material, such as pieces of polystyrene (styrofoam) or broken pots, and a potting compost (soil mix) and replant one large tuber 5cm (2in) below the surface. Cover with more soil and water well.

3 Place the pot outdoors on your windowsill or in a group with other winter-flowering specimens on a patio table where they will give welcome colour to the winter garden. After blooming, they can be replanted in the garden borders or in short grass.

POTTING UP SNOWDROPS

1 Dig up a clump of snowdrops from your garden, divide and return half to the border where it came from, first splitting it into two or three smaller clumps.

2 Divide the remaining half and plant in small containers in well-drained soil-based compost (soil mix). After the flowering season return them to a new part of the garden.

3 Snowdrops make a wonderful display on a windowsill where they will flower from mid- to late winter with no worries about frosty or snowy weather.

if it is a relatively small plant, for a hanging basket. It is hardy, evergreen and produces a mass of pink-tinged buds, which open to white flowers any time from late autumn through to spring. White, mauve or purple winter-flowering heathers can be planted around the sides so that when they come into bloom, just after midwinter, they will soften the edge of the basket and give extra colour. Choose large specimens with plenty of flower buds. Trailing ivies can also be planted around the edge. As they cascade over the sides, peg them into the moss to stop them spoiling in the winter wind. As they touch the moss, they will take root and within a season you will have a

With their intricate patterning and sweet scent, snowdrop flowers deserve close inspection. Enjoy the varied but distinctive green markings.

well-established ivy ball. Another excellent hardy foliage plant is the evergreen *Euphorbia myrsinites*, with its long, architectural, grey trail, which produce bright yellow flowers in early spring.

For the highlight of a winter container or hanging basket, plant some specimen bulbs, corms or tubers. You might dig up a clump of snowdrops or snowflakes from your own garden (never from the wild) or just a few winter aconites. However, if you want to start with new bulbs, try some dwarf irises. *Iris danfordiae*, with its golden-yellow flowers, shows up brilliantly, but there are lots of irises to choose from, including all the Reticulata irises, such as 'Harmony' and 'Joyce', both of which have sky-blue flowers with yellow on the falls, and 'Pauline', which is a marvellous dusky violet with flecks of white on the falls. They will flower from late winter to spring, doing best in a sunny position. Planted in a hanging basket, the flowers can be enjoyed at eye level, and at this height they can also be appreciated for their lovely sweet scent. Hang the basket in a sunny, sheltered spot, but in severe weather take it off its bracket and keep it in a porch or garage. Keep the soil moist but never water in

frosty conditions. To extend the season of interest, you might like to plant early dwarf tulips or daffodils to follow on in early spring.

Mid- to late winter bulbs for containers

Anemone blanda
Crocus chrysanthus
Crocus tommasinianus
Cyclamen coum
Eranthis hyemalis
Galanthus nivalis
Iris danfordiae
Iris 'Katharine Hodgkin'
Iris 'Pauline'
Leucojum vernum
Narcissus 'Rijnveld's Early Sensation'
  syn. *N.* 'January Gold'

Planting partners

Erica arborea 'Albert's Gold' (tree
  heather)
Erica carnea 'Springwood White'
  (winter-flowering heather)
Euonymus fortunei 'Emerald 'n' Gold'
Euonymus japonicus
  'Albomarginatus'
Euphorbia myrsinites
Hedera (ivy)
Helleborus foetidus (stinking
  hellebore)
Helleborus niger (Christmas
  hellebore)
Primula vulgaris (primrose)
Viburnum tinus
Viola

Early spring containers

Nearly all the early spring bulbs are extremely easy to grow in confined conditions and, because many of them are dwarf by nature, they have the perfect proportions for growing in containers of all descriptions.

Growing bulbs in containers is a wonderful opportunity to show plants off as specimens in their own right. When they are grown in a pot or urn that is sited on a wall or on the patio table, the plants become features in their own right, to be admired and enjoyed. A simple pot of crocus can look stunning just on their own, basking in the sun with their petals opened and orange style exposed. A small pot of hyacinths can give untold pleasure, seen at close quarters, when the intricate nature of the bells can be admired and the sweet scent enjoyed.

Double-planting

Although the planting space in a small- to medium-sized pot may be limited, it is possible to double-plant

Instead of allowing crocuses to get spoiled in bad weather, when the flowers remain closed, keep them on a windowsill indoors.

Dwarf early multiheaded daffodils, such as Narcissus 'Tête-à-tête', are excellent in pots and hanging baskets.

the bulbs, thereby achieving a much greater impact at flowering time. It is, for example, possible to plant six bulbs of Narcissus 'February Gold' in a lower layer in a small glazed ceramic pot, 20cm (8in) across and 18cm (7in) deep, with, after the addition of a little more soil, six more on their shoulders. Crowded by garden standards, this is not important for container-grown bulbs, which will be grown in these

circumstances for only one season. White crocuses, planted in a smaller matching glazed pot, could be planted to flower at the same time, so that their yellow stamens would provide the perfect partnership for the golden-yellow daffodils.

After flowering, transfer the contents to the garden where they should be carefully separated and planted at three times the depth of the bulb.

DOUBLE-PLANTING BULBS

1 Double-planting in autumn helps to create impact in a relatively small pot. Add drainage material, such as pieces of polystyrene (styrofoam) or broken pots, and a small covering of well-draining compost (soil mix). Plant the lower layer of bulbs, close to each other, but not touching. In this case, the bulbs used are Narcissus 'February Gold'.

2 Add more soil so that just the noses of the bulbs show, and plant the second layer on the shoulders of the first. Again, they should be close but not touching. Cover with more soil, bringing the level to within 2.5cm (1in) of the rim of the pot.

3 Plant a smaller, similarly coloured pot with crocus bulbs. Add a layer of drainage material and soil before placing the bulbs close together, but not touching. Depending on the number of bulbs in the package, single- or double-plant them.

A small pot of blue grape hyacinth *Muscari armeniacum* 'Heavenly Blue' would look good with the pots of narcissi and crocuses.

Other schemes could include *N.* 'Jetfire', which is another of the cultivars of *N. cyclamineus* with its characteristic swept-back petals, although here the trumpet is golden orange. *N.* 'Jenny' has a similar form but with a creamy white flower. A small pot of blue grape hyacinth *Muscari armeniacum* would provide a fitting contrast to either of them, both in colour and form; so would a planting of *Scilla siberica*. Alternatively, try a simple collection of pastel violas or primroses, which

could be planted up either in the autumn or in early spring to make an instant arrangement.

Front to back

Another idea to maximize space is to plant the front of a pot with early spring-flowering bulbs and the back half with mid-spring bulbs. When the first show is over, turn the pot round and enjoy the next display.

Early spring bulbs for containers

Anemone blanda
Chionodoxa
Crocus (large Dutch flowered)
Hyacinthus (hyacinth)
Narcissus cyclamineus cultivars (daffodil)
Narcissus 'Jumblie'
Narcissus 'Rip Van Winkle'
Narcissus 'Tête-à-tête'
Narcissus 'Topolino'
Muscari armeniacum (grape hyacinth)
Muscari botryoides 'Album'
Scilla siberica
Tulipa Kaufmanniana hybrids
Tulipa Double Early

Planting partners

Bellis perennis (double daisy)
Erica arborea 'Albert's Gold' (tree heather)
Erica carnea 'Springwood White' (winter-flowering heather)
Hedera (ivy)
Helleborus foetidus (stinking hellebore)
Helleborus niger (Christmas hellebore)
Euonymus fortunei 'Emerald 'n' Gold'
Euonymus japonicus 'Albomarginatus'
Euphorbia myrsinites
Primula vulgaris (primrose)
Saxifraga x *urbium* 'Variegata'
Sedum acre 'Aureum' (golden stonecrop)
Tanacetum parthenium 'Aureum' (golden feverfew)
Viburnum tinus
Viola

Narcissus 'February Gold' flowers at the same time as the delicate *Crocus sieberi* 'Albus' (formerly known as 'Bowles' White') or any of the large white, purple or blue Dutch crocuses. The result is a glorious early spring association.

An excellent daffodil for inclusion in a hanging basket, *Narcissus* 'Quince' has a sturdy, short stem and a flowering height of only about 15cm (6in). It produces several flowers on each stem, and each one has delicate pale yellow petals and a miniature broad golden cup.

Narcissus 'Quince' associates well with blue *Anemone blanda* and the creamy variegations of the ivy leaves.

Multiheaded daffodils

Dwarf, multiheaded daffodils are an excellent choice if impact is needed but space is limited. *Narcissus* 'Tête-à-tête' is a justifiably popular daffodil, for one bulb will provide two or three, well-proportioned flowers on each stem, each with a golden head and cup to match. *N.* 'Jumblie' may be less well known, but it too will provide a mass of flowers. The cups are slightly longer and appear to look in all directions, hence its name. Another great favourite is the cultivar 'Quince', which has pale yellow petals and a broad golden cup. All three are short, sturdy growers, and these qualities make them excellent choices for early spring pots, window boxes and, especially, hanging baskets.

Plant the daffodils with *Anemone blanda*, in white or shades of blue or mixed colours, underplant them with large crocuses, such as *Crocus vernus* 'Remembrance', or with single tulips, such as the Kaufmanniana *Tulipa* 'Shakespeare'. Together these bulbs can create a beautiful early-spring picture. Violas, double *Bellis perennis* (daisies) and primroses, combined with winter-flowering heathers and ivies, will make pretty partners.

Evergreen trails of ivy can be used to clothe the outside of an early spring basket. Use a few wire staples to peg the ivy into the moss sides and encourage it to make a complete ball of greenery to form the basis of the spring bulb display. This has an added advantage of preventing the ivy from being tossed about in cold winter winds, which will damage the tip ends. Plant the basket in autumn, choosing one with a diameter of 35cm (14in). Use three ivies and a mixture of 15 dwarf multiheaded daffodils, such as dainty *Narcissus* 'Quince', and 15 pretty blue *Anemone blanda*.

Maintaining hanging baskets

All hanging baskets that are outside in late winter to early spring should be hung in a sunny, sheltered position. Check that the soil is kept moist, especially in autumn and spring, but never water in frosty conditions. Although all the plants are hardy, play safe and, when severe weather is forecast, take the basket off the bracket and keep it in a less exposed position on the ground or in a porch or garage for a day or two, until milder conditions return.

Double Early tulips

As the days lengthen the Double Early tulips begin to flower. They have wide heads, full of vibrantly coloured petals. Short and sturdy, these tulips make good subjects for a container standing on the ground as well as for a hanging basket. They can be purchased as single colours, including red, orange, yellow, white and pink, or in mixed bags or boxes. *Tulipa* 'Peach Blossom' is one of the prettiest, with flowers that start as a pale pastel pink, sometimes revealing streaks of green or red. It always makes a winning combination when it is grown with blue *Muscari* (grape hyacinth), but any blue violas and pansies would look equally attractive.

These hybrids of *Narcissus cyclamineus*, with their swept-back petals, look beautiful with an underplanting of crocuses. Here, the fiery orange cups of *N*. 'Jetfire' bend as if to caress the bright orange stamens of *Crocus tommasinianus* 'Ruby Giant'.

Chionodoxa forbesii 'Pink Giant' has been planted with Double Early *Tulipa* 'Peach Blossom'. The blue *Muscari armeniacum* (grape hyacinth) in the background is yet to come into its full glory.

For an eye-catching hanging basket plant a mixture of Double Early tulips with grape hyacinths, surrounded by a frill of bedding plants, such as violas and pansies. The bedding plants will provide a certain amount of colour, even in autumn, but by the time the bulbs flower in early spring they will be in full array, providing a lively and colourful background. Give this basket a sunny, sheltered position. The more sheltered the position, the better the bedding plants will thrive.

Hyacinths

By now hyacinths are in flower, too. Many beautiful shades – pink, blue, amethyst, yellow and white – are available, and all the colours seem to have their equivalent or contrast in primroses, with which they associate so well. Strong on impact and perfume, hyacinths also associate beautifully with other bulbs, such as the rich blues of *Scilla sibirica* and *Muscari armeniacum* (grape hyacinth),

as well as all the Double Early tulips. A lovely combination would be white hyacinths such as *Hyacinthus orientalis* 'L'Innocence' or 'Ben Nevis' with dwarf yellow Double Early *Tulipa* 'Monte Carlo' and small white *Muscari botryoides* 'Album'. Creamy violas or primroses alongside *Tanacetum parthenium* 'Aureum' (golden feverfew) would make wonderful bedfellows underlining the fresh white, cream and yellow theme. There are so many beautiful associations possible with these groupings. Imagine salmon pink *Hyacinthus orientalis* 'Gypsy Queen' with orange Double Early *Tulipa* 'Nassau' planted in a trough with a carpet of rich blue *Muscari armeniacum* 'Heavenly Blue'. The addition of two-toned blue and violet violas or primroses would provide a strong contrast – the possibilities are endless. This is one of the joys of container gardening and bulbs provide one of the most important contributions for they are so varied in colour and form.

Mid-spring containers

Many of the short daffodils can be used in mid-spring containers. Although they are not all as dwarf as those that flower in early spring, there are several that are suitable for growing in hanging baskets, window boxes and tubs.

Some of the short daffodils are multiheaded and are valued by gardeners for providing a beautiful display where planting space is at a premium. *Narcissus* 'Hawera' is one of the most delicate of all, and the tiny, lemon-yellow flowers seem to last and last. Although there may be three or five flowers per stem, it is dainty in appearance, and its wiry, sturdy stem will withstand strong winds. This lovely little daffodil, which grows only 25 cm (10in) high, is excellent in hanging baskets, window boxes and small pots.

The cultivar *Narcissus* 'Segovia' is another winner with its pure white petals and creamy little centre. It, too, grows only 25 cm (10in) high. It should be used more, extending the season and offering a purity of flower that is to be treasured.

Daffodils such as the glistening white *Narcissus* 'Thalia', white 'Silver Chimes' and the fresh-faced, white-streaked, lemon-yellow 'Pipit' are, perhaps, rather too tall for a hanging basket, but they are perfect for pots, window boxes or troughs. They would look charming with heathers, such as *Erica carnea* 'Springwood White' or *E. arborea* 'Albert's Gold', and winter-flowering pansies.

Mid-season tulips

There are so many mid-season tulips that it is hard to know where to begin. Most of them grow to 35–50 cm (14–20in) in height and are best suited to medium-sized or large containers. All the Apeldoorn varieties, for example, with their mainly yellow, orange and scarlet blooms, are excellent, being strong in growth, reliable and long lasting. The Fosteriana tulips, such as *Tulipa* 'Orange Emperor', 'Yellow Emperor' and 'Red Emperor', are also firm

Mid-spring bulbs for containers

Fritillaria meleagris
Iris bucharica
Muscari armeniacum 'Valerie Finnis'
Muscari latifolium
Narcissus 'Hawera'
Narcissus 'Pipit'
Narcissus 'Segovia'
Narcissus 'Thalia'
Darwin Hybrid tulips
Double Late tulips
Single Early tulips
Mid-season tulips
Tulipa tarda
Tulipa urumiensis

Planting partners

Bellis perennis (double daisy)
Erysimum cheiri (wallflower) with taller tulips
Euphorbia myrsinites
Myosotis (forget-me-not)
Pansy
Polyanthus
Sedum acre 'Aureum'
Tanacetum parthenium 'Aureum' (golden feverfew)
Viola

Narcissus 'Segovia' always looks fresh with its glistening white petals. Here it is planted in a hanging basket with *Tulipa saxatilis* Bakeri Group 'Lilac Wonder' and *Viburnum tinus*.

Both teacup and teapot are planted with *Narcissus* 'Hawera', which is a neat little daffodil with a multitude of dainty lemon-yellow flowers.

The Single Early *Tulipa* 'Christmas Marvel' looks cheerful in its blue pot with the silver-grey foliage of *Senecio cineraria* 'Silver Dust'. It is perfect in a container in its own right or used as an extra in the herbaceous border to add height and focus to the forget-me-nots.

TULIPS AND PANSIES

1 Cover the base of the pot with a 5cm (2in) layer of drainage material, such as broken pieces of polystyrene (styrofoam) or old pots. Half-fill the pot with a soil-based compost (soil mix) containing lots of grit.

2 If preferred, use a peat-based compost (soil mix) with a layer of grit mixed thoroughly in the bottom half. The advantage is that the pot will be slightly easier to move planted in this way.

3 Plant ten tulip bulbs in two circles, spacing them so that they are not touching each other or the sides of the pot.

4 Bring the compost level to within 2.5cm (1in) of the top of the pot. Plant four blue winter-flowering pansies.

favourites. They do not grow quite as tall as the Apeldoorn group, but they are still suitable for medium to large pots. Pansies, which are available in a vast range of rich tones, including deep blue, golden yellow, yellow and red or purple, will make an excellent carpet beneath the strongly coloured blooms. The ever-reliable *Tanacetum parthenium* 'Aureum' (golden feverfew), polyanthus or *Erysimum cheiri* (wallflower) will also make good planting partners.

If pink is your preferred colour, consider the pretty *Tulipa* 'Gordon Cooper' or cherry-pink 'Christmas Marvel'. For a more subtle effect, try 'Ester', which looks charming in association with delightful *Dicentra spectabilis* in a large container or in separate pots. Another excellent choice would be the glorious, double, pink 'Angélique', which is very long

lasting in flower, spanning the season into late spring. The soft blues and whites of violas, pansies and polyanthus as well as pale blue *Myosotis* (forget-me-not) will make ideal companions for these tulips. If you can find pansies with distinctive markings, they will add extra interest to the scheme. The silver foliage of *Senecio cineraria* 'Silver Dust' will make an attractive partner. A pair of carefully co-ordinated pots, arranged symmetrically, could be especially striking, or place a planted pot in the middle of a border where dahlias or cannas might be planted later.

5 The result is a spring triumph of glorious soft pink tulips and winter-flowering pansies in shades of blue.

Single planting schemes

When they are in the right place you will find that just a few bulbs of a single species or cultivar planted on their own can have a major impact. *Muscari armeniacum* 'Blue Spike', with its spikes of lovely blue, double flowers, looks stunning in a small pot against a simple background. Alternatively, try the gorgeous pale blue *M. armeniacum* 'Valerie Finnis', which is a relatively recent discovery that has become readily available.

Iris bucharica, which is native to north-eastern Afghanistan, is an ideal specimen bulb for a medium to large pot, at least 25cm (10in) deep. Use a soil-based compost (soil mix) with about one-third extra grit mixed in. Each stem produces up to six blooms, and there is a profusion of glossy leaves, so there is no need to plant anything else in the same pot. However, *Narcissus* 'Pipit' flowers at the same time as the iris and is of a similar colour, so a few separate pots of these two bulbs make an attractive display. Their flowers will bridge the gap between mid- and late spring.

Long-term plantings

Many of the more flamboyant tulips do not flower reliably if they are left in a container for a second season. It is usually best to start again with new bulbs in fresh compost. Some of the smaller species and cultivars will perform well another year, however, as will many narcissi and grape hyacinths. Plan ahead so that you can enjoy a more mature planting scheme in subsequent years.

Remember to feed the bulbs either just before, during or after flowering so that they are able to rebuild resources for the next year. Keep them watered at this time and until their leaves have died down naturally, which usually takes about

The flowers of *Iris bucharica* and *Narcissus* 'Pipit' are a similar colour, and they make good neighbours planted in separate pots. They will both flower again another year.

six weeks after flowering. Deadhead all bulbs so that energy is not wasted in producing unnecessary seeds. Even when you have looked after the bulbs, you will get better results if you completely empty the container every two or three years and divide the bulbs into fresh groups. Use the new bulbs in a fresh arrangement and plant the extras in borders, where they should continue to flower.

Long-term container plantings often work best when a simple combination is used. Dwarf daffodils associate well with polyanthus, cowslips or double (single for early spring) primroses. Cowslips look lovely with dainty *Narcissus* 'Segovia'. A special cultivar, such as a polyanthus primula from the Gold-laced Group, with its golden eye and gold-laced petals, would be excellent with long-lasting *Narcissus* 'Hawera'. This daffodil also looks lovely with red-laced primulas. All herbaceous plants will benefit from being lifted and divided every second year, which is best done in early autumn.

A simple planting of white tulips can look stunning, just on their own.

Narcissus 'Hawera' makes a colourful combination with red-laced primulas in a terracotta pot. With care, these two plants can remain partners for many years.

Daffodil bulbs should also be divided at this time. Carefully separate the clumps and replant in two or three pots. They will not come to any harm if they are left for two years, but after that their flowering will diminish as they become overcrowded. When you are repotting make sure you use fresh soil-based compost (soil mix).

Narcissus 'Roseworthy' is a striking pink-trumpeted daffodil, which is both reliable and a good naturalizer. It makes an excellent choice for a border but can also be seen to advantage in a raised container, which allows you to enjoy it to the full. An easy long-term arrangement could include *Saxifraga x urbium* 'Variegata', which is commonly known as variegated London pride. This has the benefit of providing an evergreen covering that deters mice, squirrels and voles, which might otherwise dig up and eat the bulbs.

The saxifrage is a neat partner to many bulbs, forming low rosettes of foliage that mat well and soon produce a welcome frill to soften the edge of the container. Best of all, it provides delicate flowers in late spring and early summer, just when the daffodils have finished flowering but need moisture to complete their growth cycle. The saxifrage provides the pot with an added six weeks of colour. After this time, its flowering stems can be cut down and the daffodils' leaves removed. For the rest of the summer the pot returns to its evergreen capping while the daffodils lie dormant below. Unfortunately, both the saxifrage and all members of the primrose family are very susceptible to damage from vine weevil grubs, so take precautions in the autumn and again in spring with either beneficial nematodes or imidacloprid, which acts as a systemic insecticide. Alternatively, apply some barrier glue around the rim of the container to prevent adult vine weevils from laying eggs in the compost.

A raised trough

An arrangement in a raised trough can work well and last for many years if you select low-growing subjects with relatively small bulbs so that the shallow nature of the container is not a problem. Daintiness is another factor to consider here. Miniature daffodils, such as *Narcissus* 'Minnow', 'Segovia', 'New-baby' or 'Sun Disc', would be perfect in this situation, as would *N.* 'Hawera' and 'Bell Song'. Try a few grape hyacinths, such as the pretty white *Muscari botryoides* 'Album'. Add some slightly taller *M. latifolium* with its lower band of dark blue, almost black flowers topped with an upper band of paler blue. Together these bands make an interesting flower spike. Ordinary *M. armeniacum* and its paler selection 'Valerie Finnis' would also be good.

An alternative arrangement might include *Fritillaria meleagris* (snake's head fritillary), which has beautiful chequered flowers dangling on the lightest of stems. The flowers are sometimes pinkish, sometimes white, and either would be exquisite, raised up so that they could be enjoyed to the full. A raised container has the advantage that rabbits are unlikely to find them. Long-term partners could be auriculas, *Sedum acre* 'Aureum' (golden stonecrop) or some of the many low-growing herbs, such as thymes, marjorams and even rosemary. Despite the shallow nature of most stone troughs, these plants will flourish if there is an adequate drainage hole (cover with a tile if it is large). Use half soil-based loam and half horticultural grit. It is probably best to site a trough in partial sun and shade, so that it does not bake too much in summer.

Many years after planting, these prize daffodils, *Narcissus* 'Roseworthy', are still growing well. They are planted with *Saxifraga x urbium* 'Variegata' (variegated London pride), which provides the perfect foil as well as year-round interest.

Late spring to early summer containers

With a little careful planning, late-flowering tulips can look sensational in large pots underplanted with forget-me-nots or pansies.

Any of the Parrot tulips are excellent treated in this way. Look out for *Tulipa* 'Apricot Parrot', which could be combined with mahogany-brown pansies, or *T.* 'Black Parrot', which could be planted with white or black pansies. *T.* 'Fantasy' looks charming with a true blue pansy. The two dark, late-flowering tulips, 'Queen of Night' and 'Black Hero' always look attractive with forget-me-nots, whether blue, pink or white.

Orange-coloured varieties of wallflower are among the most strongly scented. By late spring they are joined by the *Tulipa* 'Blue Heron' – tall, strong and beautifully shaped, with fringed petals.

Tulips and wallflowers

Late tulips can also look excellent with old-fashioned red, yellow, orange, purple, rose-pink or white *Erysimum cheiri* (wallflower). Some brilliant colour schemes can be devised, with both bright, eye-catching plants and gentler, more subtle shades. The Fringed tulip 'Blue Heron', which has lilac-coloured petals, creates a strong contrast, for example, with rich orange wallflowers, whose scent is welcome on a warm sunny evening. A more restful colour scheme could be achieved by substituting a pale primrose-coloured wallflower or even a rose-pink or purple form.

Wallflowers are usually treated as biennials – that is, they are sown in late spring one year and the flowers are seen the next. They are normally sold in autumn, either as growing plants in bedding boxes or in bunches of eight or ten with just a little soil attached to their bare roots. They should be thoroughly watered and planted as soon as possible in a sunny position, where they will start to flower the following spring. Once they begin to flower the show will continue for many weeks, contributing an informal, cottage-garden style to your pots and containers.

For a combination of tulips and wallflowers, prepare the container in the usual way, using drainage material and a soil-based potting compost (soil mix). Plant ten tulip bulbs so that their eventual depth

Tulipa 'Fantasy' is one of the delightful Parrot tulip group. Here it has been simply underplanted with the blue pansy, *Viola* x *wittrockiana* 'True Blue'.

below soil level is about three times their own height, allowing for a 5cm (2in) gap at the top of the container. Plant seven or eight wallflowers in a wide circle, choosing those plants with the best root systems – discard the rest. Firm in the plants and water well. Place the container in a sunny, sheltered position.

Plantings of anemones

Anemone coronaria cultivars, with colours ranging from brilliant red to rich blue and pure white, also make excellent container displays, and they can be used to produce many different effects. *A. coronaria* De Caen Group 'Mr Fokker' has attractive blue petals, and 'Die Braut' ('The Bride') has pure white flowers. *A. coronaria* St Bridgid Group 'Lord Lieutenant' has deep blue, double flowers. The fern-like foliage of these anemones is attractive in its own right. Judicious planting at intervals in spring and early summer will give a succession of blooms, while planting two or three pots at the same time will give a sumptuous display. The knobbly tubers are best

Some anemones are blue, including the multi-petalled *Anemone coronaria* St Bridgid Group 'Lord Lieutenant'.

rehydrated by being soaked overnight before planting. Plant so that the buds point upwards and at a depth of about 7.5cm (3in) and 7.5cm (3in) apart, and allow at least three months between planting and early-summer flowering.

An earlier planting in late winter will take longer to produce blooms. Allow the tubers to dry off completely after the lifecycle is complete, ready for flowering again the following year.

A DISPLAY OF ANEMONES

1 The knobbly hard tubers of *Anemone coronaria* benefit from being soaked overnight in a tumbler of water to plump them up before planting.

2 Where possible, plant the anemone tubers with their protruding knobs pointing upwards (this is not apparent on all of them), 7.5cm (3in) deep and about 7.5cm (3in) apart.

3 Enjoy the brilliant colour of *Anemone coronaria* St Bridgid Group 'The Governor'. Successive plantings of tubers will provide colour for weeks on end.

Planted as a single specimen, *Scilla peruviana* makes a wonderful container plant with its glorious flowers. Its leaves may be untidy at this stage, but the intense blue colouring makes up for this.

Long-term arrangements

Scilla peruviana is a glorious bulb to grow in a raised container where its brilliant blue flowers can be isolated and enjoyed to the full. It is only borderline hardy so it needs a cool winter refuge away from frost, but if you can manage to protect it, you will be rewarded year after year by a show-stopping display, which will be perfect for a sunny spot on a patio table or besides the door. Linnaeus was misled, because the bulb did not originate in Peru, as the specific name suggests, but from Portugal, Spain, Italy and North Africa. It is almost evergreen, with new basal leaves developing in autumn as the old ones fade. In late spring the leaves are quite large and strappy, but then the large bud begins to open and by early summer the gorgeous conical heads of up to a hundred starry flowers are revealed. You might have only one flower or be lucky and have two as the bulb matures in years to come. There is a white form, *S. peruviana* f. alba, but unless you are planning an all-white scheme, the blue is hard to beat.

Although it is shallow, a raised sink or trough can be planted as a long-term arrangement with a succession of interest and colour. Fortunately, many miniature bulbs are suitable for this purpose. Late-flowering species tulips will bridge the gap between mid- and late

In sun or partial shade *Hyacinthoides hispanica* (Spanish bluebell) will create a splash of colour, but do not grow them where they could cross-pollinate with *H. non-scripta* (English bluebell).

Tulipa tarda, with its starry white and yellow flowers, is a good companion for *T. urumiensis*, which has yellow flowers with bronze-green undersides. Both are multiheaded and are excellent in a trough or hanging basket.

The seedheads of *Allium unifolium* provide extra interest even after flowering, especially when they are seen at close quarters in a raised sink or trough. Like many alliums, it will self-seed readily.

In a raised trough the distinctive white flowers of *Allium neopolitanum* Cowanii Group (syn. *A. cowanii*) can be enjoyed at waist level.

spring, to follow on from the miniature daffodils, *Fritillaria meleagris* (snake's head fritillary) and *Muscari* spp. (grape hyacinth), which have already flowered. Any daffodil seedheads should be removed, but those of the fritillaries and grape hyacinths can look attractive as they mature and finally show off the seeds. With luck, they will self-seed and the display will multiply.

Later-flowering varieties

For later flowering include dainty yellow and white *Tulipa tarda*, which is native to Central Asia, or bronze-green and yellow *T. urumiensis*, which is native to north-eastern Iran. Both tulips look attractive in bud as well as in flower, and because they are multiheaded you will have a pretty display from even one or two bulbs planted in the middle of the trough or around the sides.

For a further succession include some little alliums. *Allium neopolitanum* Cowanii Group (syn. *A. cowanii*), which originated in southern Europe and North Africa bears loose umbels of pure white flowers on slim stems about 30cm (12in) high. Just a little shorter, *A. unifolium* has papery, clear pink flowers, and shorter still, at only 15cm (6in), *A. oreophilum* (syn. *A. ostrowskianum*) bears a profusion of

Planted in a raised trough edged with golden marjoram and strawberries, the dainty flowers of *Saxifraga x urbium* (London pride) provide a pretty foil for the bright pink flowers of *Allium schoenoprasum* (chives).

dainty carmine pink flowers. Meanwhile, *A. schoenoprasum* makes another easy and attractive option. Commonly known as chives, it is native to a wide area in Europe, Asia and North America, and both its leaves and flowerheads can be used in cooking. It is worth noting that planted in the restricted soil of a

container the foliage will not be as prolific as in border soil, but there will still be plenty of both flowers and leaves for the kitchen. A white-flowered form is also available. Like the earlier bulbs, the allium flowers look beautiful when they are seen raised up in the trough, and they all have attractive seedheads.

Mid- to late summer containers

Many hardy summer-flowering bulbs make excellent container plants and they will perform well year after year. *Zantedeschia* (arum lily), agapanthus, lilies and triteleia can all be grown in containers and are best planted in a gritty, soil-based compost (soil mix).

Container-grown lilies

Lilies can remain in the same container for many years if they are potted on into new compost every

Lilium 'Sweet Kiss' is a double lily, which is sterile. Because it produces no pollen it is the perfect choice for gardeners who suffer from pollen allergies.

two or three years; repot in autumn. *Lilium regale* (regal lily) does really well in containers, as do some of the Asiatic hybrids, such as 'Enchantment'. The Oriental lily hybrids, which are derived from *L. speciosum* and *L. auratum* (golden-rayed lily), are later flowering and make brilliant pot plants too. 'Star Gazer', which has deep red petals, is especially suitable for a container. The double-flowered 'Kiss' lilies are suitable for gardeners who are allergic to pollen. Their flowers are not as elegant as the singles, but they are prolific in bloom and great naturalizers, so they will create a great massed effect in a large container.

Plant three lily bulbs together to create a good display and, for extra colour and contrast, underplant with gorgeous blue triteleias. These look particularly attractive with yellow lilies. Choose a larger pot for medium to tall lilies, at least 30cm (12in) deep, and use a well-drained growing medium. Some lilies require acid soil, and for this group, which includes 'Star Gazer' and the other Oriental hybrids, use a ericaceous compost (soil mix) and extra grit (two-thirds compost, one-third horticultural grit).

Lilium 'Star Gazer' has deep red, white-edged flowers, and although they are not fragrant, this is one of the most popular lilies, flowering in midsummer.

Many lilies tolerate a wide range of conditions, including alkaline soils. This group includes the species *L. henryi*, *L. martagon* and *L. regale*, the Asiatic hybrids and the 'Kiss' hybrids. For these, use a soil-based compost and add a handful of extra grit beneath the bulb itself.

All lilies will respond to a low-nitrogen but high-phosphate and high-potash feed, applied for six to eight weeks from the first opening of buds. Deadhead and allow the leaves to die back before removing

A DISPLAY OF LILIES

1 *Lilium* 'Sweet Kiss' is of medium height and is ideal for containers where it needs no support. It multiplies well to form clumps in just a few years. Tidy stems in autumn.

2 Several small bulbs will form on top of the soil. Remove these carefully so as not to disturb the roots and carefully separate the little bulbs.

3 Transplant the bulblets to a small pot, so that you can move them on later to another container or plant them out to enjoy them elsewhere in the garden.

A WICKER BASKET WITH *HIPPEASTRUM*

1 In spring plant three *Hippeastrum* 'Yellow Goddess' in a wicker basket, with just their necks showing above the soil-based compost.

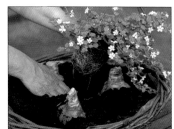

2 Plant three young *Sutera cordata* 'Snowflake' (syn. *Bacopa* 'Snowflake') plants around the edge of the basket.

3 The hippeastrum flowers are creamy yellow with striking lime green throats. There may be four to a stem, opening in succession and prolonging the display.

the stem. Lilies are hardy but need extra protection in severe winters when they are grown in containers. Move the pots into a sheltered spot and wrap them in bubble wrap if necessary to protect the rootball. Do not entirely cover the pot or condensation may lead to rot.

If arum lilies are grown in water, use an aquatic soil and an aquatic planting basket, with perforations around the outside and plenty of gravel on top.

Ornithogalum dubium

Available in white or orange form, *Ornithogalum dubium* can be planted in autumn and kept in frost-free conditions over winter, in which case it will flower in midsummer, or it can be purchased and planted in mid- to late spring to flower in late summer. Whichever approach you prefer, this bulb makes a long-flowering specimen for a small to medium-sized pot, and despite the rather untidy leaves it makes a valuable contribution to the patio.

Hippeastrum

Like the bulbs of *Ornithogalum dubium*, those of *Hippeastrum* may also be available until late spring, when they, too, can be planted to flower in midsummer. Buy firm bulbs and plant them as soon as possible in soil-based compost. These plants (often, but wrongly, known as amaryllis) are familiar flowers for indoor containers in midwinter, but their natural flowering time is closer to spring than midwinter, and by planting late the flowering can be delayed so that they can be grown outdoors in wicker baskets, window boxes or pots. Plant them with summer bedding plants, grasses or exotics, overwinter in frost-free conditions while they are dormant and enjoy for years to come.

A POT OF *ORNITHOGALUM DUBIUM*

1 *Ornithogalum dubium* bulbs are suitable for a small to medium container. Choose firm plump bulbs and if any are soft simply discard them.

2 Don't forget to put a layer of drainage material in the base of the pot. Add gritty, soil-based compost and plant four or five bulbs in each pot.

3 Place the pot in a sunny position where a succession of flowers will provide many weeks of colour. Allow to dry off after flowering and keep frost-free until the following spring.

Triteleia laxa 'Koningin Fabiola' is a useful summer-flowering corm to add in autumn to a spring-flowering bulb display with daffodils, for example. The narrow, grass-like leaves appear before the blue blooms. Here *Helleborus foetidus* will act as an excellent anchor plant, not only to show off the daffodils, but also the dainty blue *Triteleia* flowers. *Triteleia* also make a delightful display under dwarf yellow lilies. Both partnerships can remain in the container for several years.

Begonias

Tuberous begonias are probably the most colourful and versatile of all summer container plants, and they are ideal for pots, hanging baskets, wall-pots and window boxes. Although they are usually available as growing plants in early summer, you will have a much wider choice of colour if you select tubers in late winter, and plant them in late winter or early spring so that they are ready to plant out after the frosts have finished in early summer. Look out for *Begonia* 'Picotee', which makes a magnificent plant that looks beautiful in a hanging basket. Also in this group are *Begonia* 'Picotee Lace Pink' and 'Picotee Lace Red', both of which have flowers with distinctive white ruffled edges. The cultivar 'Picotee Lace Apricot' makes a memorable partnership as an

A BEGONIA HANGING BASKET

1 Line the basket with moss and plastic sheeting. Cut slits for drainage. Add potting compost (soil mix), mixed with water-retaining crystals and a long-term pelleted feed.

2 Plant the upright begonia in the centre of the basket.

5 The hanging basket is splendid in its summer glory. Easy to look after and very colourful, all the tubers can be saved for next year with or without the need for a greenhouse.

3 Plant the trailing begonias and yellow *Bidens* around the edge. Top up with compost. Choose a sheltered site in sun or partial shade.

4 Water every other day, or every day in hot weather, taking care not to splash the leaves if the sun is shining, otherwise they scorch.

Begonia 'Picotee Lace Apricot' has ruffled, rich apricot flowers dusted with white. It makes an excellent underplanting to orange *Fuchsia* 'Thalia'.

Mid- to late summer bulbs for containers

Agapanthus
Begonias
Cannas
Dahlias (especially short patio
   varieties)
Eucomis bicolor
Eucomis comosa 'Sparkling Burgundy'
Freesias (prepared)
Lilium regale
Oriental lily hybrids
Ornithogalum dubium
Pelargonium 'Schottii'
Triteleia 'Koningin Fabiola'
Tulbaghia

Planting partners

Coleus with begonias and *Canna*
   'Tropicanna'
Fuchsia 'Thalia' with orange and
   apricot begonias
Lobelia with any of these bulbs
Sutera with *Ornithogalum* and *Triteleia*
Tropaeolum (nasturtiums) with
   begonias and red, yellow or orange
   dahlias

underplanting to orange or salmon fuchsias, such as *Fuchsia* 'Thalia'.

If you decide to save the tubers for the next year, before the first frost of autumn lift the plant and move it into a frost-free place. Gradually withhold water and allow the foliage to die down. After two or three weeks, remove the tubers and store them in a dry, cool place until the following spring, when they can be brought into growth once more. Alternatively, if you have a greenhouse, move the entire container under cover. As the compost dries out and the stems die off, the tubers can remain in the compost with no further disturbance

necessary. This is ideal for hanging baskets or for arrangements in which begonias are planted with fuchsias. They will break into growth in the spring when watering begins again.

Begonia tubers are especially susceptible to being eaten by vine weevil larvae in early autumn. To avoid this, use a natural predator, such as beneficial nematodes, or a systemic insecticide, called imidacloprid, which stops the grubs maturing. Nematodes have to be watered into warm compost, and spring and late summer are ideal times for carrying out the treatment. Such action will ensure flowers the following year.

Begonia 'Giant Flowered Pendula Yellow' is an excellent choice for a summer hanging basket. It flowers from midsummer to early autumn and has 20cm (8in) long trails.

Early to mid-autumn containers

As late summer turns to autumn the begonias will still be at their best, with all their glorious reds, oranges and yellows creating an explosion of fiery colours. By now the cannas, too, will be in full flower, revealing a mixture of orange, yellow, red and salmon, but their large, paddle-shaped leaves can be as exciting as the flowers, showing vivid combinations of glowing green and gold or brilliant bronze and pink. To capitalize on the drama, position the pots in a sunny position where they will be backlit by the sun.

Container-grown cannas

Canna rhizomes can be purchased in garden centres in late winter and planted into a smaller pot for starting into growth in spring. They can be potted on in early summer into their permanent summer containers. Coleus and dark blue

Canna 'Tropicanna' (syn. *C.* 'Phaison', *C.* 'Durban') has striking deep bronze-purple leaves, which are veined with pink, making this an exciting foliage plant for a container.

The flowers of *Canna* 'Tropicanna' are a bonus to the drama of the leaves, which they fully complement. They are a warm orange, and open in succession.

Trailing yellow and orange begonias flourish throughout the summer and early autumn in a shady spot. Exotic *Begonia* 'Marginata Crispa' enhances the picture with its yellow and red-edged flowers together with nasturtiums and *Fuchsia* 'Thalia'.

Early to mid-autumn bulbs for containers

Agapanthus
Begonia
Canna
Cyclamen 'Miracle Series'
Cyclamen 'Silverado'
Dahlia (especially short patio
  varieties)
Eucomis bicolor
Eucomis comosa 'Sparkling Burgundy'
Nerine bowdenii 'Blush Beauty'
Nerine bowdenii 'Mark Fenwick'
Nerine bowdenii 'Pink Triumph'
Pelargonium 'Schottii'
Tulbaghia

Planting partners

By now the bulbs etc. are fully grown, with little extra room for secondary partnerships, though *Coleus* associates well with begonias and *Canna* 'Tropicanna' while *Fuchsia* 'Thalia' will still look wonderful with orange and apricot begonias lobelia make good plant associations depending on whether you like single or mixed planting schemes.

By midsummer cannas will need daily watering when the weather is hot. Deadheading will encourage further flowering. The plants grow rapidly, so be prepared to divide the rhizomes the following spring or pot them on into a bigger container. This task will be easier if your pot is flared or has straight sides; because

canna rhizomes can grow so large, avoid containers with narrow necks, which are difficult to empty and replant. Move the pots into a heated greenhouse as soon as frost threatens and leave them there until early summer temperatures are safe for them to be moved outside once more. The longer they grow on under cover of glass in late spring to early summer, the sooner they will come into flower.

Canna 'Striata' has large green leaves which are veined with gold, creating an eye-catching combination. The flower spikes have plum-coloured stems, and the flowers themselves are orange.

Early autumn containers can be filled with cannas, begonias and eucomis as well as fuchsias, aeoniums and felicias. Soon they will all have to be moved into a frost-free place, but for now they make a major contribution to the garden.

Canna 'Rosemond Coles' has large green leaves and vibrant red flowers edged with yellow. It makes an impressive container plant.

Pelargoniums

There are a few *Pelargonium* species that have tuberous roots and that may die back completely in winter, coming into life again in the warmer spring weather. *Pelargonium* 'Schottii' (syn. *P. x schottii*) is one of the most beautiful, and although it is tuberous, it remains evergreen throughout the winter. Its foliage is softly hairy, giving it a grey-green appearance that complements the simple wine-coloured flowers, with their dark purple stripes, which are borne from midsummer through to mid-autumn. Treat it as a specimen plant, alone in an attractive container. A porch or veranda would be an ideal situation. The foliage and flowers tend to create a dome shape, with blooms semi-prostrate rather than upright. Move the container indoors before the first frost and keep it on a sunny windowsill where you can continue to enjoy the blooms for a while at least.

The tuberous-rooted *Pelargonium* 'Schottii' has velvety grey-green foliage and attractive wine-coloured petals with dark purple stripes.

Eucomis

Bulbs of eucomis are generally available in late winter and should be planted in a soil-based compost (soil mix) immediately on purchase or in early spring if they can be stored in dry, frost-free conditions. They look good as single specimen plants but also look wonderful in groups of three, five or seven or even more if you have a large enough container. They produce long, strap-like leaves, which are sometimes wavy at the edges. From the centre of the leaves emerges a tall flower spike, covered with starry flowers all the way to the top, and this is crowned by a group of leafy bracts, which is why the plant is commonly called pineapple lily. It is an easy bulb to grow in a container, providing weeks of interest from the attractive leaves, then the flowers and, finally, the fleshy seedheads. Cut and brought inside these will continue to give pleasure through the winter. A drawback is that the flowers have quite a strong foetid smell, but this is only discernible close to. Once they have gone to seed, there is no smell.

Eucomis are borderline hardy, and in cold climates they will need the protection of a frost-free area through the winter months. Move

AN ARRANGEMENT OF EUCOMIS

1 Appearing in late summer and autumn, the tall stem of *Eucomis bicolor* bears racemes of pale green flowers with purple margins, topped with a crown of pineapple-type bracts. The stems are flecked with maroon, and the lower leaves are attractively wavy.

2 In early to mid-autumn, cut off the old flower stems of eucomis that have now been pollinated. The seedpods at the top will be fat, green and fleshy, while those at the bottom of the spike will be ripe, with shiny, round seeds visible inside.

3 Place the flowered stems in water and use them as an indoor arrangement. Once the water has been absorbed, enjoy the seedheads as a dry arrangement. Any seeds can be potted up and will produce flowering bulbs in just two or three seasons.

the pots into the shelter of a potting shed or greenhouse before or immediately after the first frost. Here they can remain dry until growth begins in the spring, when watering should begin again. Give only a little water at first, then more regularly as the leaves begin to grow. The large leaves lose water through transpiration, so when they are in full growth these are thirsty plants. Their native habitat is near streams in southern Africa, and as well as moisture-retentive soil, they prefer a position in partial shade.

There are many types of eucomis to choose from. *Eucomis bicolor* has green flowers edged with maroon or purple and blotches of a similar colour on the stem. *E. bicolor* 'Alba' has greenish-white flowers. *E. comosa* exhibits a wider variation in its colouring; it has a purple-spotted flower stem but the flowers are pinkish-purple and the leaves may be striated with purple, varying to intense deep purple. It does not have such a distinctive set of bracts at the top of its flower spike.

Nerines

For outdoor containers nerines are a good choice or, if you choose the less hardy cultivars or the late-

For an outdoor container, try *Nerine undulata* or choose one of the cultivars of *Nerine bowdenii* that flowers in early or mid-autumn.

flowering forms, they may be grown in a conservatory. For an outdoor container try *Nerine bowdenii* or any of its cultivars that flower in early or mid-autumn before the first frosts. In a container, even these nerines will be only borderline hardy and will need the shelter of a greenhouse in winter.

Winter protection

As autumn nights get colder, the summer exotics will be at risk from frost, so all the containers in which you have been growing begonias, cannas, dahlias, eucomis, tulbaghias and nerines will need to be moved to a greenhouse. Of these, the begonias will be most at risk, so act as soon as frost is likely. The first frost may blacken or damage the foliage of dahlias and cannas, but it will rarely damage their tubers and rhizomes, so they can remain outside for a little longer while there is still a chance to enjoy the last flowers.

The greenhouse will provide protection for all these plants from warmer climates, which cannot cope with freezing winter temperatures.

Move pots of tulbaghias into the greenhouse, together with cannas, begonias and eucomis, as soon as autumn frosts are forecast.

During periods of severe frost provide warmth in the greenhouse with a thermostatically controlled electric heater or a paraffin heater.

Late autumn to early winter containers

The weeks of late autumn to early winter are not the easiest for showy bulb containers, especially after the wealth of colour that has been seen in the garden in early autumn. However, there is a vast choice of bulbs that can be planted for late winter and spring flowering, with a wide choice of accompanying foliage to provide interest throughout the whole autumn and early winter.

Many bulbs are available for planting in autumn, including small crocuses, irises, grape hyacinths, chionodoxas and scillas. The rewards will come a few months later, with both bulbs and bedding plants in full flower.

Cyclamen Miracle Series

In recent years breeding programmes have been undertaken with *Cyclamen persicum*, which is best known for its use as a winter indoor plant, to produce a miniature cyclamen that will flower throughout autumn and early winter and will be hardy enough to withstand just light frosts. The result is the aptly named Miracle Series, which can be planted out in borders as well as used to great effect in containers. The flower colour varies from white, to white with a carmine pink mouth, wine red,

A POT OF *IRIS RETICULA* WITH A VIOLA

1 Choose a small pot and place some drainage in the base, top up with 5cm (2in) of soil-based compost (soil mix) and plant bulbs of *Iris reticulata* 'Katherine Hodgkin' with their noses pointing upwards.

2 Cover the bulbs with a little more soil and, for extra interest, add a viola, which will also remind you when the pot needs watering. *Viola* 'Hobbit Pippin Took' is a perfect colour match for this *Iris reticulata*.

rose, purple, salmon and scarlet. They are sweetly scented plants, but the best fragrance seems to emanate from the white forms. The leaves have different amounts of silvery mottling, but most, if not all, exhibit some degree of veining. The combination of flowers and foliage makes this little plant a winner. It lends itself to many lovely planting arrangements, being suitable for

wall-pots, window boxes, troughs and hanging baskets. A more recent introduction, *Cyclamen* 'Silverado' is slightly taller, at 20cm (8in), and makes a greater mound of foliage.

Weather protection

On frosty nights in late autumn the leaves of both *Cyclamen* Miracle Series and 'Silverado' will go limp, but by midday, as the temperature

Late autumn to early winter bulbs for containers

Cyclamen Miracle Series
Cyclamen 'Silverado'

Planting partners
Ajuga reptans 'Burgundy Glow'
Euphorbia myrsinites
Hedera (ivy)
Senecio cineraria 'Silver Dust'
Skimmia japonica
Stipa tenuissima

Miniature cyclamen are excellent subjects for a container or hanging basket display along with ivies and other foliage plants.

Viburnum tinus, winter-flowering heather and grasses provide year-round foliage interest while the bulbs are not in flower.

rises, the leaves should revive and show no ill-effects. Cyclamen planted in containers on an outdoor windowsill will be slightly protected by the building, but those in a hanging basket will be more exposed, and if prolonged periods of frost are forecast it may be safer to cover the plants with newspaper or move the basket to a cool, sheltered place, such as an outbuilding, garage, porch or even indoors. They will often survive the entire winter outdoors, but there is always an element of risk for plants in exposed containers, especially hanging baskets, where the rootball does not have the same protection as plants growing in deep garden soil.

Freezing temperatures present one type of problem. Another difficulty is posed by wet conditions. These cyclamen do not relish heavy rainfall, and the tell-tale sign that something is amiss will be pink blotches on the flowers where botrytis has become established. Extreme wet will also affect the tubers, causing rot. The shelter afforded by the house or even by a nearby tree may be sufficient

Some cyclamen have particularly attractive leaves. The silver markings on his plant look striking besides the lacy, almost white, leaves of *Senecio cineraria* 'Silver Dust'. It is ideal for a sheltered veranda or porch.

Euphorbia myrsinites makes an architectural partner for this little pink cyclamen, which shares its grey-green foliage. This pot has an underplanting of *Fritillaria michailovskyi*, which will flower in spring.

protection, but the more these plants are protected from frost and rain, the longer they will last.

Planting partners

Despite the potential problems, these small cyclamen have a great deal to offer early-winter containers.

They mix well with a host of other foliage and flowering plants and make excellent companions for ivies, particularly those with silver variegations. Another perfect partner is *Euphorbia myrsinites* with all its strange spirals, or, for a softer look, *Senecio cineraria* 'Silver Dust' with its silver intricacy. For an altogether different type of arrangement, plant *Ajuga reptans* 'Burgundy Glow' with its glossy, dark red leaves. Even the wispy leaves of *Stipa tenuissima* and the bronze buds of *Skimmia japonica* 'Bronze Knight' make handsome companions. Plant scarlet red cylamen with a selection or all of these and you will have a container full of interest for months on end.

Apart from the cyclamen, all the other plants mentioned here are fully hardy, so you can simply replace the cyclamen in late winter with pot-grown daffodils, such as *Narcissus* 'Tête-à-tête' or 'Hawera'. They will give your container an instant spring face-lift and it will still look charming.

Plants in the *Cyclamen* Miracle Series have richly coloured flowers, including pink, purple and red as well as white.

The indoor bulb garden

The range of bulbs available for growing indoors is extensive, with the opportunity to develop flower displays that are widely spread throughout the year.

Colour in the cooler months is achieved by maintaining frost-free conditions and providing gentle heat for a wonderful range of miniature and fringed cyclamens, as well as gorgeous *Hippeastrum* (amaryllis). Meanwhile, by growing *Narcissus papyraceus* (syn. *N*. 'Paper White') and commercially prepared hyacinth bulbs, we can enjoy colour and scent in the middle of winter.

In the hotter, brighter months, indoor planting schemes can produce exotic results with the climbing *Gloriosa superba* 'Rothschildiana', shapely eucomis, colourful achimenes and *Sinningia* syn. Gloxinias. Yet more plants can be grown either inside or outside in summer, such as freesias, the St Bridgid or De Caen hybrids of anemones, begonias, cannas and *Zantedeschia* (arum lily).

Available in many different colours, freesias multiply well over the years and soon provide a fantastic array of colour.

Growing techniques

Packets of commercially prepared crocuses, hyacinths, hippeastrums (amaryllis) and *Narcissus papyraceus* (syn. *N.* 'Paper White') are common sights in garden centres and supermarkets in autumn, inviting us to buy one to take home and plant.

These bulbs have been specially treated to flower early, providing indoor colour in mid- to late winter. They can also be purchased by mail order, and will withstand the rigours of the postal service. This resilience is one of the reasons why they have been so successfully marketed over the centuries.

Providing protection

Some species of bulb do require careful treatment. *Pleione* bulbs, for example, must be handled gently because they can sometimes send up shoots even before planting, and they are, therefore, usually sold individually in packets, surrounded by wood shavings. Completely

Although sturdy in physique, hyacinth bulbs are susceptible to virus diseases and fungus problems. They are, therefore, often treated with a special chemical to maintain their health. Touching the bulbs can produce a mild allergic reaction, so people who have susceptible skins should wear gloves when they handle them.

different to look at are the poisonous tubers of *Gloriosa superba* 'Rothschildiana', which are long and tapering and could be easily damaged in transit. They are often wrapped in tissue. The rhizomes of achimenes are not only brittle but tiny, so are often sold in little plastic pots surrounded by peat.

Choosing a container and compost

Many indoor containers do not have drainage holes at the base of the pot, which makes it essential that the type of compost (soil mix) and the frequency of watering are carefully monitored. With most displays of winter bulbs it is advisable to use a specially formulated indoor bulb compost, which will help to maintain the balance of the soil and prevent souring. This is particularly true when you use one of the containers that are sold especially for forcing crocus, hyacinths and daffodils but that have no drainage holes.

Containers with drainage holes make it possible to grow a wide range of bulbs, corms and so forth and to use different kinds of compost. They are ideal for plants that prefer a well-drained soil, such as freesias and nerines. Use a growing medium such as a soil-based potting compost (soil mix) with plenty of grit added for good drainage. Remember to put a glazed or plastic tray beneath the pot so that water seeping through does not spoil the windowsill or furniture.

Where it's necessary to combat summer drought, use a container without drainage holes and find a lightweight plastic pot that does have holes that will fit inside. Put some gravel in the base of the outer container so that the inner pot sits at the right height and add a shallow

Hyacinths cope with a shallow container, only 7.5cm (3in) deep, although they are happy with a deeper root run.

layer of gravel to the surface of the inner one. This way the plant will have its own water reservoir, although care will still be needed not to over- or underwater. A soil-based compost or peat-based compost, depending on the plant, can be used in these circumstances.

The choice of container gives rise to a number of other considerations, the chief of which is the size of the container you should use. The tall, midwinter-flowering daffodils, such as *Narcissus papyraceus* (syn. *N.* 'Paper White'), make a lot of root growth and need a container that is at least 15cm (6in) deep. However, hyacinths can cope with shallower containers, needing a minimum of 7.5cm (3in), although they will also be happy with a deeper root run.

Stem-rooting lilies need a much deeper container, so choose a pot that is at least 20–25cm (7.5–10in) deep. When you are choosing a container, consider the overall height and width of the fully grown plant and make sure that the container's dimensions are in proportion to the size of the plant.

GROWING CROCUSES INDOORS

1 These crocus corms are specially prepared to bloom indoors. Each of the many shoots will produce flowers.

2 The corms are planted in special indoor bulb compost. White chippings add interest to the top of the compost.

3 The pretty Dutch bowl has no drainage holes, but this is not a problem if you do not overwater.

Getting started

Once planted, crocuses, hyacinths and the later flowering daffodils, such as *Narcissus* 'Cragford' or *N.* 'Bridal Crown', need cool conditions and a period of darkness when they will make root growth, not topgrowth. This simulates the conditions they would experience outside, where they would be growing buried in soil, and though they will not appreciate freezing temperatures, they should be kept in cool conditions at around 7–10°C (45–50°F). Eventually, shoots will begin to emerge, and after about ten weeks they should be around 12cm (4¹/₂in) long. At this stage the plants can be moved into the light and into warmer conditions. Do not, however, put them in a position next to a radiator or on a south-facing windowsill.

Narcissus papyraceus (syn. *N.* 'Paper White') and its close relatives 'Omri' and 'Ziva' will grow on immediately they are given moisture, being quick to make root growth as well as topgrowth. They need light and warmth, but avoid extremes of either. *Hippeastrum* (amaryllis) needs warmth to get started, so a warm airing cupboard is ideal, the degree of light or darkness being irrelevant.

Growing on water

Although compost can always be used, hyacinths, *Narcissus papyraceus* and hippeastrums can be grown on top of water with no compost at all. This is possible only with bulbs that are quick to produce their flowers and only if you do not wish to use the bulbs for a second flowering the following year, because all the food reserves will have been used up and not replenished.

Hyacinths have been grown in this way for many years, and special glass hyacinth vases are available. These have an upper cup in which the bulb is held so that it does not sit actually touching the water. The taller plants, such as *Narcissus papyraceus* and hippeastrums, need the addition of small stones in the water to help anchor the roots and stabilize the plants. Many colours of gravel and chippings are available for landscaping and for use in fish tanks, and these are suitable for use with all bulbs grown on water, as are coloured glass nuggets.

Special glass hyacinth vases with an upper cup mean that the bulb can sit above the water.

Narcissus papyraceus (syn. *N.* 'Paper White') grows well on water as long as it is given the support of a few stones.

Finishing touches

Moss or coloured stones can be added over the surface of the growing medium at the time of planting or once the bulbs have started to shoot, to give the bowl that final finishing touch.

Ordinary lawn moss makes a soft, green topping, but, if you want a more vibrant colour, choose some dyed reindeer moss, which is obtainable from florists. Gravel or horticultural grit give a natural finish, but for a more colourful display that perhaps tones in with your indoor decorations use coloured stones, such as those sold for fish tanks, as a more exciting alternative. A thin layer scattered on the surface of the compost (soil mix) will make a neat addition, especially while you wait for the bulbs to flower.

To give bulbs that are being brought into flower for Christmas or the New Year festivities a seasonal look, you might like to add nuts or fir cones or even decorate pots with silver-painted walnuts or glittery fleece. Starry wire decorations, glass

An alternative approach is to use crushed horticultural grit with some of your favourite shells arranged on top.

droplets and gift wrapping tape are all possible extras. Look around your cupboards, there's sure to be something you can use!

Another possible decorative addition are candles, which will add atmosphere to any dark winter's night and can even make the container pretty long before all the flowers open. Fit them into a simple candle holder with a plastic spike on the end – these are readily available from florists – and gently push them into the compost. Never leave lit candles unattended.

Providing support

Although it is not always necessary, some bulbs and corms – freesias, for example – will benefit from the support of canes or twigs to prevent the foliage and flowers from flopping over. Act at the first sign of any waywardness.

Many taller subjects, including *Narcissus papyraceus* and its relatives, will benefit from the support of small beech clippings, which are sturdy and offer many smaller twigs for support, low down as well as

Plain beech twigs provide useful supports for floppy freesia foliage. Put them round the edge of the pot.

higher up. They can be left uncoloured or sprayed with paint to match the container. Whichever finish you prefer, they will do the job well and look attractive.

Another good support is *Ribes sanguineum* (flowering currant), which has strong, sturdy stems and can be sprayed silver or any other colour. Use it where the narcissi are flowering after, rather than before,

Crushed horticultural grit on top of compost gives a neat finish, while the additional green slates provide extra interest.

Starry decorations on thin wire stems add seasonal appeal. They also offer interest to the arrangement even before flowering begins.

early winter. *R. sanguineum* has fewer sideshoots than beech, but it has the advantage that when it is brought indoors and stuck into moist compost, it continues to live and will produce pretty white flowers. By the time the narcissi have finished blooming, the twigs may well have rooted and be producing buds.

Hyacinths can be supported by pieces of cane or long chopsticks tied with string or raffia. You may even find that a long cocktail stick (toothpick) is all that's required.

The beautiful *Gloriosa superba* 'Rothschildiana' is a scrambling herbaceous plant, climbing to 1.8m (6ft) in just one summer. Give it the support of a wall frame or a free-standing willow frame to which the tendrils can cling. The flamboyant flowers will be seen to good effect against the background of stems.

Bulbs that need support

Freesia	Hyacinthus
Gloriosa superba	Narcissus
'Rothschildiana'	papyraceus

Reindeer moss dyed bright green or red is available from florists and garden centres.

Hyacinths put on lots of root growth before flowering and this is shown off well when they are grown in water. Red glass beads add a touch of warmth as well as seasonal drama.

White marble chippings make an attractive finish to any display, including these forced crocus corms, which are just beginning to emerge. Soon they will reveal glorious papery purple flowers.

Cyclamen

With their swept-back petals and pouting mouths, cyclamen would appear to have a flare for drama. Like garden cyclamen, the cyclamen sold as indoor houseplants in autumn grow from tubers, which root both from the base and the sides.

They are all derived from *Cyclamen persicum*, which is a spring-flowering plant native to the countries of the eastern Mediterranean and Rhodes, Crete and Libya. In the wild the flowers are white, pale mauve, pale pink or deep pink. The leaves are variable but often have intricate silver zoning, spotting or margins.

Many cultivars have been bred from these beautiful plants, which means that forms are now available with blooms in white and many shades of salmon-pink, scarlet and purple as well as pink, and they often have a distinctive darker central spot. In addition, the flowers vary in shape and may be ruffled, double, single or twisted. They are often scented. In recent decades, attention has been given to breeding miniature flowers, more akin to the

Ruffled cyclamen flowers have a distinctive flair, and they are often combined with intricate leaf markings. Always choose a healthy plant. Look for one with stiff foliage, avoiding plants with any limp-looking leaves, and check that there are plenty of flower buds emerging from the base.

Remove any damaged leaves or fading flowers with a simple sharp tug close to the base of the stem.

The miniature cyclamen are floriferous, producing a mass of flowers with the fly-away petals that make them so endearing.

species found in the wild, which is a welcome move. Hybridizers have also emphasized foliage colour and form, with pride of place being given to intricate markings and contrasting patches of silver and green.

In the past few years, there has also been a move to breed plants that will thrive at lower temperatures and serve the dual purpose of flowering in outdoor containers in autumn as well as in indoor containers in winter. The resulting Miracle Series is a great bonus to all gardeners, both outdoor and indoor.

Another positive development has been the increased attention paid to producing highly fragrant flowers. A plant in full flower will quickly fill an entire room with its sweet perfume.

Cyclamen will thrive in light, airy conditions, but they should be kept away from draughts and too much direct sunlight. They abhor both drought and high humidity. Too much or too little water will cause serious damage. Never water over the flowers and foliage, because this will encourage rot. It is far better to water around the plants at soil level, especially where several cyclamen are planted in a single container, or to water into a saucer below the plant if the container has drainage holes. Use soft water or clean rainwater.

Do not place pots of cyclamen close to a radiator or behind a closed curtain in the evening. A temperature of 18–21°C (64–70°F) is ideal, with a night-time temperature kept above 10°C (50°F). The plants will stay in flower for longer if they are fed once a fortnight with a weak liquid fertilizer.

Keep the plants clean and tidy by removing any fading flowers and yellowing leaves. You need to remove the entire stem, along with the dying flower or leaf, because a cut or a broken stem will encourage rot. Take firm hold of the stem near the base of the plant and give a quick, sharp tug.

After flowering has finished the plants should be allowed to go into a state of natural dormancy. Gradually reduce the amount of water you give until all the growth has died down. Then keep the plant completely dry for two or three months. Modest watering can start again. The tubers will not need repotting for a couple of years because they flower best with a restricted root run. When repotting is necessary, do it during the period of dormancy and use a soil-based planting medium.

Displaying cyclamen

Cyclamen look charming when they are shown off as a single specimen, and they will suit nearly every room in the house, adding scent and delicacy. The miniature hybrids are often sold in small plastic pots, which can be quickly disguised or easily made to fit into more attractive containers, including coloured flower vases and small china bowls.

For greater impact make a massed display by planting three or four plants together in a medium-sized bowl or terrine or even a wire table centrepiece. Lighted candles will provide the final touch. Once planted, water only at soil level, remembering never to water directly over the tops of the tubers. It is, in fact, better to wait until the leaves go slightly limp and then to water only moderately.

A WIRE TABLE CENTREPIECE

1 Choose a medium-sized container, such as this wire basket, which is 23cm (9in) across and 13cm (5in) deep. Line it with moss.

2 Cover the moss with a circle of black plastic cut from a bin liner (trash bag), and fill two-thirds full with potting compost (soil mix).

3 Plant the cyclamen around the edge of the container, taking care to add compost right around the root ball of each plant. Leave a distinct gap in the centre for watering.

4 Add some matching candles as a finishing touch, but take care never to leave the lit candles unattended.

Indoor winter-flowering hyacinths

Commercially prepared bulbs allow us to enjoy hyacinths out of season. Hyacinths normally flower in spring, but special treatments, such as early lifting and subjecting them to artificially high and low temperatures, mean that they will flower in early winter.

When choosing bulbs, make sure that you buy only those that are labelled as having been prepared for forcing and remember that you need to allow about three months between the planting and flowering of a forced hyacinth.

There are several cultivars available for forcing, all of which are derived from the species *Hyacinthus orientalis*: 'Anne Marie' is light rose-pink, 'Pink Pearl' is a slightly deeper shade of pink, 'Bismarck' is sky-blue, 'Delft Blue' is more porcelain-blue, 'L'Innocence' is white, 'Jan Bos' is a carmine red, and 'City of Haarlem' is lemon-yellow. All are fragrant.

Almost any container can be used for hyacinths, which adapt easily to shallow rooting conditions. For general purposes, however, choose a container that is at least 7.5cm (3in) deep. Terracotta pots, a small

galvanized bucket, a china bowl or even a vase are ideal. Hyacinths can be grown on water or on potting compost (soil mix).

To grow them on compost, put a layer of grit in the bottom of the container and add some moistened indoor bulb fibre. Plant the bulbs on the top, with just the bottom half of the bulb sitting in the compost and the top half exposed. Arrange them so that the bulbs are not touching either each other or the sides of the container and make sure that they have about half their own width between them. Add grit, chippings or moss over the compost to retain moisture, and put the container in a cool, dark place for between eight and ten weeks, until the bulbs have made good root growth. The temperature at this stage should not exceed 7–10°C (45–50°F). Check from time to time to make sure the compost is still moist, watering as necessary.

GROWING HYACINTHS ON COMPOST

1 Place a thin layer of grit at the bottom of your chosen container. If the container has no drainage holes, use a specially prepared indoor bulb fibre.

2 Use ordinary potting compost (soil mix) if there are adequate drainage holes in the container. Add bulb fibre or compost to within 5cm (2in) of the rim.

3 Plant the hyacinth bulbs with the bottom half of the bulb in compost and the top half exposed. Space the bulbs so that they are touching neither each other nor the container. They should have about half their own width between them. Moisten the compost, but avoid watering the bulbs directly.

4 Add grit or moss in order to retain moisture, and then put the container in a cool, dark place for about 8–10 weeks until the bulbs have made good root growth. The temperature at this stage should not exceed 7–10°C (45–50°F).

5 Return the bulbs to the light when the new shoots are about 5cm (2in) long. Expose them only gradually to increased temperatures and sunlight, as the flower stem emerges. Keep the compost moist; the coloured grit darkens when damp.

Bring the hyacinths out into the light when the tips of the new shoots are about 5cm (2in) long. The shoots will be bright light green in colour but will quickly turn darker when they are exposed to the light. Expose the hyacinths only gradually to increased temperatures and levels of sunlight as the flower stem emerges. Too much heat or dryness will cause stunted growth. After flowering, apply a liquid feed and keep the compost moist as the leaves die down naturally, thus allowing the bulbs to regenerate for another year. Plant them out in the garden in early spring. Do not keep these bulbs for forcing a second year.

Growing on water

Hyacinths have been grown on water for many years, including in plain glass jars with narrow necks, and as long as you can ensure that the base of the bulb will not actually touch the water into which the roots grow, you can use almost any type of container, including the specially made vases that have a cup-shaped compartment in which the bulb can sit securely above the water. You can add coloured stones or shells to support the bulb, and it is a good idea to add a small amount of charcoal to the water to keep it fresh and "sweet". When necessary, top up the water level so that it is just below the base of the bulb. If the base of the bulb sits in the water the bulb will rot. Put the bulb in a dark, cool place, at a temperature no higher than 7–10°C (45–50°F), as for those growing on compost. Within a matter of weeks the small roots will begin to grow down into the water beneath, soon followed by the thrusting shoot above the neck of the glass. When the shoot is about 5cm (2in) long, move the

GROWING BULBS ON WATER

1 You will need water, charcoal, a hyacinth bulb and a special glass. You will need a larger glass for bulbs such as *Hippeastrum*.

2 Insert a small piece of charcoal into the glass. Bring the water level to just below the neck of the glass.

3 Insert the bulb, ensuring that the base is just above water level. Place the bulb in a cool, dark room, and when the roots are well formed and the shoot is about 5cm (2in) long, bring it out to a light spot, gradually increasing the level of sunlight and temperature. Avoid strong, direct sunlight.

4 Growing hyacinth bulbs in glass vases shows off their beauty to full effect. It is fascinating to see the mass of delicate roots that is produced, an effect that can rarely be seen otherwise. Do not allow the base of the bulb to sit in the water, because this will cause it to rot.

glass into a light, warmer position ready for flowering. Gradually increase the temperature and light as the bud lengthens. The drama of the roots is seen best where light comes from behind; so choose a place in front of the winow where you can enjoy the extra sparkle. But in order to prolong the life of the flowers, avoid direct sunlight and put them in a cooler room at night. The bulb should be discarded after flowering; having used up its food reserves, it will not produce flowers a second time.

Conditioned bulbs for early flowering

Crocus	Hyacinthus
Freesia	Narcissus
Hippeastrum	papyraceus

Hippeastrum

The massive bulbs of hippeastrums can be bought in late summer and forced into flower before midwinter. However, most are available from early autumn until early winter, and these will flower after midwinter until spring, depending on the planting time.

Commonly available at this stage are the deep red 'Red Velvet' and 'Red Lion', the brilliant red and white 'Christmas Star', the orange 'Florida' and the pink and white 'Flamingo'. Rather more unusual is 'Yellow Goddess', which has creamy yellow flowers with a lime-green throat. Doubles are sometimes to be found as well, including the white, pink-edged 'Mary Lou'. A more recent introduction has been the Cybister types with their wispy petals such as 'Merenque' and 'Tango'.

It might still be possible to buy bulbs in mid-spring, when they will probably be cheaper. If the bulbs are firm, they will still flower. Indeed, the later they are planted, the more quickly they will spring into growth.

When planted in autumn or winter, the bulbs need warmth to come to life again after their dormant period. Choose a pot that is only about 2.5cm (1in) wider than the bulb itself. Use a soil-based potting compost (soil mix) if the pot has drainage holes, or an indoor bulb fibre if the pot has no holes. Some heavy grit at the base of the pot will help to stabilize the bulb when it is in flower and also assist with drainage.

Place the potted bulb in a warm spot – an airing cupboard, for example – where the temperature is 20–25°C (68–77°F). When the shoot has begun to emerge, expose it to moderate warmth and good light. Keep the compost moist during the growing period and apply a liquid feed, such as tomato fertilizer, every week or ten days once the bud has begun to open.

If you remove the first flowering stem you may find that another one soon emerges. The leaves will begin to grow at this stage. It is important to keep the bulb watered and regularly fed so that it can complete its cycle

'Yellow Goddess' is a sumptuous choice for any container whether grown on water or in compost (soil mix). Mature bulbs will each produce two or three flower spikes.

of growth. Some months later, when the leaves begin to yellow and wither, gradually withhold water and allow the bulb to go into a dormant period. Do not attempt to repot in

GROWING *HIPPEASTRUM* IN CONTAINERS

1 Plant two bulbs for a dramatic display. Add 5cm (2in) grit to the base of a container that is about 2.5cm (1in) wider than the bulb.

2 Add indoor bulb fibre and then plant the bulb so that the neck and shoulders sit just above the rim of the container.

3 Add a little more indoor bulb fibre around the neck, still leaving the shoulders exposed. Firm down the compost.

The bulbs of the *Hippeastrum* (amaryllis) are exceptionally large.

marbles or small stones to cover the small jar. Include a small piece of charcoal with the marbles to keep the water "sweet". Add a few more marbles and carefully place the bulb so that it rests inside the neck of the container with its roots barely touching the marbles. Add enough water to bring the level just below the base of the bulb. You might like to dress the container with pretty

red beads or brightly coloured curly canes, which are available from florists. A single bulb will flower beautifully for weeks and may even produce two dramatic flowering spikes, by which time the bulb will have shrunk because it has used up all its food reserves. Bulbs planted in compost can be kept and encouraged to flower again another year, but it is best to discard those grown on water.

the first years, because hippeastrums resent root disturbance. After three or four years it will be necessary to repot, and this should be done in late summer. Leave the bulb outside in a dry, sheltered spot until autumn when it can be brought indoors again and given moisture and warmth to start the flowering cycle again. It might not flower at exactly the same time as it did the first year, but the results will still be good.

Growing on water

Hippeastrum bulbs can be grown on water in a similar way to prepared hyacinths and *Narcissus papyraceus*. Start the bulb into growth as already described, planted on moist compost, and keep it in a warm place for a short period. As soon as the bud begins to emerge, carefully wash off the compost. Plant the bulb on top of coloured stones, pebbles, marbles or glass beads, with the water level kept below the base of the bulb.

Hippeastrum bulbs are huge, so use a wide-necked glass container within which it can sit. Find a small, clean, empty glass jar with a light-coloured screw lid to fit inside the container. This allows more light to be reflected and cuts down on the number of marbles or beads that will be needed. Place the jar inside the larger container and add enough

These *Hippeastrum* 'Red Velvet' are blooming for a second time in the same container. It is important to feed them after flowering and to continue to water until the leaves show signs of yellowing. Then gradually withhold moisture and allow the leaves to die down, thus allowing the bulbs to complete their life-cycle. Do not disturb the roots; simply begin to water again when the first signs of new growth are seen. The bulbs can be allowed to flower in the same compost (soil mix) for three seasons.

Indoor winter-flowering narcissi

The species *Narcissus papyraceus* is native to south-eastern France, south-western Spain and Portugal, where it flowers outdoors in winter, although many of the commercially available bulbs actually come from Israel. It is not surprising that when given warmth and moisture, the bulbs burst into growth after being planted indoors in autumn.

Closely related and behaving in the same way are the cultivars 'Ziva', 'Omri' and 'Galilee'. Grow these narcissi in a warm, well-lit place where a temperature of 16°C (60°F) can be maintained. Other narcissi that are suitable for forcing indoors are the cultivars 'Cragford' and 'Bridal Crown', both of which are easily available but later flowering. As a rule, the later they flower, the more important it is to give the bulbs a cool period of several weeks after planting. So if you are growing bulbs of either 'Cragford' or 'Bridal Crown' indoors, place them in a cool, dark place for about ten weeks, when the shoots should be around 5cm (2in) high.

Once flowering has begun, then the cooler the room temperature the longer the flowers will last, but do not allow the temperature to fall below freezing. If you have a balcony or veranda, you may even wish to place them outside in mild weather. This is also useful if you find the perfume too strong.

Narcissus papyraceus (syn. *N.* 'Paper White') and its forms produce stems with eight or ten flowers each, which means that just two or three bulbs will produce a really worthwhile display. They look equally attractive grown on compost (soil mix) or on water.

Narcissus papyraceus (syn. *N.* 'Paper White') looks festive surrounded by seasonal stars, which highlight the shape of its flowers.

You may choose to grow several different types of cultivar, keeping to a single type in each bowl, and by doing this you will be able to have blooms from early winter through to midwinter, and beyond.

If you use a container without drainage holes – a painted, metal or glazed pot, for instance – use specially formulated free-draining bulb fibre. This will give the bulbs a good growing medium and will help prevent the compost (soil mix) from becoming sour over the ensuing months. If you use a traditional plant pot with drainage holes, you can use a soil-based potting compost (soil mix), but place a saucer beneath it to protect your furniture or the windowsill.

Forcing narcissi

Narcissus papyraceus (syn. *N.* 'Paper White') is the easiest of all the narcissi to bring into flower in late autumn or winter. It usually flowers only six weeks after planting and, unlike the later flowering and other related daffodils, it requires no special period of cool or darkness to persuade it to grow and flower indoors. Decide when you want the bulbs to bloom and then work backwards. You may wish to try a succession of flowers by planting a number of pots over several weeks in order to have a supply of fragrant blooms. Each stem produces many flowers, so a display can quite easily include as many as five or six bulbs or as few as two or three. Whatever you choose, the results will be excellent. These bulbs do not tolerate frosty conditions outside, so unless you live in a mild climate, they are best discarded after flowering and new ones purchased for the following season, when the whole cycle can begin again.

Growing on water

Narcissus papyraceus and its cultivars also grow well on top of water because they are so quick to start into growth and then flower. Use a pretty bowl filled with gravel to stabilize the roots, or choose a glass container and fill it with coloured stones or glass nuggets. Gravel and chippings are available in a range of colours and grades for garden landscaping and for indoor fish tanks. A pattern of red and white stones or some seashore stones and shells would look interesting.

Add a small piece of charcoal among the stones to help keep the water fresh. The bulbs will use all their food reserves by growing on water and should be discarded after flowering. They will not produce flowers again.

FORCING NARCISSI

1 Choose firm, plump bulbs, and plant in compost (soil mix), allowing for about six weeks before flowering. Do not worry if the bulbs already have existing shoots, but take care that they are not damaged. Grit at the base of the container is not essential, but it is useful to aid drainage.

2 Fill the container with moistened bulb fibre, bringing the level to within 5cm (2in) of the rim. Plant the bulbs so that they are close together, but away from the sides of the container. A distance apart of about half their width is ideal. Approximately half the top of each bulb should be left exposed.

3 Mulch with moss to retain the moisture as well as to add an attractive finish. Natural moss available from a florist (or maybe the garden) has been used here, but coloured reindeer moss would make an attractive and more vibrant alternative.

4 You may need to support the leaves and stems with twigs. Only do so if you notice that the stems are beginning to flop, but then act immediately. Beech twigs are ideal, as they branch well all the way up the stem and offer support from top to bottom.

Spring bulbs indoors

Several bulbs are suitable for planting in small pots before being kept in cool but sheltered conditions outside – such as next to a house wall or in an open porch – and then being brought indoors once the flower buds first show, to flower a week or two earlier than they would otherwise.

Crocuses, *Eranthis hyemalis* (winter aconite), *Muscari* (grape hyacinths), dwarf daffodils, dwarf tulips and hyacinths will all bring pleasure if they are treated in this way.

The large *Crocus vernus* (Dutch crocus) are excellent candidates for growing in this way. If the corms are to be planted in containers with no drainage holes, add a layer of grit to the base of each pot and use specially formulated indoor bulb fibre to fill the pot. For a maximum show, five crocus corms can be planted in a circle near the bottom of each pot, with another layer of five corms planted above them. Make sure that the corms are not directly on top of each other. The pots should be kept in a light place, such as a potting shed or unheated

greenhouse, in winter and watered occasionally to keep the compost (soil mix) just moist. When the shoots just begin to show colour, they can be brought indoors. The display can then be appreciated at close range, with no danger of wind or rain spoiling the delicate petals.

Prepared hyacinths for midwinter flowering are available in a limited range of colours, but bedding hyacinths, which are grown in the garden or in outdoor pots, are available in an enormous number of delicate shades, including apricot as in *Hyacinthus orientalis* 'Gipsy Queen'; violet, lilac, mulberry and burgundy as in 'Violet Pearl', 'Amethyst', 'Mulberry Rose' and 'Woodstock'; blue and white as in 'Blue Jacket'; deep blue as in 'Blue Magic'; and many others. There are also some double-flowering forms, including white 'Ben Nevis', red 'Hollyhock', violet 'King Codro' and pink 'Rosette'. Any of these hyacinths can be grown in groups of three or more or as a single specimen in a simple terracotta pot. Hyacinths like good drainage so where they are grown outdoors, open to the winter rain, it

is advisable to choose a pot with drainage holes and to use a soil-based potting compost (soil mix).

Using spring bulbs already in growth

One of the easiest ways to enjoy bulbs indoors in late winter is to buy small pots of growing bulbs. Use a pretty coloured pot or a plain terracotta pot for display purposes and place it in a light but cool position to prolong the flowering period as much as possible. Too much heat or too much direct sunlight will mean that you will enjoy only the briefest of blooms.

Dwarf irises, scillas, *Fritillaria meleagris* (snake's head fritillary), hyacinths and dwarf tulips are among the many plants that are readily available, but of them all, the miniature *Narcissus* 'Tête-à-tête' is probably the most often grown. This is a dwarf, sturdy, multiheaded, hybrid daffodil with rich yellow flowers. After flowering, deadhead each flower and plant them out in the garden in spring so that the bulbs can complete their lifecycle and flower again year after year.

Some cultivars of *Crocus vernus* (Dutch crocus) have wonderfully bold purple flowers with strongly contrasting orange stamens.

A small, metal window box planted with narcissi is perfect for a kitchen windowsill or for the conservatory.

You will need secateurs (pruners), a florist's foam ring, a large plate or dish to display the arrangement, three or four pots of dwarf *Narcissus* 'Tête-à-tête', some foliage, such as *Euonymus japonicus* 'Aureus', long stems of *Corylus avellana* 'Contorta' (corkscrew hazel) and a few sprigs of flowering forsythia and viburnums, including white *Viburnum tinus* and pink *V.* x *bodnantense* 'Dawn'.

Growing *Narcissus* 'Tête-à-tête'

An effective method of displaying these little daffodils is to find a simple coloured container that is slightly larger than the pot in which they are already growing. Use grit or stones as necessary in the outer pot to get the level right, insert the pot of daffodils and add a covering of moss to disguise the inner pot and the surface of the compost (soil mix). Keep the bulbs moist and deadhead the flowers to keep them neat.

Another way of using them is to place the pot-grown plants in a small metal window box, again raising the levels with grit or stones and topping up with moss between each pot. Reindeer moss provides a lime-green finish or you could use a coloured moss from a florist. Keep the compost (soil mix) moist and deadhead the daffodils to keep them neat.

Wet the foam ring thoroughly and give the cut foliage a good long drink in water. Place the ring on a large plate or dish and arrange the pots of bulbs to sit inside. Cut small sprigs of foliage and arrange them in groups, pushing the stems into the foam. Add some flowering forsythia and viburnum in groups and a few single stems of the hazel to give extra height. Bear in mind that within a few days the narcissi will probably grow to about 20cm (8in) or more. If you keep the foam and bulbs moist, the arrangement should stay fresh for ten days or more.

Alternatively, incorporate these daffodils into a flower and foliage arrangement. Potted bulbs will last much longer than a bunch of cut flowers, so mix them with other late-winter foliage and flowers to create a vibrant indoor display. The choice of cut foliage in autumn and winter will depend on what is available. The variegated foliage of *Euonymus japonicus* 'Aureus' would be a good choice, as would the white flowers of *Viburnum tinus* or the long, twisted stems of *Corylus avellana* 'Contorta' (corkscrew hazel). Simple ivy leaves and berries are equally attractive.

Achimenes

These plants produce long, tubular flowers, ranging in colour from rose, scarlet and blue to violet, and the flowers, which have contrasting throats of gold or white, are sometimes blotched or spotted.

The rhizomes, which resemble miniature pine cones, are small and easily broken, so they are often sold, four or five at a time, in little plastic tubs surrounded by peat. For all their fragility, however, they are easily grown in shallow containers, and the cascading types are delightful in hanging baskets, where they will tumble over the sides. Successive plantings in winter and spring will produce flowers throughout summer and autumn.

Plant the rhizomes about 2.5cm (1in) deep and 5cm (2in) apart. Water sparingly at first, but as shoots appear keep the compost (soil mix) moist at all times. It is important to water regularly because a dry period will initiate dormancy, and there will be no flowers. Apply a liquid feed every two weeks when

Achimenes 'Prima Donna' has rich salmon-pink flowers that look beautiful planted on their own or mixed with a trailing form.

Achimenes 'Cascade Fairy Pink' has pretty light pink flowers. The dark green foliage has bronze-red undertones.

plants are in full growth. Pinch out shoots to encourage bushiness and provide supports if necessary. Provide bright light, but keep the plants shaded from strong, direct sunlight. In hot weather, spray the foliage with a mister to maintain humidity. You can improve humidity around plants by standing pot-grown specimens on a gravel-covered tray and keeping the gravel damp.

As the flowering period comes to an end, gradually withhold water until the soil has dried out. Remove the dead foliage and store the rhizomes in dry peat at a minimum temperature of 10°C (50°F). The rhizomes can be propagated when next planted. Do not worry too much if they break: every single scale will produce a new plant which can be used to propagate new plants.

PLANTING ACHIMENES IN A BASKET

1 Line a wicker basket with black plastic (unless it is already pre-lined), add drainage material, such as polystyrene (styrofoam), broken pots or grit, and cover with a multi-purpose compost (soil mix), to within 2.5cm (1in) of the rim.

2 This basket has a 30cm (12in) diameter and contains eight rhizomes, planted about 5cm (2in) apart and 2.5cm (1in) deep. Two different types of achimenes can be alternated, such as *Achimenes* 'Cascade Violet Night' and *A.* 'Violet Charm'.

3 Mist to maintain humidity. Warmth, semi-shade and a damp atmosphere are ideal. The plants will flower for months on end and give endless pleasure.

Freesia

Freesias grow from corms, which may be planted indoors to flower in succession from late spring through to early summer, so that their perfume can be enjoyed over many weeks. They can also be purchased as "conditioned" bulbs and planted in pots indoors, before being moved outdoors, where they will flower in mid- to late summer.

Indoor freesias should be planted in early spring in moist, soil-based potting compost (soil mix), about 7.5cm (3in) apart and deep. Keep the compost moist throughout the growing period and apply a liquid feed every two weeks as soon as the buds show. Keep in cool to warm conditions but avoid too high a temperature, or the flowering period will be short.

There are both single- and double-flowered forms of freesia, and the plants vary in height from 10 to 30cm (4–12in). Many, though not all, freesias are exquisitely fragrant. But one of the drawbacks is their rather untidy foliage, especially at the time of flowering, so a wire ring support can be useful. For larger, more mature plants, beech twigs are ideal supports.

Freesias are sometimes unpredictable in their willingness to flower – you might be fortunate and have a wonderful pot filled with blooms, or you might have only one or two flowers. Regular moderate watering and regular fertilizer should ensure good results.

It is worth taking trouble with these plants because the scent is heavenly, with the yellow forms being best of all. Recent hybridization programmes have produced cultivars that are more reliable in terms of flowering and with even better scent.

Freesia flowers are a firm favourite in the florist shops both for their scent and delicate colours. Grow your own at home and you will be rewarded, year after year.

Conditioned freesia corms can be planted in pots indoors to flower in succession from late spring through to early summer.

Pure white *Freesia* 'Miranda' and light yellow *F.* 'Beethoven' in pots decorated with African animal-skin patterns.

Eucomis

Eucomis **is commonly called the pineapple lily or pineapple flower because it produces a tuft of leafy bracts above the flower spike. It is native to southern Africa, where it grows in grassy, often damp, areas.**

This is an easy bulb to grow indoors. In spring plant individual bulbs in a small pot, 10cm (4in) deep, in a well-drained, soil-based potting compost (soil mix), or mass the bulbs in groups of three or more in a larger pot. Water sparingly until shoots emerge and, as growth progresses, keep the compost moist at all times. After flowering, allow the plant to complete its lifecycle and gradually withhold water so that

it can rest during the dormant period before bringing it into growth again the following spring. In mild areas the bulb can be grown outside.

Eucomis autumnalis 'White Dwarf' is a particularly attractive plant with distinctive wavy foliage. It has a column of white flowers with yellow stamens, which open in succession, starting at the base; at the top the leafy hat brings the height to just over 30cm (12in). For a taller plant try *E. comosa* 'Sparkling Burgundy', which is memorable for the intense deep colour of its emerging leaves and later flower spike. This eventually reaches about 70cm (28in) with a generous number of dark pinkish-purple flowers.

Eucomis autumnalis 'White Dwarf' has a wonderful silhouette with its wavy foliage, its narrow column of scented flowers and its leafy top. This is an easy bulb to grow indoors.

Eucomis comosa 'Sparkling Burgundy' is an exciting plant to watch from the moment it first sends up its new leaves to the time its flower spike emerges, and, later, as the flowers open.

Eucomis flowers last for several weeks, opening at the bottom of the flower spike first and progressively higher up as the weeks pass by. This undemanding plant is rewarding both in its longevity and its simplicity.

Sinningia

Although the botanical name for this group of plants is *Sinningia*, the term gloxinia is better known among florists and flower arrangers. The plants are originally native to tropical areas of Brazil, Argentina and Mexico, where they have adapted to seasonal rainfall and periods of intervening drought, during which the tubers become dormant for a time.

The large, velvety flowers grow from tubers, which are shaped rather like those of begonias. They should be planted in late winter or early spring on top of moist, multipurpose compost (soil mix). Given gentle warmth and only moderate moisture at first, they soon start into growth and produce colourful plants, about 20cm (8in) in height and spread.

Flowers may be self-coloured or speckled, such as the lovely pink-spotted white 'Blanche de Méru', crimson 'Etoile de Feu', violet 'Hollywood', ivory and red Tigrina Group and purple and white 'Kaiser Wilhelm'.

Pot individual tubers into small containers with drainage holes in the base and use a multipurpose compost (soil mix). It is important to use containers with drainage holes because the leaves dislike being splashed with water and will quickly mark, so the plants should be watered from below. Keep the temperature at 21–23°C (70–73°F) until flowering and move to cooler conditions when flowering begins. The plants will have become quite leafy and take up a surprisingly large amount of space.

Alternatively, plant several tubers in one container mixing the colours to make a really colourful display. Provide the plants with well-lit conditions but do not stand in direct sunlight. Deadhead flowers to prolong flowering and apply a dilute liquid feed every two weeks. After

Sinningia 'Hollywood', with its gorgeous violet blooms, is a real show-stopper, and *S.* 'Etoile de Feu' is a glorious velvety crimson. The two together make a sumptuous display in a simple wicker window box.

flowering is over gradually withhold water and allow the rootball to go quite dry. Store in a cool, dry place at about 7°C (45°F) until the following season.

A DISPLAY OF SINNINGIAS

1 Choose a small plastic pot with drainage holes and find a slightly larger, ornamental pot for display purposes. Grit is useful in the base of the outer pot for raising the inner pot to the right height. It also provides a damp reservoir beneath the base of the plant, enabling the plant to be kept damp, which is particularly important in hot weather.

2 Use a moist, multipurpose compost (soil mix) to fill the pot to within 3cm (1¼in) of the rim. Create a small hollow, and plant the tuber so that it rests on top of the compost. Keep the temperature at 21–23°C (70–73°F) until flowering, and move to cooler conditions when flowering begins. Keep in well-lit conditions but avoid direct sunlight.

3 Avoid watering directly on top of the leaves. It is much better to water from below, occasionally removing the plant and sitting it in a saucer of water. Alternatively, remove the plant and add water to the base of the outer pot but take care not to leave the roots sitting in a pool of water. They will quickly fail if the compost is kept too sodden.

Summer bulbs indoors

Many summer-flowering bulbs, tubers and rhizomes are offered for sale as growing plants, often much earlier in the year than would be possible if they were grown on, at home, from their dry state.

Begonias and lilies, therefore, are available from spring onwards, with dahlias following on soon afterwards. They are happy kept inside, in warm, light conditions, but do not put them in a position where they will be in full, direct sun, or the flowers will last for only a few days, not weeks.

Terracotta containers always look warm and attractive, but there are many other ways of displaying plants. Silver or silver-coloured containers will give a more modern appearance indoors, and can look extremely elegant, especially if the plant is tall and beautifully shaped, such as a *Zantedeschia* (arum lily).

Do not forget to feed the plants every week to ten days with a liquid feed and keep them well watered. Frequent deadheading will help to prolong the flowering time of arum lilies, dahlias and begonias. After they have finished flowering, the

Here, dahlias are displayed individually in highly coloured containers. Just make sure there are drainage holes in the base of each inner pot.

Two or three Non-Stop begonias look marvellous in a pure white window box. There are so many delightful colours to choose from, including these soft pink shades or much stronger reds and oranges. Remember to deadhead regularly and apply a liquid feed every week.

Non-Stop begonias are so called because they continue to flower over a long period. They make excellent indoor plants.

lilies can be planted out in a sheltered part of the garden, where they will overwinter and come into flower again the following year. Begonia and dahlia tubers can be allowed to go into a dormant state, and then should be kept cool and dry until they can be brought into growth again the following spring.

Short-stemmed lilies are ideal for displaying indoors or on a balcony or veranda. 'Orange Pixie' grows to only 30cm (12in), while 'Peach Pixie' reaches 45cm (16in). Often lilies have a heady fragrance. For those suffering from pollen allergies, look out for the 'Kiss' lily types, which are double and pollen-free.

Zantedeschia 'Dusky Pink' is one of the many modern cultivars of the arum lily that have these beautifully shaped tubular flowers.

Zantedeschia (arum lily), with their boldly shaped flowers, look elegant displayed in a series of tall, modern silver containers.

Lilies make a wonderful statement with their brilliantly coloured flowers and attractive leaves. Find an old fruit or vegetable box and lightly colour-wash or spray it with paint to give a warm and interesting texture. Place the pots inside and use a little green or coloured moss to disguise the rims. After flowering, the lilies can be planted out in the garden, where they will overwinter and come into bloom again the following year.

Autumn bulbs indoors

Autumn-flowering nerines and hedychiums bring welcome colour into our lives when chilly days make life outdoors rather less enticing.

Nerine

The frilly pink flowers are one of the main characteristics of nerines, making them a favourite for the garden as well as the conservatory and indeed an important part of the cut-flower industry.

Although they are often known as the Guernsey lily, an island where they now grow in abundance, nerines actually originate from southern Africa. They are thought of as borderline hardy and some species, including the well-known *Nerine bowdenii* and its cultivars, are often grown in sheltered, sunny borders or in pots outdoors where they flower in early autumn. However, some species, such as *N. masoniorum*, are tender, and some forms are later to flower, including the purple-red cultivar 'Ancilla', white and purple 'Konak', fuchsia-pink *N. bowdenii* 'Pink Triumph', and *N. flexuosa* 'Alba', which has delightful, white, crinkly-edged petals. It is safer to enjoy all these nerines indoors.

Nerine bulbs have long necks. Purchase bulbs when they are

Nerines like to be planted with the neck above soil level. The leaves follow in late winter.

available, usually in late summer, and plant three bulbs to a pot, making sure that the top of the neck is just above soil level. Water freely when the flower buds appear but allow to become dry during the summer dormancy. The flowers will appear in autumn, with the leaves following in late winter. Remove any seedheads, unless wanted for propagation. Apply a low-nitrogen liquid feed in late winter, although not all growers recommend this treatment.

Do not divide the bulbs until it is absolutely necessary because they prefer to be congested. Eventually, however, flowering will decrease and you will need to separate the bulbs and replant them. Be aware that recently divided bulbs may not flower for the first year, because they resent being disturbed. The modern treatment of new bulbs, which are produced on a commercial scale, means that these will mostly likely bear flowers.

Planting several pots with different cultivars or species will give you colour in the conservatory for many weeks, varying from the palest pink to deep pink to purple red.

Nerine bowdenii 'Pink Triumph' has spectacular fuchsia pink flowers. Flowering in late autumn, it is one of the last nerines to flower and so is best treated as a conservatory plant where it can be protected from frosty weather.

Hybridization means that many more shades are becoming available, so the future should bring even more choice.

Hedychium

More commonly known as ginger lilies or garland lilies, hedychiums originate in lightly wooded areas of Asia, where they revel in the summer warmth and moisture. They may be grown outdoors as late summer- to autumn-flowering container plants or as cool conservatory specimens, when their ebullient foliage and scented flowers can be fully appreciated. They are rhizomatous plants, related to the edible ginger root from the genus *Zingiber* which is so highly prized in cooking, but species in the *Hedychium* genus are more showy with their flowers.

The best known of all the gingers is probably *Hedychium coronarium* (garland flower, white ginger lily), which is native to India. It can reach 3m (10ft) in height. The pointed buds eventually open to reveal long, terminal racemes, to 20cm (8in) long, of butterfly-like, white flowers with amber-yellow basal marks. *H. flavescens* (yellow ginger) is similar to *H. coronarium* but its flowers are yellow not white. The flowers of *H. densiflorum*, native to the Himalayas, have a more bottlebrush appearance, reaching 20cm (10in) long. It can grow 5m (15ft) high in ideal conditions, but is more likely to grow to 1.8m (6ft) in a conservatory. The cultivar *H. densiflorum* 'Assam Orange' has deep orange, fragrant flowers. *H. ellipticum*, a species native to northern India, has pointed leaves and a flower that appears as a 10cm (4in) spike with white and yellow-lobed flowers and purple filaments. It grows to about 1.8m (6ft) high.

Plant hedychiums in soil-based compost (soil mix) with the rhizomes just on the surface. They will cope well with confined conditions but growth is rapid, and as with many rhizomatous plants they are best divided in spring or potted on into a larger container. Remember that

Hedychium gardnerianum is one of the best known of all the ornamental ginger family, producing long racemes of butterfly-like creamy yellow blooms. These flowers are used in garlands in Nepal and Hawaii.

hedychiums will grow to 1.8m (6ft) tall or more, so choose a heavy pot that will not fall over. They enjoy warm, moist conditions, so place a gravel-filled tray beneath the pot which can be used as a water reservoir on sunny days when the temperature in the conservatory is likely to be high.

The rhizomes of hedychiums are stout and fleshy and leaf spikes are usually prominent, soon emerging into a leafy shoot. Growth is rapid and soon the shoot will be 2–3m (6–10ft) tall. Repot or divide in early spring so that the plant is poised ready to mature well.

Fleshy berries are characteristic of *Hedychium spicatum*. Although its flowers are not the most highly scented of the genus, the dried rhizomes are burned as incense, a derivative oil is used in perfumery and a powdered form is used for scenting tobacco.

Most hedychiums will grow to 1–3m (3–10ft) high, although the average is around 1.8m (6ft). Not all spiky shoots produce flowers, but the foliage is handsome in its own right. *Hedychium coronarium* is particularly attractive with its elliptical glaucous leaves.

Calendar
of care

Most bulbs are relatively easy plants to look
after and many will give years of pleasure with
very little extra need for care and attention.
Snowdrops and aconites, little cyclamen and
most of the early daffodils, scillas, grape
hyacinths and bluebells will continue without
stint with only the occasional need to divide.
There are others, however, which need rather
more care, simply because they originate from
warm climates where there is no threat of winter
frosts. In these circumstances, the bulbs either
have to be planted in a sunny sheltered site, in
very well-drained conditions where winter cold
will have a minimal effect with the help of a
thick mulch of ashes or grit, or they need to be
lifted before the winter starts and kept either
dry in frost-free temperatures or in containers in
the shelter of a heated greenhouse. Feeding and
the need for moisture are common to all plants
although some have greater need than others.
Planted in the right positions with regard to
sun or shade, and with either free-draining or
moisture retentive soil, is half the battle.
Trilliums need moist shade, nerines need sunny,
freely drained soil. Choose your plants with care
and reap the rich rewards.

Irises and alliums create a worthwhile partnership, enjoying a sunny
border, both similar in height, yet providing a valuable contrast in
flower shape.

Winter

Many of the summer- and autumn-flowering bulbs are available to buy at this time of year, including low-growing to medium begonias, *Anemone coronaria*, freesias and taller dahlias, lilies, crinums, nerines, chasmanthe and gladioli. Of these, lilies can be purchased in both autumn and late winter. They are perfectly hardy, and as long as soil conditions allow deep digging to take place, they can be planted at either time.

Most of the bulbs, corms, tubers and rhizomes that are offered for sale in late winter are tender plants, which come from warmer climates where there are no winter frosts. They should be planted in spring, so that when the foliage emerges, all risk of frost has passed. It is possible, however, to cheat the season, because some tubers and corms, such as begonias and dahlias, can be started into growth in pots in late winter, under the protection of glass, so they are ready to plant out in early summer. This method leads to earlier blooms and therefore a long flowering season.

Start dahlias into growth in pots in late winter, under the protection of glass, ready to plant out in early summer.

Galanthus (snowdrop) can be bought in late winter in pots or as loose clumps of plants with the leaves still attached to the bulbs. These are known as snowdrops "in the green". Plant them directly into borders or grassland, where they will establish and flower for years to come.

Bringing on

Cannas, begonias and dahlias are available in a wonderful array of colours and can be started into growth in late winter or early spring so that they produce a mass of flowers throughout summer. Cannas and dahlias should be planted into, and begonias should be placed on top of, barely moist compost and kept in a light, cool to warm place until growth begins at the roots. Increase the available moisture once leaves begin to emerge.

Planting in borders or containers

In mild spells, when the ground can be well dug, plant lilies in the border, either singly or in groups of three or more. Alternatively, plant them in deep containers. They thrive on well-drained soil, so add a layer of grit beneath the bulbs in both borders and containers.

Watering

This is a time when attention to watering is crucial, especially with container-grown plants. Moisture is necessary to bulbs at all stages of growth, and it is important to check that the compost (soil mix) is moist in all pots, troughs, window boxes and hanging baskets from autumn right through to spring. Pots and troughs will probably fare best, but window boxes and hanging baskets tend to dry out quickly. Lack of moisture in late autumn and early winter will inhibit root growth, and lack of water in late winter, when the leaves and buds are emerging, is also detrimental. Keep an eye on the compost and water as necessary. Do not, however, be tempted to water if frost threatens, as bulbs will not appreciate having their roots in wet, frozen conditions. It is much better to ignore any bright sunny days when nights are likely to be frosty, and water only on overcast days when the nights will be milder.

Feeding

This is not a major task at this time of year, although care should be given to any bulbs, tubers, rhizomes and corms in pots if you want to keep the plants for another display next season. Feed at flowering time or once thereafter, so that the foliage is kept healthy and the goodness can go back into the bulbs as the leaves die down. Border bulbs benefit from a general-purpose feed, which should be applied to the border in late winter or early spring. Many of the summer bulbs will still be in the greenhouse, so the best time to feed them will be when they are planted out.

Eranthis hyemalis (winter aconite) makes a welcome splash of yellow in late winter.

Protection against frost

All the hardy, autumn-planted bulbs that have been given homes in grassland or borders should not come to any harm in frosty weather. Those such as nerines and crinums, which may be considered borderline in colder areas, will benefit from a mulch of dry leaves. Bulbs and other plants that are in containers are at far greater risk. Hanging baskets should be taken off their brackets if temperatures drop below freezing for any prolonged length of time. A degree or two of frost overnight will not do any harm, but two or three nights and days of continued frost will pose greater problems. Place the baskets in the protection of a porch, garage or greenhouse. Pots and troughs should be given the protection of a house wall, where the temperatures will be less extreme, or put in a garage, porch or greenhouse. Sometimes they are too large and heavy to move easily, in which case they should be wrapped in a cloak of bubble wrap before the temperature

Galanthus (snowdrop) multiply persistently where they are growing in damp woodland, and will eventually spread to carpet vast areas. Plant them under shrubs and enjoy a similar, if scaled-down, effect.

drops to freezing. This will at least provide a little protection. Never water in frosty weather, when it is better to keep the compost (soil mix) on the dry side.

Deadheading

Removing dead flowerheads means that a plant's energy is not wasted on the production of seed at the expense of increasing the size of the bulb. However, if you want to increase from seed, you should allow the full cycle of growth to continue unabated. Many of the late winter bulbs and corms, including snowdrops, *Eranthis hyemalis* (winter aconite), *Crocus tommasinianus*, cyclamen and *Anemone blanda*, naturalize well by seed propagation.

Propagation

Collect seeds from winter aconites in late winter and early spring, and sprinkle them where you want them to flower, either in special

propagation boxes or direct on border soil or grass. Divide clumps of snowdrops and *Leucojum vernum* (spring snowflake) and replant.

Pest watch

Squirrels and mice might dig up newly planted bulbs. Snails might attack early daffodils, while birds might eat crocus flowers.

Enjoy

Now is the time to enjoy the flowers on many winter bulbs, such as the many different kinds of snowdrops. *Galanthus nivalis* and all its relations, *Leucojum vernum*, commonly known as spring snowflakes, early daffodils such as *Narcissus* 'Rijnveld's Early Sensation' (syn. 'January Gold') and 'February Gold', and the early tulips. Enjoy the flowers on winter corms such as the dwarf *Iris danfordiae*, crocus, and also on tubers such as those of the winter aconites, *Anemone blanda* and *Cyclamen coum*.

Iris 'Pauline' has dark violet flowers with distinctive white markings on the falls. This Reticulata iris is sweetly scented. Plant in an individual pot or with winter greenery in a hanging basket.

Spring

Some of the summer-flowering bulbs that were available in late winter will still be on sale, but choose those that are still plump and firm and have not been dried out by over-exposure on the garden-centre shelves. As spring progresses, cannas, begonias and dahlias in growth will go on sale, but the choice of colour and size will be more restricted than if you had bought dormant tubers and rhizomes.

Bringing on

Cannas and dahlias should be planted into, and begonias placed on top of, barely moist compost and kept in a light, cool to warm place until growth begins at the roots. Increase moisture once leaves begin to emerge. Plant outside when all risk of frost has passed.

Planting in borders, grass or containers

Gladioli, *Anemone coronaria* (single De Caen hybrids and semi-double St Bridgid varieties), *Zantedeschia*

(arum lily), tigridia, sparaxias, crinums and lilies should be planted now. You might like to try a succession of anemones which flower about three months after planting.

Transplanting

Dichelostemmas, ornithogalums and lilies that were potted earlier and now have good root formation should be transplanted. Either transfer from the pot or simply bury the pot in the garden borders.

Galanthus (snowdrop) and *Eranthis hyemalis* (winter aconite) can be purchased in spring as growing plants with their leaves intact. They might be sold in pots or in loose groups after flowering, but whichever kind you obtain, they will successfully transplant and flower well the following season.

Lifting

The life-cycle of a bulb normally continues for at least six weeks after flowering has finished, so do not be tempted to lift and dry off bulbs,

Dahlia tubers are now showing sustained new growth. New shoots can be used for propagation material.

rhizomes and so on until well after this date. Do not mow grassy areas until six weeks after snowdrops, crocuses or daffodils have finished flowering, or the following year's blooms will be greatly inhibited.

Watering

This is essential for container-grown specimens, especially if other bedding plants have been added to the scheme. Take special care with hanging baskets, which tend to dry out quickly, and with window boxes, which often receive little rainfall. Border bulbs, corms and so forth will normally receive adequate natural rainfall, although in exceptionally dry seasons they may benefit from additional moisture.

Feeding

Feed at flowering time or once thereafter so that the foliage is kept healthy and the goodness can go back into the bulbs as the leaves die down. Grassland and border bulbs will benefit from a general-purpose

The sumptuous blue of *Muscari* (grape hyacinth) is set off perfectly by an underplanting of *Senecio cineraria* with all its light silvery foliage.

feed applied in late winter or early spring. Container-grown specimens will benefit from a liquid feed.

Protection against frost

Hardy bulbs are unlikely to suffer in frosty spring weather, but keep an eye on the temperature in your greenhouse where you might be bringing on cannas, begonias and dahlias. Keep the plants away from the glass, where temperatures drop fastest, and maintain the temperature above freezing. Keep the compost on the dry side.

Deadheading

Hyacinths, daffodils and tulips should be deadheaded to avoid energy being wasted on seed production, but if you want to propagate bulbs such as *Scilla siberica*, *Muscari armeniacum*, *Chionodoxa luciliae* and *C. forbesii*, allow the seedheads to develop. Collect the seed and sow in propagation boxes or allow them to self-seed in situ.

Tulipa 'Blue Parrot' is just one of the many Parrot tulips available, all exhibiting the fullness of flower that makes them so popular.

Do not worry about hardy spring-flowering bulbs such as tulips, hyacinths and daffodils being harmed by late spring frosts.

Propagation

Collect ripe seed from winter aconites and, in due course, from *Muscari armeniacum* (grape hyacinth) and scillas. Sow in propagation boxes or simply allow them to self-seed in situ.

Pest watch

Slugs and snails adore succulent growth and will attack the young foliage on tulips and alliums, lilies and daffodil flowers. General garden cleanliness is important in keeping the slug and snail population at bay, and some gardeners use chemicals against certain pests with varying degrees of success. Rabbits, mice and birds are a nightmare as far as many bulbous plants are concerned, greedily eating off all the new shoots or flowers. Rabbits, fortunately, won't touch daffodils. Buried wire fences can stop rabbits, but there is little you can do to frighten off birds, mice and squirrels.

Enjoy

This is a really wonderful season for bulbs and corms of all kinds, and there is a multitude of daffodils, tulips, hyacinths, *Erythronium* (dog's tooth violet), fritillaries, irises, *Leucojum* (snowflake), grape hyacinths and trilliums coming into flower in grasslands, borders and containers. While you are enjoying them all, now is the time to search out your favourite colours for planting next autumn.

Summer

Gladioli might still be on sale, and late plantings now will give colour in autumn. Purchases of growing dahlias and begonias, cannas and *Zantedeschia* (arum lily) will allow you to obtain lots of colour this summer, although the range of colours will be more restricted than with dry tubers, rhizomes and so forth purchased in late winter.

Bringing on
Late plantings of dahlias and begonias are still possible, and, given warmth and moisture, they will soon grow on and produce good plants for planting out once the roots are well developed.

Planting in borders, grass or containers
Gladioli and anemones (single De Caen hybrids and semi-double St Bridgid varieties) can still be planted, although they will be later to flower than if they were planted in spring. Anemones will flower about three months after planting, while gladioli might take up to four months.

Allium seedheads are just one of the many delights of summer. They can be enjoyed in the garden or used in dried flower arrangements.

You will need to deadhead begonia blooms regularly to encourage production of flowers.

Transplanting
This is a major task now. Once all risk of frost has passed, the dahlias, cannas and begonias that were started into growth earlier can be planted out in the garden. They will be suitable for sunny borders or containers. Add slow-release food granules or well-rotted manure to the prepared holes before planting.

Lifting
If you want to remove tulips and daffodil bulbs from the borders, now is the time to lift them carefully so that they can be dried off, cleaned, sorted, labelled and stored for use again in the autumn. The best time is when the leaves have withered but are still visible.

Watering
Depending on the weather, be prepared to water. Dahlias are thirsty plants, especially in the early stages of growth.

Feeding
Once the buds have formed on dahlias, begonias and cannas, they will benefit from a regular liquid feed during the summer.

Protection against frost
This should no longer be necessary.

Deadheading
Regular deadheading of begonias, dahlias and cannas will ensure longer flower production and bigger blooms. It will also make the plants look much tidier. Gladioli and lilies should be deadheaded to conserve energy for next year's display.

Propagation
In midsummer, seeds of *Fritillaria meleagris* (snake's head fritillary) should be collected when ripe and sown in a propagating box. In late summer, small black bulbils will form up the stems of some types of lily, including those derived from

Tall-growing lilies can be supported with a special metal stake and detachable hoop.

Lilium lancifolium (formerly *L. tigrinum*; tiger lily). These will eventually fall off and propagate themselves at the foot of the parent plant, or they can be collected and planted in a propagating box.

Mowing grasslands where bulbs have flowered earlier

Normally it is best to leave growth intact for at least six weeks before mowing, or the lifecycle of the bulbs will not be completed and next year's flowering will be seriously impaired. Grassed areas with late-flowering daffodils and camassias should not be mown until midsummer.

Staking

All tall-growing lilies, gladioli and dahlias will need support. Single canes or special metal-hooped supports are adequate for lilies and gladioli, but dahlias, which grow much wider and have many strong branches, will need greater support, either from a metal stake and wider circle, substantial peasticks or from three or four stakes surrounding the plant and linked by string.

Pest watch

Slugs, snails and earwigs think dahlias are wonderful fodder. Look out for vine weevil damage to begonia tubers. The grubs can be killed by beneficial nematodes, which are watered on in late summer, or by using a systemic insecticide.

Enjoy

In early summer, rich purple is still present in the flowerheads of alliums, while gorgeous blue is possible with tall camassias, which emerge from the borders and grasslands. Later blues are rarer, but they are still possible with freesias, anemones and triteleia. The mid- to late summer range of tubers, rhizomes, bulbs and corms is dazzling. Dahlias and gladioli are available in dozens of brilliant hues, ranging from red, yellow, orange, pink and purple to white, while begonias and cannas light up the border with fiery yellows, oranges and reds. Kniphofias add another tier to the drama, and with their long tapering racemes provide a rich source of colour.

The seeds of *Fritillaria meleagris* (snake's head fritillary) will be ready for collection in midsummer. They should be sown in a propagating box.

Autumn

The autumn months bring a deluge of dry bulbs into garden centres and stores, some pre-packaged in groups of three, five and sometimes ten at a time, while others, such as the common types of daffodil, tulip and hyacinth, are sold loose so that they can be picked up in any quantity. The pre-packs can be more expensive, but the range is usually far greater. Buy early if you want to obtain special named varieties. Look out for some of your favourite colours in tulips, pick out dwarf daffodils for pots and baskets, and buy hyacinths for scent.

Bringing on

Some genera, such as calochortus and dichelostemma, are best planted in pots and kept in a frost-free potting shed, ready for transplanting or plunging into the garden the following summer.

Planting direct in borders, grass or containers

Autumn-flowering colchicums and *Lilium candidum* (Madonna lily) should be planted as soon as they are

Continue to deadhead the flowers of begonias, cannas and dahlias.

available. All the late winter- and spring-flowering varieties, including daffodils, tulips and hyacinths, should be planted direct into borders, grasslands or containers as soon as convenient, so they can form good roots in autumn and early winter. Summer-flowering lilies should also be planted now, although some will also be available in late winter.

Lifting

Tender specimens, such as begonias, dahlias, cannas and gladioli, should be lifted, dried, cleaned, labelled and stored for the winter in frost-free conditions, ready for planting the following year.

Watering

This will not be necessary for border or grass-grown plants, but take care with containers, such as hanging baskets and window boxes, which are apt to dry out quickly and may receive little rainfall.

Protection against frost

Dahlias can be left outside until blackened by the first frost, but then they should be lifted and kept frost-free or left in situ and mulched.

Deadheading

Continue to deadhead cannas, begonias and dahlias so that they still provide welcome colour for as long as the weather allows. The first frosts might vary, in some years striking in early autumn while in others it might be several weeks later.

Bulbs, such as these tulips, can be planted in formal lines using taut lengths of string as a guide. Space the tulip bulbs at 15–20cm (6–8in) intervals underneath the string.

So many different varieties of bulb are available to buy and plant now, there is bound to be something to suit everyone. Just make sure that the bulbs are plump and firm and reject any that are not perfect.

Dark-leaved cannas still make an impact in the late autumn border but they are best lifted before the first frosts.

Propagation

On replanting daffodils and tulips lifted in early summer, the main large bulb can be replanted to create a flowering clump, while smaller bulbs and corms can be planted out in rows, ready to bulk up in size for flowering in two or three years' time.

Pest watch

Earwigs, slugs and snails will still take their toll on growing plants. Look out for vine weevil damage to begonia tubers. The grubs can be killed by beneficial nematodes or by using a systemic insecticide, which is watered on in late summer. Mice and squirrels might try to dig up newly planted bulbs and corms. Be sure to firm in the soil around them.

Enjoy

This is the time to enjoy the glory of all the dahlia, begonia and canna flowers, which will bloom well until the first frosts sadly curtail the show. Late gladioli and sprays of schizostylis will also give pleasure now, as well as the glorious funnel-shaped blooms of pink or white crinums. Frilly pink nerines will come into bloom, and it is always surprising to see such vivid pink flowers at this time of year.

Much shorter specimens will also be in flower now, including the goblet shaped colchicums, either white or lilac, yellow sternbergias, and the delicate pink or white flowers of tiny autumn-flowering *Cyclamen hederifolium*.

Once autumn frosts have blackened dahlia foliage, it is time to cut down the stems and lift the tubers or mulch.

PLANT
DIRECTORIES

A directory of annuals

This directory offers a comprehensive array of annual plants – all the familiar favourites plus some rarer specimens – among which gardeners of all levels will find ample choice to help them make the most of their garden space.

The initial introduction for each entry is either for the whole genus or the main species grown. Beyond this the entry is split between more common species and cultivars and those which are less common. The advent of the internet has meant that it is often possible to obtain seed, including that of very rare plants, from around the world. Growing rarer species can be rewarding as they are often particularly beautiful. On the other hand they may be less common because they are more difficult to grow and thus create a challenge. If no temperatures are given, seed can be germinated in a cool greenhouse or even in pots left outside.

Where seed is listed as being available from seed merchants, this can be purchased directly from the merchants using their catalogues or from a store or garden centre. Some unusual varieties are available mail order only from a catalogue. Many specialist societies make seed available to their members – a good way of obtaining rarer seed. Check catalogues carefully as some seed merchants have idiosyncratic or very out-of-date ways of naming plants that may be at variance with botanical names and with those that have been used in this book.

Begonia semperflorens has long been a very popular gardener's choice and offers a wide selection of attractively coloured cultivars.

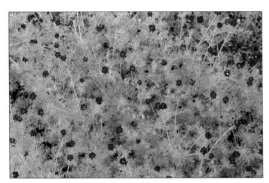

Adonis aestivalis

ADONIS
Pheasant's Eye

This is a genus containing about 20 species of annuals and perennials. Of these, only a couple of the annuals are generally grown. These are so similar that the gardener might not notice the slight botanical difference. They are thin and upright plants with feathery foliage. The flowers are bright red and cup-shaped; they look like the red buttercups to which they are related. These plants thrive in disturbed ground; they were once widespread among crops in cornfields but they are rarely seen growing wild today. They are attractive enough to be used in borders, particularly when planted in large drifts, but they are more commonly seen in beds devoted to wild flowers. They are hardy. H 45cm (18in) S 15cm (6in).

How to obtain These plants can generally only be obtained as seed. This is widely available from good seed merchants as well as from specialist societies.

Cultivation Thin the plants to about 15cm (6in) to produce a dense mass. They need a soil enriched with plenty of well-rotted organic material. It should be free draining. A position in full sun is needed. Z6.

Propagation Sow directly into the soil where the plants are to grow in either autumn or in spring. An autumn sowing produces more vigorous plants.

Uses Adonis look good in mixed beds and borders, especially in wild-flower gardens.

Adonis aestivalis

This is the most commonly seen plant. It has very finely cut leaves which set off the bright crimson flowers with a darker centre. These are produced over a very long period from midsummer to well into autumn. If you can find it there is a rare variety of *A. aestivalis* called *citrina* which has yellow flowers.

Adonis annua

This plant is very similar to the previous species but the flowers are a deeper red.

Other plants There is also a species called *A. flammea* which is worth seeking out. It is similar to the ones described above except that the flowers are larger.

AGERATUM
Floss flower

This moderately large genus contains about 40 species of perennials and shrubs as well as annuals. There is only one annual that is in general cultivation, namely *A. houstonianum*, but fortunately it has plenty of cultivars so the gardener does not lack choice. The plants are rounded and produce fluffy sprays of blue flowers. Over the years pink and white cultivars have also been introduced. Ageratum have long been used as bedding plants, and are often grown in swathes in a bed or as ribbon-like edging along a path or around beds. H and S 20–30cm (8–12in), although some cultivars reach up to 75cm (30in).

How to obtain Ageratums can be bought as seed from most seed merchants and they are available as young plants in spring from garden centres and nurseries. Plants may be sold as "Ageratum" without any cultivar being given.

Cultivation Plant out after frosts have passed in a fertile soil in full sun. Z10.

Propagation Seed can be sown under glass at 16–18°C (60–64°F) in spring. For larger plants sow in late autumn and overwinter the resulting plants in warm conditions.

Uses Ageratums make excellent bedding plants, grown in blocks or lines. They are good in window boxes and other containers. Some are good for cutting.

Ageratum houstonianum 'Bavaria'

This pretty cultivar has fluffy flower heads in blue and white. H up to 25cm (10in).

Ageratum houstonianum 'Blue Danube'

This is a short form which produces attractive pale blue flowers. H 20cm (8in).

Ageratum houstonianum 'Blue Horizon'

This is a tall variety with purple-blue clusters of flowers, which is good for cutting. H 45–60cm (18–24in) or more.

Ageratum houstonianum Hawaii Series

These short plants produce flowers either in a mixture of colours ('Hawaii Mixed', 'Hawaii Garland') or in individual colours such as 'Hawaii White'. H 15cm (6in).

Ageratum houstonianum 'Swing Pink'

This is another dwarf form, which produces pretty pink flowers. H 15cm (6in).

Ageratum houstonianum 'Purple Fields'

The flowers of this cultivar are purple. H 25cm (10in).

Ageratum houstonianum 'Red Sea'

Bright red buds open to purple-red flowers. They are good for cutting. H 45cm (18in).

Ageratum houstonianum

Agrostemma githago 'Milas'

AGROSTEMMA
Corn cockle

This is a small genus of annuals of which only a couple are generally cultivated. They grow naturally on disturbed or waste ground, and as their name implies they were once often seen growing in fields of corn.

Corn cockles are tall plants which have thin, wiry stems and open funnel-shaped flowers. These are purple with a white centre, and appear in summer. Although they work well in drifts in a mixed border they are often grown in wild-flower gardens. H 1m (3ft) in good conditions, S 30cm (12in).

How to obtain Corn cockle is usually available as seed from seed merchants or from specialist societies. Plants are rarely offered for sale, but they can occasionally be found.

Cultivation Corn cockles grow in a fertile soil in a sunny position. Plants are shown at their best when they are tightly planted together, so do not thin too vigorously. They need support in exposed positions. Z8

Propagation Sow the seed in spring where the plants are to grow. If left to set seed, corn cockles will usually self-sow.

Uses Corn cockles are best grown in either mixed borders or a wild area of the garden.

Agrostemma githago and *A. gracilis*
These species are similar to each other, and produce the purple flowers described above. The seed of *A. githago* is more common, and there are some cultivars.

Agrostemma githago 'Milas'
This is the cultivar most widely grown. It has pinker flowers than the species.

Agrostemma githago 'Milas Cerise'
This is very similar to the previous cultivar, except that the flowers are cerise.

Agrostemma githago 'Ocean Pearl'
This is a beautiful cultivar with pure white flowers. It is a must for the white garden.

ALCEA
Hollyhock

This genus produces the much-loved hollyhock. This is *A. rosea*, a perennial that is now generally grown as a biennial. Hollyhocks are very tall plants, but there are shorter cultivars that are more suitable for smaller gardens. They have one or more tall stems on which appear open funnel-shaped flowers. Some cultivars have double flowers. The flowers are produced over most of the summer and into autumn. The plants are hardy. H 2.5m (8ft).

How to obtain Hollyhocks can be purchased as seed from seed merchants or as plants from garden centres and nurseries. The plants may be sold simply as "Hollyhocks" with no colour given. The seed can be mixed or one colour. *Alcea* may be listed as its former name *Althaea*.

Cultivation Plant or thin out seedlings to intervals of 60cm (24in). They like a deep, rich soil that is well-drained. Plants may need staking in exposed areas. Hollyhocks can suffer from rust so remove them after flowering and raise new plants from seed rather than keeping old ones for subsequent years. Z4.

Propagation Sow seed where the plants are to grow. Plants left to seed will self-sow.

Uses Hollyhocks are excellent plants for either mixed or herbaceous borders.

Alcea rosea 'Black Beauty'
As its name suggests this is a black-flowered variety.

Alcea rosea 'Chater's Double'
This cultivar produces fully double flowers that look like pompoms. They come in a wide range of colours. The seed is sold as mixed or individual colours.

Alcea rosea 'Majorette Mixed'
This cultivar produces semi-double blooms in mixed pastel shades. H 1m (3ft).

Alcea rosea 'Chater's Double'

Alcea rosea 'Nigra'
This is an ancient cultivar known for at least 400 years. It carries very dark red flowers that are almost black. There is a rarer double form of the same colour, called 'Nigra Plena'.

Alcea rosea 'Peaches 'n' Dreams'
This plant produces very frilly double flowers in a soft peach-pink colour.

Alcea rosea 'Zanzibar'
Flowers in a range of pastel shades are produced on tall plants. H 2m (6ft).

Other plants *Alcea ficifolia* is another hollyhock treated as a biennial. It is similar to the above except that the leaves are more lobed. The flowers are yellow or orange, single or double. 'Antwerp Mixed' is a mix of pastel shades.

Alcea rosea

Tall annuals

Agrostemma githago 'Milas'	Helianthus annuus
Alcea rosea	Lavatera trimestris
Amaranthus caudatus	Moluccella laevis
Centaurea americana	Nicotiana affinis
Cleome spinosa	Nicotiana sylvestris
Consolida ambigua	Oenothera biennis
Cosmos	Ricinus communis
Dahlia	Tithonia rotundifolia
Datura	Zea mays
Gilia rubra	Zinnia

Amaranthus caudatus

Anchusa capensis 'Dawn Mixed'

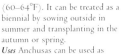

AMARANTHUS
Love-lies-bleeding

A large genus of half-hardy annuals and short-lived perennials. *A. caudatus* is of most interest to the general gardener. It has dangling flowers that look like bunches of lambs' tails or ropes, mainly in crimson or purple. They have an old-fashioned look about them and are not seen as often in gardens as they once were. They can be used in small groups in general borders or in bedding schemes. They are long flowering through summer and autumn.
How to obtain The main way to acquire these is as seed from merchants. Occasionally plants are available from garden centres.
Cultivation Plant out after the threat of frosts has passed in a soil with plenty of well-rotted organic material. It should be moisture-retentive but free-draining. Z5.
Propagation Sow the seed under glass in the spring at 16–18°C (60–64°F).
Uses These plants are best grown in general mixed borders or in bedding schemes.

Amaranthus caudatus

This, the main species grown, can reach 1.2m (4ft), but is often less. S 60cm (24in). The tassels are red or purple, although there is a cultivar 'Viridis' or 'Green Tails' with greenish flowers.

Amaranthus cruentus

Known as Prince's Feather, this plant has more upright spikes in a variety of reds and yellows.

There are a large number of cultivars available, including 'Red Cathedral' which has attractive scarlet foliage.

Amaranthus hypochondriacus

Upright spikes of flowers, mainly in shades of red. 'Green Thumb' has green flowers and 'Pygmy Torch' is a dwarf variety only 45cm (18in) high.

Amaranthus tricolor

This is Chinese spinach, grown for its decorative foliage which comes in several colours. 'Joseph's Coat' has a mixture of red, yellow, brown and green leaves, while 'Illumination' has bright pinkish-red, gold and brown leaves.

ANCHUSA
Anchusa

This is a genus of about 35 species of which a number are annuals or biennials. One in particular is of interest to the annual gardener, namely *A. capensis*. This is strictly speaking a perennial but it is usually grown as an annual. It is a clump-forming plant with long, narrow leaves that are rough with bristles, and sprays of shallow funnel-shaped flowers that flower in summer. The flowers are generally blue with a white throat although there are other cultivars with a range of colours. H up to 45cm (18in) S 20cm (8in).
How to obtain These plants are available as seed from seed merchants and specialist societies.
Cultivation Plant out or thin the young plants at 30cm (12in) intervals. Any reasonable garden soil will do but a well-draining, moisture-retentive one is preferred. Plant in full sun. Z9.
Propagation When treated as an annual, sow the seed under glass in early spring at 16–18°C

(60–64°F). It can be treated as a biennial by sowing outside in summer and transplanting in the autumn or spring.
Uses Anchusas can be used as bedding plants or grown in a mixed border.

Anchusa capensis

The species is less popular than in the past, but it is still an excellent blue-flowered plant.

Anchusa capensis 'Blue Angel'

This is an attractive cultivar which produces flowers that are bright blue in colour.

Anchusa capensis 'Blue Bird'.

Indigo-blue flowers. This is an old variety but it is probably still the most popular.

Anchusa capensis 'Dawn Mixed'

The flowers are in a mixture of colours – mainly blue with white, pink, red and purple.

Anchusa capensis 'Dwarf Mix'

These plants are smaller and more compact with blue flowers. The seed is more difficult to find.

Anchusa capensis 'Pink Bird'

As its name suggests, this cultivar has pink flowers.

ANGELICA
Angelica

This genus of about 50 species is known mainly to gardeners for the herb *A. archangelica*. However, there is a species that has only recently entered general

Anchusa capensis

Angelica gigas

cultivation that makes an excellent biennial for the border. This is *A. gigas*, a native of Japan. It has gorgeous heads of maroon flowers which are perfect for the mixed border, or for the edge of a woodland or shrub bed. It can be dramatic and eyecatching. The plants are monocarpic, that is they may grow for one, two or more years before they flower, but once they have flowered they die. Fortunately angelicas make good foliage plants so their growing time is not wasted. H 2m (6ft) S 1–1.2m (3–4ft). They are completely hardy.

How to obtain The seed is available from some seed merchants. The plants are available from nurseries and some garden centres.

Cultivation Any reasonable garden soil will do, but the richer and more moist the soil, the more splendid the plants will be. Plant out as soon as possible in either spring or autumn, in either full sun or partial shade. Z4.

Propagation Angelicas are grown from seed which is sown in autumn or spring.

Uses Angelicas look very good in borders or in woodland settings. They are excellent for wilder, more exotic plantings.

Angelica gigas

This is a truly splendid towering plant. The flowers are carried in domed heads produced on black stems above dissected, bright green leaves. The large heads are a fabulous dark crimson in colour. H 2m (6ft) S 1–1.2m (3–4ft).

Antirrhinum 'Coronette Bronze'

Other plants *Angelica archangelica* is mainly grown as a herb but it is decorative enough to deserve a place in the border, especially in a wild-flower garden. The flowers are white, and the stems and leaves dullish green. *Angelica atropurpurea* is similar to the previous plant, also having white flowers, but the stems are a contrasting purple. You will have to hunt a little further to find the seed and plants.

ANTIRRHINUM
Snapdragon

Surely all gardeners know these excellent garden plants. Quite a number of the 40 species are in cultivation but most gardeners grow just *A. majus*, which is the common snapdragon. These are bushy plants producing several spikes of curiously shaped flowers. Plants are now available in a wide range of colours and sizes. There are some forms with double flowers and others with variegated foliage. One impressive breakthrough is the trailing varieties, which look wonderful in hanging baskets. H 25–60cm (10–24in) S 45cm (18in).

How to obtain All seed merchants offer several varieties and plants can be bought from garden centres, both as colour mixtures or separate colours. The plants are available either in trays or individual pots.

Cultivation Antirrhinums will grow in any good garden soil. Plant or thin to about 45cm (18in). Z7.

Propagation Grow from seed sown under glass at 16–18°C (60–64°F) in early spring. The seed can also be sown in open ground in spring for late-flowering plants.

Uses Antirrhinums are excellent for mixed borders or for bedding. They are also very good plants for children's gardens. Some varieties are suitable for containers including hanging baskets. Taller varieties make good cut flowers

Antirrhinum majus 'Chinese Lanterns'

This is one of the new trailing forms. It produces flowers in a mixture of colours.

Antirrhinum majus Coronette Series

This attractive plant series carries flowers in a mix of colours. They are also available as individual

Antirrhinum 'Coronette White'

colours, as in the cultivars 'Coronette Bronze' and 'Coronette White'. H 60cm (24in).

Antirrhinum majus 'Floral Showers'

A dwarf collection, with plants growing up to 20cm (8in) tall.

Antirrhinum majus Mme Butterfly Series

These plants produce double flowers in a mixture of colours. H 75cm (30in).

Antirrhinum majus Rocket Series

As its name suggests, this is a very tall range. Plants reach up to 1.2m (4ft) in good conditions.

Other plants These include 'Sonnet Light Rose' and 'Black Prince'. Check seed catalogues for a better idea of the complete range.

Antirrhinum majus 'Black Prince'

Antirrhinum 'Sonnet Light Rose'

Arctotis 'Flame'

ARCTOTIS
African daisy

This is a genus of some 50 species from South Africa. There are several annual and short-lived perennials that are used as bedding plants. They are rather splendid daisies, generally having white or orange petals with a dark ring round the central black or brown disc. They are bright and gay but have the disadvantage that they shut up if the sun is not shining and generally shut half-way through the afternoon. However, the flowers of some newer cultivars stay open longer. H 60cm (24in) S 30cm (12in).
How to obtain The best way is to obtain these plants as seed since the main seed merchants sell them. They can also be bought as plants from many garden centres.

Arctotis × hybrida 'Apricot'

Cultivation A well-drained soil in full sun is essential. Plant out after frosts have passed. Z9.
Propagation Sow the seed in early spring under glass at 16–18°C (60–64°F) and prick out into individual pots.
Uses These make excellent bedding plants so long as they have plenty of sunshine. They are also good for very well-drained border, such as a gravel garden. They can be used as cut flowers.

Arctotis fastuosa
One of the easiest species to obtain. It has large 10cm (4in) flowers with orange petals and a black inner band. It provides one of the best-known cultivars, 'Zulu Prince', whose flowers have gleaming white petals with black and orange inner bands.

Arctotis Harlequin Hybrids
A mixed strain of seed with daisies in white, orange, pink, red or apricot. The Harlequin New Hybrids have the same range of colours and sometimes also have inner black bands. They also include some individual cultivars such as 'Apricot'.

Arctotis venusta
The flowers of this attractive plant are creamy-white in colour, with a blue central disc.

Other plants Arctotis hirsuta is a hairy plant, with orange, yellow or white flowers with a yellow inner band and a black central disc.

ARGEMONE
Prickly poppy

A genus of about 30 species of which there are a number of annuals in cultivation. The name prickly poppy refers to the fact that the large seed heads are covered in vicious spines, as are the leaves. Although this makes weeding and seed collecting a dangerous occupation, the flowers are absolutely delightful and so these plants are worth growing. The flowers, like many poppies, look like crumpled tissue paper. They are either glistening white or a wonderful yellow with a contrasting central boss of red stamens. The prickly leaves are an

Argemone grandiflora

attractive colour; a bluish-green with silvery markings. These are rather open, sprawling plants, so they are not suited to bedding schemes. They look good mixed with other plants in the front of a herbaceous border. Most are short-lived perennials and may last into a second year. The plants will flower all summer and continue into autumn if they are deadheaded regularly. They can reach up to 1.5m (5ft) but are usually no more than 45cm (18in) in most garden situations.
How to obtain The seed for prickly poppies can be obtained from some of the more specialized seed merchants as well as from specialist societies. The plants can occasionally be found in nurseries.
Cultivation Plant out after frosts have passed in a well-drained soil that is not too rich. Prickly poppies tolerate poor soils. Z8.
Propagation Sow seed at 16–18°C (60–64°F) under glass in the early spring.
Uses These plants are best used in a mixed border. They are excellent for gravel gardens.

Argemone mexicana

Argemone grandiflora
This has white or yellow flowers up to 10cm (4in) across. The leaves have white veining.

Argemone mexicana
This is very similar to the previous plant except that the flowers are slightly smaller and are generally yellow. There is a creamy-yellow variety *ochroleuca*, as well as the white forms 'Alba' or 'White Lustre' and a deeper, orange-yellow form 'Yellow Lustre'. These are more difficult to find than the species but they are worth looking out for.

Other plants A. pleiacantha has large white flowers up to 15cm (6in) across. Otherwise it is very similar to *A. grandiflora. A. polyanthemos* is not so prickly; the large flowers are either white or pale lilac.

ARGYRANTHEMUM
Argyranthemum

A genus of 23 species which were once classified as *Chrysanthemum* to which they have a great visual resemblance. They have daisy-like

Argemone platyceras 'Silver Charm'

Argyranthemum 'Jamaica Primrose'

Argyranthemum 'Vancouver'

flowers either with an outer ring of petals and a yellow central disc or an outer ring of petals with a similar coloured pompom of petals in the middle. The colours are white, yellow or pink. These flowers are produced over a long period, through the summer and up to the first frosts. They are tender perennials, which are usually treated as annuals. H 60–100cm (2–3ft) S 60cm (24in).

How to obtain Argyranthemums are usually purchased as plants in individual pots. They are available from garden centres and nurseries.

Cultivation Plant in a well-drained fertile soil after frosts are over. They need a sunny position. Z9.

Propagation Take basal cuttings from plants in spring or tip cuttings in summer; overwinter the resulting plants under glass.

Uses Argyranthemums are versatile plants that can be used in mixed borders, as bedding plants and in containers.

Argyranthemum **'Blizzard'**
This cultivar produces double flowers which have narrow, shaggy white petals.

Argyranthemum **'Cornish Gold'**
The flowers of this cultivar are yellow with yellow centres. H 60cm (24in).

Argyranthemum frutescens
This is one of the *Argyranthemum* species from which many of the cultivars are derived. It is also grown in its own right, and has yellow flowers.

Argyranthemum **'Jamaica Primrose'**
One of the best, with soft primrose-yellow petals and a golden central disc.

Argyranthemum **'Mary Cheek'**
Pink outer petals surround a pink pompom of petals. This is a smallish plant. H 45cm (18in).

Argyranthemum **'Mary Wootton'**
This plant is similar to the previous one but it is much larger. H 1.2m (4ft).

Argyranthemum **'Petite Pink'**
The flowers of these plants have pink outer petals and a yellow central disc. H 30cm (12in).

Argyranthemum **'Snowstorm'**
Another short plant with white outer petals and a yellow central disc. H 30cm (12in).

Argyranthemum **'Vancouver'**
This is a pink-flowered cultivar. which is similar to 'Mary Wootton'.

Other plants *Argyranthemum gracile* 'Chelsea Girl' is one of the finest cultivars to use in containers; it is often overwintered and grown as a standard. It is also used as a bedding plant. The flowers are white and the foliage is very fine and hair-like.

ATRIPLEX
Red orache

A large genus of plants that are mainly weeds or plants of no consequence. However, there is one that is important to gardeners, namely *A. hortensis*. This is often grown as a spinach substitute in the vegetable garden, but the red form 'Rubra' is widely grown as a very decorative plant. It is very tall and makes a positive statement in the border. H 1.5m (5ft) S 75cm (30in).

How to obtain Red orache is best grown from seed which is widely available. You occasionally see plants but they rarely grow to their full potential because they tend to be starved in small pots.

Cultivation Transplant any seedlings when they are very young or they will not thrive. Thin or transplant to 75cm (30in) intervals. Red oraches will grow in any garden soil but they do best in a rich, well-fed one. A sunny site is best; in shade the leaves turn green. Z6.

Propagation Sow the seed where the plants are to grow in autumn or in spring.

Uses These plants work well in mixed borders but they can also be used as a tall centrepiece in a bedding scheme.

Atriplex hortensis **'Rubra'**
This is the most commonly grown plant. Its leaves, stems and spikes of small but numerous flowers are all a deep purplish-red. This colour looks rather leaden in dull light but it turns a fabulous blood-red against a setting sun. The young leaves are a colourful addition to salads. The plant self-sows madly, so cut it down before the seed is shed. H 1.5m (5ft) S 75cm (30in).

Other plants The Plume series is a newer strain of seed that includes 'Copper Plume', which has deep red flowers, 'Gold Plume' (straw-coloured flowers), 'Green Plume' (bright green flowers) and 'Red Plume' (deep, rich red flowers and foliage). These plants are rather more difficult to track down, but they are undoubtedly worth seeking out for their decorative quality.

Atriplex hortensis 'Rubra'

Long-flowering annuals

Ageratum	Nicotiana
Argyranthemum	Pelargonium
Begonia	Petunia
Brachyscome iberidifolia	Portulaca grandiflora
Calendula officinalis	Salvia
Heliotropium arborescens	Tagetes
Impatiens	Thunbergia alata
Lobelia erinus	Tropaeolum majus
Matthiola incana	Verbena × hybrida
Mimulus	Viola × wittrockiana

Barbarea vulgaris 'Variegata'

BARBAREA
Barbarea

This is a small genus of plants, most of which are of no interest to the gardener. The exception is *B. vulgaris* which is known as winter cress and commonly grown as a salad ingredient. This is of no consequence in the flower garden but it has a variegated form 'Variegata' that is widely grown as a foliage plant. The leaves are darkish green and are splashed with golden-yellow. It is a member of the cabbage family and the flowers are the familiar four-petalled yellow ones which add little to the border and so are usually removed. It is worth leaving some on the plant, however, so that you have seed for the following year. The plants are biennial. They are tall and narrow, so quite a number of plants are needed to make an impact.
H 45cm (18in) when grown in good soil, S 20cm (8in) across.
How to obtain You can get barbareas as individual plants but this is an expensive way of buying them if you need a lot. You may have to search for seed but it is available from a number of seed merchants. Alternatively buy one plant and collect seed from it.
Cultivation Barbareas can be grown in any reasonable garden soil, and can be used either in a sunny or in a partially shaded position. Remove flowers unless seed is required. Z6.
Propagation Sow the seed in the open, as soon as possible after it has been collected.

Uses Barbareas look good in mixed borders or bedding schemes, and help brighten up darker corners.

BASSIA
Burning bush

A genus of about 25 species of perennials and annuals of which only one is grown in gardens. This is *B. scoparia* in the form *trichophylla*. It is a foliage plant that forms a bright green bush which is attractive in its own right. However, as the summer proceeds it turns a brilliant red or orange, hence its name "burning bush". The flowers are inconspicuous and of no relevance to most gardeners. Burning bushes are truly spectacular plants but while they used to be very popular but they are seen less frequently now. This is a pity since they make excellent plants for bedding as well as for filling gaps in perennial borders. Being green in the first instance they act as a foil for more brightly coloured plants. They look and feel soft.
    Plants vary in size considerably depending on soil and other conditions. They can be anything from a modest 30cm (12in) up to 1.5m (5ft) when growing well. They are conical in shape and tend not to be so wide as they are tall. S up to 45cm (18in).
How to obtain Although it is now less frequently seen than in the past, seed is still available from many merchants. It is often listed under its old name *Kochia trichopylla*. It is also worth looking out for the plants in garden centres. Z6.

Begonia semperflorens (flower detail)

Cultivation Do not plant out until after the frosts have finished, then plant in any reasonably fertile soil in a sunny position. Larger plants need shelter from winds. Z6.
Propagation Sow under glass at 16–18°C (60–64°F) in early spring. It is also possible to sow seed directly where the plants are to grow in late spring, but the resulting bushes are not very big.
Uses Excellent for borders and bedding and are especially good as central features. They can be used as specimen plants in containers.

Other plants There are no cultivars. It would be a bonus if different coloured forms were to be bred.

BEGONIA
Begonia

This is a very large genus of some 900 species of which a number are in cultivation along with a great many cultivars. The begonia

is a plant that gardeners can become very attached to, and many people collect different varieties. Here we can only scratch the surface of this fascinating group of plants, concentrating on those that are grown in the garden. (There are many more that are cultivated in greenhouses. These are in fact perennials but are treated as annuals since they are tender.) The most common garden form are the semperflorens begonias. Another group that are often seen growing outside, especially as container plants are the tuberhybrida begonias.
How to obtain The easiest way to obtain begonias is by buying plants, which are available from garden centres. Semperflorens can be bought in trays or pots and tuberhybrida in pots. Frequently they are sold as simply 'begonias' with no cultivar name given. Trays often contain plants in mixed

Bassia scoparia

Begonia semperflorens

colours, so you will need to buy plants in flower if you want particular forms. Both can also be obtained as seed. Gardeners who want to start a collection should go to specialist nurseries for a wider selection.

Cultivation Plant out after the last frosts in a good humus-rich soil which is either neutral or acid. Begonias need a lightly shaded position. Z10.

Propagation Sow seed in early spring under glass at about 20°C (68°F). Take cuttings in early summer and overwinter the young plants under warm glass.

Uses Semperflorens are superb in bedding schemes since they are usually of uniform height and so look good when planted in blocks. They are also used a lot in all forms of containers. The tuberhybrids can be used in bedding but they are shown at their best in containers.

Begonia semperflorens

These are low bushy plants with succulent stems and waxy-looking leaves and flowers. The flowers are commonly white, pink or red. They appear in early summer and continue until the first frosts. The foliage is either green or bronzy-purple. There are many cultivars to choose from. However for most garden purposes it is simply a matter of picking a colour that suits your scheme rather than seeking out any specific variety. H and S 15–45cm (6–18in).

Begonia × tuberhybrida

The tuberous begonias produce much more blowsy flowers. They are usually, but not always doubles in a wide variety of colours, often coming as picotees (edged in a different colour). These are generally too delicate for bedding, but they make good container plants. H 25–45cm (10–18in) S 30cm (12in).

BELLIS
Daisy

The humble common daisy may be the bane of gardeners' lawns but it is nevertheless a very pretty flower and there are some excellent varieties for use in borders and bedding. To many modern gardeners they look old-fashioned and have a quality reminiscent of cottage gardens. As a result, they are not seen quite so much nowadays as previously. There are about 15 species but it is the only the common daisy, *B. perennis*, that is of interest. It has

Bellis perennis 'Rogli Rose'

given rise to a large number of garden varieties. The attraction of many of these is that their flowers are double. They are either white or shades of pink, sometimes both. Strictly speaking, these plants are perennials but they are usually treated as annuals because flower quality reduces in later years. H and S 20cm (8in).

How to obtain Daisies can be obtained in single pots and occasionally in trays. Some varieties are also available as seed.

Cultivation Daisies grow in any reasonable garden soil. They prefer a sunny position, but they will tolerate a little shade. Z4.

Propagation Divide existing plants in spring. Sow seed in the open ground in summer and transplant in the autumn or spring. They can also be sown in early spring under cool glass.

Uses Use in bedding schemes, along paths or border edges, or as clumps in a mixed border.

Bellis perennis

The common daisy is usually considered a weed but it can look attractive when grown in a wild meadow or lawn. Its cultivars come in white, pink or red. They include the Pomponette Series, which have large double heads; the Rogli Series, which are semi-doubles; and the Tasso Series, which have some of the biggest heads. 'Rose Carpet' has double flowers and 'Habanera' is a double with long petals.

Annuals that can be used as cut flowers

Agrostemma githago	Gaillardia pulchella
Alcea rosea	Gypsophila elegans
Amaranthus caudatus	Helianthus annuus
Antirrhinum majus	Helipterum roseum
Brachyscome iberidifolia	Hesperis
Calendula officinalis	Lathyrus odoratus
Callistephus chinensis	Limonium sinuatum
Campanula medium	Matthiola
Celosia plumosa	Moluccella laevis
Centaurea cyanus	Nigella damascena
Chrysanthemum	Reseda odorata
Clarkia elegans	Rudbeckia hirta
Consolida ambigua	Salpiglossis
Coreopsis	Scabiosa atropurpurea
Cosmos	Tagetes erecta
Dahlia	Tagetes patula
Dianthus barbatus	Tithonia rotundifolia
Digitalis purpurea	Xeranthemum annuum
Erysimum cheiri	Zinnia elegans

Bellis perennis 'Pomponette'

Beta vulgaris subsp. cicla 'Charlotte'

BETA
Beet

This is a small genus of plants that is best known for its vegetables, particularly beetroot. Some of the plants are decorative, including another vegetable, Swiss chard or ruby chard (*B. vulgaris* subsp. *cicla*), which is often grown as a garden plant. With Swiss Chard, it is not the flower that is important but the foliage and the stems. There is also the advantage that they can be eaten.
How to obtain These plants can only be obtained as seed, but nearly all merchants carry them and a number of different varieties are available.
Cultivation Beets will grow in poor soil but the more humus-rich the soil, the better. Z5.

Beta vulgaris subsp. cicla (stems)

Beta vulgaris subsp. cicla (leaves)

Propagation Sow seed where plants are to grow in early spring, or sow in late summer for winter effects.
Uses These plants are excellent in bedding schemes especially exotic-looking ones. Another perfect use for them is in potagers or decorative vegetable gardens. They look best when they are sited against the sun.

Beta vulgaris subsp. cicla
This is a biennial but it is only kept for the first year since it grows taller and goes to seed in the second. This can be quite dramatic but is difficult to mix in with other plants. There are a number of cultivars. The leaves vary from green to dark purple or red. The stems include shades of yellow, orange, red and purple, as well as green. H 45 cm (18in).

Beta vulgaris subsp. cicla 'Bright Lights'
The stems form a rainbow of different colours, while the foliage is dark green or bronze.

Beta vulgaris subsp. cicla 'Bright Yellow'
This plant produces golden-yellow stems and green leaves which have golden-yellow veins.

Beta vulgaris subsp. cicla 'Bull's Blood'
The foliage of this cultivar is an attractive dark red.

Beta vulgaris subsp. cicla 'Charlotte'
The red stems and red-tinged leaves of this plant have an attractively wrinkled texture.

Beta vulgaris subsp. cicla 'MacGregor's Favourite'
This wonderful plant is prized for its blood-red foliage.

Bidens ferulifolia 'Golden Goddess'

BIDENS
Tickseed

This is a large genus of plants that is closely related to *Cosmos*. The main annual that interests gardeners is *B. ferulifolia* and in it you can see this affinity to cosmos. The golden-yellow flowers are daisy-like with five broad outer petals and a bronze central disc. The leaves are deeply divided and fernlike, making them very decorative. Bidens stems are thin and wiry and have a sprawling habit which makes it perfect for containers. H 30cm (12in) S 60cm (24in).
How to obtain Bidens can be purchased either as seed or as bedding plants from garden centres and nurseries.
Cultivation Any reasonable garden soil will do for bedding plants. For containers a general potting or container compost (soil mix) will suffice. A sunny position is preferred. Z8.
Propagation This plant is really a perennial and it can be kept from one year to the next by taking cuttings and overwintering the young plants. However, it is more

convenient to grow new plants from seed sown in early spring under glass.
Uses Bidens can be used in the open garden, either as bedding or in mixed borders. However, their sprawling habit means that they are best employed in containers, especially hanging baskets.

Bidens ferulifolia
This species is mainly grown in its own right. The only commonly available cultivar is 'Golden Goddess' which is not greatly different from the species except that the flowers are a bit bigger.

Other plants There are one or two other species that can be found occasionally. The naming in catalogues varies but the plants are usually sound. *B. humilis* (strictly speaking, *B. triplinervia* var. *macrantha*) is sometimes seen in the form 'Golden Eye'. This is a sprawling, almost prostrate plant that is excellent for hanging baskets. It is similar in appearance to *B. ferulifolia. B. aurea* 'Bit-of-Sunshine' is also similar.

BORAGO
Borago

A small genus of plants of which only one annual, *B. officinalis*, is commonly grown. One of the perennials, *B. pygmaea*, would make an interesting plant for hanging baskets. *B. officinalis* is often grown as a herb, with the flowers being used as decoration in Pimm's cocktails. It is also now being widely used in the drugs industry

Bidens ferulifolia

and you can come across fields coloured blue with it. It is of great interest in the garden since it has a long season, with a succession of opening flowers. H 60cm (24in) S 45cm (18in).

How to obtain It is normal to buy borage as seed, which is readily available and easy to grow. You occasionally see plants in pots for sale, but they usually give poor results since borage does not do well in small containers.

Cultivation This plant will grow in most garden conditions. It prefers a sunny spot but will tolerate partial shade. Z7.

Propagation Seed can be sown in pots but it is easier to sow it outdoors in early spring where the plants are to grow. Thin them out to 45cm (18in) intervals. Borage self-sows so once you have it you usually have new plants each year.

Uses Borage makes an attractive addition to herb gardens but it is also very good in mixed borders where it can be used to fill gaps left by spring plants that have faded. It looks pretty in a wild-flower garden.

Borago officinalis

This is a sprawling plant with rough leaves and stems. It produces bright blue flowers that have white centres. They are produced continuously through the summer and into autumn. There is a form *alba* which has white flowers that look very good against the greyish-green stems and leaves. It is perfect for a white colour scheme.

Borago officinalis

Brachyscome iberidifolia

Borago pygmaea

This is a short-lived perennial which is normally grown as a border plant. However, it has a sprawling nature which might make it worth trying as a biennial in hanging baskets. It has small sky-blue flowers.

BRACHYSCOME
Swan river daisy

This is a large genus of some 70 annual and perennial species which produce daisy-like flowers. Only one of them, *B. iberidifolia*, is widely grown although a few others are occasionally seen. In recent times *B. iberidifolia* is has become one of the most popular annuals, partly because of its looks and partly because of its versatility: it can be used very

effectively in containers as well as making a good bedding plant. The flowers are mainly purple or blue, but some of the cultivars come in different colours including pink and white. H and S 45cm (18in) in good conditions, but most plants are smaller, especially when grown in containers.

How to obtain The best choice of plants comes from growing them from seed since all seed merchants carry at least one version of this. Brachyscomes are also widely available as plants but the choice of flower colour will be restricted, usually to blue. Check plants in flower if you want specific colours since plants are often labelled only as "Brachyscome", sometimes spelt "Brachycome".

Cultivation Plant out after frosts have passed. Any reasonable garden soil will do so long as it is free-draining. Z8.

Propagation Sow seed under glass at 16–18°C (60–64°F) in early spring under glass. In warmer areas the plant self-sows.

Uses Brachyscome is excellent in containers. It can also be used as a bedding plant.

Brachyscome iberidifolia

The main plants have blue or blue-purple outer petals and a yellow central disc. The daisy-like flowers are small, about 2cm (½in) wide, but are produced in profusion over a long period. The foliage is deeply cut and fernlike.

There are a number of cultivars. In 'Blue Star' the outer petals are rolled back giving the flower a star-like quality. 'Brachy Blue' is a more compact and upright plant. There are several strains with blue, violet, white and pink flowers including Bravo Series and Splendour Series.

Annuals for infilling parterres

Ageratum	Matthiola incana
Antirrhinum	Myosotis
Begonia semperflorens	Pelargonium
Bellis	Plectranthus
Erysimum	Primula
Felicia	Salvia splendens
Helichrysum petiolare	Salvia patens
Heliotropium	Tagetes
Impatiens	Verbena × hybrida
Lobelia erinus	Viola × wittrockiana

An impressive display of ornamental cabbages *(Brassica oleracea)*.

shades of green. The leaves are often fringed.

How to obtain Ornamental cabbages are widely available as seed. They can also be bought as plants in pots. However, if these plants have been in their pots for too long they will make very unsatisfactory plants when planted out.

Cultivation Any reasonable garden soil will suffice. A sunny position is best. Z7.

Propagation Sow seed in spring where the plants are to grow, or sow in a row and transplant when large enough. Brassica seed can also be sown under glass in spring and planted out as soon as possible. Do not keep them in small containers for long.

Uses These plants can be used for winter-bedding schemes when there are few other colourful plants to call on. They are also good in winter containers. Ornamental cabbages can be mixed with edible cabbages in potagers for extra colour. They look particularly effective when partially covered with snow.

Common plants Seed often comes in mixed packets, labelled 'ornamental cabbages' or 'decorative kale', (sometimes 'flowering cabbage', although the plants are on the compost heap before they flower). Common mixes include 'Northern Lights Mixed', Osaka Series, or 'Kale Sparrow Mix' but many seed merchants offer individual colours by mail order.

Other plants In potagers many of the edible brassicas can look very effective. Red cabbages or curly kale for example. Even cauliflowers (including purple ones) and romanescos are suitable.

BRIZA
Quaking grass
Briza is a genus of around a dozen annual and grasses. Perhaps the best known is *B. media* which is grown as a perennial (see page 344). However, there are also a couple of annuals which are widely grown. They are called quaking grasses because they have masses of hanging flower heads that look like lockets and which tremble at the slightest hint of a breeze. These are a straw colour; unfortunately, they do not come in the wide range of bright colours that you see in the florists since those are dyed.

How to obtain Quaking grasses are most commonly available as seed but you will occasionally find plants on sale.

Cultivation Any reasonable garden soil will do so long as it is well-drained. A sunny position is required. Z5.

Propagation Sow the seed where the plants are to grow either in the autumn or in the early spring.

Uses These are mainly used in borders where they mix well with other plants. They can be used to make a delicate edging to a path or border, or in containers. The heads are very good for cutting and drying.

BRASSICA
Ornamental cabbage
This genus is made up of about 30 species, the majority of which are of more interest to the vegetable gardener since they include cabbages, broccolis, Brussels sprouts and cauliflowers, among others. These all belong to the species *B. oleracea*. One might think that there is not much potential here for the flower garden, but in fact there are a number of decorative cabbages and kales that are well worth growing for some winter interest. The leaves come in a wide range of colours including white, cream, pink and purple as well as various

Brassica oleracea (purple-leaved)

Brassica oleracea (green-leaved)

Briza minor

Briza maxima
Sold as the species only since there are no cultivars available. This is the taller of the two annuals. The loose, dangling flower heads are pale green at first, changing to a light straw colour. They are tinged purple. H 60cm (24in) S 25cm (10in).

Briza minor
This is similar to the previous except that the flower spikelets are smaller. H 45cm (18in) S 25cm (10in).

CALCEOLARIA
Slipper flower
A large genus of some 300 species of which there are only a couple of species and a number of cultivars that are of interest to the annual gardener. Their beauty lies in their curious flowers. The lower part is an inflated pouch (giving the plant another of its names – pouch flower) which gives the flower the appearance of a slipper. In the annual varieties the flowers are carried in dense heads, in shades of yellow, gold, orange or red and frequently spotted with red. The bold colours make them ideal for bedding schemes or for bright container arrangements.
How to obtain Slipper flowers can be purchased as either plants in individual pots or as seed. As usual, seed offers a bigger range.
Cultivation Grow in a humus-rich soil that is moisture-retentive but not waterlogged. It should be acid

Calceolaria 'Kentish Hero'

rather than alkaline. Although slipper flowers will grow in sun if the soil is moist enough, they are happiest in light shade. Plant out after frosts have passed. Z9.
Propagation Sow the seed in early spring at 16–18°C (60–64°F) under glass and prick out into individual pots.
Uses These plants are good in containers or bedding, especially in shady sites where bright colours are required. Most make excellent greenhouse plants.

Calceolaria **Herbeohybrida** **Group**
This is the main group of hybrids. The flowers come in yellow, orange or red and often have spotted lips. H 20–45cm (8–18in). S up to 30cm (12in).
There are a number of strains with mixed colours including the Anytime Series, 'Bright Bikinis', the Confetti hybrids and the Pocket hybrids. There are also single-coloured varieties including 'Goldcrest' and 'Gold Fever', both with yellow flowers. These plants can be used as greenhouse annuals; in warmer areas they make good bedding and container plants.

Calceolaria integrifolia
These are shrubby perennials, but gardeners normally grow them as annual plants. As perennials they can grow to heights of up to 1.2m (4ft) but as annuals they are more likely to be in the 25–30cm (10–12in) range and about the same across. They produce yellow flowers. The Fructiohybrida Group can be purchased as a mixture or as individual varieties including

Calendula officinalis

'Goldcut', 'Golden Bunch', 'Kentish Hero', 'Midas', 'Sunset' and 'Sunshine'.

CALENDULA
Pot marigolds
There are about 20 species of pot marigolds, but only the annual *C. officinalis* is widely grown. It is commonly called a "pot" marigold because it was once widely used as a herb. Few gardeners use it as such now, although it is still often grown decoratively in herb gardens. At its simplest the flower is a daisy with orange outer petals and an orange or dark central disc. However, there are a number of forms which have semi-double and double flowers. There are also yellow versions. The flowers are up to 10cm (4in) across.
The pot marigold is a useful plant for the garden and it has a certain sturdy quality; it is not a delicate, airy plant. H 75cm (30in) S 45cm (18in). However, its stems can be rather floppy so the real height is often much less.

How to obtain Pot marigolds are best grown from seed, which is readily available. Occasionally plants for sale can be found in garden centres. The plants will self-sow. However they generally revert to the type rather than the particular cultivar planted.
Cultivation Any reasonable garden soil will be sufficient, and although pot marigolds will grow in shade, a sunny position is to be preferred. Z6.
Propagation Seed can be sown where the plants are to be grown, either in autumn or in early spring. Thin plants to intervals of 30–45cm (12–18in).
Uses Pot marigolds are best used as plants for mixed borders, although some of the more compact forms can be used in bedding schemes as well as in containers. They work particularly well in hot-coloured schemes. The flowers are good for cutting.

Calendula officinalis
The species has orange daisies but there are plenty of varieties, such as 'Lemon Queen' which produce yellow ones. The species is grown in its own right but the cultivar 'Radio' is more typical of the garden plant. It has semi-double flowers in which all the petals are orange with no central disc. There are several series including the Kablouna Series, which is tall with double flowers, and the Pacific Beauty Series. Both are mixtures of yellow, gold or orange. Single-coloured cultivars include 'Golden Princess', with golden petals and a black central disc.

Annuals for drying

Amaranthus caudatus	Helichrysum bracteatum
Atriplex hortensis	Hordeum jubatum
Briza	Limonium sinuatum
Centaurea cyanus	Lunaria annua
Centaurea moschata	Moluccella laevis
Clarkia	Nicandra physalodes
Consolida	Nigella damascena
Eryngium giganteum	Onopordum acanthium
Gomphrena globosa	Salvia hormium
Gypsophila elegans	Xeranthemum annuum

Callistephus chinensis Milady Series

Campanula medium

CALLISTEPHUS
Chinese aster

This is a single genus species with *C. chinensis* providing a wide range of flowers. It was once much more widely grown than it is now and used to be frequently seen as a cut flower. It is similar to the other asters but the flowers are much bigger, up to 12cm (4½in) or more across. They are either singles or doubles, and come in a wide range of whites, pinks, blues and purples. The singles have a yellow central disc, and they all have a distinctive fragrance. These are bushy, upright plants. H and S 45cm (18in).

How to obtain Chinese asters are more readily obtained as seed but you can still buy plants at some garden centres and nurseries.

Cultivation Chinese asters like a moisture-retentive soil and a sunny position. Z8.

Propagation They can either be sown under glass in early spring at 16–18°C (60–64°F) or in the open ground where the plants are to grow in mid-spring, but these will be later flowering.

Uses They make good bedding plants and can also be grown in mixed borders. Plant in rows in the vegetable garden or an out-of-the-way spot for cutting.

Callistephus chinensis

There is only the one species, but it does have a number of readily available cultivars. The flowers come in the wide range of colours described above, and also in a series of forms. They include the Comet Series, which are compact doubles in a variety of colours, the Giant Singles, 'Craw Krallenaster', which produces flowers with masses of thin petals and the Ostrich Plume Series, which have feathery petals. Others include the dwarf Pinocchio Series, the fine Milady Series, whose flowers have incurving petals, 'Starlight Mix' and the tall Pommax series.

CAMPANULA
Bellflowers

A large genus of more than 300 species of which most are perennials (see pages 346–7) but a number are biennials and annuals. As their name suggests they have bell-shaped flowers, although in the annuals these are often shallow and in some cases look more like saucers than bells. Bellflowers in the wild are mainly blue and occasionally white; in cultivation the annuals tend to have a wider range of colour including pink. The flowers also come as semi-doubles and doubles. They tend to be tallish plants best used in mixed borders rather than low bedding schemes.

How to obtain The best range of plants can be had by buying seed, but there are also plants available from many garden centres and nurseries. Rarer annual seed can be obtained from specialist societies.

Cultivation Any reasonable garden soil will be sufficient so long as it is free-draining. This plant needs sun or light shade. Z6–8.

Propagation Sow seed in early spring under glass. Some can be sown in the open soil where the plants are to grow.

Uses Best used in a mixed border, but some bellflowers can be used in taller bedding schemes.

Campanula incurva

This is a biennial which has low spreading stems and inflated pale blue flowers. H 30cm (12in) S 45cm (18in).

Campanula medium

Canterbury bells are very popular biennial bellflowers. They are available in white, blue or pink and come as singles or the cup-and-saucer doubles. H 60cm (24in) S 30cm (12in). Cultivars include the shorter 'Bells of Holland' and 'Chelsea Pink', with deep pink flowers.

Campanula pyramidalis

A biennial that if grown well produces stems up to 1.5m (5ft) tall, which are covered in blue or white flowers. It is good for growing in pots. S 30cm (12in).

Other plants There are a number of rarer annuals that are worth growing. *C. lusitanica* and *C. patula* form a tangle of thin wiry stems, covered with purple flowers with white centres over a long period. *C. ramosissima* is similar but has thicker stems. *C. thyrsoides* is an upright plant with, unusually, yellow flowers. All these and

Callistephus chinensis 'Ostrich Plume'

Callistephus chinensis 'Starlight Rose'

Campanula pyramidalis

Canna 'Oiseau de Feu'

Canna 'Wyoming'

Canna 'Roi Humbert'

several more attractive plants can be grown in mixed borders or in the rock garden.

CANNA
Indian shot plant

With the growing interest in exotic gardens, cannas have become very popular plants. This is a genus of about 50 species of perennial plants but because they are tender they are treated as annuals. They are dug up every autumn and stored, much in the same way as dahlias are. They are tall plants with attractive large flowers and luscious foliage. The former are carried in spikes and come in bright oranges, reds and yellows, and the latter is usually glossy and sometimes purple or variegated. H 2–3m (6–10ft) S 50cm (20in).

How to obtain Cannas are normally bought as plants or as rhizomes. Seed is available but is generally restricted to mixtures.

Cultivation Plant in a moisture-retentive rich soil in a sunny position. Do not allow them to dry out completely, and lift and store in dry peat substitute after the first frost. Z8.

Propagation Seed can be sown in early spring under glass at 21°C (70°F) after soaking in water. In spring the stored rhizomes can be cut into sections, each with a growing eye, and planted in pots in a warm greenhouse.

Uses Use cannas in exotic bedding schemes or mixed borders where a splash of colour is required.

Canna 'Black Knight'
This eye-catching plant produces a bold display of dark red flowers. H 2m (6ft).

Canna 'Endeavour'
Scarlet flowers are carried on stately plants that reach up to 2.2m (7ft) in height.

Canna indica
This canna has orange or bright red flowers. The leaves are dark green and are often tinged with bronze. There is also an attractive cultivar 'Purpurea', which has purple foliage. H 2m (6ft).

Canna iridiflora
Deep pink flowers are carried on plants that can reach up to 3m (10ft), but are usually less.

Canna 'Striata'

Canna 'Lucifer'
A shorter plant. Spikes of red blooms, touched with yellow. H 60cm (24in).

Canna 'Oiseau de Feu'
This plant has scarlet flowers and dark green leaves. H 1m (3ft).

Canna 'Picasso'
This cultivar has yellow flowers, spotted with red.

Canna 'Roi Humbert'
A dazzling display of orange-red flowers is set against purple foliage. H up to 1.5m (5ft).

Canna 'Striata'
The flowers of this canna are orange and the leaves – pale green with pronounced yellow stripes – set off the orange beautifully. H 1.5m (5ft).

Canna 'Wyoming'
Excellent plants that have purple foliage with darker veins and orange flowers. H up to 2m (6ft).

CELOSIA
Cockscomb

This genus consists of 50 species but the varieties of one species, *C. argentea*, are of most interest. The flowers are so startling that they seem almost artificial in their colouring. There are two types. The commonest (plumosa group) produces upright feathery flowering spikes that look a bit like flames. They come in a variety of reds, oranges, yellows and pinks. The other type (cristata group) produce flat, slightly domed heads with the flowers arranged in curious squiggles, again in bright colours. They can be difficult to place with other plants, but are superb in bedding schemes. H 60cm (24in) S 45cm (18in).

How to obtain Celosias are not so popular as they once were but you can still find plants in some garden centres. There is a good range of seed available.

Cultivation Plant out after the danger of frosts has passed in rich, moisture-retentive soil. A sunny position is required. Z9.

Propagation Sow the seed under glass at 16–18°C (60–64°F) in early spring.

Uses Their main use is as bedding plants in an exotic scheme, but they are also excellent for extra colourful containers.

Celosia argentea 'Apricot Brandy'
This plumosa cultivar has bright orange upright flower heads.

Celosia argentea Century Series
One of the most popular plumosa cultivars, with flowers in a mixture of bright colours.

Celosia argentea 'Fairy Fountains'
The flowers of this plumosa cultivar are less bright and consist of pastel coloured spires.

Celosia argentea 'Freshlock Red'
A plumosa celosia which produces bright red plumes.

Celosia argentea Kurume Series
These are cristata celosia in mixture of bright colours, including some bicolours.

C. argentea plumosa 'Freshlock Red'

Centaurea cyanus

CENTAUREA
Cornflowers

The cornflowers, or knapweeds as they are also known, form a large genus of some 450 species. Many are perennials that are widely grown in our gardens (see page 348). There are also a number of annuals, of which the best known is the common cornflower, *C. cyanus*. These were originally weeds of cornfields, hence the name, and other disturbed ground. They can be grown in borders but still look best when used in a wild-flower garden. They have flattish, circular heads of blue or other coloured flowers Other annual centaureas are quite similar in appearance but are not so commonly seen. H 75cm (30in) S 20cm (8in).

How to obtain The commonest way to buy these is as seed. The rarer plants need a lot more searching for but they are available from specialist catalogues and societies.
Cultivation Sow in any reasonable garden soil so long as it is free-draining. Full sun is needed. Z6.
Propagation Sow seed where the plants are to flower, in autumn for early flowering or in spring. Thin to 20cm (8in) intervals.
Uses Grow in drifts in mixed borders or as bedding plants. The blue varieties are excellent for wild-flower gardens. Dwarf forms can be used in containers.

Centaurea cyanus

This is the common cornflower. Its flowers are blue, often piercing blue. There is also a wide choice of cultivars which offer a range of flower colours from soft pinks and whites to a very dark purple that is almost black. The cultivated forms usually have a lot

more petals, making them almost double. There are also shorter forms, such as the dwarf 'Blue Baby'. 'Black Ball' is very dark purple. In 'Frosty Mixed' the petals have a white edge. Florence Series is a shorter form, and white 'Polka Dot Mixed' is another dwarf form.

Other plants C. americana is similar to the cornflower except that the petals are much more finely cut, giving the flower a very delicate appearance. The flowers are generally white and there are several cultivars. It is not so easy to find but worth the search.

CERINTHE
Cerinthe

This genus of about ten species has been in cultivation for a long time, but it has just been rediscovered and made popular by the seed companies. *C. major* is the particular species that has brought about this popularity. It is a biennial that is grown as much for its foliage as for its flowers. The blue and purple blooms are contained in a spiral, similar to that of the forget-me-not except that the flowers are partially obscured by their sheaths. The plants are quite striking and make excellent displays grown by themselves or mixed with other plants. H 60cm (24in) S 30cm (12in).

How to obtain The best way to obtain these plants is to buy seed from merchants. You can buy

Cerinthe major

plants but they are not very satisfactory as they tend to grow spindly. Once you have planted cerinthes, they will often self-sow.
Cultivation Any reasonable garden soil so long as it is free-draining. A sunny position is required. Z5.
Propagation Sow seed in autumn or spring where the plants are to flower or in pots under cool glass. Prick them out but do not leave them in small pots too long.
Uses Cerinthes can be used in a mixed border or as bedding. They are excellent for gravel gardens and can be used in containers.

Cerinthe major

This is the main species grown. It has green leaves that are often white spotted, especially when young. The form 'Purpurascens' has much bluer leaves and is the form mostly grown. The partially obscured flowers are purple.

Cerinthe major 'Kiwi Blue'

There are some new varieties appearing, such as 'Kiwi Blue', but they are not much different.

Other plants Cerinthe minor is much rarer but it makes an excellent foliage plant since its leaves are white spotted. The flowers are small and yellow. It appears as *C. minor aurea* 'Bouquet Gold' in some catalogues.

CHRYSANTHEMUM
Chrysanthemum

There can be few gardeners who do not know chrysanthemums. As well as the well-known cultivars there are 20 species, including annuals and perennials (see page 349). We do grow some annuals in our gardens but the main form – florists' chrysanthemum – is a perennial. However, because of its tender nature we treat it as an annual and replant it each year. Florists' chrysanthemums are now highly developed: there are ten basic types, each having many cultivars. They are grown as

Cerinthe major set off against a wall beautifully.

Chrysanthemum 'Southway Swan'

Chrysanthemum 'Curtain Call'

Chrysanthemum 'Glamour'

Chrysanthemum 'Primrose Allouise'

Chrysanthemum segetum 'Prado'

border or decorative plants, but the majority are cultivated either for cutting or for exhibition. Many gardeners become hooked on them and often turn over a large part of their garden to growing them. The annual chrysanthemums are grown more for their effect in the garden. With such diversity, this is a genus well worth getting to know.

How to obtain Florists' chrysanthemums are sold as small plants in garden centres and nurseries. There are several mail-order nurseries that specialize in them. There was a short period a few years ago when they were classified as *Dendranthema*. Although they are now called *Chrysanthemum* again, some catalogues may still list them under their former name. Other chrysanthemums are usually sold as seed and they can be found in most seed merchants' catalogues.

Cultivation Plant out chrysanthemums once the threat of frost has passed. They need a soil that has been enriched with plenty of well-rotted organic material. The

soil should be moist but free-draining. A sunny position is needed. Z: see individual types.

Propagation Propagate florists' chrysanthemums from cuttings taken from the newly emerging basal growth on plants that have been overwintered. Other types are grown from seed sown in early spring at 13–16°C (55–60°F) under glass. It can also be sown where the plants are to grow, but this will make flowering later.

Uses Florists' chrysanthemums, can be grown in mixed borders, but they are more often grown in rows for cutting or for exhibition purposes. They are also good plants for containers. Other chrysanthemums can be used in mixed borders or as bedding. Corn marigolds (*C. segetum*) are excellent plants for the wild-flower garden.

Florists' chrysanthemums

There are thousands of these to choose from and it is best to get catalogues from the specialist

Chrysanthemum 'George Griffiths'

nurseries to see the range available. The ten basic types have flowers that vary from singles to doubles. There are also "incurved" chrysanthemums, which have a ball of upward curving petals, and "reflexed" ones, which have petals that curve downwards. There is a wide range of colours including white, yellows, oranges, red, pinks and purples. H 1.5m (5ft) S 75cm (30in). Z4.

Chrysanthemum carinatum

These plants have single, daisy-like flowers. The outer petals come in a range of colours from white to yellow, and orange to red. There is often an inner ring of colour at the base of the petals and a central disc of brown. 'Court Jesters' is a good mixture. There are some double forms. H 60cm (24in) S 30cm (12in). Z7.

Chrysanthemum coronarium

These are bushy plants which produce single daisy-like flowers. They have yellow outer petals and yellow central discs. The green foliage is very finely cut and fern-like in appearance. These chrysanthemums look good in wild-flower meadows. H 75cm (30in) S 45cm (18in). Z7.

Chrysanthemum segetum

Corn marigolds have simple daisy-like flowers with golden outer petals and a golden central disc. They are very beautiful when seen *en masse*. Some cultivars, such as 'Prado', have extra-large flowers and a dark disc. 'Eastern Star' has paler yellow petals and a dark central disc. Excellent for wild-flower gardens. H 60cm (24in) S 30cm (12in). Z8.

Chrysanthemum tenuiloba

A plant with extremely finely cut foliage and yellow outer petals and discs. This is a sprawling plant that produces a mass of foliage speckled with yellow. It has a cultivar 'Golden Fleck'. H 30cm (12in).

Chrysanthemum 'Debonair'

Chrysanthemum 'Taffy'

Chrysanthemum carinatum

Chrysanthemum tenuiloba

Cladanthus arabicus 'Criss-Cross'

CLADANTHUS
Palm Springs daisy

This is a small genus of daisy-like flowers of which only one, *C. arabicus*, is grown. It is not often seen and yet it is excellent for hanging baskets and other containers. Fortunately it is being offered by an increasing number of seed merchants and it is worth seeking out seed.

The light green leaves have very thin leaflets and create a tangled nest for the flowers. Both the leaves and the flowers are fragrant. The flowers are daisies with yellow outer petals and a yellow central disc. They nestle right down in the foliage, a characteristic that distinguishes this plant from the annual chrysanthemums it resembles in other respects. Another distinctive feature is that from just beneath each flower emerges a few more stems, each in turn carrying more flowers so the plant gets bigger and bigger. H up to 45cm (18in) or more, S 40cm (16in).
How to obtain This plant is mainly grown from seed, which is distributed by an increasing number of seed merchants. Occasionally you will see plants for sale in some garden centres.
Cultivation Any reasonable garden soil will be sufficient, so long as it is free-draining. Centaureas need a sunny position. Z7.
Propagation Seed should be sown in early spring under glass at 13–16°C (55–60°F). It can be sown later where the plants are to grow, but flowering will be later.

Uses They work well in window boxes, hanging baskets or other containers, or they can be used in bedding schemes.

Cladanthus arabicus
This is the only species in general cultivation. It is sold both as the species, described above, and as the cultivars 'Criss-Cross' and 'Golden Crown'. These are similar to the species but produce slightly larger flowers.

CLARKIA
Clarkia

This is a medium-sized genus of 36 species of which several are grown in our gardens as annuals. They include a number of plants that were previously classified as *Godetia* and under which name many gardeners still know them.

They are a mixed bunch with some having large single or double flowers, while others are quite small but are carried in sufficient quantities to make the plants attractive. Their basic form is funnel-shaped. The predominant colour is pink although some are dark enough to be called red or purple. Many are tinged with lighter or darker colour. Clarkias produce lots of flowers over a long period, so they are good for bedding or for use in containers. H 45cm (18in) S 30cm (12in).
How to obtain Clarkias are widely available as seed although many catalogues still list some species as *Godetia*. Most garden centres also sell plants in individual pots.
Cultivation Clarkias will grow in any reasonable garden soil, but it must not be too rich and it must be free-draining. These plants grow best in a sunny position but they will also tolerate a little light shade. Z7.
Propagation Seed can be sown in early spring where the plants are to grow. For earlier flowering, the seed can either be sown in the open in autumn or under glass in early spring at a temperature of 13–16°C (55–60°F).
Uses They make excellent bedding plants especially when they are planted in blocks or drifts. They can also be used in containers such as pots or tubs.

Clarkia 'Blood Red'

Clarkia amoena
This is the satin flower, which is often listed as *Godetia amoena*. The upward-facing flowers are quite large, up to 5cm (2in) across. They are single or double, and come in various shades of soft pink. There are a number of cultivars including the Grace Series and Satin Series (dwarf), both of which have mixed shades. 'Rembrandt' is tall with rose and white flowers, 'Sybil Sherwood' has salmon-pink flowers, and 'Memoria' has pure white ones. 'Furora' has bright red blooms, and 'Blood Red' has blood-red flowers with pale centres.

Clarkia bottae
This pretty plant is not as brash as the previous species. It has simple cup-like flowers in pink

with a pale centre. It is often listed as *Godetia bottae*. There are also several cultivars.

Clarkia breweri (C. concinna)
The flowers are wide, with thin, deeply cut petals in shades of pink. The best known cultivar is 'Pink Ribbons'.

CLEOME
Spider flower

A surprising large genus with 150 species. Only one of them, *C. hassleriana*, is grown to any extent in our gardens, although with a bit of searching the enthusiast will discover several others in this intriguing genus. The flowers are carried in rounded spikes at the top of tall stems. The heads are quite unlike those of any other plant: the

Cleome hassleriana 'Helen Campbell'

Cleome hassleriana 'Pink Queen'

spikes are quite loose and open and below them are the seed pots of flowers that have already faded. They are carried on very thin stems, giving the plant its characteristic "spider" look. The flowers are scented and they come in pink, white or mauve. The heads are usually slightly darker in colour towards the top where the buds have yet to open. The foliage is a bit like that of the lupin. H 1.5m (5ft) S 45cm (18in).
How to obtain Cleomes can be bought as plants. However, they do not like to remain in pots too long so it is best to obtain them as seed, of which there is usually a greater range available.
Cultivation Plant out after the danger of frosts has passed. Cleomes need a fairly rich soil that is very free-draining in full sun. They can also be grown under glass for cutting. Z10.
Propagation Sow in early spring under glass at a temperature of 18°C (64°F).

Uses These plants look best when grown in drifts either in a mixed border or as bedding. They can be used as cut flowers.

Cleome hassleriana

This is the species that is most commonly seen. It is occasionally grown as a species, but more commonly as one of the several available cultivars. Seed catalogues often list it under all manner of names which are no longer extant. 'Colour Fountain' is a mixture of colours but there are also varieties which are restricted to one colour such as 'Cherry Queen' (carmine red), 'Helen Campbell' (white) 'Orchid Queen' (pale mauve) and 'Pink Queen' (pink).

Other plants If you search you will find a number of other cleomes being offered by one or two seed merchants and specialist societies, *C. aculeata, C. gynandra* and *C. serrulata* amongst them. These have smaller flower heads so they are not as showy as *C. hassleriana,* but the structure and colour range is roughly the same.

COBAEA
Cathedral bells

This genus contains about 20 species of perennial climbers, of which one, *C. scandens,* is of interest to gardeners. Although a perennial, it is generally treated as an annual. Its great attraction, apart from its purple bell-shaped flowers, is that it is one of the few annual climbers. It can reach up to 4.5m (15ft) in the year if started off early enough, although as a perennial it can eventually grow as tall as 20m (70ft).

Cobaea scandens growing up a willow tripod.

How to obtain Most seed merchants carry seed. Sometimes you find plants at garden centres and nurseries. These should be planted out quickly since they do not do well in small pots.
Cultivation Plant in a humus-rich soil that is neutral to alkaline. A warm sunny site is needed. Do not plant out until after the danger of frosts has passed. Z9.
Propagation Raise plants from seed, sown in early spring under glass at 25°C (77°F).
Uses Cobaea does best when planted against a warm wall, either growing up a support or through another plant. It can be also used over pergolas and trellising.

Cobaea scandens

The flowers are large, attractive bells that stick out horizontally from the stems. They open whitish-green and quickly change to a deep purple. The form *alba*

has white flowers. *Cobaea scandens* is often known as the cup and saucer plant, the cup being the flower and the saucer the green calyx around its base.

Cobaea scandens

Annuals for light shade

Begonia semperflorens	Mimulus
Cleome spinosa	Myosotis
Consolida ambigua	Nemophila menziesii
Cynoglossum amabile	Nicotiana
Digitalis purpurea	Oenothera biennis
Erysimum cheiri	Pelargonium
Lobelia erinus	Schizanthus
Lobularia maritima	Senecio cineraria
Lunaria annua	Thunbergia alata
Matthiola bicornis	Viola × wittrockiana

Collinsia bicolor 'Blushing Rose'

COLLINSIA
Collinsia

This is a genus of about 20 plants of which only one is in general cultivation. This is *C. bicolor*, or *C. heterophylla* as it is sometimes called. It is not related to the lupin, but at a quick glance it could be mistaken for one, albeit a small one. It produces spikes of flowers of which the lower lip is one colour (usually purple) and the upper another (usually white or pink). The pointed leaves are more like those of a penstemon and rise stalkless direct from the stems. Although these plants are generally upright, they can be slightly floppy. It is best to plant them closely together so that they give each other support, or you can give individual plants other support, such as short, twiggy branches. H 60cm (24in) S 30cm (12in).
How to obtain Collinsias are rarely seen as plants in garden centres and it is best to buy them as seed from one of the few merchants that stock it.
Cultivation The soil should be a humus-rich one, but it should be free-draining. Collinsias prefer full sun, but they will grow in a little light shade. Z7.
Propagation Sow seed where the plants are to grow in spring, or in autumn for earlier flowering. Thin to 30cm (12in) intervals.
Uses Collinsias can be used either in drifts as bedding or in a mixed border. They are shown to good effect in a wild-flower garden.

Collinsia bicolor

This is the main plant grown and is described above. 'Candidissima' is a form with all-white flowers. There are also mixtures on offer from some seed merchants. They include 'Blushing Rose' and 'Surprise', which produces an attractive combination of blue, lilac and rose-pink flowers.

Other plants The only other species that is sometimes offered is *C. grandiflora*. It is a shorter plant than the above and much bushier. It also has bicoloured flowers, with a blue-purple lower lip and a paler upper one.
    There are a few seed merchants that offer this species; otherwise you need to look to specialist societies in order to find it.

COLLOMIA
Collomia

A genus of about 15 species of which a couple are occasionally cultivated. The most frequently grown is *C. grandiflora*, although it is still rarely seen. Very few seed merchants carry the seed and it is mainly grown by gardeners to whom the seed has been handed down from generation to generation. It is an old-fashioned cottage-garden plant of great beauty and it is a pity it is not more readily available. Once established you rarely lose it since it is self-sowing, often forming large drifts. However, it is easy to remove if it is in the wrong place. H 1m (3ft) S 60cm (24in), when growing well.
How to obtain Collomia seed is not easy to come by, although some seed merchants do stock it now. It is also available from some specialist societies.

Collomia grandiflora

Cultivation This plant does best in a rich, moist soil, which should be free-draining. A sunny position is required. Z7.
Propagation Sow seed in early spring where the plants are to grow. After the first year it self-sows if allowed to seed. Thin plants to 30cm (12in) intervals.
Uses Collomia could be used as a bedding plant, but the flowering season is short and it is best grown as drifts in a mixed border.

Collomia grandiflora

This is an upright, branched annual with red stems that contrast well with the mid green leaves. The flowers are a creamy salmon-pink and are carried in clusters or whorls at the tips of the branches. The seed heads are somewhat sticky and it is best to let them dry before trying to extract the seed.

Other plants *Collomia biflora* is a similar, but shorter annual with smaller heads of red or orange flowers. It is more colourful than the above but has less presence.

CONSOLIDA
Larkspur

A genus of about 40 species of annuals which used to be included in the genus *Delphinium*. The naming is still in a state of flux and the main larkspur grown may be called *C. ambigua* or *C. ajacis* depending on which authority you consult. This confusion is carried on in the seed catalogues, so don't give up if you can't find the plants under the first heading you try. Whatever their names, the plants are excellent annuals. They

Consolida ajacis, mixed colours

Consolida ajacis 'Frosted Skies'

Convolvulus tricolor 'Royal Ensign'

look like miniature delphiniums but the flower spikes are much more open and delicate; the flowers seem to float like butterflies. There is quite a range of colour. Blue is the predominant one but there are also pinks and whites and some bicolors. The plants vary considerably in size from dwarf varieties that are only 30cm (12in) high to tall ones 1.2m (4ft) high. S 30cm (12in).
How to obtain Larkspurs are available both as plants in individual pots and seed from which a bigger range is available.
Cultivation Grow in any reasonable garden soil as long as it is free-draining. A sunny position is required. Taller forms may need some form of staking in exposed positions. Z7.

Consolida ajacis

Propagation Sow seeds in the position where the plants are to grow in early spring. Thin to 30cm (12in) intervals.
Uses Good for bedding and mixed borders, these plants can also be grown in pots and tubs. The taller varieties make very attractive cut flowers.

Consolida ajacis
This is the main species and it has large number of cultivars. Some are light and airy while others have much more compact, denser flower spikes, often with double blooms. There are several series which provide a mixtures of colours. For example there are the Dwarf Hyacinth Series, Dwarf Rocket Series and the Giant Imperial Series, all providing double flowers in a range of colours and heights. 'Frosted Skies' is a beautiful single with white and blue flowers. 'Sublime' is another tall variety, as is 'Earl Grey'; both come in mixture of colours. 'Kingsize Scarlet' produces very good red flowers.

CONVOLVULUS
Bindweed
An enormous genus of some 250 plants, of which many are weeds that you would not want near your garden. However there are one or two excellent garden plants. *C. tricolor* is one of these. As well as having attractive flowers it has the added bonus of being one of the few annuals that climb.

How to obtain Convolvulus are grown from seed which is very widely available.
Cultivation Grow convolvulus in any reasonable garden soil, so long as it is free-draining. A sunny site is needed. Z8.
Propagation Sow under glass in the early spring at 13–18°C (55–64°F). They can also be sown *in situ*, although the plants will then flower later, and so will not grow quite as vigorously.
Uses These plants are excellent for growing up any form of trellising or up wigwams of sticks, either in borders or in pots or tubs.

Convolvulus tricolor
This attractive plant has the typical funnel-shaped flowers of the convolvulus. Here they are a rich dark blue, with white markings at the base of the petals and a yellow eye. H 40cm (16in) S 30cm (12in). The plant is most often seen in the form 'Royal Ensign' which has very deep blue flowers. Seed can also be bought in mixtures which contain white and pink flowers as well as blue.

Other plants Convolvulus sabatius must be one of the most beautiful of all container plants. It is a tender perennial that is treated as an annual and either overwintered under glass or started again each year. It produces a profusion of small, funnel-shaped sky-blue flowers that smother the small, shrubby plant. It is usually bought as a plant rather than seed. A real gem.

Convolvulus sabatius

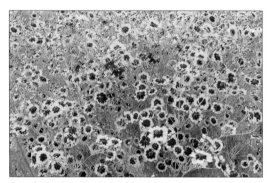

Coreopsis tinctoria

Cosmos bipinnatus 'Sonata Pink'

COREOPSIS
Tickseed

A large genus of up to 100 species of both annuals and perennials. The perennials are dealt with elsewhere (see page 350). *C. grandiflora* and *C. tinctoria* are the plants of interest to the annual gardener. The flowers are daisies with golden-yellowish outer petals and a gold central disc. The ends of the petals are usually fringed. Some plants have simple single flowers; others have semi or fully double blooms. The flowers are quite large, up to 6cm (2½in) in diameter. The plants vary in height from low-growing ones that reach only 23cm (9in) to ones that are 1.2m (4ft) tall; most reach about 45cm (18in) in height and spread.

How to obtain Annual coreopsis can occasionally be bought as plants from garden centres but they are best purchased as seed.

Cultivation Grow in any reasonable garden soil. Coreopsis prefers a sunny position, but the plants will take a little shade. Z7.

Propagation The seed can be sown in the early spring under glass at 13–16°C (55–60°F), or sown directly into the soil where the plants are to grow.

Uses They can be used in drifts in mixed borders or in bedding schemes. The shorter varieties can also be used in containers such as pots and tubs. Taller varieties are good for cutting.

Coreopsis grandiflora

This is a perennial that is usually treated as an annual. Seed of the species is commonly available but the plant is more frequently grown as one of the many cultivars including 'Early Sunrise' (semi-double flowers), 'Gold Star' (quilled petals) and 'Sunray' (double flowers).

Coreopsis tinctoria

This is similar to the previous species, but it has slightly smaller flowers. There is also more variety in the colour with the central disc often being reddish-brown and the petals flushed with red and brown. Again, it has plenty of cultivars. They include 'Tiger Flower', a dwarf only 23cm (9in) tall, and 'Mahogany Midget' a slightly taller plant which has rich mahogany-coloured flowers. Various mixed-coloured plants are also sold by some seed companies.

COSMOS
Cosmos

This is one of those annuals that has maintained its popularity over the years. There are 25 species but there are only a couple of annuals which are grown regularly. However, both have a number of cultivars, so there is plenty to interest the annual gardener. They have daisy-like flowers but the petals are wide, so producing an almost continuous disc. The petal colours are mainly white and pink in *C. bipinnatus*, the main species, but there are some yellow variants in the other species, *C. sulphureus*, as its name might suggest. Plants vary in height from the dwarf at about 30cm (12in) to the tall at up to 1.5m (5ft).

How to obtain Cosmos can be obtained as plants from most garden centres. However, they need to be purchased early on since they soon become leggy (producing long, bare stems) in small pots. It is better to raise them as seed.

Cultivation Cosmos will grow in any reasonable garden soil, but they like full sun. Z8.

Propagation Sow in early spring under glass at 16–18°C (60–64°F) or slightly later where the plants are to grow.

Coreopsis grandiflora 'Early Sunrise'

Cosmos growing in a mixed border.

Cosmos sulphureus

Uses They can be grown either as bedding plants or in drifts in a mixed border. Single colours look better in the latter. They make good cut flowers.

Cosmos bipinnatus

This is the most commonly grown species. It has a range of single colours as well as one or two varieties with bicolours: 'Candy Stripe', with its white flowers with crimson edging, is one example. The Sensation Series is one of the most popular with large flower heads up to 9cm (3½in) across. Sonata Series is a dwarf form, which grows only 30cm (12in) high. They can both be bought as a mixture or as individual colours such as 'Sonata Pink'. 'Sea Shells' has curious quilled petals. 'White Swan' is a beautiful white variety.

CREPIS
Hawk's Beard

This is a large genus of about 200 species or annuals and perennials. Most are considered weeds but some perennials are grown in the garden (see page 352) along with a couple of annuals, only one of which is in general cultivation. This one, *C. rubra*, is a gem and ought to be grown more widely than it is.

All the crepis have flower heads similar to those of the dandelion. However, unlike the dandelion, crepis are generally well-behaved and do not seed everywhere. (If the dandelion did not sow itself so prodigiously it would also be welcome since it is a magnificent

plant.) Crepis make good bedding when they are grown *en masse*, but these plants are also suitable for filling gaps in mixed borders, especially along the margins.
How to obtain These plants are usually only available as seed from seed merchants. Very occasionally you see plants for sale but do not rely on finding them.
Cultivation Plant out in any reasonable garden soil so long as it is free-draining. Z6.
Propagation You should sow the seed in pots as soon as it is ripe. No heat is required for raising these seeds.
Uses Crepis are excellent in mixed borders and in gravel gardens. They are also attractive when used as bedding plants or in a variety of tubs or pots.

Crepis rubra

This has single dandelion-like flower heads of sugary pink, which float on wiry stems above a rosette of hairy leaves for a long period during summer. H up to 40cm (16in), but often much less, S 20cm (8in). There are a few cultivars of which the white form 'Alba' is the best. There is also a darker pink form, 'Rosea'.

Other plants There are one or two more species that are occasionally grown, but it is usually not as easy to get hold of their seed. The flowers of these species are less showy. Most are yellow-flowered and look good if grown in a meadow garden. Examples include *C. biennis* and *C. capillaris*.

Cuphea ignea 'Variegata'

CUPHEA
Cuphea

Not all gardeners know this genus but it is a big one containing about 260 species. Quite a number of these are grown in gardens, usually as annuals even if they are perennials or shrubs. The best known is probably *C. ignea*, known as the cigar flower. The colours vary but red is common and gives the plants a bright cheerfulness that makes them ideal for bedding or for growing in containers. If they are plants you do not know it might be worth experimenting with one or two of them, especially if you like exotic borders.
How to obtain Cuphea is widely available from seed merchants, but check catalogues carefully since naming may vary. You sometimes see plants in garden centres.
Cultivation Cupheas will grow in any reasonably fertile garden soil,

but it needs to be free-draining. They prefer a sunny position but they will also grow in a lightly shaded one. Z9.
Propagation Sow seed in the early spring under glass at 13–16°C (55–60°F). The seed can also be sown where the plants are to grow, but flowering will be later.
Uses They make excellent bedding, especially in colourful, exotic schemes. They can also be used in containers and in mixed borders.

Cuphea cyanaea

This perennial is quite commonly grown as an annual. It has masses of orange tubular flowers with yellow tips. H 1m (3ft).

Cuphea ignea

This is the most common cuphea. It has bright red tubular flowers with a deep red and white mouth that looks rather like the ash on the tip of the cigar. It will grow up to 75cm (30in) as a perennial but is often less when grown as an annual. The variety 'Variegata' has leaves splashed with cream.

Other plants C. *hyssopifolia* (false heather) is a rounded shrub often treated as an annual. The tubes are much more flared, producing open flowers in either white or pink. H and S 60cm (24in) high.
    Cuphea × purpurea is another shrub grown as an annual. These flowers are also widely flared, making them appear larger than those of the more common varieties. The colour varies from pink to red; there are also purple varieties. H up to 75cm (30in).

Crepis rubra

Cynoglossum amabile 'Mystery Rose'

Dahlia 'Bishop of Llandaff'

Dahlia 'Lilliput'

Dahlia 'Hamari Katrina'

CYNOGLOSSUM
Hound's tongue

A genus of about 55 species, most of which are annuals or short-lived perennials (see page 354). The flowers are generally quite small but there is plenty of them and they are a lovely blue – a colour not often seen in bedding plants. They are related to the forget-me-not; as with that plant, a progression of flowers open from a spiral of buds.
How to obtain Cynoglossums are most frequently seen as seed.
Cultivation These plants are best grown in any reasonable garden soil that is moisture-retentive but at the same time free-draining. They prefer sun but tolerate a little shade. Z7.
Propagation Sow seed in pots in spring. No heat is required. They can also be sown in the open ground where they are to flower.
Uses Cynoglossums work well as bedding plants or when placed in a mixed border.

Cynoglossum amabile
This is the most commonly grown annual in the genus. As well as the blue flowers of the species, there are also varieties with white or pink flowers, some named, such as 'Mystery Rose' (rose-pink) or 'Avalanche' (white). H 60cm (24in), but often much less, S 30cm (12in).

Other plants Cynoglossum officinale is a biennial with deep purple flowers. It is best grown in the wild-flower garden.

DAHLIA
Dahlia

Most gardeners will not need to be told what dahlias are: they are very familiar to us all. While there are only 20 species there are a colossal 20,000 cultivars, which shows just how popular they are. They are not only grown in decorative situations in the garden but also for cutting and for exhibition purposes. The flowers are usually quite large and blowsy in a variety of bright colours.

The shape of the flower head has been divided into eleven groups varying from simple singles to double, spherical ones known as pompoms. There are other doubles, such as the cactus dahlia in which the narrow petals curve upwards. These plants are all perennials that are treated as annuals; they are lifted each autumn and stored overwinter before replanting in spring. There are also a few varieties which are grown from seed each year. Bedding dahlias only grow to about 45cm (18in) or so but the

perennial ones will grow up to 1.5m (5ft) in height and 60cm (24in) in spread.
How to obtain Dahlias are sold as tubers from most garden centres. They are also available from specialist nurseries which offer a much larger choice and are a must for anyone who becomes interested in these plants. Their catalogues are often a mine of information. The bedding varieties are available from most seed merchants, and most carry a good range.
Cultivation Grow dahlias in a moist humus-rich soil that is free draining. Choose a sunny position. Stake taller varieties. Z9.
Propagation The tubers can be cut in half once growth has just begun, leaving a shoot on each piece. Alternatively take basal cuttings from the emerging shoots. Seed can be sown under glass in early spring at 13–16°C (55–60°F).
Uses Many gardeners grow dahlias in separate beds or in rows in the vegetable garden for cutting or

for exhibitions. They can also be grown in mixed borders. The smaller annuals make good bedding plants and can also be grown in containers.

More common plants
There are so many varieties of dahlia that it is difficult even to start listing them. There are some, such as purple-foliaged 'Bishop of Llandaff', which are used more frequently in borders than they are for exhibition, while others, such as 'Hamari Gold', are mainly grown for exhibition purposes, but can also be used as a cut flower or even as a decorative variety in the border.

Other plants The annual bedding varieties grown from seed are offered by most seed merchants. They are usually offered as a mixture of colours. The well-known dwarf 'Redskin' has dark red or bronze foliage and flowers in a variety of colours. 'Coltness Mixed' is another old favourite.

DATURA
Thorn apple

This is a small genus from which the shrubby species have been reclassified as *Brugmansia*. The

Dahlia 'Brilliant Eye'

Dahlia 'Cactus Video'

Dahlia 'Decorative'

Dianthus barbatus 'Harbinger Mixed'

Dianthus barbatus 'Scarlet Beauty'

Dianthus chinensis 'Pluto Karminrosa'

Dianthus chinensis 'Merry-go-Round'

annual and perennial ones remain, however, as *Datura*. These plants are beautiful but they contain toxic substances; if eaten they are likely to be fatal. So plant them only if you feel confident that no one will suffer any ill effects. Their beauty lies in the very large trumpet flowers, which are white or soft pastel colours. Some have a wonderful scent. The plants are large, open plants. H 1m (3ft) S 60cm (24in).

How to obtain Most garden centres are reluctant to sell these plants because of their toxic nature. The best way to obtain them is from seed merchants.

Cultivation Plant out after the threat of frost has passed. The soil should be fertile but free-draining. The site should be sunny. Z: see individual entries.

Propagation Sow the seed under glass in early spring at 16–18°C (60–64°F). Grow the plants on in containers.

Uses Datura are mainly grown as container plants, and they are suitable for large pots or tubs.

They can be planted in the open soil. The poisonous nature of the plant means that it needs to be sited carefully.

Datura inoxia

This is another relatively common species. It has trumpets that are white, or white tinged with violet. They are very fragrant. It is slightly less hardy. Z9.

Datura stramonium

Known as Jimson weed, this is the main species grown. It has large white trumpets which are mainly white, but are occasionally purple. The seed capsules are large, green and prickly, hence its other name of common thorn apple. Z7.

DIANTHUS
Dianthus

This is a well-known genus with more than 300 species and an unknown number of cultivars. It is best known for the perennials which include carnations and pinks (see page 354). However, there are a number of annuals,

mainly used as bedding plants. Although these are not quite as popular as they once were, they are still widely grown. The flowers are either single, semi-double or double in a range of bright colours, of which only blue is missing. They are often scented. Most are annuals, the notable exception being the biennial *D. barbatus*, the sweet William, which has to be sown one year for flowering the next.

How to obtain Most annual dianthus can be purchased as either seed or plants. Seed generally offers a better range of possibilities.

Cultivation Any reasonably fertile garden soil will do but it must be free-draining. A sunny position is required. Z: see individual entries.

Propagation Sow seed of annuals in early spring under glass at 13–16°C (55–60°F), or outside where the plants are to grow, but these will be later flowering. Biennials should be sown outside in drill in early summer and moved to their flowering positions in autumn.

Uses Annual dianthus are mainly used either as bedding or in a mixed border. Some can be used as container plants.

Dianthus barbatus

This is the biennial sweet William. It is the upright plant and the tallest of the annuals. It is deliciously scented. It has flat heads of red, pink or white flowers, which are often patterned. It is good for cutting. H 70cm (28in) S 30cm (12in).

Dianthus chinensis

One of the most commonly seen annual pinks. It is variously known as the Chinese, Japanese or Indian pink. It carries single flowers that are red, pink or white with a darker central eye and often patterns. The petals are fringed. H and S 30cm (12in).

This plant has given rise to a number of cultivars with 'Strawberry Parfait' being one of the most popular. Heddweigii Group is also widely grown. Z7.

Other plants Other species that are frequently grown as annuals, often as cultivars, include *D. armeria*, the Deptford pink, and *D. superbus* which has very deeply cut petals.

Dianthus barbatus

Dianthus chinensis 'Strawberry Parfait'

Dianthus 'Can Can Scarlet'

Digitalis purpurea

Digitalis purpurea (mixed colours)

DIGITALIS
Foxgloves

This well-known genus consists of more than 20 species, most of which are perennials (see page 357) but some are annuals or treated as such. The common foxglove, *D. purpurea*, is one of these. It usually grows in the wild as a perennial in mainland Europe but, oddly enough, only as a biennial in Britain.

Foxgloves are tall, erect plants with spikes of tubular flowers that create a wonderful effect in the border. They look especially good when grown as a drift, but also look fine dotted throughout an informal planting.

How to obtain Foxgloves can occasionally be found as plants in garden centres or nurseries but they are best grown from seed which is readily available from a number of sources.

Cultivation These plants will grow in any garden soil, in either full sun or a partially shaded position. Cut off the flower spikes before they seed if you wish to prevent self-sowing. Z4.

Propagation The seed can be scattered where the plants are to grow as soon as it is ripe. Once you have foxgloves in your garden, they will continue to self-sow if they are allowed to seed.

Uses Foxgloves work best in mixed borders although the cultivars can look good used in bedding schemes. The wild forms are excellent in wild-flower gardens. Foxgloves also make very good cut flowers.

Digitalis purpurea

This is the common foxglove and it is a superb garden plant that is well worth growing. The flowers are a soft pinkish-purple with darker spots inside. There is also a white form *albiflora*. H 2m (6ft) S 45cm (18 in).

The cultivars are much brasher, with bigger flowers that are more densely packed on the stem. There is a wider range of pinks and whites and the spots are usually larger. The Excelsior hybrids (or Suttons Excelsior hybrids) provide the main range of cultivars. The Foxy hybrids are about half the size of the species.

Other plants Digitalis lanata is a perennial that is often treated as an annual. It produces small flowers, which are white with soft brown veining.

Digitalis purpurea f. albiflora

DIMORPHOTHECA
African daisy

This was once a much larger genus because *Osteospermum* was included in it and plants of that genus are still sometimes listed as *Dimorphotheca*. The plants have rather beautiful daisy-like flowers which come in a range of white and oranges, usually with a purple central disc and a central ring of violet-purple at the base of the petals. They come from South Africa and they need sunshine to open. They usually shut in the evening so they are not good plants for people who see their gardens only in the evening. They are sprawling plants so do not reach any great height. H 30cm (12in) S 45cm (18in).

How to obtain These are commonly available as plants from garden centres and nurseries. The plants often do not have any cultivar name attached to them; if you want specific colours, buy them in flower. They can also be purchased as seed from various seed merchants.

Cultivation These plants will grow in any reasonable garden soil so long as it is free-draining. They must have a warm, sunny position or the flowers will not open. Z9.

Propagation Sow African daisy seed under glass at 18°C (64°F) in the early spring.

Uses These are mainly used as bedding plants but they can also be used for filling spaces towards the front of a mixed border. They can also be used in tubs.

Dimorphotheca sinuata

This is probably the most commonly grown plant in the genus. The species itself is not often seen; it is more commonly grown as one of the hybrids. The flowers are white, orange, yellow or even pink, often with a touch of blue or purple at the base of the petals.

Dimorphotheca sinuata

Other plants *Dimorphotheca pluvalis* is known as the rain prophet because it shuts up in cloudy conditions. The flowers are white with a blue base to their petals.

DIPSACUS
Teasel

There are about 15 species in this genus which consists mainly of biennials. They are not the most colourful plants but there are a couple that are welcome in our gardens. The attraction is mainly due to the structure of the plant. It is a tall, upright, open-branched plant which has a stately architectural quality about it. The stems and leaves are covered in stout prickles and the large,

Dipsacus fullonum (foliage)

Dipsacus fullonum

opposite leaves join at the stem forming a large cup which is usually filled with water. H 2m (6ft) S 1m (3ft).

How to obtain Teasels have tap roots which means that they do not do well in pots. As a result, they are rarely seen for sale as plants. However, they are generally available as seed.

Cultivation Teasels will grow in any reasonable garden soil. They do best in sun but will also grow in light shade. Z3.

Propagation Sow the seed in the open ground where the plants are to grow in autumn or spring.

Uses These plants work well at the back of a mixed border in an informal garden, but they look best in a wild-flower garden. The seed heads make good winter decoration in the garden as well as providing winter feed for several species of bird. They make excellent dried flowers.

Dipsacus fullonum

This is the wild teasel which is the plant most commonly seen. The flower heads are egg-shaped and rather prickly with spine-like bracts. The flowers first open as a band round the middle and then expand both upwards and downwards. They are a pale purple colour, which contrasts well with the pale green of the flower head. They flower in their second year.

Other plants Dipsacus sativus This is the fuller's teasel, the head of which was used to tease out wool

Dorotheanthus bellidiformis 'Gelato Pink'

and raise the nap on cloth. The spines on the head are hooked at the end, just perfect for the job.

DOROTHEANTHUS
Livingstone daisy

A genus of about ten species which are still more commonly known under the name *Mesembryanthemum*. Only one of these is generally cultivated. It was once more widely grown than it is now, but it is very suitable for coastal gardens and is still frequently seen as bedding plants around the coast. The plants are low growing with narrow succulent fleshy leaves and masses of brightly coloured daisies. The flowers are up to 4cm (1½in) diameter. Unfortunately the flowers tend to shut up in dull weather. H 15cm (6in) S 30cm (12in) or more.

How to obtain Livingstone daisies are frequently sold as plants either in bedding packs or in individual pots. They are also readily available as seed from most merchants, and are often listed under the name *Mesembryanthemum.*

Cultivation These plants thrive in well-drained sandy soil, including pure sand, but they will happily grow in most well-drained garden soils. A sunny position must be provided or the flowers will not open. Z9.

Propagation Sow the seed under glass at 16–18°C (60–64°F) in the early spring.

Uses Excellent for bedding and borders in coastal regions where the light is bright and the soil

usually well drained. They can also be used very successfully as bedding or in containers.

Dorotheanthus bellidiformis

This is the species usually grown. The daisy flowers have a brown central disc and narrow petals in a wide range of colours including yellow, pinks, reds, purples and whites. They are often two-toned with, say, pink petals flushed with white from the centre.

There are a number of cultivars: some, like 'Magic Carpet' are a mixture of colours, while others such as 'Gelato Pink' (pink), 'Apricot Shimmer' (soft apricot), 'Cape Sunshine' (bright yellow) or 'Lunette' (also called 'Yellow Ice', pale yellow) are single-coloured varieties.

Other plants There are several other species of which seed is available if you search for it. The most frequently seen is *D. gramineus*. Its flowers are similar to *D. bellidiformis* but the leaves are narrow and grass-like.

Dorotheanthus bellidiformis

Eccremocarpus scaber

ECCREMOCARPUS
Chilean glory flower

This is a small genus containing five species of perennial climbing plants of which one, *E. scaber*, is regularly seen in gardens. It is debatable whether this should be classified in gardening terms as a perennial or as an annual since it is regularly treated as both. However, the majority of gardeners use it as an annual climber, unless it is grown in a glasshouse or conservatory, and so it has been included here. It is fast growing and so well suited for use as an annual. It will grow up through other plants or up twiggy supports up to 5m (15ft) if used as a perennial. As an annual it reaches 2–3m (6–10ft).
How to obtain Chilean glory flowers are occasionally seen in pots but they are more frequently sold as seed. Most seed merchants carry them.
Cultivation These plants will grow well in a reasonably fertile, well-drained soil. A sunny position is needed. If they are planted against a warm wall, the plants may overwinter and produce flowers for a second year. Z9.
Propagation Sow seed in early spring under glass at 13–16°C (55–60°F).
Uses Grow as a climbing plant either in borders or against walls or fences. Chilean glory flowers can also be grown in large containers if supported by a wigwam of sticks or a framework.

Eccremocarpus scaber

This is the main species grown. It is usually grown as the straight species, which has orange or flame-red tubular flower carried in loose heads. However, there are

Echium vulgare

also a number of named cultivars available. These include the Anglia hybrids which offer a range of mixed colours such as pink, red, orange and yellow. Tresco hybrids also include crimson and cream flowers. Some seed merchants just label seeds under their colours – for example, "yellow forms" – without giving a cultivar name.

ECHIUM
Bugloss

A large genus containing about 40 species, which provides the gardener with several excellent plants. They vary considerably in size from low bedding plants of about 45cm (18in) to giants reaching up to 2m (6ft) or even more. However, close examination will show that although the size and shape of the plants are different, the flowers are all basically funnel-shaped. They are

Echium vulgare 'Blue Bedder'

usually blue although they also come in other colours. This is a beautiful group of plants, especially the larger ones.
How to obtain The bedding varieties are sometimes available as plants. The others have to be bought as seed. You may have to search to find it but it is becoming more widely available.
Cultivation Plant in a fertile soil that is well drained. The larger varieties appreciate a richer soil, but, again, it must be well-drained. The smaller ones need full sun but some of the bigger ones will also do well in a dappled shade. Z: see individual entries.
Propagation Sow the seed under glass at 13–16°C (55–60°F) in early spring. The smaller ones can be sown where they are to flower.
Uses The smaller plants make excellent bedding. The taller ones are architectural in shape. They

stand out as features in borders or look good in informal planting under trees or among shrubs.

Echium vulgare

This is the most frequently seen species. The species itself is called the common viper's bugloss and is excellent for wild-flower gardens. It has a tall spike or spikes of flowers which appear from ever-expanding coils. They are blue but purple in bud. H 1m (3ft) S 30cm (12in). There are various bedding forms derived from this, including 'Blue Bedder' which has light blue flowers that darken with age. Dwarf hybrids include pink and purple flowers. Z5.

Other plants Echium wildpretii is typical of the larger species. It forms a rosette from which emerges a tall spike up to 2m (6ft) in height; it is densely covered with blue flowers and has a rather exotic appearance. S 45cm (18in). Similar species are *E. simplex*, *E. fastuosum*, *E. candicans* and *E. pininana*. These are plants for the specialist grower but well worth the effort. Z9.

EMILIA
Tassel flower

There are about 24 species of annuals in this genus, of which a couple are widely grown in our gardens. The brightly coloured flowers are carried singly or in clusters, held above the leaves. They are upward-facing and look rather like miniature tassels or paint brushes (in the past this

Emilia coccinea 'Scarlet Magic'

A particularly fine display of *Emilia coccinea*.

plant was also called Flora's paint brush). H 60cm (24in) S nearly the same as the height.

How to obtain Tassel flowers are mainly found as seed, either at garden centres or from seed merchants' catalogues. The seed is sometimes still listed under its old name of *Cacalia*.

Cultivation Any reasonable garden soil will suffice so long as the ground is free-draining. A sunny position is required. Z9.

Propagation Sow the seed in early spring at 13–16°C (55–60°F) under glass, or later directly into the soil where the plants are to grow. The latter method provides plants that are later flowering.

Uses These make good bedding plants but they also work very well in drifts of a single colour in a mixed border. They are excellent for cutting and can be dried.

Emilia coccinea

This is the most frequently seen plant. The flowers are a bright flame-red. Sometimes they are sold as cultivars such as 'Scarlet Magic' but these are not greatly different from the species.

Emilia sonchifolia

This is a bit more varied than the above. The main flower colour is reddish-purple, but there are also orange, scarlet and yellow forms available. They are usually sold as mixed colours.

Other plants There are a number of other species that are available if you search for them. They include

EE. atriplicifolia, glabra, hastata and *suavolens*. However, they do not vary greatly from the above.

ERYNGIUM
Sea holly

This is a very large genus of some 230 species of which the vast majority are perennials. However, there are a few biennials, of which one is wildly grown in gardens. This is *E. giganteum*. It is a prickly beast but a plant of such beauty that it is worth putting up with this negative aspect. Its leaves, stems and bracts are a silvery green. It is often known as Miss Willmott's Ghost: this venerable gardener had the habit of surreptitiously dropping seed in her friends' gardens and so a trail of plants were left in her footsteps – her "ghost". The name is doubly apt because the plant shows up ghostly white at night.

Eryngium giganteum 'Silver Ghost'

How to obtain This is a tap-rooted plant that does not do very well in pots. It is best to avoid buying potted plants unless they are very young, and to go for seed which is readily available.

Cultivation Any well-drained garden soil is suitable, even poor ones. Full sun is preferred. Z6.

Propagation Sow the seed in spring where the plant is to grow. It will flower the following year. Sea holly self-sows if left to set seed.

Uses This plant is best used in a mixed border where it can be grown in a drift or in single plants. It does well in a wild-flower garden and is particularly good in gravel gardens. Excellent as a dried flower.

Eryngium giganteum

This is the plant described above. The flowers are contained in dome-shaped heads which are

greenish-blue in colour. Some merchants list 'Miss Willmott's Ghost' as a cultivar name but this is the common name for the form generally in cultivation and is no different from plants or seed sold simply under the name of the species. H 1m (3ft) S 36cm (14in). The cultivar 'Silver Ghost' has been introduced relatively recently. This is an attractive plant that is much more silvery-white than the species.

Other plants Of the other biennials, *E. campestre* is the one you are most likely to find. This is a plant of dunes and dry grassy places. It is not so spectacular as other eryngiums but it is still a good plant for wild gardens and gravel gardens. It is smaller than the above, 60cm (24in) high and almost as wide. The flower heads are greenish and relatively small.

Eryngium giganteum is an excellent plant for drying.

Erysimum helveticum

ERYSIMUM
Wallflower

This is a large and popular genus of about 200 species. Most of the plants are perennials but they are not long lived so they are often treated as biennials, especially the common bedding forms. Wallflowers actually do grow well on walls, which is the nearest garden equivalent to their native cliffs; this is because they like a well-drained position. If they are given such conditions in the garden they will last for several years. The bedding varieties are very colourful and cheerful and have a very distinctive scent which is one of the pleasures of spring. H 75cm (30in) S 40cm (16in).
How to obtain The bedding varieties are widely sold as bare-rooted plants; they can be found everywhere from garden centres to petrol stations. However, it is often difficult to know what the flower colour will be. Seed merchants give a much larger choice of cultivars and allow you to be certain of the colour.
Cultivation Any good garden soil will suffice, but a well-drained one will ensure that plants overwinter better. Wallflowers prefer a sunny position. Z7.
Propagation Sow seed in rows in early summer and transfer to their flowering position in autumn.
Uses They make excellent bedding plants, and can also be used in mixed borders or in containers such as pots. They look good in cottage-garden schemes, and also combine well with bulbs.

Erysimum × allionii
This is the Siberian wallflower, which produces bright orange flowers. It is commonly available but it is not seen so often now as the following species. There are no cultivars available.

Erysimum cheiri
This is the main bedding wallflower. It is a wonderful plant, very fragrant and colourful, and the one from which most of the bedding wallflowers have been derived. Seed is mainly sold as named cultivars. Some of these, such as Bedder Series, are sold as mixtures or individual colours such as 'Orange Bedder' or 'Blood Red'.

Other plants There are several other species that can be used as annuals. One delightful little plant is *E. helveticum* which has bright yellow flowers that open from purple buds. It self-sows, so once you have it there is no need to re-sow; simply transplant the seedlings if necessary.

ESCHSCHOLZIA
Californian poppy

This small genus of about ten species produces a couple of annuals which are stalwarts of the border. They have typical poppy flowers which are shallow, funnel- or saucer-shaped, and with petals that look fragile, although they are not quite so crumpled as many of the poppies. These are cheerful flowers which come in plenty of bright colours, with orange as the base colour. The foliage is finely cut. The plants are rather sprawling and the

Eschscholzia californica 'Mikado'

flowers are carried on thin stems well above the leaves. H and S 30cm (12in).
How to obtain Californian poppies can be purchased as plants but they are best bought as seed which is readily available.

Cultivation Californian poppies can be grown in any reasonable garden soil so long as it is free-draining. They need a sunny position. Z6.
Propagation Seed can be sown in late spring where the plants are to grow. The plants will self-sow for future years. However, the cultivars are likely to revert to the basic species.
Uses These plants can either be used in bedding schemes or in mixed borders.

Eschscholzia californica
This is the main species grown. The species has mainly orange flowers but there are several cultivars which have blooms of yellow, flame-red, red and pink. There are also doubles and semi-doubles, whose flowers are more

Eschscholzia californica 'Mission Bells'

tissue-like. 'Ballerina' has double and semi-double flowers in a mixture of colours; 'Apricot Flambeau' is a pretty apricot semi-double with splashes of red; 'Mission Bells' is also semi-double but comes in a mixture of colours; 'Cherry Ripe' has red petals that get paler towards the centres; 'Mikado' has deep orange petals, which are scarlet on the reverse side; and 'Alba' is a beautiful creamy-white.

Other plants *Eschscholzia caespitosa* are similar to the above but with slightly smaller, yellow flowers. The best known cultivar is 'Sundew', which has beautiful lemon-yellow flowers.

EUPHORBIA
Spurge

This is a colossal genus with more than 2,000 species ranging from annuals to trees. The majority grown in gardens are perennials or shrubs that are treated as perennials. However, there are also two annual plants, *E. lathyris* (the caper spurge) and *E. marginata* (snow on the mountain), that make a welcome contribution to our gardens. These are both upright plants but they are quite dissimilar in other respects. Like all euphorbias, these plants produce a latex sap which can cause severe irritation to the skin and so they should only be handled wearing gardening gloves. Be sure to keep the juice away from eyes. No parts should be eaten, especially the seed of *E. lathyris* which looks a bit like capers (hence its name) but which is highly toxic.

How to obtain Both the annual species are occasionally offered as plants but they do not do very well in small pots so it is best to grow them from seed. This is readily available.
Cultivation Grow in a reasonably rich soil – the richer the soil the bigger the plants will grow. A sunny position is best. Z4–8.
Propagation Sow where the plants are to grow. *E. lathyris* will self sow if left to set seed.
Uses E. lathyris is best grown in a mixed border where its shape can be appreciated. *E. marginata* can also be used there, and it makes a good bedding plant.

Euphorbia lathyris
An upright but a much sturdier plant than the following. It produces side branches, giving it a candelabra shape and great architectural presence when fully grown. Excellent for bringing structure to a border. H 1.5m (5ft) S 45cm (18in).

Euphorbia marginata
An upright plant which has ovate leaves and tiny flowers carried among bracts at the top of the stems. These bracts and top leaves are either variegated in white or totally white, hence its common name of snow on the mountain. H 1m (3ft) S 50cm (20in). There are several cultivars including 'Summer Icicle', 'Icicle' 'Kilimanjaro' and 'Snow Top'.

EUSTOMA
Prairie gentian
A small genus of three species, of which one is increasingly being grown. Its new popularity is partly

Eustoma grandiflorum

due to the fact that it has become more readily available as a cut flower, which has prompted people to start growing it. Until recently the genus was called *Lisianthus* and the plant is still often called this. It is an erect plant bearing upward-facing flowers that are cup-shaped and often semi-doubles or doubles. The common name prairie gentian comes from the flower's blue or purple colour.
How to obtain The best way of obtaining the prairie gentian is as seed which is widely available.
Cultivation These plants are often grown under glass for cutting purposes, but they can also be grown outside once the threat of frost has passed. Grow in a reasonably fertile, free-draining soil. It should preferably be neutral to alkaline. A warm, sunny position is important. Z9.
Propagation Sow the seed under glass at 16–18°C (55–60°F) in the late winter.

Uses The prairie gentian can be used as a decorative plant in a mixed border or it can be grown simply for cutting purposes.

Eustoma grandiflorum
This, the only species grown, is sometimes called *E. russellianum* or *Lisianthus russellianus*. The cup- or bell-shaped flowers are purple or blue in the species and have a wonderful satiny texture. The centres are darker. H 1m (3ft) S 30cm (12in).
There are a number of cultivars which offer a larger range of colours including pink, white, red and even yellow. 'Echo Pink' is a double pink. 'Aloha Deep Red' is, as its name suggests, red. Heidi Series are single cultivars in a wide range of colours including salmon and various picotees. Echo Series are doubles, again with picotees. Double Eagle Mixed is another double with a mix of colours. All are good choices for cutting.

Euphorbia marginata

Fragrant annuals

Brachyscome iberidifolia	*Ipomoea alba*
Centaurea moschata	*Lathyrus odoratus*
Datura	*Lobularia maritima*
Dianthus barbatus	*Matthiola*
Dianthus chinensis	*Nicotiana*
Erysimum cheiri	*Oenothera*
Exacum affine	*Pelargonium* (foliage)
Heliotropium arborescens	*Phacelia*
Hesperis matronalis	*Reseda odorata*
Iberis amara	*Viola × wittrockiana*

Exacum affine

EXACUM
Persian violet

This is a genus containing about 25 species, only one of which is used as an annual in our gardens. This one, *E. affine*, has been used for a long time as a bedding plant and is still popular. The flowers are shallow dishes or saucers and are generally coloured a soft blue-purple with a yellow centre. Cultivars offer a slightly wider range of colours. As an added bonus the flowers are scented. These are bushy plants, which can grow up to 75cm (30in) high; the bedding or pot-plant cultivars are usually 30cm (12in) tall or less. S 15cm (6in).

How to obtain Persian violets can be purchased as plants, either in individual pots or in bedding packs. They can also be obtained as seed, where a wider range of plants is available.

Cultivation Plant out once the threat of frosts and chilly nights are definitely over. Persian violets will grow in any reasonable garden soil so long as it is free-draining. They need a warm and sunny position. Z9.

Propagation Sow seed at 18–20°C (64–68°F) under glass in the early spring.

Uses In the garden they can be used as bedding, where their uniform height can be exploited.

They can also be used as container plants for both tubs and pots, and for window boxes. In the house or greenhouse they can also be used as pot plants.

Exacum affine

This is the only species grown. The species is sometimes grown in its own right, but it usually appears in the form of one of the cultivars. The majority have soft blue-purple flowers but some are darker blue, pink and white. The bedding varieties are quite short, with many being no more than 15cm (6in) high; the height is reflected in names such as 'Midget' and 'White Midget'.

FAGOPYRUM
Buckwheat

This is genus of about 15 species of which a couple of annuals are grown both in agriculture and gardens. They are very similar to the plants that were once classified as *Polygonum* (the persicarias) and they have at times been listed as such. The flowers are small and carried in clusters and usually pink or white.

These plants have been in cultivation since the earliest agriculture as a source of grain and they are still used for green fodder and making flour. In the garden they are long flowering, lasting from midsummer well into

Fagopyrum esculentum

the autumn. Although they are perhaps not as popular as they once were, seed is still available.

How to obtain It is doubtful whether you will find buckwheat as plants, but quite a number of seed merchants carry stocks of seed. However, you may need to search for it.

Cultivation Any reasonable garden soil will suffice. A sunny position is best. Z7.

Propagation Sow the seed in spring in open ground where the plants are to grow. They are usually best sown in drifts rather than as individual plants.

Uses Their long flowering period makes these plants useful in a variety of places in the garden including informal beds and wild-flower borders. They are widely grown in the herb garden and still used to treat a variety of ailments. Bees love the flowers so they are good plants for honey producers. They also make good green manure, for which purpose they are often sold.

Fagopyrum esculentum

This has clusters of white or pink flowers carried on erect, knotted stems that also contain green, heart-shaped leaves. The flowers are fragrant. H 60cm (24in) S 30cm (12in).

Other plants *Fagopyrum tartaricum* is the Indian or Tartary buckwheat, and also known as *Polygonum tartaricum*. It is similar to the above but about half its size. It is more tolerant of drought conditions and makes excellent dried flowers.

FELICIA
Blue daisy

A large genus containing about 80 perennials and shrubs as well as a few annuals. A couple of these are among some of the most popular of bedding plants, while others are also quite widely grown. As their common name suggests they have daisy-like flowers with blue petals. The central discs are a good, contrasting yellow. They produce masses of small flowers over a long period. If grown under glass many will survive longer than a

A massed display of *Felicia amelloides*.

Felicia amelloides

year since they are strictly speaking short-lived perennials rather than annuals. Here they will grow up to 60cm (24in) high or more, but in the open they are normally much shorter. They are bushy plants and they grow about as wide as they are tall.
How to obtain Felicias can be obtained as plants from garden centres or nurseries and they are widely available as seed from all seed merchants.
Cultivation Plant out once the threat of late frosts has passed. Felicia will grow in any reasonable garden soil, although it must be free-draining. It is important to grow these plants in a warm, sunny position. Z9.
Propagation Sow seed in the early spring under glass at 16–18°C (60–80°F).
Uses Felicias have a wide range of uses. They work very well in bedding schemes but can also be used in mixed borders. They also make excellent container plants.

Felicia amelloides
A very good plant with blue flowers of varying shades. It is often sold as one of the many varieties which come in white as well as blue. 'Read's White' is a good example of the former. There is also a form with white variegations on the leaves known as 'Santa Anita Variegated'.

Felicia amoena
This is a slightly smaller plant than the previous species, but again it has bright blue flowers. Its form 'Variegata' is one of the best-known felicias; the leaves are heavily variegated with cream markings, and set off the blue flowers beautifully.

Felicia bergeriana
This is one of the lowest-growing felicias, reaching only about 25cm (10in) in height. Like the others it has blue flowers. This blue gives it its common name, the kingfisher daisy.

Felicia heterophylla
A mat-forming plant with blue daisies. However, this species also produces some pink cultivars, such as 'The Rose'. It also has a white variety 'Snowmass'.

GAILLARDIA
Blanket flower
There are about 30 species in this genus, and they comprise both annuals and perennials. There is one annual that is widely grown, as well as a perennial that is often treated as an annual. Like a large number of annuals, these plants are members of the daisy family and they exhibit the typical daisy-like flowers of an outer ring of petals and an inner disc. The petals are usually yellow in colour, flushed red towards their base and with reddish or brown central discs. These are big powerful daisies, up to 14cm (5½in) across in some plants. They are always eye-catching and more than earn their keep in the garden. H 60cm (24in) S 30cm (12in).
How to obtain Blanket flowers are available both as plants from garden centres and seed from a wide variety of sources.
Cultivation Plant out in any reasonable-quality garden soil. They should be placed in a warm and sunny position. Z: see individual entries.
Propagation Sow seed under glass in early spring at 13–16°C (55–60°F). It can also be sown where the plants are to flower, but the flowering will be much later than in greenhouse-raised plants.
Uses These make excellent bedding plants and they can also be used in a mixed border, especially one devoted to hot colours.

Gaillardia × grandiflora
This is strictly speaking a perennial and is often grown as such in warmer areas. However, it is also widely grown as an annual. It has the largest flowers. There are a number of cultivars including: 'Burgunder' (red flowers), 'Dazzler' (flame-red and yellow) and the similar 'Wirral Flame'. Z4.

Gaillardia pulchella
This is an annual which has smaller flowers than the previous but they are the same colour. There are several cultivars including 'Summer Prairie', 'Red Plume' and 'Yellow Plume'. Z8.

Red-flowered annuals

Adonis aestivalis	*Dianthus chinensis* 'Fire
Alcea rosea 'Scarlet'	Carpet'
Amaranthus caudata	*Linum grandiflorum*
Antirrhinum 'Scarlet Giant'	*Malope trifida* 'Vulcan'
Begonia semperflorens	*Nicotiana* 'Crimson'
'Lucifer'	*Papaver rhoeas*
Cleome spinosa 'Cherry	*Pelargonium*
Queen'	*Salvia splendens*
Cosmos bipinnatus 'Pied	*Tagetes patula* 'Cinnabar'
Piper Red'	*Verbena* 'Blaze'

Gaillardia pulchella 'Summer Fire'

Galactites tomentosa

Gazania 'Mini-Star Tangerine'

Gazania hybrids

GALACTITES
Galactites

This is a small genus of only three plants, of which just one, *G. tomentosa*, is grown. It is not often seen, which is surprising because it is a wonderful plant. The fact that it is a thistle may put a lot of people off, but it is a well-behaved thistle. Like other thistles it does self-sow, but only gently – in fact, there never seem to be enough seedlings to go round. This is an open, bushy plant with bluish-green leaves that are heavily marked with silver lines. The flowers are typically thistle-shaped and of a soft purple that contrasts beautifully with the variegated foliage. The foliage and stems do have sharp spines. There are no cultivars, but the flowers and variegated foliage are good enough to make them unnecessary. H up to 1m (3ft), but often only half of this. S 45cm (18in) in bigger plants.
How to obtain Galactites are not very easy to find but a few suppliers, including specialist societies, stock the seed. It is well worth seeking out.
Cultivation Any reasonable garden soil will suffice, so long as it is free-draining. The plants should have a sunny position, but they will tolerate a little light shade, for example a position in which they grow partially under a rose bush. Z6.
Propagation Sow the seed where the plants are to grow in autumn or spring, or sow in pots in an open frame. Galactites will self-sow if left to set seed, but they rarely become a nuisance.
Uses Galactites are excellent plants for the mixed border, especially if you have a garden with a silver colour scheme. They also do very well in gravel gardens.

GAZANIA
Gazania

This is a genus consisting of about 16 species of which none is commonly grown. However, between them they have produced a number of hybrids which are very popular among gardeners, especially in coastal gardens where there is bright light. This light is essential as gazanias have a habit of shutting up in dull weather.

The flowers are daisy-like with colourful ring of outer, pointed petals and a golden central disc. There is a wide range of colours from brilliant yellow through orange to various red and pinks.

There is often an inner ring of darker colour. The flowers are carried singly on stems above green foliage which is slightly frosted with silver. Gazanias make excellent bedding plants. H and S 25cm (10in).
How to obtain These are widely available as plants in garden centres and nurseries as well as seed. Seed offers the largest range of possibilities.
Cultivation Plant out after the threat of frosts has passed in a well-drained soil, preferably a light, sandy one. Gazanias require a warm, sunny position. Z9.
Propagation Sow seed under glass at 18–20°C (64–68°F) in the early spring.
Uses Gazanias are good plants for containers, such as window boxes, where they can be used to great effect. However, their main use is as colourful bedding plants.

***Gazania* Chansonette Series**
A mixture of colours including several different pinks and oranges, bronze and yellow.

***Gazania* 'Cream Beauty'**
As its name suggests, this lovely cultivar produces flowers of a creamy white colour.

***Gazania* Daybreak Series**
This is another series with a wide range of colours. Some colours are sold separately, as in the form 'Daybreak Bronze'.

***Gazania* Kiss Series**
The flower colours in this series include golden-yellow, bronze, rose and white. The colours are available separately.

***Gazania* 'Magenta Green'**
This cultivar produces flowers of deep purple.

Galactites tomentosa (foliage)

Gazania 'Daybreak Bronze'

Gazania hybrids

Gazania hybrids

Gazania Mini-Star Series
This series produces flowers in another wide range of colours including white and pink. The plants also come in single colours: for example, 'Mini-Star Tangerine' and 'Mini-Star White'.

Gazania 'Orange Beauty'
The flowers of this plant are bright orange in colour.

Gazania 'Snuggle Bunny'
This cultivar produces blooms of an unusual bronzy-orange.

Gazania 'Sunshine Mixed'
This plant carries daisies in a gay mixture of colours.

Gazania 'Talent Mixed'
This mixture produces flowers in plenty of different colours, and has attractive grey-silver foliage.

GERANIUM
Geranium

This is a very large genus of some 300 species, many of which are grown as perennials (see page 366), especially by enthusiasts. There are also a couple of annuals worth growing. They are not the most spectacular of geraniums and will probably not appeal to the average gardener, but they do

Pink-flowered annuals

Alcea rosea 'Rose'
Callistephus chinensis
Clarkia
Crepis rubra
Diascia
Dianthus
Godetia grandiflora 'Satin
  Pink'
Helichrysum bracteatum
  'Rose'
Lathyrus odoratus
Lavatera trimestris
Nicotiana 'Domino
  Salmon-Pink'
Nigella damascena 'Miss
  Jekyll Pink'
Papaver somniferum
Silene pendula 'Peach
  Blossom'

Geranium lucidum

add another couple of plants to the enthusiast's garden. They are especially suitable in a wild area, as they can spread a little too quickly in most gardens. The flowers are shallow saucers or funnels and are generally some shade of purple. Pelargoniums (see page 314) were removed from this genus more than 100 years ago, but they are still often referred to as geraniums.
How to obtain You very rarely see plants offered, although nurseries that specialize in geraniums may occasionally sell them. Seed is also difficult to find, but it is offered by specialist societies.
Cultivation Any garden soil will do. These plants will grow in either sun or shade. Z7.
Propagation Sow the seed in spring where the plants are to flower. Geranium seed can also be sown in pots and placed in an open frame without heat.
Uses These plants are quite rampant, so they are best grown in a wild garden. If used elsewhere, thin as necessary.

Geranium bohemicum
This plant forms a dense, untidy mat. The foliage is hairy and the small flowers are violet-blue. It is biennial and self-sows. H 30cm (12in) or more, S 15cm (6in).

Geranium lucidum
This is grown for its foliage, which is round and, unlike that of most geraniums, glossy and succulent-looking. The plant is excellent in shady areas since it helps to illuminate the darker

areas. In autumn it takes on reddish tints and the stems are also red. The flowers are small and pink. It is a very attractive plant, but it does seed everywhere. It is perfect for the wild or woodland garden. H 25cm (10in) S 15cm (6in).

GILIA
Gilia

A genus of about 30 species, consisting mainly of annuals. Two or three of these are in general cultivation. They vary from those with tight clustered heads of small flowers to those with loose heads of open saucer-shaped flowers. The predominant colour is blue. These look best when grown *en masse*, particularly in meadow garden. They are not seen as frequently as they once were but they are still widely available. H 60cm (24in) S 30cm (12in).

How to obtain Seed is readily available from a number of seed merchants. Occasionally you will find plants available for sale.
Cultivation Any reasonable garden soil will suffice, but it should be well-drained and not too rich. Z8.
Propagation Sow the seed in the autumn or spring in the open ground where the plants are to grow. They often self-sow if the conditions are warm enough.
Uses Gilias can be used as massed bedding or planted in drifts in mixed border. Their untidy habit makes them particularly good for wild gardens, especially meadows.

Gilia capitata
This is the main species grown. It has spherical heads (4cm/1½in across) of lavender-blue flowers, over finely cut foliage. They are sometimes known as Queen Anne's thimbles. A white form, 'Alba', is occasionally offered.

Gilia tricolor
This is called birds' eyes because the flowers have a central eye. The simple, saucer-shaped flowers have blue petals and yellow or orange shades in the throat. This, too, has a white variety, 'Alba'.

Other plants Once there were 25 or so gilia commonly available, but this has been reduced to those above. *G. achilleifolia*, which has finely cut foliage, is sometimes seen. It is a sprawling plant with spherical heads of blue flowers similar to those of *G. capitata*.

Gilia capitata

Gladiolus 'Seraphin'

GLADIOLUS
Gladiolus

A once-popular genus for which enthusiasm has dwindled in recent years. However, many gardeners still grow it so it is still widely available. There are about 180 species, some of which are treated as perennials (see page 367) while others are treated as tender annuals. Generally it is the hybrids that are grown. In spite of their decline there are still around 10,000 of these from which to choose – only a few of them are listed here. They consist of tall plants with sword-like leaves and spikes of tightly packed flowers. These are shaped like open trumpets or funnels and come in almost every colour. Some are pure colours while others are bicoloured. H 1.5m (5ft) S 15cm (6in).
How to obtain Corms are readily available from most garden centres and nurseries, usually in packs showing the colour. General bulb firms and specialist nurseries also sell gladioli, with the latter providing the biggest selection as well as offering catalogues which give advice on cultivation.
Cultivation These plants need a well-drained but reasonably fertile soil. They should have a position in full sun. Lift the corms after the leaves die back and store in a dry, frost-free place. Stake plants in exposed positions. Z8.
Propagation The small cormlets can be divided from their parents when the plants are dormant.

Uses Gladioli can be used in a decorative border but they are often grown in a special bed or in rows in the vegetable garden for cutting or for exhibition. They make excellent cut flowers.

Gladiolus 'Charm'
A fine gladiolus suitable for the border. It has simple, pinkish-purple flowers with white throats.

Gladiolus 'Elvira'
This is another simple gladiolus whose flowers come in pink. It is early flowering.

Gladiolus 'Florence C'
A large-flowered variety which produces dense spikes of glistening white, ruffled flowers

Gladiolus 'Green Woodpecker'
The spikes of greenish-yellow flowers have bright red markings in the throat.

Gladiolus 'Kristin'
The flowers of this cultivar are large, ruffled and white.

Gladiolus 'Nymph'
An early-flowering gladiolus that is suitable for the border. It has white flowers edged with red.

Gladiolus 'Prins Claus'
This is another good border variety. It has pure white flowers that have cerise markings.

Gladiolus 'Royal Dutch'
This is a large-flowered variety which carries pale blue flowers with white throats.

Gladiolus 'Seraphin'
This attractive plant has soft pink flowers with white throats.

GLAUCIUM
Horned poppy

This is a genus containing about 25 species of annuals and short-lived perennials, which are usually treated as annuals. The flowers are open and dish-shaped, with petals that look like fragile tissue paper. They come in colours ranging from yellow to orange and red. These plants are called horned poppies because of the shape of their seed pods, which are long

Glaucium flavum

and curved. They can be used as bedding, but are generally used in mixed borders. The height varies.
How to obtain Glauciums are occasionally sold as plants but they are tap-rooted and soon become starved in small pots. It is best to grow them from seed, which is quite widely available.
Cultivation Any garden soil will do, but glauciums need good drainage and full sun. Z7.
Propagation Sow the seed in autumn or spring where the plants are to flower.
Uses They are best used in mixed borders and gravel gardens. The latter suits them perfectly.

Glaucium corniculatum
This is the red horned poppy. It is a biennial and produces red or orange flowers over silvery foliage. H and S 38cm (15in).

Glaucium flavum
This is the yellow horned poppy. It is a perennial plant but is usually treated as an annual, although in well-drained conditions it will survive into a second year. The flowers are yellow or orange in colour. H 60cm (24in) S 45cm (18in).

Glaucium grandiflorum
This is another perennial grown as an annual. It has orange to deep red flowers.

GOMPHRENA
Gomphrena

A large genus containing almost 100 species, of which most are annuals although only one is in general cultivation. This, along with another couple of now-forgotten species, were once more popular than they are now. Their

Gomphrena globosa dark form

Gomphrena globosa pale form

Uses Gomphrenas have generally only been used as a bedding plant, but *G. dispersa* can be grown in hanging baskets and other containers. It can also be used in mixed borders. Gomphrena flowers are excellent for cutting and can also be dried.

Gomphrena globosa
This is the most commonly seen garden plant in the genus. It comes in a wide variety of colour, and there are an increasing number of varieties. Some, such as 'Q Formula Mixed', have mixed colours but are also issued as separate colours such as 'Q Lilac' or 'Q White'. 'Buddy' has deep purple flowers. It also has a smaller relative, 'Dwarf Buddy'. H 60cm (24in) S 30cm (12in).

Gomphrena 'Strawberry Fields'
This variety is one of the most widely available. It has bright red flower heads with tiny dots of yellow flowers showing between the brilliant bracts. It is taller than the above, reaching up to 75cm (30in) high.

Other plants Occasionally you may be able to find seed of other species, such as *G. dispersa* which is not such an upright plant. It has deep pink flowers.

GYPSOPHILA
Gypsophila
This large genus of more than 100 species provides us with a number of perennial (see pages 368–9) and annual garden plants. They are characterized by their masses of tiny white or pink flowers, which float airily on thin wiry stems, looking almost like a puff of smoke or a cloud. These are beautiful plants and they should be grown more often, particularly since they fit into so many styles of gardening. H 60cm (24in) S 30cm (12in).
How to obtain Gypsophila can sometimes be purchased as plants from garden centres and nurseries but a safer way of ensuring you get them is to order seed from one of the seed merchants.
Cultivation Gypsophilas need a light, well-drained soil and a sunny position. Z5.

Propagation Sow the seed in the spring, in open ground where the plants are to flower. Alternatively, it can be sown under glass at 13–16°C (55–60°F) at the same time of year.
Uses Gypsophilas can be used in a variety of ways including in annual bedding borders and mixed borders, where they work especially well as edging. They can also be used in most containers. They make excellent cut flowers, especially for bouquets.

Gypsophila elegans
This is the main annual *Gypsophila* that is cultivated. It produces masses of flat, star-shaped flowers in white and pink. The species itself is beautiful, but there are also a number of cultivars, many with bigger flowers. 'Covent Garden' is a good cutting form with large white flowers. 'White Elephant' (a clumsy-sounding name for an elegant plant) has the largest white flowers. 'Giant White' is tall, with slightly smaller white flowers that are good for cutting. *G.e.* var. *rosea* has soft pink flowers while 'Bright Rose', 'Carminea' and 'Red Cloud' all have much darker pink flowers.

Other plants The other major annual is *G. muralis*. This is a dwarf gypsophila which is suitable for rock gardens, containers and edging. It has pink flowers with darker veins. There are several cultivars including the darker-flowered 'Gypsy'. 'Garden Bride' has white flowers.

decline is mainly down to the reduced appeal of summer bedding. They have egg-shaped flower heads densely packed with pink, red, purple or white bracts.
How to obtain Gomphrenas are best purchased as seed from one of the several seed merchants that sell it.

Cultivation Plant out in any reasonable garden soil, but one that is free-draining. Gomphrenas should have a sunny position. Z9.
Propagation Sow the seed in early spring under glass at 16–18°C (60–64°F), or sow directly into the soil where they are to grow in late spring.

Blue-flowered annuals

Ageratum houstonianum	Limonium sinuatum 'Blue
Borago officinalis	Bonnet'
Brachyscome iberidifolia	Lobelia erinus
Campanula medium	Myosotis
Centaurea cyanus	Nemophila menziesii
Consolida ambigua	Nigella damascena
Cynoglossum amabile	Nigella hispanica
Echium 'Blue Bedder'	Nolana paradoxa 'Blue
Gilia	Bird'
Lathyrus odoratus	Salvia farinacea 'Victoria'

Gypsophila elegans 'Covent Garden'

Helianthus annuus

Helichrysum bracteatum

Helichrysum petiolare

HELIANTHUS
Sunflower

This large genus is most famous for its giant sunflower, *H. annuus*. This is an annual but there are many more garden-worthy plants which are perennials (see page 371). *H. annuus* is the only annual in the genus, but it has many cultivars. Not all of these have large heads, but the largest can reach to over 30cm (12in) across and are packed with seeds arranged in wonderful patterns. The typical sunflower is a daisy with yellow outer petals and a yellow, orange or brown central disc. There are many variations on this, with the yellow being paler or darker, and some flowers even having red or brown petals. The height varies, but the tallest plants reach 3m (10ft) or more; some are double this. These plants flower from late summer into autumn.

How to obtain You can buy plants, but they are starved in small pots. It is best to raise your own from the widely available seed.

Cultivation Plant out once the danger of frosts has passed. To get really big flowers, enrich the soil with well-rotted organic material and keep it moist. Choose a sunny position and stake plants. Z7.

Propagation Sow the seed in individual pots in early spring at 16–18°C (60–64°F) under glass.

Uses Shorter ones can be used at the backs of mixed borders. Sunflowers can be grown as specimen plants or in a line to create a summer hedge. They are good for children's gardens. Sunflowers are excellent for cutting and valuable as bird seed.

Helianthus annuus 'Italian White'
True to its name, a plant with pale-coloured blooms.

Helianthus annuus 'Music Box'
This cultivar offers a mixture of colours including yellows, reds and browns and some bicolours. A short form. H 75cm (30in).

Helianthus annuus 'Moonwalker'
The flowers of this plant are a pale lemon-yellow. H 1.5m (5ft).

Helianthus annuus 'Prado Red'
This is a red form. It reaches 1.5m (5ft) in height.

Helianthus annuus 'Russian Giant'
This is a very tall variety, which is widely grown. It has large yellow flowers. Up to 4m (12ft).

Helianthus annuus 'Sunspot'
A dwarf variety, but with large flowers. H 60cm (24in).

Helianthus annuus 'Teddy Bear'
This plant produces relatively small flower heads but they are fully double and look quite furry. They are golden-yellow in colour. H 60cm (24in).

Helianthus annuus 'Velvet Queen'
This is another tall form, with striking red flowers. A beautiful plant. H 1.5m (5ft).

HELICHRYSUM
Helichrysum

A very large genus containing a mixture of annuals, shrubs and perennials (see page 371). There are two species that are of particular interest to the annual gardener. *H. petiolare* is a shrub that is treated as an annual and grown for its foliage. The other is *H. bracteatum*. This is now called *Bracteantha bracteatum* but is still better known and distributed under its older name so it is included here. This is grown for its flower heads.

How to obtain The former is mainly bought as plants which are readily available, while the latter is usually purchased as seed.

Cultivation Helichrysums will grow in any well-drained garden soil. Z7.

Propagation Take cuttings of *H. petiolare* and overwinter the resulting plants under frost-free glass. Sow seed of *H. bracteatum* under glass in spring at 16–18°C (60–64°F).

Uses *H. petiolare* is excellent as a foliage plant anywhere in the garden but it is especially good for bedding and containers of all types. *H. bracteatum* is used for bedding. The flowers are good for cutting and drying.

Helichrysum bracteatum
This is an everlasting flower with daisy-like papery flower heads. The outer petals come in yellows,

Helianthus annuus 'Italian White'

Helichrysum 'Bright Bikini Mixed'

Helichrysum petiolare 'Goring Silver'

Hesperis matronalis var. albiflora

Hibiscus moscheutos

pinks, reds and white. The inner disc is yellow. Plants vary in height up to 1m (3ft) or more.

Bright Bikini is a series of bright doubles in red, pink, yellow or white. 'Frosted Sulphur' has pale yellow double flowers. 'Hot Bikini' is hot-red and orange. The King Size Series also have double flowers, with blooms that measure up to 10cm (4in) across and come in a variety of colours. 'Monstrosum' is another large double mixture, which is also available as single colours. 'Silvery Rose' is a particularly beautiful silvery rose-pink.

Helichrysum petiolare

This plant is grown for its silver foliage, and is particularly in demand for hanging baskets and other containers. H 50cm (20in)

Hesperis matronalis

S 1m (3ft). There are several cultivars including 'Variegatum' and 'Limelight', which has silvery lime-green leaves. 'Goring Silver' is a particularly fine silver form.

HESPERIS
Sweet rocket

This genus contains about 30 species of perennials and biennials of which only a couple are of interest to annual gardeners. The main one is *H. matronalis*, which has been grown for centuries as a cottage-garden plant. It is actually a short-lived perennial but is usually treated as an annual or biennial. It is a member of the cabbage family, but has a beautiful sweet scent that fills the evening air. The lilac or white flowers seem to glow in the evening light. H 1m (3ft) S 45cm (18in).
How to obtain You occasionally find plants of the double forms, but the single forms are usually available only as seed.
Cultivation Any reasonable garden soil will suffice. They will grow in full sun or partial shade. Z6.
Propagation Sow the seed in the autumn or spring where the plants are to flower. It can also be sown in pots placed in an open frame. If the plants are allowed to remain in the ground until they shed their seed, they will self-sow. Double forms need to be raised from basal cuttings in spring.
Uses These plants can be used in bedding, but they are best employed in a mixed border, especially in an informal one.

Hesperis matronalis

This is the sweet rocket or dame's violet. The flowers are carried in loose heads in early summer. These flowers are either lilac or

white (known as *H.m.* var. *albiflora*). Sometimes the lilac forms are deeper in colour, almost purple. The coloured flowers often become fused with white as they age. There are also double forms of the lilac, 'Lilacina Flore Pleno', and the white, 'Alba Plena'.

Other plants There is a very similar plant which is a biennial. This is *H. steveniana*. It is shorter and produces pale purple or white flowers. H 60cm (24in).

HIBISCUS
Hibiscus

This is a large genus of around 200 species of which only one or two annuals are grown in gardens, although several of the shrubs are often treated as such. The annual *H. trionum* is most commonly

grown. It is a spreading plant which carries a succession of attractive trumpet-shaped flowers up to 7cm (3in) across.
How to obtain Plants are rarely seen so it is best to obtain seed from seed merchants' catalogues.
Cultivation Plant out once the threat of late frosts has passed. Any reasonable garden soil will do but it must be well-drained. A sunny position is necessary. Z10.
Propagation Sow the seed in early spring at 16–18°C (60–64°F) under glass.
Uses Hibiscus are not suited to mass planting, but they are good in mixed borders. The spreading habit makes them excellent container plants.

Hibiscus trionum

The flowers are a beautiful cream colour which contrasts with a very dark purple central eye. H 75cm (30in) S 60cm (24in). There are several cultivars: 'Lyonia' is silvery-yellow while 'Sunnyday' has lemon flowers.

Other plants The annuals *Hibiscus cannabinus* and *H. radiatus* are sometimes offered as seed. They have creamy-white flowers, but red and purple forms are more commonly offered. Some shrubby hibiscus are occasionally used in warmer gardens in summer, being moved out from the conservatory or greenhouse in pots. They include *H. rosa-sinensis*, the Chinese hibiscus with its wealth of cultivars, and *H. moscheutos*.

Hibiscus trionum

Hordeum jubatum, with orange dahlias

Iberis crenata

HORDEUM
Barley

Although this genus contains about 20 species of grass, only one is generally grown in our gardens. This is *H. jubatum*, commonly known as squirrel tail grass. It is an annual or short-lived perennial. It has become almost a cult plant and can be seen in a wide range of elaborate bedding schemes. It is frequently bedded with seemingly unlikely partners, yet it often works. This is because it is a grass with a soft curving flower head that combines well with all kinds of plants, both flowering and foliage. The heads are pinkish-green in colour and in the sunlight they also have an attractive silvery, silky sheen. They turn straw-coloured as they age. H 50cm (20in) S 25cm (10in).
How to obtain Squirrel tail grass is occasionally available as plants. However, these are generally not worth buying as the plants are not happy in pots, and besides you need more than one or two plants for an effective display. It is much better to raise your own by sowing seed which is obtainable from a number of seed merchants and specialist societies.
Cultivation Any reasonable garden soil is suitable for hordeum. Like most grasses it needs a sunny position. Z5.
Propagation Sow the seed in spring in the open ground where the plants are to flower.
Uses Squirrel tail grass is best planted in drifts either in bedding displays or mixed borders. If possible plant them where the sun will shine through the flower heads to show off their silkiness.

Other plants Hordeum hystrix is also sometimes offered, but it is difficult to find. It is similar to *H. jubatum. H. vulgare*, the cultivated barley, can also be grown. It is not as decorative as the above but it is still interesting and makes a good dried grass.

IBERIS
Candytuft

A genus of about 40 species of which several are frequently seen in gardens. This is another plant that belongs to the cabbage family, although you would be hard-pressed to see the resemblance unless you were a botanist. They are low-growing plants with flat or slightly domed heads of mainly white flowers, although there are also pink and reddish-purple forms. They have an old-fashioned look about them but they are still popular, partly because they can be used for a variety of purposes in the garden. They rarely reach more than 30cm (12in) high, often less, and they are frequently wider than they are tall.
How to obtain These are widely available as plants, either in bedding packs or as individual plants. If you want to raise your own plants, there are plenty of sources of seed.
Cultivation Plant or sow in any reasonable garden soil. Full sun is best; they can be placed in light shade, but they may grow leggy (produce long, bare stems). Z7.
Propagation Seed can be sown where it is to flower or it can be sown under glass at 13–16°C (55–60°F) in early spring.
Uses Candytufts can be used in any form of bedding scheme or as edging or as fillers in a mixed border. They can also be grown in containers. Candytufts are good plants for children's gardens because they are easy to grow and flower quickly.

Iberis amara

This is a taller form of candytuft with plants sometimes reaching up to 45cm (18in) but often less. The flower heads are possibly more domed than in other species. They are mainly white, but there are also those that are flushed with purple. Another pleasing attribute is their attractive perfume.

There are a number of cultivars available, including 'Giant Hyacinth', 'Hyacinth Flowered', 'Iceberg', 'Snowbird' and the fragrant 'Pinnacle', all of which have white flowers.

Iberis umbellata

This is similar to the previous plant, except that there is more colour variation. As well as white there are pink, red and purple and lavender forms.

Most of the cultivars are sold in mixtures such as the Flash Series with its brightly coloured flowers, and the Fairy Series which produces flowers in softer shades. Some, however, are sold as separate colours. They include 'Flash White'.

Other plants I. crenata is a similar species to the above.

IONOPSIDIUM
Violet cress

This is a tiny genus of some five species of annual plants. Only one of them is grown to any extent and that not very frequently nowadays. This is *I. acaule*, which is variously known as violet cress or diamond flower. It is a charming low-growing plant with lilac, blue or white flowers. As it is a member of the cabbage family it has the usual four petals arranged in a cross. It flowers over a long period, from early summer well into the autumn, and is constantly covered in its star-like flowers. H 8cm (3in) high and slightly more in spread.

Iberis amara 'Giant Hyacinth'

Ionopsidium acaule

Ipomoea purpurea

How to obtain Seed is not commonly available from most merchants so you will have to search for it, but the effort is very worthwhile. Plants are only rarely seen for sale.

Cultivation Violet cress will grow in any decent garden soil, although it should be moisture-retentive but at the same time free-draining. They should be planted in full sun. Z9.

Propagation Sow the seed in spring in open ground where the plants are to flower.

Uses This is a good plant for odd places, such as crevices in pavings or walls. More formally it can be used as edging in beds or for rock gardens. It can also be grown as a small pot plant, to be placed on a wall or at the front of a group of containers.

IPOMOEA
Morning glory

This is an enormous genus, providing plenty of variety for those who would like to explore it. There are more than 500 species, and many of them are climbers. There are a dozen or so in general cultivation, but probably more to come since the plants are becoming increasingly popular. Some are annuals but most are perennials which can either be grown in a conservatory or glasshouse, or grown as annuals and used outside in the summer. Being climbers they are particularly useful since there are not a great number of annuals that grow in this way. The flowers

are mainly trumpets; they are carried in the same way as those of convolvulus, to which morning glories are closely related. The main exception is *I. lobata*, which has spikes of narrow, almost tubular flowers. Morning glories

can grow up to 6m (20ft) in height, but when used as annuals they are more likely to reach only 2–3m (6–10ft).

How to obtain Morning glories are increasingly available as plants for use under glass. The true annuals are available as seed from most seed merchants.

Cultivation Plant out after the danger of frosts has passed in any reasonable, well-drained soil. A warm, sunny position is important. Supports are necessary. Z8–10.

Propagation Sow seed under glass in spring at 18–20°C (64–68°F). Germination is improved if the seed is soaked in warm water before being sown.

Uses Morning glories can be used anywhere in the garden where height and colour are required. This can be either in the open ground or in containers. They make good patio plants.

Ipomoea lobata

This species is not quite so popular as it once was and so it is not offered so widely. However, it can still be found. It does not have the typical trumpet-shaped flowers but instead carries spikes of narrow flowers. These are orange-red in bud when they first open, but they gradually turn to cream as they age.

Ipomoea purpurea

The common morning glory is becoming increasingly popular. It carries purple trumpet-shaped flowers with white throats. It also has pink, white and striped cultivars. 'Milky Way' has white flowers with maroon stripes, while 'Scarlet O'Hara' is scarlet with a white throat.

Ipomoea tricolor

This is a very old favourite. It produces trumpets that are blue with a white eye. There are a few variations on this. 'Flying Saucers' produces blue and white flowers. 'Heavenly Blue' is still one of the most widely grown morning glories, with its sky-blue flowers and the ever-present white throat.

Other plants There are several other ipomoea species which are currently becoming increasingly popular. They include *I. coccinea*, *I. alba*, *I.* × *multifida*, *I. nil*, and *I. quamoclit*, all of which are well worth considering. They produce the typical trumpet-shaped flowers in a range of blues, purples and reds.

Ipomoea lobata

Isatis tinctoria

ISATIS
Woad

A genus of 30 plants that are mainly disregarded in the garden except for *I. tinctoria*. This was once used as a blue dye and it is still grown in herb gardens in memory of this. It is not in the frontline of decorative plants but it does produce masses of small yellow flowers on its tall upright stems in the summer. Once the flowering season is over, it is covered with masses of dangling black seed which can be very attractive, especially when they catch the sunlight. However, it will then self-sow. It probably doesn't deserve a place in borders but it fits well in wild-flower gardens where it produces a sunny display of colour. H 1.5m (5ft) S 45cm (18in).

How to obtain Woad is often available in plant form at specialist herb nurseries, but rarely elsewhere. However, seed is reasonably widely available.

Cultivation Any reasonable garden soil that is well-drained will be suitable. Woad should have a sunny position. It may need support in exposed sites. Z6.

Propagation Sow the seed in the spring where the plants are to flower. They will self-sow if left to set seed.

Uses Woad's main use is now confined to the herb garden, but it is a very good plant for wild-gardens. It would not look out of place in an informal setting, such as a cottage garden.

Other plants Just occasionally you may come across seed of *I. lusitanica* and *I. platyloba*, both of which are similar to, but shorter than, the above. Specialist societies are a good source of seed for these plants.

LABLAB
Lablab

Although this single species genus has been around in gardens for a long time it is only in relatively recent times that it has become more common. This is perhaps due to the attractive purple leaves of the main cultivar, 'Ruby Moon', which has become valued as a foliage plant. The species is *I. purpureus* which has previously been known as *Dolichos*. It is still sometimes found listed under this name in garden centres and catalogues. It is a member of the pea family and this is readily apparent from the pea-like flowers. They are big and carried in large numbers. Once flowering has finished, the plant produces large pods which provide another round of decoration. This plant has also inherited the tendency of the pea to climb, making it doubly valuable in the garden. It can get up to 6m (20ft) when grown as a perennial but as an annual it only reaches 2–3m (6–10ft) in an average summer.

How to obtain Lablab is now available in many garden centres as plants but the most reliable source is still seed which is available from most merchants.

Lablab purpureus (seed pods)

Cultivation Grow in any reasonable garden soil so long as it is free-draining. A position in full sun is required. Lablab needs some form of support to climb up. A tripod in a border is ideal, but it can be grown up any support, for example a pole or a wigwam of sticks. Z9.

Propagation Sow the seed of this plant under glass in spring at 21°C (70°F).

Uses Lablab is valuable for adding height to a mixed border or bedding scheme. The dark-leaved form is often used in more exotic plantings, where it mixes well with tropical plants.

Lablab purpureus

The flowers are pinkish-purple pea-like blooms that are tinged with paler pink. They are followed by deep purple, nearly black, seed pods. The foliage is green, tinged with purple.

The 'Ruby Moon' is more commonly seen than the species and is responsible for this plant's

revival. This has a wonderful deep purple foliage which sets off both the flowers and the seed pods beautifully.

LANTANA
Lantana

This large genus of 150 shrubs and perennials includes a few plants that have been cultivated as plants for conservatories or glasshouses for some time, but they have also increasingly been grown as outdoor annuals. The main attraction is the superb flowers which are carried in domed or rounded heads. They come in several colours, and more excitingly they actually change colour so that the younger flowers at the centre are a different colour from than those on the margins. Thus they may be flamered around the perimeter of the head and gold, tinged with orange, in the middle. Be warned though, that however pretty these plants may look they do contain toxins which can have very unpleasant consequences if eaten.

In ideal conditions lantanas will grow up to 2m (6ft) in height and spread. However, as bedding plants they will get nowhere near this, reaching more like 60cm (24in) at most.

How to obtain Lantana are most commonly bought as plants, which are available either from garden centres or from specialist nurseries. However, the seeds are becoming more widely available, usually as mixtures.

Lablab purpureus

Lantana camara 'Snow White'

Lantana camara 'Radiation'

Lathyrus odoratus 'White Supreme'

A tumbling variety of Lathyrus odoratus

Cultivation Plant out only after the danger of frosts has passed, into a soil that is reasonably rich, but free-draining. Lantanas need a warm and sunny position. Z8.
Propagation Sow seed in spring under glass at 16–18°C (60–64°F). Take cuttings in summer and overwinter the young plants under glass.
Uses These make excellent bedding plants as well as being perfect for containers of all sorts.

Lantana camara
This is the main species that is available. It has a number of cultivars. Some are single colours such as 'Snow White' which is creamy-white rather than the pure white indicated by its name, but most are bicolours such as the amazingly bright red and orange of 'Radiation'. 'Cream Carpet' is another creamy-coloured one, while 'Mine D'Or' has lovely golden flowers. 'Feston Rose' is

another bicolour with an unusual combination of pink and yellow blooms, and 'Schloss Ortenburg' is along the lines of 'Radiation' with red and orange flowers.

LATHYRUS
Pea
This is a very large genus of 150 species of which some are annuals. The best known of these is the sweet pea, *L. odoratus*, which is a climber. Traditionally it has been grown up some form over support and used in the border and for cutting. However, different forms have been bred so that there are now also low-growing ones for borders and trailing ones suitable for hanging baskets and other containers. They are prized for their colour and fragrance although the latter is missing from many modern varieties.
How to obtain Sweet peas are widely available both as plants, usually in multipacks, and as

seed. There are several specialist merchants who offer large selections of sweet peas.
Cultivation Plant out in early spring into a rich soil that is free-draining. A sunny position is required. Supports are needed for most varieties. Z6.
Propagation Sow the seed in late winter at 16–18°C (60–64°F) under glass.
Uses These plants can be used for decorative purposes in borders or grown in separate beds or in the vegetable garden for cutting and for exhibition purposes. Shorter varieties can be used in all forms of containers.

Lathyrus odoratus
The species is a magnificent plant with smaller flowers than the cultivars. They come in bright

purple and red and are highly scented. There are numerous cultivars, many aimed at gardeners who use them for cutting or exhibition. Most of the colours are much softer than the species, with soft pinks, blues and whites predominating. However, each year brighter reds and blues are introduced. Seed is most frequently sold as individual cultivars of one colour, such as the excellent 'White Supreme' or 'Jayne Amanda' which has rose-pink flowers. They are also widely sold as mixtures. Many are sold in groups, such as the Knee-hi Group, which are much shorter than usual.

Other plants There are other annual species such as the yellow *L. chloranthus* or the blue *L. sativus*.

Lathyrus odoratus

Lathyrus sativus

Laurentia axillaris 'Blue Stars'

Lavatera trimestris 'Novella'

LAURENTIA
Laurentia

This group of plants is sometimes categorized as a separate genus, Laurentia, and sometimes included in Isotoma. It is a genus of nearly 20 species of which one is commonly grown as an annual, although it is a perennial. This is L. axillaris. It is a delightful plant that has come into recent prominence. It forms a rounded hummock of finely cut foliage. Above this are carried beautiful star-shaped flowers, which are up to 4cm (1½in) across. The plant can grow up to 60cm (24in) as a perennial but when grown as an annual it is usually about 25cm (10in) in height and about the same in spread.

How to obtain Laurentia is widely available as plants, sold in individual pots, from garden centres and nurseries, and also as seed from all the seed merchants. It may be sometimes found under the name Isotoma.
Cultivation Any reasonable garden soil will do but it must be free-draining. A sunny position is important. Z7.
Propagation Sow seed in the early spring under glass at 13–16°C (55–60°F). Cuttings can be taken in summer and the young plants overwintered under glass.
Uses This plant works very well in all areas of the garden. It can be used as bedding or in a mixed border. It is also an excellent choice for all forms of container, including hanging baskets.

Laurentia axillaris

It is doubtful whether the plants and seed under this name are the species; they are more likely to be the cultivar known as 'Blue Stars'. It has starry flowers that are a lovely blue in colour. They are produced in quantity over a long period. There is also a pink form called 'Pink Stars' or 'Starlight Pink', and occasionally you find white ones. They can now also be bought as mixtures.

Other plants There are a couple of other species which can occasionally be found. L. anethifolia has white flowers in the form 'White Stars'. L. petraea also has white flowers.

LAVATERA
Mallow

This is a genus containing about 25 species, of which some are perennials and shrubs (see page 216) and others are annuals. Of the last, one in particular is widely grown. This is L. trimestris, which is prized for its showy funnel-shaped flowers. They are up to 12cm (4½in) across and are either glisteningly white or a striking pink. The pink forms often have a darker eye and radiating thin veins of darker pink. They are extremely good annuals, continuously covered in a profusion of blooms during the summer. H 1.2m (4ft) S 45cm (18in).
How to obtain Mallows can easily be found as plants in most garden centres. However, seed is also

widely available from merchants, and usually offers a greater choice of cultivars.
Cultivation Plant out in any well-drained soil. Mallows must have a sunny position to do well. Z7.
Propagation Sow seed in the early spring under glass at 13–16°C (55–60°F). For later flowering, sow directly in the ground where the plants are to flower.
Uses Mallows make excellent bedding plants as well as being of great use in mixed borders. They can also be used in large tubs.

Lavatera trimestris

This species is rarely grown in its own right, but is often seen as one of its several cultivars. 'Silver Cups' is one of the best known. This has soft silvery-pink flowers, each with darker veins and a

dollop of raspberry pink in the middle. 'Mont Blanc' is another favourite, with flowers of pure white. 'Pink Beauty' is very pale pink, with darker veins and central eye. 'Novella' is also pink.

Other plants Lavatera arborea is a biennial. While it is not in the same league as the above, it is excellent for wild-flower gardens, especially those on the coast or in sandy soils. The flowers are not as showy but they are the same funnel shape and come in a dull purply colour. This is a shrubby plant that can get quite tall. H 3m (10ft) when growing well.

LAYIA
Layia

You would be forgiven for thinking that this genus has only one plant, since that is all that most people know. In fact, there are 15 species of annual plants. The others have been grown in gardens in the past but their popularity has declined and now they are difficult to find. The one we still grow is L. platyglossa. It has also been known as L. elegans under which name it is still often sold. Its common name is tidy tips, which refers to the fact that the yellow petals have dainty white tips to them. The flowers are daisies up to 4cm (1½in) in diameter, with a ring of outer petals and an inner disc which is also yellow. The plants are upright. H 45cm (18in) S 30cm (12in). Some forms are more

Layia elegans

Limnanthes douglasii

sprawling and do not gain such a height, so they are better used in hanging baskets.

How to obtain Layias are getting more difficult to find, but some seed merchants still carry them in stock. Check under both species names.

Cultivation Any reasonable garden soil will suit these plants. Z7.

Propagation Sow the seed in spring in the open ground where the plants are to grow. They can also be sown in pots under glass at 13–16°C (55–60°F).

Uses Layia can be used as bedding or in mixed borders. They will also make a colourful addition to containers.

Other plants With determined searching, you may be able to find seed of *L. chrysanthemoides* since there is at least one merchant that still stocks it. This is a plant which carries bright yellow flowers. H 30cm (12in).

LIMNANTHES
Poached egg plant
This is one of those genera in which only one plant is generally grown, although there are up to 17 species from which to choose. The flowers look similar to those of *Layia* at first glance, although they are in no way related. *Limnanthes douglasii* is known as the poached egg plant because, as in *Layia platyglossa*, it has yellow petals with a white margin. In this case the petals are much broader and form a saucer shape. The plants

make wonderful edging to paths. They are particularly useful plants for dull days because they are so bright and cheerful they make it seem as if the sun is shining. Poached egg plants are much loved by bees. They are low-growing. They usually self-sow and can create a dense mat, making useful ground cover. H and S 20cm (8in).

How to obtain Poached egg plants are available as plants but they do not do well if confined in pots so it is best to sow your own seed. This is readily available. Once you have these plants they will produce copious amounts of seedlings, fortunately in the same area since they do not spread far.

Cultivation Any normal garden soil will do, but these plants should be positioned in the sun for the best effect. Z6.

Propagation Sow the seed where the plants are to flower in autumn or in spring.

Uses They make excellent bedding plants for the early summer, but can also be used as temporary fillers in mixed border. They are very good edging plants.

Limnanthes douglasii
This is nearly always grown as the species, described above. However, there is also a very rare variety known as *L.d.* var. *sulphurea* in which the white edging is missing, making the flowers all yellow.

Other plants Very occasionally, you may come across seed of *L. alba*. This is a white-flowered species which is similar to the above. However, it is not so attractive a plant since it is more sprawling and the flowers are smaller.

LINARIA
Toadflax
There are about 100 species in this genus which include perennials (see page 380) as well as annuals. Quite a number of these annuals are grown in gardens, but they are not widely cultivated. This may be because they are grown mainly in mixed borders and have not been developed for the bedding or container market. This also means that they are not so easy to find,

but the effort is worth it since there are some interesting plants out there. The one exception is *L. maroccana* which is facing a revival, with a number of cultivars now becoming available. Linarias vary in height from ground-hugging species to those that reach 75cm (30in) in height.

How to obtain Apart from that of *L. maroccana*, seed is difficult to find although it is available from some seed merchants and specialist societies. It is rare that you find any plants for sale.

Cultivation Any reasonable garden soil will be sufficient, but linarias prefer light soils that should be free-draining. Z6.

Propagation Sow the seed in spring in open ground where the plants are to flower.

Uses Linarias are good plants for the mixed border. *L. maroccana* can be used for bedding.

Linaria alpina
This species is strictly speaking a perennial but because it is short-lived, it is treated as an annual. It is a very low-growing plant. The small flowers are carried in short upright spikes and have a velvety texture. They are exquisite and are available in a wide range of purple-reds. Most are bicolours.

Linaria alpina is a very good plant for growing in crevices, between the cracks in paving and walls as well as on rock gardens. It self-sows without becoming a nuisance. H 8cm (3in).

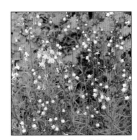

Linaria maroccana 'Bunny Rabbits'

Linaria maroccana
The multi-coloured flowers are carried in spikes and look like miniature antirrhinums. H up to 45cm (18in). There are a few cultivars including Excelsior hybrids, 'Fairy Bouquet' and 'Northern Lights', all of which produce flowers in mixed colours of blue, purple, pink and yellow. 'White Pearl' is restricted to white flowers as its name suggests. 'Bunny Rabbits' bears white, pink and yellow blooms.

Linaria reticulata
These are tall plants with very attractive foliage and deep purple flowers, which are splashed with orange or yellow on the lower lip. H 1m (3ft). There is also a mixture, called 'Flamenco', now on offer.

Other plants *Linaria elegans* is a rather beautiful, tall plant that produces purple-pink flowers. It is well worth seeking out. H 70cm (28in).

Linaria maroccana 'Fairy Bouquet'

Lindheimera texana

LINDHEIMERA
Star daisy

Lindheimera texana is the only member of this genus and it has been popular in the garden for a long time. However, it now seems to be in decline since only a few seed merchants carry it. It is an upright plant, but is generally sturdy enough to stand without staking. The flowers are up to 2.5cm (1in) across and are carried in loose heads. They are yellow, varying from soft to golden hues, and comprising five petals arranged in a star shape. They appear in profusion over a long period through the summer. The yellow is set off perfectly by the bright green foliage and bracts that surround the flowers. H 60cm (24in) S 30cm (12in).
How to obtain The plants are not commonly sold, either in garden centres or nurseries, but the seed is offered by some merchants and occasionally by specialist societies in their seed exchanges. You will need to search for this plant.
Cultivation Plant out once the danger of frosts has passed. Star daisies will grow in any soil that is reasonably rich, but it should be well drained. A sunny position is required. Z8.
Propagation Sow the seed in early spring at 16–18°C (61–64°F) under glass.
Uses Star daisies can be used as bedding as they have a long flowering season, but they work equally well in a mixed border scheme, where a splash of bright yellow is required.

LINUM
Flax

A huge genus of 200 species which contains perennials (see page 381) as well as annuals and biennials. The flaxes are characterized by their upward-facing, funnel-shaped flowers. Although generally thought of as blue, many have yellow or red flowers. There are a number of annuals for the keen gardener, but there is only one that is in widespread use. This is *L. grandiflorum*, which is a magnificent plant that is welcome in borders and bedding schemes alike. The perennial flaxes are short lived and can be used as annuals if their bright blue colour was desired. H up to 75cm (30in) S 15cm (6in).
How to obtain The seed of the main species, *L. grandiflorum*, is readily available but you will need to search carefully for any other species. Plants are rarely, if ever, offered for sale.
Cultivation Flax should be grown in any reasonably fertile soil that is well-drained. They should have a sunny position. Z7.
Propagation Sow the seed in the open ground where the plants are to flower. Thin the seedlings to 15cm (6in) intervals.
Uses These plants can be used to create spectacular blocks of colour in a bedding scheme or planted as drifts in a mixed border.

Linum grandiflorum var. *rubrum*
This plant, which is often listed as a cultivar 'Rubrum', has brilliant red flowers with a dark eye; they are quite dazzling to look at. The variety *alba* has pure white flowers. The gem of this form is 'Bright Eyes' which has glistening white flowers with a crimson base to each petal and a black centre – they are stunning. There is another form, variously listed as *caeruleum* and 'Caeruleum', which has purplish-blue flowers.

Other plants Linum sulcatum is a rarely seen annual from Eastern USA. It has pale yellow flowers and grows to 75cm (30in) in height. It is worth growing if you can find seed.

Linum usitatissimum is the common agricultural flax. Its attractive blue flowers also make it an excellent garden plant. It works particularly well in a wild-flower garden where true blue flowers are often lacking. There are some garden cultivars available, including 'Skyscraper'.

LOBELIA
Lobelia

This is an enormous genus of some 350 species. Most of those grown in the garden are perennials (see page 381) but there is one annual that is more popular then all of those put together. This is *L. erinus*. This is seen in all kinds of garden situations, from hanging baskets to the edges of pathways. It must be one of the most useful and popular of all plants and has remained so for many generations.

The flowers are basically blue, with a white dot in the throat, but there are also pink, purple and red variations. It is a bushy, sprawling little plant which grows to about 25cm (10in) and a little more across. Some varieties produce an abundance of trailing stems which makes them useful in hanging baskets.
How to obtain Lobelia is widely sold in bedding packs and in individual pots by most garden centres. Seed is also widely sold and this is offered in a better choice of cultivars.
Cultivation Any good garden soil or potting compost (soil mix) will do for these plants. Lobelia is best planted in partial shade but it can be used in full sun so long as the soil does not dry out too much. Clip occasionally to keep the plants compact. Z7.

Linum grandiflorum var. *rubrum*

Lobelia erinus 'Cambridge Blue'

Propagation Sow seed in early spring under glass at 16–18°C (61–64°F). Plants may self-sow.
Uses Lobelia looks good anywhere. It is particularly useful in containers, where it often acts as a "filler", creating a background colour for other plants.

Lobelia erinus

The species is not grown as such; it is always cultivated as one of its many cultivars. The flower colour varies from blues, such as in the 'Cambridge Blue' with its sky blue flowers and the dark blue 'Crystal Palace', to cherry-red, as in 'Rosamund'. There are a number of series which are sold either as mixtures or as individual colours. The Cascade Series has trailing stems, and is excellent for hanging baskets. It includes 'Lilac Cascade' and 'Red Cascade'. Other Series include the Palace Series and Regatta Series.

Lobularia maritima 'Snow Crystals'

LOBULARIA
Sweet alyssum

A small genus of five species from the Mediterranean area of which just one is grown in our gardens. This is sweet alyssum or sweet Alison, *L. maritima*. It is not a plant to set the world alight since it is not particularly showy. However, it is one of those plants that can act as a basic ingredient in the design of any garden. It is a perennial that is grown as an annual, although if left it may linger on in a somewhat straggly way for another year.

Sweet alyssum is low-growing, forming little hummocks of foliage which are covered with small white flowers for a very long period from summer into autumn. The flowers are sweetly scented (hence part of its name, the other part comes from the fact that the flower heads resemble those of *Alyssum*). They are carried in slightly domed heads. As well as the basic white there are cultivars that vary from pink to purple. H 5–30cm (2–12in) S up to 30cm (12in).
How to obtain These plants are frequently sold as bedding packs in most garden centres and many nurseries. Only a few of the cultivars may be available, but there should be no problem in getting white forms. For a bigger choice search the seed merchants' catalogues and grow your own.

Cultivation Any reasonable soil will do, so long as it is free-draining. It requires full sun. Z7.
Propagation Sow the seed in mid-spring in the open ground where the plants are to grow.
Uses Excellent for bedding schemes, especially where block or linear planting is required. Sweet alyssums can also be used as fillers or edging in mixed borders.

Lobularia maritima

The species is not often grown in its own right. It is more commonly found as one of its cultivars. There are several series, including the Alice Series and Easter Bonnet Series, which produce a mixture of white, pink and purple flowers. There are also individual cultivars, including 'Snow Crystals' (white flowers), 'Snowcloth' (white), 'New Purple' (purple) or 'Navy Blue' (purple, not blue as one might assume from the name). There is also a variegated form called 'Variegata', which has pale green foliage edged with white. It may occasionally be found but this plant is not widely available.

White-flowered annuals

Antirrhinum 'White Wonder'	*Iberis amara*
Argyranthemum frutescens	*Lathyrus odorata*
Clarkia pulchella 'Snowflake'	*Lavatera trimestris* 'Mont Blanc'
Cleome spinosa 'Helen Campbell'	*Lobelia erinus* 'Snowball'
Cosmos bipinnatus 'Sonata'	*Omphalodes linifolia*
Digitalis purpurea alba	*Osteospermum* 'Glistening White'
Gypsophila elegans 'Covent Garden'	*Pelargonium*
	Petunia

Lobularia maritima 'Wonderland'

Lonas annua

LONAS
Lonas
This genus has one main species, *L. annua*, also known as the African daisy or yellow ageratum. This is yet another of those annuals that was once much more popular than it is now. Indeed although a number of seed merchants still list it in their catalogues it rarely crops up in any literature about annuals. Its neglect is surprising because it is quite a showy plant and works well in borders. It is useful as a cut flower and can also be dried. The African daisy is a bushy plant with clusters of bright yellow flowers carried on reddish stems over a long period, lasting from midsummer through into the autumn. The flowers are prolific and they are also long-lasting which makes them very useful as bedding plants. H 30cm (12in) S 25cm (10in).
How to obtain Plants are very rarely seen on sale, but there are a large number of seed merchants offering lonas plants.
Cultivation Lonas will grow in any reasonable garden soil that is not too wet. It should be given a sunny position if possible. Z7.
Propagation Sow seed in early spring at 16–18°C (60–64°) under glass.
Uses Lonas makes an excellent bedding plant and can also be used to great effect in a mixed border or in containers.

Lonas inodora
The species is often grown in its own right, and there are also a couple of cultivars, 'Gold Rush' and 'Golden Yellow'. However, they are not a great deal different from the species.

LOTUS
Parrot's beak
This is a big genus containing about 150 species of shrubs and perennials. At least one of them is treated as an annual in the garden. This is *L. berthelotii*, a very beautiful plant for which everybody should be on the lookout. It is an evergreen shrub with prostrate stems. When the plant

Lotus berthelotii (foliage)

Lotus berthelotii (in flower)

is placed in a container such as a tall tub or a hanging basket, the stems hang over the edges to create curtains of foliage. The foliage is made up of narrow leaves carried in much the same way as those of lavender or rosemary. The great beauty of the leaves is that, again like those of the lavender, they are silver. This is a member of the pea family, and the relationship can be seen in the flowers. They are elongated and upward-curling, looking rather like a parrot's beak. They are scarlet and contrast beautifully with the cascades of silver foliage.
How to obtain Parrot's beak is widely available as plants, which are now carried by most garden centres as well as nurseries. It is sometimes offered as seed, but there is no advantage to be had from growing the plant from seed.

Cultivation In containers, use a loam-based potting compost (soil mix). If planted in an open garden, parrot's beak needs a free-draining soil. A sunny position is also necessary. Z8.
Propagation Take cuttings in summer from existing plants and overwinter the resulting plants under warm glass.
Uses The parrot's beak's main use is in containers from which the foliage can hang down. It can also be used in the garden, either on the flat where it can be used as bedding or on walls, down which the foliage can cascade.

Lotus berthelotii
This plant is most often grown as the species, described above. There is, however, some slight variation in colour, although this is not sufficient for cultivars to

Lunaria annua

be delineated. Some flowers contain more orange, making them a flame colour, while others are a darker red. You will need to see the plants in flower if you wish to buy one of these variants.

Other plants The only other plant worth mentioning is sometimes called *L. tetragonolobus* and sometimes *Tetragonolobus purpureus*. This is the asparagus pea, which has edible pods but can be grown as a decorative plant. It is a low-growing annual with stems that grow up to 40cm (16in). It has small pea-like flowers. They are an attractive bright red, which contrasts well with the foliage.

LUNARIA
Honesty
A genus of one species, which is a biennial that is commonly grown. This tall plant was much loved by the Victorians and it is still very popular. In the spring it has striking purple flowers and these eventually produce oval seed pods; when their outer casings are discarded, they produce a silver disc which looks superb in dried flower arrangements. If you let some plants seed they will self-sow. H 1m (3ft), S 30cm (12in).
Cultivation Any garden soil will suffice and these plants will happily grow in shade or sun. Z8.
Propagation Honesty can be propagated simply by sowing the seed where you want the plants to grow. A small plant is produced in the first year and flowering is in the following spring.
Uses Honesty is good for mixed borders and informal plantings among shrubs or trees.

Lunaria annua
This is the only species that is worth growing. The species has purple flowers but there is also a most beautiful white variety, *albiflora*. There are several variegated forms including 'Variegata', with purple flowers and white marginal variegations to the leaves, and a white-flowered form called 'Alba Variegata'. 'Munstead Purple' has darker purple flowers.

Malcolmia maritima

MALCOLMIA
Virginia stock
Of the 35 species in this genus only one, *Malcolmia* (sometimes confusingly spelt *Malcomia*) *maritima*, is in general cultivation. It is pretty little annual which is still managing to hold on to its popularity in spite of there being many showier plants around. Its thin stems are smothered with small, four-petalled flowers from spring right through into autumn. These are white, pink or purple with a white eye. Unlike the larger stocks to which it is related, this plant has no scent. Virginia stocks have an old-fashioned, prettiness, and they are ideal for bedding or for filling gaps in the mixed border. There were once several cultivars of the species, including white forms, but these are no longer sold. H 38cm (15in) S 15cm (6in).

How to obtain Virginia stocks are sometimes sold as plants. The seed is readily available.
Cultivation Sow in any reasonable garden soil, preferably one that is free-draining. Virginia stocks need a sunny position. Z7.
Propagation Sow in spring, in the open ground where the plants are to flower. If allowed to set seed they will self-sow.
Uses These plants look good in drifts, as bedding or in a mixed border. They are also good for edging paths and ideal for children's gardens, since they are easy to grow, quick to flower and stay colourful over a long period.

Other plants *M. flexuosa* is similar to the above, *M. bicolor* has pink or yellow flowers, and *M. littorea* has large purple-pink ones. You may be able to find these offered by specialist societies.

Lunaria annua var. *albiflora*

Yellow-flowered annuals

Alcea rosea 'Yellow'	Limonium sinuatum
Anoda cristata	'Forever Moonlight'
'Buttercup'	Limnanthes douglasii
Argemone mexicana	Lonas annua
Argyranthemum frutescens	Mentzelia lindleyi
'Jamaica Primrose'	Mimulus
Chrysanthemum segetum	Sanvitalia procumbens
Coreopsis 'Sunray'	Tagetes erecta
Glaucium flavum	Tagetes patula
Helianthus annuus	Tropaeolum peregrinum

Malope trifida

Matthiola longipetala subsp. *bicornis*

Matthiola Brompton Stock

MALOPE
Annual mallow

This is a small genus of four species, but only one annual is in general cultivation. Even this is less popular than it once was, but happily it is still available to those who want an attractive but not too commonly seen plant. The plant in question is *M. trifida*. The mallow part of the name comes from the fact that the flowers resemble those of the mallow (to which it is related). These are funnel- or trumpet-shaped and up to 8cm (3in) across. Their colour is purple-red, with deeper purple veins running into the centre. They appear over a long period from summer well into autumn, and contrast beautifully with the green foliage. H 1.5m (5ft) S 30cm (12in).

How to obtain Annual mallows are occasionally available as plants from garden centres and nurseries, but don't rely on finding them. It is better to obtain seed from one of the seed merchants.

Cultivation These plants will grow in virtually any reasonable garden soil so long as it is free-draining. A sunny position is best but they will grow in a little shade. Z7.

Propagation Sow the seed into open ground in spring where they are to flower or sow under glass in early spring at 13–16°C (55–60°F).

Uses Like most mallows, these are excellent for coastal gardens. They also make very attractive cut flowers.

Malope trifida

The species, described above, is grown in its own right, and there are also a few cultivars available. One of the best of these is 'White Queen', which, as its name suggests, has white flowers. 'Pink Queen' (pink flowers) and 'Red Queen' (red flowers) are also available. One of the newer cultivars is a mixture called 'Glacier Fruits' which includes pink, red and white blooms, as does 'Crown Mix'. 'Vulcan' is a larger plant which carries deep purplish-red flowers.

MATTHIOLA
Stock

This is a medium-sized genus of some 55 species of which a number are annuals or biennials. Among them are some of the best annuals for the garden. Their attraction lies partly in their magnificent compact flower heads, which come in a variety of bright or soft colours, and partly in their powerful scent. Their popularity is reflected in the fact that seed merchants sell a large range of varieties and frequently offer new ones. Looking at the dense spikes of flowers it is hard to imagine that these plants are in the cabbage family. The range of colours includes the cabbage's yellow, but generally the flowers come in a wide range of pinks, purples and reds as well as white. They are quite large, up to 2.5cm (1in) across. The scent is sweet and mainly occurs in the evening. H 60cm (24in) in some varieties, S 30cm (12in) across.

How to obtain Stocks are widely available as plants, and garden centres and nurseries sell them in packs as well as in individual pots.

Matthiola incana 'Legacy Mixed'

A larger range of varieties is available in seed form from the various merchants.

Cultivation Generally these plants are happy in any reasonable garden soil, with the usual proviso that it should be free-draining. A warm sunny position is also necessary. Z6.

Propagation Most can be sown in early spring under glass at 13–16°C (55–60°F). The night-scented stock can be sown in spring in the open ground where the plants are to flower.

Uses Stocks make excellent bedding material, but they can also be planted as drifts in a mixed border. They can also be used in containers. Site the sweetly scented ones on patios or near to sitting areas. Stocks make excellent cut flowers.

Matthiola incana

This is an upright, shrubby plant with greyish-green foliage. The dense heads of flowers come in white, or shades of pink, red or purple. The plants are generally sold in two main groups: the Brompton stocks, which are biennial, and the ten-week stocks, which are annual. The flowers are either single or double.

There are plenty of varieties of both; available either as mixtures or in single colours. Among them is the Cinderella Series, whose plants grow up to 30cm (12in) high, bearing well-scented double flowers in colours that include lavender and blue. 'Legacy Mixed' are also doubles but they are taller. The Midget Series are just 25cm (10in) high; the flowers come in a wide range of colours.

Matthiola longipetala subsp. bicornis

This is the very charming night-scented stock which produces loose heads of single flowers that are sweetly scented at night. They are especially good for planting beneath bedrooms. There are several varieties available, and these include 'Evening Fragrance' and 'Starlight Scentsation'. H 35cm (14in) S 23cm (9in).

MELIANTHUS
Honey bush

Not many annuals are used purely for foliage purposes, but *M. major* is one such plant. It is, in fact, a perennial shrub and not an annual at all, but it is usually treated in this way in gardens. It is one of a genus of six shrubby species. The great feature about it is the large leaves which are pinnate (arranged as leaflets on either side of the main leaf stalk). The foliage is a blue- or grey-green and the leaves are noticeably toothed, both features adding to the overall visual effect. In warmer areas, this plant can be treated as a perennial and kept for several years in which case it can become quite big, up to 3m (10ft) tall. As an annual, its height is about 1m (3ft) or so and the same across. If kept more than one year there is also the possibility that it will flower. The blooms are red and are produced in tall spikes.

How to obtain Available both as plants from garden centres and as seed, although the latter are becoming difficult to find since some of the major seed merchants have stopped stocking it.

Melianthus major

Cultivation Honey bushes will grow in any fertile garden soil that is moisture-retentive but at the same time free-draining. They should be planted in a sunny position. Z9.

Propagation Sow seed in early spring under glass at 13–16°C (55–60°F).

Uses This plant can be used in many places in the garden. It is attractive in its own right and can also be used as a foil to other plants. It works well as bedding but its main use is as small plantings in either mixed borders or containers.

Other plants Although *M. major* is declining in availability, other species are becoming more available if you are prepared to search for them. *M. minor* is a smaller, downy version of the above. *M. comosus*, *M. pectinatus* and *M. villosus* are sometimes available.

MENTZELIA
Starflower

This is a large genus containing some 60 species of which *M. lindleyi* is the only one generally grown. Name changes have bedevilled annuals and this is another of those that has altered. Until recently it was known as *Bartonia aurea*, under which name it is still often sold. Its attraction is the golden-yellow flowers which are flushed red at their base and produced over a long period. Each flower has five rounded petals, each of which are pointed at their tip, giving them their star-like quality. The flowers are quite large, up to about 5cm (2in) in diameter, and they produce a wonderful scent in the evening. The golden-yellow is set off beautifully by the green foliage which is finely cut. H 45cm (18in) S 25cm (10in).

How to obtain Starflowers are rarely available as plants but the seed is offered by a number of seed merchants. It is often listed under the name *Bartonia*.

Cultivation Any reasonable garden soil will be suitable for star-flowers, so long as it is free draining. These plants require a sunny position. Z9.

Propagation Sow the seed in early spring in open ground where the plants are to flower.

Uses Starflowers make excellent bedding and they can also be used successfully in a mixed border. It is also worth experimenting with them as container plants. They are best planted in a site where their evening fragrance can be appreciated, such as under the windows of living areas.

Other plants A few of the other species are occasionally grown but you will have to search to find them. *M. laevicaulis* is a biennial producing pale yellow flowers that open to twice the size of the above. It is very attractive and deserves to be more widely known. *M. involucrata* is another, this time with creamy-coloured flowers that have a satin-like texture. The flower centres are tinged with crimson. It is worth looking for among the specialist society lists.

Orange-flowered annuals

Antirrhinum majus 'Sonnet Orange Scarlet'	*Mimulus* 'Malibu'
Calceolaria 'Sunset Mixed'	*Nemesia* 'Orange Prince'
Calendula officinalis	*Papaver nudicaule*
Celosia cristata 'Apricot Brandy'	*Rudbeckia hirta*
Erysimum 'Orange Bedder'	*Tagetes erecta*
Eschscholzia californica	*Tagetes patula*
Helichrysum bracteatum	*Thunbergia alata*
	Tithonia rotundifolia 'Torch'
	Tropaeolum majus
	Zinnia haageana 'Orange'

Mentzelia lindleyi

Moluccella laevis

MOLUCCELLA
Bells of Ireland

Moluccella is a small genus of four species, of which *M. laevis* is by far the best known by gardeners. This is the famous bells of Ireland or shell flower. The second name is quite apt because the flowers do indeed look like shells. They are very small, each one cupped in a cone-shaped green bract, which gives it its shell-like appearance. The flowers are white or pale purple and they are fragrant. They are carried in upright spikes with the cones facing outward, looking rather like a modern radio mast covered with dishes. Despite its name, this plant has little to do with Ireland. In fact, it is a native plant of south-west Asia, found growing in countries such as Turkey and Iraq. H 1m (3ft) S 25cm (10in).

How to obtain This plant is normally grown from seed which is generally available from most seed merchants. The rare *M. spinosa* is very difficult to find but it is worth checking specialist society seed lists, which sometimes offer it.

Cultivation Bells of Ireland will grow in any free-draining garden soil. They must have a sunny position. Z8.

Propagation Sow seed in late spring in open ground where the plants are to flower. For earlier flowering, raise plants under glass by sowing in early spring at 13–16°C (55–60°F).

Uses This plant can be used in a variety of positions in the garden, including as bedding or in mixed borders. It makes a good cut flower and is excellent for drying.

Other plants If you are lucky, you may be able to track down *M. spinosa*. This is a pretty plant in which the white flowers are also set in cups but this time they are tipped with spines. It has red stems and is quite tall, so it needs a position at the back of a border. H 2m (6ft) S 30cm (12in).

MYOSOTIS
Forget-me-nots

This is a genus of plants that is familiar to most gardeners. The sky-blue flowers seem to have been designed to lift the spirits as winter departs and spring takes over. Several of the 50 species are in cultivation, although not all of them are annuals. They are generally small, clump-forming plants. The small flowers are carried in spikes that gradually unroll, getting longer. There are usually three stages of flowers present in each spike: seed at the bottom, open flowers above them and buds in the opening coil. The flowers come in shades of blue and have yellow centres, but there are also a few cultivars producing blooms in white and pink. H and S 30cm (12in).

How to obtain Forget-me-nots can be bought as plants, but they do not do brilliantly unless they are transplanted when young. Seed is a better bet and fortunately it is widely available.

Cultivation Any reasonable garden soil will be sufficient. Plant in full sun; these plants will also grow in shade, but will become somewhat leggy (producing long, bare stems). Remove after flowering to prevent excessive self-sowing. Z5.

Propagation Sow the seed in the open ground where the plants are to flower. Sow in summer for spring flowering and spring for summer flowering. Most plants will self-sow so there is no need to propagate after the first season.

Uses Forget-me-nots weave between and under other plants, making them perfect for mass carpeting. They can be used either

Myosotis sylvestris

in a bedding scheme – they are traditionally associated with tulips – or in a mixed scheme.

Myosotis sylvestris

This is the forget-me-not most often seen. It is usually a biennial but can be a short-lived perennial. It usually reaches 30cm (12in) in height but some forms are much less. The species has sky-blue flowers but there are cultivars with pink or white blooms. Some are sold as mixtures, such as Ball Series. This can also be obtained in single colours, including 'Snowball' (white). The Victoria Series contains 'Victoria Rose', which has rose-pink flowers. It is one of the shortest forget-me-nots, reaching a height of only 10cm (4in).

Other plants *Myosotis alpestris* is a short-lived perennial which can also be used as an annual. It produces dense heads of typical blue flowers. If you can find it *Cryptantha intermedia* is an interesting plant. Although it is not related to the forget-me-not, it looks very similar to it. It comes in white, and there are also orange and yellow variants, which look good mixed in with the true forget-me-not.

NEMESIA
Nemesia

This is a genus of about 50 species. It provides us with one of the annuals most frequently seen in the garden, *N. strumosa*. The flowers are numerous and produced over a long period. They

Nemesia strumosa 'KLM'

are about 2.5cm (1in) across and look like snapdragons, except that the bottom lip is flat and not inflated. There is a big colour range, including white, pink, red, purple, blue and yellow; there are often several flower colours mixed in one plant. H 15–30cm (6–12in) S 15cm (6in) or more.
How to obtain Nemesias are widely available in bedding packs as plants, but a greater range of options is available as seed.
Cultivation Any reasonable garden soil is suitable so long as it does not dry out completely. A sunny position is needed. In containers use a general potting compost (soil mix), preferably a loam-based one. Z9.
Propagation Sow seed in early spring under glass at 13–16°C (55–60°F).

Uses Nemesias are widely used in bedding schemes as well as for filling in gaps in mixed borders. They also suitable for containers of all types.

Nemesia strumosa

This is the main plant of the genus. It is not often sold as the species; it is much more likely to be found as one of the many varieties that are available. These include series, such as Carnival Series, and individual varieties, such as 'Danish Flag' with its red and white flowers, and 'KLM' with its blue and white blooms.

NEMOPHILA
Nemophila

A couple of unassuming and yet popular annuals belong to this genus of about 11 species. The

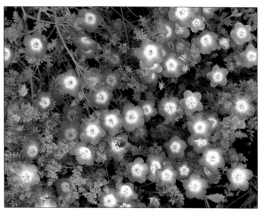
Nemophila menziesii

flowers are not remarkable but somehow they manage to catch the attention in a quiet way. They are saucer-shaped with five white petals, the tip of each having a coloured spot which is generally blue. Nemophilas flower over a long period in the summer, lasting into the autumn. The plants are fairly small. H and S about 30cm (12in) in the taller cultivars.
How to obtain Nemophilas can be purchased as plants, in bedding packs, at the majority of garden centres and nurseries. They are also widely available as seed from most seed merchants.
Cultivation Nemophilas can be grown in any free-draining garden soil. A good potting compost (soil mix) should be used for container plants. Do not let the soil dry out too much, either in the ground or in the containers, especially during very hot weather. A sunny position is best although these plants will tolerate a little shade. Z8.
Propagation The seed can be sown in spring directly into the soil where the plants are to flower. You can also sow them under glass at 13–16°C (55–60°F).
Uses The spreading nature of these plants mean that they are ideal for use in containers, especially hanging baskets and window boxes. They also make good bedding plants as well as being suitable for filling gaps in the mixed border and making good edgings to borders and beds.

Nemophila maculata

This plant is commonly known as five spot, and is the taller of the two species grown. *Nemophila maculata* is not seen quite so frequently as *Nemophila menziesii*, mainly because it has no cultivars. The flowers measure up to 4cm (1½in) across and have white petals with violet-blue spots.

Nemophila menziesii

This is popularly known as baby blue eyes. True to its name, it has blue flowers with white centres but there are some varieties that have pure white flowers. 'Penny Black' is the most startling of all the varieties since it has black flowers that are edged with white. 'Oculata' has pale blue flowers with a deep purple eye.

Nemesia strumosa

Nemophila maculata

Nicandra physalodes

soil where the plants are to flower. After the first year the plants will self-sow.

Uses These are best used as structural plants in a mixed border. They could also look quite spectacular in an imaginative bedding scheme. They can be grown in a large container, such as a tub or pot.

Nicandra physalodes

The species, described above, is grown in its own right. There is also one cultivar, namely 'Violacea'. This has darker flowers and inflated calyces which hold the flowers. These are flushed with a purple so dark it is almost black, and add to the plant's attraction.

NICOTIANA
Tobacco plant

This is a large genus of about 70 species of which a few are grown widely in our gardens. *N. alata* has long been a popular bedding plant as has its hybrid *N. × sanderae* under which name most of the cultivars are collected. *N. sylvestris* has been around for a long time but it is relatively recently that this tall plant has become so popular. The tobacco plants all have tubular flowers that flare out like trumpets. They come in a wide range of colours. Some have a wonderful scent, which is most noticeable in the evening. They tend to be long lasting, from summer well into the autumn.

How to obtain Plants are sold in bedding packs in all garden centres and many nurseries. However, a bigger range of plants can be obtained by growing them from seed which is readily available.

Cultivation Nicotiana will grow in any reasonable garden soil. If it is relatively dry or well-drained, overwinter them – many plants survive into a second year. They prefer a sunny position although they will grow in light shade. Z7.

Propagation Sow the seed in early spring under glass at 16–18°C (55–60°F).

Uses These are excellent for bedding schemes as well as being useful in mixed borders. The shorter varieties can also be used in containers.

Nicotiana sylvestris

Nicotiana alata

This plant used to be known as *N. affinis* and you will still sometimes see it being sold as such. This is a tall plant, with flowers that are pale green on the outside and white on the inside. The flowers are also fragrant. A good plant for mixed borders. H 1m (3ft).

Nicotiana 'Lime Green'

This plant is shorter than the above, reaching 60cm (24in). It has large lime-green blooms.

Nicotiana × sanderae

A range of garden hybrids with flowers in various colours,

NICANDRA
Shoo-fly flower

This is a single species genus with *N. physalodes* being the only member. It is commonly called the shoo-fly flower, presumably because of its ability to keep flies at bay. It is quite a spectacular plant when well grown since it is tall and has spreading branches. The flowers are funnel-shaped. They come in pale lilac-blue and have white centres. Individually they are not long lived, but a constant succession of them is produced from midsummer right through to the first frosts. The flowers are followed by round fruits (which give this plant its

other name of apple of Peru). These then split open to reveal hundreds of seeds, which tend to self-sow with gay abandon. H 1.2m (4ft) S 1m (3ft)

How to obtain Shoo-fly flowers are rarely seen as plants because they do not do well when confined to small pots. However, it is possible to find seed since several seed merchants carry it.

Cultivation Any reasonable garden soil will do, but the plants will do best if it is enriched with plenty of well-rotted organic material. They need a sunny position. Z8.

Propagation Shoo-fly flowers come readily from seed. It should be sown in spring, directly in the

Nicotiana 'Lime Green'

Nicotiana langsdorffii

Nigella damascena 'Miss Jekyll'

including pink and red. There are several series including the popular Domino Series, whose plants have a wide range of colours; single-coloured plants such as 'Domino Salmon Pink' are also available. This is one of the taller forms, reaching 45cm (18in) in height.

Nicotiana sylvestris
A tall species, good for the back of the border. It carries a loose head of long-tubed, white flowers, which are scented. H 2m (6ft).

Other plants *Nicotiana langsdorffii* has long, pendant flowers with a small flare at the mouth. They are lime-green. The plant used for tobacco and snuff, *N. tabacum*, has white and red flowers.

NIGELLA
Love-in-a-mist
This is a much loved genus of 20 annuals, of which a couple are regularly grown in our gardens. The flowers are really delightful. They are discs of blue with a prominent central boss, and are surrounded by a ruff of very finely cut leaves. Each flower looks rather like an exquisite brooch. There are also white and pink forms. Once the flowers are over, they produce an oval, inflated seed case, still surrounded by the filigree leaves. These plants have a wonderful old-fashioned quality and so make an ideal choice for a cottage garden. H 60cm (24in) S 25cm (10in).
How to obtain Nigellas can be seen for sale as plants, but these rarely

come to much. It is a much better option to buy seed, which is readily available.
Cultivation Any reasonable garden soil should be perfectly suitable. Nigellas tend to prefer a position in full sun but some do well in the shade. Z7.
Propagation Sow the seed in autumn or spring in the open ground where the plants are to flower. They will self-sow if left to shed their seed.
Uses These plants can be used in bedding or in mixed borders. It is a good idea to allow them to self-sow so that the plants are dotted around.

Nigella damascena
The true species has single flowers but most of those grown in the garden are a mixture of single or semi-double blooms. In the wild the flowers are pale blue. This is the most frequently seen colour in gardens but cultivars are also available in pink, violet-blue and white. 'Miss Jekyll' has soft blue flowers. The Persian Jewel Series is a mixture of colours. 'Mulberry Rose' is pink while 'Dwarf Moody Blue' is a tiny variety only 20cm (8in) high.

Other plants *Nigella hispanica* and its cultivars are similar to *damascena*.

Nigella damascena 'Persian Jewel'

Annuals with good foliage

Amaranthus caudatus	Ocimum basilicum
Atriplex hortensis 'Rubra'	'Purple Ruffles'
Bassia scoparia	Onopordum acanthium
trichophylla	Pelargonium
Beta vulgaris	Perilla frutescens
Brassica oleracea	Plectranthus
Canna	Ricinus communis
Euphorbia marginata	Senecio cinerarea
Galactites tomentosa	Silybum marianum
Helichrysum petiolare	Tropaeolum majus 'Alaska'
Melianthus major	Zea mays

Nolana paradoxa

Oenothera biennis 'Wedding Bells'

NOLANA
Nolana

This is a genus containing some 18 species, of which a couple are grown in the garden. Nolana is one of those plants that is attractive without being showy. It is not in the top league for popularity and yet it still goes on selling. The plants are low growing and make an excellent carpet of flowers during the summer. Nolanas are covered with masses of trumpet-shaped flowers. These are upward-facing so it is easy to see past their colourful bells into the throats. H 25cm (10in) S 50cm (20in).
How to obtain Nolanas are occasionally found as plants in garden centres but if you want to be sure of getting them, obtain seed from seed merchants. This is readily available.
Cultivation Nolanas will grow in any reasonable garden soil, so long as it is free-draining. They need to be planted in a sunny position. Z10.
Propagation Sow the seed in early spring under glass at 13–16°C (55–60°F). For later flowering, nolanas can also be sown in spring directly into the soil where the plants are to flower.
Uses They make excellent bedding plants and can also be used for filling gaps in a mixed border. Nolanas make good plants for edging a bed or border. Their spreading nature also makes them a natural choice for hanging baskets, window boxes and other forms of container.

Nolana humifusa

This plant is usually seen as one of its various cultivars. 'Little Bells' has lilac flowers with streaks on its white throat. 'Shooting Stars' also has lilac flowers but this time they have a dark purple eye and streaks. In both, the flowers are about 2.5cm (1in) across. The plants have quite a wide spread, which makes them an excellent choice for hanging baskets. H 15cm (6in) high S 45cm (18in).

Nolana paradoxa

This charming species produces flowers of deep blue, with the blue fading into a white throat and yellow eye. They are slighlty taller than the previous plant. H 25cm (10in).
    The cultivar 'Blue Bird' has deep blue flowers while 'Snowbird' has pure white flowers and the same yellow eye.

Other plants The plant once known as *N. lanceolata*, now *N. paradoxa* subsp. *atriplicifolia*, has silvery-haired leaves and sky-blue flowers.

NONEA
Nonea

This is one of the rarer annuals. It is not seen very often but can be found. In fact, as the author began to write this piece, a seed list arrived in the post in which offers included the very rare (in gardening terms) *N. rusica*. Although none of the 35 species is common, *N. lutea* is the plant most commonly seen. It will be of great interest to those who love the perennial pulmonarias (see page 400) as it offers them a very similar annual form. One important difference is that this plant has yellow flowers, a colour that is missing among pulmonarias. It flowers in spring. H 60cm (24in) S 25cm (10in).

Nonea lutea

How to obtain Plants and seed are very rare, though seed is slightly more common, sold mainly by specialist societies.
Cultivation Plant in moist, woodland-type soil, and ideally in light-dappled shade, although sun will be tolerated if the soil is kept moist enough. Z7.
Propagation Sow fresh seed in summer in pots and place in a shaded open frame without heat.
Uses Plant in spring bedding or, to best effect, in an informal woodland setting or shady border.

Nonea lutea

This is sometimes called yellow monkswort. The leaves are bristly and rather coarse. The flowers are small funnels of primrose-yellow. They appear in the spring.

Other plants Although rare, *N. pulla* is sometimes offered. It has deep purple flowers. *N. rusica* can also occasionally be found.

OENOTHERA
Evening primrose

This beautiful genus has 125 species, of which a surprising number are grown in gardens. The majority are perennials (see page 390) but many of these are short lived and can be thought of as annuals. There are also one or two that are true annuals or biennials. Of these, *O. biennis* is by far the most common, although it is not necessarily the most beautiful. Evening primroses are so-called because their flowers open mainly in the evening.

The flowers only last a day but there are usually plenty of buds waiting to open, which ensures a constant supply of blooms. Many of the forms in cultivation also open during the day, and some have a fine fragrance. They vary in height considerably.

How to obtain The best way to obtain these plants is from seed which is reasonably easy to find. Specialist societies offer the widest range. Plants are sometimes seen, but evening primroses do not do well if confined to small pots and so the results are often disappointing.

Cultivation Any reasonable garden soil will suffice, so long as it is free-draining. A warm, sunny position is required for these plants. Z4.

Propagation Seed can either be sown in the open ground where the plants are to flower or it can be sown in pots under glass at 13–16°C (55–60°F). Some species, *O. biennis* in particular, self-sow prodigiously.

Uses Evening primroses are mainly used in a mixed border, especially in informal plantings where they can be left to self-sow.

Oenothera biennis

This is a tall plant that produces masses of lemon-yellow flowers throughout the summer and autumn. It self-sows heavily so remove plants before too much is scattered. H 1.5m (5ft) S 60cm (24in). The cultivar 'Wedding Bells' has white flowers with yellow centres.

Oenothera deltoides

This is the desert evening primrose and as its name suggests it needs very sharp drainage. It has beautiful, glistening white flowers that fade to pink. They are up to 8cm (3in) across. H 30cm (12in) S 25cm (10in).

Oenothera glazioviana

This evening primrose produces lemon-yellow flowers, and is very similar to *O. biennis*.

Oenothera pallida

This plant is a beautiful white-flowered form whose blooms turn to pink as they age.

There is also a cultivar available, which is called 'Innocence'. H and S 50cm (20in).

Other plants The perennial species *Oenothera fruticosa* and *O. stricta* (see page 390) can be used as annuals.

OMPHALODES
Navelwort

This is a medium-sized genus containing about 28 species of which a number of perennials are grown in the garden. There is also one rather beautiful annual, *O. linifolia*. This seems to be one of those "secret" annuals; it is widely grown by those who know about it but not many gardeners do seem to know it. It is a delightful plant with powdery blue-green leaves on an upright, branching plant. The flowers are white and closely resemble the shape and size of forget-me-nots. The whole plant has a light and airy look to it. It self-sows and so once you have it, it rarely deserts you. H 30cm (12in) S 15cm (6in).

How to obtain Occasionally you see navelworts offered as plants, but these rarely do well when planted out. It is best to grow your own plants from seed, which is not too difficult to find.

Cultivation Any reasonable garden soil is sufficient so long as it is free-draining. A sunny position is required. Z7.

Propagation Sow the seed in spring in the open ground where the plants are to flower. If left to set seed they will self-sow, without becoming a nuisance.

Uses *O. linifolia* is a delightful annual for growing in gaps in a mixed border. It is perfect for a white-themed garden or border.

Other plants As well as *Omphalodes linifolia*, which is described above, other annuals you may find include *O. brassicifolia* and *O. littoralis*. They are both quite rare but they have the same attractive white flowers, so it is worth looking out for them.

ONOPORDUM
Scotch thistle

Now we come to one of the giants of the annual world – the Scotch thistle. There are just a couple of species for the gardener to consider; although there are more than 40 biennials in this genus, it would be a brave gardener who would want to grow all of these thistles. The two species that are generally grown look basically the same. They are very tall and are branched, giving them the appearance of a giant candelabra. The stems have wavy wings which have a prickle on the crest of every wave. The leaves also have spines. Both the stems and the foliage are covered with grey hairs which gives the whole plant a silvery look, especially when it catches the sunlight. On the top of each stem is a large thistle-like flower, which is just like the classic Scottish symbol: there is a purple tuft of the flower emerging from a rounded base which is covered in silvery hair and spines. H 3m (10ft) or more, S 1.5m (5ft).

Onopordum acanthium

How to obtain You occasionally see Scotch thistles being sold as plants but they dislike being kept in small pots for too long, so it is better to grow your own from seed. This is readily available.

Cultivation Scotch thistles will grow in any reasonable garden soil, but the richer it is, the larger and more impressive the plants will be. Z6.

Propagation Sow the seed in summer in a pot that can be placed in an open frame without heat. Alternatively, if the ground is available, sow where the plants are to flower in the following year. They will self-sow to provide plants for subsequent years.

Uses These plants are best used at the back of mixed borders. They could be used in bedding schemes; however, they would have to be planted on a grand scale for this to work.

Onopordum acanthium

This is one of the two main plants that are regularly grown. It is the taller of the two and the most widely available. It conforms to the description above. There are no cultivars.

Onopordum nervosum

This plant is possibly better known under its former name of *O. arabicum* and is still sometimes seen advertised as such. It is slightly smaller than the above, otherwise there is very little difference, in gardening terms, between them. Again, there are no cultivars available.

Omphalodes linifolia

Papaver nudicaule

Papaver rhoeas 'American Legend'

Papaver somniferum, double form

PAPAVER
Poppy

Poppies make up a large genus of some 70 species of which there are a number of annuals as well as perennials (see page 392) that are grown in the garden. The flowers are cup-shaped and have that crumpled tissue-paper appearance typical of poppies. The main colour is red but there are also white, yellow, orange, lilac and purple. Each flower only lasts a day but there is a succession of buds. Many plants will self-sow and will return the following year if allowed to spread their seed.
How to obtain Annual poppies are best acquired as seed, which is widely available.
Cultivation Any reasonable garden soil in a sunny position will suffice. Z2–3 or 6–7.

Propagation The majority of these plants can be sown where the plants are to flower.
Uses Poppies are good for bedding and for mixed borders. They are excellent for wild-flower gardens and borders.

Papaver commutatum

This plant is an excellent poppy with bright red flowers and a black spot at the base of each petal. Because of this colouring, it is often referred to as the ladybird poppy. H 45cm (18in), S 15cm (6in).

Papaver nudicaule

This is the Iceland poppy, which is also sometimes referred to as *P. croceum*. The flowers come in yellows, oranges, pinks and white. H 30cm (12in) S 15cm (6in).

There are a number of cultivars such as 'Garden Gnome' which is a dwarf form.

Papaver rhoeas

This is the field poppy. In its pure form, it produces bright red flowers. However, there are a number of cultivars, such as 'Fairy Wings' and the Shirley poppies, which carry flowers in a range of soft pastels, including pink and lavender-blue, as well as red. The flowers of the form 'American Legend' are red. H 1m (3ft) S 30cm (12in).

Papaver somniferum

This is the opium poppy. It is a tall plant whose flowers come in a wide range of colours and types: single, semi-double and double. The flowers are mainly shades of red, purple, pink, lavender and white. This species has given rise to a great number of named cultivars including 'Black Peony' which has dark flowers. H 1.5m (5ft) S 45cm (18in).

PELARGONIUM
Pelargonium

This is a very large genus, with some 230 species and thousands of cultivars. After 100 years of being called pelargoniums these plants are still often referred to as geraniums. However, they should not be confused with that genus (see pages 291, 366). They are mainly perennials but are usually treated as annuals in the garden. They are used both as foliage and flowering plants. The flowers tend to be carried in tight clusters, which are held on upright or trailing stems. There is a wide range of flower colour, based on shades of red, pink, orange, purple and white. The leaves are valued for their patterning or scent.

There are four basic groups of pelargonium. These are: ivy-leaved, which tend to be trailing and so are good for hanging baskets and window boxes; zonal, which have patterned leaves that are usually green and brown but also come in yellow and red; regal, with larger almost azalea-shaped flowers; and the scented-leaved varieties, which tend to have looser heads of less showy flowers. Heights and spreads are highly variable.

Papaver nudicaule 'Garden Gnome'

Papaver somniferum

Pelargonium 'Ashley Stephenson'

Pelargonium 'Shone Helena'

How to obtain Pelargoniums are widely available from many outlets. For a better selection get the catalogues of the specialist nurseries. Some varieties are available as seed.

Cultivation In containers use a good quality potting compost (soil mix). In the open garden plant in reasonably fertile soil which is free-draining. These plants need a position in sun or partial shade. Z8.

Propagation Take cuttings of plants throughout the growing season. Sow seed in early spring under glass at 13–18°C (55–64°F).

Uses Pelargoniums can be used in containers of all sorts or as bedding plants. They can also be planted in general beds.

Ivy-leaved varieties

Cultivars include 'Alice Crousse', whose flowers are cerise-pink, 'Lachsköningin' (semi-double salmon-pink), 'Mme Crousse' (soft pink), and 'Wood's Surprise' (pink and white).

Pelargonium 'Little Gem'

Zonal varieties

'Belinda Adams' has double flowers which are white, flushed with pink, 'Bird Dancer' comes in pink shades, and Century Series (seed-raised) produces red, pink or white flowers. Other good cultivars include 'Francis Parrett', which has double, purple-pink flowers, 'Irene' (semi-double, cerise blooms), 'Mme Fournier' (scarlet flowers, purple foliage) and Video Series (seed-raised, red and pink blooms).

Regal varieties

Good regal varieties include 'Ann Hoystead', which has deep red and black flowers and 'Bredon', also red and black. Other cultivars include 'Carisbrooke' (pink and red), 'Lord Bute' (red and black), and 'Sefton' (cerise and red).

Scented-leaved varieties

Recommended plants in this category include 'Attar of Roses' (mauve flowers), 'Copthorne' (mauve and purple), *P. crispum* 'Variegatum' (lemon-scented variegated leaves and mauve flowers), 'Mabel Grey' (purple), *P. tomentosum* (white flowers and peppermint-scented).

PERILLA
Perilla

A small genus of six plants, of which one, *P. frutescens*, has become very popular in recent years. This is not for its flowers but more for its foliage. The large oval leaves are green but heavily marked with purple and the margins are highly toothed. They are also fragrant. The small flowers are carried in spikes above and among the foliage. They are white or very pale pink. H 1m (3ft) S 30cm (12in) in good conditions, but is often less.

Perilla frutescens var. crispa

How to obtain Perillas are obtainable as plants from garden centres and nurseries. They are also available as seed.

Cultivation Plant out in a rich soil that is moisture retentive. Perillas can be grown in either sun or light shade. Z8.

Propagation Sow the seed in early spring under glass at 13–18°C (55–64°F).

Uses These plants are good in all forms of foliage schemes. They are very good plants for bedding, especially in exotic schemes. They can also be useful for large containers such as tubs.

Perilla frutescens

This is the plant described above. Its variety *crispa* is even better. It has deep purple leaves that are very frilled around the edge, making it an exotic-looking plant. 'Checkerboard Mixed' is a new cultivar which is a mixture of green and purple plants.

Pelargonium 'Fragaris'

Annual grasses

Agrostis nebulosa	Lagurus ovatus
Aira	Lamarckia aurea
Avena sterilis	Panicum capillare
Briza maxima	Panicum miliaceum
Briza minor	Pennisetum setaceum
Bromus briziformis	Pennisetum villosum
Chloris barbata	Setaria glauca
Chloris truncata	Setaria italica
Chloris virgita	Sorghum nigrum
Hordeum jubatum	Zea mays

Petunia 'Blue Daddy'

Petunia 'Blue Wave'

PETUNIA
Petunia

This large genus of 40 species has produced some excellent garden plants. They were originally developed as bedding plants. As containers became more popular, they were bred for that purpose as well, resulting in the magnificent plants that we see today in hanging baskets. The petunia is probably now the favourite plant for baskets, especially since new cultivars produce flowers that have not only had their colour enhanced but which have been made more weather-proof as well. The slightly hairy stems are covered for very long periods with trumpet-shaped flowers. They come in a wide range of colours, mainly based on shades of red, pink and purple, but including white and yellow. Many of them

have a contrasting coloured eye and often darker veining. H up to 45cm (18in) but usually less. The spread varies but trailing forms can grow 1m (3ft) across.
How to obtain Petunias are very widely available as plants in bedding packs or in individual pots from a large range of outlets. Seed is also easy to come by, although there is a bigger range in plant form.
Cultivation Any good potting compost (soil mix) will do for containers and a well-drained soil should be chosen for open-ground planting. Plant in full sun. Z7.
Propagation Sow the seed in the autumn under glass at 16–18°C (60–64°F).
Uses Petunias have many garden uses, but they are particularly good for hanging baskets and other containers.

Petunia **Daddy Series**
This is a good series, which produces flowers of mixed colours. Some are available as single colours. These include 'Sugar Daddy' which has pink flowers with purple veins, and 'Blue Daddy', which has bluish-purple flowers with darker veins.

Petunia **Mirage Series**
Another excellent series which has good weather-tolerance. Individual colours are available.

Petunia **Picotee Series**
The flowers of this series come in pure colours, such as blue or pink, but have a white margin.

Petunia **Storm Series**
This series includes plants with individual colours such as 'Storm Lavender' and 'Storm Pink'.

Petunia **Surfinia Series**
A magnificent modern series that has transformed hanging baskets. The purple form 'Surfinia Purple' is particularly good.

Petunia **Wave Series**
This series includes individual colours, such as 'Blue Wave' and 'Purple Wave'.

Petunia **Ultra Star Series**
Plants in this series have striped petals, giving them a star-like appearance. The colours are bright blues and reds.

PHACELIA
Scorpion weed

This is a large genus containing 150 species, of which several annuals are widely grown in our gardens. This is partly because they are attractive and partly because they are very good plants for attracting bees, hoverflies and other beneficial insects. Phacelia is now sometimes planted beside agricultural crops for this very reason. The flowers are generally blue and have protruding stamens which sometimes gives them a delightful fuzzy look. The flowers are cup-shaped and are born in clusters over a long period. The plants in this genus vary considerably in height.
How to obtain Phacelias may occasionally be found as plants but it is more common to grow them from seed.
Cultivation Any reasonable garden soil will suffice. Choose a sunny location. Z8.

Petunia 'Storm Lavender'

Phacelia campanularia

Phacelia tanacetifolia

Phaseolus 'Painted Lady' (with creeper)

Propagation Sow the seed in spring in open ground where the plants are to grow.

Uses Phacelias make excellent bedding material and can also be used to good effect in mixed borders. They are a useful addition to wildlife gardens.

Phacelia campanularia
This plant is sometimes known as the Californian bluebell. It has dark blue, upward-facing flowers. There is also a white form. H 30cm (12in).

Phacelia tanacetifolia
The best species for insects, with finely cut leaves and blue blooms. A tall plant, it may need support in exposed positions. H up to 1.2m (4ft) S 45cm (18in).

Other plants *Phacelia viscida* is a medium-sized plant, usually up to 30cm (12in) tall. It has very dark blue flowers with a white eye. There is also a cultivar, called 'Tropical Surf', but it is the same as the species.

PHASEOLUS
Runner bean
The runner bean plant, also known as the climbing bean, can be a very attractive choice for a border. As climbers, these plants are valuable in that they can bring height to a mixed border or bedding scheme. They can be grown up a wigwam of poles or a framework; the dense foliage soon covers the support. The flowers

are mainly scarlet but there are also forms that produce pink, white and purple flowers. The pods of some varieties are also very decorative. All in all, an extremely valuable plant, especially since you can eat the beans. H 3m (10ft) S 30cm (12in).

How to obtain These plants are often sold in packs or pots at garden centres. You cannot be sure what colour the flowers will be, but they are usually red. If you want to be certain, grow beans from seed; seed merchants offer hundreds of cultivars.

Cultivation Plant out after the threat of frost has passed in a soil enriched with plenty of well-rotted organic material. It should be moisture retentive. A sunny position is required. Some form of support will be needed. Z8.

Propagation Sow seeds under glass in individual pots in mid-spring or set the seed where the plants are to flower in late spring.

Uses These plants can be used as climbers up poles in a border or over a pergola. They can also be grown in containers, perhaps creating a backdrop for other plants. They can also be used as centrepieces in potagers.

Runner beans in general
These plants have scarlet flowers. They are attractive in their own right but there are plenty of alternatives, and some cultivars carry flowers of several colours, or bicoloured blooms. 'White Lady', as the name suggests, has white

flowers, while 'Painted Lady' has red and white blooms and 'Sunset' has soft pink ones. 'Summer Medley' is quite spectacular, producing an array of red, white and pink flowers. 'Relay' carries flowers of several colours. For those that like variegated foliage 'Sun Bright' has green leaves that are flushed with gold.

PHLOX
Phlox
This is a large genus of 67 species of which a number of perennials (see page 395) are in cultivation as well as one popular annual. This is *P. drummondii*. It has long been popular as a bedding plant and seems to have lost none of its appeal, mainly because it has adapted well to life in containers. It is a bushy plant with flowers that are similar in shape to those

of the perennial: flat discs on a narrow tubular base. They come in a wonderful range of colours from soft pastels to colours that hit you between the eyes. H up to 45cm (18in) but often much less, S 25cm (10in).

How to obtain These are frequently seen as plants in garden centres, but there is much more choice to be had by purchasing seed.

Cultivation The annual phlox will grow in any reasonable garden soil. Use a good-quality general potting compost (soil mix) in containers. It will grow in either part shade or full sun so long as the soil is moist enough. Z4.

Propagation Sow the seed under glass in early spring at 13–16°C (55–60°F).

Uses The traditional use for this plant is in bedding schemes, but it works equally well in mixed borders or in containers. Taller varieties are good for cutting.

Phlox drummondii
This plant is rarely sold as a species; it is more commonly seen as one of its cultivars of which there are quite a number. 'Tapestry Mixture' and 'Ethnie Pastel Shades' produce a range of soft colours while 'African Sunset' is brilliant red. 'Sternenzauber' or 'Twinkle' has unique star-like flowers with irregularly pointed petals. 'Petticoat' is a dwarf mixture with small flowers. 'Red Admiral' has luscious dark crimson flowers, while 'Grammy Pink White' has striking pink and white flowers.

Phlox drummondii 'Grammy Pink White'

Plectranthus argentatus

PLECTRANTHUS
Plectranthus

This is an enormous genus of more than 370 species. However, from the annual gardener's point of view there is only one of interest. This is *P. forsteri*, which is sometimes called *P. coleoides* and often sold as such. In fact it is a perennial, but it is treated as an annual by most gardeners. The attraction of this plant is not its flowers but its foliage. The leaves are oval and toothed, rather in the manner of nettles. They grow on trailing stems which makes this plant ideal for use in containers of all types, but especially hanging baskets. The small flowers are carried in whorls at the ends of the stems. They are tubular and resemble those of the deadnettles or thyme plants. Their colour is white or mauve. H 25cm (10in) high, S 1m (3ft).
How to obtain Plectranthus is usually purchased as a plant from garden centres. It is sometimes available from florists.
Cultivation Use a good-quality general potting compost (soil mix) if, as is very likely, you are growing these plants in some kind of container. If used in the open garden, any reasonable garden soil will suffice, as long as it is free-draining. Z10.
Propagation Take stem cuttings at any time of year and overwinter the resulting plants.
Uses The primary use for this plant is in containers. It works well in all types of container, but

especially in those where the stems can hang down, such as hanging baskets or tall pots. It can also be used as bedding and as a house plant.

Plectranthus forsteri
This plant, which is described above, has light green leaves. However, there is a cultivar which is much more commonly seen. This is *P.f.* 'Marginatus', which has attractive creamy-white margins around the leaf.

Other plants *Plectranthus argentatus* has become increasingly popular as a bedding plant. The foliage is furry and grey in colour. From this spikes of small, pale pink or bluish flowers arise. It can grow to 1m (3ft) but when used as annual bedding it reaches less than half of this height.

PORTULACA
Sun plant

This is a large genera, this time containing about 100 species. Of these there is only one annual in general cultivation. This is the sun plant, *P. grandiflora*, which is sometimes also called the rose moss. It is a native of sandy places in South America and is a perfect plant for either bedding or containers. It has bluish-green, succulent leaves and flowers that in some ways resemble poppies with their tissue-paper petals and shallow cup shape. The flowers come in a wide range of bright

colours, including oranges, reds and pinks, as well as white. H and S 20cm (8in).
How to obtain Sun plants are occasionally available as plants from garden centres but the main source is seed from the various seed merchants.
Cultivation Sun plants need a light, dry soil and a warm sunny position. If growing in a container use a free-draining compost (soil mix). Z10.
Propagation Sow the seed under glass in early spring at 13–18°C (55–60°F).
Uses These are good plants for bedding schemes if the soil is right. They are also ideal for gravel gardens. Their trailing habit makes them suitable for containers, especially hanging baskets and window boxes.

Portulaca grandiflora
Sun plants are sold as mixtures or as individual cultivars. Some mixtures can also be obtained as individual colours. The Sundial hybrids, for example, come as 'Sundial Mango' and 'Sundial Peppermint' as well as in mixed colours. Other mixtures include the Sundance hybrids and Minilace hybrids. One of the most beautiful cultivars is the pure white 'Sun State White'.

Other plants *Portulaca oleracea* is becoming increasingly available. It is a trailing plant with yellow, orange or pink flowers.

Portulaca grandiflora 'Sundial Mixed'

Reseda odorata

RESEDA
Mignonette

This is another large genus, this time containing about 60 species. One species in the genus is widely grown. This is *R. odorata*, which has been a popular plant in cottage-style gardens for centuries. It has an untidy habit, which fits in well with this type of informal gardening, but it is also very fragrant, a characteristic of so many old-fashioned flowers. The perfume is its main attraction since, while the flowers are pleasant, they are not overly decorative, or at least not when judged alongside more showy flowering plants such as the pelargonium or petunia. The blooms are very small and whitish-yellow with noticeable red anthers. They are carried in spikes which rise up from the sprawling plants. H 45cm (18in) S 30cm (12in).
How to obtain Occasionally mignonettes are seen for sale as plants, but the surest way to obtain them is to grow them from seed, available from some seed merchants and also from specialist society seed lists.
Cultivation Any reasonable garden soil will do for these plants, but it should be well-drained. A sunny position is preferred, especially if you want the scent. Z8.
Propagation Sow the seed in spring in open ground where the plants are to grow.
Uses Excellent for informal displays, including cottage-style gardens. Mignonettes can also be

used in imaginative bedding schemes. It is wonderful for wild-flower gardens and borders, and is attractive to bees.

Reseda odorata

This, the main species, is usually grown in its own right. However, there are cultivars available. These do not vary greatly from the species, but 'Red Monarch' has more pronounced red anthers. The flowers of 'Grandiflora' are more yellow, while those of 'Alba' are whiter.

Other plants There are one or two other species that are also available if you hunt hard enough. *R. alba*, which produces creamy white flowers is one, and the much taller *R. luteola*, which carries yellow flowers, is another.

RICINUS
Castor oil plant

This is a single species genus. The species is *R. communis*, which has been part of the bedding scene since Victorian times and probably before that. Although attractive, it is poisonous if eaten. The seed is particularly toxic – the deadly poison ricin is made from it. If there is any doubt as to safety – for example if children visit your garden – do not grow it. Its attraction is its foliage, although if the summer is long and hot enough it will flower. It has large palmate (like fingers radiating from a hand) leaves. In

the species these are green but there are also some excellent purple-leaved forms available. When flowers are formed, they are red or pink fuzzy balls and are carried in a spike. In the wild, this plant grows to 12m (40ft) but in the garden it is more like 1.2m (4ft) or less. S 60cm (24in).
How to obtain You can buy these as plants but do not rely on being able to find them. It is better to grow them from seed which is commonly available.
Cultivation Plant out after the threat of frosts has passed in a well-drained but rich soil. This plant requires a warm sunny position. Z10.
Propagation Sow the seed in spring: soak it in water for 24 hours first and then sow under glass at 21°C (70°F).
Uses Castor oil plants can be used as centrepieces in bedding schemes or can be added to a mixed border. They look particularly good in exotic arrangements. These plants can also be grown in large tubs or containers (they do not do well in small pots).

Ricinus communis

This is the only species and it is widely grown. However, the red or bronze-leaved forms are more commonly seen. 'Carmencita' is one of the best; it produces good red foliage and red flowers. 'Carmencita Pink' is similar but produces pink flowers. 'Gibsonii' has dark green foliage with red veins and pinkish flowers. 'Zanzibariensis' is similar but the foliage has white veins.

RUDBECKIA
Coneflower

This is a genus of about 20 species. Most of those used in the garden are perennials (see page 402). However, there is one biennial and a handful of hybrids that are very much in use. They are popular both because of their vibrant colour and because they tend to flower over a long period, including the autumn. They have daisy-like flowers which have a ring of yellow or gold outer petals. These surround a brown inner disc which is raised in a rounded cone,

Rudbeckia 'Prairie Sun'

hence the name coneflower. They can reach up to 2m (6ft) but rarely do in cultivation. Usual height 60–100cm (2–3ft) S 45cm (18in).
How to obtain Coneflowers are available both as plants and seed from garden centres.
Cultivation Coneflowers will grow in any reasonable garden soil, so long as it does not dry out too much. Conversely, the soil must also be free-draining so there is no waterlogging. Z4.
Propagation Sow the seed in the early spring under glass at 16–18°C (60–64°F).
Uses These plants can be used to good effect in either bedding or mixed borders. They are especially useful in borders that are made up of hot colours.

Rudbeckia hirta

This is the main biennial (treated as an annual) that is cultivated. It is grown as the species and there are also a number of cultivars. 'Bambi' is a short form 30cm (12in) high with attractive gold and bronze petals. 'Gloriosa' has large heads 15cm (6in) wide with golden flowers and sometimes bicolours. It has a double equivalent, 'Double Gloriosa'. 'Irish Eyes' (or 'Green Eyes') has yellow outer petals with an olive green inner ring. 'Kelvedon Star' is an old favourite with yellow flowers flushed with mahogany. 'Toto' has golden-yellow flowers with a brown centre. There are also a number of hybrids available, some of which are listed below.

Rudbeckia 'Goldilocks'

A popular long-flowering plant with semi-double or double golden-yellow flowers.

Rudbeckia 'Marmalade'

Another favourite, this time with large flowers which are yellow ageing to a rich gold.

Rudbeckia 'Prairie Sun'

This attractive plant produces golden-yellow flowers with pale green centres.

Rudbeckia 'Rustic Dwarfs'

These plants have flowers of mixed colours: yellow, gold, mahogany and bronze.

Ricinus communis

Rudbeckia hirta 'Toto'

Salpiglossis 'Splash Mixed'

Salpiglossis sinuata 'Bolero Mixed'

SALPIGLOSSIS
Salpiglossis

A small genus of two species. One of them, *S. sinuata*, is grown in gardens. There was a time when this plant was very popular but, although it is still grown, it is not seen as frequently as it once was. This is a shame since it is a very attractive plant with large trumpet-shaped flowers, rather like those of petunias. The flowers are carried in great profusion, sometimes smothering the plant. The colours include shades of red, orange, yellow and purple. The veins in the petals are either a darker version of the same colour or a contrasting colour; most of them are bicolours. The height varies between 30 and 60cm (12–24in) S 30cm (12in).

How to obtain Salpiglossis can sometimes be found as plants in garden centres, but this cannot be relied upon. If you are determined to grow them it is safer to grow your own from seed which is readily available from a number of seed merchants.

Cultivation Plant out after the threat of frost has passed. These plants do best in a fertile soil that does not dry out too much. They should have a warm, sunny position. Z8.

Propagation Sow the seed in early spring under glass at 18–21°C (64–70°F).

Uses Salpiglossis make excellent bedding plants, but they can be used to fill gaps in a mixed border. They are also suitable for large containers.

Salpiglossis sinuata

Although the species is sometimes grown in its own right, its cultivars are much more common. Many of these are sold as mixes, such as 'Casino Mixed', 'Splash Mixed' or 'Bolero Mixed'. In others, such as 'Ingrid', 'Kew Blue' and 'Ice Maiden', the colours tend to be similar in each plant although there is still a little variation, usually in the markings.

SALVIA
Sage

This is an enormous genus of 900 species that includes shrubs, perennials (see page 403) and annuals. Of the last there is only one that is grown to any extent. This is *Salvia viridis* which until recently was known as *S. hormium* and is still often listed as such in seed catalogues. This is a true annual, and there are also several short-lived perennials that are used as annuals. One such, *S. splendens* is the perfect bedding plant and is nearly always grown as an annual.

How to obtain Salvia splendens and *S. viridis* are offered in bedding packs and individual pots, as well as being widely available as seed from merchants and others. The other short-lived perennials are occasionally available as plants but can be more reliably found as seed. Seed also gives a greater choice of cultivars.

Cultivation Most will grow in any reasonable garden soil so long as it is free-draining. A warm, sunny position is to be preferred. Z9.

Propagation Sow seed of *S. viridis* in spring in the open ground where they are to flower. Sow seed of other species under glass at 13–16°C (55–60°F).

Uses Both types can be used as summer bedding. The tender perennials are often used in mixed borders or in containers.

Salvia splendens

This short-lived perennial was once the king of bedding plants. It is still used but it is nowhere

Salpiglossis sinuata 'Ice Maiden'

Salvia viridis 'White Swan'

Salvia viridis 'Pink Sundae'

Self-sowing annuals

Atriplex hortensis 'Rubra'	Limnanthes douglasii
Borago officinalis	Lunaria annua
Calendula officinalis	Myosotis
Chrysanthemum segetum	Nigella
Collomia grandiflora	Oenothera biennis
Digitalis purpurea	Omphalodes linifolia
Eryngium giganteum	Onopordum
Euphorbia lathyris	Papaver
Galactites tomentosa	Silybum marianum
Hesperis matronalis	Verbascum

near as popular as it once was. It is a bushy plant with spikes of very bright scarlet flowers. H 40cm (16in) S 30cm (12in). There are still a large number of cultivars, some of which now include other colours such as purples and creams. The Sizzler Series is one example.

Salvia viridis

This is the true annual. It is an upright plant which is grown for its spikes of pink, purple or cream bracts. The flowers are insignificant, but the uppermost leaves are coloured in this magnificent way. There are a number of cultivars to choose from including 'White Swan', which has creamy-white bracts with green veins. 'Pink Sundae' produces carmine-coloured bracts. H 45cm (18in) S 25cm (10in).

Other plants The other short-lived perennials include species such as *Salvia coccinea* and its cultivars with scarlet flowers, *S. farinacea* with deep blue flowers, and *S. argentea* with beautiful large, silver leaves.

SANVITALIA
Creeping zinnia

This is a small genus containing a mere seven species of which *S. procumbens* is the only species seen in cultivation. This is a low, creeping plant, as its common name implies. Also as the name indicates, the flowers are similar to those of the zinnia, to which it is related. They are daisy-like with an outer ring of bright yellow petals and a large inner disc which is purple-brown. The flowers are not very large, measuring only 2cm (¼in) across, but what they lack in size is more than

Sanvitalia procumbens 'Profusion Cherry'

Sanvitalia procumbens

compensated for by the quantity produced. H 20cm (8in) S 45cm (18in).

How to obtain Sanvitalias can be purchased as bedding or container plants from garden centres and nurseries. They are also available as seed from merchants, which provide a large choice of cultivars.

Cultivation Plant in any reasonable garden soil. A sunny position is to be preferred. Z8.

Propagation Sow the seed where the plants are to flower in autumn or spring. Sow under glass at 13–16°C (55–60°F) in early spring for container plants.

Uses These make excellent bedding plants. They are also suitable for containers.

Sanvitalia procumbens

This is the only species generally cultivated, and is described above. There are also a number of cultivars. These include 'Irish Eyes' whose flowers have green centres and 'Mandarin Orange' which has bright orange petals and a brown centre. 'Dwarf Carpet' reaches only 10cm (4in) in height. 'Profusion Cherry' is a lovely shade of red, and 'Sprite' is a yellow and brown semi-double.

Scabiosa atropurpurea 'Chile Pepper'

SCABIOSA
Scabious

This is a large genus containing about 80 species of perennials (see page 404) and a few annuals. Both the annuals and the perennials have a similar type of flower, which is probably best described as a pincushion. It consists of a dome of florets, with the outer ones often being larger than the inner ones. Generally the flower colour is lavender-blue but in the annuals there is some variation. The flowers are carried on slender stems above finely cut foliage, making these very attractive, delicate-looking plants. There is a certain old-fashioned quality about them that makes the scabious an ideal addition to informal schemes, such as that of a cottage garden.

How to obtain They are available as plants in individual pots from garden centres and nurseries. Seed is also widely available.
Cultivation Any reasonable garden soil will be sufficient so long as it is not waterlogged. Scabious make good cut flowers and some of the seed head can be dried. Z6.
Propagation Sow the seed in mid-spring in the open ground where it is to flower. Alternatively sow in pots under glass at 13–16°C (55–60°F).
Uses Scabious are probably best used in mixed borders although they can also be used as bedding.

Scabiosa atropurpurea

This is a superb plant with pincushion flower heads that vary from lavender to deep purple. It grows to 1m (3ft) when growing well but is often less. S 30cm (12in). There are several cultivars of which 'Chile Pepper' is the current favourite. This has very dark red flowers with speckles of white. 'Blue Cockade' has large heads twice the size of most (up to 5cm/2in across) with lavender to purple flowers.

Scabiosa stellata

This plant has pale blue pincushions. When the flower fades, these turn into spherical seed heads with each seed being framed in a ruff. They make excellent dried flowers.

Other plants Scabiosa prolifera has cream-coloured flower heads and, like the previous plant, produces papery seed heads that are good for drying. It is more difficult to find than the other species.

SCAEVOLA
Fairy fan flower

The scaevola is a large genus of about 90 species of which only one is in general cultivation. This is *S. aemula*, the fairy fan flower or the cushion fan flower. It is a curious plant that is perfect for hanging baskets but is not quite so useful in the borders. It is a low-growing, spreading plant. The flowers are lavender blue and the five petals are in the shape of a fan. H 15cm (6in) S 1m (3ft).

Scabiosa stellata

Scaevola aemula 'Blue Wonder'

How to obtain Scaevolas are generally sold as small plants by a few garden centres and by mail order. Seed can be obtained but this is not so satisfactory as named plants.
Cultivation Plant out in a moist, reasonably rich soil that is free-draining. In containers use a good general potting compost (soil mix). Scaevolas can be planted in full sun, so long as the soil is kept moist, or in light shade. Z10.
Propagation Take cuttings in summer and overwinter the young plants under glass. Seed can be sown under glass at 18–21°C (64–70°F).
Uses Its spreading habit makes the scaevola ideal as a container plant, especially in hanging baskets. It can also be used as an unusual bedding plant.

Scaevola aemula

The species can be grown from seed but the plants are not particularly floriferous. The forms 'Blue Wonder' and 'Blue Fan' produce a lot more flowers and are worth obtaining. They both have lilac-blue flowers. There is also a form called 'Mauve Clusters' in which the flowers are slightly more mauve. However, there is not a great deal to choose between the cultivars. In the wild the flowers can be white; hard searching might locate the seed of such plants.

SCHIZANTHUS
Butterfly flower

This is a genus of about 15 species of annuals and biennials. Several are in cultivation, but only one, *S. pinnatus*, and its cultivars and hybrids are used to any great extent. They are not quite so popular as they once were but they are still well worth growing since they are spectacular plants. In well-grown specimens it is impossible to see the plant for the flowers. The English name is very apt – the flowers are like butterflies. The alternative name of poor man's orchids is also true since they are very exotic looking. They are very colourful: the basic flower colouring is shades of pink with a yellow and white centre with orange spotting. H 45cm (18in) S 30cm (12in).
How to obtain Schizanthus can be bought as plants in individual pots but if you can raise them it

Scaevola aemula 'Blue Wonder' (detail)

Schizanthus pinnatus cultivars

Silene coeli-rosa 'Royal Celebration'

is better to buy seed since you will get a better choice and many more plants.

Cultivation For container plants choose a good-quality general potting compost (soil mix). In the open ground, any well-drained soil that does not dry out excessively will do. Plant in a warm sunny position. Pinch the growing tips out to make the plants bushy. Z10.

Propagation Sow seed in early spring under glass at 16–18°C (60–64°F).

Uses Schizanthus are magnificent plants for containers. They also look superb as massed bedding.

Schizanthus pinnatus

This is the main species grown, and is described above. It has several cultivars and is also one

Schizanthus pinnatus

of the parents of the next plant listed. Cultivars often come in mixed colours. They include 'Angel's Wings', 'Disco Mixed', 'Hit Parade', 'Star Parade', and the rather uninspiringly named 'Giant Hybrids'.

Schizanthus × wisetonensis

This is an excellent hybrid of the above. It also has a number of cultivars, none of which is very different from the others.

SILENE
Campion

This is one of the most important genera in gardening terms since so many of the 500 species are grown in our gardens. They include perennials (see page 243) and annuals. On the whole they are not very showy plants but they do provide a backbone to plantings. There are several annuals which are of interest. The flowers are generally five-petalled discs in various shades of pink or white. H 15–45cm (6–18in) S up to 25cm (10in)

How to obtain The plants may be seen in garden centres but they are more likely to be found in nurseries. Seed is available from seed merchants, although you may have to check out specialist society seed lists for rarer seed.

Cultivation Silene will grow in any garden soil, in either sun or shade. Z7.

Propagation Most annuals can be sown in the the spring in the open ground where the plants are

to flower. They can also be sown in pots under glass at 13–16°C (55–60°F).

Uses These plants can be used in a wide variety of garden sites. They fit well into a mixed border and some can be used in bedding or containers.

Silene coeli-rosa

This plant is commonly known as the rose of heaven and was once very popular. It looks rather like a large-flowered gypsophila. The notched petals are pink, fading to white at the base. There are several good cultivars available. The Angel Series includes 'Rose Angel' which produces rose-pink flowers and 'Blue Angel' which has lavender-blue flowers. 'Royal Celebration' carries blooms in a good mixture of colours.

Silene pendula

This attractive plant has been reintroduced in recent years in the form 'Peach Blossom'. This is a little gem which grows to no more than 15cm (6in) in height and about the same in spread. The double flowers come in shades of delicate pale pink. There is also a white form, also with double flowers, called 'Snowball', while 'Triumph' produces blooms of deep pink.

Other plants Silene armeria is a delightful plant with powdery grey-green leaves and stems and domes of small flowers in a deep rose-pink. It self-sows without becoming a nuisance. There is a free-flowering form called 'Electra' which carries flowers of a darker pink.

Silene pendula 'Peach Blossom'

Silene armeria 'Rose Angel'

Silybum marianum

Smyrnium perfoliatum

SILYBUM
Milk thistle

This is a small genus of two similar plants. The one that is most widely grown in gardens is *S. marianum*, which is known as the milk thistle or St Mary's thistle. It is valued mainly for its foliage. The leaves are large with deep lobes, each topped with a spine. They are a glossy green and covered with a random white marbling, which looks rather like spilt milk or St Mary's milk, hence the plant's name. They are very attractive leaves indeed.

The flowers are just like those of a typical thistle, with purple tufts erupting from a cup of spiny bracts. The thistle will normally spread 1m (3ft) wide when grown in good ground, but if it is in very rich soil it can grow to twice that and become huge. However, 60cm (24in) is the normal expected width and 1m (3ft) the height. If your silybum do grow very large, they can smother the surrounding plants.
How to obtain You will rarely find plants for sale, but silybum is available as seed from a variety of sources. It is usually found in specialist society seed exchanges.
Cultivation Any reasonable garden soil will do for silybum, but the richer the soil, the bigger the plants. Z7.
Propagation Sow the seed in the open ground where the plants are to grow in autumn or spring. It will self-sow if left to seed providing plants for later years.

Uses This is a magnificent foliage plant best suited to the mixed border, or it could be used as bedding in some imaginative scheme. If you are not worried about the sharp spines it can make an interesting addition to children's gardens, not least because most children find the name highly amusing.

Other plants Although it is not seen very often, the other plant in the genus, *S. eburneum*, is sometimes cultivated in gardens.

This looks very similar to *S. marianum*. The seed is available, but it is not easy to find.

SMYRNIUM
Smyrnium

This is a genus of about eight biennial plants. Of these, one is grown quite widely in gardens, while another is occasionally seen. The common one is called *S. perfoliatum*. This is not a plant for neat and tidy, formal gardens, but one that crops up in informal gardens, especially those with shady areas, or in wild-flower gardens. It is a delightful plant, looking rather like a spurge (*Euphorbia*), with its tiny yellowish-green flowers. These appear in late spring. The leaves immediately below the flowers are the same colour and it is these that give the plant its character-istic appearance. H 1m (3ft) when given good conditions, S 30cm (12in).
How to obtain Seed is available from a few seed merchants, but you will have to search for it. It is also available from the seed exchanges of specialist societies. Once you have this plant, it will self-sow.
Cultivation Any reasonable garden soil will suffice. Smyrniums will grow in sun, but they are a useful plant for light shade. Z7.
Propagation Sow the seed in the open ground where the plants are to grow. Alternatively, sow in a pot and place in an open frame without heat. Let the plants self sow for future years.
Uses These plants can be used in informal borders, including cottage gardens, but they are best used in wild-flower gardens, or in shady areas where their bright golden colour shines out.

Sutera cordata 'Snowflake'

Sutera cordata

Other plants *Smyrnium olusatrum* grows naturally around coasts, and it is good for wild-flower gardens in that kind of area. It is much bigger and more solid than the above with heavy domes of yellow flowers and large glossy leaves. It is very much like a yellow-flowered angelica. It self-sows prodigiously so be careful where you site it.

SUTERA
Sutera

This genus contains 130 species. The one that is grown in gardens is *S. cordata*, which is also known as *Bacopa* 'Snowflake'. It is one of those plants that suddenly takes the gardening world by storm. It was hardly known a few years ago and you would not have been able to find it, but now it is in most garden centres. It is a low creeping plant that is covered in a mass of white flowers, each having five rounded petals. It flowers for a long time and its sprawling habit makes it perfect for hanging baskets, for which it is mainly marketed. H 10–15cm (4–6in) S 45cm (18in).

How to obtain Suteras are available only as plants, not as seed. The cultivar *S. cordata* 'Snowflake' is readily available, but the others listed are not so frequently seen. However, they are gradually becoming more commonplace.

Cultivation Do not plant out suteras until after the threat of frost has passed. Use a good-quality general potting compost (soil mix). Pinch out the side shoots to start with so that your plant becomes bushy. Keep the compost moist; the flowers will drop if it dries out. Z10.

Propagation Take cuttings in summer and overwinter the plants under warm glass.

Uses This is an excellent hanging basket plant, which is one of the reasons it has become so popular.

It can also be used in other types of containers. There is also no reason why it should not be planted in walls and such like.

Sutera cordata

The species as such is not usually grown; it is more commonly seen in the form of one of its cultivars. The most popular of these is 'Snowflake' which has small, pure white flowers with a yellow eye. There are several new white forms on offer including 'Snowstorm' and 'Bridal Showers'. There are also a couple of lavender-coloured forms: 'Lavender Storm' and the darker-flowered 'Blue Showers'. There is a pink form, which has no specific name, and a form with golden variegated foliage and white flowers, which is known as 'Olympic Gold'.

Other plants *Sutera grandiflora* has been around for a bit longer. It is a similar spreading plant to the above, but it produces lavender-blue flowers which have a white throat. There are several cultivars.

SYMPHYANDRA
Symphyandra

This is a genus of some 12 short-lived perennials that are usually treated as annuals. They are closely related to the bellflowers, *Campanula*. Quite a few of them are in cultivation but tend to be grown by gardeners who specialize in such plants, such as alpine growers, rather than the general gardener.

There is one, however, that is not difficult to grow and is well worth the effort to find. This is *S. hofmannii*. It grows up to 60cm (24in) high and 30cm (12in) across and is covered with hanging bellflowers of creamy-white. They are each over 2.5cm (1in) in diameter. Symphyandras are not in the same league as many bedding plants, but they do remain flowering for quite a long time during the summer, an attribute which earns them their place in the garden.

How to obtain You can occasionally find symphyandras in specialist nurseries, but if you want to be certain of obtaining plants then the safest way is to get seed. This is available from a number of seed merchants as well as from the seed exchange lists of specialist garden societies.

Cultivation Symphyandras will grow in any reasonable garden soil, but they prefer light, free-draining ones. Choose either a sunny or lightly shaded position for these plants. Z4.

Propagation Sow the seed in early spring under glass at 13–16°C (55–60°F).

Uses These plants are best used in a mixed border. They make an excellent addition to a white garden or white border.

Other plants Most of the other symphyandras are available either as plants or as seed from specialist sources. Most are treated as annuals used in the mixed border or rock garden. They all have bell-shaped flowers and include blue as well as white flowers. *S. pendula* is the next most frequently seen after *S. hofmannii*. This also has white flowers. *S. armena* is a good species if you want pale blue flowers.

Annuals for hanging baskets

Begonia	Nolana humifusa
Bidens	Petunia
Brachyscome	Pelargonium
Chrysanthemum	Sanvitalia procumbens
Echium	Senecio cineraria
Felicia amelloides	Sutera cordata
Helichrysum	Tagetes
Laurentia	Tropaeolum
Lobelia	Verbena
Myosotis	Viola

Symphyandra hofmannii

Tagetes 'French Vanilla'

Tagetes patula 'Safari Tangerine'

TAGETES
Marigolds

This genus of daisy-like plants contains about 50 species. The two that are of most interest to gardeners are the French marigold (*T. patula*) and the African marigold (*T. erecta*). There are also some hybrids between the two as well as some derived from the species *T. tenuifolia*. Many marigold cultivars are in series and they are generally sold as mixtures, but some individual forms are sold.

The basic plants are daisy-like with an outer ring of petals and a central disc. However, many are doubles and semi-doubles. The predominant colour is golden-yellow but orange and mahogany-red also feature prominently. These plants have always played an important part in bedding schemes. In recent years their importance has declined, but the marigolds have retained enough popularity to remain widely available. H 15–45cm (6–18in) S 30cm (12in).

How to obtain Marigolds are available as plants, both in bedding packs and individual pots. However, buying plants restricts your choice of cultivars; growing your own plants from seed opens up hundreds of interesting possibilities.

Cultivation Any reasonable quality garden soil will be suitable so long as it is free-draining. A sunny position is best. Deadhead marigolds regularly to obtain continual flowering. Z9.

Propagation Sow the seed in the early spring under glass at 18–21°C (64–70°F). It can be sown where the plants are to flower but this will result in much later-flowering plants.

Uses These are predominantly plants for bedding schemes, but they can be used in mixed border or even in containers. They are good for children's gardens.

Tagetes Disco Series

This is a single French marigold which comes in a complete range of colours.

Tagetes 'French Vanilla'

A delightful double African marigold with large creamy-coloured flowers.

Tagetes Gem Series

This is a *T. tenuifolia* mixture, with single flowers in yellow and orange. The cultivars 'Golden Gem', 'Lemon Gem' and 'Tangerine Gem' are sold as separate colours.

Tagetes Safari Series

This is a series of double French marigolds including gold, yellow, orange and red flowers, some with mahogany markings.

THUNBERGIA
Thunbergia

This is a genus of more than 100 species. The one that is of most interest to gardeners is *T. alata*, commonly known as the black-eyed Susan. It is actually a perennial but treated like an annual. It must be said that it is welcome in the first place because of its attractive flowers, but the fact that it climbs is definitely a bonus since this is an attribute not often found in annuals. The flowers are funnel-shaped. They are orange in colour with a very noticeable black eye – hence the plant's common name. It is actually a twining plant that reaches about 2m (6ft) in height.

How to obtain Black-eyed Susans are sometimes seen for sale in garden centres and nurseries, but the way to be certain of getting plants is to grow your own from seed. This is readily obtainable from seed merchants.

Cultivation Black-eyed Susans can be grown in open ground so long as the soil is moisture-retentive but well drained. A good-quality potting compost (soil mix) should be used for containers.

Tagetes 'Golden Gem'

Tagetes erecta 'Golden Jubilee'

Thunbergia alata

Tithonia rotundifolia 'Goldfinger'

This plant needs to be sited in a warm sunny place. If you are able to keep it warm, move it inside for the winter and reuse it the following year. Z10.
Propagation Sow the seed under glass in early spring at 18–21°C (64–70°F).
Uses The black-eyed Susan can be used in any position where a climbing plant is required. It can be grown up a wigwam of branches in a bedding display or it can climb up a similar structure in a container.

Thunbergia alata
This is the climbing plant described above. The flowers are usually orange or deep yellow although they can also be cream. Most have black eyes but some lack these. It is usually grown as the species but it is sometimes offered as a cultivar such as 'Suzie Hybrids' which is not much different from the species.

Other plants Thunbergia gregorii is another climbing perennial that is treated as an annual. This is similar to the above but lacks the dark eye. It is not so commonly available.

TITHONIA
Mexican sunflower
This is a genus of about ten annuals and perennials of which one, T. rotundifolia, is grown in our gardens. This is not seen anywhere as near as often as it should be since it is a superb plant and those who grow it often rank it as one of their favourites. As with so many annuals, this has daisy-like flowers. In this case the outer ring of petals is a wonderful rich orange and the inner disc is yellow. The flowers are quite large, being up to about 7cm (3in) or more across. They appear at the end of upright stems which swell noticeably just below the flower head. The

plants are bushy and well branched. They are big plants and fill a big impressive space in the border. H 2m (6ft) when growing well, S 45cm (18in) or more.
How to obtain Mexican sunflowers are sometimes seen for sale as plants, but they do not like being confined for too long in a small pot. It is better to buy seed, which is readily available, and grow your own.
Cultivation Plant out after the threat of frosts has passed. These plants need a rich, moist, but free-draining soil and a sunny position. They may need support in exposed positions. Z9.
Propagation Sow the seed under glass at 13–18°C (55–64°F). Do not sow too early, late spring is the right time.
Uses Mexican sunflowers can be used as bedding material but they work best in mixed borders. They can be used in drifts, but a well-grown single specimen can be very impressive. They can be grown in containers, but they must be big.

Tithonia rotundifolia
The species, which is described above, is often grown. There are also a few cultivars. 'Goldfinger' is a more compact plant growing only 75cm (30in) high, making it more suited to bedding. 'Early Yellow' is the same height but with yellow flowers, while 'Torch' is double this height and has large reddish-orange flowers. 'Arcadian Blend' is a mixture of yellow, gold and orange. The single-coloured cultivars tend to look better.

TORENIA
Wishbone flower
This is a genus containing about 50 species of which, as so often happens, only one is widely grown in the garden. In this case it is T. fournieri. This is a bushy plant with masses of trumpet-shaped flowers, which can smother the plant to the extent that the leaves can hardly be seen. The flowers have a pale blue upper lip and a velvety, darker blue-purple lower one. They flower over a long period from midsummer well into autumn. H 30cm (12in) S 20cm (8in).

How to obtain Plants are not often seen for sale but seed is offered by a number of seed merchants. Torenias are not as popular as they once were, so you may have to search for them.
Cultivation Plant out in a rich moist soil in a sheltered position that is lightly shaded. Any good-quality potting compost (soil mix) is suitable for plants used in containers. Do not set these outside before the danger of frosts has been lifted. Z9.
Propagation Sow the seed in mid-spring under glass at 16–18°C (60–64°F).
Uses Torenias can be used as bedding plants in a shady position. They are also very suitable for containers.

Torenia fournieri
This is the main species grown. Seed can be obtained as the species or as one of several cultivars which have different coloured flowers. The Clown Series has pink, white and purple flowers in its mixture. Panda Series is similar except that the plants are more compact, reaching only about 20cm (8in) in height. 'Pink Panda' has pink flowers.

Other plants Torenia flava is sometimes seen on offer as seed. This is a spreading plant which is suitable for hanging baskets. It has small flowers which are a velvety-yellow colour. You may find them sold under the alternative name of 'Suzy Wong'.

Torenia fournieri Clown Series

Annuals for window boxes

Ageratum	Lobelia
Antirrhinum	Myosotis
Begonia	Nicotiana
Bidens	Nolana humifusa
Cerinthe	Petunia
Chrysanthemum	Pelargonium
Erysimum cheiri	Schizanthus
Exacum affine	Tagetes
Felicia amelloides	Verbena
Helichrysum	Viola

Tropaeolum majus

TROPAEOLUM
Nasturtium

There can be few gardeners who are not familiar with the delightful plants of this genus. There are getting on for 90 species in it, many of which are perennials that make excellent garden plants, but there is one annual in particular which is the darling of the annual grower. This is *T. majus* and its cultivars and hybrids. The typical plant has flame-red trumpet-shaped flowers, but there are quite a few variations on this. It is a trailing or climbing plant and can be used to hang from containers or scramble up through low shrubs. It is an excellent plant for covering large areas. H and S 3m (10ft) or more.

How to obtain You can buy plants but it is better to buy seed. This gives you better plants as well as a much larger choice.

Cultivation Any reasonable garden soil will be sufficient, since nasturtiums will grow in quite poor conditions. A position in full sun is best but plants often self-sow if in light shade. Z8.

Propagation Sow the seed in the spring in the open ground where the plants are to flower.

Uses Nasturtiums are versatile plants that can be used as bedding or in a mixed border. They can be allowed to spread across the ground or a support to climb up. Nasturtiums are good for covering large areas of bare earth. They can be grown in containers, but they must be large.

Tropaeolum majus

The species is often grown in its own right, but it also has a large number of cultivars and hybrids. In these the trumpets may be red, orange, yellow or cream, usually with contrasting markings in the throat. In recent times there has also been a tendency for breeders to produce plants with variegated foliage; some have splashes of pale yellow and others have darker gold markings.

Cultivars worth considering include: the Alaska Series which has creamy-white variegated leaves and a mixture of flower colours; 'Empress of India', a dwarf plant only 30cm (12in) high which has semi-double red flowers; 'Peach Melba' also with semi-double flowers but this time they are a primrose-yellow colour and have orange markings; 'Red Tiger', a semi-double with orange, red-striped flowers; and 'Milkmaid', which has creamy-yellow flowers.

Other plants Tropaeolum peregrinum is known as the canary creeper. It is a vigorous climber that grows up

Ursinia anthemoides 'Solar Fire'

to 3m (10ft), and has dainty little yellow flowers which have delicately cut petals. It is an excellent garden plant.

URSINIA
Ursinia

This is a genus containing about 40 species of perennials and a few annuals. Of these *U. anthemoides* is the main one in cultivation, although there are several others that are occasionally available. This is a plant with finely cut leaves topped by large daisy flower heads, up to 5cm (2in) or more across, carried on tall wiry stems. The ring of outer petals are deep gold or light orange with a purple spot at the base, creating an inner ring of colour. The central disc is also gold. The plants flower over a very long period. H 45cm (18in) S 30cm (12in).

How to obtain Ursinias are occasionally seen as plants for sale

in garden centres and nurseries, but they are usually purchased in the form of seed from some, not all, of the seed merchants.

Cultivation Plant out when frosts have passed in a well-drained light soil. Ursinias can also be grown in a good-quality general potting compost (soil mix). Z8.

Propagation Sow the seed under glass in the early spring at 16–18°C (60–64°F).

Uses The brightness of their colour makes ursinias very suitable as bedding plants, but they can also be used in a mixed border, especially one that is devoted to hot colours.

Ursinia anthemoides

This is the brightly coloured, bushy annual described above. Cultivars such as 'Solar Fire' and 'Sunshine Blend' are sometimes seen but they are not very different from the species.

Tropaeolum peregrinum

Ursinia anthemoides 'Sunshine Blend'

Other plants Several other species in this genus are offered from time to time. These are also yellow- or orange-flowered.

VERBASCUM
Mullein

This is an enormous genus of about 360 species. A fair number of these are in cultivation either as perennials (see page 411) or as annuals. Their great attraction is the tall spikes of flowers that they carry. Some of these are discreet and only reach 60cm (24in) or so, but others are a towering 2.5m (8ft) or more. The plants can produce just one spike or several, creating a candelabra effect. On the whole the saucer-shaped flowers are yellow, but there are also white and purple variations available. The centres of the flowers are usually purple.

How to obtain You occasionally see verbascums for sale in garden centres but they dislike being in small pots for long so it is better to grow them from seed. This is widely available.

Cultivation Plant out or sow in any reasonable garden soil so long as it is free draining. In exposed positions the taller specimens may need support of some kind. Z6.

Propagation Sow the seed in the spring, in the open ground where the plants are to flower, or sow in pots and place in an open frame without heat. Plants will self-sow.

Uses The architectural quality of verbascums makes them ideal for using as focal points, especially in a mixed border. They could also be used in an imaginative bedding scheme.

Verbascum bombyciferum

This is a biennial that overwinters as a rosette and then pushes up flower stems. The flowers are a soft yellow and the leaves are covered with silvery hairs. A magnificent plant. H 2.5m (8ft).

Other plants There are several other species available, although they are not seen as frequently. *V. thapsus*, known as Aaron's rod or great mullein, is another tall plant which will happily self-sow. It has yellow flowers. *V. sinuatum* is much shorter at about 1m (3ft), but it has many branches, each coming from the base. Again it produces yellow flowers and is a very attractive plant. *V. lychnitis*, or the white mullein, has white flowers.

VERBENA
Verbena

This is a large genus of about 250 species of annuals and perennials (see page 411). Quite a number of the perennials are tender and are treated as annuals. The annuals are generally low-growing and are often sprawling, making them ideal for containers. They are grown principally for their flowers, which are carried in flat or slightly domed heads. Individually the flowers have five petals and are tubular with an open mouth, like a disc. The colours are

Verbena 'Peaches and Cream'

generally shades of pink, red and purple, each with a white eye. There are also white flowers, which have a cream eye.

How to obtain Verbenas are usually bought as plants in individual pots from garden centres and nurseries. Most offer a good selection of varieties. Some are now offered as seed and these produce some interesting results.

Cultivation Plant out in any reasonable garden soil so long as it is free-draining. Use a good quality general potting compost (soil mix) for plants grown in containers. Z9.

Propagation Take cuttings in the summer and overwinter them under warm glass. Sow seed in early spring under glass at 16–18°C (60–64°F).

Uses Verbenas are excellent all-round plants for the garden. They can be used as bedding plants or grown in a mixed border,

and they can also be used to great effect in all types of containers including hanging baskets.

Verbena × hybrida

Most cultivars sold in garden centres come under this heading. They are often offered in series which have mixed colours, such as Derby Series, which are 25cm (10in) high and come in pink and red shades. Novalis Series are the same size but with a wider range of colours. Separate colours are available. Sandy Series and Romance Series are similar. Individual colours are also available, as in the delectable 'Peaches and Cream', which has pink and creamy flowers.

Other plants Other plants to explore include the bright red *V. peruvianna* as well as individual cultivars such as the beautiful *V.* 'Silver Anne' and *V.* 'Sissinghurst'.

Verbascum

Verbena 'Aphrodite'

Verbena 'Sandy Scarlet'

Viola tricolor

Xeranthemum annuum 'Superbissima'

VIOLA
Viola

This is a vast genus containing 500 species. Many of them are in cultivation as perennials (see pages 412–13). However, there is one that is widely grown as an annual and that is the pansy $V. \times wittrockiana$. This has long been a favourite in gardens, and was once the subject of heated competitions. Pansies tend to be rather sprawling plants with large flowers which often seem to resemble cheeky faces. Nearly all colours are represented, and usually more than one colour is present in each flower. They have long flowering periods, and there are pansies for all times of the year, including winter. Size varies but it is usually in the range of 15–25cm (6–10in) in height and up to 30cm (12in) in spread. Given the opportunity pansies will scramble up the other plants and reach greater heights.

How to obtain Plants are frequently available as bedding packs or individual pots in garden centres and nurseries as well as other outlets such as gas stations. Seed is also widely available and offers a better range.

Propagation Sow seed in early spring under glass at 13–16°C (55–60°F).

Cultivation Any reasonable garden soil will do but it must be moisture-retentive if the plants are set out in full sun. They will also grow in light shade. Trim them back if they get leggy (produce long bare stems). Z6.

Uses Pansies can be used anywhere in the garden, as bedding, in mixed borders or in containers.

Viola × wittrockiana

This is the main annual viola, although it is, in fact, a perennial. There are many cultivars available. Mixtures such as Joker Series also come as individual colours ('Jolly Joker' for example), and there are individual cultivars. These include 'Pretty', with its yellow and mahogany flowers, and 'Scarlet Orange Duet', with its red and orange flowers. The colour range is extensive, but the flowers usually have a yellow eye and frequently have black patches. The best way of looking at these plants is to get the seed merchant's catalogues, which contain hundreds of possibilities.

Other plants The tiny-flowered Viola tricolor, commonly known as heartsease, is an annual that is well worth growing. There are several cultivars. They include single-colour flowers, such as 'Bowles' Black' or bicolours. This plant self-sows.

XERANTHEMUM
Xeranthemum

This is a small genus of about six species of annuals, of which one is grown in gardens. These plants were once more widely cultivated, but like so many old-fashioned annuals they are somewhat out of fashion at the moment. This is a pity since they are very attractive, everlasting flowers.

There is quite a wide range of colours, which is based on shades of pink, red and purple. The flowers are daisy-like with an outer ring of coloured petals and a coloured central disc. H 60cm (24in) S 30cm (12in).

How to obtain Xeranthemum are occasionally seen sold as plants but the surest way to obtain them is from seed. This is offered by many seed merchants.

Cultivation Plant Xeranthemum out after the frosts have passed in any reasonable, free-draining garden soil. Give these plants a sunny position. Z9.

Propagation Sow the seed in the spring under glass at 16–18°C (60–64°F).

Uses These can be used as bedding plants or in a mixed border. They make excellent cut flowers and are perfect for drying.

Xeranthemum annuum

This species is still widely grown. It has both single and double flowers, which can be up to 5cm (2in) across, but are more often only 2cm (¾in). There are some cultivars: 'Snow Lady', which has white flowers; 'Superbissima' (rich purple); 'Lilac Stars' (lilac); and 'Cherry Ripe' (mixture of bright colours). These plants tend to flower over a very long period from midsummer well into autumn. The silvery-green leaves are covered with fine hairs.

Xeranthemum annuum

Zea mays

ZEA
Maize

This well-known genus has four species. One of them, *Z. mays*, is the much-cultivated maize which is used as a cereal crop throughout the world. Although it is widely grown in the vegetable garden, it is also grown as a decorative plant because it has both interesting foliage and colourful seed heads. The leaves are strap-like and hang down. In some cultivars they are variegated. The seed is carried in large heads, which are commonly known as corn-on-the-cob. The cases split open to display the ranks of individual corn grains. These are normally yellow but can include many other colours, making them look very decorative. The flowers are like silken tassels. These plants are tall and can reach 4m (12ft) but they are generally only half of this.

How to obtain Decorative maize is sometimes seen for sale, although it is best to grow your own plants from the wide variety of seed that is offered.

Cultivation Plant out after the last frosts in a fertile, free-draining soil. These plants require a position in full sun. Z10.

Propagation The seed can be sown, in spring, directly in the soil where the plants are to grow or sown individually in pots under glass at 18°C (64°F).

Uses Decorative maize makes a good foliage or decorative plant for the back of a mixed border. It can be used as temporary hedge.

Zea mays

This is the only species widely grown. It has been described above. It is usually sold as cultivars, either for the vegetable garden or for decorative purposes. 'Harlequin' has striped foliage in green, white and red, and corn in a deep red. Another variegated foliage plant is 'Variegata', whose leaves are striped with white. 'Strawberry Corn' has a mixture of yellow and red corn.

ZINNIA
Zinnia

The annuals of this genus of 20 species are still popular and there are many different varieties available. They are grown for their showy flowers, which are like large daisies with wide petals. They are often semi-doubles or doubles. There is a wide range of colours. Unusually, this includes green, but shades of yellow, orange, red and purple are more common. In good specimens the flowers can be up to 12cm (4½in) across. Their long stems make them suitable for cutting. H 75cm (30in) S 30cm (12in).

How to obtain Zinnias are frequently offered for sale as plants in individual pots at garden centres, nurseries and other outlets. They are also available in a wide range of seed from most seed merchants.

Propagation Sow the seed in mid-spring under glass at 13–18°C (55–64°F).

Cultivation Plant out only after all danger of frosts has passed. Choose a fertile soil to which plenty of well-rotted organic material has been added. Zinnias must have a warm and sunny position. Deadheading helps them to flower over a long period. Z10.

Uses They make excellent bedding plants or can be used in mixed borders. They can also be grown in larger containers, such as tubs.

Zinnia elegans

This is the taller of the two species commonly cultivated and the flowers are usually larger. The species is rarely grown in its own right; it is much more commonly seen as one of its many cultivars. These are generally offered as mixtures. Some, including the Profusion Series are also available as individual colours such as 'Profusion White' and 'Profusion Cherry'. The Dasher Series is similar, with 'Dasher Orange'. There are several dwarf series:

Zinnia elegans 'Profusion Cherry'

Peter Pan Series, Short Stuff Series and Small Wonder Series. Some cultivars are single coloured, such as the pale green 'Envy'.

Zinnia haageana

This is still often referred to by its former name, *Z. angustifolia*. The plants are not as big as the previous ones, but they also have broad petals. These are usually bright orange, but yellow and mahogany-red also feature among the cultivars. 'Orange Star' has pure, deep orange flowers; 'Persian Carpet' has semi-double and double flowers that are yellow or orange, splashed with mahogany.

Zinnia elegans 'Profusion White'

Zinnia elegans 'Dasher Orange'

A directory of perennials

This section provides a highly illustrated listing of the many perennials that are now available. It demonstrates very clearly just how versatile these long-lasting plants can be – providing every conceivable colour of bloom, structural shape and foliage type to help create wonderful effects in any style or size of garden.

English (common) names are given throughout this directory but increasingly the majority of plants are becoming known by their Latin or botanical names. Thus although *Agapanthus* was previously (and still is occasionally, particularly in books) known as African blue lily, it is referred to by most gardeners simply as agapanthus in the same way that *Hosta* has become hosta and *Iris* iris.

The hardiness zones given in the text refer only to the selected main plants featured and not to the whole genus. The height and spread given for each of the plants is an indication only. The dimensions will vary depending on the growing conditions and the vigour of the individual plants. The spread is particularly difficult to predict since many plants go on increasing their width throughout their lives.

One of the best geraniums for the front of a border is the colourful *Geranium cinereum* 'Ballerina', which flowers over a long period.

ACANTHUS
Bear's Breeches

There are about 30 species in this wonderful genus of which only four or five are commonly grown. The joy of these plants is their tall, architectural shapes. They are clump-forming, and produce spikes of smoky-coloured, hooded flowers. The large leaves are deeply divided and in some species are tipped with spines. These plants are ideal focal points for borders or elsewhere in the garden. They also make excellent cut and dried flowers.

Cultivation They will grow in any garden soil that is reasonably fertile in either full sun or partial shade. Z8.

Propagation From seed sown in pots in autumn or spring, or from root cuttings taken in early winter. Self-sown seedlings can also be transplanted while they are still young. Division is also possible but it can be heavy work to divide large plants.

Acanthus hungaricus
(A. balcanicus)

The flowers of this plant are pinkish-white with purple hoods, while the large leaves are dark green with narrow spineless leaflets. H and S 1.2m (4ft).

Acanthus mollis

Tall spikes of purple-hooded white flowers are carried over a clump of soft, dark green leaves with broad, spineless leaflets. H 1.5m (5ft) S 60cm (24in).

Acanthus spinosus

This produces very tall spikes of striking white flowers with purple hoods. The leaves are deeply cut

Acanthus mollis

with softish spines on the tips of the leaflets. H 1.5m (5ft) S 60cm (24in). There is a shorter form, *A. spinosissimus*, which has very deeply divided leaves with sharp spines. The leaves make this a dramatic plant, but it can be difficult to weed around.

Other plants For the keen gardener, *A. dioscoridis* (pink flowers with green hoods) and *A. hirsutus* (yellow flowers, green hoods) are well worth exploring.

ACHILLEA
Yarrow

There are 85 species of yarrow as well as a considerable number of cultivars. Not all the species are of interest to the gardener, indeed

Achillea 'Fanal'

some are weeds, but amongst their number are some first-class plants that most gardeners will appreciate. Many have a wonderful calm quality; their flat plates of flowers often seem to float above the other plants, creating a sea of tranquillity in the hurly-burly of the border. The predominant colour is yellow, but there are a number of white species and a few reds and terracottas among the cultivars. They make very good dried flowers.

Cultivation Yarrows prefer a sunny position and any reasonable garden soil. Some species need staking as they flop over. Z2–5.

Propagation Nearly all the main species and varieties can easily be increased by division or from basal cuttings taken in spring.

Achillea 'Fanal'

An attractive cultivar with brilliant red flowers. H 75cm (30in) S 60cm (24in).

Achillea filipendulina

A tall, elegant species with large flat heads of golden yellow floating 1.2m (4ft) above the ground. S 60cm (24in).

Achillea 'Moonshine'

Achillea millefolium

The species is best avoided (except in a spacious wild garden) since it is invasive, but there are a number of excellent cultivars suitable for flower beds and borders. They include 'Cerise Queen' (cerise), 'Fire King' (bright red), 'Lilac Beauty' (lilac), 'Paprika' (orange-red). H 60cm (24in) S 60cm (24in).

Achillea 'Moonshine'

This is an excellent cultivar with pale yellow flowers over soft grey foliage. However, it is not the strongest of plants and needs renewing every two or three years. H and S 60cm (24in).

Achillea ptarmica

A tall spreading plant with small heads of white flowers. It is normally grown in the attractive form 'Boule de Neige' which has double flowers. H 60cm (24in) S 1.2m (4ft).

Acanthus hungaricus

Acanthus spinosus

Achillea filipendulina

Achillea 'Taygetea'

Achillea 'Terracotta'

Achillea 'Taygetea'

This clump-forming plant has wide heads of sulphur yellow flowers carried on 60cm (24in) stems. The feathery leaves are greenish grey. S 60cm (24in).

Achillea 'Terracotta'

The best of the terracotta-coloured varieties. It has large flat heads floating 60–75cm (24–30in) above the ground and forming clumps. S 60cm (24in).

ACONITUM
Monkshood

This is a genus of about 100 species and 50 cultivars. They are very beautiful plants but unfortunately beneath this beauty is hidden poison – most parts of the plant are toxic if eaten. Avoid planting these if young children are likely to visit your garden, and in any case be careful where you site them. The plants are related to delphiniums and they have the same type of flower spikes carrying mainly bright blue flowers. The flowers are hooded, hence the plant's name, and also come in white and yellow.
Cultivation Aconitum prefer cool, partially shaded conditions but they will tolerate full sun if the soil is kept moist. They like a soil made rich with well-rotten organic material. Z3–6.
Propagation Sow seed in pots, preferably in autumn. The plants can also easily be divided in spring although they may take a while to settle down.

Aconitum 'Bressingham Spire'

A cultivar of proven track record with spikes that reach up to 1m (3ft) in height. The flowers are a rich violet blue. It flowers in late summer and into the autumn. S 30cm (12in).

Aconitum × cammarum 'Bicolor'

This is an intriguing plant with blue and white flowers that appear towards the end of summer. H 1.2m (4ft) S 50cm (20in). 'Grandiflorum Album' has large white flowers.

Aconitum carmichaelii

A long-used garden species with a number of valuable cultivars. It is a tall species, up to 1.8m (6ft), with deep blue flowers that appear from midsummer onwards. S 30cm (12in). 'Arendsii' is one of the best-known cultivars; it flowers slightly earlier than the species. 'Kelmscott' is another excellent cultivar; it has lighter blue flowers.

Aconitum hemsleyanum

This is different from the other species in that it is a climber that twines up supports or through shrubs. It has deep violet blue flowers from midsummer onwards. H 2–2.5m (6–8ft) S 1–1.2m (3–4ft).

Aconitum 'Ivorine'

One of the best of the non-blue monkshoods, this plant has beautiful pale creamy-yellow flowers that appear from spring into early summer. H 1m (3ft) S 60cm (24in).

Aconitum napellus

Aconitum 'Stainless Steel'

Aconitum napellus

A good species that has produced a number of excellent cultivars. The species has deep blue flowers but there is a cultivar 'Albiflorus' with pure white spikes. H 1.5m (5ft) S 30cm (12in).

Aconitum 'Spark's Variety'

A tall variety up to 1.5m (5ft) high with large spires of deep blue flowers that are carried from midsummer onwards. S 60cm (24in).

Other plants Other pleasing cultivars worth checking out include *Aconitum* 'Eleonara' and *A.* 'Stainless Steel'.

ACTAEA
Baneberry

Actaeas have been grown for generations, mainly for their coloured berries. However, what most gardeners have known as *Cimifuga* has now been added to the genus, giving it a group of spectacular flowering plants. The original actaeas are relatively short, clump-forming plants with little, white tufts of flowers that are followed by white, black or red berries. The cimifugas are much taller (up to 2m/6ft) and have striking, tall spikes of white flowers over attractive foliage.
Cultivation All actaeas like a woodland-type, moisture-retentive soil. The original actaeas are true woodlanders and like partial shade.

The cimifugas like partial shade, but will tolerate more sun if the soil is not dry. Z3.
Propagation The easiest method of increase is by division in spring. Actaeas can also be grown from seed as long as it is sown fresh.

Actaea pachypoda
(syn. A. alba)

An actaea that flowers in the spring and then produces a head of white berries in the late summer, when it is at its best. H 1m (3ft) S 50cm (20in).

Actaea racemosa

One of the tallest cimifugas with good green foliage and white flower spikes that resemble fire-works going off. The flowers appear in summer. H 2.5m (8ft) S 50cm (20in).

Actaea rubra

Similar to *A. pachypoda* except that it has red berries in autumn. An excellent woodland plant. H 50cm (20in) S 30cm (12in).

Actaea simplex

An excellent cimifuga type with tall white spikes of flowers in autumn and green foliage. H 1.2m (4ft) S 60cm (24in). The leaves are deep purple in some of the cultivars; 'Brunette' is a fine example of this. 'Elstead' is another attractive cultivar in which the buds are pink before they open to white flowers.

Actaea racemosa

ADIANTUM
Maidenhair fern
A romantic name for a romantic fern. The great attraction of this fern is its delicately cut fronds. They are usually carried on black or deep purple stems which set off the fresh green of the leaves perfectly. They are deciduous and when the new fronds first uncurl in spring they have a delightful pinkish tinge. These plants are best placed in a choice position where they can be easily seen.

Adiantum is a large genus of around 250 species of which 20 or so are in general cultivation. Many are frost tender but those listed below are hardy.
Cultivation These are delicate plants and so should be sited out of direct midday sunlight. They like a cool, moist root-run with plenty of leaf mould in the soil. Remove the old foliage in the late winter before the new growth begins to unfurl. Z5–8.
Propagation The plants can be grown from spore but division in spring is the easiest method.

Adiantum aleuticum
Individual leaflets are arranged in columns on either side of the black wiry midribs, giving the appearance of a long, deeply cut leaf. H 30cm (12in), slowly spreading to form a small clump (30cm/12in). The form 'Japonicum' has beautiful browny-red fronds when they first open.

Adiantum pedatum
This has similar fronds to the previous species, except that they are larger and more upright. H 45cm (18in), slowly spreading into a small clump (45cm/18in).

Adiantum venustum
The gem of the genus. It has deeply divided, filigree fronds, with the black midribs showing up in beautiful contrast to the green of the foliage. H 23cm (9in) S 30cm (12in).

Other plants In frost-free areas or for conservatory or greenhouse use try Adiantum raddianum or one of its many cultivars.

AGAPANTHUS
African blue lily
A very attractive genus of about ten species. There are many cultivars, at least one of which no garden should be without. The flowers are tubular, usually blue and carried in a globe, up to 20cm (8in) across, at the top of a tall, leafless stem. The foliage is strap-like and erupts from the base of the plant like a fountain. Agapanthus make excellent plants for the border or for containers. They flower in summer and make good cut flowers. The majority are hardy.
Cultivation They will grow in any reasonably fertile soil in full sun. Although they prefer a moist soil they will tolerate a degree of dryness. In cold areas they will appreciate a warm mulch during the winter. Z7.
Propagation Although they can be grown from seed sown in autumn they are more reliable grown from divisions taken in spring.

Agapanthus 'Castle of Mey'

Agapanthus africanus
A late-summer species with deep blue flowers. The flower stems reach 1m (3ft) tall S 50cm (20in). 'Albus' has white flowers.

Agapanthus 'Blue Giant'
Excellent blue-coloured flowers carried on tall (1.2m/4ft) stems. S 50cm (20in).

Agapanthus campanulatus
A fine species that has produced a number of popular cultivars. It produces large (up to 20cm/8in) heads of variable blue or white flowers in mid to late summer. H 60–120m (2–4ft) S 50cm (20in). 'Isis' is one of the most popular cultivars with deep blue flowers in late summer. The variety albidus has white flowers.

Agapanthus 'Castle of Mey'
This is a shorter variety that carries lovely deep blue flowers. It blooms in mid to late summer,

Agapanthus 'Dorothy Palmer'

and is excellent placed in a position at the front of a border. H 60cm (24in) S 30cm (12in).

Agapanthus 'Gayle's Lilac'
This has lilac flowers so it is good for those who want a paler form. H 60cm (24in) S 30cm (12in). A. 'Golden Rule' has yellow edges to its strap-like leaves. The flowers are light blue and appear mid to late summer. H 60cm (24in) S 30cm (12in).

Agapanthus Headbourne hybrids
This term covers a collection of hybrids of varying blues, originally selected by Lewis Palmer for their hardiness. 'Loch Hope' is an excellent tall variety. It has deep blue flowers which appear from late summer into autumn. H 1.5m (5ft) S 50cm (20in). 'Peter Pan' is a short form, suitable for small pots. H 60cm (24in) S 30cm (12in).

Other plants There are many more cultivars to explore, including 'Dorothy Palmer'. Nearly all are worth considering.

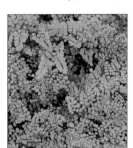
Adiantum venustum

Agapanthus campanulatus

Agapanthus 'Loch Hope'

Agastache foeniculum

Agastache 'Honey Bee White'

Alchemilla mollis

AGASTACHE
Mexican bergamot

This genus is not seen as often as it deserves to be. This is probably because the plants are short lived in moist soils. However, they self-sow and once you have them you are rarely without them. There are about 30 species but only a few are cultivated. The foliage is aromatic making this a pleasant plant to weed around. Another joy is the delightful spikes of flowers, which bloom from midsummer into autumn. Each plant sends up plenty of upright stems, the top of which is covered in whorls of bright blue, white, pink or red flowers. They are excellent for gravel gardens.

Cultivation These are plants from dry hills and so they like a well-drained soil in full sun. Z8.
Propagation They can readily be grown from seed, sown inside or scattered where the plants are to grow. They will self-sow if the conditions are right. Basal cuttings can be taken in spring.

Agastache foeniculum
(syn. *A. anisata*)
This can be a tall species when grown in a reasonably rich soil. The mint-like leaves smell of aniseed, and the flowers are a wonderful dusky dark blue. H 1.5m (5ft) S 50cm (20in). There are a number of cultivars the most popular being 'Alabaster' with white flowers. 'Blue and White' is also often grown.

Agastache mexicana
This is the other main hardy species in cultivation. It has pink to dark red flowers over a long period in late summer and often beyond. H 1m (3ft) S 30cm (12in). There are several cultivars including 'Mauve Beauty' with lilac-mauve flowers. 'Champagne' has fine fizzy spikes of creamy-white flowers.

Other plants These are the main species but it is worth exploring *Agastache rugosa* and *A. urticifolia* among others. 'Honey Bee White' is another cultivar to try.

ALCHEMILLA
Lady's mantle

A large genus of 250 species of which a number are in cultivation. Their attraction is that they are good both as flowering and foliage plants. The flowers are small but grouped in clusters; in some cases they form tight clusters, in others airy sprays. The flowers are a yellowy lime-green. This contrasts well with the green foliage which is rounded and pleated. In some species the foliage is more deeply cut. Alchemilla is a perfect plant for growing along paths or on the banks of ponds.

Cultivation Any reasonably fertile soil will do for this plant. It will grow in either full sun or partial shade. Cut back to the ground after flowering to prevent seeding and to promote new foliage. Z6.
Propagation Self-seeds, but it can be propagated from seed sown in spring or from divisions.

Alchemilla conjuncta
A mat-forming plant with very distinctive foliage. The deeply lobed leaves are green but edged with silver. It is low-growing, only reaching about 20cm (8in) unless it is scrambling through another plant. S 30cm (12in)

Alchemilla mollis
A common but excellent plant. It is floppy but reaches about 45cm (18in) in height. It has a lovely scent when you are up close. The flowers appear in early to midsummer and the plant should then be cut back. S 45cm (18in).

Other plants The above are the main species but there are plenty more that are worth growing, especially the low, mat-growing ones. Try *Alchemilla alpina*, *A. elizabethae*, or *A. ellenbeckii* with its red stems.

Perennials for seaside gardens

Artemisia
Centranthus
Crambe maritima
Crocosmia
Echinops
Erigeron
Eryngium
Geranium
Kniphofia
Lathyrus
Limonium
Linaria
Origanum
Osteospermum
Papaver
Perovskia
Persicaria affinis
Phormium
Sisyrinchium
Yucca

Agastache foeniculum 'Blue and White'

Alchemilla conjuncta

Alchemilla elizabethae

Allium cristophii

ALLIUM
Ornamental onions

This very large genus of bulbs (more than 700 species) has a deservedly popular place in hardy borders. Alliums are very decorative and are best placed so that they pop up between or through other plants. Although some have lax heads the majority of popular species have round globes of flowers, 25cm (10in) or more across.

Most have purple flowers but there are others with blue, white, pink or yellow heads. There are species that flower at all times between spring and autumn. Most have strap-like foliage. However, this can be rather ugly since it is often dying back just as the flowers are coming into bloom. Hide the plants amongst other plants in the middle of the border so that the dying leaves will not be visible.

Cultivation Alliums will grow in most soils except extremely wet ones. They are perfect for dry soils such as gravel borders. They like full sun. Z3–8.

Propagation Alliums generally increase with little help from the gardener. They can be grown from seed or from the bulbils that often appear in the flower heads. The easiest way is to divide off the little bulblets that develop around the main bulb.

Allium carinatum subsp. *pulchellum*

A beautiful flower with a shower of drooping pink to purple flowers that appear over a long period in the autumn. The grass-like foliage can be confused with weeds early in the year. H 45cm (18in) S 8–10cm (3–4in).

Allium cristophii.

Very impressive purple flowers that are large and globe-like. They make good dried flowers. H 60cm (24in) S 20cm (8in).

Allium hollandicum

A medium-sized spherical-headed onion for the spring border. The flowers are purple. This plant is best known in its form 'Purple Sensation' which has an almost luminous quality. H 1m (3ft) S 10cm (4in).

Allium roseum

A charming allium which is best grown so that it peeps up through other plants. It has lax heads of only a few flowers, but these are of a most delicate pink. They appear in summer. The plant has bulbils and can be slightly invasive. However, it rarely causes problems especially if the bulbils are removed before they ripen. H 1m (3ft) S 10cm (4in).

Allium schoenoprasum

This is the humble chive. It flowers briefly but profusely in the early summer, when it is a perfect choice for lining paths. The flowers are purple but in the form 'Forescate' they are brighter and more rosy-pink. Shear to the

ground after flowering to encourage new foliage. H 30cm (12in) S 10cm (4in).

Allium sphaerocephalon

This allium has bright reddish flowers that are compressed into a tight ball. It flowers in summer and is excellent planted amongst other plants. H 75cm (30in) S 10cm (4in).

Other plants There are many, many more species of allium to choose from and it is worth making a note of any pleasing ones that you see as you go round gardens. Be aware that some of the smaller ones can become a little invasive.

ALSTROEMERIA
Peruvian lily

Alstroemeria are known mainly as cut flowers, but increasingly, they are becoming popular as a garden plant. There are 20 species and about 100 garden-bred cultivars.

The plants are summer-flowering, producing masses of funnel-shaped flowers. They vary in colour from yellows and oranges to pinks and reds, with most having a mixture of two or more colours. The throats are distinctively streaked or spotted. As well as being suitable for growing in the greenhouse for cutting, most make good garden plants. They are ideally placed in the middle of the border.

Cultivation Alstroemerias like a moist soil with plenty of organic material added to it. They should be in full sun, although they will tolerate a little shade. Slugs can be a nuisance. Z7.

Propagation These plants can be grown from seed, but the most usual method of propagation is by division.

Alstroemeria ligtu hybrids

Alstroemeria aurea

These are the most commonly seen Peruvian lilies in gardens and possibly the hardiest. The flowers are bright orange, streaked with reddish brown. They get up to 45cm (18in) high. S 60cm (24in). There are several cultivars: 'Lutea' has flowers of bright yellow with brownish spots.

Alstroemeria ligtu

A pink-flowered hardy species that is mainly grown in the form of ligtu hybrids which come in a variety of colours. H 75cm (30in) S 60–100cm (2–3ft).

Alstroemeria psittacina

The flowers are not so flared as on other species, but they are intriguingly coloured in shades of green and red. H 1m (3ft) S 60cm (24in).

Other plants There are many other highly coloured cultivars to explore. The best way to choose between them is to go to a specialist nursery which has plenty to offer.

ANEMONE
Anemone

This is a large genus of garden plants offering several distinct forms from tall Japanese anemones to low wood anemones. There are 120 species in the genus and most are in cultivation. For the keen gardener it is a good genus to collect since it presents interesting and varying flowers from early spring through to autumn. Most are simple open flowers but there are some lovely doubles. There are anemones of all colours except black.

Cultivation All need a moisture-retentive soil, except for the bulbous species, such as the

Allium roseum

Allium schoenoprasum

Alstroemeria aurea

Anemone blanda

Anemone hupehensis 'Prinz Heinrich'

Anemone nemorosa

Anthemis punctata subsp. cupaniana

coronarias which need a well-drained soil. Shade is preferred by the small woodlanders and full sun by the bulbs. All the others like sun or partial shade. Z5–6.
Propagation All can be grown from seed preferably sown after it has ripened. Division is the other main method of increase.

Anemone blanda
A lovely woodland flower for early spring, with discs of blue, white or pink petals. It dies back after flowering and seeding. H 5–10cm (2–4in) S 10–15cm (4–6in).

Anemone coronaria
A tuberous anemone with bright red, blue or white spring flowers. Good for the front of a border or containers. H 5–25cm (2–10in) S 10–15cm (4–6in). The most common group of cultivars are the De Caens which are

Anemone coronaria 'Lord Lieutenant'

delightful. *A.c.* 'Lord Lieutenant' is also an attractive cultivar. Other bulbous species worth considering are *A. × fulgida* and *A. pavonina*, which have bright red forms.

Anemone × hybrida
(Japanese anemone)
Few gardens can wish to be without Japanese anemones which embrace several species including this hybrid. Although tall (up to 1.5m/5ft) they are wiry and do not need staking. The colours are various shades of pink and white; the white look good against green hedges. They flower from midsummer onwards. S 60cm (24in).

There are lots of good cultivars including 'Honorine Jobert' (white) and 'Königin Charlotte' (semi-double flowers).

Anemone hupehensis
(Japanese anemone)
This species is often confused with the previous one. The summer flowers are very similar in shape and colour (pinks and whites). H 1m (3ft) S 1m (3ft).

Anemone hupehensis

Again there are plenty of good cultivars including 'Hadspen Abundance' and 'Prinz Heinrich', both with deep pink flowers.

Anemone nemorosa
(Wood anemone, windflower)
A dainty white flower that grows well under deciduous trees and shrubs. It dies back after flowering and seeding. H 5cm (6in) S 30cm (12in). There are blue forms, such as 'Blue Bonnet'. There are also similar species (*A. × ranunculoides*) which have bright yellow flowers.

Other plants For the enthusiast there are plenty of other species, such as *AA. polyanthes, rivularis, sylvestris* and *trullifolia*.

ANTHEMIS
Anthemis
This genus provides some of the mainstays of the summer border: fresh-looking daisies in a range of colours from white through cream to yellow and orange. All have a yellow or golden central disc. The flowers are carried on wiry stems up to 1m (3ft) high. The foliage is generally deeply cut and in some cases very attractive. Many have a tendency to reflex (curl back) their petals at night so they are not good plants to choose if you see your garden only in the evening. For the daytime border, however, their bright cheerfulness is indispensable.
Cultivation Anthemis need a fertile, moisture-retentive soil in full sun. Some will need support unless the garden is fairly wind-free. They resent disturbance so transplant young. Z4–8.
Propagation The species can be grown from seed but cultivars are best reproduced from basal cuttings in spring.

Anthemis punctata subsp. cupaniana
A delightful species with white daisies which float above a mat of silver foliage in early summer. Cut the flower stems off after flowering so that you can appreciate it as a foliage plant for the rest of the summer. The leaves are almost ground hugging, but flower stems reach up to about 30cm (12in) or so in height. S 30cm (12in).

Anthemis sancti-johannis
This has striking orange flowers in summer. The plants are short lived, so be sure to take cuttings each year. H 60cm (24in) S 60cm (24in).

Anthemis tinctoria
A good species with a superb group of cultivars. H and S 1m (3ft). Cultivars worth looking out for are 'E.C. Buxton' (lemon-yellow), 'Sauce Hollandaise' (pale cream) and 'Wargrave' (pale yellow), but all are good.

Other plants Cultivars worth growing include *AA.* 'Beauty of Grallagh', 'Grallagh Gold', 'Susanna Mitchell' and Tetworth'.

Anthemis tinctoria 'E.C. Buxton'

Aquilegia 'Bunting'

Aquilegia 'Dove'

Artemisia ludoviciana 'Silver Queen'

AQUILEGIA
Aquilegia, columbine,
granny's bonnet

Whichever of the various English
names you prefer, these are
delightful plants. The flowers
resemble a female ballet dancer
standing on tip-toe with her arms
above her head. They vary from the
typical blue through to different
shades of white, pink, red, yellow
and even greenish-brown.

These are plants of the late
spring and early summer, and they
look delightful when scattered
among the other plants of that
time of year. There are about
70 species and many cultivars
from which to choose.
Cultivation Aquilegia will grow in
most reasonably fertile soils. They
can be grown in full sun or partial
shade. Cut off the flowering
stems after flowering as the
foliage can still be enjoyed. Z3–6
Propagation They can easily be
grown from seed, too easily
perhaps as they will self-sow

abundantly if the seed pods are
left on. Self-sown seedlings may
not come true, but you can get
some interesting results.

Aquilegia canadensis
A delicate, relatively small-
flowered variety with yellow and
red blooms. H 1m (3ft) S 30cm
(12in). Another attractive red and
yellow species is *A. formosa.*

Aquilegia fragrans
This species produces soft
pinkish-white flowers that are
occasionally tinged with blue.
They have a sweet fragrance that
you can smell when you get close
to them. The plants can become
hybridized with other species and
the scent lost. H 45cm (18in)
S 10cm (4in).

Aquilegia longissima
This is a good yellow species with
largish flowers distinguished by
their very long spurs. H 1m (3ft)
S 50cm (20in).

Aquilegia McKana Group
A group of hybrids with large,
mixed coloured flowers that have
long spurs. H 60cm (24in)
S 30cm (12in).

Aquilegia viridiflora
A delightful low-growing species
with unusual greenish-brown
flowers. It is best grown in groups
at the front of a border or on a
raised bed. H and S 30cm (12in).

Aquilegia vulgaris
The granny's bonnet
The typical plant as it grows
in the wild has blue flowers but
there are many cultivars with
blooms in a mix of colours such
as the wonderful white 'Nivea'.
H 1m (3ft) S 50cm (20in).
There are also double-flowered
forms such as 'Nora Barlow' with
green and red flowers.

Other plants The range above is
fairly wide but there are still plenty
of other plants that the enthusiast
could look out for. They include
A. flabellata (blue) and its wide
range of cultivars, *A.* 'Hensol
Harebell', *A.* 'Bunting', *A.* 'Dove'
and *A. alpina.* A related genus with
similar flowers but without the
spurs is *Semiaquilegia.*

ARTEMISIA
Wormwood

A genus of about 300 species,
many of which are weedy and
certainly to be avoided in the
garden. However, a number of
species have some excellent
cultivars that no garden should be
without. Many of these are
considered to be foliage plants,
with most gardeners removing the
flower spikes as they appear. The
appeal of the foliage is firstly the

colour, which is often a beautiful
silver, and secondly the cut, often
a delicate filigree. These are good
plants for any sunny border. They
work well with soft colours, but
can also be useful as foils between
stronger colours.
Cultivation Artemisias are sun-
loving plants and do not do well
in shade. The soil should be
fertile but well-drained, except for
A. lactiflora which likes a moist
soil. Z3–8.
Propagation Most are spreading
forms, which are easy to increase
by division. One or two are
difficult to divide and are
therefore best propagated by
taking cuttings in spring.

Artemisia alba 'Canescens'
A silver-leaved artemisia with very
fine foliage that can look rather
like unruly coils of silver wire.
The flowers are a dirty brown and
should be removed when they
appear in summer. H 45cm
(18in) S 30cm (12in).

Artemisia lactiflora
The odd man out since it is
grown for its flowers. This plant
has tall upright stems with dark
green leaves. The sprays of
flowers in late summer are creamy

Aquilegia vulgaris

Aquilegia vulgaris 'Nora Barlow'

Artemisia lactiflora

Artemisia ludoviciana 'Valerie Finnis'

white and very attractive. H 1.5m
(5ft) S 50cm (20in). It has a
popular cultivar in 'Guizhou'
which is prized for its foliage and
stems which are purple in the
early summer.

Artemisia ludoviciana
Another silver-leaved species, this
time with more solid, spear-
shaped leaves. The flowers are
dirty yellow and are usually
removed when they appear in
summer. The plant can be tall, but
tends to flop as it ages so it
should be discreetly supported if
possible. H 1m (3ft) S 60cm
(24in). There are two extremely
good cultivars: 'Silver Queen' and
'Valerie Finnis', either or both
deserving of a place in the garden.

Artemisia 'Powis Castle'
To many gardeners this is the ace
in the pack. It has deeply cut,
filigree leaves that are an intense
sparkling silver. The yellowish
flowers tend to spoil the effect
and should be removed. H 60cm
(24in) S 1m (3ft).

Artemisia schmidtiana
Yet another excellent plant with
very narrow silver foliage. It is a
lowish carpeting plant. H 45
(18in) S 60cm (24in). It has a
delightful cultivar 'Nana' which
only grows 10cm (4in) high.

Other plants Artemisia arborescens,
A. caucasica and *A. stelleriana*
'Boughton Silver' are worth
exploring if there is space.

ARUNCUS
Goatsbeard
These plants are probably suitable
only for large gardens since their
flowering season is brief and they
take up space. That said they are
very attractive and are well worth
growing if you have space near a
pond or other area where the soil
is reasonably moist. The flowers
are creamy-white and held in large,
loose pyramidal spikes in summer
for about a week or so before they
start to turn brown.
Cultivation Sun or partial shade in
a moisture-retentive soil. Cut
back in autumn. Z3–8.
Propagation Goatsbeards should be
divided in spring.

Aruncus dioicus

Aruncus aethusifolius
A dwarf form that does not get
taller than 30cm (12in). Useful
for small gardens. S 20cm (8in).

Aruncus dioicus
The most commonly grown
goatsbeard. This is a tall, clump-
forming plant that can look truly
magnificent when in flower. H 2m
(6ft) S 1.2m (4ft). Out of
flower it makes a moderate foliage
plant. It has an excellent cultivar
'Kneiffii', which is shorter
(1.2m/4ft) and has very
attractive, deep-cut leaves for
which it is mainly grown.

ARUNDO
Giant reed
A small genus of which only
one species is of interest to the
general gardener. This can grow to

Arundo donax

dizzy heights, up to 5m (15ft).
It makes a bold focal point in a
large garden, and an excellent
feature in a border if it is big
enough. However, for many
gardens it is most effective when
used as a summer screen. This is
a tall grass with strong vertical
stems and broad, strap-like leaves.
Cultivation The giant reed prefers
a fertile, moisture-retentive soil
but it will grow in any reasonable
garden soil. Like most grasses it
likes full sun but needs protection
from winds. It should be cut back
to the ground in spring before
new growth starts. Z7.
Propagation Divide the clumps in
spring just before growth begins.
The giant reed can also be grown
from seed sown in pots.

Arundo donax
This is the only species normally
grown in gardens. It is tall with
green leaves and stems, and purply
plumes of flowers in autumn.
H 3m (10ft) S 1m (3ft). Its
variety *A.d. versicolor* is shorter
(up to 2m/6ft) and has creamy
stripes running down the length
of its leaves. The cultivar
'Macrophylla' has very broad (up
to 7.5cm /3in) leaves which are
bluish-green in colour.

ASPLENIUM
Spleenwort
This is an enormous genus of
some 700 species of evergreen
and semi-evergreen ferns, and
there are also a number of
cultivars. Only a few species
are in general cultivation so
the gardener does not have too
much of a problem deciding
which to grow. They vary from
those with typical triangular, fern-
like fronds to those with wide,
strap-like foliage. They are
splendid plants for growing in
a woodland setting or in shade
and generally provide interest
throughout the year.
Cultivation These plants need to
be planted in a shady area, and
in a moisture-retentive, but
free-draining, soil.
Propagation The best method of
increase is by dividing existing
plants in spring. The species can
also be increased by sowing spore
as they ripen.

Asplenium bulbiferum
Hen and chicken fern
This plant gets its common name
because it produces young plants
along its fronds. The fronds are
typically fern-shaped; triangular
with deeply divided segments. It
prefers acid soils. In really good
conditions it can grow up to
1.2m (4ft) high. S 30cm (12in).

Asplenium scolopendrium
Hart's tongue fern
The most popular species with
the most cultivars. As its name
implies the strap-like fronds taper
towards the top, like tongues.
The margins are slightly wavy. It
prefers alkaline soils. H 60cm
(24in) S 45cm (18in).
There are a number of interesting
cultivars. The Crispum Group
have wavy margins to the foliage,
while the Cristatum Group have
crests at the top of the fronds.

Asplenium trichomanes
Maidenhair spleenwort
So called because it resembles the
delicate maidenhair fern in that
it has small dark green, elliptic
leaflets arranged either side of a
dark midrib. This plant prefers
alkaline soils. H 15cm (6in)
S 15–30cm (6–12in).

Other plants There are a number
of other species that are more
suitable for the conservatory or
heated greenhouse, as well as
other cultivars of *A. scolopendrium*
which the enthusiast can explore.

Asplenium scolopendrium

ASTER
Aster

This is a large genus of about 250 species and at least as many cultivars. It is a popular genus and many of the species are in cultivation although most gardeners grow only a few, in particular the Michaelmas daisies. Asters have daisy-like flowers with a colourful outer disc of petals and a central one of yellow. The petals cover a wide colour range from white and pink to blue and purple. Most produce multiple heads and are a mass of colour when in bloom, often for a very long time. They make very good border plants.

Cultivation Any good garden soil, preferably in sun. Many asters can suffer from mildew, but unless this is unsightly it can be ignored. Many of the floppier forms need staking, but the Michaelmas daisies are usually self-supporting, except in exposed areas. Z4–8.

Propagation Most asters are extremely easy to divide in the spring. A few like *A. × frikartii* are difficult to divide and basal cuttings is then the best method.

Aster alpinus

These are low, spreading plants which are excellent for the front of a border. The species has blue flowers which appear from the early summer onwards. H 25cm (10in) S 30–45cm (12–18in). There are a number of very good cultivars to try, including 'Dunkle Schöne' (deep blue) and 'White Beauty' (white).

Aster amellus 'Blue King'

Aster amellus

Most of the numerous cultivars make splendid plants. They have relatively large daisies, up to 5cm (2in) across. The colours are many variations on pink and blue. Flowers appear from late summer and continue well into autumn. H and S 50cm (20in). Cultivars to look out for include 'Blue King' (blue), 'Brilliant' (pink), 'King George' (violet blue), 'Rosa Erfüllung' (pale pink), 'Rudolph Goethe' (lavender) and 'Veilchenkönigin' (violet).

Aster cordifolius

This has floating sprays of small flowers on stems up to 1.5m (5ft) high. S 1m (3ft). It is best grown in one of two cultivars: 'Silver Spray' (pale pink) or 'Sweet Lavender' (lavender-blue).

Aster ericoides

Beautiful, delicate sprays of small blue or pink flowers in autumn. H 1m (3ft) S 50cm (20in). Some superb cultivars, including 'Blue Star' (blue), 'Golden Spray' (pinkish white), 'Pink Cloud' (pink) and 'Snow Flurry' (white).

Aster × frikartii

An excellent hybrid of which 'Mönch' is the gem. This has large (7.5cm/3in) blue heads that

Aster lateriflorus

continue from midsummer right through to the end of autumn. Its 75cm (30in) stems often need some support. S 45cm (18in). 'Wunder von Stäfa' is similar.

Aster novae-angliae

These rather coarse Michaelmas daisies make excellent tall plants for the back of the border. There are many good cultivars including 'Andenken an Alma Pötschke' (rose-pink), 'Barr's Violet' (violet blue), 'Harrington's Pink' (pink) and 'Herbstschnee' (white).

Aster novi-belgii
Michaelmas daisies

More refined and shorter than the previous species, these are suitable for the middle of the border. H 1.2m (4ft) S 60–75cm (24–30in). There are hundreds of excellent cultivars; look at them in flower to choose your favourites.

Other plants There are many other excellent species, including *AA. divaricatus, lateriflorus, sedifolius* and *tongolensis*.

ASTILBE
Astilbe

A small genus of only about 12 species, but supplemented with many additional garden forms. Astilbes are characterized by their flat tapering flower heads and deeply divided leaves. The colours of the flowers vary from pink to red by way of purple, and with a few whites and creams. They flower in summer. Although they grow well in full sun they are also good plants for lightly shaded areas. They are particularly good for growing next to ponds and other water features.

Cultivation Astilbes like moisture-retentive soils that should preferably remain damp all

Astilbe × arendsii 'Fanal'

through the summer. They will grow in either full sun or light shade. Z4–7.

Propagation The plants can be divided in spring.

Astilbe arendsii

A wonderful selection of cultivars from Germany. H 1m (3ft) S 60cm (24in). Among the many excellent plants on offer are 'Brautschleier' (white), 'Bressingham Beauty' (pink), 'Erica' (bright pink), 'Fanal' (dark crimson-red), 'Irrlicht' (white), 'Snowdrift' (white) and 'Venus' (bright pink).

Astilbe chinensis

This is a relatively short astilbe (up to 60cm/24in) with pink flowers. The variety *pumila* is dwarf (25cm/10in) high, making it an excellent choice for the front of a border. It has purplish-pink flowers. S 20cm (8in).

Other plants There are a large number of garden cultivars, which vary in height and flower colour.

Aster alpinus

Aster × frikartii

Astilbe × arendsii 'Venus'

Astilbe 'Aphrodite'

Astrantia major 'Rubra'

Good examples to try include
A. 'Aphrodite', A. × crispa 'Perkeo'
(pink), A. 'Red Sentinel' (bright
red), and A. 'Rheinland' (pink).

ASTRANTIA
Masterwort
Astrantia is a small genus of
about 10 species. Only two of
them are in general cultivation,
but they are excellent plants and
there are a number of garden
cultivars. The flowers are basically
greenish-white but they are
generally flushed with pink or
varying intensity, some dark
enough to be red. They resemble
pincushions surrounded by bracts.
These clump-forming plants tend
to reach up to 1m (3ft) in good
conditions. Although they will
grow in sun they are excellent
plants for lightly shaded positions
and flower over a long period
from early summer onwards.
Cultivation Masterworts prefer
moisture-retentive soil but
generally do well in any reasonable
garden soil. If the soil is on the
dry side then a shaded position is
required. Z5–8.
Propagation These plants are easy
to divide in the spring. They will
also grow readily from seed, but
the cultivars are unlikely to come
true if you use this method.

Astrantia major
This is the main species grown
with most of the cultivars derived
from it. The flowers of the
species have a pinkish tinge, but
some of the cultivars are much
stronger in colour, some even a
dark red. H 60cm (24in) S 45cm
(18in). Although the species is
worth growing in its own right,
one of the cultivars will generally
give a better effect. There are
many good ones to try, including
'Hadspen Blood' (deep blood-
red), 'Primadonna' (pink),
'Rosensinfonie' (deep pink),
'Rubra' (red), 'Ruby Cloud' (ruby
red), 'Ruby Wedding' (ruby red),
'Shaggy' (greenish white with very
long surrounding bracts) and
'Sunningdale Variegated' (creamy
variegations on the leaves).

Astrantia maxima
This is mainly grown as the
straight species, and is well worth
tracking down for its delightful
shell-pink colouration. H 60cm
(24in) S 30cm (12in).

ATHYRIUM
Lady fern
This is a large genus consisting
of about 180 species of ferns and
a number of garden cultivars. It
got its English name because of

Autumn-flowering perennials
Anemone x hybrida
Aster
Boltonia
Chelone
Chrysanthemum
Cimifuga
Helianthus
Kirenshonga
Liriope
Leucanthemella
Nerine
Ophiopogon
Rudbeckia
Schizostylis
Sedum
Solidago
Tricyrtis
Vernonia

the delicacy of the lacy, elegant
fronds of the main garden species
A. filix-femina. The plants are
deciduous ferns whose fronds
turn brown in autumn. They grow
up to 1.2m (4ft) when they are
well suited.
   Like most ferns they prefer a
shaded position and are ideal for
growing in a woodland setting or
in another shady position, such
as in a border on the north side
of the house.
Cultivation Lady ferns require a
moisture-retentive soil such as
you would find in a woodland.
They do not like an alkaline soil,
and need to be grown in light

shade. Cut back the old leaves in
spring before the new growth
begins. Z3–5.
Propagation Division in the spring
is the easiest method. Plants can
also be grown from spores.

Athyrium filix-femina
An attractive species which has
a number of cultivars and is
also worth growing in its own
right. H 60–120cm (2–4ft)
S 30–100cm (1–3ft). Among the
best cultivars are the Cruciatum
Group with crested fronds, the
intriguing 'Frizelliae' in which the
leaflets (pinnae) have been
reduced to alternate, single round
leaves on either side of the main
rib, and the 'Minutissimum' with
its smaller 30cm (12in) stems.

Athyrium niponicum
The species is in cultivation but it
is the variety pictum which is
usually seen. This is a lowish
plant with the most beautifully
coloured fronds. They are a
metallic greeny-silver flushed with
purple. H and S 30cm (12in).

Other plants There are several
tender lady ferns that can be
grown in a conservatory or heated
greenhouse as well as a few more
hardy cultivars that would make a
welcome addition to the garden if
you get hooked on ferns.

BAPTISIA
Baptisia
A genus of some 20 species of
which only one is in general
cultivation. This is B. australis
which has a loose, lupin-like head
of bright blue flowers. These
appear in early summer and are
set off against fresh green foliage.
H 1.5m (5ft) S 60cm (24in).
Cultivation A rich, moist soil in
sun or partial shade. Z5.
Propagation This is easily increased
from freshly collected seed. It can
also be propagated by division.

Astrantia major

A. major 'Sunningdale Variegated'

Athyrium niponicum

Baptisia australis

Bergenia 'Bressingham White'

Bergenia 'Sunningdale'

Brunnera macrophylla

Brunnera macrophylla 'Dawson's White'

BERGENIA
Elephant's ears

The English name is an apt description of plants in this genus of about eight species with its numerous cultivars. The key feature of the plants is the large oval leaves, which make an excellent ground cover on all types of soil and in conditions of sun or shade.

Most have shiny, evergreen leaves that glint in the sun, and many of them also turn a wonderful liverish-red during the winter. The flowers, which are produced in spikes in the early summer, are also attractive. The plants usually grow up to 45cm (18in) or sometimes a little more. S 60cm (24in).
Cultivation Bergenias prefer a moist but well-drained soil. However, they will also grow in dryish, but not drought-ridden, soils. They suit a sunny or partially shaded position. Z3–5.
Propagation You can increase these plants by division. Alternatively, place 2.5cm (1in) sections of budded rhizome in cutting compost (soil mix) until they have rooted.

Bergenia 'Ballawley'
This is a good form for winter use as the glossy green leaves take on a superb glossy purple-bronze tint throughout the winter. The spring flowers are bright red.

Bergenia 'Bressingham White'
This plant has deep green foliage surmounted by a spike of white flowers in spring.

Bergenia cordifolia
Crinkle-edged leaves that tint slightly during the winter. The flowers are an excellent magenta colour. There is a form 'Purpurea' which has darker winter leaves.

Bergenia 'Silberlicht'
Grown mainly for its flowers which are a brilliant white when newly opened but which fade to pink as they age.

Bergenia 'Sunningdale'
This is a very good winter-coloured variety with attractive carmine-coloured flowers.

Other plants There are many others to look at if you have the space. *B. ciliata* (hairy leaves) and the cultivars 'Schneekönigin' (white flowers), 'Morgenröte' (deep pink) and 'Wintermärchen' (almost red) are good choices.

BRIZA
Quaking grass

Most of the 15 species that make up this genus are annuals but there is one good perennial *B. media*, the common quaking grass or trembling grass. The English name comes from the fact that the hanging, heart-shaped heads move in the slightest breeze, giving the impression that the whole plant is trembling. The spikelets are purple changing to a golden-yellow as they ripen. The grass can grow up to 60cm (24in) high, with a spread of 10cm (4in). This plant is attractive in the garden and also works well in dried arrangements.
Cultivation Any well-drained garden soil in full sun. Z4
Propagation Can be divided in early spring just as growth begins. It can also be grown from seed.

BRUNNERA
Brunnera

A small genus of three species of which one, *B. macrophylla*, is in general cultivation. This is a gem for a lightly shaded position, either under shrubs or trees, or on the shady side of a building or fence. It has fairly large, oval leaves that are slightly coarse. The blue flowers are similar to forget-me-nots but they are carried on airy stems above the leaves. They appear in spring but the foliage continues to provide interest for most of the summer.
Cultivation A moisture-retentive soil is needed in a partial shaded position. Z3
Propagation Brunnera is easy to increase by division in spring.

Brunnera macrophylla
The species is attractive in its own right and it is certainly well worth growing. H 50cm (20in) S 60cm (24in). However, there are several cultivars with variegated leaves which makes

Bergenia 'Silberlicht'

Briza media

Brunnera macrophylla 'Jack Frost'

Winter-flowering perennials

Adonis amurensis	Helleborus
Crocus	purpurascens
Cyclamen coum	Hepatica nobilis
Eranthis hyemalis	Iris ungicularis
Euphorbia rigida	Primula vulgaris
Galanthus	Pulmonaria rubra
Helleborus niger	Ranunculus ficaria
Helleborus	Vinca difformis
orientalis	Viola odorata

Caltha palustris 'Alba'

Caltha palustris 'Flore Pleno'

them even more desirable. 'Dawson's White' has wide, irregular, white margins to the green leaves. 'Hadspen Cream' is similar except that the margins are narrower and a creamier white. 'Jack Frost' has silver foliage that looks as though the leaves have frost on them. 'Langtrees' is an intriguing cultivar which has silver spots in the middle of each leaf.

CALAMAGROSTIS
Reed grass

Calamagrostis is a large genus of grasses. It includes some species that were classed as Stipa until recently. They are all decorative grasses which can be used either as a prominent feature in a border or simply mixed in to enhance the general effect.
Cultivation Reed grasses will grow in any reasonable garden so long as they are planted in full sun. Cut back the old stems in late winter before the new growth starts. Z5
Propagation This is best carried out by division in spring just as growth is beginning.

Calamagrostis × acutiflora

A tall grass with narrow leaves and plumes of purplish flowers that turn silver. H 2m (6ft) S 50cm (20in). It has a couple of very good cultivars: 'Karl Foerster' has pinkish flowers that fade to beige, and the slightly shorter 'Overdam' has leaves with yellow margins that fade to white.

Calamagrostis arundinacea

This plant forms a clump of arching foliage, soon topped with masses of fine-stemmed drooping flowers that create a lovely hazy effect. H 1m (3ft) S 1.2m (4ft).

Calamagrostis brachytricha

A splendid grass with green leaves that are often tinged with bronze in spring and autumn. The flowers are pinkish-grey. H 1.2m (4ft) S 75cm (30in).

Other plants C. emodensis and C. epigejos are two more interesting species that grass enthusiasts might like to look at.

CALAMINTHA
Calaminth

A small genus of about eight species, of which only two are in general cultivation. They are relatively low plants, only reaching about 45cm (18in) in good conditions. Their glory is the mass of thyme-like flowers that are produced over a long period in the summer. The flowers are mainly pink but can also edge towards mauve. The leaves are aromatic when crushed or bruised. These are excellent plants for placing at the front edge of borders or along paths.

Calamintha nepeta subsp. nepeta

Cultivation Plant in any good garden soil in full sun. Z6.
Propagation Divide plants in spring, or sow seed, also in spring.

Calamintha grandiflora

This is a larger plant, which has flowers of a bright pink. H 45cm (18in) S 45cm (18in).

Calamintha nepeta

About the same size as *grandiflora*, this has flowers that are a paler lilac-pink, sometimes almost white. H 45cm (18in) S 60cm (24in). *C.n.* subsp. *nepeta* is often called *C. nepetoides*. It is a shorter plant and has tiny lilac-white flowers that cover the plant in a cloud – perfect for the edge of a path or patio. *C.n.* 'Blue Cloud' has, as its name suggests, many flowers with a distinct blue tinge.

CALTHA
Marsh marigold

There are about ten species of caltha, but only one of them, *C. palustris*, with its several

Caltha palustris

varieties and cultivars, is in general cultivation. This plant with its delightful large golden buttercup-like flowers is one of the glories of spring.

It does best when grown beside water but it will also grow in bog gardens and even in borders if the soil is kept sufficiently damp. Marsh marigolds are sprawling plants but they can reach 45cm (18in) in height and 30cm (12in) in width.
Cultivation The soil must be moist and, unlike many plants, the roots can be in mud or shallow water. Caltha flourishes in a sunny position but it will also grow in light shade, under deciduous trees, for example. Z3.
Propagation Increase is easily carried out by division in spring or from seed that is sown as soon as it is ripe.

Caltha palustris

Although there are good cultivars, the species is well worth growing in its own right – it makes a superb addition to any pond. 'Alba' is not quite as striking as the species, but this white-flowered form still has a lot of charm and looks particularly attractive growing along side the golden form. 'Flore Pleno' is a smaller plant than the species but its worth lies in its exquisite double flowers with their concentric rows of petals.

Caltha palustris var. palustris.

This is sometimes known as *C. polypetala*. It is a giant form of the species with large flowers. There is also an attractive double form of this larger plant with the name 'Plena'.

Camassia leichtlinii subsp. leichtlinii

CAMASSIA
Quamash

This is a small genus of bulbs that are frequently grown as part of a herbaceous border. They have also become popular for naturalizing in a meadow or wild garden. Camassias are tall-growing plants which produce tall spikes of striking, star-like flowers, usually in blue or white. The foliage is lush but not attractive; it is a good idea to plant them in the middle of the border so that the foliage is hidden but the flower spikes stand proud of surrounding vegetation. H 1m (3ft) S 20–30cm (8–12in).
Cultivation Camassias like good moist, but free-draining soil in full sun or just a light shade. Plant in autumn at a depth of about 10cm (4in). Z2.

Camassia leichtlinii subsp. suksdorfii

Campanula carpatica

Propagation Increase by dividing the bulbs in summer or by sowing seed while it is still fresh.

Camassia leichtlinii subsp. leichtlinii
This plant used to be known as *C.l.* 'Alba', the 'Alba' referring to its white flowers. These have a touch of green in them and are really very beautiful.

Camassia leichtlinii subsp. suksdorfii
Being the commonest form, this was and still often is referred to simply under the species name *C. leichtlinii*. It has blue flowers which vary in intensity from pale to very deep blue-violet. There are several cultivars to explore.

Camassia quamash
This plant is similar to the above with blue flowers. It is excellent for naturalizing.

CAMPANULA
Bellflower

This is a much loved genus of some 300 species of which many are in cultivation. They vary from ground-hugging plants to ones

Campanula 'Loddon Anna'

with tall spires of flowers. The typical bellflower is blue but there are also plenty of white and pink variants. The flowers vary from classic bell-shapes to flat, wide-open stars. The majority flower in summer, and most are excellent at forming large clumps. They should be placed anywhere from the front to the back of a border, depending on their height.
Cultivation Most bellflowers need a rich, moist, but well-drained soil. The majority also prefer full sun but there are a number that like a little shade. Z3–6.
Propagation Seed can be sown in the spring, and many of the plants can also be divided at the same time of year. Basal cuttings can also be taken from many species in spring.

Campanula carpatica
A low-growing (25cm/10in) species that is perfect for edging the path or border. The flowers are an open-dish shape and come in varying shades of blue as well as white. S 30cm (12in). There are a number of excellent cultivars including 'Weisse Clips' (white) and 'Blue Clips' (blue).

Campanula punctata

Campanula glomerata
A medium bellflower that carries its flowers in a cluster at the top of the flower stem. Excellent for borders or for naturalizing in meadow gardens. H 45cm (18in) S 60cm (24in).

Campanula lactiflora
A tall border plant with many flowers carried in loose heads. H 1.2m (4ft) S 60cm (24in). The type is well worth growing but there are also a number of very good cultivars including 'Loddon Anna' (lilac-pink), 'Prichard's Variety' (violet blue) and 'White Pouffe', which is a dwarf form with white flowers.

Campanula latifolia
A tall species with large tubular bells of intense blue. H 1.2m (4ft) S 60cm (24in). The variety 'Alba' has beautiful white flowers that brighten up a lightly shaded

Campanula lactiflora

Campanula portenschlagiana

Campanula poscharskyana

spot of the garden. 'Brantwood' (deep violet) is another excellent cultivar to try.

Campanula latiloba
This bellflower has dense heads of open bell-shaped flowers with lavender blue flowers H 1m (3ft) S 45cm (18in). Again there are several very good cultivars.

Campanula persicifolia
An attractive medium height bellflower which often needs staking to keep its upright stance. The flowers are large open cups in blue or white. H 1m (3ft) S 30cm (12in). There are some beautiful double forms, such as 'Boule de Neige'.

Campanula portenschlagiana
A low-growing campanula with bright violet purple flowers. It is excellent for edging paths. H 15cm (6in) S indefinite.

Campanula poscharskyana
A spreading campanula that will scramble up through shrubs and other plants. The pale-blue flowers are star-shaped and are carried over a long period from early summer well into autumn. This plant makes good ground cover. H 10–15cm (4–6in) S indefinite.

Other plants There are so many other campanulas that are worth pursuing, such as C. punctata or the similar C. takesimana with their large pink tubular bells. Virtually any campanula you come across in a nursery will be worth growing, and it can be fun to experiment.

CARDAMINE
Bittercress
A delightful genus of plants whose numbers have been increased by the addition of species that were in the genus Dentaria. There are some weeds – hairy bitter cress being one that gardeners especially hate – but the majority of cardamines are garden plants with great charm. They flower in spring. Since they are suited to partial shade, they are excellent for growing under deciduous shrubs or in the shade of a building.

Cardamine heptaphylla

Cultivation Most prefer a moist, woodland-type soil with plenty of added leaf mould. They will grow in sun as long as the soil is kept moist, but prefer a light shaded position. Z5–6.
Propagation Most cardamines are easy to divide in the spring. They can also be grown from seed or, in some cases, from the small reddish bulbils that are carried in the leaf joints.

Cardamine enneaphyllos
A spreading plant with clusters of creamy white flowers held above mid-green leaves. It needs to be grown in partial shade. H 30cm (12in) S 60cm (24in).

Cardamine heptaphylla
Clusters of simple white, and occasionally pink, flowers. It reaches 30cm (12in) tall, and sometimes double that. Does best in partial shade. S30 cm (12in).

Cardamine pentaphyllos
An attractive plant with clusters of pinkish-purple flowers, sometimes white. H 30cm (12in) but sometimes double that. S 60cm (24in). This plant requires a partially shaded position.

Cardamine pentaphyllos

Cardamine pratensis
This is the much-loved cuckoo flower or milkmaid. It has loose heads of delightful lilac flowers. H 45cm (18in) S 30cm (12in). There are various interesting double forms.

CARDIOCRINUM
Giant Lily
Although there are three species in the genus, only one of them, C. giganteum, is in general cultivation. It is a tall plant, reaching up to 2m (6ft), with large white trumpet flowers, creating a very striking picture. It likes a cool shaded position but the head can be in sun – making it ideal for growing amongst shrubs or at the back of borders. The dried seed capsules are amongst the most desirable of dried flowers. S 1m (3ft).
Cultivation It must have a rich soil with plenty of humus in it. Plant in partial shade. Z6.
Propagation It is best to buy bulbs. It can be grown from seed but you will have to wait seven years or more before it flowers. Established bulbs will produce offsets (offshoots) which can be divided but even these take up to five years to flower.

Cardiocrinum giganteum
A tall plant with lily-like trumpet flowers that are angled downwards. They are white and highly scented, and appear in

Cardiocrinum giganteum

summer. There is also a variety yunnanense which has shiny brown stems and flowers that are tinged with green.

Other plants Keen gardeners should look out for the similar but less frequently seen species C. cordatum, which is worth finding a supplier for.

CATANANCHE
Cupid's dart
A small genus of five species of which only one is in general cultivation. These are for the border rather than for containers and are best used in association with other plants. Catananche are perfect for gravel gardens. The buds have a curious paper-like quality and even the cornflower-like petals feel dry and papery. The flowers are carried on slender, wiry stems in summer and into the autumn. They are ideal for dried arrangements.
Cultivation These are short-lived plants but their life can be prolonged by growing them in a free-draining soil. They must have a sunny position. Z4.
Propagation Catananche are best increased from seed sown in spring. They can be divided but care is needed as they have thick tap roots. These roots can be used as cuttings, taken in the winter.

Catananche caerulea
This is the main species in cultivation and the form that one usually sees. The flowers are blue with a darker centre. H 45cm (18in) S 30cm (12in). The form 'Major' is a popular one but it often looks the same as the main species. A good alternative is the cultivar 'Bicolor' which has a violet-purple centre and white petals. The all-white form is 'Alba', which is also very attractive.

Catananche caerulea

CENTAUREA
Knapweeds

For the serious perennial gardener this is a "must-have" genus: there are many top-class plants in it. It is a large genus, containing about 450 species with about 40 being in general cultivation. They have thistle-like heads which are often quite large. They come in a variety of colours: reds, purples, blues, yellows and whites. The flowers usually appear in summer and rarely last more than a few weeks. They provide good colour for the border.

Cultivation Most will grow in any good garden soil. They prefer a sunny position. Z3–7.

Propagation The most common method of increase is by division in spring, although most species can also be grown from seed sown at the same time of year.

Centaurea dealbata

An appealing clump-forming perennial with purple-pink flowers with white centres. H 1m (3ft) S 60cm (24in). The cultivar 'Steenbergii' has deeper pink flowers and is even more attractive than the species.

Centaurea hypoleuca

Another clump-forming centaurea which is somewhat similar to the previous one, but with larger flowers. The flowers are again pink with a paler centre. H 60cm (24in) S 45cm (18in). The cultivar 'John Coutts' has dark pink flowers.

Centaurea hypoleuca 'John Coutts'

Centaurea macrocephala

This is a clump-forming plant with upright stems. These carry large heads with a papery, dark brown bud that contrasts beautifully with the bright yellow flowers. A truly wonderful plant. H 1.5m (5ft) S 60cm (24in).

Centaurea montana

A favourite of the late spring to early summer garden. A somewhat sprawling plant whose bright blue flowers each have a purple centre. H 45cm (18in) when staked, S 60cm (24in). There is a good white form *alba* and several good colour varieties.

Centaurea pulcherrima

An attractive plant with very good silvery foliage that earns it a place in the garden as a foliage plant when it is not in flower. The

Centaurea montana

exquisite flowers are pink with a creamy centre. H 75cm (30in) S 60cm (24in).

Centaurea 'Pulchra Major'

Strictly speaking, this is now called *Leuzea centauroides*. It is similar to *C. pulcherrima* but is on a much larger scale with huge flowers up to 7.5cm (3in) across. H 1m (3ft) S 60cm (24in).

Centaurea simplicicaulis

A mat-forming plant with large pink flowers. H 25cm (10in) S 60cm (24in).

Other plants There are many more for the gardener to try. *C. bella* (pink) has good foliage, *C. cheiranthifolia* (cream and purple) is exceptionally good, and *C. ruthenica* (yellow) is another cultivar worth considering.

CENTRANTHUS
Red valerian

A genus of a dozen or so plants of which one, *C. ruber*, is in general cultivation. It forms clumps of stems, which carry dense heads of tiny purplish-red flowers. The

colour varies, sometimes it is redder, sometimes pinker and occasionally it is white. These are excellent plants for growing in gravel gardens, and in spite of their height they are also good for walls and banks. H 1m (3ft) S 45–60cm (18–24in).

Cultivation Red valerian will grow in any garden soil, even impoverished ones. It likes a well-drained position in full sun. Z3.

Propagation The simplest method is from seed sown in spring. One plant will usually provide enough self-sown seedlings for most uses.

CEPHALARIA
Cephalaria

A genus of plants of which only one is in general cultivation. This is *C. gigantea* which is a clump forming plant. It forms a very tall, open plant with airy stems, each carrying soft yellow, almost creamy-yellow, flowers. The flowers are similar to those of the scabious to which it is related. It is eye-catching, especially when planted against a dark green hedge and it is a valuable border plant. H 2.5m (8ft) S 1.2m (4ft). There is a shorter (2m/6ft) species, *C. alpina*, which has similar yellow flowers, but this is less common and not quite so long lived.

Cultivation It likes a well-drained but fertile soil. Plant in a sunny position if possible, although it will take a little light shade. Cut back after flowering or it will self-sow prodigiously. Z6.

Propagation This plant is easy to grow from seed sown in either autumn or spring.

Centaurea dealbata

Centaurea macrocephala

Centranthus ruber

Cephalaria gigantea

Ceratostigma plumbaginoides

CERATOSTIGMA
Ceratostigma

A small genus that consists mainly of shrubs but there is one notable perennial, *C. plumbaginoides*. It is a spreading plant up to 45cm (18in) high and 20cm (8in) wide. The joy of it is the bright blue periwinkle-like flowers, which sparkle out of the late summer and autumn garden. The leaves take on reddish autumn tints. This is a good plant for interspersing with others towards the front of the border. The shrubby ceratostigmas fulfil the same function and have very attractive flowers that are also blue. In particular, have a look at *C. griffithii* and *C. willmottianum*.
Cultivation Ceratostigmas thrive in any good garden soil with plenty of organic material. They need a sunny position. Prune the shrubs in early spring. Z6.
Propagation Increase your stock of these plants by taking cuttings in spring or summer.

CHELONE
Turtlehead

This is a small genus of which only one species is in general cultivation. The name refers to the strange turtle-like shape of the flowers. These are dark pink and carried in a short terminal spike from late summer into autumn. The main species is *C. obliqua* which grows to about 60cm (24in) in height and has a spread of 50cm (20in). These are good plants for providing autumn colour in the middle of the border. The other species worth looking at if you can find them are *C. glabra* and *C. lyonii*.
Cultivation Turtleheads need a rich, fertile soil that is moist. They can be grown in sun or light shade. Z4.
Propagation Division is the easiest method of increase but they can also be grown from seed sown in spring or from cuttings taken at the same time of year.

CHRYSANTHEMUM
Chrysanthemum

This genus needs little introduction since it is familiar as both a cut flower and garden plant. The familiar florist chrysanthemums are perennials, but they are treated as annuals (see pages 272–3) because they are tender and need to be renewed each year. However there are a number of species and cultivars that are truly hardy and can be left outside all year. Most have a very long flowering time and will last from late summer and sometimes right into winter. Some – such as *C. rubellum* (syn. *C. zawadskii*) and its cultivars – are very similar to the single florist chrysanthemums and make good cut flowers.

The list of plants classified under the genus *Chrysanthemum* have gone through several changes. Many were moved to *Dendranthema*. They have now been

Chrysanthemum rubellum

moved back to *Chrysanthemum* but you may still come across them under the previous name.
Cultivation The hardy plants will grow in any reasonably fertile garden soil, preferably one that is well-drained. They prefer a sunny position but they will grow in light shade so long as they receive some sun. Z4.
Propagation Taking basal cuttings in spring is a reliable method of increase. The plants can also be divided at the same time of year.

Chrysanthemum rubellum
Strictly speaking, this species is now called *C. zawadskii* but it is still generally referred to as *C. rubellum*. H 75cm (30in) S 45cm (18in). The species is occasionally grown, but its many cultivars are more common. They have single, semi-double or double, daisy-like flowers in a variety of colours. Some of the best include 'Clara Curtis' (pink), 'Emperor of China' (double pink), 'Mary Stoker'

Chrysanthemum rubellum 'Clara Curtis'

(apricot-yellow), 'Mrs Jessie Cooper' (red) and 'Nancy Perry' (dark pink).

Chrysanthemum hosmariense
This is now *Rhodanthemum hosmariense* but is still often referred to by its former name. It is a delightful little plant with silver foliage and white daisy flowers that are in bloom from spring to autumn. Perfect as an edging plant in a well-drained sunny position. H 15cm (6in) S 30cm (12in).

Chrysanthemum uliginosum
Now known as *Leucanthemella serotina*, this is a wonderful plant for autumn. It is tall with white daisy flowers that appear from mid-autumn through until winter. The flowers have a habit of tilting and facing the sun, which they follow throughout the day. A good plant for the back of a border, but make sure it will face into the garden when flowering. H 2m (6ft) S 60cm (24in).

Chelone obliqua

Chrysanthemum rubellum

Chrysanthemum hosmariense

CLEMATIS
Clematis

Most people think of this genus purely in terms of woody climbing plants. The majority of the 200 species and hundreds of cultivars are just that, but there are also a number of herbaceous species that die back each year. They do not have the big blowsy quality of some of the climbers but they are still very attractive. Most need some form of support but even with this, they rarely grow very tall. Some can be left to sprawl over the neighbouring plants, perhaps covering a spring plant that has lost its freshness.
Cultivation A rich moisture-retentive soil is required. The roots should be in shade with the plant in sun, although some will tolerate a little light shade. Most need some form of support, such as pea-sticks. Cut to the ground each spring. Z3.
Propagation Take basal cuttings in spring. Most perennial clematis can also be divided, with care.

Clematis × durandii

One of the largest flowered herbaceous clematis with indigo-blue blooms. Grow through a shrub or over pea-sticks. H 1–2m (3–6ft) S 45–150cm (1½–5ft).

Clematis heracleifolia var. davidiana

A late-summer flowering species whose blue flowers have reflexed (turned back), strap-like petals. An added bonus is that this plant is highly scented. H 1m (3ft) S 75cm (30in). There are a number of cultivars of varying shades of blue.

Clematis recta

Clematis integrifolia

This has intriguing nodding flowers that hang attractively from upright stalks. They are usually blue, but there are also several forms that produce flowers in other colours, including 'Rosea' (pink) and 'Alba' (white). 'Hendersonii' has extra large flowers. The plants are sprawling and can be left to clamber over other plants; they can also be supported. H and S 75cm (30in).

Clematis × jouiniana

It is the sheer number of flowers that makes this clematis attractive: it is a mass of small mauve-blue flowers. It requires support on pea-sticks. H 1m (3ft) S 1–2m (3–6ft).

Clematis recta

Although the species is often grown in its own right it is usually the form 'Purpurea' that is

grown. This has wonderful purple foliage in spring; in early to midsummer it produces masses of small white flowers. H 1–2m (3–6ft) S 50cm (20in).

Other plants There are a few more species that can be explored including *C. texensis*, *C. addisonii* and *C. stans*. There are also myriad woody ones to grow; plants in the *C. viticella* group, in particular, go very well with herbaceous plants.

CONVALLARIA
Lily-of-the-valley

A small genus of which one species, *C. majalis* – the much-loved lily-of-the-valley – is regularly grown. This low plant is ideal for shady positions under shrubs or for growing on the shady side of a building. It spreads to form a mat of leaves surmounted in spring by short arching stems carrying fragrant white bells. In warm weather the scent can spread widely. The flowers are good for cutting for display or bouquets. H 23cm (9in) S indefinite. There is a pink form *rosea* which is identical except for the colour of the flowers. There is also 'Albostriata' in which the flowers are the same but the leaves have narrow yellow stripes running down them. In the cultivar 'Fortin's Giant' everything is doubled in size.
Cultivation A shady position in rich moist soil although it will survive drier soils. Z2.
Propagation Divide in the autumn or early spring. Plants can be grown from seed sown in spring, but the seed is not easy to find.

COREOPSIS
Tickseed

A useful genus of plants which add welcome splashes of gold to a border. It is a large genus of around 100 species but only a handful are in cultivation. They have daisy-like yellow or gold flowers, double in some cultivars, which bloom in summer. They work well towards the front or in the middle of the border where their colour stands out.
Cultivation Tickseed will grow in any reasonable garden soil. It needs a sunny position. Z3.

Coreopsis verticillata 'Moonbeam'

Propagation To increase, divide plants in spring, or take stem cuttings in summer.

Coreopsis lanceolata

Tall flower stems carry single flowers of bright gold. H 60cm (24in) S 30cm (12in). There are various forms: some have brown centres ('Sterntaler') and others are much shorter ('Baby Gold').

Coreopsis verticillata

The most widely grown of the perennial species. It is a fine plant with masses of shining gold flowers floating above delicate, narrow foliage in summer. H 75cm (30in) S 30cm (12in). There are some good cultivars: 'Grandiflora' (also known as 'Golden Shower') has warm yellow flowers, 'Moonbeam' has wonderfully soft yellow blooms and 'Zagreb' is golden yellow.

CORTADERIA
Pampas grass

A small genus of grasses of which a couple of species with their cultivars are generally grown.

Clematis integrifolia 'Hendersonii'

Convallaria majalis

Coreopsis verticillata 'Zagreb'

Cortaderia selloana 'Pumila'

These are stunning: they have fountains of narrow leaves that are surmounted by tall stems carrying great tufts of white flower heads. Unfortunately, most are so large (up to 3m/10ft tall and 2m/6ft across) that you need a large garden to do them justice. There are some dwarf forms for smaller gardens, but these seem rather to miss the point. Pampas grasses make excellent focal points, especially if they are placed so that they can be seen against the blue sky. They last well into winter before they start to look untidy.
Cultivation They will grow in any reasonable garden soil, but require a sunny position. Cut down flowering stems in late winter and shear off the leaves every three years. Do not plant pampas grass near areas where children run or play as the edges of the leaves are very sharp. Z7.
Propagation Divide off part of the plant in late winter or early spring just before growth begins.

Cortaderia richardii
A lesser-grown species than the following. It comes from New Zealand rather than South America, but looks similar. The flowering stems tend to be more arching, but they too carry huge feathery plumes.

Cortaderia selloana
This is the main species grown and it is fabulous: tall and stately with feathery flower heads. The form 'Aureolineata' (also known as 'Gold Band') has golden stripes on the margins of the leaves. 'Albolineata' is similarly variegated but with silvery-white stripes; it is slightly smaller. 'Pumila' grows to only 1.5m (5ft). 'Pink Feather' has silvery-pink flower heads. 'Sunningdale Silver' has glistening silvery-white feathers.

CORYDALIS
Corydalis
This is a large genus of 300 or more species. It is much beloved by alpine gardeners, but there are

Corydalis flexuosa

a couple that are large and robust enough for the perennial gardener to consider. These have curious tubular flowers which look rather like swarms of tiny fish, floating above the ferny leaves. They are good for naturalizing along the edge of woodland gardens, or under deciduous shrubs and trees in smaller gardens. H 30cm (12in) S 30cm (12in).
Cultivation The corydalis listed here require a moist soil in either sun or partial shade. Z5–6.
Propagation Grow from seed, which should sown while it is still fresh. Many self-sow.

Corydalis cava
This plant has white or purplish flowers which appear in the spring. It grows well in woodland type soil in partial shade.

Corydalis flexuosa
Brilliant blue flowers in spring and early summer. This species should be grown in a moist, fibrous soil in a lightly shaded position. There are several good cultivars to explore.

Corydalis lutea
One of the easiest of the corydalis to grow, this has yellow flowers. It is excellent for growing on old walls. Flowers all year.

Corydalis ochroleuca
Good for damp positions. This has a long flowering season, with creamy white and yellow blooms.

Corydalis solida
This plant produces a range of different coloured flowers, based on mauvish purple but including red especially in the fine form 'George Baker'. Spring flowering.

COSMOS
Cosmos
A small genus of annual and perennial plants of which few, mainly annuals (see pages 278–9) are in cultivation. The one perennial that is commonly grown is *C. atrosanguineus*. This has deep crimson flowers, so deep and velvety that they appear almost brown. In addition, the plant actually smells of chocolate when the weather is warm. The flowers are dish-shaped, rather like a daisy with wide petals. They are carried on wiry stems up to 75cm (30in) high. The plants are excellent for placing in a front-of-border position where they can easily be smelt. S 45cm (18in).
Cultivation Cosmos need a rich, moist soil and a warm, sunny position. They are late in appearing in spring, so hold off digging them up if you think they have died. Z7.
Propagation Increase by taking basal cuttings as soon as the plants are big enough.

Cortaderia selloana 'Sunningdale Silver'

Cortaderia selloana 'Aureolineata'

Corydalis lutea

Cosmos atrosanguineus

Crambe cordifolia

Crepis incana

CRAMBE
Crambe

Two plants in this small genus are in general cultivation. They can be spectacular but the most popular one, *C. cordifolia*, is not often seen outside large gardens because of its size. With care, though, it can be accommodated in smaller areas. The glory of this plant is the flowers which form a wonderful haze of white.
Cultivation These plants need rich, well-drained soil in full sun. They can be prone to slugs when the leaves first appear; you must control these pests at this point, or you will lose the plant. Z7.
Propagation Division is possible but awkward because of the size of the plants. The best option is to take root cuttings in winter.

Crambe cordifolia

A large plant with a great dome of white flowers, 2m (6ft) high and across in summer. It is ideal for a large herbaceous border. The multi-branching flower stems are excellent for dried arrangements if you can get them through the door. The leaves are rather coarse but since this is a plant for the

middle or rear of the border, they are rarely seen, whereas the flowers float mistily above the surrounding plants.

Crambe maritima

This is a much smaller plant, growing only about 45cm (18in) high with a spread of 60cm (24in). It also produces a mass of flowers, but not quite as delicately as its larger relative. The main reason for growing it is the foliage, which is a wonderful powdery blue. It is an excellent foliage plant for the front of border. It needs a well-drained soil and does particularly well in gravel gardens.

CREPIS
Hawk's Beard

A large genus of dandelion-like plants that includes 200 or more species. Only a handful of them are generally grown in cultivation. Some are annuals or treated as annuals (see page 279) but others are true perennials. They are clump-forming plants that are suitable for the front of a border or for naturalizing in short grass. The flowers are multi-petalled, in the manner of a dandelion. They are carried on wiry stems that reach up to 30cm (12in) above rosettes of ground-hugging leaves. S 10cm (4in).
Cultivation Hawk's beard will grow in any reasonable garden soil, as long as it is well-drained. They need a position in full sun. Z7.
Propagation Increase by sowing fresh seed. The plants often produce self-sown seedlings.

Crepis aurea

This has typical dandelion-like flowers in a rich orange-yellow; they are carried from late summer onwards. These plants are good for the front of a hot-coloured border or for growing in short grass in a meadow garden.

Crepis incana

This is a short-lived perennial that is sometimes treated as an annual. It carries a large number of sugar-pink flowers. This form is usually just used in the border where it is an ideal plant for a frontal position. It looks particularly good when planted with blue veronicas.

CRINUM
Crinum

This is a large genus of tender bulbs, most of which are suited to growing in a conservatory. There is one that is not only hardy but also very attractive. This is *C. × powellii*. It has large strap-like leaves that arch outwards, framing the tall flowering stems that carry lily-like, trumpeted flowers. These are generally pink but there is also a glistening white form 'Alba'.

Crinums are best planted behind other plants so that the leaves are hidden but the gorgeous trumpets show above their surroundings. These appear in late summer and autumn and grow to 1m (3ft) high and 60cm (24in) across.
Cultivation These plants need a rich, free-draining soil in full sun. Plant the bulbs so that the neck is above the soil level. Z7.
Propagation Increase by dividing off the offsets (offshoots) from around existing bulbs.

CROCOSMIA
Montbretia

These plants form a small genus of popular bulbous plants. They include the common montbretia (*C. × crocosmiiflora*) – which seems to occur in most gardens.

Most bulbs seem to have rather ugly foliage, but the crocosmia has long, ribbed, tapering leaves that stand upright, making a good contrast to other foliage around them. In late summer tall arching stems carry a spray of red, orange or yellow flowers, which look good against with the foliage. These plants are excellent for growing in clumps or drifts in the middle of the border or for planting in odd corners.
Cultivation Plant in any reasonable garden soil, preferably in full sun, although they will also tolerate a little light shade. Divide the plants every few years as they can get congested. Z7.
Propagation The plants are very easy to propagate: divide off the new corms in late winter or early spring, before they start to grow.

Crambe maritima

Crinum × powellii

Crocosmia × crocosmiiflora

Crocosmia 'Lucifer'

Cynara cardunculus

Crocosmia × crocosmiiflora

This is the main species cultivated. It grows up to 60cm (24in) tall and has dull-orange flowers held on upright stems. S 15–20cm (6–8in).

There are plenty of cultivars to explore. The flowers vary from the subdued, soft apricot-tinted yellow of 'Solfatare', with its soft bronze foliage, to the striking 'Emily McKenzie' which has large flowers with brown centres surrounded by a bright orange. 'Jackanapes' is another bicolour cultivar; its flowers come in yellow and rich orange. 'Star of the East' is an excellent orange form, paling towards the centre. 'Lady Hamilton' is similar but has deep yellow flowers. The many cultivars are generally much better than the species and it is worth acquiring several different ones, for a hot-coloured border.

Crocosmia 'Emberglow'

A good border plant with bright red flowers that always create a splash of colour.

Crocosmia 'Honey Angels'

This is a fine crocosmia whose appealing yellow flowers have creamy throats.

Crocosmia 'Lucifer'

One of the most spectacular of the crocosmias. It is tall, reaching up to 1.2m (4ft). The flower stems are arching and carry sprays of large bright crimson flowers that stand upright like flames. They are superb against the green foliage. S 20–25cm (8–10in)

Crocosmia masoniorum

This is similar to the previous one, but its flowers contain more orange and are not so bright. H 1.2m (4ft) S 15cm (6in).

Other plants There are many cultivars for the enthusiast to look at, all with subtle variations on the basic type. Since they are easily grown, they make ideal plants to collect.

CYNARA

Cynara

Two plants in this genus are generally grown in gardens, one for decoration (although it can be eaten) and the other for eating (although it can also be used for show). The main border plant is C. cardunculus. This is a statuesque plant: tall with silver foliage and huge purple thistle-like heads. It looks good planted singly as a focal point or in a group.

Cultivation These plants need a fertile, well-drained soil. Place in a sunny position, away from strong winds. Z7.

Propagation To increase, divide off "slips" (rooted cuttings) in spring.

Cynara cardunculus

A superb giant "thistle". It produces fountains of silver foliage surmounted by tall silver stems carrying thistle-like flowers in summer. They are excellent for drying. The base of the stems and leaf stalks can be cooked when young – when the plant is known as a cardoon. H 2m (6ft) S 1m (3ft). Occasionally you can find dwarf forms on offer which are useful for small gardens. 'Florist Cardy' is a form specially bred for use as a cut flower, but it is not a great deal different from the type.

Cynara scolymus

Now officially, but cumbrously, known as C. cardunculus Scolymus Group. This is the globe artichoke of the vegetable garden. It is the large flower bud that is eaten. It can be used in the border as a lesser version of the above. The leaves are not so attractive in shape, nor so silver, but it still makes a good foliage plant, especially early in the season. H 1m (3ft) S 60cm (24in).

Crocosmia 'Honey Angels'

Bee and butterfly plants

Anchusa	Helenium
Aster	Lythrum
Centaurea	Mentha
Delphinium	Monarda
Doronicum	Nepeta
Echinacea	Origanum
Echinops	Scabiosa
Eryngium	Sedum
Eupatorium	Solidago
Foeniculum	Trifolium

Cynara scolymus

CYNOGLOSSUM
Hound's tongue

A genus of about 55 species. Most of those with garden interest are annuals or biennials (see page 280). However, there is one, *C. nervosum*, which is perennial and worth growing in the border. This is a medium-sized plant with bristly stems and leaves. It is the flowers that are principally of interest since they are a wonderful bright blue colour. The individual flowers are quite small but they are carried in uncurling spikes – much in the same way as forget-me-nots, to which they are related. The plant flowers in early summer and is very useful for adding bright blue colour to the middle of the border at that time of year. H 60cm (24in) S 50cm (20in). *Cultivation* Plant in any garden soil that is not too rich. Choose a sunny position. This plant is short lived and needs replacing every three years or so. Z5. *Propagation* The best way to increase this plant is by sowing seed in spring.

DELPHINIUM
Delphinium

These plants are much-loved, but few gardeners know the full range of them: the flowers come in yellow and red as well as the most commonly seen blue ones. This is a fairly large genus of some 250 species of which a surprising number are in cultivation. The most popular are those that produce tall spires covered in

Delphinium 'Fenella'

flowers, but there are also shorter species whose flowers are held in loose airy clusters. Many of these are not as robust as the taller ones, but they make good garden plants if renewed every few years. *Cultivation* A deep, rich but free-draining soil is required. Delphiniums should be placed in full sun. Tall ones with heavy spikes may need staking, unless the garden is very sheltered. Watch out for slugs in the early stages of growth. Z3. *Propagation* The best way of increasing most cultivars is to take basal cuttings in spring. The species should be grown from seed, sown as soon as it is ripe.

Delphinium Belladonna Group, Elatum Group and Pacific Hybrids

These are the main groups of tall, heavily flowered delphiniums. Many are grown for cutting rather than for border display, but they can also be used in such situations. They flower in early summer and grow up to 1.5m (5ft) tall. S 60cm (24in). There is a vast range of named cultivars with flowers varying in colour from pale to dark blue, purple and white. Many have double flowers, often with white or black centres, known as "bees". They include: 'Bruce', a semi-double with deep purple flowers and brown eyes; 'Butterball', another semi-double, this time with creamy-white flowers and deeper eyes; 'Fenella', a semi-double with bright blue petals and a black eye. 'Giotto', a semi-double whose flowers are two-toned blue with light brown eyes; 'Sandpiper', a semi-double with white petals and a brown eye; and 'Tiddles', which has double mauve flowers.

Delphinium 'Sandpiper'

Delphinium 'Elizabeth Cook'

Delphinium 'Alice Artindale'
A wonderful double for the border. The little button flowers are a light blue; when dried, they retain their colour for years. H 1.2m (4ft) S 60cm (24in).

Delphinium cardinale
This unusual delphinium has bright red flowers with yellow centres. The flowers are carried in a loose spike. H 1–2m (3–6ft) S 60cm (24in).

Delphinium cashmerianum
This perennial is short lived, but it is still worth growing for its loose heads of bright blue flowers. H 45cm (18in) S 30cm (12in).

Delphinium grandiflorum
A delightful delphinium with gracefully floating bright blue flowers. It is good for the front of a border, especially if planted

Delphinium 'Southern Countryman'

Delphinium 'Clifford Sky'

in a group of three. However, it is short lived. H 45cm (18in) S 30cm (12in).

Delphinium nudicaule
Another short-lived plant, this time with loose spikes of yellow, orange or red flowers. It likes a well-drained soil. H 20cm (8in) S 5–10cm (2–4in)

Delphinium semibarbatum
Still known to many gardeners as *D. zalil*, this has loose spikes of yellow flowers. H up to 1m (3ft) in good conditions; S 30cm (12in). However, it is short lived and needs replacing regularly.

DIANTHUS
Pinks

Dianthus is a large genus of about 300 species. Many are in cultivation, and they are often grown by alpine enthusiasts. Border use is almost exclusively confined to one species, *D. caryophyllus*, or rather to the many cultivars that have been derived from it. These are known collectively as pinks. They can be roughly divided into two groups: the old-fashioned varieties which generally flower only once in the summer and are often scented; and the modern varieties which have the advantage of flowering, often continuously, throughout the summer but are in most cases scentless. Old-fashioned varieties have flowers that can be single, semi-double or double, while most modern ones are doubles. The flowers grow on stiff stems

Dianthus deltoides

Dianthus 'Garnet'

Dianthus 'Whatfield Ruby'

that emerge from a clump of narrow, silver foliage. The tallest grow to about 45cm (18in) but most are shorter. They are excellent plants for the front of borders and for lining paths. S 25cm (10in).
Cultivation Pinks need a well-drained soil that is neutral or alkaline. Full sun is essential. Z7.
Propagation Since most pinks are cultivars only vegetative methods can be relied upon. Of these, taking cuttings in summer is by far the easiest.

Dianthus deltoides
A choice plant for edging a path. The foliage is narrow and dark green, while the flowers are like tiny jewels in pink, red or white. This species is grown from seed. H 20cm (8in) S 25cm (10in).

Dianthus 'Doris'
One of the best old-fashioned pinks – a double with pink petals and a darker pink centre. It is very long-flowering and well scented.

Dianthus 'Garnet'
A low-growing pink for the rock garden or front of border with single carmine flowers with a darker centre. The foliage is compact and a good silver colour.

Dianthus 'Mrs Sinkins'
Another fine old-fashioned pink. It is a rather untidy double (the calyx which holds the petals together splits), but it is a good white and it has the most amazing scent. It is very easy to grow and will tolerate heavy soils.

Dianthus 'Musgrave's Pink'
Also known as 'Charles Musgrave'. An excellent single, old-fashioned variety with single, creamy-white flowers that have a pale green centre. It is scented.

Dianthus 'Rose de Mai'
This is a wonderful old-fashioned pink with pale mauve-pink flowers. It is fragrant and is one of the earliest to flower. The plant is rather sprawling.

Dianthus 'Whatfield Ruby'
This small, single-flowered pink produces brilliant ruby-coloured flowers. It is best placed at the front of a border.

Other plants There are about a thousand cultivars from which to choose, most of which make excellent plants. Go to a specialist nursery in summer so that you can see them in flower before making your choice.

DIASCIA
Diascia
These plants have been grown in gardens since at least Victorian times, but it is only relatively recently that they have achieved the popularity they deserve. They have a very long flowering season, producing spikes of mostly pink flowers over low-growing mounds of green, heart-shaped foliage. They grow on average to about 25cm (10in) high with a spread of 60cm (24in) and are perfect for creating mats in the front of borders. They are also excellent plants for growing in containers.
Cultivation Diascias need a moist but well-drained soil that is not too wet in winter. They prefer a position in full sun, although they will tolerate a little light shade under tall trees or shrubs. Shear occasionally to keep the plants compact. Z4–7.

Propagation These plants are easy to root from cuttings, which can be taken at any time of the year.

Diascia 'Blackthorn Apricot'
This is a good modern cultivar with apricot-pink flowers.

Diascia rigescens
One of the oldest species in cultivation. It is larger and coarser than most others but produces large spikes of deep pink flowers.

Diascia 'Ruby Field'
This is an excellent form, which produces deep pink flowers.

Diascia 'Rupert Lambert'
Another fine form. Like the previous one, it produces blooms of a deep pink.

Diascia 'Salmon Supreme'
A good modern form which has salmon pink flowers.

Diascia vigilis
One of the longest-lived forms, with soft pink flowers. It is best grown in the form 'Jack Elliott'.

Dianthus 'Doris'

Dianthus 'Rose de Mai'

Diascia 'Rupert Lambert'

Diascia vigilis

DICENTRA
Dicentra

A genus of much-loved cottage garden plants. Their main characteristic is the locket-shaped flowers that hang like jewels from arching stems. They are set against foliage which is also attractive, usually being finely cut and fern-like. There are a good number of species and cultivars around, allowing keen gardeners to make an interesting collection. All dicentra like a bit of shade making them very useful for growing under shrubs or on the shady side of buildings or fences. Some will spread, making them useful ground cover for the earlier part of the summer.

Cultivation Dicentra are basically woodland plants and so they like the type of moist soil found there. They also require a lightly shaded position. Z2–4.

Propagation Division in spring is the easiest method of increasing dicentra. The species can also be propagated by sowing seed in autumn or spring.

Dicentra 'Bacchanal'

This beautiful plant forms a large mat of green ferny foliage that is surmounted by pendants of deep crimson flowers in early summer. When given the right conditions it can grow to 45cm (18in) high. Spread starts at about 10cm (4in) but the plant continues increasing indefinitely.

Dicentra 'Brownie'

This delightful plant forms large spreads of silvery grey foliage with pearly-white flowers appearing in early summer. H 30cm (12in) with an ever-increasing spread.

Dicentra 'Brownie'

Dicentra 'Bacchanal'

Dicentra formosa

A popular species with several cultivars, each forming spreading mats of green leaves and pink lockets. H 45cm (18in) with an ever-increasing spread.

The species is worth growing in its own right but there are also several interesting forms including *alba* with white flowers. The subspecies *oregana* has pink flowers and is the parent of many of the dicentra cultivars.

Dicentra 'Langtrees'

Another spreading form, with good, silvery grey foliage and pinkish-white flowers in early summer. H 30cm (12in) with an ever-increasing spread.

Dicentra 'Luxuriant'

This cultivar has bluish foliage and bright red flowers. H 35cm (14in); again the plant continues to spread until removed.

Dicentra scandens

This is an unusual, summer-flowering dicentra. Not only does it have yellow or whitish-yellow flowers, but it is also a climber. It will scramble though or over low shrubs and other plants. H and S up to 1m (3ft).

Dicentra spectabilis

Bleeding hearts or Dutchman's breeches are both apt descriptions of the flowers of this plant. The large flowers are carried on long arching stems in spring. In the species they are rose-pink tipped

Dicentra spectabilis

with white and in the form *alba* they are pure white. This is also different from the preceding forms as it is a bigger and more robust form that forms a clump rather than a spreading mat. H and S 60cm (24in) when given good conditions.

Dicentra 'Stuart Boothman'

A very good form with beautiful blue-grey foliage that sets off well the rose-pink flowers. It flowers in early summer and reaches about 30cm (12in) or so in height and spread.

DICTAMNUS
Burning bush

A genus of which *D. albus* is the only species, although its little-grown subspecies *caucasica* is sometimes considered a separate

Dictamnus purpureus

species. It is a splendid border plant, with spikes of white flowers held high above its deeply divided, ash-like leaves (its old name was *D. fraxinella* – meaning 'resembling ash'). In the form *purpureus* they are purplish-pink, striped with darker pink. The flowers appear in the summer.

This plant is known as the burning bush because on a hot day the seed pods release gases which can be ignited with a match. The white and purple forms grow up to 1m (3ft) with a spread of 60cm (24in). Both certainly deserve their place in middle of a border.

Cultivation Any reasonable garden soil as long as it is well-drained. It is best in a sunny position, although it will also tolerate a little light shade. Z4.

Propagation The easiest method of increase is sowing fresh seed. Plants can be divided in spring but this can be tricky since they do not like to be disturbed.

DIERAMA
Angel's fishing rod

This is a beautiful genus of plants that ought to be more widely grown. There are 44 species altogether, but most gardeners only know one or two. The strange English name is derived from the fact that the flowers are hang from very slender arching stems, much in the manner of bait from a fishing rod. The flowers are bell-shaped and come in variations of pink and purple.

Dieraina dracomontanum

They appear in summer. The stems emerge from a fountain of strap-like foliage.

The flowers need space to hang so dieramas should not be surrounded by tall plants: the edge of a border is ideal or, even better, overhanging water.
Cultivation These need a moist, but well-drained soil and they should be placed in full sun. Z8.
Propagation The best method of increase is from seed sown fresh, although it may take several years to get a flowering plant. They can also be divided in spring but they will take a while to settle down.

Dierama dracomontanum
This is a short form, so it is suitable for small gardens. It has light pink flowers. H 60cm (24in) S 45cm (18in).

Dierama igneum
A short-stemmed version with unusually bright red flowers. H 60cm (24in) S 45cm (18in).

Dierama 'Merlin'
A new form with beautiful rich purple flowers that are a deep blackberry colour. H 1m (3ft) S 75cm (30in).

Dierama pulcherrimum

Dierama pendulum
One of the taller species when it is grown in good conditions. It has purplish-pink flowers. H 2m (6ft) S 15–20cm (6–8in).

Dierama pulcherrimum
This is another tall form, with attractive flowers of varying shades of pink and purple. H 2m (6ft) S 1m (3ft). There is also a white form *album*.

Other plants There are a surprising number of other species and cultivars waiting to be discovered by the keen gardener. *D.* 'Guinevere', *D. latifolium*, *D. medium*, *D. pauciflorum*, *D.* Slieve Donard hybrids and many others are certainly worth looking at.

DIGITALIS
Foxglove
Everyone knows the foxglove, but many gardeners grow only the common purple one which is in fact a biennial (see page 282). There are a surprising number of other species that are far less well-known. While most of these are perennial they tend to be short lived and so need to be replaced every two or three years. However, they are easy to propagate from seed. The flowers all have the same basic foxglove shape except some are smaller and more squat. The flowers vary considerably in colour from yellow and cream through to differing shades of soft brown, purple and pink.

Digitalis lutea

They are carried in tall spikes. Foxgloves can either be dotted around amongst other plants in a cottage garden style, or you can grow them in a drift for a more organized effect.
Cultivation Foxgloves will grow in any reasonable garden soil and will tolerate either sun or light shade, making them versatile plants. Z3–5.
Propagation These plants all come readily from seed, which should be sown in spring.

Digitalis ferruginea
A distinguished-looking plant with upright stems carrying masses of rust-brown flowers over dark green leaves during summer. H 1.5m (5ft) S 45cm (18in).

Digitalis grandiflora
A shorter plant, up to 1m (3ft) high, which produces pale yellow blooms with a slightly flattened appearance in early summer. H 1m (3ft) S 45cm (18in).

Digitalis lanata
Extremely beautiful, soft white foxgloves with brown veining. H 60cm (24in) S 30cm (12in).

Digitalis × mertonensis

Digitalis lutea
Another yellow-flowered foxglove. This one produces narrow tubes in early summer. H 60cm (24in) S 30cm (12in).

Digitalis × mertonensis
This is a hybrid with large, slightly flattened foxgloves. They are a purple-pink with a touch of light brown in them. This makes a good border plant. It reaches 1m (3ft) in height, with a spread of 45cm (18in).

Digitalis parviflora
As the botanical name implies, this foxglove has small flowers, but a lot of them. They are a wonderful rusty-brown colour. H 60cm (24in) S 30cm (12in).

Other plants There are many interesting foxgloves that are just as good as those listed above. Try, for example, *DD. davisiana, dubia, obscura, stewartii, thapsi* and *viridiflora*.

Digitalis ferruginea

Spring-flowering perennials

Ajuga reptans	Lamium orvala
Anemone blanda	Meconopsis cambrica
Anemone nemorosa	Myosotis
Bergenia	Primula
Cardamine	Pulmonaria
Dicentra	Ranunculus ficaria
Doronicum	Symphytum
Euphorbia polychroma	Trillium
Helleborus	Veronica peduncularis
Lamium maculatum	Viola

Doronicum 'Spring Beauty'

D. affinis 'Polydactyla Mappleback'

Dryopteris affinis 'Cristata'

Echinacea purpurea

DORONICUM
Leopard's bane

This genus can be easily overlooked as "yet another daisy", but they are very good daisies, especially as they appear in spring when their golden flowers are most welcome. This is a grouping of about 25 species of which only a few are in cultivation. They are simple plants with large yellow flowers that float above the mid-green foliage. They look best when planted in a large clump, rather than individually, so that they shine out from the dappled spring shade.
Cultivation Any reasonable garden soil, but preferably a moist one. Most require a light shade. Z4.
Propagation They are very easy to increase by division.

Doronicum 'Frühlingspracht' (or 'Spring Beauty')
This is a double that is beautiful but lacks the elegance of the singles. Golden-yellow flowers are carried on stems up to 45cm (18in) high. S 30cm (12in).

Doronicum 'Miss Mason'
One of the best with large (8cm/3in) heads that appear in early summer. H 45cm (18in) S 60cm (24in).

Doronicum orientale
This is a taller species with large yellow flowers. It has a particularly good form called 'Magnificum', which is slightly taller and has larger flowers. H 60cm (24in) S 1m (3ft).

Other plants There are several others worth checking out including 'Little Leo' (dwarf) and *D. pardalianches* (tall).

DRYOPTERIS
Buckler fern

A huge genus of some 200 species of ferns of which quite a number are in cultivation. These are excellent ferns for use in shady areas such as under tall shrubs or in the shade of a house or wall. They look especially good filling odd dark corners. They are deciduous but in milder areas they may stay evergreen throughout the winter. They form fountains of typical fern-like fronds. The fanatic might want to collect all the variations but to the general gardener just one or two is likely to be sufficient since the variations between cultivars are not that great.
Cultivation Like many ferns these like a moist, rich, woodland-type soil in partial shade. Z3–5.
Propagation The easiest method is to divide the plants in spring just before growth resumes. They can also be grown from fresh spore.

Dryopteris affinis
This is one of the three main species. It has fronds that are very similar to those of *D. filix-mas*: lance-shaped and about 1m (3ft) long. There are a large number of cultivars, such as 'Cristata' and 'Polydactyla Mappleback', to explore. Most of them have distorted fronds of some kind. S 1m (3ft).

Dryopteris dilatata
Similar to the above but with broader fronds. It is taller growing to about 1.5m (5ft) when happy with the conditions. Again there are a number of cultivars. S 45cm (18in).

Dryopteris filix-mas
This is the male fern. It is very similar to the *D. affinis*. An excellent garden plant with lots of poise. H 1.2m (4ft) S 1m (3ft). There are a large number of variants, including the popular 'Crispa Cristata' from which to choose.

ECHINACEA
Coneflower

A small genus of which one species, *E. purpurea*, is widely grown both as a species and in its various cultivars. It is a moderately tall plant which is

Doronicum 'Miss Mason'

Dryopteris filix-mas 'Crispa Cristata'

Echinacea purpurea 'Green Edge'

Echinops ritro

Elymus magellanicus

Epilobium angustifolium album

ECHINOPS
Globe thistle

A large genus of more than 100 species of which only a few are worthy of general cultivation. Most of those are very similar, mainly varying in the colour of the thistle. This flower is spherical and held on stiff stems above slightly spiny foliage. Most of these plants are best grown in the middle of a border; their foliage is not particularly attractive and is best hidden behind surrounding plants.
Cultivation These will grow in any reasonable, well-drained garden soil. They prefer a sunny position, but tolerate light shade. Z3.
Propagation The species come readily from seed and will often produce self-sown seedlings. It is possible to divide the plants but it is not easy. Root cuttings can be taken in winter.

Echinops bannaticus

This has blue heads above a greyish-green foliage. The heads are up to 5cm (2in) across and are in flower from midsummer onwards. H 1.2 (4ft) S 1m (3ft).
There are some good cultivars of which 'Taplow Blue' is the best, although 'Blue Globe' and the white form 'Albus' are also well worth growing.

Echinops ritro

This is the most popular species. The flowers are slightly smaller than those of the previous one; it is also a shorter plant. H 1.2m (4ft) S 75cm (30in). The subspecies *ruthenicus* and cultivar 'Veitch's Blue' are also very good.

Echinops sphaerocephalus

A tall plant for the back of the border. The flowers are an off-white. It self-sows vigorously. H 2m (6ft) S 1m (3ft).

ELYMUS
Wild rye

This is a large genus of grasses, of which a couple are of interest to the general gardener. Their main attraction is the unusual blue or silvery-blue leaves, which make them very useful for adding foliage interest to gravel beds. The plants form low hummocks

grown for its flowers. These are like large daisies with a single fringe of petals around a central cone. Being large they stand out in the border and mix well with both other herbaceous plants and with grasses. H 1.2m (4ft) S 45cm (18in).
Cultivation This plant needs a soil rich in well-rotted organic material, but it should be well drained. It can be grown in full sun or a little light shade. Z3.
Propagation The species can be grown from seed sown in spring, but the cultivars need to be increased by division in spring.

Echinacea purpurea

The flower has a cone which is a bronze colour while the petals are a deep purple-pink. The flowers are up to 12cm (5in) across and larger in some cultivars. They flower in summer and continue into autumn.
The forms 'Alba', 'White Lustre' and 'White Swan' all have white flowers; the white petals of 'Green Edge' have a delicate green edging. Other cultivars include the dwarf form 'Kim's Knee High', the large-flowered 'Magnus' and 'Rubinstern', a very good dark purple form.

Other plants There are other species which are available for the keen gardener to hunt down. *E. angustifolia* has similar flowers except that the petals are much narrower and longer. *EE. pallida* and *paradoxa* are good plants to include in a collection.

of arching blades surmounted by flower spikes which are not particularly attractive. H 20cm (8in) S 15cm (6in).
Cultivation Any garden soil that is well-drained will be suitable. Place in full sun. Z4.
Propagation The easiest method of increase is to divide existing plants just before growth begins in spring. They can also be grown from seed which should be sown at the same time of year.

Elymus hispidus

The foliage of this species grows erect and is an attractive silver-blue colour.

Elymus magellanicus

This is considered the best plant since the short blades are of an intense blue.

EPILOBIUM
Willow herb

The name willow herb strikes terror into most gardeners' hearts because the genus contains some of our worst weeds. However, it also contains a few very pleasing garden plants. They vary from tall ones that reach 1.5m (5ft) or so to very low ones. With such a variation in height their uses obviously vary, but in general they make good border plants.
Cultivation Grow in reasonable, well-drained garden soil. They do well in full sun or light shade. Z7.
Propagation Increase can be from seed sown in spring or by division at the same time of year.

Epilobium angustifolium

This is one of the worst of weeds, but the form *album* is worth growing if you have a very large wild garden where it can be kept out of harm's way. It produces tall spikes of white flowers. Since it will form attractive drifts but is not so rampant as the species, it is an excellent plant to include in a white colour scheme. H 1.5m (5ft) with an infinite spread.

Epilobium glabellum

A perfectly safe little willow herb, this forms a mat of dark green leaves which offsets perfectly the creamy flowers. Grow in partial shade at the front of a border. H 20cm (8in) S 15cm (6in).

Epilobium hirsutum

This is another species to avoid unless you have a large wild gardens where it would be welcome. It has a variegated form 'Well Creek' that is liked by some gardeners. H 2m (6ft) and an infinite spread.

Epilobium glabellum

EPIMEDIUM
Barrenwort

A genus of 30 or so species which has become quite popular of late, especially with several new species coming in from China. These are generally dual-purpose plants since they have attractive flowers and also have good foliage for the rest of the year. The spring flowers are small and hang airily from arching stems. Many are evergreen and the foliage is an elongated heart-shape with a leathery and often glossy appearance. Epimediums are essentially woodlanders and like to grow in a shady position. They are good either under shrubs or in the shade of buildings or walls, where they make the perfect, spreading ground cover.
Cultivation Best grown in a moist, typical woodland soil. These plants should also be positioned in partial shade although some will grow in full sun. Z4–5.
Propagation All the species can be grown from fresh seed, but the easiest method of increase is to divide them in spring.

Epimedium grandiflorum
The flower stems are up to 35cm (14in) high and have yellow, pink, purple or red flowers dangling from them. The foliage is often tinged with bronze or even red. S 30cm (12in).

There are many good cultivars including 'Crimson Beauty' (crimson flowers), 'Nanum' (dwarf with white flowers) and 'White Queen' (white flowers).

Epimedium × perralchicum
The floating flowers are yellow in this species, and hang from 45cm (18in) stems. The evergreen

Epimedium × perralchicum

Epimedium × rubrum

leaves are a shiny dark green with a bronze tinge. S 30cm (12in). 'Fröhnleiten' is a good form that produces large flowers.

Epimedium × rubrum
The leaves are tinged with red and bronze, while the flowers are a wonderful mixture of yellow and bright red. H 30cm (12in) S 20cm (8in).

Epimedium × versicolor
A dainty-flowered plant: the outer parts of the flowers are pink and the inner are yellow. The foliage is tinted with reddish-brown. H and S 30cm (12in). There are several good cultivars including the yellow-flowered 'Sulphureum'.

Other plants Plants in this genus are such an interesting bunch that many gardeners collect them. Other species to check out include *EE. acuminatum, alpinum, davidii, diphyllum, leptorrhizum, perralderianum, × warleyense* and many more.

EREMURUS
Foxtail lily

It would be a strange gardener who was not immediately struck by these plants, with their huge, colourful spikes of flowers. There are more than 40 species, of which half a dozen plus a few cultivars are in cultivation.

They are all splendid and very eye-catching. In late winter thick shoots emerge from the fleshy roots and tall stems up to 2m (6ft) develop. The large flowering spikes begin to bloom from the bottom and seem to fizz away like giant fireworks. There is a good range of colours from white and yellow to pink of various shades. These plants are excellent for a position in the middle or back of the summer border.

Eremurus himalaicus

Cultivation These need a well-drained soil that is rich in well-rotted organic material. Place in a sunny position, sheltered from wind. Protect the emerging buds from severe frosts. Z4–6.
Propagation The easiest method is to dig up the fleshy roots and divide into individual crowns once flowering is over.

Eremurus himalaicus
This stunning plant produces long heads of pure white flowers. H 1m (3ft) S 1.2m (4ft). 'Himrob' has flowers of pale pink.

Eremurus × isabellinus
This is a group of very interesting cultivars with a good range of colours including 'Cleopatra'

Eremurus × isabellinus 'Oase'

Eremurus stenopyllus

(orange), 'Feuerfackel' (flame red), 'Moonlight' (pale yellow) 'Oase' (apricot), 'Obelisk' (white) and 'Pinokkio' (orange). H 1.5m (5ft) S 60cm (24in).

Eremurus robustus
A slightly shorter plant at 1.2m (4ft) or so. It produces spikes of pale pink flowers. S 1m (3ft).

Eremurus stenophyllus
A 1m (3ft) high plant with spikes of dark yellow flowers. Excellent. S 45cm (18in).

Other plants There are a number of other species and cultivars that will repay the effort spent seeking them out from specialist catalogues and nurseries. However, don't fill the whole garden with them as this will overdo the dramatic effect they create.

ERIGERON
Fleabane

Daisies may not be as exotic as, say, lilies, but they do form the backbone of many of our borders. Erigeron is a large genus with a large number of daisy-like species and their commonly grown cultivars. They are clump-forming plants, usually of low stature, making them ideal for carpeting the front of a border. The tall ones are good for mid-border situations. The flowers come in a range of colours and often appear over a very long season.

Erigeron glaucus

Cultivation Any reasonable garden soil is suitable but one that has been enriched with well-rotted organic material will suit these plants best. A sunny position is required, although many will tolerate a little light shade. The taller varieties may need support as they can be floppy. Z3–6.
Propagation The clump-forming varieties are best divided in the spring. Seed can be sown for the species and basal cuttings can be taken from some in spring.

Erigeron aurantiacus
A clump-forming plant whose bright orange flowers have a yellow central disc. H 30cm (12in) S 30cm (12in).
'Azurfee' is a taller form reaching 45cm (18in), this time with light blue, semi-double flowers with yellow centres. 'Dignity' has purple daisies with a yellow centre; again it grows to 45cm (18in) or more. 'Dimity' is a semi-double with bright pink flowers; H 30cm (12in) S 45cm (18in). 'Dunkelste Aller' is a very

Erigeron karvinskianus

good semi-double form with deep violet-blue flowers which have yellow centres. It is one of the taller forms, growing to 60cm (24in) S 60cm (24in). 'Foerster's Liebling' is another excellent form with pinkish-purple, semi-double flowers. It grows to 45cm (18in). S 60cm (24in).

Erigeron karvinskianus
This is a superb, airy plant for growing on banks, in walls or in crevices in paving or containers. It produces masses of small white and pink daisies on thin wiry stems over a very long season from spring until winter. It grows in clumps. It deserves a place in almost any garden. H 30cm (12in) S 45cm (18in).

Erigeron 'Quakeress'
This is a taller form which produces pale bluish-pink flowers. H 45cm (18in) S 60cm (24in).

Other plants There are several other species and cultivars, including E. glaucus to investigate. All produce a good number of flowers and are easy to grow.

ERYNGIUM
Sea holly
No garden should be without at least one of these wonderful plants. The foliage and flowers generally have a bluish tinge to them, although some also have a silvery appearance. The flowers form tight domed heads, which are surrounded by blue, silver or greenish bracts, rather like a collar. They retain their colour for a long time and are very useful for drying. These flower heads are often very spiky. The leaves can also be spiky and are usually attractive in their own right.

There are around 200 species, many of which are in cultivation. They are very good border plants, usually best sited in a middle position, and they are especially good in gravel beds.
Cultivation Most sea hollies grow in any garden soil so long as it is free-draining. It is important to plant them in full sun. Z3–7.
Propagation Species will come quite readily from seed sown fresh. They can also be divided,

Eryngium alpinum

although this is not easy since most are tap-rooted. Taking root cuttings in winter is usually easier.

Eryngium agavifolium
A tall plant with stems carrying clusters of pale green flower heads. The leaves that spring from the rosette at the base are spiny. An eye-catching plant but the spines mean that you need to take care when weeding nearby. H 2m (6ft) S 60cm (24in).

Eryngium alpinum
Large heads of silvery blue, which are touched with purple and surrounded by narrow, soft bracts. E. × oliverianum is similar except that the stiff bracts are prickly. H 1m (3ft) S 60cm (24in).

Eryngium × oliverianum

Eryngium bourgatii
This much-branched plant has masses of small blue heads. The leaves are dark green, veined with silver. It is a good foliage plant. H 45cm (18in) S 30cm (12in).

Eryngium × tripartitum
A splendid plant with a haze of small violet-blue flower heads. If well treated it can grow to nearly 1m (3ft). This is an excellent plant for mid border but it is often short lived. S 50cm (20in).

Other plants There are many other wonderful eryngiums, including EE. amethystinum, eburneum, horridum, maritimum, pandanifolium and planum with all its wonderful cultivars.

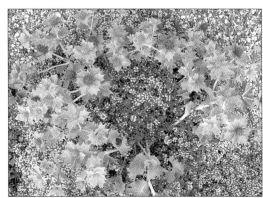

Eryngium maritimum

ERYSIMUM
Wallflowers

A large genus related to the cabbage family – but don't let that put you off since they are superb garden plants and every garden should include several of them. The most commonly grown wallflowers are treated as biennials (see page 286) but there are also a selection of excellent plants that, although short lived, are grown as perennials. The small, flat flowers are carried in loose spikes or clusters in early summer, often well into summer and even beyond. Most colours are represented except for blue. They are usually bright and cheerful-looking plants, making them good for the front of a border. Most grow from 45–75cm (18–30in) S 45cm (18in).

Cultivation Any garden soil will do, but the plants will last longer in a well-drained soil. A sunny position is required. Z3–6.

Propagation The species can be grown from seed, but most cultivars are best increased by cuttings taken in early summer.

Erysimum 'Bowles' Mauve'
What a wonderful plant this is. A great dome of airy stems carries purple flowers from spring through to autumn. Up to 1m (3ft) in height.

Erysimum 'Bredon'
This is a shorter form (up to 30cm/12in or less) with bright yellow flowers.

Erysimum 'Bowles' Mauve'

Erysimum 'John Codrington'

Erysimum 'Constant Cheer'
A lovely mixture of colour: the flowers open a brownish-orange and then slowly change to purple.

Erysimum 'John Codrington'
Another excellent form. This time the flowers come in a mixture of yellow, soft purple and brown creating a tapestry of colour.

Erysimum 'Moonlight'
This is a low-growing cultivar that forms a mat some 25cm (10in) high. The pale yellow flowers open from red buds.

Erysimum 'Rufus'
This has flowers of a good rusty brown colour. However, it isn't very strong and needs replacing every or every other year.

Erysimum 'Wenlock Beauty'
'Wenlock Beauty' is possibly the best of the bunch. It carries masses of sparkling flowers in a mixture of reds, mauves, browns and apricots. It grows to 45cm (18in) or so.

Other plants Other wallflowers worth considering include *E. linifolium*, which can be grown from seed. It produces a number of cultivars, basically with a lilac or purple base colour. *E. mutabile* is similar with mixed colours. Other cultivars include 'Butterscotch' (yellowish-orange), 'Jacob's Jacket' (mixed colours), 'Golden Jubilee' (golden yellow) and 'Golden Gem' (golden yellow).

EUPATORIUM
Hemp agrimony

A large genus of which only a handful of plants are widely grown in gardens. They are valued

Eupatorium p.m. 'Album'

for their late summer and autumn flowering. Many are large and they create a good block of colour at that time of year. They are also attractive to butterflies and bees. The main species and cultivars produce flattish heads of pink flowers, while others have loose heads of small button-like white flowers. They can be invasive, so they are usually only grown in large borders. There are some smaller versions that are suitable for smaller gardens.

Cultivation These plants need a moisture-retentive soil. They do best in sun although they will take some light shade.

Propagation The easiest method of propagation is to divide the plants in spring.

Eupatorium cannabinum
This is not the most attractive of the eupatoriums, but it is good for attracting butterflies and insects. Place in a damp site in a wild garden. H and S 1.2m (4ft).

Eupatorium purpureum
This is the main plant for border use. It is tall at 2m (6ft) or more. Again it is very attractive to butterflies. It is probably most frequently grown in the form *E.p. maculatum* 'Atropurpureum' which has good purple colouration both

Eupatorium purpureum

in its flowers and stems. S 1.5m (5ft). Its companion *E.p.m.* 'Album' has white flowers. The form *E.p.* 'Purple Bush' is lower-growing, reaching up to around 1m (3ft), so it is better suited to smaller gardens.

Eupatorium rugosum
This is species with flattish heads of up to 30 round, white flowers. It looks good in the evening light. H 1.5m (5ft) S 30cm (12in). A similar white-flowered species is *E. perfoliatum*.

EUPHORBIA
Spurge

An enormous genus of over 2,000 species, which vary from trees to ground-hugging plants. Fifty or more herbaceous species are in regular cultivation. The flowers are insignificant, but they are surrounded by colourful bracts, usually in yellowish-green. These last longer than the flowers giving the plants greater staying power. They make good border plants, planted singly or in groups. Some of the bigger ones make good focal points. The sap can be irritating to the skin and eyes.

Cultivation Any good garden soil is suitable, but preferably one that is not too dry. They do best in sun but most tolerate light shade.

Propagation Sow seed in spring. Some self-sow, producing enough seedlings for most purposes. Some spreading species can be divided. Those that grow from one basic stem can be increased by taking basal cuttings in spring.

Euphorbia amygdaloides
The species is best grown in a wild woodland garden. Its variety *robbiae* is an excellent plant for shady areas, even quite dense and dry ones. The short-lived form 'Purpurea' has good purple foliage and bracts in spring and is more suitable for the border. H 60cm (24in) S 30cm (12in).

Euphorbia characias
A tall rounded clump of radiating stems each topped with a club-shaped spike of yellowish-green "flowers". There are many forms, of which *wulfenii* is the most important. This is similar to the

Euphorbia characias wulfenii

Euphorbia dulcis 'Chameleon'

Filipendula rubra

species but the flower heads are often larger and yellower. Both the species and *wulfenii* have a lot of cultivars, with only marginal differences between them. They make superb border plants and a large clump makes an eye-catching feature when planted on its own. H and S 1.5m (5ft).

Euphorbia griffithii
A spreading, single-stemmed plant with reddish stems, leaves and bracts. The forms 'Dixter' and 'Fireglow' are excellent. It can be rampant in light soils. H 1m (3ft) S 50cm (20in).

Euphorbia polychroma
An excellent species that forms a rounded hummock 45cm (18in) high. It has bright yellow "flower" in spring. S 50cm (20in).

Other plants There are many species from which to choose. Good ones to consider include *EE. dulcis* (especially 'Chameleon'), × *martinii, mellifera, myrsinites. nicaeensis, palustris* and *sikkimensis*.

FILIPENDULA
Meadowsweet
This is a small genus with a few worthy garden plants. Their attraction comes from the sprays of white, pink or purple flowers, held on strong purple stems above attractive, deep-cut foliage. Many are good border plants; others are perfect for the wild or meadow garden. Some filipendulas are moisture-lovers and they are therefore good for growing next to water features or in bog gardens. They generally grow to about 1m (3ft) although some

reach double that height. They flower from midsummer onwards. S 1m (3ft).
Cultivation A soil with plenty of well-rotted organic material is ideal, although it should be free draining. Plant in either full sun or partial shade. Z2–3.
Propagation Division is by far the easiest method of propagation for all of them.

Filipendula camtschatica
A tall plant with large, divided leaves and sprays of white or pinkish flowers. H 2m (6ft) S 1m (3ft).

Filipendula 'Kahome'
This is a smaller (45cm/18in) form, ideal for the small garden. It has pink flowers suspended above a bronze foliage. An excellent plant. S 30cm (12in).

Filipendula purpurea
A fine plant with several very good cultivars. It has sprays of magenta flowers. H 1.2m (4ft)

S 60cm (24in). The cultivar 'Elegans' is worth considering since it is a more refined version. The form *albiflora* has beautiful white flowers.

Filipendula rubra
A good garden form, especially in the variety 'Venusta' which produces bright cerise flowers that become pink as as they age. It grows to about 2m (6ft) or even higher under good conditions. S 1.2m (4ft).

Filipendula ulmaria
The species can be grown in a border but it is not a top-class plant. However, it is perfect for naturalizing in a meadow garden, especially in damper areas or along a ditch. H and S 30cm (12in). The form 'Aurea' has yellow foliage that changes to a yellowish green with age. It is often placed in borders as a foliage plant.

Euphorbia polychroma

Euphorbia × martinii

Filipendula ulmaria

Foeniculum vulgare

FOENICULUM
Fennel

For some gardeners fennel is
something confined to the
vegetable garden, but *F. vulgare* is a
splendid plant for the border. It is
usually grown in the form
'Purpureum'. It is mainly grown
as a foliage plant, but the flat
heads of tiny yellow flowers are
beautiful in their own right
especially when seen floating
above the delicately cut foliage.
The plant is very upright-growing
and gets up to 2m (6ft) tall. The
foliage is very fine and feathery.
When freshly opened the leaves
are a dark bronze colour,
becoming purplish-green as they
age. This is a superb plant, grown
either by itself or in groups, for
the middle or towards the back
of a border. S 75cm (30in).

Francoa sonchifolia

Cultivation Any good garden soil
will do, but moister and richer
soils produce better plants. A
sunny position is needed. Fennel
can self-sow prodigiously so cut
back the flowering stems before
seed is produced. Z4.
Propagation The easiest and best
method of increase is from seed
sown in autumn or spring. There
are usually enough self-sown
seedlings for most uses but move
them into position while they are
still small as they are tap-rooted.

FRANCOA
Bridal wreath

A quiet and relatively unassuming
plant that always adds a touch of
quality to a border. *Francoa* is a
small genus of plants of which
only three are regularly grown in
gardens. Their attraction is the
arching stems that are topped
with cylindrical spikes of small,
star-like, pink flowers with
reddish markings. In good
conditions these spikes will reach
1m (3ft) but they are usually less.
There is little to choose between
the species except in the density
of the pink colouration. They
make excellent plants for the first
or second row of the border,
placed so that the stems arch over
other plants that have already
flowered or have yet to flower.
S 45cm (18in).
Cultivation These plants prefer a
humus-rich soil that is well-
drained but they will grow in
most reasonable garden soils. Sun
is preferable but they tolerate a
little shade. They may need winter
protection in cold areas. Z7.
Propagation Francoas come readily
from seed sown in spring.

Francoa appendiculata
This plant has pale pink flowers
with darker makings.

Francoa ramosa
Very pale pink, almost white
flowers with deep pink markings.

Francoa sonchifolia
Pink flowers with purplish-pink
markings. There is an almost
pure white form, 'Alba', of this.
There is also 'Rogerson's Form' in
which the flowers are much
darker, appearing almost purple.

Fritillaria imperialis

FRITILLARIA
Fritillary

A large genus of bulbs of 100
species. Most are of interest to
the alpine enthusiast, with only a
handful being suitable for the
perennial garden. They vary in
size from a few centimetres to
1.2m (4ft). They have pendant
bell-shaped flowers in many
colours, including green and
almost black. True blue is the
only colour missing. Some are
worthy of the spring border but
others are better in a wild garden.
Cultivation Conditions vary and
are given under individual species
below. Z3–6.
Propagation Seed is readily
produced and this is an easy if
lengthy method of reproduction.
Division of the small bulblets, or
"rice", is also very easy.

Fritillaria acmopetala
A small-belled form suitable for
choice spots at the front of a
border where it will not get
swamped. The bells are green

Fritillaria meleagris

Fritillaria persica

suffused with purple. It needs a
well-drained soil that does not get
too wet in winter. H 30cm (12in)
S 5–8cm (2–3in). *F. gracea* is
similar but with bigger bells.

Fritillaria imperialis
A very impressive plant. It has
clusters of orange or yellow
flowers at the top of each tall
stem just beneath an upright tuft
of green leaves. It needs similar
conditions to the previous plant,
and is good for the middle of the
border where its dying foliage will
be covered by summer plants.
H 1.2m (4ft) S 30cm (12in).

Fritillaria meleagris
A beautiful plant with large bells
hanging from thin stems. The
flowers are chequered purple
and white, although there are also
white forms which have a light
chequering of green. These can be
grown in a border but are also
ideal for naturalizing in grass,
particularly if the soil is damp. H
30cm (12in) S 5–8cm (2–3in).

Fritillaria verticillata

Green-flowered perennials

Alchemilla mollis
Anemone nemorosa
 'Viridiflora'
Aquilegia viridiflora
Dianthus 'Charles
 Musgrave'
Euphorbia
Galtonia viridiflora
Helleborus argutifolia
Helleborus foetidus

Hemerocallis 'Lady Fingers'
Iris 'Green Halo'
Iris 'Green Spot'
Kniphofia 'Green Jade'
Kniphofia 'Percy's Pride'
Lilium 'Limelight'
Primula auricala (several)
Ranunculus 'Green Petal'
Zantedeschia aethopica
 'Green Goddess'

Gaura lindheimeri 'Siskiyou Pink'

Gentiana acaulis

Fritillaria persica

This plant is another tall form. It produces clusters of very dark purple, almost black flowers. It needs dry conditions and a hot place to do well. *F. persica* often does not live long in borders but it is so beautiful that it is worth trying to grow. H 75cm (30in) S 10cm (4in).

Fritillaria verticillata

A delightful plant with pale green and white flowers. It soon forms a large clump. It is best planted near shrubs to which its tendrils can cling. It will grow in most well-drained borders. H 45cm (18in) S 10cm (4in).

GALEGA
Goat's rue

A small genus of herbaceous plants of which four are in general cultivation. These are tall, open plants with many branches, the tips of which carry short, upright spikes of small, pea-like flowers. The colours are generally white, blue or pinkish-purple, and the pretty flowers are often bicoloured. Galegas flower in early summer when they produce

a good mound of blooms for the back of the border. H 1.5m (5ft) S 1m (3ft).
Cultivation Any good garden soil will do, but a richer, moister soil will provide the best results. These plants do best in full sun, but they will also tolerate a little light shade. They may need some form of support.
Propagation Galegas can be divided in spring, although this is not easy. They can also be grown from seed sown at the same time.

Galega × hartlandii

This is one of the better plants, most commonly represented by two of its cultivars. 'Alba', as its name suggests, has white flowers. The other is 'Lady Wilson', which is a bicolour whose flowers come in white and mauvish-blue.

Galega officinalis

There is not much to choose between the two species. Again this has bicoloured flowers in white and pale blue. It also has an all-white form 'Alba'. The form 'His Majesty' has white and mauve-purple bicoloured flowers.

GAURA
Gaura

A genus of about 20 species of which only one is in general cultivation. This is *G. lindheimeri*. It has several cultivars but the species itself is as good as any of them. It has tall, thin stems from which dance delightful butterfly-like flowers. These are white with a touch of pink. H 1.2m (4ft) S 1m (3ft). 'Siskiyou Pink' is the most popular cultivar. Here the flowers are a dark pink, but they

are less effective than the white and the plant is not very robust. 'Corrie's Gold' has gold-edged leaves which do little to increase the attraction of the plant.
Cultivation Gaura will thrive in any reasonable garden soil as long as it is well drained. It must have a sunny position. Z5.
Propagation They can be divided with care in the spring, but this is not the easiest of tasks. It is easier to take basal cuttings at the same time of year. The species can also be grown from seed, which is sown in spring.

GENTIANA
Gentian

The 400 species of gentians provide some of the bluest plants in nature. There are a number that are of interest to the alpine gardener, but there are only one or two that are suitable for use in the perennial garden. The flowers are trumpet-shaped. The majority of gentians are ground-hugging plants that like moist, even boggy conditions. The taller border varieties are more accommodating and will grow in any soil that has humus in it. They are ideal plants for shady areas in the garden.
Cultivation Grow in rich moisture-retentive soil. They prefer partial shade, although full sun will be tolerated if the ground does not dry out. Z5.
Propagation Divide gentians in spring or sow the seed as soon as it is harvested.

Gentiana acaulis

This is not the easiest plant to grow but when it is happy, it is wonderful. Very large, upward-

facing trumpets appear in late spring and early summer. H 10cm (4in) S 10cm (4in).

Gentiana asclepiadea

This is the willow gentian, a tallish plant that produces long arching stems, the tips of which often touch the ground. They carry blue, upward-facing flowers on either side. A perfect plant for a choice position in the shady garden. It flowers in late summer. H 1m (3ft) S 60cm (24in).

Gentiana lutea

This is an unusual yellow gentian. It is a tall, upright plant which carries whorls of bright yellow, starry flowers in midsummer. Ideal for naturalizing in grass, such as in a meadow garden. H 1.2m (4ft) S 60cm (24in).

Gentiana sino-ornata

A ground-hugging plant with brilliant blue trumpets facing upwards. There are many cultivars and similar species, all of which are suitable for moist ground in light shade where they will not get swamped by other plants. H 5cm (2in) S 30cm (12in).

Galega × hartlandii

Gentiana asclepiadea

Geranium 'Ann Folkard'

Geranium clarkei 'Kashmir White'

Geranium 'Johnson's Blue'

GERANIUM
Hardy geraniums

Many people get confused between these plants and the pelargoniums, the red-flowered plants that are still commonly referred to as geraniums more than 100 years after their name was changed. Geranium is a large genus with more than 300 species. Some are tender but a surprising number of the remainder are in cultivation. There are many gardeners who have been bitten by the collecting bug and have a large number in their garden. Even if you don't collect them it can be surprising how quickly the number of different geraniums that you own increases, which shows how good and versatile they are.

They have open, dish-like flowers in a variety of colours, mainly based on pink and purplish-blue colour schemes. They vary in height from ground-hugging to 1.2m (4ft). Most flower in early summer but some are later and others flower over a

long period. Geraniums are very versatile: there is a geranium for every position in the garden in both sun and shade.

Cultivation Most geraniums grow in any reasonable garden soil, but they prefer it laced with plenty of well-rotted organic material. Some are sun lovers, others prefer shade. Cut early-blooming forms after flowering to the ground to get fresh foliage. Z2–6.

Propagation Species can be grown from seed sown in spring. Cultivars can be divided or cuttings taken in spring.

Geranium 'Ann Folkard'

A sprawling plant that clambers between and over other plants. The foliage is yellowish early on, while the flowers are magenta with a dark eye. This geranium has a long flowering season. H 60cm (24in) S 1m (3ft).

Geranium × cantabrigiense

An excellent carpeting geranium that makes perfect ground cover. The leaves are slightly shiny and

set off the pink flowers perfectly. 'Biokovo' has flowers of such a pale pink as to be almost white. 'Cambridge' is another good pink form. H 15cm (6in) with an infinite spread.

Geranium cinereum

This is a dwarf plant that is usually grown as one of its cultivars such as 'Apple Blossom' (pale pink flowers) or 'Ballerina' (purple-veined pink flowers). Both have a long flowering season and are perfect for placing at the edge of borders. H 15cm (6in) S 30cm (12in).

Geranium clarkei

This species is grown only in the form of its cultivars. These make excellent plants although they only flower once. 'Kashmir Purple' has perfect mauvish-pink flowers with reddish veins, while 'Kashmir White' has white flowers with paler veins. They grow in a rounded hummock, and make excellent border plants. H and S 45cm (18in).

Geranium himalayense

A good border plant. The flowers are a light purple, darker towards the middle and with a whitish centre. There are several good forms. 'Plenum' ('Birch Double') has attractive double flowers and 'Gravetye' has larger flowers with more purple in them. H 30cm (12in) S 60cm (24in).

Geranium magnificum

A good old-fashioned cottage-garden plant with soft leaves and blue flowers. It tolerates some shade. H and S 60cm (24in).

Geranium 'Johnson's Blue'

A good single form, this has blue flowers with whitish centres. H 45cm (18in) S 60cm (24in).

Geranium macrorrhizum

A superb plant for shade (although it will also grow in sun). The leaves are aromatic when crushed and are semi-evergreen. The pink flowers are produced in early summer. There are several good forms with flowers of varying pinks. H 38cm (15in) S 60cm (24in).

Geranium oxonianum

This and its many cultivars make excellent ground cover in either sun or shade. The clump-forming plant will scramble up through shrubs given a chance. The flowers are bright pink. H and S 75cm (30in).

Geranium phaeum

Another excellent clump-forming plant. This time the flowers are relatively small with reflexed (bent back) petals held in airy sprays on thin stems. The flowers vary from

Geranium cinereum 'Ballerina'

Geranium phaeum

Geranium psilostemon

Geranium sanguineum striatum

Geum rivale

Gillenia trifoliata

pink to purple to white. There are many good cultivars including 'Samobor' which has large chocolate blotches on the leaves. H 75cm (30in) S 45cm (18in).

Geranium psilostemon
A superb plant that forms a large round hummock of airy stems bearing magenta flowers with dark centres. Perfect for larger borders. H and S 1.2m (4ft).

Geranium sanguineum
This is a superb species with lots of cultivars, many of which flower over a long period. It has purpled-red flowers over a hummock of foliage. The variety striatum and its cultivars have pink rather than red flowers, with prominent veins. H and S 30cm (12in).

Other plants There are many more species and cultivars to explore including all the forms of *G. pratense* and *G. sylvaticum*.

GEUM
Avens

A genus of about 50 species, a number of which make good garden plants. Although several species are grown it is mainly

their cultivars that grace our borders. Geums are low clump-formers with thin, wiry stems that carry brightly coloured flowers well above the foliage. The flowers are flat discs, usually with a golden central boss. Some forms are double. The colours are mainly reds, oranges and yellows although there are some with more subtle colours. They mainly flower in early summer although some are repeat flowering.
Cultivation Geums will grow in most reasonable garden soils as long as they are free-draining. They need a sunny position. Z5.
Propagation The species can be increased from seed sown in spring, but division is the easiest method and an essential one for the cultivars.

Geum 'Borisii'
This is a wonderfully bright plant with vivid orange-red flowers that are produced over a long season. H 45cm (18in) S 30cm (12in). Another excellent cultivar is 'Coppertone', a lowish-growing (30cm/12in) geum with soft coppery-coloured flowers which are more bell-shaped. 'Lemon Drops' has lemon-yellow flowers

which look particularly good planted near blue violas.

Geum rivale
A plant with pinkish-orange flowers which are bell-shaped rather than disc-shaped. The species is attractive but the cultivars are more often grown. H 45cm (18in) S 20cm (8in). 'Leonard's Variety' is the most famous. It is a more refined plant than the species with lots of reddish-apricot flowers. 'Album' has greenish-white flowers.

There are lots of other cultivars to explore including 'Mrs Bradshaw' (large, semi-double red), 'Georgenberg' (flame orange), 'Prinses Juliana' (orange) and 'Rubin' (semi-double flowers in flame-red).

GILLENIA
Gillenia

A small genus of two, of which one, *G. trifoliata*, is in general cultivation. This is a shrubby perennial with a mass of wiry stems carrying very delicate, butterfly-like flowers. These are pure white with red bud sheaths. It makes a delightful plant, which is not seen as frequently as perhaps it should be. The flowers last throughout the summer. H 1m (3ft) S 60cm (24in).
Cultivation Any reasonable garden soil except alkaline ones. It needs a sunny position lightly shaded at the hottest time of day. Z4.
Propagation Grow from seed sown in spring. The plants can be divided at the same time, although this is not that easy.

GLADIOLUS
Gladiolus

This is a large genus of bulbs that is well known to gardeners. Most are tender and are treated as annuals (see page 292), but there are a few exceptions which are of interest to the perennial gardener. One in particular, *G. byzantinus*, is hardy and commonly grown. This has not got the big blowsy flowers of the annuals; its blooms are simpler and in many ways much more refined. Gladioli are excellent plants for a late-spring border. Plant in-between emerging summer plants so that the gap

left when flowering is over is covered by the new foliage.
Cultivation Any reasonable garden soil will do. Site in full sun; they can tolerate light shade. Z7–8.
Propagation Dig up the corms and divide off the new ones. They can also be grown without much problem from seed sown in spring. They do not need staking.

Gladiolus communis subsp. byzantinus
This is still known mainly as *G. byzantinus* by most gardeners. It has vivid magenta flowers down one side of a slightly arching stem. It has long sword-like leaves. H 1m (3ft) S 15cm (6in).

Other plants There are a few other gladiolus that can be grown in the open garden although they may be a problem in colder areas. *G. papilio* is probably the best of these with wonderful smoky yellow flowers. *G. × colvillei* has some good cultivars in particular the white 'The Bride'.

Geum 'Lemon Drops'

Geum 'Rubin'

Gladiolus communis subsp. byzantinus

Gunnera manicata

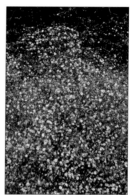

Gypsophila paniculata 'Bristol Fairy'

Gypsophila repens 'Fratensis'

GUNNERA
Gunnera

This is a genus consisting of about 45 species. Several of them are of interest to the gardener but only a couple are cultivated to any extent. Although these have similarities in terms of their leaf and flower shape, they are very different in form and size: one is ground-hugging and grows only to 10cm (4in) or so, while the other towers to at least 2m (6ft) and sometimes double that across. It is the latter that is usually of most interest to most gardeners.
Cultivation Gunneras, particularly the larger ones, require a deep, rich soil with plenty of well-rotted organic material. You need to protect the crowns over the winter. Z6–8.
Propagation Division is the easiest method for smaller species. However, their sheer size makes this impractical for the large ones, although small rooted pieces can be detached. Instead, take basal cuttings from the buds that emerge in spring.

Gunnera magellanica
A low creeping plant with rounded leaves. The flowers are green but are given colour when the flame red berries are formed. They are held in upright heads, only a few centimetres high. These plants are not really suitable for the perennial border but can be grown over a rock garden or down a bank. They need covering in winter. S indefinite.

Gunnera manicata
This is the main species grown. It is a giant with leaves that can reach more than 2m (6ft) across. They look like giant rhubarb leaves and are tall enough for children to shelter under. The stems are rough with coarse prickles. These rub in the wind producing a rasping sound. Although these plants are mainly for the large garden it has been known for them to be used as ground cover in a small suburban front garden. They are best sited next to medium to large ponds. The flowers would be insignificant if it wasn't for the size of the flower head. They are green and are carried on a thick clumps below the leaf canopy. H and S at least 2m (6ft).

Gunnera tinctoria
This plant is less frequently seen than the previous one, but is becoming more popular. It is similar but slightly smaller and more compact. It is not so hardy and will require winter protection. H and S 1.5m (5ft).

GYPSOPHILA
Gypsophila

It is hard to image any plant that differs so much from the heavy presence of the Gunnera above. These plants are lightness itself, with large airy sprays of small flowers that create a misty effect. This is a large genus with around 100 species. A handful of these are in cultivation, providing the gardener with plants that are not only beautiful in their own right but contrast well with many of those around them Some are annuals (see page 293).
Cultivation Any good garden soil will do so long as it is not too acid. It should have plenty of grit incorporated so that it is very free-draining. Z3.
Propagation Increase stock by sowing seed in spring. These plants are difficult to divide so take root cuttings in early winter.

Gypsophila cerastioides
This is really the province of the alpine growers. However, it can be used on the edge of raised beds or next to paths so long as it is not swamped by larger neighbours. It is mat-forming, and the flowers are white with pinkish centres. H 7.5cm (3in) S 10cm (4in).

Gypsophila paniculata
This is the main plant for the border. In summer it forms a cloud of small white flowers and is often called baby's breath because of this. The mass of wiry stems form a mound up to 45cm (18in) high or so. It needs a position towards the front of the border. S 1m (3ft).

There are several cultivars of which 'Bristol Fairy' is still the best. This has larger flowers than the species. There is a smaller plant with double flowers: 'Compacta Plena'.

Gypsophila repens
This is much shorter than the previous plant. It tends to be more spreading and is ideal for planting on the edge of a raised bed so that it can spill over the edge. The flowers are white, or

Gypsophila cerastioides

Gypsophila tenuifolia

white tinged with pink. H 25cm (10in) S 30cm (12in). The best known form is 'Dorothy Teacher' which is more compact with pink flowers that darken as they age. Another is 'Fratensis'.

Gypsophila 'Rosenschleier'
Also known as 'Rosy Veil', this plant is one of the best gypsophilas for the border. It forms a large, rounded haze of pale pink flowers that are white when they first open. H 45cm (18in) S 45cm (18in).

Gypsophila tenuifolia
A tufted plant forming a mat over which float plenty of small white or pink flowers. It grows up to 20cm (8in) high and 60cm (24in) across.

HAKONECHLOA
Hakonechloa
This is just one species in this genus. It is *H. macra*, which is sometimes grown in gardens but it is usually as one of its two main cultivars that it is grown. It forms a clump with arching stems. The plant reaches about 45cm (18in) high and 60cm (24in) across. 'Aureola' is the form most commonly seen. It is variegated, with alternating bright golden and green stripes running down the length of the leaves. 'Alboaurea' is similar but has touches of white.
Cultivation These plants will grow in most reasonable garden soils but they do best in richer soils so

Hakonechloa macra 'Alboaurea'

long as they are free-draining. They will grow in either sun or light shade, but the colour is best in the latter. Z6.
Propagation Increase is by division which should be carried out in spring as the new growth begins.

HEDYCHIUM
Ginger lily
A genus of around 50 species, which in spite of their tenderness have become increasingly popular for use in the border as well as in containers. The plants have a tropical appearance with large, shiny green leaves and a terminal spike of butterfly- or orchid-like flowers which add to their exotic appearance. One of the attractions is their sweet scent. These plants generally grow to between 1 and 1.5m (3–5ft) but some of the more vigorous ones can reach 3m (10ft) if they are given the right conditions. These are plants for exuberant colourful borders, especially those with a tropical feel about them – mix them in with other large-leaved and colourful plants. S 1m (3ft).
Cultivation These need a rich soil with plenty of well-rotted organic material. It should be well-drained. The position can be in either sun or partial shade. Plant the rhizomes just below the surface of the soil. Mulch deeply in the autumn to protect them from the frosts. Z8.
Propagation Ginger lilies should be propagated by dividing the rhizomes in spring.

Hedychium coccineum
This is one of the most colourful of the ginger lilies. The flowers are about 5cm (2in) long, and they may be white, pink, coral red

Hedychium densiflorum

or orange with red stamens. In good conditions, the plant can grow to 3m (10ft) but it usually reaches only half this height. It has a very good form 'Tara', which has orange flowers. S 75cm (30in).

Hedychium densiflorum
This species has yellow or orange flowers. It is one of the tallest but rarely grows to its full potential height, usually reaching only 2m (6ft) with a spread of 60cm (24in). It is reasonably hardy. There are number of good cultivars including 'Assam Orange', which has bright orange flowers, and 'Stephen' (primrose yellow with red anthers).

Hedychium gardnerianum
This is a spectacular plant, producing clear yellow flowers with red stamens. It is tender and can only be grown in frost-free positions unless it is grown inside in containers and moved out after frosts have passed. H 2m (6ft) S 75cm (30in).

Other plants There are a number of other species and cultivars that are widely grown but their hardiness is doubtful. If you want to try, they are best grown in a warm, sheltered position or they can be cultivated under glass.

HEDYSARUM
Hedysarum
This is a large genus of around 100 species. Only one is in general cultivation, although there are a couple of others that are worth looking out for. They are members of the pea family and have spikes of small pea-like flowers, which provide a good splash of red in the spring or summer borders.
Cultivation Grow in any reasonable garden soil that is well-drained. A sunny position is needed. Once in position, avoid disturbing. Z7.
Propagation They come readily from seed sown in spring. They can be divided at the same time of year, but this is not easy.

Hedysarum coronarium
This is the species most commonly seen in gardens. It has bright red flowers which appear in the spring and early summer. H and S 1m (3ft).

Hedysarum hedysaroides
Similar to the previous plant but it is a bit smaller and the flowers are more purple. The blooms are produced in the summer. H 60cm (24in) S 60cm (24in).

Hedysarum multijugum
This is a bigger plant with erect spikes of red-purple flowers throughout the summer. H 1.5m (5ft) S 60cm (24in).

Hedychium gardnerianum

Hedysarum coronarium

Helenium 'Moerheim Beauty'

Helenium 'Waldtraut'

Helianthemum 'Henfield Brilliant'

HELENIUM
Sneezeweed

A genus of about 40 or so species of which only two or three are in cultivation. There are a large number of cultivars and these are most welcome since they add colour to our borders from summer onwards. They are upright, clump-forming plants that reach between 1–1.2m (3–4ft) in height. The flowers are daisy-like with red, yellow, orange or brown outer petals and a brown or gold inner disc.

Cultivation Heleniums do best in full sun and in a soil that does not dry out too much; add plenty of well-rotted organic material. Slugs can be a nuisance when new shoots are emerging. Z3.

Propagation The simplest method of increasing heleniums is to divide them in spring.

Helenium autumnale
This plant is parent to many of the cultivars. However, it is still worth growing in its own right.

The flowers have yellow petals and a brown central disc. H 1.5m (5ft) S 45cm (18in).

Helenium bigelovii
This is the other plant that is responsible for many of the colourful hybrids. It is shorter than the previous, getting up to about 60cm (24in). It has yellow petals and a brown or yellow central disc. S 30cm (12in).

Helenium 'Bruno'
This has bright reddish brown petals and a brown disc.

Helenium 'Butterpat'
A plant with bright butter-yellow petals and a golden disc.

Helenium 'Moerheim Beauty'
One of the most attractive of the heleniums. It has brownish-red flowers touched with yellow, with brown discs.

Helenium 'Riverton Beauty'
This plant has petals of a lovely soft yellow with a reddish-brown central disc.

Helenium 'Rotgold'
Distinctive colouring features red flowers streaked with yellow, and a brown disc.

Helenium 'Waldtraut'
A plant with mahogany and yellow petals and a brown central disc.

Helenium 'Wyndley'
'Wyndley' has flowers that are yellow streaked with red. It has brown disc florets.

HELIANTHEMUM
Rock roses

These are really shrubs but they have always had a place in the perennial border and so are included here. This is a large genus of more than 100 species but it is the many cultivars that are of interest to gardeners. These form rounded hummocks of grey or green foliage against which round, flat flowers are displayed. The blooms come in many shades of red, pink, orange, yellow and white. They have a yellow centre. There is a quiet simplicity about these flowers that makes them perfect for the edge of a border, or grown to hang down a wall or sprawl onto a path or patio. They flower in early summer; some, especially the doubles, last into late summer. H 30cm (12in) S 45cm (18in).

Cultivation Any garden soil as long as it is free-draining. A sunny position is important. Sheer over the plant once it has flowered to keep it compact. Z5.

Propagation Helianthemums are increased by cuttings taken in either spring or early summer.

Helianthemum 'Amy Baring'
A superb form with deep golden flowers and orange in their centres.

Helianthemum 'Butterball'
'Butterball' is double-flowered form with buttery yellow flowers as its name implies.

Helianthemum 'Cerise Queen'
This plant carries double flowers which look like powder puffs of cerise petals.

Helianthemum 'Chocolate Blotch'
A delightful plant whose orange petals have chocolate brown blotches at the base.

Helianthemum 'Henfield Brilliant'
This gorgeous cultivar has flowers of such a bright red that they can seem to hit you between the eyes with their brilliance.

Helenium 'Riverton Beauty'

Helianthemum 'Wisley Pink'

Helianthemum 'Raspberry Ripple'

One of the brashest of the rock roses. The flowers are white with splashes of raspberry red and with a yellow boss of stamens.

Helianthemum 'Wisley Pink'

Strictly speaking, this is now called 'Rhodanthe Carneum' but it is still generally known as 'Wisley Pink'. It is a wonderful plant with soft pink petals set off against soft grey foliage. Possibly the best of the bunch.

Helianthemum 'Wisley Primrose'

Another superb plant whose primrose-yellow flowers look charming against soft grey foliage.

Helianthemum 'Wisley White'

An excellent plant which has wonderful white flowers touched with yellow.

HELIANTHUS
Sunflower

Most people are aware of the large sunflowers that are grown as annuals (see page 294) but many do not realise that there are also a number of perennial species. These might not be as big and brazen as the dinner-plate-sized annuals, but they still make a good splash of bright colour, especially during the autumn. They have daisy-like flowers, with an outer ring of bright yellow petals surrounding an inner disc of similar colour. Some of the cultivars are double forms where the disc is replaced by a pompom of petals. The flowers are carried on stiff, upright stems, which vary in height from 1m (3ft) or so up

Helianthus 'Loddon Gold'

to 2.5m (8ft). They soon make a decent-sized clump. Most are best sited at the back of the border and look particularly good against a dark green hedge.
Cultivation Add plenty of well-rotted organic material to the soil before planting in a sunny position. The taller varieties may need staking in exposed positions.
Propagation Division in spring is by far the easiest method of propagation.

Helianthus atrorubens

In late summer this vigorous sunflower produces yellow flowers with a deep red central disc. H 1.5m (5ft) S 1m (3ft).

Helianthus × laetiflorus 'Morning Sun'

Helianthus 'Capenoch Star'

A good plant which has large yellow-petalled flowers with a yellow centre. H 1.2m (4ft) 60cm (24in).

Helianthus × laetiflorus

A popular hybrid that has produced some good cultivars. It has yellow flowers with yellow disc. H 2m (7ft) S 1.2m (4ft). 'Miss Mellish' is a semi-double form with yellow petals and a more golden-coloured disc. 'Morning Sun' is similar.

Helianthus 'Lemon Queen'

A fine variety with lemon-yellow petals and a yellow centre. It is a tall variety that needs to be grown at the back of the border where it can peep over the other plants. H 1.8m (6ft) S 60cm (24in).

Helianthus 'Loddon Gold'

A old variety that has stood the test of time. It is a double with a mass of golden-yellow flowers. H 1.5m (5ft) S 60cm (24in).

Helianthus 'Monarch'

A tall plant with semi-double flowers with narrow yellow petals and green-brown centre. H 2.5m (8ft) S 60cm (24in).

Helianthus salicifolius

Before the flowers appear in autumn this can be a difficult plant to identify: its upright stems carry a large number of narrow leaves which droop down, looking just like those of a tall lily. But the idea of a lily is quickly dispelled when the bright yellow flowers appear. This is a tall plant growing to 2.5m (8ft), S 60cm (24in).

Other plants There are a number of other species and cultivars to explore, although most are variations on the same theme.

HELICHRYSUM
Helichrysum

A very large genus of over 500 species, which like the last genus is mainly known for the plants grown as annuals (see pages 294–5). However, there are a number of perennials that are worth growing. They are perhaps

Helianthus salicifolius

not in the top league of plants but they do add unusual colour combinations to the border, mainly through their grey foliage. The felted leaves do not like wet climates, especially winter wet. They do well in gravel beds.
Cultivation Helichrysums grow in any reasonable garden soil but it must be really well drained. A sunny position is essential. Z6–8.
Propagation Division is possible in spring. Alternatively, cuttings can be taken in summer.

Helichrysum splendidum

This is a shrubby plant with upright stems carrying narrow grey leaves. They are topped with small yellow flowers in late summer. H and S 1.2m (4ft).

Helichrysum 'Schwefellicht'

Also known as 'Sulphur Light', this is one of the best helichrysums for the perennial border. The foliage is an attractive grey-green overlaid with white. The bunches of upward-facing flowers are bright sulphur yellow fading to orange or brown as they go over, which creates a delightful two-toned effect. They flower in late summer. H 40cm (16in) S 30cm (12in).

Other plants There are several other species and varieties worth checking out if you like to include plenty of grey in your borders.

Helichrysum 'Schwefellicht'

Helleborus foetidus

Helleborus × hybridus Double

Hemerocallis 'Stafford'

HELLEBORUS
Hellebore

This is an extremely popular genus. There are about 15 or so species, most of which are in cultivation, along with a host of cultivars. Their popularity may be partly due to the fact that they flower in late winter when not much else is around. At that time of year they certainly brighten up the garden. They have flat or cup-shaped flowers which come in a wide variety of colours. Doubles and picotee varieties with flowers edged in a different colour have extended the range available. These are mainly woodland plants. Place where they can be seen in winter and spring, but hidden during the rest of the year. *Cultivation* A soil kept moist with plenty of organic material is required for most species. Partial shade is preferable. Z4–6.
Propagation Species can be grown from seed, which should be sown as soon as it is ripe. Species and cultivars can also be divided in spring after flowering.

Helleborus argutifolius
These are tall plants that often need support. The dark green leaves are noticeably toothed and

the flowers are cup-shaped and a delicate pale green. H 1.2m (4ft) S 45cm (18in).

Helleborus foetidus
A leggy plant with narrow leaves and bell-shaped flowers. The flowers are green, often with a purple lip. H and S 45cm (18in). 'Wester Fisk' is a good form.

Helleborus × hybridus
These plants used to be known as the oriental hybrids. The flowers are flat and dish-shaped and there is a wide mixture of colours; some are spotted and others are doubles. There are many named varieties from which to choose. All are good, so try to see them in flower before you buy. H 45cm (18in) S 45cm (18in).

Helleborus niger
The Christmas rose produces flat flowers which are white, but usually infused with a little pink. It is not the easiest plant to grow and it can be a martyr to slugs. H and S 30cm (12in).

Other plants There are a great number of other species and cultivars that are worth exploring, such as *H. × sternii*. Visit specialist

nurseries in spring so that you can see them in flower before making your choice.

HEMEROCALLIS
Daylily

A genus of around 15 species, but it is the thousands of cultivars that are of most interest to the perennial gardener. This vast quantity is well beyond the needs of even the keenest, but there is a surprising amount of variation between them. The basic plant is a clump of strap-like leaves arching out in a fountain, from which emerge stiff stems carrying a mass of buds. These open a few at a time but only for a day (hence the plant's English name). The flowers are shaped like flaring trumpets and are coloured in mainly yellow, orange or red as well as occasional pinks and whites. They are one of the mainstays of the summer border. H 75cm (30in) S 60cm (24in).
Cultivation Plant in any reasonable garden soil that has been enriched with organic material. A sunny position is best but most will take some light shade. Staking is not usually required. Z2–4.
Propagation Although they are heavy plants to dig up, division is the best method of increase.

Hemerocallis 'Catherine Woodberry'
This is a very beautiful plant which produces flowers of an unusual lilac-pink.

Hemerocallis 'Corky'
One of the most refined of the daylilies. It produces small trumpet-shaped flowers that are

mahogany on the outside and bright golden yellow on the inside. A superb plant to grow.

Hemerocallis 'Golden Chimes'
This has quite open trumpets with reflexed (turned back) petals of clear gold. It is good against a background of green foliage.

Hemerocallis 'Lark Song'
The flowers of this cultivar are a delightfully clear yellow with distinctive green throats.

Hemerocallis 'Red Rum'
This produces yellow-throated flowers of a lovely flame-red. They are quite startling.

Hemerocallis 'Stafford'
The flowers are deep red, almost mahogany, with yellow in the throat and up the centre of petals.

Hemerocallis 'Stella de Oro'
Here the broad petals that make the flower are more circular. They are a good golden-yellow colour.

Other plants There are hundreds of other excellent daylilies, including 'Eenie Weenie' (short, yellow), 'Frans Hals' (mahogany red), 'Green Flutter' (yellow and

Helleborus niger

Helleborus × sternii

Hemerocallis 'Lark Song'

Hemerocallis 'Wind Song'

green), 'Marion Vaughn' (clear yellow), 'Prairie Blue Eyes' (lavender blue), 'Wind Song' (creamy yellow) and many more.

HEUCHERA
Coral flower

A genus of 55 species and an increasing number of cultivars. The plants used to be grown for the erect, airy stems of tiny flowers, but they are now often cultivated as foliage plants as more plants with attractive leaves have been bred. The leaves are basal and circular. They are green or purple and often have silver markings. The spikes of flowers are green, white, pink or red and usually appear in early summer. They are perfect at the front of the border. H 60cm (24in) S 45cm (18in).
Cultivation Any reasonable moisture-retentive soil in sun or shade will be suitable. Z4.
Propagation Heucheras should be propagated by division in the autumn or spring.

Heuchera cylindrica

Green leaves with a silverish, mottled effect. The spikes of flowers are cream. It is best grown in the form of one of its cultivars; they include 'Chartreuse' (yellow-green flowers), 'Greenfinch' (green flowers) or 'Hyperion' (pink and green flowers).

Heuchera 'Firefly'

This plant produces wonderful spikes of bright scarlet flowers.

Heuchera 'Helen Dillon'

One of the best, this has silvery-grey leaves with green veins. The spikes of flowers are red.

Heuchera micrantha 'Palace Purple'

This attractive foliage plant has purple leaves with a metallic sheen. The flowers are buff.

Heuchera 'Pewter Moon'

Another good foliage plant. The leaves are purple with silver markings. Pinkish-buff flowers.

Heuchera 'Rachel'

This plant has purple leaves similar to those of 'Palace Purple' but the flowers are pink.

Other plants There are many other cultivars, which are mainly variations on the above themes.

HOSTA
Hosta

A genus of about 40 species and many thousands of cultivars. They are grown mostly for their foliage, but they also have spikes of attractive small lily-like flowers in white, blue, or pale purple. The green leaves are generally heart- or spear-shaped. There are many variations: some are heavily pleated or puckered; some have cream or yellow variegations; some are golden and others are blue. This gives the gardener tremendous scope when adding foliage to the borders. Hostas will grow in full sun or partial shade so long as the soil is moist. They will often make dense drifts. The foliage usually reaches about 30–45cm (12–18in) with the flower spike reaching twice that height. S 1m (3ft).
Cultivation Plant hostas in an organic-rich soil which retains moisture well. They can be placed

Hosta 'Frances Williams'

either in sun or partial shade. They are very susceptible to slugs, so will need protection.
Propagation The cultivars are increased by division, which can be hard work if clumps are large.

Hosta 'Big Daddy'

Large, puckered leaves that are a good bluish-green. White flowers.

Hosta crispula

Wavy-edged leaves are green with white variegations round the margins; the flowers are pale blue.

Hosta fortunei

An attractive species with many excellent varieties. The species has pointed, dark green leaves and lavender flowers. The leaves of the variety *albopicta* have pale yellow centres and green margins; in *aureomarginata* they are green with golden-yellow margins; *hyacinthina* has grey-green leaves edged in white and dark blue flowers.

Hosta 'Frances Williams'

An old favourite and still considered one of the best. The leaves are puckered and a bluish-

green with a wide, irregular margin of creamy-white or yellow. The flowers are pale lavender.

Hosta 'Halcyon'

This is a choice plant which has superb leaves of a dusty blue. The flowers are also blue.

Hosta 'Honeybells'

Large, pale green leaves with wavy margins. The fragrant flowers are white, streaked with lavender.

Hosta 'Hydon Sunset'

The leaves are small, opening a fresh yellow-green and then going to a darker green. The flowers are deep purple.

Hosta 'Sum and Substance'

This has very large leaves that are lime green and can be yellow when the plant is sited in full sun. The flowers are very pale lavender.

Other plants The plants listed above make up only a fraction of those available. The only way to see anything approaching the whole range is to find a specialist nursery or its catalogue.

Heuchera micrantha

Hosta crispula

Hosta 'Halcyon'

Hosta 'Hydon Sunset'

Houttuynia cordata 'Chameleon'

HOUTTUYNIA
Houttuynia

The only species in this genus is *H. cordata*. This is widely grown in gardens, but it is more frequently seen in either its variegated or double forms. The species is low growing, and its heart-shaped leaves make good ground cover, especially for shady areas. The flowers are four white bracts (petal-like leaves) with a central flower cone, which show up well against the leaves. H 25cm (10in) S indefinite.

The variety 'Chameleon' has similar flowers but variegated foliage which is green with creamy-yellow margins touched with red. 'Flore Pleno' has green leaves and double flowers. Houttuynias are excellent for woodland areas or under shrubs. They are also very good for growing in bog gardens or around water features.
Cultivation Any reasonable garden soil although it prefers moist conditions. It is best in the shade but will grow in sun. Z5.
Propagation The best way to propagate houttuynias is to divide them in spring.

HUMULUS
Hop

Only one hop is grown in the decorative garden. This is *H. lupulus* 'Aureus', the golden form of the one used for brewing beer. It is a climber that ascends by twining around its host. It dies back to the ground each winter so it has to climb its 5m (16ft) or so from scratch each year, which it normally does by midsummer. The leaves and stems are very rough in texture and can cause burns on the skin if heavily brushed against. The foliage is golden yellow. The female plants

Humulus lupulus 'Aureus'

produce 'hops', which are the green flowers, in early autumn. Hops are good for growing over frameworks or up through trees.
Cultivation Grow in any reasonable garden soil, although the plants will do better in richer conditions. They are best grown in full sun and will need some support: a framework, trees, or strings or wires attached to poles. Z6.
Propagation Divide the plant carefully in spring.

INULA
Inula

A large genus of daisy-like plants. Of the 100 or so species, only a handful are in cultivation, but these provide some stunning plants. They vary from low-growing plants of only 15cm (6in) to towering giants of 2.5m (8ft) or more. The foliage is generally quite coarse but the flowers are more refined. They are golden-yellow or light orange, with slender petals and central golden disc. Most appear from late summer onwards.

Depending on the plants' height, they can be used at any point from the front to the back of a border.
Cultivation Inulas like a rich soil with plenty of well-rotted organic material. They also like a sunny position. Z5.
Propagation The easiest method of increase is to divide in the spring, although the species can also be readily grown from seed sown at the same time of year.

Inula ensifolia

Inula ensifolia

This is a short, clump-forming plant that is perfect for the front of a border. H 45cm (18in) S 30cm (12in). It has a few cultivars, of which 'Goldstar' is the best. 'Compacta' is only 15cm (6in) high.

Inula helenium elecampagne

This is excellent for naturalizing in a wild or meadow garden. H 1.2m (4ft) S 60cm (24in).

Inula hookeri

The best of the bunch, with wonderful buds that open to flowers whose petals look like threads of gold. The flowers are carried singly at the tip of each stem. The plant may be cut back by late frosts but recovers. H 75cm (30in) S 45cm (18in).

Inula magnifica

This is a taller species suitable for growing in the middle to the back of the border. The flowers are carried in heads of up to 15 blooms. H 2m (6ft) S 1m (3ft).

Inula orientalis

A medium-height species for the middle of a border. The flowers are carried singly. H 1m (3ft) S 60cm (24in).

Inula hookeri

Inula magnifica

Inula racemosa

The tallest of the garden varieties reaching up to 2.5m (8ft) in good conditions. It may need support in exposed positions. The flowers are pale yellow and are carried singly up the tall stems, often effectively forming a spike. Best grown at the back of a border or as an impressive clump at the end of a path. S 1.2m (4ft).

Inula royleana

A medium-height plant for the middle of the border. The leaves are large and coarse. The orange flowers are carried singly. H 1m (3ft) S 60cm (24in).

IRIS
Iris

A very large genus of about 300 species, of which many are in cultivation. They are a diverse collection since they vary from dwarf to tall plants. They flower at almost all seasons of the year including winter and they like conditions from dry soil to standing in water. However, the flowers all bear a close resemblance to each other: they have three "standard" petals that stand upright and three "falls" that hang or arch downwards. Standing up in the centre of all these are three small "stigma flaps". Most colours are represented in one cultivar or another. They are wonderful plants for a border; their one disadvantage is that they flower only once in a season. On the

Iris 'George'

other hand, their sword-like leaves make them into an effective foliage plant for the remainder of the time. There are many specialist irises, which are grown under glass by alpine growers.
Cultivation The majority like a well-drained garden soil that is not too rich but not too spare either. They need a sunny position, especially the *germanica* ones which like to have the tops of their rhizomes exposed to the sun. Plant in late summer or autumn. Z3–5.
Propagation For all species the easiest method of increase is to divide them after flowering.

Iris chrysographes
A delicate iris with small dark purple, almost black, flowers with gold markings. It prefers a moist soil. H 45cm (18in) S indefinite.

Iris danfordiae
A small bulbous iris that flowers in late winter. It has yellow flowers. H 15cm (6in) S 5cm (2in). There are several other dwarf bulbous species worth growing such as *I. histrioides* (blue) and *I. reticulata* (blue, purple). There are also lots of named varieties such as 'George' (purple), 'Harmony' (blue and

Iris pallida

yellow) and 'Joyce' (blue). They are all about the same height and flower in late winter.

Iris ensata
This species and its more than 100 cultivars like a damp position that never dries out. They can be grown in borders with plenty of moisture-retaining material in the soil. H 1m (3ft) S indefinite. The flowers are variations on purple, although there are white forms such as 'Alba' and 'Moonlight' as well as some blues.

Iris foetidissima
A useful iris for shady places and woodland. The flowers are purple suffused with yellow. They have prominent red seeds in winter. H 30–100cm (1–3ft) S indefinite.

Iris unguicularis

Iris germanica
A portmanteau name that covers an extremely large number of cultivars such as 'Chantilly'. These are the border irises with thick rhizomes. The flowers are generally large and come in many colours. Specialist dealers or their catalogues are the only way to find your way around these plants if you are interested. Most gardeners are content with one or two chosen at random. H 60–120cm (2–4ft) S indefinite.

Iris laevigata
This is similar to *I. ensata* in both its appearance and preferred conditions. There are plenty of cultivars from which to choose, the colours mainly based on purple or white. H 60–120cm (2–4ft) S indefinite.

Iris pallida
A very beautiful species with pale grey-green leaves that set off beautifully the misty blue flowers. It has two variegated cultivars: 'Argentea Variegata' with silver-

Iris 'Purple Sensation'

striped leaves and 'Variegata' with gold stripes. H 70–100cm (2½–3ft) S indefinite.

Iris sibirica
A clump-forming iris with narrow leaves. The flowers are based on the violet-blue of the species. There are many good cultivars from which to chose. H 50–120cm (1½–4ft) S indefinite.

Iris unguicularis
A must in every garden. This is a winter-flowering iris with delicate soft mauve flowers and a lovely scent. It is good for picking but beware: slugs love it. There are several cultivars with flowers of varying degrees of purple. It likes poor soil conditions and a sunny spot. H 20cm (8in) S indefinite.

Other plants Each of the above species has masses of cultivars and there are also many other species including *II. douglasiana, innominata, japonica, setosa, xiphium* (Spanish irises and Dutch irises such as *I.* 'Purple Sensation').

Iris germanica

Iris sibirica

Iris 'Chantilly'

Knautia macedonica

KNAUTIA
Knautia

A small genus of about 60 species of which only one is in general cultivation. These plants are related to the scabious. They have flowers that look like miniature pincushions, carried on tall airy stems. They tend to have a long flowering period, which makes them useful although the flowers at the end of the year are noticeably smaller than those in midsummer. They are very good plants for the middle of the border, especially if you like the effect of one clump of plants merging with the next since they tend to be a bit floppy.

Cultivation Knautia can be planted in any good garden soil and in a sunny position. Z6.

Propagation These are easy to increase either from basal cuttings in spring or seed sown at the same time of year.

Knautia arvensis
This is not frequently seen, but it is still a delightful plant with lavender-coloured flowers. It is good for the meadow garden. H 1.2m (4ft) S 45cm (18in).

Knautia macedonica
This is the most commonly grown plant in the genus. Its great virtue is the deep crimson flowers, a colour that is not often seen in herbaceous plants. This was the only colour available until recently when pastel-coloured varieties were introduced. These are generally referred to as Melton

Pastels. It is a floppy plant that can be staked, but this must be done at an early stage of growth. H 75cm (30in) S 60cm (24in).

KNIPHOFIA
Red hot poker

A very distinctive genus of flowering plants, of which there are about 70 species and many cultivars. The plants form dense clumps of narrow, sword-like foliage that arches out like a fountain. Erect stems rise out of the foliage, each carrying a dense club-like spike of flowers. Initially most garden forms were flame-red, hence the English name, but variations on red, orange, yellow and green are now being grown.

When in full flower the plants are stunning, but they can look tatty once they start to go over; at this point it is best to remove the flower stems. They vary in height from dwarf forms of about 45cm (18in) to tall ones that reach about 1.5m (5ft). Most flower in summer, and some last into the autumn.

Cultivation Kniphofias need a deep, free-draining soil to which plenty of well-rotted organic material has been added. They prefer a sunny position although they will tolerate a little light shade. Z7.

Propagation The best way of propagation is by division.

Kniphofia 'Alcazar'
This is a flame red poker of medium height. H 75cm (30in) S 45cm (18in).

Kniphofia 'Bees' Sunset'
Soft orange flowers bloom from mid to late summer. H 1m (3ft) S 60cm (24in).

Kniphofia 'Buttercup'
Yellow flowers are produced by this cultivar in early summer. H 75cm (30in) S 60cm (24in).

Kniphofia 'Candlelight'
This is a short form. There is green tip to the flower head, which turns greenish-yellow as the flowers open. H 60cm (24in) S 60cm (24in).

Kniphofia 'Little Maid'
This is a superb small kniphofia with pale yellow flowers that turn cream as they age. H 60cm (24in) S variable.

Kniphofia 'Percy's Pride'
A good kniphofia for the autumn garden. The flowers are yellowish-green. H 1m (3ft) S 50cm (20in). Another good green is 'Green Jade'.

Kniphofia 'Prince Igor'
Perfect for the hot border, the poker of this tall variety is a wonderful rich orange. H 1.5m (5ft) S 60cm (24in).

Kniphofia rooperi
This is a late-flowering species which produces its poker in the autumn, often late autumn. The flower heads are much fatter and rounder than usual. They are a flame-orange that ages to golden

Kniphofia 'Candlelight'

yellow. These plants are taller than most others. H 1.2m (4ft) S 75cm (30in).

Kniphofia 'Royal Standard'
A typical poker with an orange tip and yellow base where it is ageing. H 1.2m (4ft) S 60cm (24in).

Kniphofia 'Sunningdale Yellow'
A good all-yellow kniphofia. H 1m (3ft) S 60cm (24in).

Kniphofia 'Toffee Nose'
An intriguing form with flowers of a toffee colour that fades to an attractive cream further down the flower head. H 45cm (18in) S 30cm (12in).

Kniphofia 'Wrexham Buttercup'
A rich golden-yellow poker that illuminates a border. H 1.2m (4ft) S 60cm (24in).

Kniphofia 'Alcazar'

Kniphofia 'Prince Igor'

Kniphofia 'Toffee Nose'

Lamium maculatum 'Roseum'

Lamium maculatum 'Beacon Silver'

Lathyrus tingitanus

LAMIUM
Dead nettle

The leaves of some species may worry gardeners as they look like those of stinging nettles, but they are harmless. There are about 50 species in all. Most of them are weeds but a few make good garden plants. In some the leaves are marked or mottled in silver while in others it is the cluster of large thyme-like flowers in white, purple or yellow that are the attraction. Most flower early on, from spring to early summer, but those with attractive leaves can double as foliage plants for the rest of the season. Most are spreading, making them good ground cover for the front of the border, where they will weave their way between other plants.
Cultivation Lamium should grow well in any reasonable garden soil so long as it does not dry out completely. They can be grown in either sun or light shade. Z3–4.
Propagation They can easily be divided in spring. If you do not want to disturb the plants, basal cuttings can be also taken at the same time of year.

Lamium galeobdolon
The yellow archangel of the woodlands. A tall species with mid-green leaves that are often splashed with silver and with spikes of yellow flowers. It is attractive but it can become a nuisance so it is best suited to wild plantings; plant one of its cultivars in more regulated areas. H 60cm (24in) S indefinite. 'Hermann's Pride' is a more compact plant. It has dark green leaves with prominent silver markings. 'Silberteppich' ('Silver Carpet') is a popular variety with leaves that are greyish-green but so overladen with silver that the green can hardly be seen. The flowers are yellow. 'Silver Angel' is another well-loved silver variety worth trying.

Lamium maculatum
This is a delightful old-fashioned, cottage-garden plant. It produces spreading carpets of green foliage, usually with white or silver markings. From these arise short spikes of pink flowers. After flowering the plants tend to get a bit straggly; they are best cut back

to regenerate the foliage and induce second flowering. H 20cm (8in) S 1m (3ft).
   There are a number of very good forms. 'Roseum' is an old one with darker, purplish flowers. A white-flowered form is 'Album' but this has been superseded by 'White Nancy' which not only has white flowers but very silver leaves, touched with green around the margins. 'Pink Pewter' is a pink-flowered version of this, while 'Beacon Silver' is similar but with pale pink flowers. 'Aureum' and 'Cannon's Gold' both have pink flowers and golden foliage, the former with silver patches.

Lamium orvala
This is a delightful plant that is not seen as often as it should be. It flowers in spring, when it forms a well-rounded clump of stems. Peering from the large nettle-shaped leaves are smoky purple-pink flowers. The plant dies back once its flowering season finishes. H 60cm (24in) S 30cm (12in).

LATHYRUS
Everlasting pea

Although not as well known as the annuals (see page 299), the perennials in this genus are very pretty. Some are climbers, while others are scramblers and yet others form a bushy plant. They all produce pea-like flowers of differing sizes. Their colours are all generally are based on purple. They can be used in the border or on the edge of shrubby areas.
Cultivation These plants will do best in a soil that has had plenty of organic material added to it.

They prefer a sunny position, but many everlasting peas will grow in light shade. Z5.
Propagation Grow from seed sown in the spring. Those that spread underground can be divided.

Lathyrus grandiflorus
One of the best, this has large rounded flowers in two-tone pink. It scrambles through shrubs. H 1.2m (4ft) S 60cm (24in).

Lathyrus latifolius
This everlasting pea is a bit coarse but it produces a show of pink or white flowers. Let it sprawl or tie it to supports. H 1.5m (5ft) S 2m (6ft).

Lathyrus vernus
A wonderful clump-former, which blooms in early spring. H 45cm (18in) S 30cm (12in).

Other plants Look at *L. aureus* (orange flowers), *L. nervosus* (blue) and *L. tingitanus* (pink).

Some purple perennials

Aster (various)	Lythrum salicaria
Centaurea montana 'Parham'	Lythrum virgatum
Echinacea purpurea	Penstemon 'Burgundy'
Erigeron 'Dunkelste Aller'	Penstemon 'Russian River'
Erodium manescavii	Phlox 'Le Mahdi'
Erysimum 'Bowles' Mauve'	Salvia viridis
Geranium (various)	Senecio pulcher
Liatris spicata	Stachys macrantha
Linaria purpurea	Thalictrum delavayi
Lobelia × gerardii 'Vedrariensis'	Verbena bonariensis

Lamium orvala

Lathyrus vernus

Lavatera thuringiaca

Lavatera cachemiriana

LAVATERA
Mallow

This is a genus of about 25 species, of which a few are perennial. There are also some shrubs that are often thought of as perennials in the border context. What distinguishes this group of plants is the funnel-shaped flowers, which usually come in soft, delicate shades of pink. The most popular species tend to be quite tall. They add bulk to a border and often bring continuity since they flower for a long time.
Cultivation Mallows will grow in any reasonable garden soil so long as it is well drained. They should have a sunny, sheltered position protected from winds. Z6–8.
Propagation Species can be grown from seed sown in spring. Cultivars need to be propagated from cuttings taken in summer.

Lavatera cachemiriana
This is a true perennial. It has tall, upright stems from which grow delicate pink flowers. These are flatter and not so funnel-

shaped as some other varieties. It is not a long-lived plant but it is easy to increase from seed, of which it produces masses. H 1.5–2m (5–6ft) S 1m (3ft).

Lavatera × clementii
A collection of shrubby hybrids that make good background plants or centrepieces in a border. H 2m (6ft) S 2m (6ft). One of the best known of these hybrids is 'Barnsley' which has white flowers, each with a prominent blotch of red in the centre. 'Bredon Springs' is another popular variety. This has purplish-pink flowers with prominent purple veins. 'Kew Rose' is similar with bright pink flowers with purple veining. 'Candy Floss' has very pale pink funnels.

Lavatera maritima
This is a true perennial. It naturally grows near the sea but it can be also used to good effect in inland gardens. It has pink or white flowers with prominent carmine veins. H 1.5m (5ft) S 1.5m (5ft).

Lavatera thuringiaca
This is a shrubby plant which will fill a large space. It produces bright purple-pink flowers. H and S 2m (6ft). In the form 'Ice Cool' the flowers are a wonderful pure white.

LEUCANTHEMUM
Shasta daisy
A genus of 25 species that were once known as *Chrysanthemum* and indeed they resemble those plants. There are only a couple of species that are grown regularly in the garden, both having typical daisy-like flowers with a ring of outer white petals and a central yellow disc. They are not refined plants, and look their best in a cottage-garden setting. Shasta daisies are very tough. In a neglected garden, they will be virtually the last cultivated plants to disappear.
Cultivation These will grow in any reasonable garden soil, but they do best if it has been enriched with well-rotted organic material. They need a sunny position. Z5.
Propagation The easiest method of increase is to divide these plants in the spring.

Leucanthemum × superbum
The shasta daisies are rather coarse plants growing to about 1m (3ft) high, and eventually making a large clump. They need staking at an early stage. The white flowers are large, up to 10cm (4in) or more across and are often rather untidy looking, especially in the doubles. All this makes them sound undesirable but in fact they create a very

Leucanthemum × superbum 'Sonnenschein'

pleasing splash of white in the border and are easy to look after. S 60cm (24in).

There are a number of cultivars including several doubles: 'Horace Read', 'Esther Read', 'Fiona Coghill', 'Cobham Gold', 'T. E. Killin' and 'Wirral Supreme'. 'Aglaia' is an excellent semi-double. There are also plenty of very good singles including 'Phyllis Smith', 'Silberprinzes-schen', 'Alaska', 'Mount Everest' and many more. The flowers all have subtle differences. The cultivar 'Sonnenschein' has primrose-yellow flowers, and is worth growing.

Leucanthemum vulgare
This is the ox-eye daisy or marguerite of the roadside and meadow. It is a much more delicate plant than the above, with flowers that are usually about 5cm (2in) across. It is not particularly brilliant in the border but it is a must for a wild or meadow garden. H 45cm (18in) S 60cm (24in).

Lavatera × clementii 'Barnsley'

Leucanthemum maxicum

Liatris spicata

LIATRIS
Gayfeather

A genus of 35 species of which only a few are in cultivation. The difference between the various species in cultivation is botanical rather than visual and so there is little difference between them from a gardener's point of view. Liatrises are readily available from nurseries but they are not as widely grown as perhaps they ought to be. Their beauty is in the dense spikes of purple flowers that rise above a mass of narrow leaves: they look a bit like bottle brushes. A clump of these plants is always most colourful and makes a welcome addition to any border, so it is worth tracking them down.

Cultivation A moisture-retentive soil is needed for these plants, so make sure that there is plenty of well-rotted organic material in the soil. The soil should also be well-drained. A place in full sun is required. Z3.

Propagation The easiest method of increase is to divide the plants in spring. However, they can also be grown from seed sown at the same time of year.

Liatris aspera
This species has pinkish-purple flowers that are further apart in the spike. It flowers in summer. H 1m (3ft) S 30cm (12in).

Liatris pycnostachya
A tall species. The long-lasting flower heads are long, often over 30cm (12in). They are a reddish-purple and occasionally white. The plant blooms from summer into autumn. H 1.5m (5ft) S 30cm (12in).

Liatris spicata
This can also grow up to 1.5m (5ft) but does not usually reach this height in gardens. The flower spikes are pinkish-purple. This plant flowers from late summer onwards. S 30cm (12in).

There are several garden cultivars. 'Alba', as its name suggests, has white flowers as has the popular 'Floristan Weiss'. 'Floristan Violett' is similar but with violet-purple flowers. 'Kobold' is another popular form, especially in smaller gardens since it is a much more compact plant. It has violet-purple flowers.

LIGULARIA
Ligularia

This is a large genus of 180 species. About 20 are in cultivation, although only a few are generally available. They vary in appearance from plants with large orange, daisy-like flowers to those with tiny flowers held in a

Ligularia dentata 'Desdemona'

large airy spike. Most of the garden forms are tall. Many are rather coarse and are best placed in wild areas of the garden; others are more refined and make good border plants.

Cultivation Ligularia generally like a moist soil, so plenty of well-rotted organic material should be added before planting. They will grow in sun or partial shade. Some are susceptible to slugs. Z3.

Propagation Division in spring is the easiest method of increase, although species can also be grown from seed sown at the same time of year.

Ligularia dentata
One of the shorter species. It has orange daisies from late summer onwards. H 1.2m (4ft) S 60cm (24in). It is grown mainly as one of two cultivars: 'Desdemona', which has deep orange flowers and large, heart-shaped leaves that are purple underneath; and 'Othello' which is similar except that the leaves are also purplish on the top. Both are grown as foliage plants as well as for their attractive flowers.

Ligularia 'Gregynog Gold'
A tall species that bears heads of deep golden flowers, each with a browner centre. H 2m (6ft) S 60cm (24in).

Ligularia × palmatiloba
A medium height species with yellow flowers and lobed leaves. H 1m (3ft) S 75cm (30in).

Ligularia przewalskii
Tall spikes of small yellow flowers rise on black stalks from attractive divided foliage. This makes a good border plant. H and S 1m (3ft).

Ligularia 'The Rocket'
One of the best ligularias, this is similar to the previous one. The flower spikes resemble a rocket with trail of golden sparks. It is excellent for the back of a border since it is very tall. It also looks very impressive when grown as a large clump or drift. H 2m (6ft) S 1m (3ft).

Other plants If you have a large garden, especially with wild areas, then you might consider looking at some of the other species such as: *L. hodgsonii, L. sibirica, L. veitchiana,* and *L. wilsoniana.*

Ligularia 'The Rocket'

Flowers with good heads for drying

Acanthus	Humulus
Achillea	Liatris
Allium	Limonium
Anaphalis	Miscanthus
Catananche	Persicaria
Cortaderia	Rheum
Delphinium	Scabiosa
Eryngium	Solidago
Gypsophila	Stipa

Lilium auratum

Lilium 'Cover Girl'

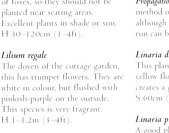

Lilium regale

LILIUM
Lily

Everybody knows the lilies. This is a magnificent genus with more than 100 species and innumerable cultivars. They are bulbous plants. Most reach about 1m (3ft) in height but they are often much taller. They have a spread of up to 30cm (12in). The flowers vary in shape from trumpets, flared funnels and bowls to pendulous turkscaps and bells. There is also a wide range of colours with pure blue being about the only one missing. Many are fragrant. Lilies are excellent plants for the border, with different varieties growing in sun and shade. They can also be grown in containers. They are very good for cutting.
Cultivation A soil enriched with organic material is ideal for lilies, but it must be free-draining. Species vary: most like the sun and a few prefer shade. Slugs can be a nuisance and increasingly the scarlet lily beetles are becoming a real pest. It is important to check daily and kill these pests whenever they are seen or you will lose the plants. Z3–7.

Propagation There are several ways of increasing lilies. For the amateur the easiest method is simply dividing off the new bulbs that form around the old. Seed can be sown from the species. The brown or black bulbils that form on the stem can also be "sown".

Lilium auratum
A species which has wide-open, flared flowers. They are white with a golden centre and usually spots. This plant is the parent of several cultivars and a number of hybrids. H 1m (3ft).

Lilium candidum
This is the Madonna lily. It is a choice plant with pure white trumpets. H 1.5m (5ft).

Lilium lancifolium
Also known as *L. tigrinum*, or the tiger lily, this has orange turkscap flowers with reddish-brown spots. H 1m (3ft).

Lilium longiflorum
Long trumpet flowers in pure white. Prefers light shade. A good cut flower. H 1m (3ft).

Lilium martagon
A delightful turkscap lily for a woodland or shady setting. The flowers dangle airily from the stem and are purple. There are also white forms. H 1.5m (5ft).

Lilium pyrenaicum
A superb turkscap lily with masses of very narrow, bright green leaves and pendant yellow flowers with brown spots. Unfortunately the flowers smell of foxes, so they should not be planted near seating areas. Excellent plants in shade or sun. H 30–120cm (1–4ft).

Lilium regale
The doyen of the cottage garden, this has trumpet flowers. They are white in colour, but flushed with pinkish-purple on the outside. This species is very fragrant. H 1–1.2m (3–4ft).

Lilium speciosum
This large lily has white turkscap flowers with crimson spots. They have a delightful fragrance. The plant requires a shady position. H 1.5m (5ft).

Other plants Most species are in cultivation and there are many elegant cultivars – including 'Chinook', 'Cover Girl' and 'Enchantment'. Go to specialist nurseries to see the full range.

LINARIA
Toadflax

This large genus of more than 100 species has several that are garden-worthy. The attraction is the small antirrhinum-like flowers which are carried in erect spikes. These vary in colour from yellow to purple; some are bicoloured. Linaria are not in the top league of plants but they fill the spaces between other plants with a certain charm. Another advantage is that they are easy to grow.
Cultivation Any reasonable garden soil that is free-draining. They prefer a sunny position. Z7.
Propagation By far the easiest method of increase is from seed, although some of the linarias that run can be divided.

Linaria dalmatica
This plant carries spikes of large yellow flowers in summer. It creates a good drift. H 1m (3ft) S 60cm (24in).

Linaria purpurea
A good plant that self-sows but does not become a nuisance. The stems can rise to 1m (3ft) but are often shorter. They carry spikes of tiny purple flowers over a long period. There is a superb pink form, 'Canon Went' and a

Lilium 'Chinook'

Lilium 'Enchantment'

Lilium pyrenaicum

Lilium lancifolium

Linaria purpurea

white one, 'Springside White', both of which usually come true from seed. S 60cm (24in).

Linaria triornithophora
A slightly ungainly plant with large yellow and purple flowers. Good for the general border. H 1m (3ft) S 60cm (24in).

Linaria vulgaris
This is rather like a smaller and paler version of *L. dalmatica* except that it runs vigorously. It can become invasive in a border but earns its keep in a wild garden. H 75cm (30in) S 10cm (4in).

LINUM
Flax
A very large genus of more than 200 species of which only a few are in general cultivation. Those that are, however, are well worth

Linum narbonense

Linum perenne

their place in the garden. Some are annuals (see page 302). The flowers are usually funnel-shaped, although some are so flared as to be almost flat. They come in yellow, red or blue; the blues being a good intense colour. The flowers often only last a day and the ground is frequently covered in colourful petals where they have dropped. The stems are rather thin but they are wiry and do not usually need support. Linums are excellent border plants.
Cultivation These plants will grow in most garden soils but they are longer lived if the soil is free-draining. A sunny position is essential. Z5.
Propagation The easiest method of increase is from seed sown in spring. Tip cuttings can also be taken from some species.

Linum narbonense
This is one of the two main border flaxes. It is a plant of great beauty: hundreds of blue flowers float on very thin stems in a hazy cloud. It is not long lived so it is worth propagating some spares every other year. H 45cm (18in) S 45cm (18in).

Linum perenne
This is very similar to the previous plant, except that it is even shorter-lived. Although it is a perennial, winter damp often kills it off, so have some spares. H 30cm (12in) S 15cm (6in).

LOBELIA
Lobelia
Most gardeners are familiar with the blue annual lobelia that is seen hanging from baskets and other containers. However, few

realize just how many lobelia there are to choose from: there are 370 species in the genus. Many are tropical. These are very tall and cylindrical, with some resembling the rotating brushes found in car washes. However, there are also a handful of perennials that are a welcome addition to temperate gardens. These include some that produce the reddest of all garden flowers. Most need damp conditions and are happiest near water features.
Cultivation A humus-rich soil that doesn't dry out is required for most perennials. They prefer a sunny position but also grow well in shade. Most are on the tender side and suffer in damp winters so give them some protection in colder, wetter areas. Z2–3.
Propagation Most of the perennial lobelias should be propagated by division in spring.

Lobelia 'Bees' Flame'
A superb plant. It has rich purple foliage and tall spikes of the most brilliant scarlet flowers. A clump of them makes a stunning sight. H 75cm (30in) S 30cm (12in).

Lobelia cardinalis
This is similar to the previous plant, except that it is taller. The foliage is not quite so dark, except in some of the cultivars. H 1m (3ft) S 23cm (9in).

Lobelia 'Cherry Ripe'
Spikes of cherry-red flowers are set off against dark green foliage that is suffused with purple. H 1m (3ft) S 23cm (9in).

Lobelia 'Dark Crusader'
Another deep red-flowered variety with deep purple-red foliage. H 1m (3ft) S 23cm (9in).

Lobelia × gerardii 'Vedrariensis'
A wonderful border plant, this lobelia is upright, with a loose spike of purple flowers. The flowering season is long, and starts in the summer. H 1m (3ft) S 30cm (12in).

Lobelia 'Pink Elephant'
This has sugary pink flowers and green foliage. H 1.5m (5ft) S 30–35cm (12–14in)

Lobelia cardinalis

Lobelia 'Queen Victoria'
One of the best of the red forms, this carries bright scarlet flowers above purple leaves and stems. H 1m (3ft) S 23cm (9in).

Lobelia siphilitica
This plant produces a tall spire of blue flowers. Although it will grow in the sun, it is perfect for a shady position. H 1m (3ft) S 23cm (9in).

Lobelia tupa
This is a more tender (Z8) plant but it is well worth growing in warmer areas. It can be very tall and has a loose spike of red flowers that have an exotic quality about them. The foliage is unlike the other forms in that it is slightly furry. This plant needs a well-drained soil and a warm position. H 2m (6ft) S 1m (3ft).

Lobelia 'Cherry Ripe'

Lupinus polyphyllus

LUPINUS
Lupins

There is something tranquil about a clump of lupins. They are the quintessential plant of herbaceous borders and a vital ingredient in the cottage garden. There are more than 200 species, of which a handful are grown in gardens. The flowers are dense spires of pea-like blooms in either one or two colours. They have a gorgeous peppery fragrance. The leaves are also attractive; they are deeply divided, like fingers on a hand.
Cultivation A deep humus-rich soil is ideal, but it should be well-drained. A sunny position is needed. Modern lupins do not seem to last long and need replacing every two or three years to perform satisfactorily. Watch out for the grey lupin aphid. Z4.

Lupinus Russell hybrids

Propagation The simplest way to propagate is to grow lupins from seed, but for specific cultivars it is best to take cuttings in spring.

Lupinus 'Chandelier'
A delightful bicolour with dark and light yellow flowers. H 1m (3ft) S 60cm (24in).

Lupinus 'The Chatelaine'
This is a bicolour with rose-pink and white flowers. H 1.2m (4ft) S 45cm (18in).

Lupinus 'The Governor'
This is a bicolour with flowers of deep blue and white. H 1m (3ft) S 60cm (24in).

Lupinus 'My Castle'
This is a single-coloured, rose-pink lupin. A very satisfying plant when at its peak. H 1m (3ft) S 60cm (24in).

Lupinus 'The Page'
A single-coloured form whose blooms are a lovely carmine. H 1m (3ft) S 60cm (24in).

Lupinus polyphyllus
The species from which many garden hybrids have been bred. It is interesting to grow but the numerous cultivars derived from it are much better. H 1m (3ft) S 60cm (24in).

Lupinus Russell hybrids
Originally introduced in 1937, these are a wonderful selection of cultivars. Many of those currently available may not be descended from the original stock but they are still very good. H 1.2m (4ft) S 75cm (30in).

Other plants There is a similarity between many cultivars, with the main difference being the colour. So it may simply be a matter of choosing a strain that fits in with your colour scheme, rather than trying to obtain particular plants.

LYCHNIS
Lychnis

A small genus that is related to the garden pinks. There are a dozen or so species available for garden use. They are quite a diverse collection of plants, the

Lychnis × arkwrightii

majority being pink or white with a few being orange or flame-red. All the garden forms make good border plants and are especially good for informal or cottage-garden style borders.
Cultivation Any reasonable garden soil will do. However, the better the soil, the better the plants will do. Most prefer it to be well-drained. Place in full sun or light shade. Z3–4.
Propagation Most come readily from seed sown in the spring, but many of the clump-formers can also be divided in spring. Basal cuttings can be taken at the same time of year.

Lychnis × arkwrightii
A lowish plant with large flat flowers that are a superb bright orange. The foliage is brownish-purple and sets off the orange beautifully. This is a perfect plant for the hot border. It flowers in early to midsummer. H 45cm (18in) S 25cm (10in). There is a good cultivar, 'Vesuvius'.

Lychnis chalcedonica

Lychnis coronaria 'Alba'

Lychnis chalcedonica
Flat heads of flame-red are set off against a brightish green foliage. This plant grows tall but it needs support. An early to midsummer species. H 1m (3ft) S 45cm (18in). There are also a dirty-white form *albiflora* and muddy-pink form 'Rosea'; neither are as stunning as the species.

Lychnis coronaria
A frequently seen lychnis with furry silver stems and foliage, and the most vivid magenta flowers which appear during summer. There is a white form, 'Alba', and a white form with pink centres known as the Oculata Group. H 1m (3ft) S 45cm (18in).

Lychnis flos-cuculi
The ragged robin. It is not a good border plant since the flowers are too slight but it is excellent for damp areas such as bog gardens or areas beside natural streams, especially in meadow gardens. Flowers in early summer. H 45cm (18in) S 20cm (8in).

Lychnis flos-jovis
A small version of *L. coronaria*, except that the flowers are more refined and the plant more

Lychnis flos-jovis

compact. The main flower colour is a rose-pink to red but there are also white forms. H 75cm (30in) S 45cm (18in).

Lychnis × haageana

Another orange-flowered species, this time of moderate height. It flowers in early to midsummer but it is not long lived. H 75cm (30in) S 30cm (12in).

LYSICHITON
Skunk cabbage

Only two species make up this genus, both of which are grown in cultivation. These are not plants for small gardens (unless you like things on a grand scale). They both flower in early spring when there is not much else around. The flowers are relatively modest in size, but as the leaves get bigger the plant increases rapidly until it reaches 1m (3ft); it looks rather like a giant cos lettuce. One would be enough for most gardens, but they spread quite freely and soon create a grove of such monster lettuces. However, they are spectacular plants and if you have the space and the right conditions where they can grow alongside a stream or in a bog garden, then they are certainly worth having.

Cultivation A damp, rich soil, preferably near water. Plant in sun if possible but they will tolerate a little light shade. Z6.

Propagation The easiest method of increase by division of the small side growths. Alternatively sow the fresh seed in a compost that is kept wet, or sow directly into mud.

Lysichiton americanus

The most popular of the two species. This has bright yellow spathes or hoods, enclosing a spike of small yellow flowers on 30cm (12in) stems. The spathe adds another 15–20cm (6–8in) to the height. They have an unpleasant smell. S 75cm (30in).

Lysichiton camtschatcensis

Similar to the previous in shape and size but the spathe is pure white and the flower spike greenish-yellow. A sweetish scent. H 75cm (30in) S 60cm (24in).

Lysichiton americanus

LYSIMACHIA
Loosestrife

This is a large genus of about 150 species, a number of which are in cultivation. It should not be confused with the next genus, *Lythrum*, which is also commonly known as loosestrife. Plants in this genus have yellow or white flowers that are carried in tall spikes. They generally like moist conditions but as long as the borders have plenty of organic material they can be successfully grown there. They look most effective when grown in drifts. Most gently spread, forming large clumps. However, they are not difficult to control if they exceed their allotted space. The flowers consist of a shallow cup of five petals forming a star-shape. The plants vary in height from ground-hugging mats which are suitable for winding between plants at the front of a border to tall, 1.2m (4ft) ones, which are best placed at the middle or back.

Cultivation Lysimachia like a humus-rich soil in full sun or partial shade. Z3–5.

Propagation By far the easiest method of increase is to divide the plants in spring.

Lysimachia ciliata

A tall plant with loose spikes of slightly hanging, lemon-yellow flowers. It flowers in summer. H 2m (6ft) S 60cm (24in). There is an extremely good cultivar called 'Firecracker'. It has

Lysimachia ephemerum

brownish-purple foliage which sets the yellow off wonderfully. It also makes a good foliage plant, especially in spring.

Lysimachia clethroides

This species has curious crooked spikes of small white flowers from midsummer onwards. It is a beautiful plant. H 1.2m (4ft) S 60–100cm (2–3ft).

Lysimachia ephemerum

Tall plants with spikes of small white flowers with pinkish centres in summer. The leaves are bluish-green. H 1m (3ft) S 30cm (12in).

Lysimachia nummularia

This is normally grown in its golden-leaved form 'Aurea'. It is a running, mat-forming plant that

Lysimachia nummularia 'Aurea'

makes excellent ground cover, especially between other plants. The yellow flowers are individual rather than held in spikes, and appear through summer. This is a good foliage plant. H 2.5–5cm (1–2in) S indefinite.

Lysimachia punctata

This plant carries spikes of deep yellow flowers which are carried tightly against the stems and nestle amongst the leaves. It is very attractive but can be aggressive so it should be planted either where it can be controlled or in a wilder area, where it can rampage at will to make a large drift. H 60–75cm (24–30in) S 60cm (24in).

Lysimachia vulgaris

This plant is very similar to the last species but its flowers grow in loose spikes that arise from the axils (joints) of the leaves. It spreads and is best used in the wild garden. H 60-75cm (24–30in) S 60cm (24in).

Lysimachia punctata

Lythrum salicaria 'Feuerkerze'

LYTHRUM
Purple loosestrife

A genus of about 40 species, of which only one or two are deemed garden-worthy. Those that are grown make excellent border plants since they form clumps of bright pink-purple flowers over a long period. The flowers are carried in long spikes and the plants grow up to 1.2m (4ft) high. They can be placed in any border but they are particularly useful for planting in a bog garden, or beside a water feature.

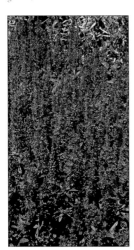

Lythrum salicaria 'Robert'

Cultivation Lythrums need a moisture-retentive soil, so dig in plenty of well-rotted organic material before planting. They like a position in full sun. Z3.
Propagation The simplest way to increase your stock is to divide the clumps in spring. It is also possible to take basal cuttings, also in spring.

Lythrum salicaria

This plant gets its name from its narrow, willow-like leaves. It is one of the main border plants that is grown extensively in its own right but also in the form of a wide number of cultivars. It grows to about 1.2m (4ft) high and has tall spikes of pinkish-purple flowers from midsummer onwards over a long period. S 45cm (18in).

The cultivars are all variations on the same theme, the intensity of the pink or purple being the main varying factor. Good forms include 'Blush', 'Feuerkerze', 'Lady Sackville', 'Morden Pink', 'Robert' and 'Zigeunerblut'.

Lythrum virgatum

This is very similar to the previous species, except that it is not quite so tall and the flower spike is generally shorter. The flowers are purple, with those of some cultivars paler and others darker. H 1m (3ft) S 60cm (24in).

Again there are several cultivars. 'Dropmore Purple', 'Rose Queen', 'Rosy Gem' and 'The Rocket' are all worthy of a place in the border, but one or two of them would be enough for most gardeners.

MACLEAYA
Plume poppy

A small genus of which all three species are in cultivation. These are wonderful plants for the back of a large border. They can rise up to 2.5m (8ft) when given the right conditions, so they are not plants for a small garden. Another problem for the small garden is that macleayas tend to run and can become invasive, so they do need to be given plenty of room. However, there is no doubt that these plants are beautiful enough to earn their place in the large garden, because both their

Macleaya cordata

Macleaya × kewensis

foliage and flowers. The flowers are tiny and petalless. They are carried in airy sprays, creating an off-white or pinkish-coral haze. This is set off by the unusual greyish-green foliage, the colour of which is almost impossible to describe. The leaves are heart-shaped and lobed.
Cultivation Macleayas will grow in any reasonable garden soil, so long as it is well-drained. They require a sunny position. Watch out for slugs, which can be a problem with this plant. Another

M. microcarpa 'Kelway's Coral Plume'

hazard is late frosts, which will cut them back although they will reshoot. Z3.
Propagation These plants can be divided in spring but they take a while to settle down again and do not always take. Alternatively use the thick roots as cutting material in early winter.

Macleaya cordata

A tall species, with whitish flowers that create a dangling haze. The flowers appear from midsummer onwards. This is possibly the least invasive of the macleayas. H 2.5m (8ft) S 60cm (24in). There is a very good cultivar, 'Flamingo', in which the flowers are pinker.

Macleaya × kewensis

This plant is similar to the above except the flowers are cream or buff in colour.

Macleaya microcarpa

A slightly short form but it is also the most invasive. The species is sometimes grown, but it is mainly cultivated as 'Kelway's Coral Plume', probably the most popular of all the plume poppies. It has coral-pink flowers which are carried throughout the summer. H 2–2.5m (6–8ft) S 1–1.2m (3–4ft). A more recent cultivar, 'Spetchly Ruby', has darker coloured flowers.

Malva moschata alba

MALVA
Mallow

This genus contains around 30 plant species, and is closely related to the genus *Lavatera*. This relationship is evident in the similar shape of the flowers, but mallow blooms are nowhere near as brash as those of their near-relations. Although still funnel-shaped, they are flatter and more open. The *Malva* genus also offers gardeners a wider range of colour, which not only includes pink and white but also purple and blue.

The plants are shorter and more herbaceous. They tend to grow between 45cm (18in) and 1.2m (4ft). They make good border plants and some are also perfect for naturalizing in the meadow garden.
Cultivation Mallows will grow in any reasonable garden soil. They prefer a place in full sun. Z3.
Propagation These are not easy plants to divide but they can be increased from basal cuttings in

spring. Alternatively the species can be grown from seed which should be sown in spring.

Malva moschata

This, the musk mallow, is one of the gems of the genus. When happy with its conditions it will grow up to 1m (3ft) but it is often shorter. It produces masses of candy-pink flowers, which always seem to have a freshness about them. The plant continues producing flowers from the early summer right on into the autumn. It can be naturalized in grass. S 60cm (24in). It has an equally delightful form – *alba* – with white flowers.

Malva sylvestris

This is the other main garden species. It can grow a bit taller than the previous, up to 1.2m (4ft), but often flops rather than growing upright. The flowers are a pinkish-purple, usually with deeper coloured veins, and, again, are produced over a very long

Malva sylvestris 'Primley Blue'

season. S 1.2m (4ft). There are several cultivars, the most famous of which is 'Primley Blue' in which the flowers, as the name suggests, are blue, with pronounced darker veins. It tends to be prostrate rather than upright. Another excellent form, this time very upright, is the subspecies *mauritanica*. This has large, dark purple flowers. 'Brave Heart' is very similar.

MALVASTRUM
Malvastrum

There are number of species in this genus but only one of them, *M. lateritium*, is generally in cultivation. This plant is somewhat tender and so it is usually only grown in frost-free areas. It will last longer if the soil drainage is good, and makes an ideal candidate for the gravel or Mediterranean garden.

M. lateritium is a prostrate, sprawling plant that grows as tall as 25cm (10in) and up to 1m (3ft) across. It carries 5cm (2in)

saucer-shaped flowers which are white with a narrow pink ring surrounding the yellow centre. The fresh-green leaves are shaped like those of the maple.
Cultivation This plant needs a well-drained position in full sun. It needs winter protection in colder areas. Z8.
Propagation Increase by taking softwood cuttings in summer. Malvastrum can also be grown from seed sown in spring.

MATTEUCCIA
Matteuccia

This is a small genus of ferns, of which only one species is frequently grown in our gardens. This is *M. struthiopteris*, the ostrich fern. It is so called because its large fronds resemble the tail feathers of the ostrich. Another name is the shuttlecock fern because the whole plant with its ring of fronds looks like a shuttlecock. When it is growing well, the plant reaches up to 1.5m (5ft) in height, with a spread of 75cm (30in). A space in a woodland area is the ideal setting. *M. orientalis* is occasionally also grown. This is similar but it only grows to H 60cm (24in) S 45cm (18in), making it more suitable for smaller gardens.
Cultivation Matteuccias grow well in moist, humus-rich soil in sun or partial shade. Z2.
Propagation The simplest method is division of the small plants that form around the main one. It can also be grown from spore.

Grasses and ferns

Grasses	Pennisetum
Arundo	Phalaris
Briza	Stipa
Calamagrostis	**Ferns**
Cortaderia	Adiantum
Elymus	Asplenium
Hakonechloa	Athyrium
Milium	Dryopteris
Miscanthus	Osmunda
Molinia	Polystichum

Matteuccia struthiopteris

Meconopsis cambrica

Meconopsis grandis

Mentha × piperita f. citrata

MECONOPSIS
Meconopsis

This is a genus of some 45 species of poppy-related plants. This relationship can be seen in the tissue-paper-like petals. Most of the flowers come in one of a range of wonderful blues, while others are yellow. There are also a few reds. Most of the species are in cultivation, but the majority are tricky to grow and are really the province of specialist growers.

With one exception, *M. cambrica*, these plants need a moist, buoyant atmosphere and so are best grown in damp, maritime areas where they do not dry out. They are most difficult in dry, hot areas. They are among the most beautiful of garden plants and look especially good in a woodland setting or planted amongst shrubs.

Cultivation Meconopsis need a deep, rich soil that remains moist and, if possible, a moist atmosphere around them. They like a partially shaded position. A special plot with plenty of well-rotted organic material that is regularly sprayed with water but which does not contain sitting water is necessary in dry, hotter areas. Z5–7.

Propagation They can be grown from seed sown as soon as it is ripe. Some species can be divided.

Meconopsis betonicifolia
The best-known of the blue poppies. It grows to a magnificent height and has large blue flowers,

which appear in early summer. This is a really stunning plant when grown well. Unfortunately it is not long lived and so it is best to propagate it every year from seed to ensure its continuance. There are white forms. H 1.2m (4ft) S 45cm (18in).

Meconopsis cambrica
The Welsh poppy is the easiest meconopsis to grow. It is an attractive plant with yellow or orange flowers. They appear mainly in spring and early summer but continue sporadically throughout the summer. The plant will grow in sun or shade; the brightly coloured flowers look especially effective in a shady area. It needs deadheading regularly since it self-sows. H 45cm (18in) S 30cm (12in).

Other plants The above species are the two most popular plants, although *M. grandis* and *M. × sheldonii*, which are similar in appearance to *M. betonicifolia*, are also widely grown. If you have the right conditions and like meconopsis, there are plenty of other wonderful plants that you can search out.

MENTHA
Mint

The one thing most gardeners know about mint is that it runs. However, there is quite a bit more to them than that. There are about 25 species in the genus and quite a number of these are in

cultivation. Many are for the herb garden and are of no real interest to the perennial gardener, but others are suitable for the border. They are mainly grown for their foliage, which adds flavour and fragrance to cooking, but the scents can also be appreciated in the garden. The flowers are not conspicuous but they attract bees and butterflies, which are a welcome addition to any garden.

Cultivation Any reasonable garden soil will do. Choose a sunny position. Most mints are inclined to be invasive so be careful with your choice of position. Either restrict their root run by planting in a pot or dig round them each year and remove questing roots.

Propagation Mints are very easy plants to increase by division at any time of year.

Mentha × gracilis
The species, ginger mint, is not of interest in the border but the form 'Variegata' is more attractive. This has darkish green foliage with bright gold markings, making it a useful foliage plant. H 45cm (18in) S 60cm (24in).

Mentha longifolia
This is one of the best border mints, although it is still invasive. It has greyish-silver foliage which can be very attractive, and spikes of lilac flowers. H 1.2m (4ft) S indefinite. A good form for border use is the so-called Buddleia Mint Group. There is also a variegated form.

Mentha × piperita f. citrata
A special mint that smells of eau de cologne. H 20cm (15in) S indefinite.

Mentha suaveolens
This plant has quite large, round, hairy leaves. The form 'Variegata' is a good foliage plant: pale green leaves with nicely contrasting creamy blotches. H 30–45cm (12–18in) S 60cm (24in).

MILIUM
Milium

A small genus, of which only the marvellous *M. effusum*, in its golden form 'Aureum', is of interest. Known as Bowles' golden grass, this plant reaches just 30cm (12in), with a spread of 30cm (12in), but it has arching leaves in a lovely shade of yellow. Arising from the spring foliage are stems with delicate flower spikelets, both of which are also yellow. Use it to add a splash of sun to shady areas.

Cultivation Bowles' golden grass will grow in any good garden soil, but it prefers a woodland-type

Mentha longifolia Buddleia Mint Group

Milium effusum 'Aureum'

soil with plenty of leaf mould. It also likes a lightly shaded position. Z5.

Propagation It will grow easily from seed and can also be divided in early spring as new growth gets under way.

MIMULUS
Musk

Mimulus is a large genus of some 150 species, some of which are perennials and are regularly grown in our gardens. They have tubular flowers that flare out at the end. The inner parts of the tubes are usually heavily spotted, sometimes resembling a monkey's face; monkey flower is another common name for the plant. The flowers are yellow, red, pink or orange and often a mixture of these. The plants generally like moist conditions and are ideal for lightening the edges of ponds or streams, or in a bog garden.

Cultivation Grow in a moist, humus-rich soil that never dries out. Some will thrive in shallow water. They like full sun or just a little light shade. Z3–7.

Propagation Most mimulus are easy to divide and cuttings can also be taken.

Mimulus 'Andean Nymph'

A wonderful plant with rose-pink tubes diffused with cream. The inside is lightly spotted red. It has a long flowering season. H 23cm (9in) S 25cm (10in).

Mimulus lewisii

This is a very good border plant that can be grown away from water. It forms a loose clump which is speckled with rose-pink flowers with pale throats over a long period. H 60cm (24in) S 45cm (18in).

Mimulus aurantiacus

Mimulus luteus

A yellow-flowered monkey flower with red spots in the throat. It spreads to make a dense mat and is perfect for the side of streams or ponds. H and S 30cm (12in).

Other plants There a many more attractive species and cultivars. Those in bright reds and oranges, such as 'Wisley Red', 'Fire Dragon' (gold and red), 'Western Hills' and 'Whitecroft Scarlet' as well as the taller *M. cardinalis*, are very good for hot borders, as are the red and orange forms of *M. aurantiacus* and *M. guttatus*.

MISCANTHUS
Miscanthus

This is an important genus of grasses to the gardener. It consists of about 20 species of which a number are in cultivation. They are grown mainly for their size and stunning appearance. Most are tall, up to 3m (10ft) or more when in flower. Then, they make a fountain of narrow leaves and

Miscanthus sinensis 'Gracillimus'

are topped with tall stems carrying elegant silky tufts of flowers. They are excellent plants for creating a focal point, either in a border or by themselves. They look particularly good next to water.

Cultivation These plants are usually happy in any reasonable garden soil, but they need a sunny position. Cut down the old foliage and flower stems in late winter. Z5.

Propagation Miscanthus need to be increased by division in early spring as new growth begins.

Miscanthus floridulus

A giant plant. The arching leaves are light green and rough along the margins. The flowers are white, but are only reliably produced in warmer areas. H 2.5m (8ft) S 1.5m (5ft).

Miscanthus sacchariflorus

This is very similar to the previous species, except that it is taller and produces its white

Miscanthus sinensis 'Variegatus'

flowers more reliably. It can be slightly invasive. H 3m (10ft) S indefinite.

Miscanthus sinensis

This is the species that is usually of most interest to gardeners. *M. sinensis* is widely grown in its own right but there are now more than 100 cultivars all varying by a small degree. H 3m (10ft) S 45cm (18in). Some of the cultivars are much smaller than the species, providing those with small gardens a welcome opportunity to grow these graceful plants. Some of the best cultivars are 'Flamingo', 'Gracillimus', 'Kleine Fontaine' (dwarf), 'Pünktchen', 'Silberfeder', 'Variegatus' and 'Zebrinus' (variegated), but there are many others to check out.

Mimulus guttatus

Miscanthus sinensis 'Flamingo'

Miscanthus sinensis 'Kleine Fontaine'

Miscanthus sinensis 'Zebrinus'

Molinia caerulea

Molina caerulea 'Edith Dudszus'

Monarda 'Cambridge Scarlet'

MOLINIA
Molinia

A tiny genus of two species of which only one, *M. caerulea*, is of interest to gardeners. However, there are also a large number of cultivars so the keen gardener does not go short of choice.

The main species has thick clumps of narrow arching leaves from which arise stiff stems carrying an airy array of upright flowers. They look particularly effective when covered with rain drops or dew. The top of the flower stems reach to about 1.5m (5ft), while the clump of leaves is about 60–75cm (24–30in). This versatile plant looks good in a border or in a lone position, especially by water.

Cultivation Molinia grows in any reasonable garden soil and, like most grasses, it needs a sunny position. Cut to the ground in late winter before the new growth begins. Z4.
Propagation The species can be grown from seed while the cultivars should be increased by division in spring, just before growth begins.

Molinia caerulea
This has been described above. The cultivars vary mainly in height and colour and all belong to one of the two subspecies described below. H 3m (10ft) S 60cm (24in).

Molinia caerulea subsp. arundinacea
This subspecies is generally taller and more airy than the next. The main cultivar is undoubtedly the magnificent 'Karl Foerster'. It can grow to 2.2m (7ft) and has delicate open flower heads. Both these and the leaves turn a wonderful golden-yellow in autumn. S 60cm (24in). Other cultivars that are worth looking at include 'Fontäne', 'Transparent' and 'Windspiel'.

Molinia caerulea subsp. caerulea
There are several cultivars here that are well worth checking out. They include 'Edith Dudszus' (dark flowers), 'Heidebraut' (yellow flowers), 'Moorhexe' (black stems),

'Strahlenquelle' (arching stems) and 'Variegata', which has variegated foliage.

MONARDA
Bergamot

This is a small genus of around 15 species. About half of them are in cultivation, and their number is greatly exceeded by the many cultivars available. One of the first things you notice about monardas is the strong scent that the bruised foliage gives off: it is a real pleasure weeding near them. The next is the curious shape of the flowers. They look like large thyme flowers and are arranged in dense whorls around the stem. The colours of the flowers vary from bright red to softer pinks

Molinia caerulea subsp. arundinacea

Monarda 'Prärienacht'

and purples and they appear in summer. These are perfect border plants and a large clump of them is always eye-catching. Some are quite tall, but the average height is about 1m (3ft), with a spread of 45cm (18in).
Cultivation These plants need a moist, humus-rich soil, otherwise they will dwindle and eventually die and they are also likely to suffer from mildew. They do best in a position in full sun. Z3.
Propagation The easiest method of increase is by division in spring, but basal cuttings can also be taken at the same time of year.

Monarda 'Beauty of Cobham'
This attractive plant has purplish-green foliage that nicely sets off the dense whorls of pale pink flowers held in purple bracts.

Monarda 'Cambridge Scarlet'
This is an old form, but is still one of the best. The flowers are bright scarlet.

Monarda 'Croftway Pink'
Another old cultivar. As its name suggests, it produces pink flowers.

Monarda didyma
One of the main garden species. It is from this that many of the cultivars are derived. The flowers are red or pink held with red-tinged bracts.

Monarda 'Petite Delight'
A lavender-rose form. It is short, reaching only half the height of most, at about 45cm (18in).

Monarda 'Petite Pink Supreme'
This is another short form, this time with red flowers and purple bracts. H 45cm (18in).

Monarda 'Prärienacht'
The flowers of this form are a wonderful clear purple.

Monarda 'Schneewittchen'
A good form with white flowers, which work well in a border with an all-white colour scheme.

Monarda 'Scorpion'
This one has purple flowers. It is a little taller than the others at about 1.2m (4ft).

Monarda 'Scorpion'

Monarda 'Squaw'
Another red-flowered form, but this has the advantage of being a little more mildew-resistant than the previous one.

Other plants There are quite a number of other species and cultivars that are well worth looking out for. Most are in the same colour range as those that have been listed above.

MYRRHIS
Sweet cicely
The only member of the genus is *M. odorata*. It was once widely used as a herb but it is now mainly grown for its decorative quality, although some cooks still use the leaves for flavouring fruit dishes. The delicate fern-like leaves are very finely cut. Above them in early summer are flat heads of tiny white flowers, much in the style of cow parsley, another hedgerow plant. The plant grows to about 60cm (24in) or more in

Myrrhis odorata

favourable conditions, with a similar spread. It looks good growing against a green hedge or against an old wall. Although it can be used to good effect in a border it makes an excellent plant for the wild garden.
Cultivation Any reasonable garden soil will suffice and a place in light shade seems to be best. It will self-sow if the seeds are allowed to be shed. Z4.
Propagation The simplest method of increase is from seed sown in spring. The plant can also be divided but this is not easy.

NEPETA
Catmint
A very large genus of around 250 species of which more than 40 are grown in gardens. However, there are only a few that are of specific interest to the general gardener. Most of these plants produce a haze of tiny, soft blue flowers carried on stiff arching stems; one produces blooms of pale yellow. The leaves are often aromatic.
    Nepetas can be one of the mainstays of a romantic garden, and are at their best at the height of summer. Their pastel flower colours work very well with other soft shades, and can also be used to soften stronger neighbouring colours. Their love for well-drained soils makes the grey-leaved forms good for gravel or Mediterranean gardens. Generally nepetas grow no taller than about 1m (3ft) and they have a spread of 60cm (24in).
Cultivation Any good garden soil will do so long as it is free draining. Nepetas must have a sunny position. Cut them back after their first flush of flowers and then fresh foliage and more flowers will appear. Cats like the smell of some of these plants and will often lie on them crushing them to the ground.
Propagation Nepetas can be increased from basal cuttings in spring or by division at the same time of year.

Nepeta cataria
This is a coarser plant than the others. It has dirty-white flowers and greyish-green foliage. This species is the favourite for cats.

Nepeta clarkei

Nepeta clarkei
A nepeta with stiff upright stems and flowers of pure blue, which are accentuated by a white spot. H 80cm (32in).

Nepeta × faassenii
An excellent clump-forming plant with silvery-grey, aromatic foliage and pale blue flowers. It is a bit floppy but that adds to its hazy charm. H 45cm (18in).

Nepeta govaniana
The odd one out since it has pale yellow flowers carried loosely on stems up to 1m (3ft) high.

Nepeta nervosa
A much lower plant than other border species. It has upright stems containing spikes of blue flowers. It is a good front-of-border plant. H 45cm (18in).

Nepeta racemosa
This is similar (it is one of its parents) to *N. × faassenii* with the same soft blue flowers and ethereal appearance. However, it is a bit shorter. It is a good plant for flopping over the edge of paths. H 45cm (18in). 'Walker's Low' is a good compact variety. 'Snowflake', as its name suggests, has white flowers.

Nepeta govaniana

Nepeta racemosa 'Walker's Low'

Nepeta sibirica
A good plant for the mid-border. It has upright stems carrying pale blue flowers. H 1m (3ft).

Nepeta 'Six Hills Giant'
A cultivar with grey-silver leaves. It is similar to *N. × faassenii*, but the flowers are darker and it is much taller. H 1m (3ft).

Nepeta 'Souvenir d'André Chaudron'
This is similar to *N. sibirica*, but half the size. H 45cm (18in).

Nepeta subsessilis
A tall species with upright stems carrying bright blue flowers from midsummer. H 1m (3ft).

Nepeta 'Six Hills Giant'

Oenothera fruticosa

Oenothera fruticosa subsp. glauca

Oenothera speciosa

Origanum laevigatum

OENOTHERA
Evening primrose

A large genus containing 125 or so species, of which a number are in cultivation. Their main attraction is the flat saucer-like flowers that open mainly towards evening, which makes these plants ideal for commuters who only see their gardens at that time. Their colour is usually yellow although there are some white and pinks. Summer is their flowering time.

The plants vary considerably in their heights: there are prostrate ones whose stems crawl across the ground and tall ones that can reach 1m (3ft) or more. They are often short lived, especially in wetter soils.

Cultivation Evening primroses will grow in most garden soils so long as it is free draining – this is essential. They need a sunny position. Z4.

Propagation The species all come readily from seed but the cultivars generally need to be divided.

Oenothera acaulis

A plant for the front of a border or perhaps for a rock garden since it has quite prostrate stems. These carry flared funnel-shaped flowers that are white, turning to

pink as they age. This plant must have good drainage. H 15cm (6in) S 20cm (8in).

Oenothera caespitosa

Another low-growing species. It has white-cupped flowers that are fragrant. They also turn pink as they age – a feature of many oenotheras. They are short lived. H 12cm (5in) S 20cm (8in).

Oenothera fruticosa

This is the main perennial border species. It is an upright plant reaching up to 1m (3ft), although some of its cultivars are only half this tall. It has spikes of yellow or gold flowers. This plant will take a little light shade. S 45cm (18in).

'Fyrverkeri' is the best-known cultivar. The flowers open from red buds and the leaves are flushed with purple, making a beautiful plant. Another good cultivar is 'Yellow River'. There is a subspecies *glauca* (previously known as *O. tetragona*) which has pale yellow flowers.

Oenothera macrocarpa

This vibrant plant was previously known as *O. missouriensis*. It is a prostrate, species whose sprawling

stems produce flowers that are brilliant yellow. H 30cm (12in) S 40cm (16in).

Oenothera speciosa

This is a delightful species that tends to run among other plants. It is mainly prostrate. The flowers are white or pale pink with darker pink veins. H 30cm (12in) S 30cm (12in).

Oenothera stricta

A wonderful species with tall, gangling stems carrying yellow flowers opening from red buds. H 1.2m (4ft) S 30cm (12in). 'Sulphurea' is a delicate soft yellow. The flowers of both age to coral pink.

ORIGANUM
Marjoram

A genus with several species in cultivation, although many of the smaller ones are really only suitable for the alpine grower. The perennial ones have fragrant foliage and thin stems carrying sprays of purple flowers. They make excellent front-of-border plants but they do tend to spread by self-sowing. They can become a nuisance unless they are dead-headed before the seed is spread.

Cultivation These will grow in any reasonable garden soil. They prefer full sun, but will take a little light shade. Z7.

Propagation The species can be grown from seed sown in spring, and the cultivars are easily divided at the same time of year.

Origanum 'Kent Beauty'

A wonderful plant that will attract much attention. It is low in the ground, but it has flower heads that resemble very attractive hops.

The small pink flowers are tucked inside whorls of deep pink and green bracts. It likes a well-drained soil in a sunny position. Ideal for the front of a border. H 15cm (6in) S 30cm (12in).

Origanum laevigatum

Probably the main origanum for the perennial border. The flowers appear in sprays on the top of wiry stems. The flowers are pinkish-purple and have dark purple bracts around them, which make them appear to be in flower for a longer period than they really are. H 60cm (24in) S 20cm (8in). There are several good forms, of which 'Herrenhausen' is possibly the best.

Origanum vulgare

This is the wild marjoram. It is similar in many respects to the last, with sprays of pink flowers reaching up to 60cm (24in) in height but often less. It has several cultivars of which 'Aureum' is possibly the best. This has golden leaves and they remain golden for most of the season, making it a valuable foliage plant. This plant self-sows prodigiously so be sure to remove flower heads before it seeds. S 45cm (18in).

Oenothera fruticosa 'Yellow River'

Oenothera macrocarpa

Origanum vulgare 'Aureum'

Osmunda regalis

OSMUNDA
Royal fern

This is a genus of about 12 fern species of which only one, *O. regalis*, is in general cultivation. This splendid fern grows as high as 2m (6ft) when well suited but is often much shorter. The fronds are not as delicately cut as many garden ferns but still have a good shape and their vivid green sets off the central cluster of smaller flowering stems, which are covered with rusty brown spores. This fern likes a permanently damp position: a bog garden or a spot beside a stream or pond. S 1m (3ft).

   O. cinnamomea and *O. claytoniana* are also worth checking out if you can find them.

Cultivation These need a damp position that does not dry out. The soil should contain plenty of humus. They grow in shade but will also grow in full sun if the situation is moist enough. Z2.

Propagation The easiest way to increase your stock of royal ferns is to divide the plants in the spring, just before the new growth begins. They can also be grown from spore.

OSTEOSPERMUM
Osteospermum

This is a delightful genus of roughly 70 species of which a number of the more hardy are in cultivation. Osteospermums are colourful daisies that always make a splash in the border. Colours of the outer petals include white, yellow and shades of pink through to purple, while the centres are yellow, purple or brown. They are wonderful plants for the front of a border or even for containers. Their only disadvantage is that they often shut up in dull weather and during the evening. Some are marginally tender so take cuttings each year to safeguard your stock.

Cultivation Any good garden soil as long as it is well drained. A sunny position is vital. Z8.

Propagation Take cuttings in spring or early summer.

Osteospermum 'Buttermilk'

As you would imagine from the name, the outer petals are very pale yellow, darkening towards the ends. The central disc is bluish-purple. This is a very good plant that flowers over a very long period. H 60cm (24in) S 30cm (12in).

Osteospermum 'Cannington Roy'

This is another gem. The outer petals are white with purple tips to them. As they age they become flushed with pink. The central disc is purple. This is shorter than the previous plant with a height of 25cm (10in). S 45cm (18in). There are several other Cannington hybrids covering the full range of colours.

Osteospermum jucundum

A very good plant with masses of flowers that have pinkish-purple petals and blue central discs. It is a late flowerer, producing blooms from late summer onwards. H 45cm (18in) S 30cm (12in). It has a number of cultivars. One of the best is the excellent 'Blackthorn Seedling', which has darker flowers in a rich purple.

Osteospermum 'Lady Leitrim'

This plant has white petals that fade to pink as they age. The central disc is blue. H 45cm (18in) S variable.

Osteospermum 'Nairobi Purple'

This is one of the lower-growing osteospermums. It carries flowers that have dark purple petals and a black central disc. It flowers over a long period from early summer onwards. H 25cm (10in) S 30–45cm (12–18in).

Osteospermum 'Whirlygig'

This cultivar is one of the most intriguing members of the genus.

Osteospermum 'Lady Leitrim'

The petals are pure white and the central disc is blue. Its attraction lies in the fact that the petals fold in half-way down their length. This makes the ends look like paddles, while the whole flower has the appearance of the ripples made in still water after a pebble has been dropped in – a truly wonderful shape. H 60cm (24in) S 30–45cm (12–18in).

Osteospermum 'White Pim'

The identification of this plant has still not settled down: it is still familiar to most gardeners as *O. eklonis prostratum* or to some as *O. caulescens*. This is one of the hardiest plants in the genus and it survives well in most gardens. The petals are white and the central disc varies but is often bluish. Flowers appear over a long season. H 60cm (24in) S variable.

Osteospermum 'Cannington Roy'

Osteospermum 'White Pim'

Paeonia lactiflora 'Bowl of Beauty'

Paeonia lactiflora 'Alice Harding'

Papaver orientale 'Curlilocks'

Papaver orientale 'Khedive'

PAEONIA
Peony

One of the most popular of all perennial species, these beautiful plants suit almost any type of garden, from old-fashioned cottage gardens to modern formal ones. There are only about 30 species of peony, most of which are in cultivation, but hundreds of cultivars have been bred from them. The typical peony has a bowl-shaped flower in varying shades of red, pink or white. There are also some rather fine yellows. As well as single flowers there are also semi-doubles and doubles. While the doubles are beautiful they do have the problem of being top-heavy, especially when filled with rain water, and they often sag miserably to the ground. The foliage of peonies is also very attractive, especially when it first emerges and some have very good autumn colour.
Cultivation Peonies need a deep rich soil, so add plenty of well-rotted organic material. They will grow in either sun or a light shade. They often take a while to settle down after being disturbed so try not to move them once established. Z3–5.

Propagation They can be divided in spring but this is not easy and they will take a while to settle down. Root cuttings taken in early winter is the easiest method.

Paeonia lactiflora
This white-flowered species is grown in its own right, but it is known mainly in the form of one of its hundreds of cultivars. There are far too many to mention but one exceptional one is given separately below and other ones to look out for include 'Adolphe Rousseau' (semi-double deep red flowers), 'Alice Harding' (pale pink double), 'Duchesse de Nemours' (double white), 'Félix Crousse' (double cerise), 'Festiva Maxima' (double white) and 'Monsieur Jules Elie' (double red).

Paeonia lactiflora 'Bowl of Beauty'
Deep rose-red petals and a large central boss of yellow make this a superb peony. H 75cm (30in) S 1m (3ft).

Paeonia mlokosewitschii
This is one of the most beautiful of peonies. It blooms in spring, making it one of the earliest to flower. The single flowers are

lemon-yellow. The foliage has reddish tints when it first appears and again in the autumn. As a bonus the plant also produces colourful seedpods in autumn. A great plant for any garden. H and S 75cm (30in).

Other plants There are so many other good peonies. Take a look at *PP. cambessedesii, mascula, tenuifolia,* and *veitchii,* as well as many of the other cultivars. If you get hooked, seek out a specialist nursery or get its catalogue.

PAPAVER
Poppy

This is another popular genus with many in cultivation, although many of these are annuals or short-lived perennials. The main perennial is *P. orientale,* which is one of the mainstays of the early summer border. The floppy coarse stems rise up to 1m (3ft) in height when supported. The flowers are great bowls of paper tissue in a variety of reds, pinks, oranges and white. They are not attractive once flowering is over, so place in the middle of the border where other plants will cover them or the gap they leave when cut back. S 1m (3ft).

Cultivars that are well worth growing include: 'Allegro' (scarlet with black basal markings on the petals), 'Black and White' (white with deep crimson basal markings), 'Cedric Morris' (pink with black basal markings), 'Curlilocks' (bright orange with frilled petals), 'Effendi' (orange), 'Goliath' (huge flowers, deep red, black basal marks), 'Khedive' (pale pink), 'Mrs Perry' (salmon-pink with black basal marks), 'Patty's Plum' (plum coloured), 'Perry's White' (white), 'Picotée' (white petals with an orange edge to them), 'Prinzessin Victoria Louise' (deep salmon-pink with black basal marks), 'Türkenlouis' (scarlet with black basal marks) and 'Turkish Delight' (soft pink).
Cultivation Choose a deep rich soil that is well drained and give them a sunny position. Give the plants some support in spring when they are about half-grown. Z2.
Propagation These plants can be divided with difficulty in spring but it is much easier to take root cuttings in the early winter.

PENNISETUM
Fountain grass

This is a large genus of grass, which has produced a number of very decorative plants for our gardens. The main characteristic as far as gardeners are concerned is the soft cylindrical flower heads, which look especially delightful when they have dew on them. These are flower heads to run your fingers through, so plant them near paths or at least at the front of a border. Pennisetums form rounded clumps from which the thin flowering stems arch. The flowers are buff or pink. They are not completely hardy so

Paeonia lactiflora 'Adolphe Rousseau'

Paeonia mlokosewitschii

Papaver orientale 'Effendi'

Pennisetum alopecuroides

Pennisetum villosum

Penstemon 'Sour Grapes'

Penstemon 'Russian River'

in colder areas it is important to propagate them regularly. Another problem is that they can look like grass weeds when they first appear in spring so take care not to weed them out.

Cultivation Pennisetums will grow in any reasonable garden soil as long as it is well drained. A sunny position is essential. Cut back the dead growth in early spring before the new growth appears. Protect in cold winters. Z6–8.

Propagation The easiest method of increase is from seed sown in spring. It is also possible to divide these plants just before the new growth starts in spring.

Pennisetum alopecuroides

A tall grass whose flower stems reach up to 1m (6ft) in height and 45cm (18in) in spread if conditions are favourable. The flowers are deep pink-purple and are held in long (20cm/8in) cylindrical spikes. They appear in late summer. This is a very attractive plant and there are also a number of cultivars. 'Hameln' is

interesting as it is a much shorter form (H 60cm/24in) and it flowers earlier. 'Little Bunny' is even smaller at H 40cm (16in).

Pennisetum orientale

This plant is similar to the previous one, but smaller with violet-pink flowers. H 45cm (18in) S 30cm (12in).

Pennisetum villosum

Another very attractive grass. It has arching stems carrying shorter and fatter cylinders of flowers that are a buff colour. H 45cm (18in) S 50cm (20in).

PENSTEMON
Penstemon

An invaluable genus for the garden. It contains more than 250 species. Many are of interest to the specialist grower, but only a few appeal to the perennial gardener. It is the many cultivars that make this such an important group of plants. The flowers are carried in loose spikes from early summer through to the frosts and beyond. They are tubular and often flared. The colour varies from pink to red and purple and also includes white. Most have at least two colours in them. The flowers of the species come in a wide range, including blue and yellow. These are excellent plants for growing singly or as drifts.

Cultivation Any reasonable garden soil will do, but better results will be achieved in a fertile soil. It should also be free draining. Penstemons need full sun. Z4–6.

Propagation The plants are easy to propagate from cuttings taken at any time of year, even winter.

Penstemon 'Alice Hindley'

This has widely flared tubes shaded in soft pinkish-blue and white. H 1m (3ft) S 30cm (12in).

Penstemon 'Andenken an Friedrich Hahn'

One of the hardiest, this produces wine-red flowers over a long period. Also known as 'Garnet'. H 1m (3ft) S 60cm (24in).

Penstemon 'Apple Blossom'

The flowers are large, with pink tips merging into a white throat. H 75cm (30in) S 60cm (24in).

Penstemon 'Burgundy'

This is a tall penstemon, carrying burgundy-red flowers. H 1.5m (5ft) S 60cm (24in).

Penstemon heterophyllus

A smaller-flowered plant with electric-blue flowers that are especially bright in the cultivar 'Heavenly Blue'. A superb plant. H 45cm (18in) S 25cm (10in).

Penstemon 'Hidcote Pink'

This has rose-pink flowers with crimson pencilling in the throat. H 1m (3ft) S 30cm (12in).

Penstemon 'Sour Grapes'

The flowers of this cultivar are tubes of purple. H 60cm (24in) S 60cm (24in).

Other plants Amongst others, look at 'Cherry' (red), 'Chester Scarlet' (scarlet), 'Pennington Gem' (pink), 'Russian River' (deep purple), 'Schoneholzeri' (scarlet) and 'White Bedder' (white), and the species P. hirsutus (white and mauve).

Pennisetum orientale

Penstemon 'Pennington Gem'

Penstemon hirsutus

Persicaria affinis (summer)

PEROVSKIA
Perovskia
This genus of seven species is little known, possibly because only one is in general cultivation. This is the delightful plant *P. atriplicifolia*. Strictly speaking it is classed as a sub-shrub rather than a perennial but it is usually treated as the latter by gardeners. From its shrubby base it throws up tall stems carrying airy spikes with soft violet-blue flowers. The small foliage is a soft grey and so the plant has a misty quality about it. It is perfect for a romantic setting, especially when mixed with other pastel colours. It grows to about 1.2m (4ft) with a spread of 1m (3ft), and the flowers appear from late summer onwards. The foliage is aromatic. There is a shorter cultivar, 'Little Spire', and a couple of other hybrids of which 'Blue Spire' is the most popular. It is essentially the same as *P. atriplicifolia*, except for the deeply divided leaves.

Perovskia 'Blue Spire'

Persicaria affinis (autumn)

Cultivation Any reasonable garden soil will do but it must be well-drained. It is important to plant in full sun. Prune each year's growth back to old wood near the base. Z6.
Propagation The easiest method of increasing perovskias is to take cuttings in summer.

PERSICARIA
Persicaria
This genus was until relatively recently part of what was known as *Polygonum*. About 70 species were moved to this genus, quite a number of which are worthy of cultivation. The flowers of most are small and carried cylindrical spikes, the majority being pink of one shade or another. They are normally held well above the foliage. This is dense, making good ground cover. The plants are useful for creating a mat between other plants, either in a border or in some odd corner where ground cover is needed simply to suppress weeds. The foliage of some species also has the advantage of producing good autumnal colours which in some cases continues well into the winter. These are easy, obliging plants and yet add colour to the borders at most times of the year.
Cultivation Persicarias will grow in any reasonable garden soil and they can thrive in either sun or partial shade. Z3–6.
Propagation The easiest method of propagating persicarias is by division in the spring.

Persicaria affinis
This is a wonderful ground-cover plant. It is low growing: up to 25cm (10in) to the top of the flowers with the mat of foliage reaching half that. The spikes of

Persicaria amplexicaulis

flowers are pink, and age to red then brown. The leaves similarly age to red and brown, and make good winter cover. S 30cm (12in). There are several good cultivars including 'Dimity', 'Donald Lowndes' and 'Superba'.

Persicaria amplexicaulis
A clump-forming plant, which is ideal for the middle or back of a border. It has large leaves, which are topped by a narrow cylinder of flowers on thin stems: these seem to whiz out of the foliage like fireworks. H and S 1.2m (4ft).
    The main colour is red but there are cultivars with other colours such as 'Alba' (white), 'Firetail' (bright red, very thin spikes), 'Inverleith' (dark red) and 'Rosea' (pink).

Persicaria bistorta
Although this will grow in a border if the soil is moist enough, it is primarily a plant of damp places and so it does well in bog

gardens or beside water. The large leaves form a low (30cm/12in) mat above which the flower spikes rise. The flowers are a sugary pink and contrast well with the leaves below. They appear in spring. It makes excellent groundcover, and will spread gently without becoming a nuisance. S indefinite. There is a good form 'Superba', which produces bigger flower spikes.

Persicaria virginiana
Although the species is often grown in its own right, it is mainly found in the form 'Painter's Palette'. The attraction here is the large leaves, which are splashed with green, cream, brown, pink and red. As with the main species, the loose flower spikes are greenish, aging to red. H and S 60cm (24in).

Other plants Cast an eye over *PP. campanulata*, *capitata*, *milletii* and *vaccinifolia* if you can find them.

Persicaria bistorta

Phalaris arundinacea

Phlox divaricata 'Chattahoochee'

Phlox paniculata 'Mother of Pearl'

PHALARIS
Phalaris

This is a genus containing about 15 species of which the majority are far too weedy for the garden. The only one that is generally grown can also be considered a weed since it can become very invasive. It is so beautiful, however, that a special place should usually be found for it. It is *P. arundinacea* var. *picta*, which is known as gardener's garters. The attractive feature of this plant is the leaves which are pale green striped with silvery white and with occasional pink flushes. It does run, so be sure to contain it in some way or plant it where it can romp freely. The greenish flower stalks can reach 1m (3ft) but are often less. S indefinite. There is another form *P.a.* 'Feesey' which has pinkish-purple flushes and is not quite so rampant.
Cultivation Any garden soil will be sufficient for this plant, but it must have a sunny position. Plant

it in a sunken bucket or surround in some other way to prevent it from spreading too far. Cut down old growth before the new starts in spring and trim it over again in early summer. Z4.
Propagation Its invasive habit means that this plant is very easy to propagate by division in spring.

PHLOX
Phlox

There are 67 species of phlox, a number of which are in cultivation. There are three different forms: the tall border phloxes, the low cushions for use on rock gardens and border edges, and an intermediate-height group which are good for woodlands and shady places. They all have the same shaped flowers. These consist of a disc of five petals, which are narrower in some species than others. They are all colourful, some intensely so. They range from soft pinks and mauves to bright reds, taking in purples and whites. The main border species is *P. paniculata* which has a large number of cultivars.
Cultivation The majority of these plants need a rich, moist soil, although it should be well drained. Most grow in full sun or light shade. Z4.
Propagation They can be divided or basal cuttings can be taken in the spring. However, the taller species can suffer from stem eelworm and so it is best to propagate them from root cuttings taken in early winter.

Phlox carolina

This is mainly grown in the excellent form of 'Bill Baker' which has pink flowers in early summer. It makes a very good plant for the edges of woodland gardens, or for areas of light shade with a woodland-type soil. H 45cm (18in) S 30cm (12in).

Phlox divaricata

Another woodlander growing in moist soil. This has pale blue or white flowers on stems growing up to 45cm (18in) high. There are a number of cultivars, the most spectacular of which is 'Chattahoochee' whose lavender flowers have a rose-pink centre. The plant is not long lived and needs regular replacement. H 45cm (18in) S 30cm (12in).

Phlox douglasii

A low mat-forming species with small flowers in spring. It is excellent for the front of the border. H and S 20cm (8in).

There are many colourful cultivars, including 'Crackerjack' (magenta) and 'Red Admiral' (bright crimson).

Phlox paniculata

This is the main border phlox. The elegant flowers are often subtly perfumed, and appear from midsummer onwards. H 1.2m (4ft) S 60cm (24in).

The many cultivars include 'Blue Ice' (pale blue), 'Bright Eyes' (pale pink with red eyes), 'Eventide' (pale blue), 'Fujiyama' (pure white), 'Hampton Court' (lilac-blue), 'Le Mahdi' (violet with darker eyes), 'Mother of Pearl' (pink-tinged white) and 'Norah Leigh' (variegated leaves and pale mauve flowers with dark centres).

Phlox subulata

Like *P. douglasii*, this is low growing and covered with masses of flowers in spring. H 10cm (4in) S 20cm (8in). A good variety is 'Marjorie' (deep pink).

Phlox douglasii

Phlox paniculata 'Hampton Court'

Phlox paniculata 'Norah Leigh'

Phormium tenax 'Variegatum'

PHORMIUM
New Zealand flax

The two species of this genus are important garden plants. They are clump-forming plants on a grand scale, producing a huge fountain of wide sword-like leaves and, occasionally, towering sprays of red or yellow flowers. There is a surprising number of cultivars, mainly with different coloured foliage. The flower stems can reach up to 5m(16ft) in height, and the clump of leaves are up to 2.5m (8ft) tall. These impressive architectural plants make ideal focal points either in a border or freestanding at some other point in the garden. Their size dictates that they are really only suitable for larger gardens, but there are some smaller cultivars that would suit those with less space. They are excellent for seaside gardens.
Cultivation These plants need a well-prepared free-draining soil and a sunny position.
Propagation Although it is a struggle with such a large plant, division is the best method of increase. Fortunately it is possible to break off a small piece without digging up the whole plant.

Phormium cookianum

This is the smaller of the two species with leaves that reach up to 1.5m (5ft) and flower stems that are a little taller. It has yellowish flowers. S 30cm (12in). The form *P.c.* subsp. *hookeri* 'Tricolor' is the most popular cultivar. Its green leaves have red and yellow stripes.

Phormium 'Sundowner'

This is a gem of a plant, which is about the same height as the previous one. It has erect bronze-coloured leaves attractively striped in pink and yellow. H 1.5m (5ft) S 1.2m (4ft).

Phormium tenax

This is the big one. Although some leaves are arching, the majority tend to stand up giving it a good shape. H 3m (10ft) S 1–2m (3–6ft). There are a number of cultivars of which the Purpureum Group, with its purple foliage, is the most popular. 'Variegatum' with cream stripes is also a good cultivar.

PHUOPSIS
Phuopsis

The only species of this genus, *P. stylosa*, is a low-growing spreading plant carrying beautiful balls of pink flowers over a long period in the summer. The spreading stems root as they go so it can be a nuisance in the wrong place. However, it is very attractive placed at the front of a border where it can weave between other plants. It has a slight foxy smell, to which some people object. H and S 30cm (12in).
Cultivation Any reasonable garden soil is suitable. It will grow in full sun or light shade. Cut back after flowering reduce spreading. Z6.
Propagation Phuopsis can easily be propagated by dividing the plants in the spring.

PHYGELIUS
Phygelius

Both species of this genus are in cultivation and there is also a hybrid between them. They are actually shrubs but they are

Phuopsis stylosa

usually considered perennials by gardeners. They are grown for their tall stems carrying loose sprays of pendant tubular flowers. These are red, pink or yellow, and appear over a long period, from early summer to autumn. The plants can get very tall, up to 3m (10ft) or more, but generally they are around 1–1.5m (3–5ft) tall, with a spread of 2m (6ft). They are not startling plants but more than earn their keep in a border.
Cultivation Phygelius need a reasonably rich soil which is free-draining yet moisture-retentive. They need a sunny position. Z8.
Propagation The best method of increase is to take softwood cuttings in early summer.

Phygelius aequalis

This plant has dusky-pink flowers. It has a few cultivars of which 'Yellow Trumpet' is one of the best, with pale yellow flowers.

Phygelius × rectus 'African Queen'

Phygelius capensis

This is a slightly bigger plant than the previous species, and has orange-red flowers.

Phygelius × rectus

This is the hybrid between the two species above. There are a number of interesting forms. 'African Queen' is one of the best known, with its red flowers. 'Moonraker' has pale yellow flowers. 'Pink Elf' is shorter at H 75cm (30in) and has pink flowers with deeper coloured tips. 'Salmon Leap' has salmony-orange flowers and 'Winchester Fanfare' has deep reddish-pink flowers.

PHYSOSTEGIA
Obedient plant

One species of this small genus is grown in the garden. *P. virginiana* is called the obedient plant because

Phygelius aequalis

Phygelius × rectus 'Moonraker'

Physostegia virginiana subsp. speciosa
'Bouquet Rose'

P.v.ssp. 'Variegata'

Platycodon grandiflorus

when the flowers are pushed to one side, they stay in position instead of springing back. The spikes of flowers are tubular and flared at the end, rather like those of antirrhinums. They are either pink or white and appear from midsummer onwards on stems up to 1.2m (4ft) high. The plant has a spread of 60cm (24in).

There are several cultivars. 'Alba', 'Crown of Snow' and 'Summer Snow' are white as their names suggest. *P.v.* subsp. *speciosa* 'Variegata' has whiter margins to the greyish leaves and cerise flowers. Another *speciosa* cultivar is 'Bouquet Rose', which has pale mauve-pink flowers. *P.v.* 'Vivid' has bright purple-pink blooms.
Cultivation Grow in any reasonable garden soil so long as it does not dry out too much; add plenty of well-rotted organic material. They like full sun or light shade. Z4.
Propagation Increase is by division in early spring. The species can be grown from seed.

PLATYCODON
Balloon flower

A genus with *P. grandiflorus* as its only species. The English name refers to the flower which inflates itself like a balloon just before it fully opens. It is closely related to the bell flowers and resembles them when open. The five petals form a shallow dish with the tips bent back. The colour is a wonderful violet-purple. These are not big plants, reaching only 60cm (24in) in height and with a spread of 30–45cm (12–18in) but they make excellent plants for the centre of a bed in late summer when the flowers open. There is a white form 'Alba' as well as pink forms such as 'Perlmutterschale' and 'Fuji Pink'. 'Apoyama' and 'Mariesii' are possibly the best blue forms, the latter being a more compact plant.
Cultivation Any well-drained garden soil will do, but it must be capable of retaining some moisture throughout the summer. Either a sunny or partially shaded position will suffice. Z4.
Propagation Taking basal cuttings in spring is probably the easiest method of increasing your stock.

Platycodons can also be divided but this can be tricky since they do not like to be disturbed.

PODOPHYLLUM
Podophyllum

A small genus of plants of which two or three are in cultivation, although they are not frequently seen. They are woodland plants and are best planted in such areas since they are not really border plants. The foliage has the curious habit of emerging through the ground like a folded umbrella before opening. At least one species hides its flowers beneath these leaves which is intriguing, but does not help its popularity. In spite of this shyness they make good shade plants and they do at least have attractive leaves. The flowers are followed by large, plum-sized coloured fruit. These are plants for those who want to grow something different. They will spread to form a large clump for those who have space.
Cultivation Podophyllums like a deep moist soil, such as a woodland soil with plenty of leafmould or other organic

material. They will grow in sun but are better suited to dappled shade under trees or amongst shrubs. Z3–7.
Propagation These plants spread by underground rhizomes so they can easily be divided. They can also be grown from seed, which should preferably be sown as soon as it is ripe.

Podophyllum hexandrum

This plant used to be known as *P. emodii*, a name which is still more familiar to many people than its new one. It produces solitary white flowers on each stem before the leaves unfold from their furled umbrella. When the leaves do open they are large and mid-green with brownish-purple mottling that makes them rather attractive. The ensuing red fruit are large and plum-shaped. H 45cm (18in) S 30cm (12in). There is a variety *chinense* which has pink flowers and deeper divisions in the leaves.

Podophyllum peltatum

This is the other major podophyllum grown in our gardens. In contrast to the previous one, the leaves open before the flowering. This is a shame since the 5cm (2in) cup-shaped flowers hang down and are obscured by the leaves. They are a rather attractive pale pink or white, and are followed by yellowish-green, or sometimes reddish, fruit. H 30–45cm (12–18in) S 30cm (12in).

Physostegia virginiana 'Summer Snow'

Red-hot perennials

Canna 'Assault'	Lobelia tupa
Canna 'Endeavour'	Lychnis chalcedonica
Crocosmia 'Lucifer'	Mimulus cupreus 'Whitecroft Scarlet'
Dahlia 'Bishop of Llandaff'	
Geum 'Mrs Bradshaw'	Mimulus 'Wisley Red'
Hemerocallis 'Berlin Red'	Papaver orientale 'Glowing Embers'
Hemerocallis 'Little Red Hen'	
Hemoracallis 'Stafford'	Penstemon 'Flame'
Kniphofia 'Prince Igor'	Potentilla 'Gibson's Scarlet'
Leonotis leonurus	Tropaeolum speciosum

Podophyllum hexandrum

Polemonium caeruleum

POLEMONIUM
Jacob's ladder

This genus of about 25 species includes 20 or so that are cultivated, although there are only a handful that are really popular. It is a delightful group; the flowers are generally blue or pink and have a decidedly fresh look about them. The majority are funnel-shaped blooms, with some being flatter than others. They flower in spring or early summer, making them perfect plants for the early border. Their foliage is often composed of leaflets on either side of the stem, resembling a primitive ladder, hence its English name.
Cultivation These will grow in any reasonable garden soil, but they do best in a moisture-retentive one. They will grow in either full sun or partial shade. Z4.
Propagation The species can be easily grown from seed (some will self-sow). Alternatively, they can all be divided in spring.

Polemonium carneum

Polemonium foliosissimum

Polemonium caeruleum

This is the species that best exhibits the Jacob's ladder foliage. It is a tall, upright plant topped with loose clusters of blue flowers. It flowers in early summer. H 1m (3ft) S 60cm (24in). The form *album* has white flowers as does 'Everton White'. 'Brise d'Anjou' has variegated foliage; *P. foliosissimum* is similar.

Polemonium carneum

This is a delightful plant with saucer-shaded flowers of the most delicate pink. It is a loose, clump-forming plant which flowers in early summer. It makes a good front-of-border plant. H 40cm (16in) S 45cm (18in). It has a variety 'Apricot Delight', which produces flowers of that colour.

Polemonium 'Lambrook Mauve'

A loose, clump-forming plant with masses of beautiful mauve flowers from late spring. A superb plant for the front of border. H 30cm (12in) S 30cm (12in).

Polemonium pauciflorum

This is the odd one out since it produces long tubular flowers that are pale yellow flushed with red and appearing in midsummer. It is a tallish plant making it suitable for mid border use. H 45cm (18in) S 15cm (6in).

Polemonium reptans

A low-growing, rather sprawling plant but one that is blessed with fine flowers especially in its numerous cultivars. Those of the species are blue. H 30cm (12in) S 30cm (12in). 'Blue Pearl' is a good blue form, while 'Virginia White' is white. 'Pink Dawn' is, as its name suggests, pink.

Polygonatum × hybridum

POLYGONATUM
Solomon's seal

These are graceful plants with an air of tranquillity about them. There are about 50 species in all but only a few are in general cultivation. They are characterized by arching stems from which dangle creamy-white bells, usually hanging in pairs; the pointed oval leaves are held stiffly above them like wings. Although these can be grown in sun they often do best planted in cool, dappled shade, such as under trees or shrubs. They are plants to look at individually rather than in a crowded border where their effect is lost.
Cultivation If possible, plant in a moisture-retaining, woodland-type soil. They do best in light shade, but full sun is all right if the soil is kept moist. Z4.

Polygonatum hookeri

This is a gem. It is also unusual owing to its bluish-pink flowers. It spreads between other plants. H 10cm (4in) S 30cm (12in).

Polygonatum × hybridum

This is probably the main garden species. It forms large clumps or drifts but is not invasive. The creamy-white flowers hang in fours. They appear in spring. H 1.2m (4ft) S 1m (3ft).

Polygonatum multiflorum

This is the other main garden species. It is similar to the previous except the flowers are possibly whiter and it is shorter growing. H 1m (3ft) S 30cm (12in). There is also a variegated form called 'Striatum'.

Other plants There are a number of other species worth looking at, especially *P. hirtum* with its broader leaves, *P. biflorum*, and the variegated form *P. odoratum* var. *pluriforum* 'Variegatum'. If you are interested in Solomon' seals then there is a closely related but little-known genus *Disporum* that you may want to check out.

POLYSTICHUM
Shield fern

This is a large genus of some 200 evergreen species of fern. About 20 of these are in cultivation although only a couple of these are seen with any frequency. These have a typical fern shape with lance-shaped fronds that arise from a central crown, reminiscent of a shuttlecock, and unrolling as they emerge. The fronds are deeply cut and make attractive plants for a shady position, either under trees or shrubs, or in the

Polygonatum odoratum var. *pluriforum* 'Variegatum'

P. setiferum 'Pulcherrimum Bevis'

shade of a house. Dappled shade is the best place to show them off. They add a cool tranquillity to the scene and make a good contrast to bright golden flowers of, say, *Meconopsis cambrica*.
Cultivation They need a deep woodland-type soil, well supplied with rotted organic material. They should be grown in the shade. Z5.
Propagation Shield ferns can be divided in spring, just before growth starts. Alternatively they can be grown from spore.

Polystichum acrostichoides
This fern has narrow fronds that are up to 60cm (24in) long with a spread of 45cm (18in).

Polystichum aculeatum
A popular polystichum, this is also called the hard shield fern. Its narrow, dark green fronds are up to 60cm (24in) long.

Polystichum munitum
This is rather different from the rest since the fronds are not soft but leathery and somewhat glossy, making them good for reflecting light in dull areas. They are narrow and up to 1m (3ft) long, with leaflets that are not subdivided. S 30cm (12in).

Polystichum setiferum
This is the most popular species and it has 30 or so cultivars, all varying slightly from the species, which has long fronds. These may be up to 1.2m (4ft) in ideal conditions but are more usually

around 1m (3ft). S 45cm (18in). There are various groups of cultivars that are worth considering. These include the Divisilobum Group, the Plumosodivisilobum Group and the Plumosum Group. Other attractive cultivars include 'Dahlem', 'Herrenhaussen' and 'Pulcherrimum Bevis'.

Other plants If you get hooked on ferns it is a good idea to visit specialist nurseries and browse through their catalogues.

POTENTILLA
Cinquefoil
This is a very large genus containing more than 500 species. The majority of garden-worthy plants fall into two camps, the shrubs and the perennials. The latter are of interest here, although it must be said that the shrubs are very useful in mixed borders. They have flat or saucer-shaped flowers with five petals (sometimes they are doubles) in various colours from white through to the most vivid of reds. They tend to be sprawling plants that wend their way pleasingly around and through other plants. They bring splashes of colour to the front and mid border.
Cultivation Cinquefoils will grow in any reasonable garden soil. They prefer a sunny position. Z4.
Propagation The best way of increasing your stock is to divide potentillas in spring.

Potentilla alba
A mat-forming plant with large leaves and loose sprays of white flowers in spring. H 10cm (4in) S 8cm (3in).

Potentilla neumanniana

Potentilla atrosanguinea
The foliage often has silver hairs, especially on the underside. The flowers are red, orange or yellow. They appear over a long period in the summer. H 45cm (18in) S 60cm (24in).

Potentilla 'Gibson's Scarlet'
This is a real show-stopper. It carries flowers of the most brilliant scarlet throughout the summer. H and S 45cm (18in).

Potentilla nepalensis
One of the best, with excellent cultivars. It is loose and sprawling with masses of crimson, orange or pink flowers. H 50cm (20in) S 60cm (24in). Some of the cultivars are bicoloured. Among the best are 'Miss Willmott' (reddish pink flowers with a

darker centre), 'Ron McBeath' (carmine with a darker centre) and 'Roxana' (bright pink with a darker centre).

Potentilla neumanniana
Another mat-former for the front of a border. It has yellow flowers. H 10cm (4in) S 30cm (12in).

Potentilla recta
An erect plant that is good for scrambling through other plants. It has yellow flowers. H 60cm (24in) S 60cm (24in). 'Warrenii' is the best-known form, again with yellow flowers. *P.r.* var. *sulphurea* has beautiful soft yellow flowers.

Potentilla 'William Rollison'
This is a startling semi-double with bright orange suffused with yellow. H and S 45cm (18in).

Potentilla 'Gibson's Scarlet'

Potentilla nepalensis 'Ron McBeath'

Potentilla 'Blazeaway'

Primula bulleyana

Primula japonica

Primula vialii

Pulmonaria saccharata

PRIMULA
Primula

One of the most delightful genera of all garden plants. It is surprisingly large with more than 400 species and innumerable cultivars. Most are in cultivation, but mainly with specialist growers. However there are still a large number that are grown in the general garden. They vary from those that are only a few centimetres high to tall candelabra types up 1m (3ft) tall. Most prefer shade and so they make excellent plants for under trees or shrubs. They are also good for damp positions beside streams or ponds and in bog gardens.
Cultivation All the perennial garden types need a moist soil. They prefer light shade but will grow in sun. Z4–7.
Propagation Most will come easily from seed and many can also be easily divided in spring.

Primula bulleyana
A candelabra primula with tall stems carrying whorls of red flowers that eventually fade to

orange. The flowers are produced in the summer. H 60cm (24in) S 30cm (12in).

Primula denticulata
Known as the drumstick primula. Its stems carry a terminal ball of purple flowers. Spring flowering. H 45cm (18in) S 30cm (12in).

Primula florindae
This is a very tall primula. Its stems carry a terminal cluster of flowers which hang down. They are yellow and appear in summer. H 1m (3ft) S 60cm (24in).

Primula japonica
A candelabra primula which carries whorls of red or white flowers in late spring and early summer. It is very easy to grow. H and S 45cm (18in).

Primula pulverulenta
A tall candelabra primula with stems carrying whorls of purple-red flowers in early summer. H 75cm (30in) S 45cm (18in).

Primula veris
The cowslip is a meadow plant and likes an open position. It is ideal for the wild garden. It flowers in late spring. H and S 15–20cm (6–8in).

Primula vialii
A orchid-like primula with stems carrying a pyramidal cluster of smaller flowers. They are mauve when open but the buds above them are crimson, giving a wonderful two-toned effect. The flowers appear in the summer. H 45cm (18in) S 30cm (12in).

Primula vulgaris
It seems impossible to imagine a garden without primroses growing in it. These ones are low, with stems that carry a single soft yellow flower in the spring. H and S 20cm (8in).

PULMONARIA
Lungwort

A small genus of about 15 species of which a number are in cultivation. These are late-winter and spring-flowering plants. They produce small funnel-shaped blooms in blue, pink, red and white. They are carried in clusters on top of stems which rise up to 30cm (12in) above the ground, with a spread of 30cm (12in). The foliage is rough with bristly hairs and in many cases has silver blotches. If the stems and leaves are cut to the ground after flowering new foliage appears. It remains fresh for the rest of the summer, and the lungwort earns its keep as a foliage plant. They will grow in sun but do best in light shade and are excellent for growing under shrubs.
Cultivation Pulmonaria need a fertile soil that does not dry out too much. As long as the soil is

kept moist they can be grown in full sun, otherwise a position in light shade is best. Z3.
Propagation The plants are easily divided in spring.

Pulmonaria angustifolia
This species produces attractive blue flowers and foliage that is a plain green but which is often edged in brown.

Pulmonaria 'Beth's Pink'
A excellent fresh-looking form with deep pink and blue flowers. There is a light silver spotting on the leaves.

Pulmonaria 'Lewis Palmer'
A fine-looking form with long spotted leaves and pink flowers that age to blue.

Pulmonaria rubra
This has plain, light green leaves that contrast well with the brick-red flowers. There are several good cultivars including 'Bowles' Red' and 'Redstart'. 'David Ward' has coral-red flowers and excellent cream-coloured variegations on the leaves.

Pulmonaria saccharata
Violet or red and blue flowers and spotted leaves. There are several excellent cultivars including 'Frühlingshimmel' (blue flowers) and 'Mrs Moon' (pink/blue).

Pulmonaria 'Sissinghurst White'
This is a very good white-flowered form, which has silver spots on the foliage.

Primula japonica

Primula vulgaris

RANUNCULUS
Buttercup

The buttercup family is a large one, covering 400 species. Many are weeds but there are also a number of excellent border plants as well as many smaller ones grown by alpine specialists. The general conception of buttercups is that they are yellow but there as many, if not more, white-flowered species. One thing that most have in common is the shallow, saucer-shape of the flowers, although there are also a number of button-like double-flowered cultivars. Ranunculus like varied conditions: there are some for the open border, others for the shade of trees and shrubs while still more prefer the moisture of a bog garden. On the whole the garden varieties are not as invasive as the more weedy species.

Cultivation Most buttercups that the perennial gardener will be concerned with require a fertile, reasonably moist soil, with plenty of well-rotted organic material. Plant in a sunny or partially shaded position. Z3–5.

Propagation Many buttercups can be divided. They will also come from seed, preferably sown as soon as it is ripe.

Ranunculus aconitifolius

Possibly the most important buttercup for the perennial gardener. It is a clump-forming plant, producing white flowers in early summer. H 60cm (24in) S 50cm (20in). The best known form is the double-flowered 'Flore Pleno'. It does best in shade.

Ranunculus acris

This is the meadow buttercup. It is not recommended for the normal border but it is excellent

Ranunculus amplexicaulis

in meadow gardens. 'Farrer's Yellow' (pale yellow) and 'Flore Pleno' (double) are sometimes grown in borders. It will grow in sun or shade. H and S 45–60cm (18–24in).

Ranunculus amplexicaulis

A delightful species with white flowers that are flushed with pale pink. It likes a gritty soil and should be planted at the front of a border. It produces its flowers in early summer. H 30cm (12in) S 10cm (4in).

Ranunculus ficaria

The lesser celandine can become invasive but its leaves are only above ground during the spring so it is not a real nuisance. It is very low-growing with shining yellow flowers. H 10cm (4in) S 20cm (8in). There are also forms with orange (*R.f.* var. *aurantiacus*) and near white ('Salmon's White') flowers as well as some with decorative foliage such as 'Brazen Hussy' (deep purple leaves). They are all excellent for growing under shrubs.

Ranunculus gramineus

This is a clump-forming species with large glistening yellow flowers and thin grass-like leaves.

Ranunculus gramineus

It flowers in spring and makes a good border plant. H 30cm (12in) S 8cm (3in).

RODGERSIA
Rodgersia

A small genus of plants with all six species in cultivation. The great thing about these is that they have both attractive foliage and flowers. In good conditions they will grow up to 2m (6ft) and they form quite large clumps (up to 2m/6ft), so they are plants for a larger garden. The foliage is palmate (like fingers on a hand), large, deeply veined and with a slight gloss on it. It is often purple or purple-tinged. The flowers are carried well above the leaves in clusters of white, cream or pink in summer.

Cultivation These plants need a soil that does not dry out, so add plenty of organic material to it. They do best in a lightly shaded position.

Propagation The simplest method of increase is to divide these plants in spring.

Rodgersia aesculifolia

The foliage of this species is palmate, and looks like that of a horse chestnut. The flowers are white or pink.

Rodgersia aesculifolia

Rodgersia pinnata

This is similar to the previous species, with palmate leaves and slightly darker flowers. The form 'Superba' is excellent. It has good purple foliage when it first appears, and bright pink flowers.

Rodgersia podophylla

This is slightly smaller than the previous, reaching about 1.2m (4ft). It has similar palmate foliage, although the leaflets are broader and divided at the tips giving a jagged appearance. It produces clusters of white flowers. Good autumn colour.

Rodgersia sambucifolia

This is the shortest species, at only 1m (3ft). The leaves are more pinnate, with leaflets arranged opposite each other as in an ash. The flowers are white or pink.

Ranunculus acris

Ranunculus ficaria, double form

Rodgersia pinnata

Rodgersia podophylla

ROMNEYA
Tree poppy

The only member of this genus, *R. coulteri*, is widely grown in gardens. It is a somewhat woody perennial, which runs below ground to form large clumps when it is happy with the conditions. It is related to the poppies and has the characteristic paper-tissue flowers. In this case they are glisteringly white with a wonderful golden boss of stamens in the middle. They are large, up to 20cm (8in) across. The flowers are set off well against the grey-green foliage. The plants are a bit untidy and sprawling but the quality of the flowers more than makes up for this. They are suitable for borders where there is space, otherwise they can be grown on their own. They grow up to about 2.5m (8ft) but are often less, especially when they are sprawling. Spread is 1m (3ft). There is a variety *trichocalyx* which in gardening terms is not much different from *coulteri* itself. However, its form 'White Cloud' is more free-flowering and the foliage better.

Cultivation Any reasonable garden soil will do but it must be well drained and in a sunny warm position. Z7.

Propagation Tree poppies can be divided but this is quite difficult. It is much easier to take basal cuttings in spring.

RUDBECKIA
Coneflower

This is a genus of about 20 species, of which a number are annuals (see page 319). There are also a number of perennials, which are well worth growing in your autumn borders. They add a welcome touch of brilliant gold and have the habit of flowering over a long period, often starting in the summer and going on until the frosts arrive.

Coneflowers are daisies and get their name from the cone-like central disc in the flowers. This disc is usually a brown or green colour, while the outer ray petals are yellow or gold, sometimes verging on orange. The flowers measure 8cm (3in) or more across. The majority of these plants grow up to about 1m (3ft) but some that will reach 3m (10ft). S 60cm (24in).

Cultivation Rudbeckias do not like soil that dries out too much, so add plenty of well-rotted organic material. At the same time it should not be waterlogged, so add grit to keep it free-draining. Z3.

Propagation Most can easily be increased by division in spring. Species can be grown from seed sown at the same time of year.

Rudbeckia fulgida var. *deamii*

Commonly known as black-eyed Susan, this is a very popular plant for borders, especially hot-coloured ones. It has orange-yellow flowers that appear from midsummer onwards. H 75cm (30in). Another well-known and popular rudbeckia

Rudbeckia 'Herbstsonne'

is *R.f.* var. *sullivantii* 'Goldsturm'. This grows to about 60cm (24in) and has very large flowers. The third variety that is commonly grown is var. *speciosa*.

Rudbeckia 'Goldquelle'

This is a popular cultivar with double flowers that are a bright lemon-yellow. H 1m (3ft).

Rudbeckia 'Herbstsonne'

This is a plant for the back of the autumn border since it grows to 2m (6ft). It produces flowers of bright gold. They are large, up to 12cm (5in) across. The central cone is green.

Rudbeckia laciniata

This particular species makes an excellent plant for the back of a border. It can grow up to 3m (10ft) in height when it is given the right conditions, although it is usually shorter than this, at about 2–2.5m (6–8ft). The flowers are a paler yellow than the previous species and are very wide, measuring up to 15cm (6in) – often the petals droop under their own weight. Like the other rudbeckias, this plant has a long flowering season – from midsummer right through to the end of autumn.

'Hortensia' is currently the best-known of this species' cultivars. It is a vigorous plant, and one that looks very similar to the species, except that its flowers are doubles.

Rudbeckia occidentalis

The species itself is not often grown but there are two cultivars – known as 'Black Beauty' and 'Green Wizard' – that are becoming increasingly popular with gardeners. Basically, these consist simply of the dark brown central cone, surrounded by green bracts or leaves. The effect is as though somebody has pulled off all of the petals. Although these are undoubtedly rather intriguing-looking flowers, few people could honestly describe them as being beautiful.

Romneya coulteri

R.f. var. *sullivantii* 'Goldsturm'

Rudbeckia fulgida var. *deamii*

SALVIA
Sage

This is a huge genus, of almost 900 species. The gardener is only concerned with about a tenth of these, which is still a lot of plants, especially since some species have plenty of cultivars. Sage grown as a garden plant is characterized by its tubular flowers, with an upper and lower lip. Their colour varies from bright red to bright blue, with lots of shades in-between. The flowers are carried in whorls, in spikes held well above the foliage, which can be aromatic. Generally these plants are grown for their flowers, although there are shrubby species (*S. officinalis*), with variegated foliage. Flowering starts in summer and continues into autumn. Some of the salvias are marginally tender and may need overwinter protection. They all make excellent border plants; some can be used in containers.
Cultivation Salvias like a fairly rich, well-drained soil and prefer a sunny position, although some will take a little light shade. Z5–8.
Propagation Species can be grown from seed sown in spring. Most can be grown from basal cuttings taken in spring and many can also be divided at the same time.

Salvia argentea
This is one perennial definitely grown for its foliage. It produces large woolly leaves that are a

Salvia involucrata 'Bethellii'

Salvia sclarea

wonderful silver. It also produces spikes of pink or white flowers. It is not keen on winter wet. H 1m (3ft) S 45cm (18in).

Salvia buchananii
The large flowers produced by this sage are magenta. H 60cm (24in) S 30cm (12in).

Salvia cacaliifolia
An attractive plant which carries piercing blue flowers. H 1m (3ft) S 30cm (12in).

Salvia fulgens
Bright red flowers held in loose spikes. H 1m (3ft) S 1m (3ft).

Salvia guaranitica
This is a tall plant with deep blue flowers. H 1.5m (5ft) S 30cm (12in). There are several excellent cultivars including 'Blue Enigma' with large fragrant flowers.

Salvia involucrata
A good late-flowering plant for the border. It has purplish-red flowers. The form 'Bethellii' is the best with well-coloured flowers. H 75cm (30in) S 1m (3ft).

Salvia nemorosa
A regular plant in the garden border, with spikes of purple flowers. H 1m (3ft) S 45cm (18in). There are some excellent cultivars, which include 'Amethyst', 'Lubecca', 'Ostfriesland' and 'Pusztaflamme'.

Salvia sclarea
This sage is normally grown in gardens as the variety *turkestanica*. It is tall, with dense spikes of white and pink flowers. It is an excellent plant but needs to be replaced regularly. H 1.2cm (4ft) S 30cm (12in).

Salvia sylvestris
A shrubby plant with purple flower spikes. H and S 45cm (18in). Its many superb cultivars include 'Blauhügel' (blue), 'Mainacht' (deep blue) and 'Rose Queen' (pink).

Other plants There are plenty more salvias for the interested gardener to discover and enjoy.

SANGUISORBA
Burnet

Sanguisorbas tend to be grown as specialist plants. There are about 18 species, most of which are in cultivation, but not often seen. They are mainly tall plants, with thin waving stems that carry the

Sanguisorba obtusa

flowers in terminal bottlebrushes. These vary in colour from white to deep red. They make good plants for the summer border. H 1.5m (5ft) S 45cm (18in).
Cultivation Any reasonable garden soil will do so long as it is not barren. Burnets like sun, but will tolerate a little light shade. Z4.
Propagation The plants will come readily from seed and can also be divided in spring.

Sanguisorba armena
This is grown mainly for its foliage which is a powdery blue-green, much in the mould of *Melianthus*. The flowers are pink. H 1.2m (4ft) S 45cm (18in).

Sanguisorba canadensis
Cylinders of white flowers are held 1.2m (4ft) or more above the ground. S 60cm (24in).

Sanguisorba hakusanensis
A beautiful plant whose terminal spikes of flowers are a deep pink colour with an underlying white. H 75cm (30in) S 60cm (24in).

Sanguisorba menziesii
These tall plants produce tight cylinders of deep red flowers. H 2m (6ft) S 60cm (24in).

Sanguisorba officinalis
Similar to the previous burnet, except that the flower cylinders are shorter, almost rounded. It is best grown in the wild garden. H 1.2m (4ft) S 60cm (24in).

Sanguisorba obtusa
Similar to the previous two species, but shorter at 60cm (24in). S 45cm (18in).

Scabiosa 'Blue Butterfly'

Schizostylis coccinea

Sedum middendorffianum

SCABIOSA
Scabious

A large genus of around 80 species, of which a number are grown in gardens both as annuals (see page 322) and perennials. They are delightful plants that deserve to be grown in all gardens. The flowers look like round pincushions and are carried above the foliage on wiry stems. They are in pastel colours, mainly mauves as well as creams and white, and flower over a long period through the summer.
Cultivation Scabious grow in any reasonable garden soil but they need a sunny position. Z3.
Propagation The simplest way to increase the perennials is to divide or take basal cuttings in spring.

Scabiosa 'Blue Butterfly'

This is a fine cultivar with lavender-blue flowers. H 45cm (18in) S 30cm (12in).

Scabiosa caucasica

A clump-forming plant with plenty of 'pincushions' that come in various shades of pale blue and lavender. The flowers are up to 8cm (3in) across. H and S 60cm (24in). There are also some excellent cultivars including 'Clive Greaves' (lavender) and 'Miss Willmott' (white).

Scabiosa columbaria

This is similar to the above except that the flowers are about half the size. H and S 1m (3ft). It has a smaller form 'Nana' and a variety *ochroleuca* with wonderful creamy yellow flowers.

Scabiosa prolifera

A rarer scabious but one worth considering if you can find it. It has cream flowers which are surrounded by green bracts. H 60cm (24in) S 30cm (12in).

SCHIZOSTYLIS
Kaffir lily

This genus contains just one species, *S. coccinea*, with several good cultivars. It is a bulbous plant, producing narrow, strap-like leaves and tall spikes of cupped, star-like flowers in autumn. The flowers are shades of pink, white or flame-red. They are valuable plants for the autumn border or for odd corners. In the wild it is usually found growing next to water. H 60cm (24in) S 30cm (12in). Its variety *alba* has white flowers. Other plants include: 'Jennifer' (pink blooms); 'Maiden's Blush' (pink); 'Major' (large and red); 'Sunrise' (salmon-pink); 'Viscountess Byng' (the palest of pink); and 'Zeal Salmon' (salmon-pink).

Cultivation They grow in any reasonable garden soil, but prefer one that does not dry out completely. A sunny position is needed. Z6.
Propagation Kaffir lilies are very easy plants to lift and divide in the spring.

SEDUM
Stonecrop

This is a very large genus of some 400 species. A surprising number of these are in cultivation but there are only a handful that are of direct interest to the perennial garden. They vary considerably in size from ground-huggers only a centimetre or so high to border plants of 60cm (24in). They are all characterized by their succulent, fleshy leaves. The flowers are small and star-like and carried in clusters. There is a wide range of colours from yellows and oranges to pinks and reds. For the border types it is mainly the reds that are of interest. Their main flowering period is autumn.
Cultivation Any reasonable garden soil will do for sedums so long as it is well-drained. A place in the sun is to be preferred to get the best out of the plants. Z3.
Propagation The easiest method of increase is to root individual leaves in a cutting compost.

Sedum cauticola

This is a low-growing sedum that needs to be placed at the front of the border. The grey-green leaves set off well the pretty purplish-

Sedum cauticola

pink flowers which deepen in colour as they age. H 10cm (4in) S 20cm (8in).

Sedum 'Herbstfreude'

Better known as 'Autumn Joy', this is an old favourite for the border. It is one of the taller forms, and has flat heads of pink flowers that turn brownish-red as they age. The foliage is green, flushed with icy white. H 60cm (24in) S 30cm (12in).

Sedum middendorffianum

Another plant for the front of the border. It has dense heads of yellow flowers which rise above the glossy green foliage. H 15cm (6in) S indefinite.

Sedum 'Ruby Glow'

A superb front-of-border plant. The ruby flowers really do seem to glow and they are set off well by the purple-flushed foliage. H 25cm (10in) S 25cm (10in).

Sedum spectabile

This is the main border species with several excellent cultivars. It has flat heads of pink flowers. H and S 60cm (24in). Good cultivars include 'Brilliant' (bright pink flowers), 'Carmen' (bluish-pink), 'Iceberg' (white) and 'Septemberglut' (pink).

Scabiosa prolifera

Schizostylis coccinea 'Sunrise'

S.t. maximum 'Atropurpureum'

Sedum telephium

This species has green leaves and pink flowers. It is mainly grown in the gorgeous form *S.t. maximum* 'Atropurpureum', which has dark purple stems and foliage as well as pink flowers. H 60cm (24in) S 30cm (12in).

SIDALCEA
Sidalcea

This is a genus of about 25 species. Although only a couple are grown in general cultivation they are important garden plants. They are related to the mallow and hollyhock and have the same saucer-shaped flowers. They are usually a shade of pink and appear in early and midsummer. The flowers grow on spikes carried on tall stems, up to 1.2m (4ft) when the plant is growing well. The leaves are rounded, and become more deeply lobed further up the stem. These are perfect plants for the middle of the border and the clear pink forms have a wonderful serenity about them. The darker purple-pinks are a bit more difficult to place, but they still make very good plants.
Cultivation Any reasonable garden soil will do for the sidalcea. A sunny position is preferred but it will grow in partial shade. Z5.
Propagation Species can be increased from seed, but cultivars need to divided in spring.

Sidalcea candida

This is a wonderful species, producing lovely white flowers that are often carried in a dense

Sidalcea malviflora

spike. It is not as tall as the following species, *S. malviflora*. H 1m (3ft) S 60cm (24in).

Sidalcea malviflora

This is the main species from which most of the cultivars have been derived. It has pink flowers, which vary in intensity from a pale to a purplish pink. There is also a white variety 'Alba'. The flowers are produced from early to midsummer. H 1.2m (4ft) S 30cm (12in).

These excellent cultivars are often listed directly under *Sidalcea*: 'Croftway Red' (reddish-pink flowers), 'Elsie Heugh' (a wonderful purplish-pink), 'Loveliness' (pale pink), 'Mrs Borrodaile' (another purplish-pink), 'Oberon' (rose-pink), 'Rose Queen' (dark rose-pink), 'Sussex

Beauty' (a really lovely shade of pink) and 'William Smith' (very deep pink).

SILENE
Campion

A very large genus with some 500 species. Almost 50 of these are available to gardeners, though not that many as garden perennials. They are related to the dianthus and many have the same flat-disc-like flowers, each with five petals, sometimes with a notch in the centre of the outer edge. They are good reliable plants rather than startling border features. Some are better in a wild or meadow garden.
Cultivation Any garden soil as long as it is reasonably moisture-retentive. Most will grow in either full sun or light shade. Z5.
Propagation Sow seed in spring or early autumn or take softwood cuttings in spring.

Silene acaulis

This is the moss campion, a low carpeting plant with delightful flowers carried on very thin stems in spring. This is really a plant for the alpine gardener, but they also make such excellent edge-of-border plants for a shady place. The flowers are pink, white or red. There are a number of cultivars worth exploring. H 5cm (2in) S 15cm (6in).

Silene alpestris

This is another rock-garden plant but, again, it is eminently suited to the front of a border so long as it is not swamped by larger plants.

Silene dioica

It produces masses of pure white flowers in the early summer. H 15cm (6in) S 20cm (8in).

Silene dioica

The red campion of hedgerows and open woodland. This is an attractive plant with rose-pink flowers. It can be grown in the border but it is better used in a wild garden, especially under light shrubs or in a damp meadow. H 75cm (30in) S 25cm (10in). The double forms 'Flore Pleno' and 'Rosea Plena' are more suitable for the border.

Silene schafta

Another rock-garden plant that is suitable for the edge of a border. This produces masses of magenta flowers from the late summer onwards, much later than most other silenes. H 25cm (10in) S 10cm (4in). There is a good cultivar 'Shell Pink', which has pale pink flowers.

Silene uniflora

A low-growing, mat-former that is ideally suited to the rock garden, but also does well on the edge of a border. This is the sea campion. It has white flowers and an inflated calyx (sheath round the base of the flower) with intricate veining. H and S 20cm (8in). The double form 'Robin Whitebreast' is especially popular. The excellent variegated form, 'Druett's Variegated', has greyish green leaves splashed with cream.

Sidalcea 'Elsie Heugh'

Sidalcea malviflora 'William Smith'

Sisyrinchium striatum

Smilacina racemosa

Solidago cutleri

Stachys byzantina

SISYRINCHIUM
Sisyrinchium

This is a genus of about 90 species. There is only one, *S. striatum*, which is of general use to the perennial gardener although there are several grown by alpine enthusiasts. These plants are related to the irises and this can be seen in the leaves, which are stiff and sword-like. From these fans of leaves erupt spikes of yellow or blue flowers in summer.
Cultivation Any reasonable garden soil will do but a free-draining one will see the best results. The plants self-sow prodigiously so deadhead after flowering. Z4.
Propagation These are extremely easy to divide in spring and they also come readily from seed sown at the same time of year.

Sisyrinchium 'Biscutella'
A rock-garden plant that can be used in the front of a border so long as it does not get swamped. It has yellow flowers diffused with brown and purple. Also good for gravel beds. H 30cm (12in) S 20cm (8in).

Sisyrinchium 'E.K. Balls'
Similar to the previous plant, except that it is slightly shorter with deep lilac flowers. H 25cm (10in) S 20cm (8in).

Sisyrinchium graminoides
This plant has deep violet-blue flowers with a yellow throat. It is good for the front of borders and gravel beds. H 45cm (18in) S 8cm (3in).

Sisyrinchium striatum
The main border plant. It has dull green foliage and masses of star-like creamy-yellow flowers. They

can be impressive in a drift. H 1m (3ft) S 30cm (12in). 'Aunt May' is a variegated form with soft grey foliage striped with creamy-white. This cultivar is not long lived and it is worth dividing each year to have some plants in reserve.

SMILACINA
Smilacina

A genus of 25 species of which only one is regularly grown in gardens, although others are occasionally seen. The main one is *S. racemosa*. It is related to the Solomon's seal (*Polygonatum*) but although the foliage is similar it is has more upright stems. The creamy-white flowers are carried in dense spikes at the top of each stem, and are set off well by the dark green foliage. This is an excellent plant for a lightly shaded position, but the flowers do not last long and soon go brown. H 1m (3ft) S 45cm (18in). *S. stellata* is the only other relatively common species. The flowers are smaller and it forms large clumps which are best sited in a wild woodland garden.
Cultivation A woodland-type soil with plenty of leaf mould or other organic material. A lightly shaded position is best. Z3.
Propagation This is easy to divide in spring, but can also be grown from seed.

SOLIDAGO
Golden rod

A genus of about 100 species, but most are too weedy for the garden. However, there are a few exceptions, which make excellent border plants. They carry golden-yellow sprays of small aster-like daisies, which appear from the late summer. They work well in mid to rear border positions, and

are especially useful for hot-coloured borders. H 1m (3ft) S 30cm (12in).
Cultivation Any reasonable garden soil, but it should be well-drained. Sun is best although some will take a little light shade. Z4.
Propagation Golden rods are very easy to propagate by division in the spring.

Solidago 'Crown of Rays'
A medium-height solidago with flattened heads of golden flowers. H 60cm (24in) S 25cm (10in).

Solidago cutleri
A shorter front-of-border plant. It reaches 45cm (18in) in good conditions. S 30cm (12in).

Solidago 'Golden Wings'
Another excellent form, this time with flattened sprays of golden flowers. It is a much taller plant. H 2m (6ft) S 1m (3ft).

Solidago 'Goldenmosa'
One of the best. It has upright sprays of golden flowers. H 75cm (30in) S 45cm (18in).

Solidago 'Goldenmosa'

Solidago 'Linner Gold'
An old favourite with conical heads rather than sprays of golden yellow flowers. H 1m (3ft) S 45cm (18in).

Other plants A hybrid between *Solidago* and *Aster* has produced × *Solidaster luteus*. These hybrids have clusters of flowers rather than sprays and are a fresh-looking mixture of gold and pale yellow. They grow to about 1m (3ft) with a spread of 45cm (18in) and are excellent border plants.

STACHYS
Stachys

A very large genus of plants, containing up to 300 species. Most are too weedy for the garden, but there are one or two excellent border plants. They have thyme-like tubular flowers, usually in variations of pink. The foliage in some is more important than the flowers, indeed some gardeners actually remove the flower-stems of *S. byzantina* as they feel it spoils the effect of the attractive silver foliage.
Cultivation Stachys will grow in any reasonable garden soil as long as it is free-draining. Choose a sunny position. Z4.
Propagation These clump-forming plants can easily be divided.

Stachys byzantina
This is the species that most gardeners grow. It has soft furry leaves with a silvery tinge, which gives its English name of lamb's ears. The leaf stems are prostrate and creep gently across the surface of the soil. The flower stalks, which are also furry, are upright and carry tiny pink flowers. These are perfect for the foliage but many gardeners cut them off. The

Stachys byzantina 'Primrose Heron'

Stipa arundinacea

Stipa tenuissima

flower stems reach up to 45cm (18in) with a spread of 60cm (24in). There are several cultivars. 'Big Ears' has extra large leaves. In 'Cotton Boll' the flowers are covered with silvery hairs. 'Primrose Heron' is a variegated form in which the silver is infused with yellow. 'Silver Carpet' is a good non-flowering form with intense silver foliage.

Stachys candida
Another silver-leaved plant. This one forms a more rounded shape and carries white flowers that are spotted with purple. It is short, so it is more suited to the front of the border or raised bed. H 15cm (6in) S 30cm (12in).

Stachys citrina
A second short form, it also has woolly leaves but carries spikes of pale yellow flowers. H 20cm (8in) S 30cm (12in).

Stachys macrantha
This species is an excellent early-summer plant which produces dense spikes of large, bright

purple flowers. It makes a good splash of colour. H 45cm (18in) S 30cm (12in).

Stachys officinalis
This is the wild betony. A midsummer flowerer which has smaller heads than the previous but is nonetheless still very noticeable. The flowers are deep reddish-purple. It can be grown in the border but it does self-sow rather viciously so it is best grown in the wild garden, possibly on a bank where it looks good. H 45–60cm (18–24in) S 30–45cm (12–18in).

STIPA
Stipa
A very large genus of some 300 grasses of which there are two or three that are of interest to the gardener. These are clump-forming plants that are well-behaved and do not spread too far. They are mainly grown for their flower heads rather than the foliage. The heads are carried on stiff, upright stems and form a hazy effect. These are excellent

plants to position where they catch the evening sun: they seem to sparkle and glow if placed with the sun behind them. Some are tall and statuesque and make an excellent feature. Others are humbler and fit well in a border.
Cultivation Stipas can be grown in any free-draining soil, but they should be given a sunny position. Cut back before the new growth begins in spring. Z6.
Propagation To increase, divide these plants in spring as soon as the new growth starts.

Stipa arundinacea
This produces a fountain of flowering heads from midsummer onwards. These are not carried on stiff stems but arch over, often touching the ground. Good for the front of a border, especially next to pathways. H 1m (3ft) S 1.2m (4ft).

Stipa calamagrostis
Arching sprays of flowers appear in summer. Their silvery colour makes them look rather like jets of water being sprayed out from the centre of the plant. Excellent. H 1m (3ft) S 1m (3ft).

Stipa gigantea
This is the one that every one knows. It can grow very tall and has stiff stems carrying open heads of straw-coloured flowers. These move in the slightest breeze and glisten in the sun. Give it sheltered position. H 2.5m (8ft) S 1m (3ft).

Stipa tenuissima
A much shorter grass. This is an erect grass with very fine flowers that create a beautiful hazy effect in the summer. H 60cm (24in) S 60cm (24in).

Stachys macrantha

Stipa calamagrostis

Stipa gigantea

Stokesia laevis 'Blue Star'

STOKESIA
Stokesia

This is a genus of only one species, *S. laevis*. It is not seen that often in general gardens but it is much more common in those of plant enthusiasts. As a result, it has gradually built up a number of cultivars, although the species itself is still well worth growing. It is not a very tall plant, 60cm (24in) at the most and often less as it can be rather sprawling. The foliage is noteworthy, but the flowers are even better. They are carried singly on the end of each stem and are about 10cm (4in) across. They face upwards and look rather like large cornflowers, with the outer florets being purple and the inner ones either darker or paler shade. These are plants for a position towards the front of the border. 'Alba' and 'Silver Moon' have white flowers. 'Blue Danube' is deep blue. 'Blue Star' is a light lilac blue. 'Wyoming' is an old form with good purple flowers.

Cultivation Stokesia prefer a neutral or acid soil which should be fertile and free-draining, especially during the winter. They should be sited in full sun. Z5.

Propagation The plants should be divided in spring, or take root cuttings in early winter.

SYMPHYTUM
Comfrey

This genus consists of about 30 or so species. Most of them are weeds, but in spite of this we still insist on growing them in our garden. They are rampant, but in the right place they can be magnificent. Generally the right place is not the border (unless you can contain the plants) but in a wild garden where they can rampage. They are grown both for their foliage and their flowers. The foliage is coarse and often bristly, but in some cultivars it is pleasantly variegated. The tubular flowers are carried at the ends of the stems in a coil which unfurls further as each flower opens. They are blue, red and white (and often a combination of these), as well as creamy-yellow. They flower mainly in spring or early summer.

Cultivation Any good garden soil will do but they do best in rich, fertile soils that do not dry out too much. They grow in sun or partial shade. They are invasive through underground rhizomes so give them plenty of space. Z3.

Propagation Comfreys can easily be propagated by dividing the plants in spring.

Symphytum asperum
This is a tallish plant with flowers that open pink and age to blue or a mixture of both. Invasive. H 1.2m (4ft) S indefinite.

Symphytum caucasicum
A medium-height plant of about 60cm (24in) with floppy stems. The flowers are a true blue and

Symphytum rubrum

appear over the summer. An invasive plant. H 60cm (24in) S indefinite.

Symphytum 'Goldsmith'
A good variegated form with red, white and blue flowers. H 30cm (12in) S indefinite.

Symphytum 'Hidcote Blue'
An excellent plant with very colourful flowers. These are multicoloured, containing red, white and blue. H 45cm (18in) S indefinite.

Symphytum 'Hidcote Pink'
This is similar to the previous plant, except that the flowers are pink and white. It is also known as *S.* 'Roseum'. H 45cm (18in) S indefinite.

Symphytum ibericum
A plant with cream flowers and a floppy habit. H 45cm (18in) S indefinite. It has several cultivars, including 'Blaueglocken' and 'Wisley Blue' (blue flowers).

Symphytum officinale
A tall plant, which does not have a lot to recommend it to general gardeners. However, its leaves can be used for making excellent compost or liquid fertilizer. The flowers are generally purple but they can also be cream. It is best grown in a wild garden where there is plenty of space. H 1.5m (5ft) S indefinite.

Symphytum rubrum
This is one of the better forms for gardeners. It can be used in the border so long as an eye is kept on its spread. It produces good red flowers. H 60cm (24in) S 1m (3ft).

Symphytum × uplandicum
This hybrid is the tallest of all the comfreys. It has flowers that start off pink and then age to blue and purple. H 2m (6ft) S 60cm (24in).

There are some good variegated forms: 'Variegatum' and 'Axminster Gold'.

Stokesia laevis 'Wyoming'

Symphytum ibericum

Pink perennials

Anemone H hybrida	Malva moschata
Aster	Monarda didyma 'Croftway
Astilbe	Pink'
Dianthus	Papaver orientalis 'Cedric
Diascia vigilis	Morris'
Dicentra	Penstemon 'Hidcote Pink'
Erigeron 'Charity'	Persicaria
Filipendula	Phlox paniculata
Lamium roseum	Sedum spectabile
Lychnis flos-jovis	Sidalcea

TELLIMA
Fringe cups

This is a genus with only one species, namely *T. grandiflora*. This is a good plant for the spring border. Its flowers are pale green at first, making the plant almost inconspicuous, although they age to red. They are carried in loose spikes on tall stems above lobed, rounded leaves. The plant has a fresh quality about it, making it well suited to the spring and early-summer garden scene. It looks good planted in the shade, from where the light green can shine out. Fringe cups are excellent plants for growing under shrubs or trees or in the shade of a house. H and S 1m (3ft).

The redness is brought out in some of the cultivars, such as 'Perky', which is a shorter plant with red flowers. Several have purple or purple-tinged foliage including 'Purpurteppich' and Rubra Group.
Cultivation Fringe cups can be grown in any reasonable garden soil but do best in a moisture-retentive one. If the soil is moist enough they will grow in sun but their preferred position is in a light shade. They self-sow, so either deadhead once flowering has finished or dig up the seedlings. Z4.
Propagation These plants come very easily from seed sown in spring. Larger plants can be divided, also in spring.

Thalictrum aquilegiifolium

THALICTRUM
Meadow rue

Thalictum is a large genus of around 130 species. About 50 or so of these are in cultivation, although not all are of direct interest for the perennial gardener. The fascinating thing about the thalictrum is that the flowers do not have any petals; the fluffiness of the tuft of stamens is what gives them their interest; fortunately this tuft is very prominent. There are a group of very colourful plants, with the flowers varying in colour from lilac and purple to creamy white and yellow, that bring a great deal of delight to our borders. They vary in height from just a few centimetres to 2m (6ft); however, the small ones are of little use in the general border.

Thalictrum flavum subsp. *glaucum*

Cultivation Any decent garden soil with a good humus content. They will grow in sun or in a light shade. Z4–5.
Propagation Sow seed as soon as it is ripe. The plants can be divided in spring, but this can be tricky.

Thalictrum aquilegiifolium
This is a spring-flowerer. The flowers are either creamy-white or purple and appear in wonderful fluffy clusters. The dangling seedpods are also very attractive. H 1m (3ft) S 30cm (12in). 'Thundercloud' is a good cultivar with darker purple flowers.

Thalictrum delavayi
An excellent border plant with a haze of purple flowers in summer. H 1.2m (4ft) S 60cm (24in). The superb 'Hewitt's Double' has no stamens; instead it produces a double purple flower of the sepals (the bud sheath).

Thalictrum flavum subsp. glaucum
A tall plant with powdery blue-green leaves and clusters of bright yellow flowers in summer. H 2m (6ft) S 60cm (24in).

Thalictrum lucidum
Similar to the previous, with greenish yellow flowers but shining green foliage. Up to 1.2m (4ft) tall. S 30cm (12in).

Thalictrum rochebruneanum
An elegant plant with lavender or white flowers in the summer. H 1m (3ft) S variable.

TRADESCANTIA
Tradescantia

A large genus best known for its house plants. However, one group of cultivars, *T. Andersoniana* Group, is widely grown in gardens. Long, pointed leaves arch out of an untidy clump, and three-petalled brightly coloured flowers shine out like jewels from the leaf joints. The plants make good-sized clumps for the front of a border. H 45cm (18in) S 30cm (12in). Good cultivars include 'Iris Prichard' (white and blue), 'Isis' (dark blue), 'J. C. Weguelin' (light blue), 'Karminglut' (magenta), 'Osprey' (white and blue) and 'Purple Dome' (purple).
Cultivation Chose a moisture-retentive soil containing plenty of well-rotted organic material. They thrive in sun or light shade. Z7.
Propagation The simplest method of increase is to divide existing plants in spring.

Tellima grandiflora

Thalictrum lucidum

Tradescantia Andersoniana Group

TRICYRTIS
Toad lily

These are intriguing plants which are more frequently grown by the specialist grower than the general gardener. This is a shame because they are attractive and are not difficult to grow. They are not showy at a distance but close up they are fascinating. The star-shaped flowers are either white or yellow, heavily spotted in purple and with a central column of stamens and stigmas. The flowers appear in late summer or autumn on plants that grow to about 1m (3ft) high and spread 45cm (18in). These plants are shade-lovers and should be grown under shrubs or tree, or in the shade of a house. They need to be grown in a drift to have any impact.
Cultivation A moist, woodland-type soil with plenty of organic material is required. Plant in a shady position. Z4.
Propagation The best method of propagation for toad lilies is by division in spring.

Tricyrtis formosana
White or pink flowers heavily spotted with reddish purple. The plants are fairly high and the dark leaves also have purple spotting. The Stolonifera Group is similar. H 80cm (32in) S 45cm (18in).

Tricyrtis hirta
Another of the main toad lilies. They have white flowers with purple spots. H 80cm (32in)

S 45cm (18in). There are a number of cultivars including 'Alba' with white flowers, 'Albomarginata' which has variegated leaves and 'Miyazaki' which has light spotting on the white flowers and is a taller plant.

Other plants If you get hooked on tricyrtis there are a number of other species and cultivars to look at. *T. macrantha* has deep yellow pendant flowers and *T.* 'White Towers' has pure white flowers.

TRILLIUM
Wake robin

This is a genus containing about 30 species of woodland plant. They are grown mainly by specialist growers. However, they also have a lot to offer the general gardener so long as they are grown in a shady area. The main characteristic is that each stem carries three leaves as well as a flower that consists of three petals. The flower colour varies from white, through pink to red and purple as well as yellow. The plants vary in height from just a few centimetres to 60cm (24in). They flower in spring.
Cultivation Grow in a woodland-type soil with plenty of humus that does not dry out. These plants need a shady position under shrubs or trees. Z4.
Propagation Division is a method of increase but they are often slow to re-establish. Seed can be sown when still fresh.

Trillium grandiflorum

Trillium cuneatum
A tall plant, with tall mottled leaves and upright petals in a glossy deep maroon. H 60cm (24in) S 30cm (12in).

Trillium grandiflorum
These are one of the most beautiful of the trilliums. The flowers are upward-facing and have wide glistening white petals. The plant spreads slowly to form a clump. H and S 30cm (12in).

There is a beautiful double form 'Flore Pleno' and a rare pink form 'Roseum'.

Other plants Gardeners can become fanatical about trillium. If you like them it is worth finding specialist nurseries and seeking out the more unusual ones.

Trollius europaeus

TROLLIUS
Globeflower

A small genus of about 24 plants of which a couple are suitable for the perennial border. They are closely related to the buttercups as shown by the globe-like yellow flowers. Globeflowers flower in late spring and early summer. H 1m (3ft) S 45cm (18in).
Cultivation Globeflowers need a deep, humus-rich soil that retains plenty of moisture. They prefer sun but tolerate light shade. Z4
Propagation Existing plants can be divided in spring, or seed can be sown as soon as it is ripe.

Trollius × cultorum
This is a collection of hybrids with 'Alabaster' being one of the best. Its flowers are a very delicate

Tricyrtis formosana

Trillium cuneatum

Trillium grandiflorum 'Roseum'

Veratrum nigrum

Verbena bonariensis

shade of pale yellow. 'Feuertroll' and 'Orange Princess' have orange-yellow flowers. H 60cm (24in) S 30cm (12in).

Trollius europaeus
This is a little shorter than the previous plant and produces golden flowers. 'Canary Bird' is a pale yellow form. H 60cm (24in) S 45cm (18in).

VERATRUM
Veratrum

A specialist genus of 45 species which should be grown by more general gardeners. The plants take several years to reach flowering size, but during that time the pleated leaves provide great interest. Once flowering size is reached, a large stem up to 2m (6ft) rises up and its side branches are festooned with masses of star-like flowers in white or brownish-red. It is a truly remarkable sight, especially if seen against the sun. These are mainly plants for a woodland or shade garden.
Cultivation A deep, humus-rich soil is required and either a shady position, or a sunny one that does not dry out. Z6.
Propagation The quickest method is to divide in spring, but these plants can also be grown from seed sown when fresh.

Veratrum album
This veratrum produces white or greenish-white flowers in summer. H 2m (6ft) S 60cm (24in).

Veratrum nigrum
The choicest species, which has mahogany-red flowers in summer and superb pleated foliage. H 1.2m (4ft) S 60cm (24in).

Veratrum viride
This plant has plainer foliage than the above but it is still impressive. It grows to 2m (6ft) and has greenish flowers. S 60cm (24in).

VERBASCUM
Mullein

This is a glorious genus of about 45 species of annual (see page 329) and perennial plants without which many gardens would be impoverished. The attractive thing about them is the tall spikes, which are densely covered with flowers. Sometimes these spikes rise up 2.5m (8ft)

Verbascum nigrum

or more. The colours of the flowers are basically yellow, but there are also white, pink and purple cultivars. These plants add structure and shape to a border. Even the shorter ones are eye-catching when planted in drifts. They flower throughout the summer and into autumn.
Cultivation Any reasonable garden soil will do but it should be free-draining. A sunny position is best. Deadhead unless you want them to self-sow. Z5.
Propagation Mulleins all come easily from seed sown in spring. Root cuttings can be taken in early winter.

Verbascum chaixii
A plant producing several main stems. The flowers are yellow with red centres. H 1m (3ft) S 60cm (24in). There is a white form 'Album'.

Verbascum 'Cotswold Queen'
Spikes of yellow flowers with purple centres. The spikes are not so densely packed as those of the previous species. H 1.2m (4ft) S 30–60cm (12–24in).

Verbascum 'Gainsborough'
Similar to the previous plant but with softer yellow flowers. H 60–120cm (2–4ft) S 30–60cm (12–24in).

Verbascum 'Letitia'
This is a shrubby plant with lots of woolly, wiry stems carrying bright yellow flowers. H and S 30cm (12in).

Verbascum nigrum
Similar to *V. chaixii* with yellow and white forms. H 60cm (24in) S 60–120cm (2–4ft).

Verbascum olympicum
Although a perennial this dies after eventually flowering in its third year. It is an excellent foliage plant with glistening silver-white stems and leaves. The flowers are yellow. H 2m (6ft) S 1m (3ft).

VERBENA
Verbena

A very large genus of tender perennials (see page 329) and perennials. Although there are

only a few of the latter, it is still an important genus for the general gardener, with at least three excellent species to choose from. All the plants listed below have very long flowering seasons, which mainly start in midsummer and last well into the autumn. They all make very good border plants, needing little attention.
Cultivation Verbenas will grow in any good garden soil as long as it is free-draining. A sunny position is preferred. Z8.
Propagation They all come readily from seed and *V. corymbosa* can easily be divided.

Verbena bonariensis
This is superb plant with tall wiry stems carrying small clusters of purple flowers. Although tall, this is a "see-through" plant which can be placed anywhere in the border including the front. It is short lived but readily self-sows. H 2m (6ft) S 60cm (24in).

Verbena corymbosa
A lowish, floppy plant. It creeps gently to form a large clump. It has blue flowers, which seem to shine out in the twilight. H 1m (3ft) S 25cm (10in).

Verbena hastata
A delightful upright plant without the wiriness of the others and with more foliage. It has purple flowers. H 1m (3ft) S 30cm (12in). There is an excellent pink form ('Rosea') and a very good white one ('Alba').

V. austriaca subsp. teucrium 'Blue Fountain'

Veronica peduncularis

VERONICA
Speedwell

A large genus of some 250 species and many cultivars. This is an important genus in the garden, providing us with many valuable plants, especially blue-flowered ones. They vary considerably in height, so there are plants for all parts of the border; the taller ones provide excellent vertical emphasis in the middle or back. The majority of speedwells carry their flowers in distinct spikes. The flowers appear mainly during the summer and are various shades of blue with the occasional pink or white cultivar. They are very easy plants to grow and every border should include at least one.

Cultivation Veronicas like a moist, humus-rich soil and will immediately show distress if the ground dries out too much (a good early indicator of drought). They prefer a sunny position but will grow in light shade. Z4.

Propagation Most can be divided in spring and species also come readily from autumn-sown seed.

Veronica austriaca
The species is rarely grown, but its many cultivars make this a popular plant. They are all roughly 20–30cm (8–12in) high with a similar spread. They have dense spikes of blue flowers throughout summer. 'Ionian Skies' has sky-blue flowers. The subspecies *teucrium* contains most of the notable cultivars, most of which have dark blue flowers. They include 'Blue Fountain', the traditional favourite 'Crater Lake Blue', 'Kapitan', 'Shirley Blue' and 'Royal Blue'.

Veronica cinerea
A low prostrate species with silver woolly foliage and short spikes of blue flowers. It is ideal for the front of border. H 15cm (6in) S 30cm (12in).

Veronica gentianoides
A taller species which produces loose spikes of pale blue flowers. The forms 'Alba' and 'Tissington White' have white flowers. H and S 45cm (18in).

Veronica spicata 'Alba'

Veronica longifolia
A good border plant, forming large clumps of drift. The blue flowers are densely packed into spikes. This plant self-sows prodigiously so always deadhead once flowering is finished. There is a pink form 'Rosea'. H 1.2m (4ft) S 30cm (12in).

Veronica peduncularis
A spreading mat-former. It is mainly grown in the form 'Georgia Blue' which has purple foliage and deep blue flowers. H 12cm (5in) S 1m (3ft).

Veronica spicata
A good species for the front of border with lots of interesting cultivars. The subspecies *incana* is fantastic. It has very silvery foliage and stems topped with vivid blue flowers. H and S 45cm (18in). Other *V. spicata* cultivars worth looking at include 'Alba' (white), 'Heidekind (pink flowers), 'Icicle' (white), 'Rotfuchs' (dark reddish-pink) and 'Wendy' (bright blue).

VIOLA
Viola

For the gardener, the genus *Viola* can be split into three types. There are the species, then there are the pansies which are considered as annuals (see page 330) and finally there are the violas. The violas have larger flowers than those of the species, and are of most interest to the perennial gardener. However, do not write off the species since there are several excellent plants which carpet the ground in spring and are well worth growing. Violas are usually low plants. The flowers are carried on single stems arising from the foliage. The flowers are either single or multicoloured.

Cultivation Violas must have a moisture-retentive soil or they will die out. As long as they are moist enough they will grow in sun, but light shade is the best position. Z5.

Propagation The species can be grown from seed, but any perennial cultivar needs to be increased by taking basal cuttings in the spring.

Viola 'Ardross Gem'
This is, indeed, a real gem, with blue and yellow flowers. H 15cm (6in) S 20cm (8in).

Viola cornuta
A species that flowers from spring to autumn, producing lilac or blue flowers. It will scramble through low shrubs. There are several cultivars, all of which make excellent border plants. H and S 20cm (8in).

Viola 'Irish Molly'
An attractive plant with yellowy-bronze flowers. H 10cm (4in) S 20cm (8in).

Viola 'Jackanapes'
This plant produces cheeky gold and red-purple flowers. H 8–12cm (3–5in) S 20cm (8in).

Viola odorata
The sweet violet, which starts to flower in mid-winter. It is ideal for a shady spot under shrubs. The small flowers vary from violet

Veronica longifolia

Veronica spicata

Viola 'Ardross Gem'

Viola 'Elizabeth'

Zantedeschia aethiopica

blue to pale blue, pink and white, and are highly scented. H 7cm (3in) S 15cm (6in).

Other plants There are hundreds of viola cultivars, including the delightful 'Elizabeth'. Check out the several nurseries that specialize in them if you become enthused and want more of them.

YUCCA
Yucca

A genus of about 40 species, of which half a dozen are in general cultivation. Some might argue that these are shrubs but they are widely included in perennial borders and so are included here. They have pointed, sword-like leaves coming either from the base or from a woody stem. Above these rise huge spikes of bell-shaped, cream flowers. These are plants for dry areas and they do very well in gravel beds. They are always striking and can be grown in association with other plants or singled out by themselves as focal points in the garden. They can be grown in containers.

Cultivation Any garden soil will do as long as it is very well-drained. Add plenty of grit to wetter soils. Grow in full sun. Z5.

Propagation Take off the rooted suckers and transplant them. Alternatively, take root cuttings in early winter.

Yucca filamentosa
Known as Adam's needle, this stemless species has dark green leaves that grow directly from a rosette on the ground. Along the margins of the leaves are thin, curly threads – the filaments of its name. Tall spikes up to 2m (6ft) high carry nodding white bells from midsummer onwards.

S 1m (5ft). There are three variegated forms 'Bright Edge', 'Color Guard' and 'Variegata'.

Yucca flaccida
This plant is similar to the previous since it is almost stemless and the leaves again come from basal rosettes. It has thin threads on the margins of the leaves. Large bell-shaped, white flowers appear from midsummer onwards. H and S 1m (3ft). Again there is a variegated form, 'Golden Sword'. 'Ivory' has creamy-ivory flowers.

Yucca gloriosa
A stemmed species with pointed leaves that are arching rather than stiffly erect. It produces large amounts of flowers from late summer onwards. These are cream but may be flushed with purple. H 3m (10ft) S 2m (6ft).

ZANTEDESCHIA
Arum lilies

These are superb plants. Most people know the blooms but few realize that the plants can be grown in the garden. There are six species in the genus but only Z. aethiopica is grown in the open. This forms large clumps of shiny, dark green, arrow-shaped leaves. They set off beautifully the glistening white spathes (sheaths) that surround the true flowers, which are modest and are carried on a spike inside the spathe.

This plant must have moist soil. It is marginally tender and may need winter protection in some areas. The form 'Crowborough' is reputedly more hardy than others but most seem to come through most winters. Arum lilies can be grown in an ordinary border so long as it is kept moist, but they do best next to or in a water feature or bog garden. It grows well in shallow water up to 30cm (12in) deep; the water is likely to remain below freezing, protecting the plant. H 1m (3ft) S 60cm (24in).

Cultivation A wet or moist soil that does not dry out. A sunny position is required. Z8.

Propagation Increase your stock of arum lilies by dividing the plants in spring.

ZAUSCHNERIA
Zauschneria

A small genus of plants. There is only one that is worth growing in the perennial border. This is Z. californica which is valuable because of its late flowering. This starts in the autumn, but continues right through to the first frosts. It is a spreading plant, which runs underground but it is not too difficult to prevent it from travelling too far. It has grey foliage and brilliant orange flowers, which certainly pep up the late border. In spite of coming from California, it is hardy. H and S 30cm (12in). The subspecies cana 'Dublin' has red flowers.

Cultivation This needs full sun and a well drained soil, but it need not be too fertile. Z7.

Propagation Zauschnerias can be increased by dividing existing plants in spring.

Yucca filamentosa

Yucca flaccida

Zauschneria cana 'Dublin'

A directory of bulbs

The bulb garden list is extensive, with plenty of choice for many different situations, whether your garden is in sun or shade, whether your soil is moist or well drained, whether you need dwarf or tall plants, whether you like fine foliage as well as flowers, whether you seek special colours such as vibrant oranges and reds, or soft salmons, creams and pale yellows, for example, not to mention a whole range of blues and deep dark purples. Here you will find details of the origins and correct growing conditions, propagation, pests and diseases, the flowering time, size of plant, colour, whether a flower is scented, hardiness rating and much more besides – all displayed in an easy-to-follow alphabetical list with scores of beautiful illustrations.

Advice is also given as to whether a plant is best suited to the garden beds and borders, or if it can be grown in grass, if it is suitable for containers on the terrace or patio, or if it is best grown indoors where temperatures are consistently warm. Some genera such as *Narcissus* will thrive in all these situations, whilst others are more selective and will only cope with a limited range of habitats. This bulb directory will enable you to select those plants you require for your own garden and home. Many of them are really easy to grow and you may be assured that in this list will be some of the most dramatic plants available to any gardener.

Agapanthus 'Loch Hope' is an evergreen perennial that flowers from July to September. It has extra-large beautiful blue flower-heads.

Bulb planner

Type of bulb	planting time	depth	spacing	flowering time
Achimenes	spring	2.5cm (1in)	2.5cm (1in)	summer and autumn
Agapanthus	spring	10cm (4in)	45–60cm (18–24in)	midsummer to early autumn
Allium	autumn	5–15cm (2–6in)	15–30cm (6–12in)	late spring to early autumn
Amaryllis	late summer	15cm (6in)	10cm (4in)	autumn
Anemone blanda	autumn	5cm (2in)	10cm (4in)	late winter to spring
Anemone coronaria	early spring	8cm (3in)	10cm (4in)	midsummer
Arum	autumn or spring	5cm (2in)	15cm (6in)	early summer
Asphodeline	autumn	8cm (3in)	30cm (12in)	late spring to summer
Begonia	spring	at soil level	20cm (8in)	summer to early autumn
Brimeura	autumn	5–8cm (2–3in)	2.5cm (1in)	spring
Calochortus	autumn	8cm (3in)	8cm (3in)	late spring to early summer
Camassia	autumn	10cm (4in)	10cm (4in)	late spring
Canna	spring	5cm (2in)	60cm (24in)	midsummer to autumn
Cardiocrinum	autumn	at soil level	60–90cm (24–36in)	late summer
Chionodoxa	autumn	5cm (2in)	5cm (2in)	late winter to mid-spring
Colchicum	late summer	10cm (4in)	10–15cm (4–6in)	autumn
Corydalis	autumn	8cm (3in)	10cm (4in)	spring
Crocosmia	spring	8–10cm (3–4in)	8cm (3in)	mid to late summer
Crocus, spring	autumn	8cm (3in)	5cm (2in)	autumn
Crocus, autumn	late summer	8cm (3in)	5cm (2in)	autumn
Cyclamen	autumn	2.5–5cm (1–2in)	10cm (4in)	autumn to early spring
Dactylorhiza	autumn	8cm (3in)	15cm (6in)	spring to late summer
Dahlia	early spring	15cm (6in)	30–90cm (12–36in)	summer to autumn
Dierama	autumn	5–8cm (2–3in)	30cm (12in)	summer
Eranthis	early autumn	5cm (2in)	8cm (3in)	mid- to late winter
Eremurus	autumn	just below soil	60cm (24in)	early to midsummer
Erythronium	autumn	10cm (4in)	10cm (4in)	spring
Eucomis	spring	15cm (6in)	20cm (8in)	late summer
Freesia	early spring	8cm (3in)	5–8cm (2–3in)	midsummer
Fritillaria	autumn	10–20cm (4–8in)	8–45cm (3–18in)	mid-spring to early summer
Galanthus	early autumn	8cm (3in)	10cm (4in)	mid- to late winter
Galtonia	spring	13cm (5in)	10cm (4in)	late summer

Allium oreophilium

Dahlia 'Kidd's Climax'

Begonia 'Picotee'

Lilium 'Her Grace'

Cyclamen coum

Type of bulb	planting time	depth	spacing	flowering time
Gladiolus	spring	8–10cm (3–4in)	10–15cm (4–6in)	midsummer
Gloriosa	spring	2.5cm (1in)	30cm (12in)	summer to autumn
Hedychium	spring	2.5cm (1in)	90–200cm (3–7ft)	late summer to early autumn
Hippeastrum	autumn onwards	neck above soil	20cm (8in)	winter onwards
Hyacinthoides	autumn	8cm (3in)	10cm (4in)	spring
Hyacinthus	autumn	10cm (4in)	20cm (8in)	spring
Iris reticulata	autumn	5cm (2in)	10cm (4in)	late winter
Kniphofia	spring	crown at soil level	60cm (24in)	summer to early autumn
Leucojum	autumn	8cm (3in)	8cm (3in)	late winter to autumn
Lilium	autumn	10–15cm (4–6in)	15–45cm (6–18in)	late spring to late summer
Muscari	autumn	5cm (2in)	5cm (2in)	spring
Narcissus	autumn	10–15cm (4–6in)	15cm (6in)	late winter to late spring
Nectaroscordum	autumn	5cm (2in)	10cm (4in)	late spring to early summer
Nerine	spring	2.5–8cm (1–3in)	8cm (3in)	early to late-autumn
Ornithogalum	autumn or spring	10–15cm (4–6in)	10–15cm (4–6in)	spring or mid- to late summer
Oxalis	autumn	5cm (2in)	10–15cm (4–6in)	early to late summer
Pelargonium	spring	2.5cm (1in)	30cm (12in)	summer to early autumn
Pleione	late winter	5cm (2in)	5cm (2in)	spring
Puschkinia	autumn	5cm (2in)	5cm (2in)	spring
Ranunculus	late winter to spring	5cm (2in)	8cm (3in)	late spring or summer
Schizostylis	spring	8cm (3in)	15–20cm (6–8in)	autumn
Scilla	early autumn	8–10cm (3–4in)	15–20cm (6–8in)	spring to early summer
Sinningia	spring	at soil level	13cm (5in)	summer
Sternbergia	late summer	15cm (6in)	8cm (3in)	autumn
Tigridia	spring	10cm (4in)	10cm (4in)	summer
Trillium	autumn or spring	10cm (4in)	30cm (12in)	mid-spring to early summer
Triteleia	autumn	8cm (3in)	10cm (4in)	early to midsummer
Tritonia	autumn	8cm (3in)	20cm (8in)	summer
Tulbaghia	spring	8cm (3in)	8cm (3in)	summer to early autumn
Tulipa	late autumn	8–15cm (3–6in)	8–20cm (3–8in)	spring
Veltheimia	autumn	top above soil	30cm (12in)	spring
Veratrum	spring	nose at soil level	60cm (24in)	early to midsummer
Watsonia	spring	15cm (6in)	10cm (4in)	late spring to late summer
Zantedeschia	spring	15cm (6in)	30–45cm (12–18in)	midsummer

Hippeastrum 'Mary Lou'

Narcissus cyclamineus

Tulipa 'Angelique'

Colchicum 'Violet Queen'

Erythronium 'Pagoda'

ACHIMENES
Hot-water plant, cupid's bower

This small but showy plant is often known as the hot-water plant because it used to be grown on top of the hot-water pipes in Victorian greenhouses, where it would thrive in the warmth and shade before being brought into the house. It is a genus of about 25 species of winter-dormant perennials from the subtropical forests of Central America. The many cultivars bear trumpet-shaped flowers in a wide range of colours, including dark and light pink, blue and primrose yellow. They may be vigorous upright or trailing perennials. The tiny rhizomes are quite fragile.
Cultivation In frost-prone areas grow indoors in a conservatory or as houseplants; in frost-free gardens they may be grown in a border. The plants enjoy light shade but not direct sunshine. The trailing forms are well suited to hanging baskets; the others may be grown in containers. Bring into growth in the spring at 16–18°C (61–64°F) and water sparingly at first. Plant rhizomes 2.5cm (1in) deep, allowing about one rhizome to 2.5cm (1in) of container – i.e. 10 rhizomes to a 25cm (10in) pot – in a soil-based compost (soil mix) or a proprietary loamless compost (soil-less mix). Water freely in summer. Apply a weekly liquid fertilizer. In autumn remove dead topgrowth and store in containers at 10°C (50°F) in completely

Achimenes 'Friendship'

dry conditions until spring.
Propagation Divide rhizomes or take stem cuttings in spring.
Pests and disease Aphids, thrips and red spider mites.

Achimenes 'Cascade Fairy Pink'
This trailing cultivar has solitary light pink flowers, 5cm (2in) across borne in generous numbers throughout summer and autumn. It makes an ideal partner for *A.* 'English Waltz'. H 20cm (8in) but will trail to 40cm (16in) S 20cm (8in). Tender/Z10.

Achimenes 'Cascade Violet Night'
This trailing cultivar has striking purple-blue flowers, 5cm (2in) across, which are borne in generous numbers throughout summer and autumn. It makes an ideal partner for *A.* 'English Waltz', 'Prima Donna' or 'Violet Charm'. H 20cm (8in) but will trail to 40cm (16in) S 20cm (8in). Tender/Z10.

Achimenes 'English Waltz'
The large, funnel-shaped, pink flowers look stunning against the dark green foliage with its bronze-red undertones. H 20cm (8in), S 20cm (8in). Tender/Z10.

Achimenes 'Friendship'
The rich lilac-pink flowers look wonderful in an indoor hanging basket or as a table houseplant. H 20cm (8in) S 20cm (8in). Tender/Z10.

Achimenes 'Prima Donna'
The rich salmon-pink flowers look beautiful planted on their own or mixed with a trailing form. H 20cm (8in) S 20cm (8in). Tender/Z10.

Achimenes 'Violet Charm'
The deep violet-blue flowers create a sumptuous picture whether planted on their own or mixed with a trailing form. H 20cm (8in) S 20cm (8in). Tender/Z10.

Flowers with salmon or apricot pink flowers

Achimenes 'Prima Donna'	*Hyacinthus orientalis* 'Gipsy Queen'
Begonia 'Picotee Lace Apricot'	*Narcissus* 'Bell Song'
Crocosmia 'Lady Hamilton'	*Narcissus* 'Romance'
Crocosmia 'Solfatare'	*Narcissus* 'Roseworthy'
Dahlia 'Gerrie Hoek'	*Narcissus* 'Salome'
Dahlia 'Zingaro'	*Schizostylis coccinea* 'Sunrise'
Eremurus 'Oase'	*Tulipa* 'Apricot Beauty'
Eremurus 'Sahara'	*Tulipa* 'Apricot Parrot'
Gladiolus (several)	*Zantedeschia* 'Cameo'

AGAPANTHUS
African blue lily, lily of the Nile

The genus, which contains about 10 species of vigorous, clump-forming perennials with thick, fleshy roots, originates in southern Africa. The plants produce strap-shaped, arching leaves and rounded umbels of blue or white flowers, followed by decorative seedheads.
Cultivation Grow in full sun in moist but well-drained soil in borders or in containers. Plant so that the green portion of the stem appears just above soil level. Where grown in borders mulch in winter as added protection against frost. If grown in containers, use a large, deep pot and a soil-based potting compost (soil mix), with plenty of drainage at the base, and overwinter in a frost-free greenhouse. Overcrowding seems to encourage more generous flower production, so only divide when absolutely necessary. Newly planted specimens will appreciate additional moisture while they are in full growth. Apply a liquid feed monthly from spring until flowering.
Propagation Sow seed at 13–15°C (55–59°F) when ripe, or in spring. Seedlings take 2 to 3 years to flower. Divide in spring.
Pests and diseases Slugs, snails and viruses.

Agapanthus 'Ben Hope'
This cultivar has rounded umbels of open, trumpet-shaped, rich blue flowers, which make a magnificent display from mid- to late summer. H 1.2m (4ft) S 60cm (24in). Hardy/Z7–10.

Achimenes 'Cascade Fairy Pink'

Achimenes 'Prima Donna'

Agapanthus 'Ben Hope'

Agapanthus 'Castle of Mey'

Agapanthus 'Blue Giant'
This cultivar has rounded umbels of open, bell-shaped, rich blue flowers from mid- to late summer. H 1.2m (4ft) S 60cm (24in). Hardy/Z7–10.

Agapanthus 'Blue Moon'
This cultivar has rounded umbels of open, bell-shaped, pale blue flowers, which make a magnificent display in late summer and early autumn. H 60cm (24in) S 45cm (18in). Hardy/Z7–10.

Agapanthus 'Castle of Mey'
This is one of the daintier hybrids, producing rich dark blue flowers from mid- to late summer. H 60cm (24in) S 30cm (12in). Hardy/Z7–10.

Agapanthus 'Headbourne White'
Variable in colour, these summer to late-summer-flowering hybrids are amongst the hardiest grown. They are named after a garden at Headbourne Worthy near Winchester, England. It is a form of *Agapanthus campanulatus*, which originated from a packet of mixed agapanthus seed from the Kirstenbosch Gardens in South Africa. H 90cm (36in) S 50cm (20in). Hardy/Z7–10.

Agapanthus 'Loch Hope'
The deep blue flowers of this agapanthus, which is one of the tallest in the group, appear in late summer and early autumn above grey-green leaves. H 1.5m (5ft) S 60cm (24in). Hardy/Z7–10.

Agapanthus praecox subsp. **maximus 'Albus'**
This is a beautiful white form of the evergreen species from South Africa, flowering from late summer to early autumn. Best grown in containers in frost-prone sites. H 1.50m (5ft) S 60cm (24in). Borderline hardy/Z9.

Agapanthus praecox subsp. **orientalis**
(syn. A. orientalis)
This subspecies, native to South Africa, has bright blue flowers that in late summer make a striking contrast with the dark green leaves. In frost-prone areas it should be grown in containers. H 60–90cm (24–36in) S 60cm (24in). Half-hardy/Z9–10.

Agapanthus 'Snowball'
A shorter cultivar, with a strong stem and large, rounded umbels of white flowers, which appear in late summer and make a striking contrast with the dark green leaves. It is good beside border paths or in containers. H 40cm (16in) S 40cm (16in). Hardy/Z7–10.

Agapanthus 'Snowy Owl'
The rounded umbels of white flowers are decidedly different in appearance, with each flower being narrow and flared. The flowers open in late summer and are set off beautifully by the dark green leaves. Good for borders or containers. H 1.2m (4ft) S 60cm (24in). Hardy/Z7–10.

Agapanthus 'Headbourne White'

Agapanthus praecox subsp. maximus 'Albus'

ALLIUM
Ornamental onion

This is a large genus of about 700 species of perennial spring-, summer- and autumn-flowering bulbs, and some rhizomes, which originate in dry and mountainous areas of the northern hemisphere. Those described here are mainly late-spring- or early-summer-flowering bulbs. Alliums are commonly referred to as ornamental onions because of their distinctive smell. In fact, all parts generally smell of onions, including the leaves, which often wither by flowering time. They can look untidy so plant the taller varieties behind herbaceous plants such as geraniums, hostas and hesperis so that they are hidden. Alliums produce short to tall, globe-like umbels of blue, white or yellow flowers, which are usually followed by decorative seedheads. Both the flowers and seedheads are often used for indoor flower arrangements. It is best to remove only the top part of the stem. The flowers are a rich source of nectar for bees. Contact with bulbs may irritate the skin in some people or aggravate some skin allergies.

Cultivation Best grown in full sun, in moist but well-drained soil in garden borders, although they will tolerate partial shade. Borderline hardy species, such as *A. caeruleum*, *A. cristophii*, *A. nigrum*, *A. schubertii*, *A. tuberosum* and *A. unifolium*, should be mulched in winter to provide extra protection, especially where soils are not so free-draining. Plant bulbs in autumn. As a general guide, aim to plant at a depth which is four times the diameter of the bulb: for *A.* 'Purple Sensation' this would be around 15cm (6in) deep, and for *A. sphaerocephalon* around 8cm (3in). Remove the old stems and leaves once they have withered.

Propagation Sow seed at 13–15°C (55–59°F) when ripe or in spring. Many alliums will self-seed, including *A. hollandicum* and *A. karataviense*; to avoid this, deadhead after flowering. Divide clumps in autumn.

Pests and diseases White rot, downy mildew and onion fly.

Allium caeruleum (syn. A. azureum)
Blue garlic

This species from north and Central Asia flowers in summer.

The dense umbels, 2.5cm (1in) across, are composed of 30–50 bright blue, star-shaped flowers, which sway on slender stems. The leaves die back before the flowers appear. Best in a dry situation. H 20–80cm (8–32in) S 2.5cm (1in). Borderline hardy/Z7–10.

Allium carinatum subsp. pulchellum (syn. A. pulchellum)

This allium originated in central and southern Europe, Russia and Turkey. It flowers in summer, but unlike *A. carinatum*, it does not produce bulbils, so that although it rapidly forms clumps, it is not invasive. It is almost evergreen. The loose umbels, 5cm (2in) across, have up to 30 rich purple, bell-shaped flowers. The outer ones are pendent. *A. carinatum* subsp. *pulchellum* f. *album* is the white form. H 30–45cm (12–18in) S 5cm (2in). Hardy/Z7–10.

Allium cernuum
Nodding onion, wild onion

This dainty species is native to North America. In summer the stiff stem bends over sharply at the tip and bears pendent umbels, 6cm (2¹⁄₂in) across, consisting of 25–40 nodding, bell-shaped, pink flowers. H 30–60cm (12–24in) S 5cm (2in). Hardy/Z4–10.

Allium cristophii
(syn. *A. albopilosum*, *A. christophii*)

This extremely popular allium species is native to Iran, Turkey and Central Asia. Flowering in early summer, the umbels are up to 20cm (8in) across and consist of about 50 star-shaped, lilac-purple flowers, which have a lovely rich, metallic sheen in sunlight. Foiled by hardy geraniums, it is perfect for planting beneath a wisteria arch or among early-flowering roses. H 30–60cm (12–24in) S 25cm (10in). Borderline hardy/Z7–10.

Allium 'Firmament'

This recently introduced cultivar, which is a hybrid between *A. atropurpureum* and *A. cristophii*, has dark purple flowers, borne in early summer. The umbels, to 20cm (8in) across, consist of about 50 star-shaped flowers. This is showy but expensive! H 80m (32in) S 25cm (10in). Hardy/Z4–10.

Allium cristophii

Allium neapolitanum

Allium × hollandicum

Allium flavum

This smaller but quite showy species is native to Europe and western Asia. In summer it bears loose umbels, only about 1cm ($\frac{1}{2}$ in) across, of up to 60 bell-shaped, bright yellow flowers. The flowers bend downwards as they open. It self-seeds readily in a sunny spot. H 10–35cm (4–14in) S 5cm (2in). Hardy/Z4–10.

Allium giganteum

This tall species, which is native to Central Asia, flowers in late spring and early summer. The umbels are to 12cm (5in) across and consist of about 50 star-shaped, lilac-pink flowers. It makes a lovely feature on its own or mixed with A. × hollandicum and A. 'Purple Sensation' in a border with wisterias close by. H 1.2m (4ft) S 25cm (10in). Hardy/Z4–10.

Allium 'Globemaster'

This stately allium flowers in late spring and early summer, a second flush following the first and thus extending the season. For this reason, the leaves persist longer than on most alliums. It certainly lives up to its name with flower globes 15–20cm (6–8in) across. They consist of about 50 showy star-shaped, deep purple flowers. H 80cm (32in) S 25cm (10in). Hardy/Z4–10.

Allium × hollandicum
(syn. A. aflatunense of gardens)

This species is native to Central Asia and flowers in late spring and early summer. The globes, which are to 10cm (4in) across, consist of about 50 star-shaped, purplish-pink flowers held in dense umbels. Bees love them. It is perfect for planting beneath laburnums and wisterias. H 70–90cm (28–36in) S 25cm (10in). Hardy/Z4–10.

Allium karataviense

Also native to Central Asia, this species flowers in late spring. The globes are 5–8cm (2–3in) across and consist of 50 or more small, star-shaped, pale pink flowers with purple midribs, borne on stiff stems. The pair of broad, grey, elliptical, almost horizontal leaves, 15–23cm (6–9in) long, are a special feature, so do not plant medium to large perennials nearby and obscure them. This allium will self-seed, producing a pleasing massed effect. H 20cm (8in) S 10cm (4in). Hardy/Z4–10.

Allium karataviense 'Ivory Queen'

This cultivar is closely related to the species that grows in Central Asia, but it differs in having ivory white flowers with protruding yellow anthers. Flowering in late spring, the globes are 5–8cm (2–3in) across. As with the parent, the leaves are a special feature. H 20cm (8in) S 10cm (4in). Hardy/Z4–10.

Allium × moly
Golden garlic

This small but showy species is native to southwestern and southern Europe. In summer it bears loose umbels, only 5cm (2in) across, of up to 30 bright yellow, star-shaped flowers. H 15–25cm (6–10in) S 5cm (2in). Hardy/Z4–10.

Allium moly 'Jeannine'

This is slightly taller than the species and is regarded as an improved form. It flowers in summer, bearing loose umbels, only 5cm (2in) across, of up to 30 bright yellow, star-shaped flowers. H 30cm (12in) S 5cm (2in). Hardy/Z4–10.

Allium neapolitanum
(syn. A. cowanii)

This species is native to southern Europe and North Africa. It flowers in summer, bearing globes 5cm (2in) across of up to 30 small, star-shaped, pure white flowers. It is an attractive plant and is excellent in raised troughs. H 20–40cm (8–16in) S 5cm (2in). Borderline hardy/Z7–10.

Allium karataviense

Allium 'Purple Sensation'

Allium oreophilium

Allium schubertii

Allium nigrum
(syn. *A. multibulbosum*)
This species is native to the Mediterranean. The umbels, 8cm (3in) across, consist of about 30 creamy white, cup-shaped flowers, each with a dark green ovary. The flowers are borne in late spring to early summer, and it is excellent under laburnum or white wisterias. H 70cm (28in) S 25cm (10in). Borderline hardy/Z7–10.

Allium oreophilum
(syn. *A. ostrowskianum*)
This species is native to the Caucasus and Central Asia. It flowers in early summer, bearing small, loose umbels, just 4cm (1¹/₂in) across, which consist of up to 15 long-lasting, bell-shaped, bright carmine-pink flowers. It makes an easy and effective plant for a sunny spot at the front of a well-drained border. H 20cm (8in) S 5cm (2in). Hardy/Z4–10.

Allium paniculatum
This species is native to Europe and Central Asia. Flowering in summer, the ovoid umbels are just 5cm (2in) across and consist of up to 40 bell-shaped, pink, white or yellowish-brown flowers with prominent stamens. The flowers become pendent as they open. It

provides a long-lasting display and is best in a sunny, open site that is not too damp. H 30–70cm (12–28in) S 5cm (2in). Hardy/Z4–10.

Allium 'Purple Sensation'
This popular cultivar flowers in late spring and early summer. The umbels are up to 10cm (4in) across and consist of about 50 star-shaped, deep violet flowers. It is a spectacular species either planted on its own or mixed with *A. × hollandicum* and *A. giganteum*, where it will create a lovely mixture of lighter and darker shades and a variety of heights. It is one of the best of all alliums. H 60–90cm (24–36in) S 25cm (10in). Hardy/Z4–10.

Allium rosenbachianum
This species is native to Central Asia. It flowers in summer, bearing globes that are 10cm (4in) across and consist of 50 or more star-shaped, deep purple flowers with protruding violet stamens. H 90cm (36in) S 15cm (6in). Borderline hardy/Z7–10.

Allium roseum
Rosy garlic
This species is native to southern Europe, North Africa and Turkey and flowers in summer. The tiny umbels are just 1cm (¹/₂in) across and consist of cup-shaped, pale pink flowers, often with bulbils present. These bulbils may be invasive and are best removed. H 10–65cm (4–26in) S 5cm (2in). Hardy/Z4–10.

Allium sativum
Garlic
This species is thought to have originated in Central Asia, but its use in cooking has meant that it is now so commonly grown that its origins are obscure. It is made up of ovoid bulbs, each of 5–18 bulblets enclosed in a papery tunic. Flowering in summer, the umbels are just 2.5–5cm (1–2in) across and consist of white, bell-shaped flowers, often with bulbils present. H 90cm (36in) S 25cm (10in). Hardy/Z4–10.

Allium schoenoprasum
Chives
This species is native to a wide area in Europe, Asia and North America. Flowering in late spring and early summer, it bears small but showy globes, 2.5cm (1in)

Allium nigrum

Allium schoenoprasum

Allium sphaerocephalon

across, consisting of 30 or more small, bell-shaped, pale purple (sometimes white) flowers borne on stiff stems. The dark green leaves are cylindrical and hollow and are commonly used in cooking, as are the flowers. H 30–60cm (12–24in) S 30cm (12in). Hardy/Z4–10.

Allium schoenoprasum 'Forescate'
More vigorous than the common chive, this cultivar is taller and produces a brighter purplish-pink flowerhead. As with the species, both the leaves and flowers can be used in cooking. H 60cm (24in) S 40cm (16in). Hardy/Z4–10.

Allium schubertii
This species is native to the eastern Mediterranean and Central Asia. The large, rounded umbels, borne on stiff stems, are about 20cm (8in) across.

They have inner and outer zones of small, star-shaped, mauve-blue flowers, just like fireworks. The flowers appear in early summer. Plants need full sun to flower well but are definitely a talking point! H 40cm (16in) S 25cm (10in). Borderline hardy/Z7–10.

Allium sphaerocephalon
Round-headed leek
This species, which is known for its drumsticks, is native to Europe, northern Africa and western Asia. Unlike many other alliums, it has ovoid umbels, 2.5cm (1in) across, which are formed from densely packed, pink to reddish-purple flowers and are borne in early to midsummer. It looks attractive with bronze foliage and is good as a cut flower for indoor arrangements. H 60cm (24in) S 8cm (3in). Hardy/Z5–10.

Allium triquetrum
Three-cornered leek
This species is native to southern Europe but is now naturalized in Britain, making its home in milder areas in damp, shady conditions. It can be invasive, so keep it for wilder areas of the garden. Its Latin and common names reflect its characteristic triangular stems, which carry clusters of pendent white flowers, each with a green midrib. It flowers from mid- to late spring. H 35cm (14in) S 8cm (3in). Borderline hardy/Z7–10.

Allium tuberosum
Chinese chives
The species is native to Southeast Asia. It flowers in late summer to autumn, bearing globes 5cm (2in) across which consist of many small, star-shaped, fragrant white flowers. The leaves, which are up to 35cm (14in) long, are edible, as are the flowers. H 25–50cm (10–20in) S 8cm (3in). Borderline hardy/Z7–10.

Allium unifolium
This species is native to Oregon and California, USA. The globes, which are borne in spring, are 6cm (2¹/₂in) across and consist of up to 20 small, open bell-shaped, purple-pink flowers, making a lovely border display in the garden. H 30cm (24in) S 10cm (4in). Borderline hardy/Z7–10.

Allium ursinum
Ramsons, wild garlic, wood garlic
A common woodland plant, this species is native to Europe and Russia, where it thrives in damp shady places. It may be easily recognized by its distinctive garlicky smell. Flowering in late spring, the globes are to 6cm (2¹/₂in) across and consist of 6–20 small, starry white flowers. H 30cm (24in) S 10cm (4in). Hardy/Z4–10.

Allium vineale 'Hair'
False garlic, stag's garlic
This is closely related to the species, which is native to Europe, North Africa and western Asia. It is a distinctive form of allium, with hair-like protuberances giving a twisted appearance. Flowering in summer, it produces long stems with just a few flowers and many green bulbils. Beware: it self-seeds readily, so you may want to avoid it altogether. H 70cm (28in) S 8cm (3in). Hardy/Z4–10.

Allium unifolium

Amaryllis belladonna

AMARYLLIS

This is a genus of just one species of autumn-flowering, deciduous, perennial bulbs. They originally came from coastal hills and besides streams in the Western Cape, South Africa. The true amaryllis is often confused with the tender hippeastrum, which is commonly known and sold as amaryllis and to which it is distantly related. However, the true amaryllis has a solid stem, whereas the hippeastrum (from South America) has a hollow stem. The amaryllis is one of the stars of the autumn border, its wonderful pink, trumpet-shaped flowers creating a focal point when other plants may be over. The strappy leaves appear after flowering.

Cultivation The amaryllis is only borderline hardy so choose a warm, sunny site beneath a sheltered wall and make sure that the soil is well drained. Plant in late summer, when the large, round bulbs are dormant. Plant them so that their necks are just at soil level. Protect the foliage from frost with bracken or straw when temperatures fall below freezing. Alternatively, plant in

deep containers, using soil-based compost (soil mix) with additional leafmould and sand. Enjoy them outside or in a porch or conservatory, where you will be rewarded with the rich fragrance.

Propagation Sow seed at 16°C (61°F) when ripe. Grow on under glass for 1 or 2 seasons before planting in their final position outdoors. Remove offsets in spring after leaves die down or in late summer before growth begins.

Pests and diseases Slugs, narcissus bulb fly; under glass, aphids and red spider mite can be a problem.

Amaryllis belladonna
Belladonna lily, Jersey lily
The species is native to the Western Cape, South Africa. In autumn it produces umbels of 6 or more scented, pink, funnel-shaped flowers, 6–10cm (2½–4in) long. The strappy, fleshy leaves appear after flowering. It looks especially effective planted among low-growing shrubs. In cooler areas it should be grown against a warm wall. This is a truly glorious bulb, which will add drama to any border scheme. H 60cm (24in) S 10cm (4in). Borderline hardy/Z7–10.

ANEMONE
Windflower

This is a genus of about 120 species, some of which have perennial rhizomatous or tuberous rootstocks, mainly flowering in spring and summer. The Greek word *anemos* means wind, which helps to explain why the anemone is commonly known as the windflower, for the delicate petals quiver in the breeze.

Cultivation Grow in sun or partial

shade in well-drained soil; plant in garden borders, in the eye of a tree or in outdoor containers. *A. nemorosa* prefers light shade. Plant the tubers of *A. blanda* 5cm (2in) deep as soon as they are available in autumn. Because they should not be allowed to dry out too much, soak them overnight before planting. As the tubers mature, they will grow to about 10cm (4in) across, producing many flowers. These will self-seed to create large colonies. The knobbly, misshapen tubers of *A. coronaria* De Caen Group and St Bridgid Group are also best soaked overnight before planting and then planted with the buds pointing upwards, 8cm (3in) deep, in autumn (with a mulch) or in spring. Allow to dry off after flowering. Plant the rhizomes of *A. nemorosa* 5cm (2in) deep in autumn.

Propagation Separate the tubers when dormant; plants will self-seed readily.

Pests and diseases Caterpillars, slugs, leaf spot and powdery mildew.

Anemone apennina
Originating from southern Europe, this is a particularly worthy garden plant for dry areas beneath deciduous trees in fine grass. It flowers in early to mid-spring. The pale blue flowers, 2.5cm (1in) or more across, are occasionally white or pink flushed. H 12cm (4½in) S 30cm (12in). Hardy/Z6–9.

Anemone blanda

Anemone coronaria St Bridgid Group

Anemone nemorosa

Anemone blanda

Originating from the eastern Mediterranean, this is a very worthy garden plant, flowering for 6–8 weeks from late winter to mid-spring. The starry flowers, 2.5cm (1in) or more across, have 10–15 white, pale blue or dark blue, occasionally mauve and pink, petals. The attractive leaves are fern-like. They associate beautifully with primroses and all early dwarf daffodils and are excellent in garden borders or beneath the eye of a tree, where they will self-seed. They are also good for containers. H 10–15cm (4–6in) S 15cm (6in). Hardy/Z6–9.

Anemone blanda 'Radar'

This is a brightly coloured form, with magenta flowers and contrasting white centres. Like the species, it flowers for 6–8 weeks from late winter to mid-spring. The leaves are darker green than those of its parent. H 10–15cm (4–6in) S 15cm (6in). Hardy/Z6–9.

Anemone blanda 'White Splendour'

This is a particularly robust and welcome A. blanda, with its large, starry, bright white flowers that create a wonderfully welcome sight in early spring and last well into mid-spring. The attractive leaves are fern-like. The flowers show off well in front of dark foliage plants, and they associate beautifully with white-barked birches. H 15–20cm (6–8in) S 15cm (6in). Hardy/Z6–9.

Anemone coronaria De Caen Group and St Bridgid Group

Both groups derive from the original species, A. coronaria, which is found in the Mediterranean area. Plants in the De Caen Group bear single white, red, pink, mauve or blue flowers. These are 2.5–8cm (1–3in) across and have 6–8 petals. A. 'The Bride' is a stunning white. The St Bridgid Group includes plants with semi-double flowers with a mass of petals. Colours vary from red, pink, violet, blue to white. A. 'Lord Lieutenant' is a splendid blue. All these anemones should be grown in a sheltered spot near the front of a border or in containers. The flowers appear from late spring to early summer, depending on planting time. Generally allow 3 months between planting and early or midsummer flowering, but longer for a late-spring show. They make ideal cut flowers but should be picked while in bud. H 25cm (10in) S 15cm (6in). Hardy/Z8–10.

Anemone nemorosa
Wood anemone

Originating in the woodlands of Europe, this is a vigorous, carpeting plant, which flowers from spring to early summer. It bears dainty, demure white flowers, sometimes with a pink flush, about 2.5cm (1in) across and with 6–8 petals. It is useful for naturalizing in light shade beneath deciduous shrubs or in woodland areas. H 8–15cm (3–6in) S 30cm (12in). Hardy/Z4–8.

Anemone nemorosa 'Robinsoniana'

This is a lovely wood anemone with large, pale blue petals, named in 1870 at the Oxford Botanic Gardens. H 15cm (6in) S 30cm (12in). Hardy/Z4–8.

Anemone nemorosa 'Rosea'

This pale pink form of the wood anemone is very pretty and much sought after. Plant in a small colony where it can be treasured on its own. H 8–15cm (3–6in) S 30cm (12in). Hardy/Z4–8.

Anemone coronaria De Caen Group

Arum italicum 'Marmoratum'

ARUM
Cuckoo pint, lords and ladies

The genus contains 26 species of mainly spring-flowering, tuberous perennials found in partially shady locations as far afield as southern Europe, North Africa and western Asia to the Himalayas. All parts if eaten can cause severe discomfort, and contact with the sap may irritate the skin.

Cultivation Plant tubers 10–15cm (4–6in) deep in autumn or spring. Choose a well-drained site in sun or partial shade.

Propagation Sow seed in a cold frame in the autumn, first removing the outer pulp from the berries. Divide clumps of tubers after flowering.

Pests and diseases Trouble free.

Arum italicum 'Marmoratum'
(syn. *A. italicum pictum*)
This cultivar is related to a species that originates in southern Europe, Turkey and North Africa. The species is renowned for its glossy, arrow- or spear-shaped leaves, which have distinctive cream veins, and the leaves of this cultivar are veined with pale green or cream. It flowers in early summer and needs an open, sunny site to do best, when it will produce white spathes, 15–40cm (6–16in) long, each enclosing a spike of rich red berries in late summer. However, it is the foliage that is the main attraction, and grown in partial shade it will produce bigger leaves. These emerge in late autumn or winter, and their striking distinctive shape and markings make them particularly sought-after for flower arrangements. This is a useful plant for the winter garden, where it creates a fine backdrop for snowdrops and winter aconites. H 30cm (12in) S 15cm (6in). Hardy/Z7–9.

ASPHODELINE
Jacob's rod

This genus of up to 20 species of biennials and perennials originated in sunny, rocky meadows from the Mediterranean to the Caucasus. They grow from rhizomes and produce tall racemes of yellow or white flowers, with grass-like, basal and stem leaves.

Cultivation Grow in moderately fertile, well-drained soil in full sun.

Mulch in autumn in cold areas.

Propagation Sow in a cold frame in spring. Divide in late summer or early autumn by teasing apart the fleshy rhizomes and replanting.

Pests and diseases Slugs, snails and aphids.

Asphodeline liburnica
This species is native to Austria, Greece, Italy and the Balkans. It forms neat clumps with slender stems and fine, linear, grey-green foliage. The bright yellow flowers appear in summer and are fragrant. H 25–60cm (10–24in) S 30cm (12in). Hardy/Z6–9.

Asphodeline lutea
King's spear, yellow asphodel
This perennial, native to central and eastern Mediterranean and western Turkey, is clump-forming and larger than *A. liburnica*. In late spring and summer it produces tall, dense racemes to 20cm (8in) long. The bright yellow flowers associate well with a foreground of lime-green foliage such as that of golden marjoram *Origanum vulgare* 'Aureum' and a background of bronze foliage such as *Cotinus* 'Grace'. H 1.2m (4ft) S 30cm (12in). Hardy/Z6–9.

Asphodeline lutea

Begonia 'Can-can'

BEGONIA

The genus was named in honour of Michel Bégon (1638–1710), a French botanist and governor of French Canada. It is a huge genus, containing about 900 species, some of which are tuberous-rooted. The tuberous begonias, whose tubers are dormant in winter, include the Tuberhybrida, Multiflora and Pendula types, which derive from species growing in the Andes. They may be found under the headings Fimbriata begonias, which bear carnation-type petals, Exotic begonias, whose flowers are two-toned, the Non-Stop flowering kinds, which are generally compact and good for bedding, and the Pendulous or Cascading types, which are useful in hanging baskets or raised beds. **Cultivation** Grow in sun or partial shade in garden borders or containers. Start the tubers into growth in spring indoors, placing them on the surface of the compost (soil mix), the hollow side upwards, at 16–18°C (61–64°F). Move outside into summer flowering positions after all risk of frost has passed. Allow to dry after flowering. Lift tubers in autumn, dry off, dust with fungicide and store in cool, dry conditions at 5–7°C (41–45°F). **Propagation** Sow seed and root basal cuttings in spring. **Pests and diseases** Vine weevil is a major problem in late summer.

Begonia 'Billie Langdon'
Flowering from midsummer until early autumn, this *B.* × *tuberhybrida* cultivar is a large, upright begonia with pure white flowers, each to 18cm (7in) in diameter. The mid-green leaves can reach 20cm (8in) in length. It is best planted on its own in a heavy container. H 60cm (24in) S 45cm (18in). Tender/Z10.

Begonia 'Can-can'
Flowering from midsummer until early autumn, this is a *B.* × *tuberhybrida* cultivar with an upright habit. It has rich yellow flowers, to 17cm (6½in) across. The petals have a ruffled red edge, which makes a beautiful combination. Ideal for a single-specimen container. H 90cm (36in) S 45cm (18in). Tender/Z10.

Begonia 'Champagne'
Flowering from midsummer until early autumn, this is a *B.* × *tuberhybrida* cultivar. The double flowers, 5–8cm (2–3in) across, have creamy white petals and form generous clusters of cascading colour around the plant, trailing to 20cm (8in). This begonia is ideal for planting in wall pots, window boxes or hanging baskets, either on its own or combined with other summer-flowering bedding plants such as *Lobelia* and *Impatiens*. H 20cm (8in) S 20cm (8in). Tender/Z10.

Begonia 'Giant Flowered Pendula Yellow'

Begonia 'Flamboyant'
Flowering from midsummer until early autumn, this is a *B.* × *tuberhybrida* cultivar with an upright habit. It was first grown in 1911. It has single, dark scarlet-red flowers and is ideal for a container. H 30cm (12in) S 15cm (6in). Tender/Z10.

Begonia 'Giant Flowered Pendula Yellow'
Flowering from midsummer until early autumn, the double and single yellow flowers are 5cm (2in) across. This pendulous begonia, a *B.* × *tuberhybrida* cultivar, trails to 20cm (8in); it is ideal for hanging baskets and window boxes. There is also an attractive 'Giant Flowered Pendula Orange' as well as pink, white and red forms. H 20cm (8in) S 20cm (8in). Tender/Z10.

Begonia grandis subsp. *evansiana*
Flowering from midsummer until early autumn, this species is native to China, Malaysia and Japan. It has notched, olive-green leaves, 10cm (4in) long, which are pale green, sometimes red, on the underside. The pink or white flowers are fragrant. H 50cm (20in) S 30cm (12in). Half-hardy/Z10.

Bulbs with creamy flowers

Begonia 'Champagne'	Hippeastrum 'Yellow Goddess'
Camassia leichtlinii subsp. leichtlinii	Lilium 'Roma'
	Lilium 'Belle Epoque'
Crocus 'Cream Beauty'	Narcissus 'Topolino'
Crocus 'E.A. Bowles'	Narcissus 'Silver Chimes'
Galtonia candicans	Tulipa 'Peaches and Cream'
Gladiolus 'Charming Beauty'	Tulipa 'Spring Green'

Begonia 'Non-stop Orange'

Begonia 'Picotee Lace Apricot'

Begonia 'Helene Harms'

Flowering from midsummer until early autumn, this old cultivar, dating back to 1902, is an upright begonia with many semi-double, yellow flowers, 5–8cm (2–3in) across. The mid-green leaves are 20cm (8in) long. H 13cm (5in) S 15cm (6in). Tender/Z10.

Begonia 'Marginata Crispa'

Flowering from midsummer until early autumn, this B. × tuberhybrida cultivar has an upright habit. The yellow petals have ruffled red edges, which makes a delightful combination. Ideal for window boxes or containers. H 20cm (8in) S 20cm (8in). Tender/Z10.

Begonia 'Non-stop Orange'

Flowering from midsummer until early autumn, this is a B. × tuberhybrida cultivar. It is an upright begonia, with double orange flowers to 10cm (4in) across, and it looks wonderful in a container or window box. There are also double yellow, pink, red and white Non-stop begonias. H 18cm (7in) S 20cm (8in). Tender/Z10.

Begonia 'Pendula Cascade White'

Flowering from midsummer until early autumn, the flowers of this trailing begonia are finer than those of the Giant Flowered cultivars. They reach 5cm (2in) in diameter, but are held on slender stems. The plant will trail to 18cm (7in), making it ideal for hanging baskets and window boxes. There is also an attractive 'Pendula Cascade Orange' as well as yellow, pink and red forms. H 18cm (7in) S 20cm (8in). Tender/Z10.

Begonia 'Picotee'

Flowering from midsummer until early autumn, this cultivar is upright in habit, but its large, heavy flowers create a natural fountain effect, which provides colour all around the margins of the plant as well as in the centre. The rich yellow-orange flowers show patches of yellow, giving a two-toned effect, but the edges are deep orange, making a strong contrast. The colour will vary according to summer temperatures at both day and night. It is an excellent choice for large hanging baskets, window boxes, pots or troughs. H 20cm (8in) S 20cm (8in). Tender/Z10.

Begonia 'Picotee Lace Apricot'

Flowering from midsummer until early autumn, this cultivar is upright in habit. The rich apricot flowers are ruffled and edged in white. They make an excellent underplanting to orange fuchsias, such as 'Thalia'. H 20cm (8in) S 20cm (8in). Tender/Z10.

Begonia 'Roy Hartley'

Flowering from midsummer until early autumn, this cultivar has double pink flowers, to 10cm (4in) across, tinged with salmon-pink. It flowers from mid- to late summer. H 60cm (24in) S 40cm (16in). Tender/Z10.

Begonia sutherlandii

This elegant spreading species, which originates in South Africa and Tanzania, is an ideal subject for a hanging basket or window box and is perhaps best grown on its own where it can be shown to greatest advantage. The pendent, clear orange flowers are produced in succession throughout summer, providing a really colourful display. H 15–30cm (6–12in) S 45cm (18in). Half-hardy/Z10.

Begonia 'Picotee'

Brimeura amethystina

BRIMEURA

This is a genus of only 2 species of bulbs coming from the mountain meadows and garigue of south-east Europe and the Pyrenees.
Cultivation Grow in sun or partial shade but choose a well-drained, humus-rich soil. Where temperatures fall below −10°C (14°F) provide a winter protection of bracken or leafmould. Plant the bulbs 5–8cm (2–3in) deep and 2.5cm (1in) apart.
Propagation Sow seed in pots in a cold frame as soon as it is ripe. Plant out after 2 years. Divide clumps when dormant in summer.
Pests and diseases None.

Brimeura amethystina
(syn. *Hyacinthus amethystinus*)
This late-spring- to early-summer-flowering bulb has narrow, semi-erect leaves. Each flowering stem bears up to 15 pendent, tubular, blue flowers, at first sight similar to those of a diminutive bluebell. H 10–25cm (4–10in) S 2.5–5cm (1–2in). Hardy/Z5–9.

CALOCHORTUS
Butterfly tulip, cat's ears, fairy lanterns, globe lily
This is a genus of about 60 species of bulbs from grasslands and open woodland of western North America and Mexico. The botanical name originates from the Greek words *kalós* (beautiful) and *chortos* (grass). The flowers are, indeed, beautiful, and the leaves are grass-like. The many common names also reflect the shape and habit of the flowers.
Cultivation Plant the bulbs 8cm (3in) deep and 8cm (3in) apart in pots containing soil-based compost (potting mix). Then they are best overwintered under cover to guard against rain. In late spring the pots can be buried in garden soil, where they can be allowed to flower. In mild, sunny areas plant direct into well-drained soil in sheltered borders in autumn. Whether the bulbs are in containers or garden soil, choose a site that is in full sun. After flowering, the bulbs divide and do not flower again the following year but miss 1–2 seasons.

Propagation Sow seed in pots in a cold frame as soon as ripe, or remove offsets in late summer.
Pests and diseases None.

Calochortus luteus 'Golden Orb'
This cultivar is derived from the species *C. luteus*, which grows in California, where it is known as the yellow mariposa. Tall, thin but sturdy, branched stems bear 1–7 deep yellow, open bell-shaped

Calochortus luteus 'Golden Orb'

flowers, 4–6cm (1½–2½in) across, each with reddish-brown marks towards the base of the petals. The flowers appear in late spring to early summer. H 50–60cm (20–24in) S 5–10cm (2–4in). Borderline hardy/Z5–10.

CAMASSIA
Quamash
This is a genus of about 5 species of bulbs which thrive in damp meadowland. The common name was given by the Native Americans of the Pacific Northwest, where the plants originate. They are also sometimes known as wild hyacinths, which they resemble. They make an excellent choice for a natural garden where they will flower at the same time as buttercups and cow parsley.
Cultivation In autumn plant the bulbs in borders or grassland at a depth of 10cm (4in) and 10cm (4in) apart and allow to naturalize. They will form good groups. Grow in sun or partial shade.
Propagation Sow seed in pots in a cold frame as soon as ripe, or remove offsets in late summer.
Pests and diseases Trouble free.

Camassia cusickii
This species comes from northeastern Oregon. It flowers in late spring to early summer, bearing long racemes of cup-shaped, pale to deep blue flowers. It will cope with a fairly shady position. H 60–80cm (24–32in) S 10cm (4in). Borderline hardy/Z3–8.

Camassia cusickii

Camassia leichtlinii subsp. suksdorfii

CANNA
Indian shot plant

This is a genus of 50 species of rhizomatous herbaceous perennials from moist open areas of forests in Asia and the tropical parts of North and South America. The genus name comes from the Greek word *kanna* (reed).

Cultivation In spring plant the rhizomes under glass in large containers, 5cm (2in) deep and 60cm (2ft) apart. If required, move outside from early to midsummer. Choose a sunny, sheltered spot on the patio or if you wish, transplant from containers into sunny, sheltered borders. Alternatively, grow them in or near water. Deadhead to promote continuity of flowering. Apply a liquid feed every month. Before the foliage turns black with frost in autumn, remove the stems, dig up the roots and store in barely moist peat or leafmould in frost-free conditions. In just one season a single rhizome will produce a root system to 50cm (20in) across.

Propagation Sow seed at 21°C (70°F) in spring or autumn. Chip seed or soak for 24 hours in warm water before sowing. In early spring divide rhizomes into short sections, each with a prominent eye. Pot on and start into growth at 16°C (61°F), watering sparingly at first.

Pests and diseases Outdoors, slugs and caterpillars; indoors, red spider mite.

Canna 'Black Knight'
Flowering from midsummer to early autumn, this cultivar has attractive bronze foliage and luscious dark red flowers. H 1.8m (6ft) S 50cm (20in). Half-hardy/Z7–10.

Canna 'King Midas'
Flowering from midsummer to early autumn, this canna has dark green leaves and golden-yellow flowers with orange markings. H 1.5m (5ft) S 50cm (20in). Half-hardy/Z7–10.

Canna 'Louis Cottin'
Flowering from midsummer to early autumn, this is a cultivar with bronze foliage and yellow flowers spotted with red. Both the leaves and the flowers are apt to bleach so avoid planting it in full sun. H 1.2m (4ft) S 50cm (20in). Half-hardy/Z7–10.

Canna 'Lucifer'
Flowering from midsummer to early autumn, this is a short but free-flowering cultivar. It has racemes of bright red flowers, each edged with yellow, and attractive mid-green foliage. H 60cm (24in) S 50cm (20in). Half-hardy/Z7–10.

Camassia leichtlinii subsp. leichtlinii
(syn. *C. leichtlinii* 'Alba')
Indian lily
This subspecies comes from western North America, from California to British Columbia. It flowers in late spring, bearing tall racemes of star-shaped, creamy white flowers, each 5–8cm (2–3in) across. H 60–130cm (30–54in) S 10cm (4in). Borderline hardy/Z5–9.

Camassia leichtlinii subsp. suksdorfii
Indian lily
The species, which also comes from western North America, from California to British Columbia, bears tall racemes of star-shaped, blue to violet flowers, each 5–8cm (2–3in) across. Flowering in late spring, it associates well with *Narcissus poeticus* var. *recurvus* (pheasant's eye narcissus). H 60–130 (30–54in) S 10cm (4in). Borderline hardy/Z5–9.

Camassia quamash
Common camassia
This late-spring-flowering bulb bears a spike of star-shaped white, violet or blue flowers, each measuring 7cm (3in) across. It originates in North America, from Canada to Montana, and the bulbs were once an important source of food for Native Americans, who used to pit-roast or boil them. H 20–80cm (8–32in) S 10cm (4in). Borderline hardy, Z4–10.

Canna 'Durban'

Canna 'Roi Humbert'

Canna 'Lucifer'

Canna 'Monet'
Flowering from midsummer to early autumn, this canna has blue-green leaves and soft salmon-pink flowers. H 90cm (36in) S 50cm (20in). Half-hardy/Z7–10.

Canna 'Orange Perfection'
Flowering from midsummer to early autumn, this is another short cultivar. The flowers are a beautiful soft orange. H 60cm (24in) S 50cm (20in). Half-hardy/Z7–10.

Canna 'Picasso'
Flowering from midsummer to early autumn, this cultivar has blue-green leaves and yellow flowers spotted with red. Both flowers and leaves are apt to bleach so avoid a position in full sun. H 90cm (36in) S 50cm (20in). Half-hardy/Z7–10.

Canna 'President'
Flowering from midsummer to early autumn, this canna has long racemes of red flowers, 5cm (2in) wide, to accompany the mid-green foliage. This is a taller cultivar. H 90cm (36in) S 50cm (20in). Half-hardy/Z7–10.

Canna 'Roi Humbert'
Formerly known as *Canna* 'Red King Humbert', this canna flowers from midsummer to early autumn. It is a tall cultivar, with large racemes, 20–30cm (8–12in) long, of orange-scarlet flowers, which show up well against the leaves. The colour associates well with other bronze-foliage plants, such as grasses or *Foeniculum vulgare* 'Purpureum' (bronze fennel). H 2.1m (7ft) S 50cm (20in). Half-hardy/Z7–10.

Canna 'Rosemond Coles'
Flowering from midsummer to early autumn, this cultivar has long racemes of large red flowers, 8cm (3in) across, each edged with yellow and with yellow-spotted throats. The undersides of the petals are golden-yellow. H 1.5m (5ft) S 50cm (20in). Half-hardy/Z7–10.

Canna 'Striata'
Flowering from midsummer to early autumn, this cultivar has long racemes of orange flowers 8cm (3in) wide, and light green foliage striped with yellow veins. H 1.5m (5ft) S 50cm (20in). Half-hardy/Z7–10.

Canna 'Striped Beauty'
Flowering from midsummer to early autumn, this cultivar is shorter than most. It has creamy white veining in its foliage, and the flower buds open to reveal red flowers. H 80cm (32in) S 50cm (20in). Half-hardy/Z7–10.

Canna 'Tropicanna'
(syn. *C.* 'Phaison', *C.* Durban)
Flowering from midsummer to early autumn, this canna has tall spikes of orange flowers 5cm (2in) wide. They are set off by the wonderfully deep bronze foliage, which has striking pink veins. H 90cm (3ft) S 60cm (2ft). Half-hardy/Z7–10.

Canna 'Wyoming'
Flowering from midsummer to early autumn, this cultivar has pretty frilled orange flowers showing up well against the dark brown-purple leaves. H 1.8m (6ft) S 50cm (20in). Half-hardy/Z7–10.

Canna 'Picasso'

Canna 'Rosemond Coles'

Canna 'Wyoming'

Chionodoxa sardensis

Cardiocrinum giganteum

CARDIOCRINUM

This is a genus of 3 species of summer-flowering bulbous perennials, the most commonly grown of which is *Cardiocrinum giganteum*. The bulbs are grown for their lily-like flowers and attractive, heart-shaped leaves.
Cultivation Requires partial shade and moist, humus-rich soil. Avoid excessive dryness. They are ideal for growing in a woodland garden. In autumn plant bulbs just below the soil surface. Protect emerging growth in spring with a dry mulch. Water well in summer and provide a mulch of organic matter to prevent water evaporation.
Propagation The bulbs die after flowering, but offsets or daughter bulbs are produced and will flower in 3–5 years. Ripe seed may take seven years to flower.
Pests and diseases Lily viruses and slug damage.

Cardiocrinum giganteum
Giant lily
This species originates in the Himalayas, northwest Burma, southwest China and Japan. The leaves are broad and strongly veined. In late summer the magnificent tall racemes bear up to 20 fragrant, trumpet-shaped, cream flowers, streaked with purplish-red inside, which grow to 15cm (6in) long and are followed by decorative seedheads. Do not allow the soil to dry out. H 1.5–4m (5–13ft) S 45cm (18in). Hardy/Z7–9.

CHIONODOXA
Glory of the snow
This is a genus of 6 species of bulbs found on open mountain sides and forests in Crete, western Turkey and Cyprus. They are closely related to scillas.

Cultivation Choose a site in full sun and in autumn plant 5cm (2in) deep and 5cm (2in) apart.
Propagation Sow seed in pots in a cold frame as soon as they are ripe. Remove offsets in summer. They will naturalize easily.
Pests and diseases Largely trouble free.

Chionodoxa forbesii
Native to western Turkey, this species flowers in early spring, the racemes bearing up to 12 star-shaped, blue flowers, each with a white centre. H 10cm (4in) S 3cm (1¼in). Hardy/Z3–9.

Chionodoxa forbesii 'Pink Giant'
Derived from a species growing in western Turkey, 'Pink Giant' is a most garden-worthy cultivar, producing long racemes of 4–12 star-shaped, pale pink flowers, 1–2cm (½–¾in) wide, with white centres. The flowers are borne from early to mid-spring, so plant in the border or put several in a container in association with violas and dwarf daffodils. H 15cm (6in) S 4cm (1½in). Hardy/Z3–9.

Chionodoxa sardensis
Also from western Turkey, this species is slightly smaller than *C. luciliae*. In early spring racemes bear 4–12 star-shaped, deep clear blue flowers with blue centres, perfect for associating with blue *Anemone blanda*. H 10cm (4in) S 3cm (1¼in). Hardy/Z3–9.

Chionodoxa forbesii 'Pink Giant'

Colchicum speciosum 'Album'

Colchicum 'The Giant'

COLCHICUM
Autumn crocus, naked ladies

Colchicums are commonly known as autumn crocus because of their resemblance to the better known spring-flowering crocus and as naked ladies because they flower before the leaves emerge. In the United States they are known as naked boys. The genus contains about 45 species, which are native to alpine and sub-alpine meadows and stony slopes of Europe, north Africa, western and central Asia, northern India and western China.
Cultivation Grow in well-drained soil in full sun. In summer or early autumn plant corms 10cm (4in) deep in open ground in borders or grassland.
Propagation Sow seed in pots in a cold frame as soon as ripe or separate corms when dormant in summer. Increases freely.
Pests and diseases Grey mould and slugs.

Colchicum autumnale
Meadow saffron

This species grows in the sub-alpine meadows of Europe. In autumn each corm produces 1–6 goblet-shaped, lavender-pink flowers, with petals 3–5cm (1–2in) long. The flowers soon flop over. The broad leaves, 25cm (10in) long, appear after flowering, growing most in spring. The leaves might dwarf other spring-flowering bulbs, so take care with the position. This is a good choice for naturalizing in grass. H 10–15cm (4–6in) S 10–15cm (4–6in). Hardy/Z4–9.

Colchicum bivonae

This species grows in the sub-alpine meadows of southern Europe, from Corsica and Sardinia to western Turkey. Large, funnel-shaped, pinkish-purple flowers, chequered with dark purple, appear in late summer and autumn. The leaves are produced in spring. H 10–15cm (4–6in) S 10–15cm (4–6in). Hardy/Z4–9.

Colchicum speciosum 'Album'

The species originated in Caucasus, northeastern Turkey and Iran, and this is the most widely grown cultivar. In autumn 1–3 goblet-shaped, weather-resistant, white flowers, with petals 5–8cm (2–3in) long, appear long before the glossy leaves, which emerge in late winter or early spring. This is an excellent plant in open ground in borders or grassland. Left undisturbed, the corms will eventually produce large clumps. H 20cm (8in). S 20cm (8in). Hardy/Z4–9.

Colchicum 'The Giant'

This hybrid is one of many cultivars, and in autumn it produces a succession of up to 5 large purplish-violet flowers, each with the typical goblet shape. H 20cm (8in) S 20cm (8in). Hardy/Z4–9.

Colchicum 'Pink Goblet'

The pretty pink goblet-shaped flowers are produced in early autumn. They are perfect for planting in open spaces between shrubs where they can be left to naturalize. H 20cm (8in) S 10cm (4in). Hardy/Zone 4–9.

Colchicum 'Violet Queen'

One to five pretty pinkish-violet flowers with pointed tepals are produced in early autumn. They are funnel-shaped and fragrant. H 15cm (6in) S 10cm (4in). Hardy/Zone 4–9.

Colchicum 'Waterlily'

This hybrid is unusual in that it has tightly double flowers, with pinkish-lilac petals. In autumn it produces a succession of up to 5 blooms. The heads are heavy, so it is best grown where it will be supported by surrounding plants such as violas and lamiums. H 10–15cm (4–6in) S 15–20cm (6–8in). Hardy/Z4–9.

Colchicum 'Violet Queen'

CORYDALIS

The flowers of corydalis are an unusual shape. Each bears a long spur on the upper petal, and this gave rise to the name of the genus, for the Greek word *korydalis* means lark, and the spur on the flowers was thought to resemble the spur of the lark. This is a genus of about 300 species of fleshy- or fibrous-rooted annuals and biennials and tuberous or rhizomatous perennials. Most are herbaceous, although a few are evergreen. Many are from wooded or rocky mountain sites in northern temperate regions.
Cultivation Grow *C. solida* in full sun (although it will tolerate partial shade) and *C. cava* and *C. fumariifolia* in partial shade. In autumn plant tubers 8cm (3in) deep in borders or beneath trees and shrubs, where they will quickly colonize.
Propagation Sow seed in pots in a cold frame as soon as ripe. Divide spring-flowering species in autumn. Plants increase freely.
Pests and diseases Snails and slugs.

Corydalis cava
(syn. *C. bulbosa* of gardens)
Native to Europe, this corydalis has dense spikes of dark purple or white flowers, each up 2.5cm (1in) long, with downward-curving spurs. It flowers in spring and dies down in summer. H 10–20cm (4–8in) S 10cm (4in). Hardy/Z6–8.

Corydalis fumariifolia
(syn. *C. ambigua* of gardens)
This species originates in Russia, China and Japan. The bright blue or purplish-blue flowers, about 2.5cm (1in) long, have flattened, triangular spurs. It flowers in spring and dies down in summer. H 10–15cm (4–6in) S 10cm (4in). Hardy/Z7–8.

Corydalis solida
Fumewort
This spring-flowering species, native to northern Europe and Asia, bears dense racemes of pale mauve-pink to red-purple or white flowers, each to 2cm (¾in) long, with downward-curving spurs,

Crinum × powellii 'Album'

held above grey foliage. *C.* 'George Baker' AGM has deep reddish-pink flowers. Fumewort looks pretty with daffodils and other spring bulbs, all of which make ideal bedfellows. For those planted in partial shade, taller *Lilium martagon* (martagon lilies) can be planted to follow on later. H 18cm (7in) S 10cm (4in). Hardy/Z7–8.

CRINUM

The botanical name for the genus comes from the Greek word *krinon* (lily). It includes about 130 species of deciduous or evergreen bulbs, found near streams and lakes throughout tropical regions and South Africa. Contact with the sap may irritate the skin.
Cultivation Best grown in full sun outdoors in a sheltered border or in pots under glass. The bulbs are extremely large with long necks and can measure to 20cm (8in) in length. In spring plant so that the neck of the bulb is just above soil level. In a conservatory plant in soil-based compost (soil mix) with added sand and fertilizer, and grow in full or bright but filtered light. Water freely when in growth and keep moist after flowering. Provide a deep mulch in winter for plants in the garden.
Propagation Sow seed at 21°C (70°F) as soon as ripe. Remove offsets in spring.
Pests and diseases None.

Crinum × powellii 'Album'
This hybrid of two South African species has umbels of up to 10 widely flared, fragrant white flowers, to 10cm (4in) long. These are borne in late summer or early autumn above broad leaves, which may reach to 1.5m (5ft). It is an impressive plant, and grown well in moist but well-drained soil, it makes a beautiful garden specimen. *C. × powellii* AGM is pink. H 1.5m (5ft) S 30cm (12in). Borderline hardy/Z6–10.

Corydalis solida

Crocosmia 'Emberglow'

Crocosmia 'Solfatare'

CROCOSMIA

The name of the genus derives from *krokos*, the Greek word for saffron, and *osme* (smell), because the dried flowers smell of saffron when they are immersed in warm water. This is a small genus of only 9 species of clump-forming corms from grasslands in South Africa. The name montbretia is generally applied to all crocosmias, but strictly speaking montbretia is the hybrid *C. × crocosmiiflora*.

Cultivation Grow in sun or partial shade. In spring plant corms 8–10cm (3–4in) deep among shrubs or in a herbaceous border, but mulch during the first winter and in subsequent severe or prolonged frosty spells. In marginal areas plant beneath a sheltered, south-facing wall. Tall growth will benefit from support in early summer. Lift and divide clumps in spring to retain vigour.

Propagation Sow seeds in pots as soon as ripe. Divide in spring just before growth begins.

Pests and diseases Red spider mites may be a problem.

Crocosmia 'Bressingham Blaze'
Appearing in late summer, the brilliant orange-red flowers contrast with the yellow throats to make colourful, arching sprays. The leaves are strappy, pleated and mid-green. H 75–90m (30–36in) S 8cm (3in). Borderline hardy/Z5–9.

Crocosmia 'Emberglow'
The dark red flowers, which are borne in summer, make an impressive array on their arching stems. The leaves are strappy, pleated and mid-green. H 60–75cm (24–30in) S 8cm (3in). Borderline hardy/Z5–9.

Crocosmia 'Emily McKenzie'
In summer this smaller cultivar produces downward-facing, bright orange flowers, with attractive mahogany throat markings. The leaves are strappy and mid-green. H 60cm (24in) S 8cm (3in). Borderline hardy/Z5–9.

Crocosmia 'Firebird'
Flowering in summer, this cultivar has upward-facing, bright orange-red flowers. The leaves are strappy and mid-green. H 80cm (32in) S 8cm (3in). Borderline hardy/Z5–9.

Crocosmia 'George Davison'
Appearing in late summer, the lemon-yellow flowers of this cultivar make a lovely display on their slightly arching stems. The leaves are strappy and mid-green. H 60–75cm (24–30in) S 8cm (3in). Borderline hardy/Z5–9.

Crocosmia 'Lady Hamilton'
Flowering in late summer, this attractive cultivar has golden-yellow flowers with apricot centres. The leaves are strappy and mid-green. H 60–75cm (24–30in) S 8cm (3in). Borderline hardy/Z5–9.

Crocosmia 'Lucifer'
Flowering in midsummer, this cultivar has upward-facing, bright red flowers, 5cm (2in) long, on tall, slightly arching stems. The leaves are strappy, pleated and mid-green. H 1.2m (4ft) S 8cm (3in). Borderline hardy/Z5–9.

Crocosmia masoniorum
Flowering in midsummer, the upward-facing orange flowers are borne okn tall arching stems. H 1.2cm (4ft) S 8cm (3in). Borderline hardy/Z5–9.

Crocosmia 'Solfatare'
Flowering in midsummer, this cultivar has bronze foliage with apricot yellow flowers borne on arching stems. H 60cm (24in) S 8cm (3in). Borderline hardy/Z5–9.

Tall flowering bulbs over 70cm (28in)

Agapanthus 'Loch Hope'	Dahlia (many)
Allium giganteum	Eremurus 'Oase'
Allium 'Purple Sensation'	Eremurus × isabellinus
Asphodeline lutea	Galtonia candicans
Canna (most)	Lilium (most)
Crinum × powellii	Nectaroscordum siculum
Crocosmia 'Lucifer'	Tulipa 'Blue Heron'

Crocosmia 'Lucifer'

CRCCUS

The name is derived from the Greek *krokos* (saffron), and the genus includes the species *Crocus sativus*, cultivated for the spice saffron, which is obtained from its stigmas. The genus embraces more than 80 species of dwarf corms, found in a wide range of locations, from central and southern Europe, northern Africa, the Middle East, Central Asia and western China. Hundreds of cultivars have been produced from the original species. The crocus is one of our best-known late-winter and early-spring flowers, but there are several species that flower in autumn, as well as the true autumn crocus, which is quite distinct from, and not to be confused with, colchicums, which are sometimes referred to as autumn crocus.

Cultivation Grow in full sun. Plant corms 8cm (3in) deep in borders or containers in autumn for late winter- to spring-flowering crocuses and in late summer for autumn-flowering ones.

Propagation Many crocuses self-seed naturally. Remove baby corms during dormancy.

Pests and diseases Squirrels, mice and voles eat the corms; birds will pick off the flowers.

Crocus 'Blue Pearl'

Flowering in late winter to early spring, this hybrid is derived from a species that grows in southeastern Europe. The flowers have a soft blue outer colour, with white inner petals with yellow throats. The delicate colouring is superb. H 8cm (3in) S 5cm (2in). Hardy/Z3–8.

Crocus 'Cream Beauty'

Appearing in late winter to early spring, the flowers have a soft blue outer colour, with white inner petals with yellow throats. H 8cm (3in) S 5cm (2in). Hardy/Z3–8.

Crocus 'E. A. Bowles'

This spring-flowering crocus has beautiful pale cream flowers, brushed with a hint of darker grey on the reverse side of the petals. H 8cm (3in) S 5cm (2in). Hardy/Z3–8.

Crocus 'Snow Bunting'

This is a late-winter- and early-spring-flowering crocus with ivory-white flowers with a yellow base and purple feathering on the outside of the petals. It looks wonderful planted with *Anemone blanda*. H 8cm (3in) S 5cm (2in). Hardy/Z3–8.

Crocus 'Blue Pearl'

Crocus 'Zwanenburg Bronze'

Appearing in early spring, the pale yellow flowers are bronze on the outside. Plant them near purple violets or show them off by surrounding them with a gravel mulch. H 8cm (3in) S 5cm (2in). Hardy/Z3–8.

Crocus × luteus 'Dutch Yellow' (syn. C. 'Dutch Yellow')

The sterile flowers, which appear in winter to early spring, are a rich golden-yellow and associate well with other early-spring

Crocus chrysanthus

flowers, such as dwarf daffodils, *Anemone blanda* and violas. This cultivar also looks effective planted in grass. Increase by dividing the clumps. H 8cm (3in) S 5cm (2in). Hardy/Z3–8.

Crocus niveus

This is an autumn-flowering crocus from southern Greece which produces one or sometimes two flowers when the leaves are just emerging. The flowers vary from white to lilac, with yellow throats and prominent orange styles. It thrives best in full sun with a gritty, poor to moderately fertile soil as it needs summer dormancy to flower well. H 10–15cm (4–6in) S 10cm (4in). Hardy/Zone 4–9.

Crocus nudiflorus

This autumn-flowering crocus from south-west France, north and eastern Spain produces just one rich purple flower before the leaves emerge. H 15–25cm (6–10in) S 10cm (4in). Hardy/Zone 4–9.

Crocus speciosus

Flowering in autumn, this species is found across a wide area from Turkey, the Crimea, the Caucasus and into Central Asia. The scented, violet-blue flowers are veined with darker blue and have prominent orange styles. The leaves follow in spring. H 10–12cm (4–4¹/₂in) S 5cm (2in). Hardy/Z3–8.

Crocus nudiflorus

Crocus tommasinianus

Crocus tournefortii

Bulbs for naturalizing

Anemone blanda
Anemone nemorosa
Camassia
Colchicum
Crocus tommasinianus
Cyclamen hederifolium
Eranthis hyemalis
Erythronium
Galanthus nivalis
Hyacinthoides non-scripta
Narcissus poeticus var.
  recurvus
Trillium

Crocus sieberi subsp. *sublimis* f. *tricolor*

The species from which this hybrid has been developed originates in Greece. Flowers appear in late winter to early spring. Each petal has 3 bands of colour: yellow at the centre, then white, then blue-purple. The colouring is exquisite. H 5–8cm (2–3in) S 5–8cm (2–3in). Hardy/Z3–8.

Crocus sieberi 'Violet Queen'

The flowers appear in late winter to early spring. The petals are pale lilac-pink, which contrasts with the yellow at the centre. This is easy to grow and increases well. H 5–8cm (2–3in) S 5–8cm (2–3in). Hardy/Z3–8.

Crocus tommasinianus

Flowering in late winter to early spring, the species originates from woods and shady hillsides in southern Hungary, the former Yugoslavia and north-western Bulgaria. The flowers vary from pale silvery lilac to reddish-purple. On dull days the slender flowers are rather modest, but in sun they open to create a wonderful display. They are suitable for naturalizing in grass. H 8–10cm (3–4in) S 5–8cm (2–3in). Hardy/Z3–8.

Crocus tommasinianus 'Ruby Giant'

Appearing in late winter to early spring, the slightly rounded, deep violet-blue flowers, which are sterile, associate well with white *Anemone blanda* and early primroses. H 8–10cm (3–4in) S 5–8cm (2–3in). Hardy/Z3–8.

Crocus tommasinianus 'Whitewell Purple'

The slightly rounded purple-red flowers, which appear in late winter to early spring, are paler towards their base and contrast wonderfully with the orange anthers. H 8–10cm (3–4in) S 5–8cm (2–3in). Hardy/Z3–8.

Crocus tournefortii

The leaves appear from late autumn to winter, at the same time as the flowers, which are pale lilac-blue, with orange stigmas and white anthers. The species is native to southern Greece and Crete, and it requires a warm, sunny site. H 5–8cm (2–3in) S 5–8cm (2–3in). Borderline hardy/Z5–8.

Crocus vernus 'Jeanne d'Arc'

Flowering in early spring, this is a Dutch hybrid with large white flowers. It associates beautifully with early dwarf daffodils and early species tulips. H 10cm (4in) S 5–8cm (2–3in). Hardy/Z3–8.

Crocus vernus 'Pickwick'

Flowering in early spring, this Dutch hybrid has large white flowers streaked with lilac and dark purple. It is an eye-catching crocus, which associates well with early dwarf daffodils and early species tulips. H 10cm (4in) S 5–8cm (2–3in). Hardy/Z3–8.

Crocus vernus 'Remembrance'

Flowering in early spring, this Dutch hybrid has large, glossy violet flowers. It makes a perfect partner for early-flowering, dwarf, golden-yellow daffodils in borders, naturalized in grass or in containers. H 10cm (4in) S 5–8cm (2–3in). Hardy/Z3–8.

Crocus 'Zephyr'

Appearing in autumn, the pale silver-blue flowers, veined with dark blue, have yellow throats and white anthers. Leaves follow in spring. H 10–12cm (4–4¹/₂in) S 5cm (2in). Hardy/Z3–8.

Crocus sieberi subsp. sublimis f. tricolor

Crocus vernus 'Remembrance'

Cyclamen coum

Cyclamen cilicium

CYCLAMEN
Sowbread

The name of the genus derives from the Greek word *kyklos* (circle), probably in reference to the fact that the seed stalks of some species twist after flowering. The fruiting capsule is drawn down to soil level. The genus includes 19 species of tuberous perennials, found in a wide range of habitats from the eastern Mediterranean to Iran and south to Somalia, where there is winter rainfall and a dryish summer dormancy period. The rounded to heart-shaped leaves often have attractive silver markings.

Cultivation In autumn plant tubers 3–5cm (1¼–2in) deep in border soil. They do best in sheltered conditions and in partial shade beneath trees and shrubs.

Propagation Sow seed as soon as ripe, in darkness, at 6–12°C (43–54°F) or, for *C. persicum*, at 12–15°C (54–59°F). Soak seed for 10 hours before sowing and then rinse. *C. hederifolium* will self-seed naturally.

Pests and diseases Squirrels, mice and voles eat the tubers. Cyclamen are also prone to vine weevils, red spider mites, cyclamen mite and, under glass, grey mould.

Cyclamen cilicium

This species comes from southern Turkey and flowers in autumn. The pink or white flowers, with a darker maroon stain towards the mouth, appear at the same time as the leaves, which are rounded or heart-shaped and often patterned. It is perfect for under a spreading evergreen tree or shrub, where it will be protected from excess moisture and colder temperatures. H 12cm (4½in) S 5–8cm (2–3in). Borderline hardy/Z5–9.

Cyclamen coum

This species comes from Bulgaria, the Caucasus, Turkey and Lebanon. Appearing in late winter and early spring, the nodding, white to pale pink or pale purple flowers have darker staining towards the mouth. The rounded leaves often have silver markings. This cyclamen associates well with snowdrops. H 5–8cm (2–3in) S 10cm (4in). Hardy/Z5–9.

Cyclamen coum subsp. *caucasicum* 'Album'

This is the white form of the species, flowering in late winter and early spring. Its only colouring is the pink nose or staining towards the mouth of the flower. H 5–8cm (2–3in) S 10cm (4in). Hardy/Z5–9.

Cyclamen coum subsp. *caucasicum* Pewter Group 'Maurice Dryden'

The foliage is most distinctive: the pewter-silver leaves have a dark green midrib and edge. The large flowers are white tinged with pink, appearing first in late winter and lasting to early spring. H 5–8cm (2–3in) S 10cm (4in). Hardy/Z5–9.

Cyclamen hederifolium
(syn. *C. neapolitanum*)

This species is native to Europe from Italy to Turkey. Appearing in autumn, the pink fly-away flowers have a maroon stain towards the mouth. The flowers are sometimes scented. The ivy- or heart-shaped leaves are often patterned and normally appear after the flowers. These leaves make an excellent display throughout the winter months, making it a very valuable, though diminutive, garden plant. *C. hederifolium* var. *hederifolium* f. *albiflorum* has pure white flowers without basal markings. H 10cm (4in) S 5–8cm (2–3in). Hardy/Z5–9.

Cyclamen hederifolium

Cyclamen persicum

Dactylorhiza praetermissa

Cyclamen mirabile

This species comes from southwestern Turkey. Appearing in autumn, the attractive pale pink flowers have delicately serrated petals, with purple-stained mouths. The leaves are heart-shaped and patterned with silver blotches. H 10cm (4in) S 5–8cm (2–3in). Borderline hardy/Z5–9.

Cyclamen persicum

This species comes from the southeastern Mediterranean to northern Africa. The pink, red or white flowers have darker staining towards the mouth, and the heart-shaped leaves are often attractively patterned. Many

cultivars have been bred, and there are forms in various shades and sizes to choose from. Among the many florist's cyclamens are the ruffled-petalled, white-flowered 'Victoria', which is 30cm (1ft) high. They are normally grown as pot plants and are ideal for cool conservatory planting schemes or a north-facing windowsill indoors, when they flower from midwinter to early spring. The scented, miniature Miracle Series, which are only about 15cm (6in) high, are suitable for planting out in a sheltered spot in the garden, where they will flower from autumn right through to spring. H 10–30cm (4–12in) S 15cm (6in). Borderline hardy, Z5–9.

DACTYLORHIZA
Marsh orchid, spotted orchid

This is a genus of about 30 species of tuberous orchids, which are not widely grown but deserve a place in woodland gardens, where they will flower from late spring to midsummer.
Cultivation Plant the long, narrow tubers 8cm (3in) deep in moisture-retentive but well-drained soil in partial shade. They will appreciate being in a sheltered corner and will benefit from an annual mulch of leafmould.
Propagation In autumn lift and divide tubers, making sure each piece has a shoot.
Pests and diseases Slugs and snails.

Dactylorhiza maculata
Heath spotted orchid

The variable species, in both size and colour, is native to Europe and North Africa. From mid-spring to late summer it bears spikes of flowers, which may be shades of pink, red or purple or even white. The leaves may be plain green or have red-brown markings. They prefer less fertile, slightly acidic soil. H 15–60cm (6–24in) S 15cm (6in). Hardy/Z6.

Dactylorhiza praetermissa
(syn. *D. majalis* subsp. *praetermissa*)
Southern marsh orchid

In late spring to early summer this plant, which is native to northwestern Europe, produces a dense spike of purple-red flowers, which are often streaked and spotted with black. Plant in moisture retentive but not boggy soil. Additional grit is helpful in heavy clay. H 30–70cm (12–28in) S 15cm (6in). Hardy/Z6.

Dactylorhiza maculata

Bulbs with distinctive leaves

Allium karataviense
Arum italicum 'Marmoratum'
Canna 'Striata'
Canna 'Tropicanna'
Cardiocrinum giganteum
Cyclamen coum 'Maurice Dryden'
Dahlia 'Bishop of Llandaff'
Dahlia 'Yellow Hammer'
Erythronium californicum 'White Beauty'
Tulbaghia violacea 'Silver Lace'
Tulipa 'New Design'
Tulipa 'Red Riding Hood'
Zantedeschia 'Cameo'

DAHLIA

The genus was named in honour of the Swedish botanist Dr Anders Dahl (1751–89), who was a pupil of Linnaeus. It includes about 30 species and some 2,000 cultivars of bushy, tuberous-rooted perennials from mountainous areas of Mexico and Central America to Colombia. The dahlia is one of the showiest flowers in the summer border. There is a wide range of colours, including both strident and pastel shades of yellow, orange, red, lavender, deep purple and pink as well as white, and some forms combine more than one colour. They vary in flower size from 5cm (2in) across, as with the Pompon dahlias, to enormous, dinner-plate-sized flowers, almost 30cm (12in) across. They are also available as dwarf patio cultivars and large exhibition dahlias.

Cultivation Start tubers into growth under glass in early spring but do not plant out until all risk of frost has passed in early summer. Choose a sunny site with rich, well-drained soil. Most medium to tall dahlias will need staking or a sturdy support. In autumn cut off the topgrowth, lift the tubers and store them in dry, frost-free conditions. In warmer, sheltered areas dahlias may be left in the ground over the winter, particularly if a dry mulch is applied before temperatures drop below freezing.

Dahlia 'Omo'

Propagation Start tubers into growth in early spring and either take basal shoot cuttings or divide tubers into smaller sections, making sure each has a shoot.
Pests and diseases Caterpillars, slugs and earwigs may cause problems outdoors; stored tubers may rot.

All the following dahlias will flower from midsummer to autumn. They are all half-hardy.

Single-flowered dahlias (Division 1)

A central disc is surrounded by 1 or 2 rows of petals. Mostly dwarf, these dahlias are suitable for bedding and container use. No staking is required.

Dahlia 'Dark Desire'

An attractive but unusual cultivar, this has rich, dark chocolate-purple petals, set off by a central yellow disc. The wiry stems are dark and slim, making this a good choice for a border or raised bed where the plant as a whole can be fully appreciated. H 90cm (36in) S 30cm (12in). Half-hardy/Z8–10.

Dahlia 'Ellen Houston'

The orange-red flowers contrast beautifully with the purple-tinged foliage of this plant. H 30cm (12in) S 30cm (12in). Half-hardy/Z8–10.

Dahlia 'Omo'

This pretty dahlia is white with a yellow disc. H 45cm (18in) S 45cm (18in). Half-hardy/Z8–10.

Dahlia 'Yellow Hammer'

This is a distinctive, bushy dwarf bedding dahlia with yellow blooms held above dark bronze foliage. H 60cm (24in) S 45cm (18in). Half-hardy/Z8–10.

Dahlia 'Ellen Houston'

Dahlia 'Yellow Hammer'

Dahlia 'Hillcrest Regal'

Dahlia 'Clair de Lune'

Anemone-flowered dahlias (Division 2)
The flowers are double, with one or more rings of petals around a central group of tubular florets.

Dahlia 'Freya's Paso Doble'
This well-known dahlia has white outer petals and a raised central yellow cushion of much shorter petals. H 90cm (36in) S 60cm (24in). Half-hardy/Z8–10.

Dahlia 'Scarlet Comet'
The vivid red flowers have upright central petals. H 1.2m (4ft) S 60cm (24in). Half-hardy/Z8–10.

Collerette dahlias (Division 3)
These dahlias have an outer ring of ray-florets which may overlap, surrounding an inner ring of shorter florets forming a collar around a central disc. Flowerheads are 10–15cm (4–6in) across.

Dahlia 'Clair de Lune'
The inner collar of cream petals is surrounded by an outer ring of lemon-yellow petals. This dahlia can be grown in borders or containers, and it looks lovely against bronze or pale green foliage. H 1.1m (3ft 6in) S 90cm (36in). Half-hardy/Z8–10.

Dahlia 'Hillcrest Regal'
This dahlia has maroon flowers with a white-tipped collar, which contrast well with the central yellow disc. H 1.1m (3ft 6in) S 60cm (24in). Half-hardy/Z8–10.

Waterlily-flowered dahlias (Division 4)
The flowers are classified as large, medium, small or miniature, and are fully double and flattened.

Dahlia 'Figurine'
The small flowers have petals that are a blend of pink and white, fading towards the centre. H 1.2m (4ft) S 60cm (24in). Half-hardy/Z8–10.

Dahlia 'Gerrie Hoek'
This charming dahlia has small flowers with pale pink outer petals and darker pink inner petals. H 1.2m (4ft) S 60cm (24in). Half-hardy/Z8–10.

Dahlia 'Zingaro'
This pretty compact dahlia has petals blending from pink through warm orange-pink to yellow. It is suitable for a medium to large container. H 60–75cm (24–30in) S 35cm (14in). Half-hardy/Z8–10.

Bulbs with pink flowers

Allium cernuum
Allium roseum
Amaryllis belladonna
Begonia (many)
Chionodoxa forbesii
 'Pink Giant'
Colchicum autumnale
 'September'
Dahlia 'Figurine'
Dahlia 'Kidd's Climax'

Hyacinthus orientalis 'Pink
 Pearl'
Lilium 'Pink Perfection'
Nerine bowdenii 'Pink
 Triumph'
Nerine undulata
Nerine 'Zeal Giant'
Schizostylis coccinea 'Jennifer'
Tulipa 'Angélique'
Tulipa 'Ester'

Dahlia 'Figurine'

Dahlia 'Alva's Supreme'

Dahlia 'Kidd's Climax'

Decorative dahlias (Division 5)

The flowers are classified as giant, large, medium, small or miniature. They are double and the tips of the petals are bluntly pointed.

Dahlia 'Alva's Supreme'

The giant flowers, 25–30cm (10–12in) across, are pale yellow. H 1.1m (3ft 6in) S 60cm (24in). Half-hardy/Z8–10.

Dahlia 'Arabian Night'

The small flowers have velvety red petals that are long, broad and gently rounded, and they look attractive against its dark green foliage. It is a popular dahlia, which can be grown in borders but also looks effective in large half-barrels. H 1m (3ft 3in) S 1m (3ft 3in). Half-hardy/Z8–10.

Dahlia 'David Howard'

The miniature flowers are golden-orange and look delightful against the lovely bronze foliage. H 75cm (30in) S 75cm (30in). Half-hardy/Z8–10.

Dahlia 'Kidd's Climax'

This is one of the most beautiful dahlias of all time. It is a delicate blend of pink suffused with golden yellow, making it an old favourite that has been winning prizes for over 50 years. H 1.1m (3ft 6in) S 60cm (24in). Half-hardy/Z8–10.

Dahlia 'Smokey'

The small flowers are a wonderful mixture of purple and white. H 1.1m (3ft 6in) S 90cm (3ft). Half-hardy/Z8–10.

Ball dahlias (Division 6)

The globe-shaped flowers are small or miniature and all are fully double.

Dahlia 'Barberry Carousel'

The small globe-shaped flowers are lavender blended with white, making a delightful combination. H 90cm (36in) S 60cm (24in). Half-hardy/Z8–10.

Dahlia 'Cherida'

The small globe-shaped flowers are bronze-tinged lilac. H 1m (3ft 3in) S 60cm (24in). Half-hardy/Z8–10.

Dahlia 'Cryfield Rosie'

The small yellow flowers are tinged with red. H 1m (3ft 3in) S 60cm (24in). Half-hardy/Z8–10.

Dahlia 'Jomanda'

The small globe-shaped flowers are terracotta red. H 1m (3ft 3in) S 60cm (24in). Half-hardy/Z8–10.

Dahlia 'Regal Boy'

The small ball-shaped flowers are an exciting rich royal purple. H 1m (3ft 3in) S 60cm (24in). Half-hardy/Z8–10.

Dahlia 'Robin Hood'

Small globe-shaped flowers with warm orange-bronze blends. H 90cm (36in) S 60cm (24in). Half-hardy/Z8–10.

Dahlia 'Sunny Boy'

Orange perfectly formed petals create a small ball-shaped dahlia. H 90cm (36in) S 60cm (24in). Half-hardy/Z8–10.

Dahlia 'David Howard'

Dahlia 'Jomanda'

Dahlia 'Noreen'

Dahlia 'Brilliant Eye'

Pompon dahlias (Division 7)

The flowers are fully double and more globose than ball dahlias (Division 6). The petals are round or blunt at the tips. Although the plants are to 90cm (36in) high, the flowers are only 5cm (2in) across.

Dahlia 'Brilliant Eye'

The bright red, rolled petals make neat flowers. This dahlia looks lovely in association with blue caryopteris or asters (Michaelmas daisies). H 90cm (36in) S 60cm (24in). Half-hardy/Z8–10.

Dahlia 'Moor Place'

A good exhibition cultivar, its flowers are maroon purple, and the leaves are glossy and dark green. H 90cm (36in) S 60cm (24in). Half-hardy/Z8–10.

Dahlia 'Noreen'

A good exhibition cultivar, this dahlia has pinkish-purple flowers. H 90cm (36in) S 60cm (24in). Half-hardy/Z8–10.

Dahlia 'Rhonda'

A good exhibition cultivar, this has perfect pale lilac-pink flowers. The leaves are glossy and dark green. H 90cm (36in) S 60cm (24in). Half-hardy/Z8–10.

Dahlia 'Small World'

This is regarded as one of the best white dahlias. The flowers are sometimes flecked with purple. It associates well with plants with silver foliage. H 90cm (36in) S 60cm (24in). Half-hardy/Z8–10.

Cactus-flowered dahlias (Division 8)

The flowers are classified as giant, large, medium, small or miniature. They are fully double and have rolled, pointed petals.

Dahlia 'Doris Day'

This small cactus-flowered dahlia has long, dark red petals and makes a compact bush. The flowers are ideal for cutting. H 90cm (36in) S 60cm (24in). Half-hardy/Z8–10.

Dahlia 'Kiwi Gloria'

This is a small cactus-flowered dahlia with delicate lilac and white blooms. It is a top exhibition dahlia but needs "stopping" (the removal of the growth centre) to perform well, and it is not regarded as easy for the average gardener. H 1m (3ft 3in) S 60cm (24in). Half-hardy/Z8–10.

Dahlia 'Summer Night'

The flowers of this attractive dahlia have deep red, long, narrow, pointed petals and almost black centres, making a memorable combination. It makes an excellent choice for the border as well as being a favourite cut flower for the house. H 1m (3ft 3in) S 60cm (24in). Half-hardy/Z8–10.

Dahlia 'Doris Day'

Dahlia 'Hayley Jane'

Dahlia 'Nargold'

Semi-cactus-flowered dahlias (Division 9)

As with cactus-flowered dahlias, the flowers are classified as giant, large, medium, small or miniature, but the petals are rolled to only half their length.

Dahlia 'Belle of the Ball'

This is a large lavender-pink dahlia, raised in the United States, with heavily fimbriated (with fringed edges) petals. It is excellent for garden, cut flower and show use. H 1.2m (4ft) S 60cm (24in). Half-hardy/Z8–10.

Dahlia 'Geerlings Indian Summer'

A medium dahlia, with pointed and rolled red petals. This is an ideal dahlia for growing in a container, such as a large half-barrel, as well as at the front of a border. H 1.2m (4ft) S 60cm (24in). Half-hardy/Z8–10.

Dahlia 'Hayley Jane'

This eye-catching plant is a small dahlia with white petals that are tipped with purple. H 1.2m (4ft) S 60cm (24in). Half-hardy/Z8–10.

Dahlia 'Kenora Sunset'

A medium dahlia, this has brilliant red and yellow blooms. It makes a showy border plant. H 1.2m (4ft) S 60cm (24in). Half-hardy/Z8–10.

Dahlia 'Lemon Elegans'

This is a lovely pure yellow small dahlia with fully curving blooms on long stems. H 1.2m (4ft) S 60cm (24in). Half-hardy/Z8–10.

Dahlia 'Nargold'

Originating in South Africa in 1994, this medium cultivar is fimbriated with deeply split petals, so that the overall effect is of a frilled flower. It has an unusual blend of deep bronze tips suffused with deep golden yellow. H 1m (3ft 3in) S 60cm (24in). Half-hardy/Z8–10.

Dahlia 'Piper's Pink'

This is a small cultivar with pink flowers, dating back to 1964. It is a dainty dahlia and would be pretty beside blue Perovskia. H 90cm (36in) S 60cm (24in). Half-hardy/Z8–10.

Dahlia 'Purple Gem'

The long, narrow, pointed, recurved petals are rich purple. This is a good dahlia for a border, and the flowers are ideal for cutting. H 1m (3ft 3in) S 60cm (2ft). Half-hardy/Z8–10.

Bulbs with orange or bronze flowers

Begonia 'Non-stop Orange'
Dahlia 'Art Deco'
Dahlia 'Ellen Houston'
Dahlia 'Nargold'
Dahlia 'Small World'
Lilium 'Fire King'
Lilium 'Orange Pixie'
Tulipa 'Oranje Nassau'

Dahlia 'Purple Gem'

Dahlia 'Piper's Pink'

Dahlia 'Art Deco'

Dahlia 'Bishop of Llandaff'

Miscellaneous dahlias (Division 10)
This group includes a wide range of hybrids, which are sometimes described as peony-flowered, orchid-flowered, mignon or gallery. Not all these designations are universally accepted.

Dahlia 'Art Deco'
One of the gallery-type dahlias, this is a relatively recent introduction from the Netherlands. It is a striking orange with an even deeper orange centre. It is useful for borders or patio containers. H 25–30cm (10–12in) S 25–30cm (10–12in). Half-hardy/Z8–10.

Dahlia 'Bishop of Llandaff'
This dahlia bears scarlet red flowers with yellow anthers and dark bronze-green leaves. Its warm hues make a valuable contribution to summer and autumn borders. H 85cm (34in) S 90cm (36in). Half-hardy/Z8–10.

Dahlia 'Jescot Julie'
This double orchid-type dahlia has orange-purple flowers with purple-backed petals. H 60–90cm (24–36in) S 60–90cm (24–36in). Half-hardy/Z8–10.

Dahlia 'Ragged Robin'
This is an attractive but unusual cultivar. The flowers, which are held high above the foliage, have a profusion of deep red petals surrounding the central yellow disc. The wiry stems are dark and slim. This makes a choice plant for a border or raised bed, where the plant as a whole, not just the flowers, can be fully appreciated. H 90cm (36in) S 30cm (12in). Half-hardy/Z8–10.

Dahlia 'Tally Ho'
This is a single dark-leaf dahlia with warm red flowers that has been rather underestimated but is as good as 'Bishop of Llandaff'. H 75cm (30in) S 60cm (24in). Half-hardy/Z8–10.

Dahlia 'Tally Ho'

DIERAMA
Angel's fishing rod

This is a genus of 44 species of evergreen perennials, which grow from corms. They originated in moist mountainous grassland in Ethiopia, eastern and southern tropical Africa and South Africa.
Cultivation Choose a sheltered site, in full sun, with reliably moist but well-drained soil. Winter protection may be necessary in cold areas. Plant corms 5–8cm (2–3in) deep in spring.
Propagation Sow seed in a container as soon as ripe, or divide in spring.
Pests and diseases Trouble free.

Dierama pulcherrimum

This forms large, dense tufts of rush-like leaves and produces lots of arching flower stems along which papery pink flowers open in sequence throughout the summer. This is a graceful plant and is perfect for softening the edge of a hard patio landscape or for placing besides a pool. It may be hard to establish, but once happy it requires little attention. *D. pulcherrimum* 'Blackbird' has deep wine purple flowers. H 1–1.5m (3–5ft) S 60cm (24in). Borderline hardy/Z7.

Eranthis hyemalis

ERANTHIS
Winter aconite

This is a small genus of about 7 species of small, hard, knobbly tubers from woodlands and shady habitats in Europe and Asia. They prefer alkaline or neutral soil to acidic conditions.
Cultivation Grow in full sun or light shade; they are ideal beneath deciduous trees. Plant the small, pea-like tubers 5cm (2in) deep. They can be difficult to establish if they are too dry, so plant the tubers as soon as they are available in autumn, soaking them overnight before planting; alternatively, buy aconites growing 'in the green' in spring. They are ideal for a cultivated eye beneath a tree, where they will flower just before snowdrops, then overlap with them for a time. They will also naturalize in grass. They form large clumps and colonize quickly in ideal conditions, especially in alkaline soils.
Propagation Sow seed in a cold frame when ripe in late spring. Dig up and separate tubers in spring after flowering.
Pests and diseases Prone to smuts.

Eranthis hyemalis

Originally from southern France to Bulgaria, this is one of the first flowers to emerge after midwinter has passed. The golden-yellow petals are surrounded by a collar of deeply dissected green leaves. If you can remember where they have become established in the garden, try digging up a few tubers in mid- to late autumn and pop them into a small container, where they will flower from mid- to late winter. They can always be replanted in garden soil after flowering. H 5–8cm (2–3in) S 8cm (3in). Hardy/Z4–9.

Eremurus 'Oase'

EREMURUS
Foxtail lily, desert candle

The genus name is descriptive: *eremos* is a Greek word meaning solitary, and *oura* means tail, which refer to the tall flower spikes that emerge far above the foliage. This is a genus of 40 to 50 species of clump-forming, fleshy-rooted perennials, which splay out from a central crown. They originate in dry areas of western and central Asia.
Cultivation Choose a sunny, well-drained spot in the border, and plant the crowns in autumn, just below the soil surface; take care not to disturb the roots thereafter. Protect young growth, which is susceptible to frost, with a dry mulch in spring. Offer supports for plants in exposed sites. The long, strappy leaves can look unsightly, but die back soon after flowering.
Propagation Sow seed in a cold frame in autumn or carefully divide established clumps in autumn and replant.
Pests and diseases Prone to damage from slugs.

Dierama pulcherrimum

Erythronium dens-canis

Eremurus × isabellinus Ruiter hybrids

Flowering in early and midsummer, this group of perennials has long, narrow leaves and tall racemes of mixed orange, copper and pink flowers. Similar to the Ruiter hybrids are the cultivars 'Cleopatra' (bright orange), 'Image' (clear yellow), 'Parade' (clear pink) and 'Sahara' (copper). Well-established plants will form a striking picture in the garden. H 1.5m (5ft) S 90cm (3ft). Hardy/Z5–8.

Eremurus 'Oase'

Also flowering in early and midsummer, this is a shorter version of its towering cousins, but it, too, has long, narrow leaves and impressive racemes of yellow flowers, which fade to apricot and orange-brown. H 90–120cm (3–4ft) S 60cm (2ft). Hardy/Z5–8.

Eremurus robustus

This species, which is native to Central Asia, flowers in early and midsummer. It is an especially tall plant, with long, narrow leaves and massive racemes of pale pink flowers, which are enhanced by golden-yellow stamens. H 2.1m (7ft) S 90cm (3ft). Hardy/Z5–8.

Eremurus stenophyllus subsp. stenophyllus

This tall perennial originated in Central Asia, Iran and western Pakistan, and it flowers in early and midsummer. It has long, narrow leaves and tall racemes of

clear yellow flowers, which fade to orange-brown. H 1.5m (5ft) S 75cm (30in). Hardy/Z5–8.

Flowers with recurved petals

- Cyclamen coum
- Cyclamen hederifolium
- Erythronium
- Lilium martagon
- Lilium speciosum
- Narcissus cyclamineus
- Narcissus poeticus var. recurvus

ERYTHRONIUM
Dog's tooth violet

The genus contains about 22 species of bulbous perennials from Europe, Asia and North America. The bulbs are unusually long, whitish in colour and rather pointed, which has given rise to the common name of dog's tooth violet. The other common names of erythronium, trout lily and fawn lily, refer to the mottling on the leaves.

Cultivation Grow in partial shade in humus-rich, well-drained soil. Plant bulbs 10cm (4in) deep. They can be difficult to establish if they are too dry, so look for bulbs packaged in moist peat. Leave undisturbed so that they can form a large clump. Mulch with leafmould each year.

Propagation Divide established clumps in spring after flowering.

Pests and diseases Prone to damage from slugs.

Erythronium californicum 'White Beauty'

The species to which this cultivar belongs originates in California, USA. The delicately mottled leaves are a beautiful foil for the white flowers, which appear in spring. Each flower has a dark orange ring at the centre. H 20–30cm (8–12in) S 15cm (6in). Hardy/Z4–9.

Erythronium dens-canis

Native to Europe and Asia, this is one of the prettiest of spring flowers, with dainty, swept-back petals which may be white, pink or lilac. The leaves have attractive blue and green markings. Plant it in borders or among short, fine grasses. H 10–15cm (4–6in) S 10cm (4in). Hardy/Z3–9.

Erythronium 'Pagoda'

This is a vigorous cultivar derived from a Californian species, *E. tuolumnense*. Flowering in spring, it has yellow, swept-back petals and prominent, deep yellow anthers, with 2 or more flowers on each stem. The glossy leaves are plain deep green. A well-established clump could be displayed to advantage against a background of dark green foliage. H 15–35cm (6–14in) S 10cm (4in). Hardy/Z4–9.

Erythronium revolutum
American trout lily

Originally from north California, this plant bears pale to dark pink, pendent flowers with most distinctive and attractive reflexed petals. The flowers, which appear in mid-spring, look striking above the green leaves, which are mottled with brown. H 20–30cm (8–12in) S 10cm (4in). Hardy/Z4–9.

Erythronium 'Pagoda'

Eucomis autumnalis 'White Dwarf'

Eucomis bicolor

Eucomis comosa 'Sparkling Beauty'

EUCOMIS
Pineapple lily

This is a genus of about 15 species of bulbs found in southern Africa. The name is derived from the Greek words *eu-* (beautiful) and *kome* (head), which refer to the tuft of small bracts growing out of the top of the flower, a feature that makes it instantly recognizable as the pineapple lily.

Cultivation Grow indoors or, in warm, sheltered areas, beneath a sunny wall. Plant the large, rounded bulbs 15cm (6in) deep. Grow in a medium container, using a soil-based potting compost (soil mix) with added grit, and place in full light. Keep dry and frost-free in winter and start into growth in spring. Apply a liquid feed at regular intervals throughout summer. Repot every year. Alternatively, in warm, sheltered districts, where the risk of frost is negligible, plant outdoors in a warm, sunny spot beneath a wall; mulch in severe winters.

Propagation Remove offsets in spring after flowering, at the time of repotting, or sow seed at 16°C (61°F) in autumn or spring.

Pests and diseases None.

Eucomis autumnalis 'White Dwarf'

The small, white, star-shaped flowers are carried in a dense spike, which is topped with the distinctive crown of bracts. The flowers appear in late summer and last well into the autumn. The light green leaves have wavy margins. H 30cm (12in) S 20cm (8in). Borderline hardy/Z8–10.

Eucomis bicolor

Appearing in late summer and early autumn, the tall stems bear racemes of pale green flowers with purple margins, topped with a crown of pineapple-type bracts. The stems are flecked with maroon. The lower leaves are attractively wavy. H 40cm (16in) S 20cm (8in). Borderline hardy/Z8–10.

Eucomis comosa 'Sparkling Beauty'

With its deep burgundy leaves and stem and generous number of dark pinkish-purple flowers, this dramatic eucomis has become extremely popular. Flowering in late summer and autumn, the plant is grown as much for the intense, deep colour of its emerging leaves as its exciting flower. The deep colouring eventually fades as the flower spike ages and the seed pods are formed. This is a beautiful and dramatic specimen plant that is excellent for pots whether outside or in the conservatory. H 75cm (30in) S 20cm (8in). Borderline hardy/Z8–10.

Eucomis pallidiflora
Giant pineapple flower, giant pineapple lily

This late-summer-flowering bulb bears spikes of star-shaped, greenish-white flowers, with a crown of bracts. The flowers have an exotic air, especially when seen against the long, strappy leaves, which reach to 70cm (28in) and have wavy margins. Plant in containers or in borders. H 75cm (30in) S 20cm (8in). Borderline hardy/Z8–10.

Eucomis pallidiflora

FREESIA

This is one of the best-loved cut flowers, renowned for its perfume and beautiful array of colours. The genus was named by the German plant collector, C. E. Echlon, who died in South Africa in 1868, in honour of his student Friedrich Heinrich Theodor Freese (d.1876). It includes six or more species of corms from rocky upland sites to lowland sandy parts of South Africa, mainly from Cape Province. The first species to be sent to Britain, in 1816, had white flowers, and it was not until 1898 that a yellow-coloured species was introduced, whereupon selective hybridization began.

Cultivation Grow indoors or use outdoors as a summer bedding plant. Indoors, specially conditioned corms may be planted in early spring, 8cm (3in) deep and 5–8cm (2–3in) apart. Choose a medium to large container and use a soil-based potting compost (soil mix) with added grit. Shade from sun and keep moist until established. Position in full light and water freely. Keep temperatures below 13°C (55°F). Apply a liquid feed at regular intervals throughout summer once flower buds appear. Gradually reduce watering after flowering until the compost is dry. Leave dormant until repotting in autumn. Alternatively, plant specially conditioned corms outside in late spring to a depth of 8cm (3in) in a warm, sheltered border for

Freesia 'Dijon'

Freesia 'Wintergold'

flowering in late summer. Keep well watered through their growing period. Either discard corms at the end of the season and start again with treated corms the following season or dry them off and overwinter in a frost-free environment.

Propagation Remove offsets in autumn or sow seed at 13–18°C (55–64°F) in autumn or winter.

Pests and diseases Red spider mite, aphids, dry rot and fusarium wilt.

Freesia 'Blue Heaven'
The flowers of this species are almost transparent, with bluish-mauve petals combining beautifully with the pretty yellow throats. H 40cm (16in) S 10cm (4in). Half-hardy/Z9–10.

Freesia 'Dijon'
The blooms of this freesia are semi-double, with yellow flowers and throats. They make a pretty contrast to F. 'Blue Heaven'. H 40cm (16in) S 10cm (4in). Half-hardy/Z9–10.

Freesia 'Duet'
This species has semi-double white flowers that make a charming group either on their own or mixed with F. 'Blue Heaven or F. 'Everett'. H 40cm (16in) S 10cm (4in). Half-hardy/Z9–10.

Freesia 'Everett'
The familiar funnel-shaped flowers are pinkish-red in colour. They are also fragrant. Flowering

time varies, but treated corms planted in pots under cover in early spring will flower in midsummer, and those planted out in the borders from mid- to late spring will flower in late summer. H 30cm (12in) S 10cm (4in). Half-hardy/Z9–10.

Freesia 'Wintergold'
The fragrant, funnel-shaped flowers are yellow and make a beautiful cut flower. Flowering time varies, with treated corms planted in pots under cover in early spring will flower in midsummer, and those planted out in the borders from mid- to late spring will flower in late summer. H 25cm (10in) S 10cm (4in). Half-hardy/Z9–10.

Freesia 'Blue Heaven'

Freesia 'Duet'

Fritillaria imperialis 'Maxima Lutea'

Fritillaria imperialis 'The Premier'

rise to the common name; alternatively, the name may derive from the snake's head appearance of the seedhead, which appears soon after the petals have dropped. Grown in grassland, they are perfect companions for cowslips and ladysmock. In a container they look dramatic beneath white *Narcissus* 'Thalia'. H 20cm (8in) S 8cm (3in). Hardy/Z3–8.

FRITILLARIA
Fritillary

This is a genus of about 100 species of bulbs offering a wide range of flowering types, from giant, showy crown imperials to the small but much-loved snake's head fritillaries. They are found throughout the temperate regions of the northern hemisphere, from the Mediterranean through southwestern Asia and also western areas of North America.
Cultivation In autumn plant the large bulbs of *F. imperialis* and *F. persica* 20cm (8in) deep in garden soil where they will not be disturbed, or in large containers in compost (soil mix). *F. meleagris* has much smaller bulbs and should be planted 10cm (4in) deep. Fritillaries benefit from a layer of grit beneath the bulb at the time of planting and extra

lime, unless the soil is alkaline. Bulbs of *F. imperialis* are large and prone to rotting, so plant them tilted to one side to prevent water accumulating in their centres. They like a hot, dry summer after flowering. The smaller fritillaries may be grown in clumps, and the larger ones can be grouped or spaced 90cm (36in) apart so that each plant can be fully appreciated.
Propagation Divide the offsets in late summer.
Pests and diseases Prone to damage from slugs and lily beetle.

Fritillaria imperialis
Crown imperial

The species is native to areas from southern Turkey to Kashmir. It is a large bulb, which in late spring produces a stout stem topped by impressive umbels of

3–6 pendent bells, which may be orange ('The Premier'), yellow ('Maxima Lutea' AGM) or, more often, red ('Rubra'), out of which a crown of glossy, leaf-like bracts emerges. Both the bulbs and the flowers have a distinctive foxy smell. Introduced into Europe before 1592, this has long been a favourite plant, both in the grand, formal garden and in the cottage garden. H 70cm (28in) S 25cm (10in). Hardy/Z5–9.

Fritillaria meleagris
Snake's head fritillary

Originally native to an area extending from Britain to western Russia, in mid-spring the small bulb produces a wiry stem with 1 or 2 broadly bell-shaped flowers in pink, purple or white, each with strong chequerboard markings. The patterning may have given

Fritillaria michailovskyi

This fritillary is native to northeastern Turkey. The bulb produces a short stem with 1–4, sometimes even 7, broadly bell-shaped flowers, which are brown-purple on the outside but are tinged with green. The tips have an attractive yellow rim. They appear in late spring. Plant them at the front of a sunny border, where they will not be crowded out by taller plants. H 10–20cm (4–8in) S 5cm (2in). Hardy/Z5–8.

Fritillaria persica 'Adiyaman'
Persian lily

The species from which this cultivar has been developed originated from southern Turkey to Iran. The cultivar is rather taller than the species, and it flowers more generously. In late spring the bulb produces a stout stem with more than 30 dark purple, bell-shaped flowers, each covered with a waxy bloom. They look exquisite beside bright red *Tulipa* 'Apeldoorn' and the later dark purple *T.* 'Queen of Night'. H 1.5m (5ft) S 15cm (6in). Hardy/Z7–8.

Fritillaria uva-vulpis

This species is native to southeastern Turkey, north Iraq and west Iran. The bulb produces a short stem with a single, sometimes 2, narrowly bell-shaped flowers, 5cm (2in) long, which are brownish-purple, yellow within and yellow at the recurving tips. They appear in late spring and early summer. Plant them near the front of a sunny border, where they will not be overcrowded by taller plants. H 20cm (8in) S 5cm (2in). Hardy/Z7–8.

Fritillaria michailovskyi

Fritillaria persica 'Adiyaman'

GALANTHUS
Snowdrop

The genus name is derived from the Greek words *gala* (milk) and *anthos* (flower), a description for one of our most familiar bulbs, which is better known as the snowdrop. This is one of the first bulbs to flower after midwinter, growing taller as the days lengthen. The genus includes 19 species of bulbs from Europe to western Asia, mostly in upland wooded sites. They associate well with *Eranthis hyemalis* (winter aconite), winter-flowering heathers and dwarf Reticulata irises.

Cultivation Grow in sun or partial shade in moist soil that does not dry out in summer. Plant the bulbs 5cm (2in) deep in garden soil or short grass as soon as they are available in early autumn. They can be difficult to establish, although once they have settled down they will form good clumps and may self-seed. Alternatively, buy snowdrops 'in the green' – that is, those that have already flowered but still have their leaves. Plant them immediately after purchasing, and they should establish well. Plant groups of single and double snowdrops near each other in a border or in grassland. They will establish more quickly in border soil than in grassland, but even here, given time, they will form large groups.

Propagation Lift and divide clumps of bulbs after flowering. They will self-seed.

Pests and diseases Narcissus bulb fly and grey mould.

Galanthus 'Atkinsii'

This is a vigorous, comparatively tall snowdrop, which comes into flower in the late winter. It has elongated white flowers 3cm (1¼in) long. The three outer petals open to reveal three shorter inner petals, with a heart-shaped green tip to each inner petal. The flowers have a strong honey scent. H 20cm (8in) S 8cm (3in). Hardy/Z3–9.

Galanthus elwesii

This species is native to the Balkans and Turkey, and although it is less well known than the common snowdrop G. *nivalis*, some people think it is the superior species. It is a larger plant, with broad, rather glaucous leaves. The honey-scented flowers, which have large green spots on the inner petals, appear in late winter. H 12–23cm (4½–9in) S 8cm (3in). Hardy/Z3–9.

Galanthus nivalis
Common snowdrop

Originally from Europe in an area stretching from the Pyrenees to Ukraine, the species may also be native to Britain. In late winter it bears small, pure white, single flowers, 1–2cm (½–¼in) long, which fall like little drops of snow. The three outer petals open to reveal three shorter inner petals, each with an inverted, V-shaped, green mark at the tip. They have a delicious honey scent which is worth investigating. H 10cm (4in) S 10cm (4in). Hardy/Z3–9.

Galanthus 'S. Arnott'

Galanthus nivalis 'Flore Pleno'

The double form of the common snowdrop bears small, double, pure white flowers, 1–2cm (½–¼in) long, which hang from the stems, showing irregular outer petals and heavily marked, green and white smaller petals inside. They are sterile but will multiply from offsets. They look beautiful with a curtain of dark green ivy to set them off. H 10cm (4in) S 10cm (4in). Hardy/Z3–9.

Galanthus 'S. Arnott'

Named after the nurseryman Sam Arnott, this comparatively tall snowdrop flowers in late winter and early spring. The large, rounded, pure white flowers, 2–4cm (¼–1½in) long, fall like rounded drops of snow from a slender stem. The 3 outer petals open to reveal 3 shorter inner petals, each with green markings at the base and apex. They have a strong honey scent. H 20cm (8in) S 8cm (3in). Hardy/Z3–9.

Dwarf flowers

Allium karataviense
Anemone blanda
Colchicum speciosum
Crocus
Cyclamen coum
Cyclamen hederifolium
Eranthis hyemalis
Galanthus nivalis
Iris danfordiae
Iris reticulata
Muscari 'Valerie Finnis'
Narcissus 'Topolino'
Narcissus 'Tête-à-tête'
Tulipa (various species)

Galanthus nivalis 'Flore Pleno'

Galanthus 'Atkinsii'

Galtonia candicans

GALTONIA

The genus is named after Sir Francis Galton (1822–1911), a British scientist who travelled widely in South Africa where the 3 species of bulbs in the genus originate. They grow mainly in moist grasslands in their native home, but only one species is commonly grown in gardens.
Cultivation Grow in full sun in moist soil that does not dry out in summer. Plant the bulbs in early spring, 13cm (5in) deep, in well-drained garden soil among shrubs or in a herbaceous border. Add grit to heavy soils. They are borderline hardy, and it is advisable to mulch ground where frost occurs, and in areas where the ground freezes solid it is best to lift the bulbs in winter and store them in a frost-free place.

Propagation Remove offsets in early spring or sow seeds in spring (keep seedlings frost-free for the first 3 years).
Pests and diseases None.

Galtonia candicans
Cape hyacinth, summer hyacinth
The species originates from the Orange Free State, Eastern Cape, Natal and Lesotho. It is a tall plant, bearing up to 30 pendent, creamy white flowers, each up to 5cm (2in) long, on tall, sturdy stems in succession over several weeks in late summer. They are best planted in the border in bold groups and they show up well against plants with dark green foliage or against a wall. They may need replacing in their fourth year. H 1.1m (3ft 6in) S 10cm (4in). Hardy/Z7–10.

GLADIOLUS
The name of the genus derives from the Latin word *gladius* (sword), a reference to the shape of the leaves. There are about 180 species of corms in the genus, with more than 10,000 hybrids and cultivars. The species are found principally in South Africa, but they also occur in Mediterranean countries, north-western and eastern Africa, Madagascar and western Asia.
Cultivation Grow in full sun in moist soil that does not dry out in summer. In spring plant the corms 8–10cm (3–4in) deep in garden soil. Lift and dry off in autumn. Divide the new corms from the old ones, discarding the latter, and replant the new ones the following spring.
Propagation Remove cormlets when dormant. Alternatively, sow seed of hardy species in a cold frame in spring; sow seeds of half-hardy to tender plants at 15°C (59°F) in spring.
Pests and diseases Grey mould, thrips, aphids and slugs.

Gladiolus communis subsp. byzantinus
(syn. *Gladiolus byzantinus*)
This gladiolus originates from Spain, northwestern Africa and Sicily. It produces up to 20 funnel-shaped, magenta-pink flowers, each to 5cm (2in) across. From late spring to early summer they are borne in succession on tall flower spikes, starting at the base. It is borderline hardy, and it is best to mulch the ground where frost occurs, and in areas where the ground freezes solid it is best to lift the bulbs during winter. H 90cm (36in) S 8cm (3in). Hardy/Z6–10.

Gladiolus papilio
Originating from eastern South Africa, this species flowers from mid- to late summer. It produces hooded flowers, which range from yellow to yellow-green and are heavily flushed with purple. It spreads by means of stolons. It is borderline hardy, so it is advisable to mulch ground where frost occurs, and in areas where the ground freezes solid it is best to lift and store the bulbs in winter. H 90cm (36in) S 8cm (3in). Hardy/Z6–10.

Gladiolus hybrids
A vast number of hybrids have been bred over the last hundred years, but they fall into 3 main groups. Grandiflorus Group hybrids, which have one flower spike only, are mainly classified according to flower size: giant, large, medium, small and miniature. This group includes the Butterfly gladioli, which have ruffled petals and, often, a contrasting patch of colour on the lower petals. Nanus Group hybrids produce several slender spikes with loosely arranged flowers. Primulinus Group gladioli have a single thin, whip-

Gladiolus communis subsp. *byzantinus*

Gladiolus 'Seraphim'

Gladiolus 'Charming Beauty'

Gladiolus 'Nymph'

GLORIOSA

This genus of only one species is unusual because it is one of the few tuberous perennials to climb. It is native to tropical Africa and India. All parts of the plant are poisonous.

Cultivation Grow indoors in full sun. In early spring plant tubers 8–10cm (3–4in) deep in a large container, using a soil-based potting compost (soil mix) with added grit. Place in full light. Water well when growth begins and apply a liquid feed every 2 weeks. Offer support for the plant to climb up. Keep tubers dry in winter.

Propagation Separate the tubers in spring. Alternatively, sow seed at 19–24°C (66–75°F) in spring.

Pests and diseases Aphids.

---

like flower spike and bear triangular flowers. All hybrids are half-hardy/Z7–10.

Gladiolus 'Charming Beauty'
This is a Nanus gladiolus with rose-coloured, funnel-shaped flowers, to 5cm (2in) across, which are blotched with creamy white. It flowers from mid- to late summer. It can survive relatively mild winters in a border, if well mulched. H 60cm (24in) S 8cm (3in). Half-hardy/Z7–10.

Gladiolus 'Green Woodpecker'
This medium-sized Grandiflorus hybrid has funnel-shaped, greenish-yellow, ruffled flowers, to 5cm (2in) across, with wine-red marks on the throats. They are borne on a tall, upright stem. The flowers appear from mid- to late summer. H 1–1.5m (3–5ft) S 8cm (3in). Half-hardy/Z7–10.

Gladiolus 'Leonore'
This is a Primulinus gladiolus, which bears buttercup yellow flowers on a single flower spike, to 55cm (22in) long. It flowers in midsummer. H 90cm (36in) S 8cm (3in). Half-hardy/Z7–10.

Gladiolus 'Nymph'
This is a Nanus gladiolus with dainty white flowers, to 5cm (2in) across, each with a red mark on the throat. They are borne in succession on 25cm (10in) flower spikes. It looks dainty in a border and is a good partner for grey foliage. H 70cm (28in) S 8cm (3in). Half-hardy/Z7–10.

Gladiolus 'Seraphim'
This is a medium-sized Grandiflorus hybrid with pretty, pink, ruffled flowers, to 5cm (2in) across, each with a white throat. The blooms are borne in

succession on tall flower spikes in midsummer. It should be grown in a border and looks lovely near lime-green foliage. H 70cm (28in) S 8cm (3in). Half-hardy/Z7–10.

Gladiolus 'Zephyr'
This is a large-flowered Grandiflorus hybrid with ruffled light lavender pink flowers and small ivory throats, produced in midsummer. H 1.7m (5ft 6 in) S 15cm (6in). Half-hardy/Z7–10.

Gloriosa superba 'Rothschildiana'
The graceful flowers, 8–10cm (3–4in) across, have bright red petals edged with yellow. They are borne from the upper leaf axils from summer to autumn. The bright green leaves are glossy. This plant is excellent for growing in a conservatory. Handling the tubers may irritate the skin. H 1.8m (6ft) S 30cm (12in). Tender/Z10.

Gloriosa superba 'Rothschildiana'

Bulbs that require full sun

Agapanthus	Gladiolus
Allium schubertii	Iris bucharica
Allium karataviense	Iris danfordiae
Amaryllis belladonna	Iris reticulata
Canna	Nerine
Chionodoxa	Ornitholgalum dubium
Crinum × powellii 'Album'	Schizostylis
Dahlia	Sternbergia lutea
Eremurus	Tigridia
Galtonia candicans	Tulipa

Hedychium coccineum

Hedychium spicatum

HEDYCHIUM
Ginger lily

This genus of about 40 species of perennial rhizomes is found at the edge of forests and in damp places in tropical Asia, the Himalayas and Madagascar. The flowers are often sweetly fragrant and can be used in cooking. The roots, sap and flowers are mostly scented of ginger.

Cultivation In warmer areas some hedychiums can be grown permanently in borders outdoors. Grow in moist but well-drained soil, in sun or partial shade, with shelter from cold winds. Mulch in winter. In frost-prone areas, they can be bedded out into borders or grown in containers and treated as conservatory plants or summer patio plants. Use a tall, heavy pot

and a soil-based compost (soil mix), with added grit. Keep in a warm spot until the first signs of a new bud appear at the top of the rhizome, water freely in the growing season and provide high humidity and indirect light. Apply a liquid fertilizer every 4 weeks through the flowering season. Cut down after the first autumn frosts and move to a frost-free place for the winter months. Keep barely moist until early spring. Plants given the early warmth of growth under glass will flower earlier.

Propagation Divide the rhizomes in spring. Alternatively, sow seeds at 21–24°C (70–75°F) as soon as they are ripe.

Pests and diseases Aphids and red spider mite may be a problem if the plants are grown indoors.

Hedychium coccineum
Red ginger lily, scarlet ginger lily

This is a species from the Himalayas. It produces sharply pointed mid-green leaves and, in late summer and early autumn, racemes of tubular red, pink, orange or white flowers with prominent red stamens. Despite its status as half-hardy, it has been known to survive cold winters with a mulch. In frosty areas, however, it is better to grow it in a container which can be moved into frost-free conditions for the winter. H 1.8m (6ft) S 1m (3ft 3in) or more. Half-hardy/Z9–10.

Hedychium coccineum 'Tara'

The flowers of this cultivar are orange with red stamens. H 1.8m (6ft) S 1m (3ft 3in) or more. Borderline hardy/Z8–10.

Hedychium coronarium
Garland flower, white ginger lily

This species is native to India. It has sharply pointed mid-green leaves and in late summer and early autumn bears clusters of fragrant, white, butterfly-like flowers. H 90–120cm (3–4ft) S 90cm (36in) or more. Half-hardy/Z9–10.

Hedychium densiflorum 'Assam Orange'

The species, which comes from the Himalayas, was collected by Frank Kingdon-Ward in 1938. Like the species, this cultivar has sharply pointed, glossy, mid-green leaves, but in late summer it produces clusters of fragrant, deep orange flowers in dense racemes like bottle brushes. H 1–1.8m (3–6ft) S 1.8m (6ft). Borderline hardy/Z8–10.

Hedychium gardnerianum
Kahili ginger

This species is native to Northern India and the Himalayas. It produces long stems with broad grey-green foliage, crowned in late summer with wonderful butterfly-like, creamy-yellow flowers with red stamens. It is superbly fragrant. It could be grown in a pot or, in warm areas, near a pond. H 2m (6ft) Borderline hardy/Z8–10.

Hedychium spicatum

This is a species from the Himalayas. It has sharply pointed, glossy, mid-green leaves and in late summer produces large white flowers with a prominent lip and red to orange blotches. They are delicately scented. H 1–1.5m (3–5ft) S 1.8m (6ft). Borderline hardy/Z9–10.

HIPPEASTRUM

This genus of about 80 species of bulbs, found in Central and South America, is associated with many colourful large-flowered hybrids, which are often – incorrectly and confusingly – known as amaryllis. Each bulb will produce consecutively, 1–3 flowerheads, each on a hollow stem. Each flowerhead will normally have 2–5 individual flowers. The flowerheads are frequently as large as 20cm (8in) in diameter, although those of the miniature cultivars will be around 12.5 (5in) across. There are many exciting new developments, including the introduction of the Cybister types, which have tapering spidery petals in combinations of several exotic colours. Note that all parts are mildly toxic if ingested.

Cultivation In warmer areas, including zones 9–10, the bulbs can be grown permanently outdoors in borders or containers. In frost-prone areas bulbs are usually available throughout autumn until the following spring, and it is possible to grow them outdoors as summer container plants as long as planting is left until spring. Place them outside, after all risk of frost has gone, in sun or light shade and they will flower in 4–6 weeks. In frost-prone areas hippeastrums are more usually grown indoors in pots as houseplants. From autumn to winter plant the bulbs so that the neck and shoulders are above the surface of the compost. Take care that you do not damage the long, fleshy roots. Use a tall, heavy pot and a soil-based compost (soil mix) with added grit. Keep in a warm spot until the first signs of a new bud appear at the top of

Hedychium gardnerianum

Hedychium densiflorum 'Assam Orange'

Hippeastrum 'Christmas Star'

Hippeastrum 'Mary Lou'

the bulb. Bring into full light and keep the soil moist, applying a liquid fertilizer every 2 weeks. After flowering, allow the leaves to complete their life-cycle and then keep the compost dry while the bulbs are dormant. Bring bulbs into growth again the following autumn. They resent root disturbance, so it is best to pot on every 3–5 years at the end of the dormancy period. Often, the later the bulbs are started into growth, the quicker they will come into flower. Try growing them on pebbles and water in late winter (but discard the bulbs after flowering).
Propagation Remove offsets in autumn. Alternatively, sow seeds at 16–18°C (61–64°F) as soon as ripe and keep seedlings growing without a dormant period until they eventually come into flower.
Pests and diseases Aphids.

Hippeastrum 'Apple Blossom'
This cultivar produces white flowers with pink tinges to the tips of the petals. The flowers reach 10–15cm (4–6in) across. It will flower in midwinter or later depending on time of planting. H 30–50cm (12–20in) S 30cm (12in). Tender/Z10.

Hippeastrum 'Christmas Star'
Grown as a houseplant, this cultivar is a great favourite for a cheerful midwinter show with its rich red petals and white centres. It produces 4–6 umbels of funnel-shaped flowers, about 25cm (10in) across. The flowers are borne on stout, leafless stems. Often 2 or 3 flowerheads are produced in succession on new stems. The leaves tend to follow later. H 50cm (20in) S 30cm (12in). Tender/Z10.

Hippeastrum 'Mary Lou'
This cultivar has glorious double, white flowers, but each petal is edged with pink, which produces an exquisite effect. The total width of all the flowers is about 25cm (10in). They are borne on stout, leafless stems. Often 2 or 3 flowerheads are produced in succession on new stems. As a houseplant, it will flower in midwinter or later depending on the time of planting. Buy two or three bulbs and plant in the same container for a sumptuous display. The leaves will follow later, although they might begin to emerge soon after the flowers have opened. H 50cm (20in) S 30cm (12in). Tender/Z10.

Hippeastrum 'Merengue'
This cultivar is a recent introduction of the Cybister type, with its spidery flowerheads and exotic combination of deep red and brown flowers. These are borne on stout, leafless stems. Often 2 or 3 flowerheads are

Hippeastrum 'Apple Blossom'

Hippeastrum 'Red Velvet'

Hippeastrum 'Tango'

Hippeastrum 'Yellow Goddess'

produced in succession on new stems. As a houseplant, it will flower in midwinter with the leaves following later. H 45cm (18in) S 30cm (12in). Tender/Z10.

Hippeastrum 'Red Lion'
This cultivar produces scarlet flowers, which can reach 15cm (6in) in diameter, with a total width of 25cm (10in). When it is grown as a houseplant, the flowers provide a welcome burst of colour in midwinter. H 30–50cm (12–20in) S 30cm (12in). Tender/Z10.

Hippeastrum 'Red Velvet'
This cultivar produces bright red flowers on tall stems. Individual flowers may reach 15cm (6in) in

diameter, with a total width of 25cm (10in). As a houseplant, they give seasonal cheer in midwinter. H 60cm (24in) S 30cm (12in). Tender/Z10.

Hippeastrum 'Tango'
This cultivar is another recent introduction of the Cybister type, and it has wispy flowerheads of a striking combination of cherry red and green flowers. These are borne on stout, leafless stems. Often 2 or 3 flowerheads are produced in succession on new stems. Grown as a houseplant, it will flower in midwinter, with the leaves following later. Left until a late-spring planting, the flowers can be delayed until midsummer. H 45cm (18in) S 30cm (12in). Tender/Z10.

Hippeastrum 'Yellow Goddess'
The creamy yellow colouring is unusual among hippeastrum cultivars, and the flowers are made all the more attractive by their lime-green throats. The flowers are borne on stout, leafless stems. Often 2 or 3 flowerheads are produced in succession on new stems. Grown as a houseplant, it will flower in midwinter with the leaves following later. Left until a late-spring planting, the flowering can be delayed until midsummer. H 45cm (18in) S 30cm (12in). Tender/Z10.

Bulbs with green in the flowers

Eucomis bicolor
Galanthus nivalis 'Flore Pleno'
Gladiolus 'Green Woodpecker'
Hippeastrum 'Yellow Goddess'
Leucojum aestivum
Leucojum vernum
Nectaroscordum siculum
Ornithogalum nutans
Ornithogalum thyrsoides
Ornithogalum umbellatum
Tulipa 'Spring Green'
Tulipa urumiensis
Veratrum album
Zantedeschia aethiopica 'Green Goddess'

HYACINTHOIDES
Bluebell
This is a much-loved genus of 3 or 4 species of bulbs from deciduous woods and moist meadows of western Europe and northern Africa. There is nothing more enchanting in mid- to late spring than the sight of a mass of bluebells on a grassy bank or creating a sea of blue in the dappled shade of a wood. It is best to avoid planting them in a border because they are invasive and will eventually take over.
Cultivation Grow in partial shade under shrubs or trees in border soil or short grass. In autumn plant bulbs 8cm (3in) deep. Allow to self-seed, or deadhead flowers to prevent this from happening. Bluebells can also be successfully planted beneath hedgerows, in borders, grass or containers, although their favourite home will be beneath deciduous trees where the canopy of leaves is light.
Propagation Sow seed in containers in a cold frame as soon as ripe. Remove offsets from mature bulbs during the summer dormancy. They will self-seed. The English bluebell and the Spanish bluebell flower at the same time and will often hybridize naturally in the garden if planted close to each other. If you want to protect the English bluebell, avoid planting the Spanish bluebell altogether.
Pests and diseases None.

Hippeastrum 'Red Lion'

Hyacinthoides hispanica

Hyacinthus orientalis 'Amethyst'

Hyacinthoides hispanica
(syn. *Endymion hispanicus, Scilla campanulata, S. hispanica*)
Spanish bluebell
Found growing in woods and among shady rocks in Portugal, Spain and northern Africa, this spring-flowering bulb bears single blue, mauve or pink flowers on erect racemes of up to 15 bell-shaped, unscented flowers all the way around the stem. The leaves are broader than those of the English bluebell. Plant them among rhododendrons and azaleas for good colour associations or with small silver-foliage plants in a container. H 40cm (16in) S 10–15cm (4–6in). Hardy/Z4–9.

Hyacinthoides non-scripta
(syn. *Endymion non-scriptus, Scilla non-scripta, S. nutans*)
English bluebell
This species is found in woods and meadows of western Europe, beneath hedgerows or in oak and beech woods in spring. It bears single blue, sometimes pink or white, flowers in graceful racemes, which bend over at the tip. Up to 12 pendent, narrow, bell-shaped, scented flowers are borne on one side of the stem. To naturalize, plant 50–100 bulbs to 1 square metre (1 sq yd). The white-flowered form is *H. non-scripta* 'Alba'. H 20–40cm (8–16in) S 8–10cm (3–4in). Hardy/Z6–9.

HYACINTHUS
Hyacinth
This is one of the most fragrant of all spring-flowering bulbs. The genus contains only 3 species, found on limestone slopes and cliffs in western and Central Asia, but the many well-known cultivars have been bred from *H. orientalis*, which is native to central and southern Turkey, north-western Syria and Lebanon. It is an excellent bulb for indoor and outdoor use. Note that touching the bulbs can cause skin irritation, so wear gloves when handling.
Cultivation Outdoors grow in sun or partial shade in borders or in containers. Good drainage is important, so when planting in pots use a soil-based compost (soil mix) with extra grit. Flowers appear in early to mid-spring and combine beautifully with white or blue *Anemone blanda*, Double Early tulips, primroses, polyanthus and violas. Bedding hyacinths (ordinary hyacinths) should be planted in autumn, at a depth of 10cm (4in). Use soil-based compost in containers, with extra grit to ensure good drainage. For indoors choose specially treated (prepared) bulbs, which are available in late summer and early autumn. A wide range of colours is available, but not as wide as that available for bedding out.

Prepared bulbs should be planted in early autumn so that the flowers will appear in early winter. From planting to flowering normally takes about 12 weeks. Where the bowl or pot has no drainage holes, use a special bulb compost (planting medium). Alternatively, place the bulb on top of water in a special hyacinth glass (with a narrow neck to support the bulb). Keep the bulbs in a dark, cool place at 10°C (50°F) for about 8 weeks to allow the roots to develop. Bring into a light but not sunny spot until the flower bud is visible. Thereafter, take into a warm room and allow to flower. After flowering, discard bulbs that have been grown on water. All other container-grown hyacinths can be transferred to the garden, where they will flower for many years.
Propagation Remove offsets from mature bulbs while dormant in summer.
Pests and diseases None.

Hyacinthus orientalis 'Amethyst'
The distinctive lilac-amethyst flowers, which are borne in early to mid-spring, are richly scented and combine well with pink primroses and grey-foliage plants. H 20–30cm (8–12in) S 8cm (3in). Hardy/Z6–9.

Hyacinthoides non-scripta 'Alba'

Hyacinthus orientalis 'Blue Jacket'

Hyacinthus orientalis 'City of Haarlem'

Hyacinthus orientalis 'Ben Nevis'
This is a double hyacinth with white, delightfully scented flowers. Plant with white violas for a stunning all-white effect. The flowerheads are heavy and may need support. H 20–30cm (8–12in) S 8cm (3in). Hardy/Z6–9.

Hyacinthus orientalis 'Blue Jacket'
This is an excellent dark blue hyacinth, with fragrant flowers, which would combine well with rich blue *Muscari armeniacum* to make an all-blue effect. H 20–30cm (8–12in) S 8cm (3in). Hardy/Z6–9.

Hyacinthus orientalis 'Carnegie'
The racemes consist of up to 40 waxy, single, pure white, tubular, bell-shaped flowers, which are richly scented and borne on stout, leafless stems. They combine beautifully with Double Early tulips. H 20–30cm (8–12in) S 8cm (3in). Hardy/Z6–9.

Hyacinthus orientalis 'City of Haarlem'
This is one of the cultivars that is available as both prepared and ordinary bedding bulbs, so check before buying. The beautiful single, pale lemon-yellow flowers are wonderfully scented and look lovely grown indoors, where they flower in midwinter, or outdoors, where they flower from early to mid-spring, especially when they are partnered with blue *Muscari armeniacum* and violas. H 20–30cm (8–12in) S 8cm (3in). Hardy/Z6–9.

Hyacinthus orientalis 'Delft Blue'
This cultivar is available as both prepared and ordinary bedding bulbs. The soft blue flowers are wonderfully scented and look charming grown indoors, when they flower in midwinter, or outdoors, when they flower from early to mid-spring, with pale blue or white *Anemone blanda* or violas. H 20–30cm (8–12in) S 8cm (3in). Hardy/Z6–9.

Hyacinthus orientalis 'Gipsy Queen'
The delightful salmon-pink flowers of this hyacinth are richly scented and look striking planted in old terracotta pots, where they will flower from early to mid-spring. They combine wonderfully with pale yellow, blue or white primroses. H 20–30cm (8–12in) S 8cm (3in). Hardy/Z6–9.

Hyacinthus orientalis 'Hollyhock'
The double, crimson-red, tubular, bell-shaped flowers are borne on stout, leafless stems from early to mid-spring. It will combine beautifully with blue polyanthus or with *Tanacetum parthenium* 'Aureum' (golden feverfew). H 20–30cm (8–12in) S 8cm (3in). Hardy/Z6–9.

Hyacinthus orientalis 'Jan Bos'
This cultivar is available as both prepared and ordinary bedding bulbs. The single, richly-coloured cerise-red flowers are scented and look festive grown indoors, when they flower in midwinter, or outdoors, when they flower from early to mid-spring. They are an excellent partner for black violas. H 20–30cm (8–12in) S 8cm (3in). Hardy/Z6–9.

Hyacinthus orientalis 'L'Innocence'
This old favourite is available as both prepared and ordinary bedding bulbs. The single white flowers are scented and look wonderful indoors, when they flower in midwinter, or outdoors, when they flower in mid-spring. They are a good planting partner for pale yellow primroses and pastel-coloured violas. H 20–30cm (8–12in) S 8cm (3in). Hardy/Z6–9.

Hyacinthus orientalis 'Pink Pearl'
This cultivar is available as both prepared and ordinary bedding bulbs. The single rose-pink flowers are deservedly popular. They are scented and look great indoors, when they flower in midwinter, or outdoors, when they flower in mid-spring. Plant with blue primroses and violas. H 20–30cm (8–12in) S 8cm (3in). Hardy/Z6–9.

Hyacinthus orientalis 'Woodstock'
The unusual, single, deep burgundy flowers combine well with grey-foliage plants or pink primroses in early to mid-spring. H 20–30cm (8–12in) S 8cm (3in). Hardy/Z6–9.

Hyacinthus orientalis 'Jan Bos'

Hyacinthus orientalis 'Woodstock'

Hyacinthus orientalis 'Pink Pearl'

Iris 'Blue-eyed Brunette'

Iris 'Chantilly'

Iris 'Dancer's Veil'

IRIS

This is a large genus containing more than 300 species of winter-, spring- and summer-flowering bulbs, rhizomes and fleshy-rooted perennials, found in a wide range of habitats throughout the northern hemisphere. The name means "rainbow", an apt description given the many colours – from primrose-yellow to indigo – of the flowers.

Cultivation The bearded iris (growing from rhizomes) and the bulbous iris are best grown in full sun. The beardless iris (see *Iris sibirica* below) will grow in sun or partial shade. Most of the bearded and beardless iris prefer a neutral to acid soil, whereas the bulbous varieties thrive in a neutral to alkaline soil. Rhizomes of the bearded iris are best planted so that they rest on top of the soil, but those of the beardless irises are best planted below soil level. Bulbs of *Iris danfordiae* should be planted only 5cm (2in) deep; other bulbs should be planted 8cm (3in) deep in the border or containers in autumn, although the Xiphium Iris hybrids can also be planted in spring.

Propagation Separate rhizomes and bulb offsets from midsummer to early autumn.

Pests and diseases Slugs and snails are the main problems.

Bearded Irises

These are grown from fleshy rhizomes, which produce sword-like leaves and large flowers with higher erect petals, which are known as standards, and lower petals, referred to as the falls. There are conspicuous hairs on these lower petals, referred to as the beard.

Iris 'Annabel Jane'

This is a vigorous, rhizomatous, tall bearded iris, which has lilac-blue flowers from late spring to early summer. H 1.2m (4ft) S 60cm (24in). Hardy/Z4–9.

Iris 'Batik'

With fluted petals of royal purple, this bearded rhizomatous iris has eye-catching flowers that are wildly streaked with white on both standards and falls. They appear from late spring to early summer. H 60cm (24in) S 50cm (20in). Hardy/Z4–9.

Iris 'Blue-eyed Brunette'

This is a vigorous, rhizomatous, tall bearded iris, which has rich red-brown flowers with gold beards from late spring to early summer. H 1m (3ft 3in) S 50cm (20in). Hardy/Z4–9.

Iris 'Chantilly'

This is a vigorous, rhizomatous, tall bearded iris, which has pale lavender flowers from late spring to early summer. H 1m (3ft 3in) S 50cm (20in). Hardy/Z4–9.

Iris 'Dancer's Veil'

The lightly ruffled flowers are predominantly white with violet blue markings at the margins of the gently waving petals. They appear from late spring to early summer. H 90cm (36in) S 60cm (24in). Hardy/Z4–9.

Beardless Irises

Like bearded irises, these are also grown from fleshy rhizomes, which produce the characteristic iris flower but without any beard on the lower petals. The group includes *I. pseudacorus* as well as *I. sibirica* and its many hybrids.

Iris pseudacorus
Yellow flag

This species is found in a wide area, from Europe through to western Siberia, Turkey and Iran. It is a vigorous rhizomatous beardless iris, with ribbed grey-green leaves and yellow flowers, which appear from early to midsummer. It is suitable for damp places, such as boggy areas or the margins of ponds. H 90–150cm (3–5ft) S 1.8m (6ft) or more. Hardy/Z4–9.

Iris 'Batik'

Iris pseudacorus

Iris sibrica 'Tropic Night'

Iris danfordiae

Iris sibirica
Siberian iris

This species, which is native to central and eastern Europe, northeastern Turkey and Russia, is a rhizomatous beardless iris with narrow, grass-like leaves. In early summer it bears violet-blue petals with white splashes on the falls. H 60–90cm (24–36in) S 8cm (3in). Hardy/Z4–9.

Iris sibirica 'Tropic Night'

Like its parent, this cultivar is a rhizomatous beardless iris. It has rich blue flowers with white splashes on the falls. H 60cm (24in) S 8cm (3in). Hardy/Z4–9.

Bulbous Irises

Irises in this group are mainly grown from small bulbs, although those of *I. bucharica* are significantly larger. They flower in late winter through to summer, depending on the species.

Iris bucharica

This is a vigorous species, native to northeast Afghanistan and Central Asia, which produces long glossy leaves and in late spring to early summer masses of pretty yellow and white flowers. H 20–40cm (8–16in) S 10cm (4in). Hardy/Z4–9.

Iris danfordiae

This small species from Turkey has scented lemon-yellow flowers, 5cm (2in) across, with green markings. Flowering in late winter, they look effective with winter-flowering heathers and in small pots. H 10cm (4in) S 5cm (2in). Hardy/Z6–9.

Reticulata Irises

The species *I. reticulata*, from the Caucasus, is one of the first bulbs to flower in the New Year. A number of hybrids have been raised, and although excellent for rock gardens and small containers, including hanging baskets, they will not flower reliably a second year, so it is best to replant.

Iris 'George'

A Reticulata iris with fragrant, rich purple flowers, 4–6cm (1½–2½in) across, which have a yellow stripe down the centre of the fall petal. H 15cm (6in) S 5cm (2in). Hardy/Z6–9.

Iris 'Joyce'

A Reticulata iris with sky blue flowers, 5cm (2in) across, with orange on the falls. They look pretty on their own in a small pot. H 10–15cm (4–6in) S 5cm (2in). Hardy/Z6–9.

Iris 'Pauline'

A Reticulata iris with sweetly scented, dark purple flowers, 5cm (2in) across, with white crests on the falls. They look really wonderful in a container with *Viburnum tinus* (laurustinus) or *Euphorbia myrsinites*. H 10–15cm (4–6in) S 5cm (2in). Hardy/Z6–9.

Iris bucharica

Iris 'George'

Iris 'Joyce'

Iris 'Bronze Beauty'

Iris 'Silvery Beauty'

Xiphium Irises

This is a large group derived from the bulbous *I. xiphium* (known as the Spanish iris) hybridized with *I. tigitana* (from northwest Africa) by horticulturists in the Netherlands, hence the common name, Dutch irises. They are beautiful flowers, available in a wide range of colours. As well as being excellent cut flowers, they make wonderful plants for the herbaceous border, where they flower in late spring to early summer. The ones listed below are slightly shorter than most. They look sumptuous beneath wisteria arches and marvellous partnering

herbaceous poppies and alliums, where they will bloom year after year. H 45cm (18in) S 8cm (3in). Hardy/Z5–8.

Iris 'Bronze Beauty'
The flowers of this lovely iris combine deep bronze and gold. H 45cm (18in) S 8cm (3in). Hardy/Z5–8.

Iris 'Gypsy Beauty'
The flowers are deep blue and bronze. H 45cm (18in) S 8cm (3in). Hardy/Z5–8.

Iris 'Oriental Beauty'
The flowers are a wonderful combination of lilac and yellow. H 45cm (18in) S 8cm (3in). Hardy/Z5–8.

Iris 'Sapphire Beauty'
The flowers are a rich blue with orange on the fall and look great besides alliums or poppies. H 45cm (18in) S 8cm (3in). Hardy/Z5–8.

Iris 'Silvery Beauty'
The flowers combine pale blue and silver-grey. This delightful Xiphium iris flowers alongside white or purple alliums such as *A. nigrum*, *A.* 'Purple Sensation' and *A. cristophii*. H 45cm (18in) S 8cm (3in). Hardy/Z5–8.

Iris 'Symphony'
This iris combines white standards with primrose-yellow and orange falls. H 50cm (20in) S 8cm (3in). Hardy/Z5–8.

KNIPHOFIA

Red-hot poker, torch lily
The genus, which is native to southern Africa, contains about 70 species, from which many cultivars have been developed. They are mostly tall plants, bearing dense racemes of flowers on sturdy, erect stems, which rise from clumps of grassy leaves. Some species are evergreen.
Cultivation Grow in sun in fertile, well-drained soil. Plant rhizomes.
Propagation Sow seed in spring and keep the pots in a cold frame until ready to plant out. Divide clumps in late spring.
Pests and diseases Thrips and root rot.

Kniphofia **'Percy's Pride'**
This tall perennial produces racemes of green-tinged, yellow flowers in late summer and early autumn. H 1.2m (4ft) S 60cm (24in). Hardy/Z6–9.

Kniphofia rooperi
(syn. *K.* 'C.M. Prichard')
The flowers, which are borne from early to late autumn, are a mixture of autumnal shades of orange and yellow. In contrast to the tapering flower spikes of most red-hot poker plants, this one has flowers that form a wedge-shape. It is a robust, hardy, evergreen perennial with broad, strappy, dark green leaves. H 1.2m (4ft) S 60cm (24in). Hardy/Z6–9.

Iris 'Oriental Beauty'

Species for summer

Agapanthus	Gladiolus
Allium caeruleum	Hedychium coronarium
Allium carinatum subsp.	Iris bearded
pulchellum	Iris sibirica
Allium cernum	Iris pseudacorus
Allium cristophii	Kniphofia 'Percy's Pride'
Allium flavum	Lilium 'Moneymaker'
Allium roseum	Lilium regale
Allium sphaerocephalon	Lilium candidum
Begonia	Ornithagalum thyrsoides
Canna	Pelargonium schottii
Cardiocrinum giganteum	Tigridia pavonia
Dahlia	Tritonia
Eucomis	Tulbaghia
Galtonia candicans	Zantedeschia

Kniphofia rooperi

Lilium 'Admiration'

Leucojum aestivum

LEUCOJUM
Snowflake

The name is derived from the Greek words *leukos* (white), a clue to the colour of the flowers, and *ion* (violet), a reference to their delicate fragrance. The genus includes about 10 species of bulbs found in a range of habitats from western Europe to the Middle East and northern Africa. The species grown most often in gardens are the spring and summer snowflakes. They look similar to snowdrops, but the petals are of equal length (the snowdrop has 3 long and 3 short petals).

Cultivation *L. aestivum* and *L. vernum* can be grown in full sun or partial shade but the soil must be reliably moist. Both species will naturalize well in damp grass and damp woodlands. *L. roseum* prefers a sunny, well-drained site and will need protection in winter from prolonged frost and dampness. In autumn plant the bulbs 8cm (3in) deep in the border where they can form a good-sized clump.
Propagation Separate bulb offsets from midsummer to early autumn.
Pests and diseases Slugs and narcissus bulb fly.

Species for spring

Anemone blanda	Muscari armeniacum
Anemone nemorosa	Muscari azureum
Camassia leichtlinii	Leucojum aestivum
Chionodoxa forbesii	Narcissus bulbocodium
Chionodoxa luciliae	Narcissus poeticus var.
Chionodoxa sardensis	recurvens
Corydalis solida	Ornithogalum nutans
Fritillaria imperialis	Scilla peruviana
Fritillaria meleagris	Trillium undulatum
Hyacinthoides non-scripta	Tulipa tarda
Iris bucharica	Tulipa urumiensis

Leucojum aestivum
'Gravetye Giant'
Summer snowflake
The parent species is native to northwestern, central and eastern Europe and the Middle East. This cultivar, which is taller and more robust than the species, bears 2–8 white, bell-shaped flowers, with a distinctive green tip at the end of each petal, on each stem. They look lovely near water, where their reflection can be fully enjoyed. Despite the common name, the flowers appear in mid- to late spring. H 90cm (36in) S 8cm (3in). Hardy/Z4–9.

Leucojum roseum
The species originates in Corsica and Sardinia. The solitary, pale pink flowers, 1cm (½in) long, open in early autumn and look lovely with autumn crocuses or colchicums. The narrow leaves appear with, or a short while after, the flowers. H 10cm (4in) S 5cm (2in). Borderline hardy/Z6–9.

Leucojum vernum
Spring snowflake
This species comes from southern and eastern Europe. It has white, bell-shaped flowers with a distinctive green tip at the end of each petal, borne singly, or occasionally two on each stem. It flowers in midwinter and early spring. It will naturalize well in damp grass where left undisturbed and look wonderful as a large display beneath deciduous trees. H 20–30cm (8–12in) S 8cm (3in). Hardy/Z4–8.

LILIUM
Lily

The genus name *Lilium* is an old Latin name, akin to *leirion*, which was used by Theophrastus to refer to *Lilium candidum* (Madonna lily), one of the oldest established plants in gardens. The Greeks admired it for its beauty and food value, and it was used on many ceremonial occasions. The Romans took it with them as they conquered neighbouring lands. In the Christian era it became a symbol of Christ's mother and was grown in monastic gardens throughout Europe. Although historically this one species has been of major importance, there are more than 100 species of bulbs in the genus, which come mainly from scrub and wooded areas of Europe, Asia and North America. A large number of garden hybrids have been developed from the species, giving today's gardeners an enormous choice of colour and form.
Cultivation Most lilies prefer acid to neutral soil, but some, such as *L. candidum* and *L. henryi*, like alkaline soils, and the Asiatic hybrids, *L. pyrenaicum*, *L. regale* and *L. martagon* will certainly tolerate alkaline conditions. Lilies require shade at their base and sun at the top. Although a few tolerate light overhead shade, none thrives in full shade. In early autumn plant plump, firm bulbs on a bed of sand or grit to facilitate good drainage if the soil is heavy. Some bulbs are much bigger than others, and as a rule plant at a

Lilium 'Concorde'

Lilium 'Enchantment'

Lilium 'Eros'

depth 2–3 times the height of the actual bulb. Stem-rooting lilies should be planted deeper, at around 3 times the height of the bulb. Exceptions are *L. candidum* and *L. × testaceum*, which need to be planted close to the soil surface. Grow in a border where they can be left undisturbed for many years and form a good-sized clump. Alternatively, plant in containers, for which dwarf lilies are ideally suited. Some bulbs, including all Division 4 lilies and most Division 7 lilies, require ericaceous compost. All will benefit from extra horticultural grit in the mix, at a ratio of 2 parts compost to 1 part grit, with an extra layer of grit just beneath the bulbs.

Propagation Sow seed as soon as it is ripe in containers in a cold frame. Remove scales and offsets or bulblets from dormant bulbs as soon as the foliage dies down.

Lilium 'Bronwen North'

Detach stem bulbils, where produced, in late summer.

Pests and diseases Lily beetle, slugs and aphids. Grey mould can be a problem in a cool, wet spring.

Asiatic Hybrids (Division 1)
Derived from Asiatic species and hybrids, these are sturdy, stem-rooting lilies. They produce dark purple bulbils in the axils from which new bulbs can be propagated. They will tolerate a range of soils, including alkaline. There are 3 subdivisions: 1a upward-facing flowers (the group includes the double, pollen-free lilies and several much shorter pot and border lilies); 1b outward-facing flowers; and 1c pendent flowers.

Lilium 'Admiration'
Division 1a. This lily produces large, upward-facing, scentless flowers; the tepals are creamy yellow. H 40cm (16in). Hardy/Z4–8.

Lilium 'Apollo'
Division 1a. This short lily has unscented, white flowers in midsummer. It is excellent for containers. H 60cm (24in). Hardy/Z4–8.

Lilium 'Aphrodite'
Division 1a. This is a double form with upward-facing pink flowers. It is sterile and has no pollen, so is the perfect choice for gardeners who suffer from pollen allergies. It is medium height and ideal for containers. H to 70cm (28in). Hardy/Z4–8.

Lilium 'Bronwen North'
Division 1c. This is a striking, easily grown lily for the mixed border. In early summer, medium, slightly scented, turkscap flowers hang from the stems; the tepals are pale mauve-pink, spotted and lined with purple. H to 90cm (36in). Hardy/Z4–8.

Lilium 'Concorde'
Division 1a. A wonderful border plant, this has unscented, lemon-yellow flowers, greenish at the base, from early to midsummer. It associates well with grey foliage. H to 90cm (36in). Hardy/Z4–8.

Lilium 'Enchantment'
Division 1a. In summer this lily has showy, vivid orange, cup-shaped, unscented flowers, 12cm (4¹/₂in) across, which are marked with dark purple spots. The dark spotting on the petals combines well with deep bronze foliage plants in the border. It is a good lily for containers, where it can stay for 2–3 years. H 60–90cm (24–36in). Hardy/Z4–8.

Lilium 'Eros'
Division 1c. 'Eros' is an easily grown lily that associates well with cottage garden plants. In midsummer it produces fragant turkscap flowers; the tepals are pinkish-orange, spotted maroon. H 1.2m (4ft). Hardy/Z4–8.

Lilium 'Fata Morgana'
Division 1a. This is a double form with upward-facing yellow flowers, which are slightly

speckled red. It is sterile and has no pollen, so is suitable for gardeners with pollen allergies. It is medium height and ideal for containers. H to 70cm (28in). Hardy/Z4–8.

Lilium 'Fire King'
Division 1b. This is a vigorous lily with orange-red, shallowly funnel-shaped, unscented flowers, marked with purple spots. They open in midsummer. It is excellent for containers, where it can stay for 2–3 years. H 1–1.2m (3–4ft). Hardy/Z4–8.

Lilium 'Gran Sasso'
Division 1a. This is an excellent variety for general garden use. In early and midsummer, it produces large, upward-facing, unscented flowers, up to six per stem. The tepals are rich orange, heavily spotted with maroon. H 1–1.2m (3–4ft). Hardy/Z4–8.

Lilium 'Gran Sasso'

Lilium 'Her Grace'

Lilium 'Maxwill'

Lilium 'Peggy North'

Lilium 'Silhouette'

Lilium 'Her Grace'

Division Ia. In midsummer, this lily produces large, upward-facing, unscented, bowl-shaped flowers; the tepals are rich clear yellow. It is excellent for general garden use, can be planted in a container and used in flower arrangements as a cut flower. H to 1.2m (4ft). Hardy/Z4–8.

Lilium 'Karen North'

Division Ic. This is an elegant, prolific lily. In midsummer, it produces medium, lightly scented turkscap flowers; the tepals are orange-pink, lightly spotted with darker pink. It is excellent for planting in containers and for general garden use. H to 1.2m (4ft). Hardy/Z4–8.

Lilium 'Maxwill'

Division Ic. This lily produces a tall, stout stem with racemes of unscented turkscap-shaped

flowers which are a brilliant orange-red with black spots. It is ideal for growing in front of shrubs in well-drained soil in full sun or partial shade and looks lovely with other midsummer-flowering plants, such as *Crocosmia* 'Lucifer' and yellow achilleas. H 1.5–2.1m (5–7ft). Hardy/Z4–8.

Lilium 'Orange Pixie'

Division Ia. This short lily bears unscented bright orange flowers with darker spots in early to midsummer. It is excellent for containers. H 30cm (12in). Hardy/Z4–8.

Lilium 'Peach Pixie'

Division Ia. This short lily has unscented, orange to rose-pink flowers in early to midsummer. It is perfect for terracotta containers or raised beds around the patio or terrace. H 45cm (18in). Hardy/Z4–8.

Lilium 'Pink Tiger'

Division Ib. This is a vigorous lily with beautiful shallowly funnel-shaped, unscented, salmon-pink flowers, streaked with deeper apricot and marked with purple spots. They open in midsummer. It is excellent for containers. H 1.3m (4ft 6in). Hardy/Z4–8.

Lilium 'Peggy North'

Division Ic. In midsummer this lily produces medium-sized, lightly scented, turkscap flowers; the tepals are glowing orange, spotted with dark brown. It is an excellent lily for a mixed or herbaceous border. H to 1.5m (5ft). Hardy/Z4–8.

Lilium 'Red Carpet'

Division Ia. This short lily bears unscented cherry-red flowers in midsummer. It is excellent for containers. H 35cm (14in). Hardy/Z4–8.

Lilium 'Roma'

Division Ia. This lily produces fragrant, creamy white flowers, lightly spotted with maroon, on a tall stem from early to midsummer. It associates well with lime-green or grey foliage. H to 1.2m (4ft). Hardy/Z4–8.

Lilium 'Silhouette'

Division Ia. This lily produces large, upward-facing, scentless flowers; the tepals are white, flushed creamy yellow at the base, and spotted and edged maroon. Its unique markings are best appreciated in flower arrangments. H to 1m (3ft 3in). Hardy/Z4–8.

Lilium 'Sun Ray'

Division Ia. This short lily has unscented, bright yellow flowers with dark spots in early to midsummer. It is a good colour for terracotta containers. H 50cm (20in). Hardy/Z4–8.

Lilium 'Karen North'

Lilium 'Orange Pixie'

Lilium 'Roma'

Lilium 'Sweet Kiss'

Lilium 'Shuksan'

Lilium 'Sweet Kiss'

Division 1a. This double form has upward-facing yellow flowers. It is sterile and produces no pollen so is a perfect choice for gardeners with pollen allergies. It is medium height and ideal for containers, where it needs no support, and multiplies well to form large clumps in just a few years. H to 70cm (28in). Hardy/Z4–8.

Lilium 'White Kiss'

Division 1a. This double form has upward-facing white flowers, which are spotted brown. It is sterile and produces no pollen so is a good choice for gardeners who have pollen allergies. It is medium height and ideal for containers, where it needs no support and multiplies well. H to 70cm (28in). Hardy/Z4–8.

Martagon Hybrids (Division 2)

Derived mainly from *L. martagon*, a species that is native to a large area from Europe to Mongolia, and *L. hansonii*, which is native to Russia, Korea and Japan, these hybrids are mainly stem-rooting lilies with turkscap flowers (with highly recurved petals). They are suitable for dry shade or woodland and will tolerate a range of soils. All are hardy/Z4–8.

Lilium 'Mrs R.O. Backhouse'

This well-known lily is one of the oldest cultivars in cultivation, dating from the end of the 19th century. It has unscented, turkscap flowers, which hang from the stem in early to midsummer. The sepals are orange-yellow with maroon spotting and are flushed pink on the outside. H 1.3m (4ft 6in). Hardy/Z4–8.

Candidum Hybrids (Division 3)

Derived from *L. chalcedonicum*, *L. candidum* and other European species (but not *L. martagon*), this is a small group of lilies with turkscap flowers that are sometimes scented. They are usually not stem-rooting. They tolerate alkaline conditions.

Lilum × testaceum Nankeen lily

This lily bears fragrant turkscap flowers from early to midsummer. The petals are light apricot-pink, spotted with red. Grow in full sun or partial shade. H 1–1.5m (3–5ft). Hardy/Z4–8.

American Hybrids (Division 4)

Derived from American species, these are rhizomatous lilies, bearing sometimes scented, usually turkscap flowers. They are not stem-rooting. The group includes the Bellingham hybrids, which date from the 1920s; these have occasionally fragrant turkscap flowers, which vary from yellow to orange to orange-red, all spotted with deep brown, and all appearing in early to midsummer. They are excellent for naturalizing in light shade, and good for informal situations such as open woodland or the back of a border. They need acidic, preferably moist soil.

Lilium 'Shuksan'

This selected form has lightly scented tangerine-yellow flowers tipped with red and spotted with black or reddish-brown. H to 1.2m (4ft). Hardy/Z4–8.

Longiflorum Hybrids (Division 5)

Derived from *L. formosanum*, native to Taiwan, and *L. longiflorum*, from southern Japan and Taiwan, this is a small but growing group that includes fragrant, trumpet- or funnel-shaped flowers, which are usually grown for the cut-flower trade. They will tolerate a range of soils, including alkaline.

Lilium 'Centurion'

This lovely lily produces large, outward-facing, sweetly scented, funnel- to trumpet-shaped flowers, up to four per stem, that open flat; the tepals are creamy salmon, with heavy spotting towards the base. H to 90cm (36in). Hardy/Z4–8.

Trumpet and Aurelian Hybrids (Division 6)

Derived from Asiatic species (but not *L. auratum*, *L. japonicum*, *L. rubellum* or *L. speciosum*), these are mostly hardy, fragrant, stem-rooting lilies. They tolerate alkaline conditions. There are four subdivisions: 6a trumpet-shaped flowers; 6b (usually) outward-facing, bowl-shaped flowers; 6c shallowly bowl-shaped flowers, which often open flat; and 6d flowers which have distinctly recurved petals.

Lilium African Queen Group

Division 6a. This is a wonderful group of cultivars with large, fragrant, outward-facing to nodding, trumpet-shaped flowers, which are brownish-purple on the outside and yellow or orange-apricot on the inside. The flowers appear in mid- to late summer. Simply sumptuous, but plants might need support. H 1.5–1.8m (5–6ft). Borderline hardy/Z4–8.

Lilium Pink Perfection Group

Division 6a. This is another marvellous group of cultivars with large, scented, outward-facing to slightly nodding, trumpet-shaped flowers, which are at eye level. They are pink with a combination of purple and soft yellow, and are excellent in pots, flowering in midsummer. Plant with *L.* African Queen Group for sheer effect and continuity of colour. Plants might need support. H 1.5–1.8m (5–6ft). Hardy/Z4–8.

Lilium Golden Splendor Group

Division 6a. Cultivars in this group produce vigorous, slightly variable flowers on strong stems in midsummer. The blooms are large, scented, outward-facing and somewhere between trumpet-shaped and bowl-shaped. They are various shades of yellow, with dark burgundy-red colouring on the outside. They are good for pots or the border, where they might need support. H 1.2–1.8m (4–6ft). Hardy/Z4–8.

Lilium 'Centurion'

Lilium 'White Henryi'

Lilium 'Belle Epoque'

Lilium 'Royal Class'

Lilium 'Star Gazer'

Lilium 'White Henryi'
Division 6d. This has large, fragrant flowers, which open flat in late summer. They are white, flushed deep orange at the base. H to 1.5m (5ft). Borderline hardy/Z4–8.

Oriental Hybrids (Division 7)
Derived from species from the Far East, such as L. auratum, L. japonicum and L. speciosum, these lilies flower mostly in late summer and are often scented. Most are lime-hating and require acid soil. There are four subdivisions: 7a trumpet-shaped flowers; 7b bowl-shaped flowers; 7c flat flowers; and 7d flowers with distinctly recurved petals.

Lilium 'Acapulco'
Division 7d. This lily has fragrant, rich pink flowers with recurving petals. H to 1m (3ft 3in). Hardy/Z4–8.

Lilium 'Belle Epoque'
Division 7b. This lily produces large, outward-facing, bowl-shaped scented flowers, up to 8 per stem; the tepals vary in colour from white to soft pink, with a central cream band. H to 1m (3ft 3in). Hardy/Z4–8.

Lilium 'Casa Blanca'
Division 7b. The fragrant, pure white flowers have orange-red anthers. H 1.2m (4ft). Hardy/Z4–8.

Lilium 'Cosmopolitan'
Division 7b. This hybrid lily has fragrant, bowl-shaped flowers in midsummer; tepals are pink to red. H 1m (3ft 3in). Hardy/Z4–8.

Lilium 'Hotlips'
Division 7c. This is a sensational and popular lily. The fragrant white flowers, which are streaked and spotted with red, appear in late summer. H to 90cm (36in). Hardy/Z4–8.

Lilium 'Imperial Gold'
Division 7c. The large, fragrant, star-shaped, glistening yellow flowers have a yellow stripe in the centre. The flowers appear in late summer. H 1.8m (6ft). Hardy/Z4–8.

Lilium 'Journey's End'
Division 7d. This lily bears racemes of large, unscented, broad turkscap flowers. They are deep pink with maroon spots and white tips and appear in late summer. H 1–1.8m (3–6ft). Hardy/Z4–8.

Lilium 'Mona Lisa'
Division 7c. The white flowers are heavily spotted with red and have a broader stripe of red in the centre. They are borne from mid- to late summer. H to 90cm (36in). Hardy/Z4–8.

Lilium 'Omega'
Division 7d. This lily has short stems with racemes of large rose-pink flowers with yellow centres and sparse red spotting. It flowers in late summer. H 60–80cm (24–32in). Hardy/Z4–8.

Lilium 'Royal Class'
Division 7b. The fragrant flowers vary from white to soft pink and have a central yellow band and prominent papillae. H to 90cm (36in). Hardy/Z4–8.

Lilium 'Star Gazer'
Division 7c. This lily has deep rose-red flowers edged with white.
It is suitable for deep containers but needs ericaceous compost. This is not a fragrant lily, yet it is one of the most popular species. It flowers in midsummer. H 70–100cm (28–39in). Hardy/Z4–8.

Lilium 'White Mountain'
Division 7c. This lily has beautiful white flowers with a yellow band right down the centre of each petal. It flowers in late summer. H to 80cm (32in). Hardy/Z4–8.

Other Hybrids (Division 8)
This diverse division includes all the remaining hybrids that are not included in the other groups.

Lilium 'Moneymaker'
This bears up to 6 sweetly scented, clear pink flowers in midsummer. H 90cm (36in). Hardy/Z4–8.

Lilium 'Cosmopolitan'

Lilium 'Moneymaker'

Lilium auratum

Lilium davidii

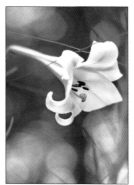

Lilium formosanum

Lilium longiflorum

Species Lilies (Division 9)

This group includes all true species and their forms.

Lilium auratum
Golden-rayed lily

Native to Japan, this lily has the largest flowers of all. From late summer to autumn it bears up to 20, and sometimes as many as 30, sweetly scented, white and gold flowers with crimson spots, to 30cm (12in) across. It requires acid soil and full sun, with light shade provided by low-growing plants. H 1–1.8m (3–6ft) S 10cm (4in). Hardy/Z4–9.

Lilium candidum
Madonna lily

This lily is native to southeastern Europe and countries of the eastern Mediterranean. It bears 5 or more white, faintly scented, trumpet-shaped flowers, 5–8cm (2–3in) long, with bright yellow anthers. They have a sweet scent and appear in midsummer. This is the only lily to produce overwintering basal leaves. It requires neutral to alkaline soil. H 1–1.8m (3–6ft), S 10cm (4in). Hardy/Z4–9.

Lilium davidii

This species is native to western China. In summer it produces up to 12 nodding turkscap flowers, borne on long stalks. The flowers are vermilion-orange, spotted black. It is a stem-rooting lily that tolerates a wide range of soils, including lime, but it does best in humus-rich soil. H 1–1.3m (3ft–4ft 6in) S 10cm (4in). Hardy/Z5–8.

Lilium duchartrei
Marble martagon lily

This species from western China produces up to 12 nodding turkscap flowers, borne on long stalks in summer. The flowers are white, spotted with deep purple inside and with a purple flush, aging to red, on the outside. It grows from a rhizomatous bulb and spreads by stolons; it will form large colonies in good conditions. It tolerates lime but does best in well-drained soil in a cool, lightly shaded position. H 60–100cm (24–36in) S 10cm (4in). Hardy/Z4–8.

Lilium formosanum

This elegant, stem-rooting lily, originally from Taiwan, grows from rhizomatous bulbs. It has slender, fragrant, trumpet-shaped white flowers, 12–20cm (4½–8in) long, with a reddish-purple flush on the outside. The flowers are borne from late summer to early autumn. This lily requires a moist, acid soil. H 60–150cm (2–5ft) S 10cm (4in). Borderline hardy/Z5.

Lilium hansonii

This vigorous species, originally from eastern Russia, Korea and Japan, produces racemes of up to 12 nodding turkscap flowers, gloriously orange-yellow with brown-purple spots towards the base. It is a stem-rooting lily, which tolerates a wide range of soils, but likes good drainage and a position in partial shade. H 1–1.5m (3–5ft) S 10cm (4in). Hardy/Z5–8.

Lilium lancifolium
Tiger lily

This species is native to eastern China, Korea and Japan. It bears up to 40 (but more usually 5–10) orange-red, purple-speckled flowers. It is robust, clump-forming and stem-rooting and flowers from late summer to early autumn. It prefers moist acid soil but tolerates some lime. H 60–150cm (2–5ft) S 10cm (4in). Hardy/Z4–9.

Lilium longiflorum
Easter lily

This elegant lily, which is originally from south Japan and Taiwan, is a vigorous, stem-rooting plant, which is lime tolerant. It prefers partial shade. In midsummer it produces short racemes of 1–6 fragrant, trumpet-shaped, pure white flowers, to 18cm (7in) long, with yellow anthers. This is a flower that is often grown to decorate churches at Easter-time. H 40–100cm (16–39in) S 10cm (4in). Half-hardy/Z5.

Lilium candidum

Lilium duchartrei

Lilium martagon

Lilium martagon
Martagon lily, turkscap lily
This lily, which is native to a wide area stretching from Europe to Mongolia, has glossy, nodding, pink to purplish-red flowers with dark purple spots. The flowers, which appear in early and midsummer, are in the shape of a Turk's cap and are 5cm (2in) across. It is ideal among shrubs in well-drained soil in full sun or partial shade. It will tolerate a range of soils. *L. martagon* var. *album* AGM is white. H 1–1.8m (3–6ft) S 10cm (4in). Hardy/Z4–8.

Lilium pyrenaicum
Originally from the Pyrenees, this is a stem-rooting, clump-forming lily, which bears racemes of up to 12 unpleasantly scented yellow flowers with dark maroon spots. The flowers, which appear in early and midsummer, are turkscap type and are 5cm (2in) across. It is ideal growing among shrubs in well-drained soil in sun or partial shade. It needs neutral to alkaline soil. H 30–90cm (12–36in) S 10cm (4in). Hardy/Z4–8.

Lilium regale
Regal lily
This lily, which originated in western China, enjoys a position in full sun. In summer it bears large, trumpet-shaped, scented, white flowers, 13–15cm (5–6in) long, with purple streaking on the reverse. It can be grown in the border, although it may need support. It will tolerate a range of soils, although excessively alkaline soils should be avoided. It is excellent growing among deep red

Lilium regale

or white, late-flowering, old-fashioned roses. It is also suitable for large, deep containers. It is a wonderful, easy-to-grow lily. H 60–180cm (2–6ft) S 10cm (4in). Hardy/Z4–9.

Lilium speciosum var. rubrum
Originally from eastern China, Japan and Taiwan, this lily is admired for its carmine-red flowers, which appear in late summer. Each flower, to 18cm (7in) across, has darker crimson spots and is turkscap in shape. This lily needs moist, acid soil and a position in partial shade. It might need staking. It is excellent in deep containers. A number of selected forms have been developed, including *L. speciosum* var. *album*, which has white flowers, while var. *roseum* has deep pink flowers. H 90cm (36in) S 10cm (4in). Hardy/Z5–8.

Lilium speciosum 'Uchida'
This is a lily of garden origin, a selection of a species from eastern China, Japan and Taiwan. In late summer and autumn, erect stems carry large, fragrant, outward-facing or hanging turkscap flowers; the tepals are brilliant crimson, spotted with green or darker red, with white tips. H to 2m (6ft 6in). Hardy/Z5–8.

Lilium tsingtauense
This is a species from China and Korea. It is a distinctive lily, flowering in midsummer, when it produces elegant, upward-facing, unscented, bowl-shaped flowers that open flat. The flowers have orange or vermilion-orange petals spotted with purple. Planted in sun or partial shade, it thrives in moist, acid soil but will tolerate some lime. H 90cm (36in) S 10cm (4in). Hardy/Z5–8.

Lilium speciosum 'Uchida'

Lilium wallichianum
Originally from the Himalayas, this is a fragrant lily with white or cream trumpet-shaped flowers, which flare to 20cm (8in) across and are tinged with green on the exterior. The flowers are borne in late summer to autumn. It is stem-rooting and needs moist, acid soil. It is not hardy but will grow in deep containers. H 1–1.8m (3–6ft) S 10cm (4in). Half-hardy/Z5–8.

Lilium wilsonii
This lily originates in Japan. It flowers in summer, bearing large, upward-facing, unscented, bowl-shaped flowers. The blooms are orange-red, striped yellow at the base and spotted with dark brown. This lily needs well-drained soil in sun or partial shade. H 1.1m (3ft 6in) S 10cm (4in). Hardy/Z5–8.

Lilium speciosum

Lilium tsingtauense

Lilium wilsonii

MUSCARI
Grape hyacinth

The name of this genus derives from the Latin word *muscus* (musk scent), the fragrance carried by some of the species. The genus contains 30 species of bulbs from the Mediterranean to south-western Asia, the best known of which is *Muscari armeniacum*, whose cultivars are so useful in borders, grassland and all types and sizes of containers.

Cultivation Plant in full sun, although they will also tolerate partial shade in pots. In autumn plant bulbs 5cm (2in) deep in small to large groups. They will multiply rapidly.

Propagation Sow seed in containers in a cold frame in autumn. Remove offsets in summer.

Pests and diseases Viruses can be a problem.

Muscari armeniacum

The species comes originally from south-eastern Europe to Caucasus. For many weeks from early to mid-spring dense racemes, 2–8cm (¾–3in) long, of beautiful blue flowers are borne in grape-like bunches at the top of the stem. This is one of the prettiest of all the blue bulbs, and it looks sumptuous as a mass planting beneath roses or along a path. It makes an excellent association with all Double Early tulips and is especially delightful with pink *Tulipa* 'Peach Blossom'. The only drawback is that the foliage can grow long and untidy, but the exquisite colouring and long duration of flowering make up for any waywardness. H 20cm (8in) S 5cm (2in). Hardy/Z2–9.

Muscari armeniacum

Muscari armeniacum 'Valerie Finnis'

Muscari armeniacum 'Blue Spike'

This is one of several cultivars available derived from *Muscari armeniacum*. It has double, soft blue flowers on a spike that reaches 15cm (6in), making it a little shorter than the species. It also flowers slightly later in mid-spring. It is good in the border or in a small container. H 15cm (6in) S 5cm (2in) Hardy/Z2–9.

Muscari armeniacum 'Valerie Finnis'

This is a recent introduction, which was found in the Northamptonshire garden of plantswoman Valerie Finnis. Derived from *Muscari armeniacum*, it produces lovely pale blue flower spikes. It is so easy to grow that it promises to become a favourite for mid-spring gardens. It is perfect for a window box, hanging basket or small pot along with mid-spring-flowering miniature daffodils and violas. H 15cm (6in) S 5cm (2in). Hardy/Z2–9.

Muscari aucheri

The species is native to Turkey. In mid-spring dense racemes of beautiful bright blue flowers are borne. They have constricted white mouths and, usually, are crowned with paler blue sterile flowers. H 10–15cm (4–6in) S 5cm (2in) Hardy/Z2–9.

Muscari azureum

This is another species that originated in Turkey. In mid-spring it bears racemes of bright blue flowers with a darker stripe on each lobe. H 10cm (4in) S 5cm (2in). Hardy/Z2–9.

Muscari botryoides f. album
Pearls of Spain

The species is native to France, Germany and Poland southwards throughout central and south-eastern Europe. This muscari has slender racemes of scented, white flowers in mid-spring. They are borne in bunches at the top of the stem like tiny grapes. It is daintier than *M. armeniacum* and has much neater leaves. H 15–20cm (6–8in) S 5cm (2in). Hardy/Z3–9.

Muscari comosum
Tassel grape hyacinth

The species is native to southern Europe, Turkey and Iran. In late spring and early summer it bears racemes of creamy brown flowers with violet-blue, upper sterile flowers borne in tassels on top. *M. comosum* 'Plumosum' has feathery heads made up of entirely purple sterile threads. H 20–60cm (8–24in) S 5cm (2in). Borderline hardy/Z2–9.

Muscari latifolium

This species is originally from the open pine forests of northwestern Turkey. The slender racemes of dark violet flowers have a crown of paler sterile flowers on top. This bulb produces one broad leaf, hence its specific name *latifolium*. It is an excellent bulb for containers if they can be kept in a sheltered place in winter. H 20cm (8in) S 5cm (2in). Borderline hardy/Z2–10.

Muscari neglectum
(syn. M. racemosum)

This species is native to North Africa and southwest Asia. The slender racemes of blue-black flowers with constricted white mouths are borne in spring on dense racemes. It has many mid-green leaves, channelled to almost cylindrical. It is good in containers or for a special place at the front of a border. H 20cm (8in) S 5cm (2in). Hardy/Z2–10.

Muscari latifolium

NARCISSUS
Daffodil

This group of bulbs is sometimes known by its Latin name, *Narcissus*, and sometimes by its common name, daffodil. There are about 50 species, originally growing in a wide range of habitats in Europe and North Africa, where they are found in meadows and woodlands and even in rock crevices. As a harbinger of spring, this is one of the best-loved of all bulbs, and many thousands of cultivars have been grown over the years. The predominant colour is yellow but many are white. Sometimes the outer petals are one colour and the trumpet another, giving rise to bicolour plants; pink and orange are additional colour variations.

The length and shape of the trumpet can vary considerably. Sometimes it is long and narrow, as in the species *N. cyclamineus*; sometimes it is shorter, when it becomes known as the eye, as in *N. poeticus* var. *recurvus*. Sometimes the trumpet is frilly around the edge, and it may even be split, as in the butterfly daffodils, such as 'Cassata'. Usually the flowers are held singly but occasionally they are multiheaded – 'Hawera', for example, can have as many as 3 or 4 blooms – and some, including 'Paper White Grandiflora', might

have 8–10 or even more. Occasionally, the flowers are double, even in the species, but double flowers are more often seen in the cultivars, such as 'Ice King' or 'Tahiti'. Some daffodils have a strong scent, particularly those derived from *N. poeticus*, such as the cultivars 'Sir Winston Churchill' and 'Cheerfulness'. Fragrance is also common in indoor midwinter-flowering bulbs, such as 'Paper White Grandiflora'.

Most cultivars reach 40cm (16in) or more when in flower, but there is a group of dwarf daffodils, which have become increasingly popular. They are derived from species such as *N. bulbocodium, N. cyclamineus, N. jonquilla, N. minor* and *N. triandrus* and forms like *N. tazetta* subsp. *lacticolor* (syn. *N. canaliculatus*). Of these, the cultivars originating from *N. cyclamineus* and *N. triandrus* are exceptionally useful and reliable. These are generally sturdy and will stand up well to wind. They are eminently suitable for borders and look pretty in small-scale gardens with confined space. They are also ideal for pots and windowboxes where the proportions are good, and the bulbs are quite small so they do not take up too much planting space. These bulbs will grow to great effect in open grassland too.

Narcissus 'Golden Harvest'

The early-spring flowerers are particularly suitable in this respect, their flowering time coinciding with a period when the grass is short early in the season.

All daffodils make good cut flowers. Cutting the flowers will not weaken the flowering ability in the following season, although removing the leaves will have a detrimental effect.

Cultivation All narcissi grow well in sun or partial shade, where the soil is moist in autumn and the spring growing season. Daffodils are tolerant bulbs that will grow in any reasonable garden soil as long as it is well drained, but the species and cultivars of *N. cyclamineus, N. triandrus* and *N. bulbocodium* prefer acidic to neutral conditions and *N. jonquilla* and *N. tazetta* prefer slightly alkaline soil. If they are in containers use an ericaceous mix. The cultivars of *N. cyclamineus* are not choosy and will grow well in any good garden soil. If they are in containers use an ordinary soil-based potting compost (soil mix). Those planted for midwinter flowering indoors will benefit from being in a proprietary indoor bulb compost.

For groups planting distance is usually about 15cm (6in) in each direction. Planting depths depend on the size of the bulbs, but as a rule plant the bulb so that its nose is twice the depth of the bulb below soil level. With larger bulbs this might be 15cm (6in) deep or more, whereas for the dwarf daffodils, of which the bulbs are often much smaller, the depth is usually about 10cm (4in). The only exception is in the treatment of indoor midwinter-flowering bulbs, which are planted so that the top of each bulb is level with the compost.

To promote healthy bulbs for the following year's flower production, deadhead after flowering so the plant does not waste energy on producing seedheads. If the daffodils are planted in grass, allow the leaves to die down naturally for at least 6 weeks after flowering before you mow. When they are planted in borders, simply remove

Narcissus 'Dutch Master'

yellowing leaves once the natural dying process is complete. On poor soils and in containers apply a high-phosphate feed in spring to allow the bulb to build up energy for the following season.
Propagation Seed can take up to seven years to produce a flowering bulb. Remove offsets as leaves fade in summer or early autumn.
Pests and diseases Narcissus bulb fly, narcissus eel worm, slugs, fungal infections and viruses may be a problem.

Trumpet Daffodils (Division 1)
The trumpet is the same length as, or longer than, the petals. All narcissi in this group are hardy/Z3–9.

Narcissus 'Arctic Gold'
This is a vigorous and free-flowering daffodil with mid-green foliage and smooth, waxy, rich golden-yellow flowers almost 10cm (4in) wide, which appear in mid-spring. The trumpets are widely flanged and deeply notched. H 40cm (16in).

Narcissus 'Dutch Master'
This is a uniform soft yellow daffodil with a large cup. Flowering in early spring, this is a typical daffodil for borders or grassland. H 35cm (14in).

Narcissus 'Golden Harvest'
This is one of the leading golden-trumpet daffodils. Early to flower in spring, it makes a welcome addition to any border or grassland. H 35cm (14in).

Narcissus 'King Alfred'
This daffodil is golden-yellow. One of the best known of all daffodils, it flowers in mid-spring. Plant in borders or grassland, although its large cup makes it susceptible to flopping in rain. H 35cm (14in).

Narcissus 'Little Gem'
This is a well proportioned, dwarf miniature trumpet daffodil. It flowers in early spring and is perfect for hanging baskets, small pots, raised troughs and windowboxes or for the front of a border. H 20cm (8in).

Narcissus 'Carlton'

Narcissus 'Pinza'

Narcissus 'Mount Hood'
This lovely daffodil is ivory-white both in its trumpet and perianth. Flowering in late spring, it makes an attractive daffodil to extend the season. Plant in borders or grassland. H 35cm (14in).

Narcissus 'Rijnveld's Early Sensation' (syn. *N.* 'January Gold')
This daffodil, which will stand up to cold weather, is one of the earliest to flower. It has a yellow trumpet and petals. It is strong and robust and a good choice for late-winter colour. Plant in borders or grassland. H 35cm (14in).

Narcissus 'Rose Caprice'
This two-toned daffodil has white petals and salmon-pink cups. It flowers in mid-spring and is ideal for medium to large containers and borders. H 35cm (14in).

Narcissus 'Topolino'

Narcissus 'Spellbinder'
This is a special daffodil with a reverse bicolour, aging to nearly white with a yellow rim to the trumpet. It makes an attractive mid-season daffodil. Plant in borders or in grassland. H 35cm (14in).

Narcissus 'Topolino'
This little daffodil has white petals and a primrose-yellow trumpet, which looks down gently to the ground. Early to flower, it is quite excellent in containers with early primroses and violas and makes a natural grouping in grass. It is good for borders too. H 20cm (8in).

Narcissus 'W. P. Milner'
This dainty daffodil, with milky white petals and bicolour white and cream trumpet, flowers in early spring. It is pretty in small baskets and troughs and makes a lovely grouping in borders partnering white or purple violets and *Anemone blanda*. H 23cm (9in).

Large-cupped Daffodils (Division 2)
The cup is longer than one-third of, but not as long as, the perianth segments. These daffodils usually flower in mid-spring. All are hardy/Z3–9.

Narcissus 'Carlton'
This is a soft yellow daffodil with a large cup, which is frilly at the mouth. An excellent naturalizer, it is a delightful daffodil for borders or grassland, flowering in mid-spring. H 45cm (18in).

Narcissus 'Delibes'
This is an unusual daffodil, with an apricot-yellow perianth and dark red cup. It is good for planting in borders or grassland. Flowering in early spring, it is a useful daffodil to start the season. H 35cm (14in).

Narcissus 'Flower Record'
This white daffodil has a medium-sized yellow cup edged with orange. It is suitable for borders or grassland and flowers in mid-spring. H 40cm (16in).

Narcissus 'Ice Follies'
This is a popular white daffodil with a widely flared, creamy white crown, which pales with maturity. Early to flower, it makes a welcome addition to any spring border and grows well in grass. It is free to flower and increases well. H 35cm (14in).

Narcissus 'Juanita'
This is a yellow daffodil with a medium orange cup. Suitable for planting in borders or in grassland, it is a useful daffodil to start the season in early spring. H 35cm (14in).

Narcissus 'Pink Smiles'
Flowering in mid-spring, this is a white daffodil with a lovely rose-pink cup. It is suitable for planting in grassland or borders where it will associate handsomely with either lime-green or bronze foliage, as well as other white flowers. H 35cm (14in).

Narcissus 'Pinza'
This is a striking daffodil with rich yellow petals and a deep red cup. It will flower in mid-spring. It looks very attractive planted against a dark background or with rich blues. H 35cm (14in).

Bulbs with yellow flowers

Asphodeline lutea	*Erythronium* 'Pagoda'
Begonia (many)	*Freesia* 'Dijon'
Calochortus luteus 'Golden Orb'	*Freesia* 'Winter Gold'
	Fritillaria imperialis 'Maxima Lutea'
Canna 'Louis Cottin'	*Hyacinthus orientalis* 'City of
Canna 'Picasso'	Haarlem'
Crocosmia 'George Davison'	*Lilium* 'Golden Splendor'
Crocosmia 'Lady Hamilton'	*Narcissus* (most)
Crocosmia 'Solfatare'	*Sternbergia lutea*
Crocus × *luteus* 'Dutch Yellow'	*Tulipa* 'Golden Apeldoorn'
Dahlia (many)	*Tulipa* 'Honky Tonk'
Eranthis hyemalis	*Tulipa* 'Monte Carlo'

Narcissus 'Pipe Major'
This is a showy daffodil with yellow petals and a strong orange-red cup. It flowers in late spring and looks lovely in borders or grassland. H 35cm (14in).

Narcissus 'Rainbow'
This is a delicate white daffodil. It has a beautiful peach cup with a coppery pink rim. It looks stunning in borders, especially when planted near lime-green or bronze foliage. It is also excellent in grassland. Because it is later to flower, it is useful for extending the season from mid- to late spring. H 40cm (16in).

Narcissus 'Red Devon'
This daffodil has a yellow perianth and a red cup. It flowers in mid-spring, and is a striking addition in borders or grassland. H 40cm (16in).

Narcissus 'Roseworthy'
This beautifully proportioned white daffodil, with its rich pink trumpet, is lovely. It flowers in mid- to late spring and looks stunning in a medium to large container, and is even better when the container is raised and backlit with spring sunshine. This is also a good daffodil for borders. H 35cm (14in).

Narcissus 'Roseworthy'

Narcissus 'Segovia'

Narcissus 'Rip van Winkle'

Narcissus 'St Keverne'
This is a lovely golden-yellow daffodil, bred in Cornwall, with clear lemon-yellow perianth and a deeper gold cup. It is an ideal choice for the early-spring garden whether in borders or grassland. H 35cm (14in).

Narcissus 'St Patrick's Day'
This is a delicate, two-toned cultivar with creamy white perianth and lime-green trumpet. It flowers in mid-spring and looks good in borders, where its unusual colour combination can be seen to full effect. H 35cm (14in).

Narcissus 'Salome'
This beautiful white daffodil, with its delicate pink trumpet, is stunning for borders. It flowers in late spring. H 35cm (14in).

Small-cupped Daffodils (Division 3)
The cup is less than one-third the length of the petals. Hardy/Z3–9.

Narcissus 'Merlin'
This beautiful daffodil has white petals and a flattened, pale yellow cup trimmed with a band of red. It flowers from mid- to late spring. H 45cm (18in).

Narcissus 'Segovia'
This is an excellent dainty bicolour daffodil, with white petals and a pale yellow cup. Flowering from mid- to late spring, this is good for the front of the border and for small containers. H 25cm (10in).

Double Daffodils (Division 4)
The petals or the cup (or both) are double, which sometimes gives a muddled appearance. Nearly all are hardy/Z3–9.

Narcissus 'Bridal Crown'
Developed from N. tazetta (and sometimes classified as Division 8), this is a white, multiheaded daffodil. It is fragrant and makes a lovely indoor daffodil to flower in midwinter. H 35cm (14in). Half-hardy/Z8.

Narcissus × odorus 'Double Campernelle'
(syn. N. 'Double Campernelle')
This is a pretty double yellow daffodil and delightfully fragrant. It flowers in early spring and is ideal for pots and window boxes. H 25cm (10in).

Narcissus 'Rip van Winkle'
(syn. N. minor var. pumilis 'Plenus')
The parent species originated from the Pyrenees. Flowering in early spring, it has rather lax stems to support the weight of the spiky double yellow flowers, but it looks pretty in short grass or a border. H 20cm (8in).

Narcissus 'Salome'

Narcissus 'Thalia'

Narcissus 'Tahiti'

Narcissus 'Yellow Cheerfulness'

Narcissus 'Sir Winston Churchill'

This much-loved cultivar is derived from fragrant *N.* × *medioluteus* (syn. *N.* × *poetaz*). The daffodil is white and multiheaded. Sturdy in growth, it is excellent for borders or grassland and, being later to flower, is a useful daffodil to extend the season. It will follow on well from the earlier-flowering 'White Lion'. H 40cm (16in).

Narcissus 'Tahiti'

This is a double yellow cultivar with fine red segments. It is late to flower and is a useful and showy daffodil to extend the season. A prize daffodil for planting in borders rather than grassland. H 40cm (16in).

Narcissus 'Unique'

This is a double white cultivar with yellow segments. Late to flower, it makes an attractive daffodil that is a good choice for extending the season. It is best planted in borders rather than grassland. H 40cm (16in).

Narcissus 'White Lion'

This is a double white cultivar with pale lemon-yellow segments. It flowers in mid-season and makes an excellent contribution to borders or grassland where it associates well with the later-flowering 'Sir Winston Churchill'. H 40cm (16in).

Narcissus 'Yellow Cheerfulness'

A cultivar of *N.* × *medioluteus* (syn. *N.* × *poetaz*), this is a double primrose-yellow daffodil with a neat button cup. There are often several flowers on each stem. It is fragrant, sturdy and excellent for borders. It flowers in late spring, so is a useful daffodil to extend the season. H 40cm (16in).

Triandrus Daffodils (Division 5)

Derived from *N. triandrus*, which is native to Spain, Portugal and north-western France, these cultivars flower in mid-spring. Each stem usually produces 2–6 flowers. All are hardy/Z3–9.

Narcissus 'Hawera'

This is an excellent multiheaded daffodil, with dainty lemon-yellow flowers. The oval petals are reflexed. It is derived from *N. triandrus* and *N. jonquilla* and dates from the 1930s. Flowering from mid- to late spring, this daffodil is long-lasting, good for the front of a border and excellent for small containers. H 15cm (6in).

Narcissus 'Ice Wings'

Ice-white trumpets and white reflexed petals give this lovely multiheaded daffodil its name. Derived from *N. triandrus*, it flowers in mid-spring and looks lovely in borders or containers. H 30cm (12in).

Narcissus 'Thalia'

This is an excellent multiheaded daffodil, with white trumpets and white reflexed petals. It is derived from *N. triandrus* and flowers in mid-spring. It looks pretty at the front of borders and in containers. H 30cm (12in).

Bulbs with double flowers

Anemone 'Lord Lieutenant'	*Hyacinthus orientalis* 'Hollyhock'
Begonia (many)	*Narcissus* 'Rip van Winkle'
Colchicum 'Waterlily'	*Narcissus* 'Tahiti'
Dahlia (many)	*Narcissus* 'White Lion'
Galanthus nivalis 'Flore Pleno'	*Tulipa* 'Angélique'
Hyacinthus orientalis 'Ben Nevis'	*Tulipa* 'Peach Blossom'

Narcissus 'Ice Wings'

Narcissus 'February Gold'

Narcissus 'Foundling'

Cyclamineus Daffodils (Division 6)

Derived from *N. cyclamineus*, which is native to north-west Portugal and north-west Spain, these daffodils produce a single flower with swept-back petals. They usually have a long cup or trumpet, and flowers appear from early to mid-spring. The species will naturalize well in damp conditions, preferring acidic soils, where it will succeed in partial shade. The cultivars thrive in any garden soil. They are usually dwarf. All are hardy/Z3–9.

Narcissus 'Jetfire'

Narcissus 'February Gold'

This is one of the best of all the dwarf daffodils, with a pretty golden-yellow trumpet and fly-away petals. It flowers in early spring. Strong, sturdy and long in flower, it is ideal for grassland, borders and many containers. It will naturalize well. H 25cm (10in).

Narcissus 'Foundling'

This is a popular daffodil, with broad, white, fly-away petals surrounding a delicate deep pink cup. Flowering from early to mid-spring, it is ideal for pots and raised troughs or for a special place in the border. H 25–30cm (10–12in).

Narcissus 'Jack Snipe'

This is one of the best dwarf bicolour daffodils. It has white reflexed petals and a golden-yellow trumpet. Good for borders and grassland, where it will naturalize well, and for containers. It flowers in early spring. H 25cm (10in).

Narcissus 'Jenny'

The combination of creamy white trumpet and matching fly-away petals makes this a popular choice for the garden or small containers. It flowers in early spring. H 25–28cm (10–11in).

Narcissus 'Jetfire'

This is a striking dwarf daffodil, with a golden-orange trumpet and reflexed yellow petals. Strong, sturdy and long in flower, it is ideal for borders. It flowers in early spring and will naturalize well. H 25cm (10in).

Narcissus 'Peeping Tom'

Slightly taller than the others listed in this category, this daffodil has the reflexed petals reminiscent of its cyclamineus parent and a long golden-yellow trumpet. It flowers in early spring. It is good for borders, grassland, where it will naturalize well, and containers. H 30cm (12in).

Jonquilla and Apodanthus Daffodils (Division 7)

Derived from *N. jonquilla*, which originates in southern and central Spain and southern and eastern Portugal, these daffodils have 1–5 scented flowers on a single stem. All are hardy/Z3–9.

Narcissus 'Bell Song'

This pretty daffodil, which opens slightly lemon-yellow but then fades to ivory-white, has a neat, flat, pink crown. It flowers in mid-spring and is fragrant. It is ideal for pots, raised troughs and window boxes or for a special place in the border. H 25–30cm (10–12in).

Narcissus 'Peeping Tom'   Narcissus 'Bell Song'

Narcissus 'Pipit'

Narcissus 'Suzy'

Narcissus 'Ziva'

Narcissus 'Pipit'

This is a delightful, multiheaded daffodil with gorgeous lemon-yellow flowers, often streaked with white. The petals are reflexed. The cups reverse to near white with age. It flowers for a long time, from mid- to late spring, and is an excellent choice for larger containers and for borders. It increases well. H 30cm (12in).

Narcissus 'Quail'

This is a rich golden-yellow daffodil. It is multiheaded and fragrant, flowering from mid- to late spring. It is a good choice for small to medium containers and for borders. H 30cm (12in).

Narcissus 'Sun Disc'

This tiny daffodil has unusual flowers, which are like miniature golden-yellow discs. The crowns

are almost flat. It increases rapidly, but is so small that it needs a position at the front of a border or in small containers, such as a wall pot or hanging basket. It flowers in mid-spring. H 15cm (6in).

Narcissus 'Suzy'

This is a highly distinctive yellow daffodil with wide but shallow orange crowns. It is heavily scented. Taller than most of the others in this category, it is suitable for planting in borders and for medium to large containers. It flowers in mid-spring. H 40cm (16in).

Tazetta Daffodils (Division 8)

These are either small-flowered cultivars, with up to 20 flowers on each stem, or large-flowered cultivars, with 3 or 4 flowers on each stem. They have broad petals

and small cups. They are usually scented and make good cut flowers. 'Minnow' and 'Silver Chimes' are hardy/Z3–9, but the others are half-hardy and should be grown indoors. They flower in late autumn to mid-spring.

Narcissus 'Geranium'

This has a pure white perianth and an orange cup. It is double, multiheaded and fragrant. Sturdy and excellent for borders, this is a late-spring-flowering daffodil that is useful for extending the season. H 35cm (14in).

Narcissus 'Martinette'

This bears several yellow flowers on each stem, each bloom having a neat but striking orange cup. Fragrant and early to flower, this is useful for small to medium containers or borders. H 30cm (12in).

Narcissus 'Minnow'

Developed from *N. tazetta*, this is a multiheaded daffodil, with rounded flowers. The dainty creamy white blooms have pale yellow cups. It flowers in early spring and is good for pots, raised troughs and window boxes or for the front of the border. H 33cm (13in).

Narcissus 'Paper White Grandiflorus'

Developed from *N. papyraceus*, which is native to southern France, southern Spain and North Africa, this daffodil bears bunches of 5–10 fragrant, glistening white flowers, 1cm ($^{1}/_{2}$in) across. H 40cm (16in). 'Ziva' is similar but slightly shorter; 'Omri' is also shorter but has creamy white flowers. They are useful as indoor pot daffodils to flower in midwinter, and all are fragrant. Use a proprietary indoor bulb compost and, 6 weeks before the flowers are required, plant so that the top of the bulbs is level with the compost. Half-hardy/Z8.

Narcissus 'Silver Chimes'

This is a fragrant white daffodil with up to 6 nodding heads on each stem. The small crown has a touch of creamy yellow, which has a softening effect. Flowering in mid-spring, it needs a warm, dry spot at the front of a sunny border or beneath a sunny wall. It is excellent for small to medium containers in a sheltered site where it can be fully appreciated. H 30cm (12in).

Narcissus 'Minnow'

Narcissus 'Silver Chimes'

Narcissus cyclamineus

Poeticus Daffodils (Division 9)
Developed from *N. poeticus*, which originally came from a wide area extending from France to Greece, this group have spreading, pure white petals and shallow cups, rimmed with red. They appear in late spring. All are hardy/Z3–9.

Narcissus 'Actaea'
The pure white flowers, which appear in mid-spring, have a brilliant scarlet eye. This is a delightful cultivar for borders or grassland. H 40cm (16in).

Narcissus 'Actaea'

Wild Species (Division 10)
The plants in this group are species and naturally occurring. They prefer sandy or peaty soil and do best when they are planted on a sloping bank of fine grasses, where the ground is damp in spring and dry in summer, where they will self-seed. All are hardy/Z3–9.

Narcissus bulbocodium
Hoop-petticoat daffodil
This tiny species daffodil grows in southern and western France, Spain, Portugal and Northern Africa, where it flowers in mid-spring. It is a distinctive daffodil, with a funnel-shaped cup, which flares out like an old-fashioned hoop-petticoat. The leaves are like dark green needles. *N. bulbocodium* var. *conspicuus* has a rich golden-yellow trumpet, 4cm (1¹/₂) wide, and is slightly larger than *N. bulbocodium*. *N.* 'Golden Bells' is regarded as an improved form of the species, with flowers that are almost twice the size of the species. H 10cm (4in).

Narcissus tazetta subsp. lacticolor (syn. N. caniculatus)
A pretty species daffodil, flowering in mid-spring, this has 3 or 4 sweetly scented flowers on each stem. The tiny yellow cup is surrounded by reflexed white petals. It is ideal for pots, raised troughs and window boxes or for a special place in the border. H 15cm (6in).

Narcissus bulbocodium

Narcissus cyclamineus
This is a species daffodil whose characteristic swept-back petals give it a distinctive shape, reminiscent of a cyclamen, hence its name. It is native to north-west Portugal and north-west Spain, and it is a parent of many dwarf hybrids. Flowering in early spring, it will naturalize well in damp conditions, preferring acidic

Narcissus 'Cassata'

Narcissus 'Quince'

soils, where it will succeed in partial shade. The cultivars thrive in most types of garden soil. H 15–20cm (6–8in).

Narcissus poeticus var. recurvus
Old pheasant's eye, pheasant's eye
Widely naturalized in the alpine meadows of southern Europe, this produces stunning flowers with tiny yellow, red-edged, flattened cups surrounded by glistening white recurved petals. This is an exceptionally good naturalizer and is one of the best-loved daffodils. It is also one of the last to flower in late spring. H 45cm (18in).

Split-corona Daffodils (Division 11)
The flowers are usually solitary with cups that are split for more than half their length. All are hardy/Z3–9.

Narcissus 'Cassata'
This is known as one of the butterfly daffodils with white perianth and lemon split corona. Flowers appear in mid-spring, and it is a showy plant for a prime spot in a spring border. It is not a good naturalizer in grass. It is a really choice plant for flower arrangers. H 35cm (14in).

Miscellaneous (Division 12)
These are daffodils that do not fit easily into any of the other categories. The following are hardy/Z3–9.

Narcissus 'Jumblie'
This is a memorable little golden-yellow daffodil, which is multi-headed and has little trumpets facing randomly in different directions, hence its name. It flowers in early spring. Short and sturdy, it is ideal for hanging baskets, small pots, raised troughs and window boxes or for the front of a border. H 20cm (8in).

Narcissus 'Quince'
This is a pretty little daffodil, with several flowers on each stem, each one with a deep golden-yellow trumpet surrounded by primrose-yellow petals. It flowers in mid-spring and is a good choice for small containers and borders. H 15cm (6in).

Narcissus 'Tête-à-tête'
This is an excellent multiheaded daffodil, with golden-yellow trumpet and petals. Early to flower, it is an excellent choice for the front of a border or for small containers. H 15cm (6in).

Narcissus poeticus var. recurvens

Narcissus 'Tête-à-tête'

NECTAROSCORDUM
Honey lily

This is a genus of just 3 species of bulbous, onion-scented, herbaceous perennials, similar to alliums, found in damp or shady woodlands and dry mountain slopes of southern Europe, west Asia and Iran. The flowers have large nectaries on the ovary, which gives rise to the name from the Greek word *nectar*; the Greek word *skorodon* refers to the plants' garlic scent, particularly of the leaves.
Cultivation Grow in any moderately fertile soil in full sun or partial shade. Plant bulbs 5cm (2in) deep in autumn. They may self-seed, particularly in light soils.
Propagation Sow seed in a cold frame in autumn. Remove offsets in summer.
Pests and diseases Trouble free.

Nectaroscordum siculum
(syn. *Allium siculum*)

Originally from France and Italy, this produces unusual but attractive flowerheads, which are recognizable by the loose umbels of bell-shaped flowers that appear in late spring and early summer. The flowers themselves are white or cream with a pink flush, tinted green at the bases. Although pendulous as flowers, they become erect as seedheads, which remain attractive for several weeks. The leaves die down soon after flowering. *N. siculum* subsp. *bulgaricum*, which comes from south-eastern Europe, north-eastern Turkey and Ukraine, is similar in height but has off-white flowers, flushed green and purple-red. H 1.2m (4ft) S 10cm (4in). Hardy/Z7–10.

NERINE

This is a genus of about 30 species of bulbs found on well-drained sites on cliffs, rocky ledges and mountain screes in southern Africa. Although all species in the genus are sometimes referred to as the Guernsey lily, this common name is properly applied only to *N. sarniensis* (see below). In 1659 a ship of the East India Company, bound for the Netherlands, was shipwrecked in the English Channel off the island of Guernsey. Boxes of bulbs, among them *N. sarniensis*, were washed ashore, and the islanders noted that the bulbs had taken root in the sand and began to cultivate them. Because the ship had come from the Far East, they thought the bulbs had originated from Japan. The real origin was not established for more than a hundred years, when they were recognized as those growing on Table Mountain in South Africa. All parts of the plant may cause mild stomach ache if ingested.
Cultivation Nerines require full sun and a well-drained site. Plant bulbs outdoors in early spring so that the noses are just above soil level and the shoulders well below.

Nerine bowdenii 'Blush Beauty'

Indoors bulbs should be planted in autumn or early spring in pots in soil-based compost (soil mix), again with the noses just above soil level. The flowers appear in autumn, the leaves follow in late winter, and the plant is dormant in summer, when it likes a dry, warm period. They flower best when congested. After flowering, apply a low-nitrogen liquid fertilizer.
Propagation Sow seed at 10–13°C (50–55°F) as soon as ripe. Divide clumps after flowering.
Pests and diseases Slugs.

Nerine bowdenii

Originally from Eastern Cape Province, Orange Free State and northern KwaZulu/Natal in South Africa, this nerine bears umbels of up to 7, sometimes more, funnel-shaped, slightly scented, pink flowers, each to 8cm (3in) across. The flowers, which are borne on stout stems, have wavy-edged, recurved petals. The flowers appear in autumn and are followed by the leaves in late winter. The plant goes dormant in summer, when it likes a dry, warm period. It soon forms large clumps. In cold areas provide a dry mulch in winter. *N. bowdenii* 'Alba' has white flowers occasionally tinged pink. H 45cm (18in) S 8cm (3in). Borderline hardy/Z8–10.

Nerine bowdenii 'Blush Beauty'

The flowers are borne on tall stems, bearing slender pale pink blooms. This is an unusual but attractive cultivar that is good for borders and for containers; pale blue glazed ones would be most attractive. For best results, allow the bulbs to become congested, then they will be more floriferous. H 1.2m (4ft) S 8cm (3in). Borderline hardy/Z8–10.

Species for autumn

Amaryllis belladonna	*Cyclamen hederifolium*
Colchicum autumnale	*Cyclamen mirabile*
Colchicum bivonae	*Nerine bowdenii*
Crocus niveus	*Nerine sarniensis*
Crocus sativus	*Sternbergia lutea*
Crocus speciosus	*Tulbaghia violacea*
Cyclamen cicilium	

Nectaroscordum siculum

Nerine bowdenii 'Pink Triumph'

Nerine bowdenii 'Mark Fenwick'

Nerine bowdenii 'Codora'

This cultivar of *N. bowdenii* flowers in early and mid-autumn. It bears vibrant red flowers on strong stems. Leave undisturbed in the container and allow it to become congested, when it will flower all the better. H 45cm (18in) S 8cm (3in). Borderline hardy/Z8–10.

Nerine bowdenii 'Mark Fenwick'

This is one of the taller cultivars of *N. bowdenii*, and it has longer, darker stems and broader pink flowers than the species. Leave undisturbed in the container and allow to become congested, when it will flower all the better. H 60cm (24in) S 8cm (3in). Borderline hardy/Z8–10.

Nerine bowdenii 'Pink Triumph'

Like other cultivars of *N. bowdenii*, this is borderline hardy, but because of its later flowering period – usually late rather than mid-autumn – it is safer to grow it in a container and enjoy it in a cool conservatory. It produces rich fuchsia-pink flowers with wavy margins, borne on strong stems. Leave undisturbed in the container and allow it to become congested, when it will flower all the better. H 45cm (18in) S 8cm (3in). Borderline hardy/Z8–10.

Nerine sarniensis
Guernsey lily

This nerine is native to South Africa's Northern Cape and Eastern Cape Province. It bears a distinctive spherical head of up to 20 deep orange-pink flowers with wavy margins to the petals. It flowers in early autumn. H 45–60cm (18–24in) S 12–15cm (4¹/₂–6in). Half-hardy/Z9–10.

Nerine 'Stephanie'

This cultivar flowers in early autumn. It produces pretty, creamy white flowers with a pale lilac-pink flush. Leave undisturbed in the container and allow it to become congested, when it will flower all the better. H 45cm (18in) S 8cm (3in). Borderline hardy/Z8–10.

Nerine undulata
(syn. *N. crispa*)

This nerine comes from low altitudes in South Africa's Eastern Cape Province and the Orange Free State. In autumn it produces umbels of 8–12 funnel-shaped, mid-pink flowers, to 5cm (2in) across, with characteristic narrow, crinkled petals. H 30–45cm (12–18in) S 10–12cm (4–4¹/₂in). Half-hardy/Z9–10.

Nerine 'Zeal Giant'

This is another of the taller cultivars of *N. bowdenii*. It has long stems and broad pink flowers. Leave undisturbed in the container. It takes a long time to form a good clump, but be patient. Allow it to become congested and eventually it will flower even better. H 60cm (24in) S 8cm (3in). Borderline hardy/Z8–10.

Nerine 'Zeal Giant'

Nerine undulata

Ornithogalum nutans

Ornithogalum dubium

ORNITHOGALUM
Star-of-Bethlehem

This genus contains 80 species of bulbs from a wide range of locations, from dry and rocky areas to meadows and woodlands in central and southern Europe, the Mediterranean, the former USSR, western and south-western Asia, tropical Africa and South Africa. Note that all parts may cause severe stomach ache if ingested and the sap may irritate the skin.

Cultivation Ornithogalums grow best in well-drained alkaline soil in full sun. In spring plant the bulbs of *O. arabicum* and *O. thyrsoides* 15cm (6in) and 10cm (4in) deep, respectively, in borders outdoors. After flowering lift them, and keep them dry and frost-free in winter. Alternatively, plant in pots in autumn in soil-based compost (soil mix). Keep in a cool, frost-free place and move outside in summer. In autumn plant the bulbs of *O. umbellatum* and *O. nutans* 8cm (3in) and 5cm (2in) deep, respectively, in borders outdoors

or in thin grassland where they should naturalize.

Propagation Sow seed in a cold frame in autumn or spring. Remove offsets during dormancy.

Pests and diseases None.

Ornithogalum arabicum

Originally from Mediterranean countries, in early summer this species has tall stems with a flattish head of usually 6–12 scented, cup-shaped, cream or white flowers, each with a distinctive black ovary. H 30–75cm (12–30in) S 8cm (3in). Half-hardy/Z7–10.

Ornithogalum dubium

The species is native to Cape Province in South Africa. It produces dense racemes packed with cup-shaped, orange, red, yellow or rarely white flowers, with yellow-green ovaries. They open in long succession from late spring or later depending on planting time. A late-spring planting will bring flowers in early autumn. H 30–45cm (12–18in) S 5cm (2in). Half-hardy/Z7–10.

Ornithogalum nutans

The species, which originated in Europe and southwestern Asia, flowers in late spring. Racemes of up to 20 semi-pendent, funnel-shaped, white flowers, with recurved tips to the petals, are produced. Each flower has a green stripe on the outside so that the whole effect is of a pretty grey-green rather than pure white. They will grow happily in borders or in grass, where they will naturalize well, but they prefer partial shade. H 20cm (8in) S 5cm (2in). Hardy/Z6–10.

Ornithogalum thyrsoides
Chincherinchee

This summer-flowering bulb, which is native to the Western Cape in South Africa, produces dense racemes packed with cup-

shaped white flowers, cream or green at the base, which open in long succession. H 30–40cm (12–16in) S 10cm (4in). Half-hardy/Z7–10.

Ornithogalum umbellatum
Star-of-Bethlehem

Native to Europe, Turkey, Syria, Lebanon, Israel and northern Africa, from mid- to late spring this bulb produces corymb-like racemes of 6–20 star-shaped white flowers on long stalks. Each flower has a green stripe down the outside. The long leaves wither as the flowers open. Although they like a sunny spot, they will tolerate partial shade, but the flowers need sunshine to open out. They will colonize well. H 15cm (6in) S 10cm (4in). Hardy/Z7–10.

Ornithogalum umbellatum 'Star-of-Bethlehem'

OXALIS

This is a large genus containing about 500 species of bulbs, tubers, rhizomes or fibrous-rooted annuals or perennials, widely distributed in woodlands or open areas from South America to southern Africa. The name *Oxalis* is derived from the Greek words *oxys* (sharp) and *als* (salt), which is a direct reference to the plants' sap, which is acidic. The plants have clover-shaped leaves, which often twist and close at night or on hot days.
Cultivation Most species like a position in sun, but some will tolerate shade. In autumn plant the fibre-covered bulbs 5cm (2in) deep in sunny borders outdoors, where they will soon form large, compact clumps. Bulbs of *O. tetraphylla* can also be planted in spring. *O. triangularis* can be grown in pots in the conservatory.
Propagation Sow seed at 13–18°C (55–64°F) in late winter or early spring. Divide in spring.
Pests and diseases Prone to rust, slugs and snails.

Oxalis adenophylla

This clump-forming perennial, which is native to the Andes, Chile and Argentina, grows from fibre-covered bulbs. The bulbs produce a plethora of heart-shaped, grey-green leaves. The foliage makes an attractive backdrop for the small, cup-shaped, purplish-pink flowers, which are distinctive for their darker veins and purple throats. They appear in spring. The colouring of *O. adenophylla* 'Silver Shamrock' is particularly pleasing. H 10cm (4in) S 15cm (6in). Hardy/Z7–10.

Oxalis tetraphylla
(syn. O. deppei)
Good-luck plant, lucky clover
The species comes from Mexico and in early summer produces loose, umbel-like cymes of reddish-purple flowers, 2.5cm (1in) across, which appear above the 4 deeply lobed, clover-like leaflets. These have purple bands at the bases. It needs a sheltered site. H 15cm (6in) S 10cm (4in). Borderline hardy/Z7–9.

Oxalis triangularis
Love clover
Native to Brazil and not hardy, in summer this bulb produces loose sprays of light pink flowers, 2.5cm (1in) across. They are borne above strongly contrasting triangular, rich burgundy red leaves. Plant outside in well-drained soil and use as summer groundcover, for edging rock gardens or at the base of steps, where it will naturalize quickly in a sunny spot. Alternatively, plant in spring in a small container and keep in dry, cool conditions until the leaves appear. Then increase the levels of moisture and light. It makes a good houseplant. H 15cm (6in) S 15cm (6in). Half-hardy/Z7–10.

Pelargonium 'Schottii' syn. *P.* × *schottii*

PELARGONIUM

This is a genus of about 250 species of mainly evergreen perennials (some from tuberous roots), succulents, subshrubs and shrubs, commonly but incorrectly known as geraniums. They occur in a range of habitats, from deserts to mountains, mainly in South Africa but also in Somalia, Australia and the Middle East.
Cultivation Pelargoniums require full sun and good drainage. Use a gritty compost and make sure you give plants a well-lit, well-ventilated position with a minimum temperature of 5°C (41°F). Water carefully, avoiding the central stem and tuberous roots, and keep nearly dry during periods of low temperatures and low light levels. Some tuberous species die back entirely while dormant; *P.* 'Schottii' does not. Gradually start watering again when growth appears more active, in early spring. These are tender plants and may be grown as houseplants or outside in the summer garden.
Propagation The species will come true from seed sown at 13–18°C (55–64°F) in late winter or early spring. Take softwood cuttings in summer.
Pests and diseases Prone to vine weevils, aphids and grey mould.

Pelargonium 'Schottii'
(syn. P. × schottii)
The species from which this form has developed originated in South Africa, and it is one of the more unusual pelargoniums to grow from a tuberous root. It produces velvety grey leaves, which are deeply incised and attractive. The flowers, which are borne on long stems, are in clusters of single, wine-coloured blooms with faint black stripes. It is a lovely plant for a container in a special place outdoors during the summer or in a conservatory. H 30cm (12in) S 30cm (12in). Tender/Z9–10.

Oxalis triangularis

Pleione formosana

Ranunculus asiaticus

PLEIONE

This genus has about 20 species of small, terrestrial, deciduous orchids from high wet forest or woodlands from northern India to southern China and Taiwan. Each pseudobulb will produce a solitary flower and one folded leaf.
Cultivation Grow indoors as a houseplant in a semi-shaded position or outdoors in a container in a sheltered, partially shaded site, only after all risk of frost has passed. In late winter or early spring plant the pseudobulbs 5cm (2in) deep so that the top one-third of the pseudobulb can still be seen. Plant singly or 5cm (2in) apart in small containers or window boxes, using a peat-based compost (soil mix). When in full growth, feed with a weak fertilizer. Flowers usually appear 4–6 weeks after planting. Deadhead after flowering and eventually bring outdoor containers inside to store in frost-free conditions until spring.
Propagation Divide annually, discarding old pseudobulbs.
Pests and diseases Aphids, red spider mites, slugs and mealybugs.

Pleione formosana
The species is native to eastern China and Taiwan. The elegant rose-lilac flowers have a central white lip, which has red or brown markings and a fringed edge. It is commonly known as the windowsill orchid and will flower in spring indoors. Plants in the *P. formosana* Alba Group have glorious white flowers with a central white lip, which has striking red or brown markings and a fringed edge. H 12cm (5in) S 30cm (12in). Half-hardy/Z10.

PUSCHKINIA

This little bulb was named after a Russian botanist, Count Apollos Mussin-Puschkin, who died in 1805. It is a genus of only one species and originates in the mountains of Turkey, Syria, Lebanon, Iraq and Iran, as well as the Caucasus. It flowers in damp meadows and scrub where the snows have just melted.
Cultivation It thrives in full sun or light shade. In autumn plant the bulbs 5cm (2in) deep at the front of a border or in a stone trough. It is dainty in growth and is good among other small plants. They form large groups in nature.

Puschkinia scilloides var. libanotica

Propagation Sow seed in containers in a cold frame in summer or autumn. Remove offsets in summer as leaves die down.
Pests and diseases Viruses can sometimes cause damage.

Puschkinia scilloides var. libanotica
This spring-flowering bulb produces compact racemes, which bear 4–10 tiny pale blue flowers, just 1cm (½in) across. Each petal has a darker blue stripe down the centre and a central white cup. *P. scilloides* var. *libanotica* has slightly smaller white flowers; it comes from Turkey and Lebanon. H 20cm (8in) S 5cm (2in). Hardy/Z3–6.

RANUNCULUS
Buttercup, crowfoot

This is a widely distributed genus of about 400 species of mainly deciduous, sometimes evergreen, tuberous, fibrous-rooted or rhizomatous perennials, annuals and biennials. The name is derived from the Latin word *rana* (frog) because many of the species grow in damp places.
Cultivation Grow in full sun or light shade. Plant the tubers in late winter indoors or in spring outdoors, placing them 5cm (2in) deep and 8cm (3in) apart (claws facing downwards) in borders or containers. They like plenty of moisture while they are in growth, although too much will cause the leaves to turn yellow. Make sure the compost (soil mix) or soil is fast draining.

Propagation Divide tuberous species in spring or autumn. Sow seed of *R. asiaticus* in autumn for flowering in late spring.
Pests and diseases Slugs, snails, aphids and mildew.

Ranunculus asiaticus
Persian buttercup
This colourful plant originated in the eastern Mediterranean, north-eastern Africa and south-western Asia. It produces single or double, peony-type flowers, 5cm (2in) across, in white and a range of colours including red, pink, orange and yellow. The flowering time varies according to cultivation. As a conservatory plant it will flower in late spring, but outside in the garden it will flower in summer. H 25cm (10in) S 20cm (8in). Half-hardy/Z8–10.

Ranunculus asiaticus 'Mount Vernon'

Schizostylis coccinea 'Jennifer'

Schizostylis coccinea 'Sunrise'

SCHIZOSTYLIS
Kaffir lily

The genus takes its name from the Greek words *schizo* (to cut, to divide) and *stilis* (style), because the style is divided into 3 distinct branches. It is a genus of only one species of virtually evergreen rhizomatous plants, which live in damp places in southern Africa. The flowers are like small gladioli, with 6–10 flowers on each stem, and 2 flowers open at a time. They make excellent cut flowers.

Cultivation They thrive in moderately fertile, moist but well-drained soil in full sun. In spring plant the rhizomes, at least 3 to a group, 8cm (3in) deep and 15–20cm (6–8in) apart, in a sunny, sheltered border where the soil will remain moist throughout the growing period. Apply a mulch in winter. The protection and warmth of a south-facing wall is ideal. Leave undisturbed. They make a lovely association with small coloured grasses, such as *Festuca glauca* (blue fescue) or *Uncinia rubra*. They can also be grown in containers.
Propagation Divide rhizomes in spring.
Pests and diseases None.

Schizostylis coccinea 'Jennifer'
This is a robust cultivar derived from a species originally found in Lesotho and Swaziland in southern Africa where it thrives by streams and riverbanks. Spikes of beautiful cup-shaped, mid-pink flowers are borne on slender stems, like small gladioli. These are a truly welcome sight in autumn. H 60cm (24in) S 30cm (1ft). Borderline hardy/Z6–9.

Schizostylis coccinea 'Major'
This robust cultivar produces spikes of striking, large, cup-shaped red flowers on stiff stems in autumn. H 60cm (24in) S 30cm (12in), Borderline hardy/Z6–9.

Schizostylis coccinea 'Sunrise'
This cultivar produces spikes of cup-shaped, salmon-pink flowers, which are borne on slender stems, like small gladioli. They appear in autumn. In good, damp but well drained conditions they should clump up well to provide useful colour in the autumn border. H 60cm (24in) S 30cm (12in). Borderline hardy/Z6–9.

Bulbs with red flowers

Anemone 'The Governor'	Fritillaria imperialis 'Rubra'
Begonia 'Flamboyant'	Hedychium coccineum
Canna 'Roi Humbert'	Hippeastrum 'Red Lion'
Canna 'President'	Hyacinthus orientalis
Canna 'Rosemond Coles'	'Hollyhock'
Crocosmia 'Fire Bird'	Lilium 'Red Carpet'
Crocosmia 'Lucifer'	Lilium speciosum var. rubrum
Dahlia 'Arabian Night'	Nerine bowdenii 'Cordora'
Dahlia 'Dark Desire'	Schizostylis coccinea 'Major'
Dahlia 'Doris Day'	Tulipa 'Apeldoorn'
Dahlia 'Geerings Indian	Tulipa 'Little Princess'
Summer'	Tulipa 'Madame Lefeber'
Dahlia 'Ragged Robin'	Tulipa 'Mona Lisa'
Dahlia 'Tally Ho'	Tulipa 'Red Riding Hood'

Schizostylis coccinea 'Major'

Scilla peruviana

SCILLA
Squill

This is a genus of about 90 species of bulbs found in a variety of locations in Europe, Asia and southern Africa. It is closely related to the genera *Chionodoxa* and *Puschkinia*.

Cultivation Grow in full sun or partial shade. In early autumn plant the bulbs 8–10cm (3–4in) deep in borders or containers.

Propagation Divide clumps of established bulbs when dormant in summer.

Pests and diseases Viruses.

Scilla bifolia

This species is native to central and southern Europe and Turkey. In early spring it produces spikes of up to 10 starry, blue to purple-blue flowers. They are excellent for naturalizing and will do well under deciduous shrubs. H 15cm (6in) S 5cm (2in). Hardy/Z1–8.

Scilla bithynica
Turkish squill

The species comes from north-western Turkey and Bulgaria, where it grows in damp meadows, woods and scrub. In early to mid-spring spikes of 6–12 star-shaped, blue flowers, 2cm (¾in) across, are borne above strap-like leaves. Plant among shrubs in borders or in partially shaded grassy areas among small trees and shrubs where they will flower with *Anemone blanda* and *Crocus*. H 10–15cm (4–6in) S 8cm (3in). Hardy/Z1–8.

Scilla liliohyacinthus

Originally from south-western France and Spain, this is a small, clump-forming perennial with relatively large, lily-like bulbs, flowering in late spring with dense, conical racemes of 5–20 star-shaped, bright blue flowers. It prefers cool conditions. H 15–25cm (5–10in) S 8cm (3in). Hardy/Z3–9.

Scilla mischtschenkoana 'Tubergeniana'

This species comes from southern Russia and Iran. It flowers in late winter and early spring, producing spikes of 2–6 starry, pale blue flowers. Bulbs should be planted at the front of a sunny border or with other bulbs in containers. They also look lovely grown informally in fine grass alongside cyclamen and *Galanthus nivalis* (snowdrop). H 10–15cm (4–6in) S 5cm (2in). Hardy/Z1–8.

Scilla peruviana

This species is not native to Peru, as the specific name suggests, but from Portugal, Spain, Italy and North Africa. It is virtually evergreen, with new basal leaves developing in autumn as the old ones fade. In early summer the bloom appears, gorgeous conical heads of 50–100 star-shaped, purplish-blue flowers. It is definitely a show-stopper and worthy of being grown in a container and raised up on a sunny wall so that all can enjoy its beauty. Provide a cool winter refuge away from frost. It is only borderline hardy, so if grown in a border, choose the shelter of a south-facing wall in well-drained soil. There is a white form, *S. peruviana* f. *alba*. H 15–30cm (6–12in) S 20cm (8in). Borderline hardy/Z8–10.

Scilla siberica
Siberian squill

This species is native to southern Russia and Turkey, where it grows among rocks, scrub and woods. It produces spikes of 4–5 bell-shaped, nodding, bright blue flowers, about 1cm (½in) across. They should be planted at the front of a sunny border or with other bulbs in containers, flowering alongside *Anemone blanda* and *Crocus*. They also look charming grown informally in grass, where they establish quickly to form large clumps. Here crocus, early daffodils and anemones might also be planted. *S. siberica* 'Spring Beauty' has a darker blue flower. H 15cm (6in) S 5cm (2in). Hardy/Z1–8.

Scilla siberica

Sinningia 'Hollywood'

SINNINGIA
Gloxinia

The genus was named in honour of Wilhelm Sinning (1794–1874), who was head gardener at the University of Bonn. It embraces about 40 species of tuberous perennials and low-growing shrubs from Central and South America. The best known plant in the genus is the florists' gloxinia. It is thought that the name gloxinia was given by a Belgian nurseryman, Louis Van Houtte, who named a special new cultivar that had bright carmine, white-edged, drooping petals after his wife, Gloxinia Mina. Another theory is that it was named after Benjamin Peter Gloxin. Modern cultivars are mainly from *S. speciosa* and *S. guttata*.
Cultivation Grow in light or partial shade indoors. In spring plant the tubers on the surface of the compost (soil mix) and keep barely moist until growth is noticed. Plant one tuber in a 13cm (5in) diameter pot. Never expose the plants to direct sunlight. Apply a dilute liquid feed during the growing and flowering season. As the foliage dies down, reduce watering, and keep tubers dry in winter.
Propagation Sow seed in fine compost in late winter. Take cuttings from young shoots.
Pests and diseases Leafhoppers and western flower thrips.

Sinningia 'Etoile de Feu'
(syn. *Gloxinia* 'Etoile de Feu')
This sinningia produces wide, trumpet-shaped, carmine-pink flowers with wavy paler margins all summer long. Grow it as a houseplant. H 25cm (10in) S 45cm (18in). Tender/Z10.

Sinningia 'Etoile de feu'

Sinningia 'Hollywood'
(syn. *Gloxinia* 'Hollywood')
It produces wide, trumpet-shaped, sumptuous, violet flowers, which are sometimes edged with silver and will flower through the summer. H 25cm (10in) S 45cm (18in). Tender/Z10.

Sinningia 'Mont Blanc'
(syn. *Gloxinia* 'Mont Blanc')
The pure white, trumpet-shaped flowers appear above velvety leaves. This excellent houseplant will continue to flower through the summer. H 25cm (10in) S 45cm (18in). Tender/Z10.

STERNBERGIA
Autumn daffodil

This genus of 8 species of dwarf bulb was named after the Austrian botanist Count Kaspar von Sternberg (1761–1838). Found on stony hillsides, scrub and pine forests in southern Europe, Turkey and Central Asia, they are similar to crocuses but have 6, not 3, stamens and grow from bulbs rather than from corms. Like the crocus, some species are autumn-flowering and some flower in spring. All parts are poisonous.
Cultivation Grow in full sun. As soon as they are available in late summer (so that they do not dry out too much) plant the bulbs 15cm (6in) deep near the front of a sunny border beneath a wall. They establish best in alkaline soils. They will increase by bulb division, but do not disturb until the clump fails to flower.
Propagation Separate offsets when dormant in late summer.
Pests and diseases Prone to narcissus viruses, narcissus bulb flies and eelworms.

Sternbergia lutea
Mount Etna lily, golden crocus
The species comes originally from among the rocks, scrub and pine woods of southern Europe, from Spain to Afghanistan. Yellow, goblet-shaped flowers, 4cm (1½in) across, appear in autumn at the same time as the dark green, strap-like leaves. H 15cm (6in) S 8cm (3in). Borderline hardy/Z6–9.

Sternbergia lutea

Tigridia pavonia

TIGRIDIA
Tiger flower

This genus includes 23 species of bulbs from seasonally dry lands in Mexico and Guatemala. The genus is named after the Latin word *tigris* (tiger), a reference to the local jaguars with their spotted coats, like the central marking on the flowers. Its brilliant colouring and distinctive markings have made it a favourite plant for hybridizing.
Cultivation Grow in full sun. In spring plant the bulbs 10cm (4in) deep in a sunny sheltered border. They need lifting before winter frosts. Overwinter in dry sand, at a temperature of 10°C (50°F), and replant in spring. They make good outdoor container plants when planted in a soil-based compost (soil mix). They associate well with bronze-foliage plants.
Propagation Buy offsets when dormant. Sow seed at 13–16°C (55–61°F) in spring.
Pests and diseases Prone to viruses.

Tigridia pavonia
Peacock flower

Native to Mexico, this bulb produces a succession of orange, yellow, white, pink or red flowers, each 10–15cm (4–6in) across, with intricate and beautifully contrasting central markings. They flower through the summer. H 1.5m (5ft), though more often 50cm (20in) in cultivation in Europe, S 10cm (4in). Tender/Z8–10.

TRILLIUM
Trinity flower, wake robin, wood lily

This genus includes about 30 species of rhizomatous plants, mainly from higher altitude woodland in North America. They have a distinctive whorl of 3 broad leaves, out of which grows a flower consisting of 3 green sepals and 3 beautiful petals, hence the genus name, which is based on the Latin *tri-* (three).
Cultivation Trilliums require deep or partial shade and deep moist soil, preferably neutral to acid. In autumn or early spring plant the rhizomes 10cm (4in) deep. They spoil if they are allowed to dry out before planting, so obtain stock that has been transported in moist peat. They will take a while to recover in their new conditions, but once established they should be left undisturbed to create a bold group.
Propagation Can be grown from seed but plants take 7 years to reach flowering size. Divide rhizomes in autumn or early spring, making sure that each new section has at least one growing point.
Pests and diseases Slugs and snails may damage the leaves.

Trillium grandiflorum f. roseum

This comes from woods beside streams in eastern North America. In late spring and early summer this cultivar bears pale pink, cup-shaped flowers on top of the dark green leaves. The flowers open

Trillium grandiflorum 'Flore Pleno'

wide and have large, slightly wavy petals, 8cm (3in) wide, which grow darker as they age. It looks lovely beside the unfurling fronds of young ferns. *T. grandiflorum* 'Flore Pleno' AGM is a double white form. H 40cm (16in) S 30–40cm (12–16in). Hardy/Z5–9.

Trillium luteum
Yellow wake robin

The species grows in rich woodland areas of south-eastern North America where in spring sweetly fragrant, golden-yellow or bronze-green flowers are borne erect on top of mid-green leaves, heavily marked with paler green. The narrow flower petals are about 9cm (3½in) long.

Bluebells and lily-of-the-valley make perfect planting partners. H 40cm (16in) S 30–40cm (12–16in). Hardy/Z5–9.

Trillium undulatum
Painted trillium, painted wood lily

This rhizomatous perennial, from hemlock and spruce forests of eastern North America, has funnel-shaped flowers composed of 3 wavy, white or pink petals with a frill of red-edged, green sepals. The petals have a red stripe at the base. The single flowers appear from mid- to late spring and are carried above oval, blue-green leaves. It thrives in moist, acid soil. H 10–20cm (4–8in) S 30cm (12in). Hardy/Z5–9.

Trillium grandiflorum f. roseum

Triteleia ixioides

TRITELEIA
Californian hyacinth

This genus is composed of about 15 species of corms. Closely related to *Brodiaea*, it is mainly found in grass and woodland in the west of the United States. Its name is derived from the Greek *tri* (three) and *telos* (end), a reference to the stigma being three-lobed. It makes a good cut flower and can be dried.

Cultivation In autumn plant the corms 8cm (3in) deep in a sunny herbaceous border where they would enjoy the same conditions as autumn-flowering nerines. Alternatively, plant them in containers in a soil-based compost (soil mix) and stand them on a sunny sheltered patio, mixing them with later flowering lilies in a large container. Keep dry and sheltered in winter.

Propagation Sow seed at 13–16°C (55–61°F) as soon as ripe or in early spring. Separate corms when dormant.

Pests and diseases None.

Triteleia ixioides 'Starlight'

T. ixioides (syn. *Brodiaea ixioides*, *B. lutea*) from which this cultivar was developed is native to western North America, in California and southern Oregon. In early and midsummer its strong stems bear loose heads, 12cm (4¹/₂in) across, of up to 25 starry yellow flowers. It is pretty in a sunny border or raised up in a container where the blooms can be enjoyed for up to 6 weeks. H 25cm (10in) S 10cm (4in). Borderline hardy/Z7–10.

Triteleia laxa 'Koningin Fabiola'

The cultivar is derived from the species *T. laxa* (syn. *Brodiaea laxa*), which originates in western North America, in California and southern Oregon. In early summer its stems bear loose umbels, 15cm (6in) across, of up to 25 purple-blue flowers, each 5cm (2in) long. It is an attractive plant to mass in a border or in a large container. It is also good as a cut flower. H 25cm (10in) S 10cm (4in). Borderline hardy/Z7–10.

TRITONIA

The name derives from the Greek word *triton* (weathercock), a clue to the strange habit of the stamens in some of the species, which change directions. It is a genus of 28 species of corms, closely related to *Crocosmia* and mainly found on grassy or stony hillsides of South Africa and Swaziland.

Cultivation They like light, sandy soil and a sheltered position in full sun. In autumn plant the corms 8cm (3in) deep in a sunny, well-drained border. Provide a winter mulch. Alternatively, plant them in containers in a soil-based compost (soil mix) and stand on a sunny sheltered patio. Keep dry and frost-free in winter.

Propagation Sow seed at 13–16°C (55–61°F) as soon as ripe. Separate corms when dormant.

Pests and diseases None.

Tritonia crocata

This species is native to Western Cape and Eastern Cape, South Africa. In summer it produces spikes of up to 10 cup-shaped, orange or pink flowers, with transparent margins. There are several interesting cultivars, including *T. crocata* 'Princess Beatrix', which has brilliant orange-red flowers. H 15–35cm (6–14in) S 20cm (8in). Half-hardy/Z7–10.

Tritonia laxifolia

This is a smaller species of the plant found in Eastern Cape, South Africa, as well as in Tanzania, Malawi and Zambia. It produces colourful spikes of 10–12 cup-shaped, salmon-pink, orange to brick-red flowers in late summer to early autumn. H 20cm (8in) S 20cm (8in). Half-hardy/Z7–10.

Tritonia crocata

Bulbs with blue flowers

Agapanthus 'Ben Hope'	Crocus 'Blue Pearl'
Agapanthus 'Blue Giant'	Hyacinthoides non-scripta
Agapanthus 'Blue Moon	Hyacinthus orientalis 'Blue
Allium caeruleum	Delft'
Anemone blanda	Iris 'Sapphire Beauty'
Anemone 'Lord Lieutenant'	Scilla peruviana
Camassia quamash	Scilla siberica
Chionodoxa sardensis	Triteleia laxa 'Koningin Fabiola'

Tulbaghia violacea var. robustior

Tulbaghia sinnleri syn. T. fragrans

TULBAGHIA
Society garlic
This genus was named after Ryk Tulbagh (d.1771), who was governor of the Cape of Good Hope. It contains about 26 species of deciduous or semi-evergreen, clump-forming perennials, growing from bulbs or fleshy rhizomes, all native to South Africa.
Cultivation They like well-drained soil and a sheltered position in full sun. In areas that are not frost-free, tulbaghias are best planted in a container in soil-based potting compost (soil mix) so that they can be moved out to a sunny position once all risk of frost has passed in the late spring. Keep almost dry and frost free in winter.

Propagation Sow seed in a cold frame as soon as it is ripe, or in spring. It germinates easily and the seedlings soon reach flowering size. Alternatively, divide in spring.
Pests and diseases Outdoors none, although aphids may be a problem under glass.

Tulbaghia acutiloba
This species grows from a bulb that is native to the Eastern Cape and Transvaal in South Africa. The leaves are grey-green, erect and narrow. The scented white flowers are borne continually on small stems throughout the summer. They appear like miniature daffodils with tiny orange trumpets. H 12cm (5in) S 8cm (3in). Borderline hardy/Z7–10.

Tulbaghia 'Fairy Star'
This is an interspecific cross between *T. violacea* and *T. cominsu*, which has resulted in a slightly less robust plant but with a very pretty pale lilac-pink, open flowerhead. The leaves are grey-green, erect and narrow. The flowers are borne from midsummer until early autumn. H 30cm (12in) S 30cm (12in). Borderline hardy/Z7–10.

Tulbaghia leucantha
This small but unusual and rather variable species is native to South Africa. It produces dainty flowers, which appear like miniature daffodils with tiny, rusty orange trumpets and pale lilac petals on small stems throughout the summer. H 20cm (8in) S 8cm (3in). Half-hardy/Z8–10.

Tulbaghia natalensis
This species grows from a bulb that is native to north-east Transvaal and KwaZulu/Natal in South Africa. The leaves are grey-green, erect and narrow. The pale lilac flowers are borne on small stems throughout the summer. H 20cm (8in) S 8cm (3in). Borderline hardy/Z7–10.

Tulbaghia simmleri
syn. *T. fragrans*
From early to midsummer delicate umbels of light to deep purple flowers appear on tall slender stems. They are commonly known as sweet garlic or pink agapanthus. H 60cm (24in) S 25cm (10in). Borderline hardy/Z7–10.

Tulbaghia violacea
This species grows from a bulb-like rhizome found in the Eastern Cape and Transvaal. The leaves are grey-green, erect and narrow. The flowers are borne on tall stems from midsummer until early autumn. They appear as delicate umbels of lilac flowers smelling of garlic. H 45–60cm (18–24in) S 25cm (10in). Borderline hardy/Z7–10.

Tulbaghia violacea var. robustior
From midsummer to early autumn the delicate lilac-purple flowers of this species appear on the tall slender stems. They have the common characteristic of smelling of garlic. H 45–60cm (18–24in) S 25cm (10in). Borderline hardy/Z7–10.

Tulbaghia violacea 'Silver Lace'
This is similar to the species but has slightly larger flowers and an attractive cream stripe in the leaves. It is also slightly more tender. H 35 (14in) S 25cm (10in). Borderline hardy/Z7–10.

Tulbaghia violacea

Bulbs with lilac or purple flowers

Allium cristophii	Hyacinthus orientalis
Allium 'Globemaster'	'Amethyst'
Allium 'Purple Sensation'	Iris 'George'
Allium schubertii	Iris 'Pauline'
Crocus 'Pickwick'	Sinningia 'Hollywood'
Crocus tommasinianus	Tulbaghia simmleri
'Whitewell Purple'	Tulbaghia violacea
Dahlia 'Belle of the Ball'	Tulipa 'Blue Heron'
Dahlia 'Purple Gem'	Tulipa 'Blue Parrot'

TULIPA
Tulip

This is one of the best known of all bulb groups, loved for its range of flamboyant colours, including red, orange, yellow, pink, mauve, purple and near-black, as well as white. True blue is the one colour that is missing. The genus is made up of about 100 species, which are found on hot, dry hillsides of temperate Europe, the Middle East and, particularly Central Asia, often growing on alkaline soils.

Over the last 400 years thousands of cultivars have been raised. The name comes from the Turkish word *tulbend* (turban), perhaps reflecting the shape and colour range of the flowers. In 1554 Ghislain de Busbecq (1522–91), then ambassador of the Holy Roman Empire to Süleyman the Magnificent, confused the name with the word *tulipam*, hence the name of the *Tulipa* genus today.

Usually the flowers are held singly, but some plants are multiheaded, as is the case with the species *T. tarda*, which may have 2 to 3 flowers. Occasionally the flowers are double, like those of the cultivars 'Peach Blossom' and 'Angélique'. Sometimes the petals are fringed, for example in 'Blue Heron', and sometimes they are quite crinkled, as in the Parrot tulips.

Most cultivars reach 40cm (16in) or more when in flower, but there are many dwarf cultivars and smaller species, which are ideal for the front of the border. All tulips are excellent for pots and window boxes, and the bulbs are quite small so they do not take up too much planting space. Tulips make extremely good cut flowers. Note that all parts may cause mild stomach ache if ingested, and contact with any part may aggravate skin allergies in some people.

Cultivation Tulips like a site in full sun. They should be planted to a depth of twice the height of the bulb, which usually means around 10cm (4in) deep for the dwarfer forms and 15cm (6in) or more for the taller cultivars, which will have larger bulbs. On lighter soils

Tulipa 'Apricot Beauty'

these depths can be increased. Deadhead after flowering. Remove the old stems and leaves once they have withered.

The bulbs can be lifted for the summer dormancy period or left in the ground where the Darwin, Kaufmanniana, Greigii and Triumph hybrids in particular will form good clumps if they are left alone. Lift if required and ripen in a greenhouse. Store in a dry place out of direct sunlight for planting again in autumn. Choose only the biggest bulbs to replant in the borders. The smaller ones can be grown on in a nursery bed. An annual potash-rich fertilizer or sulphate of potash is beneficial and should be applied in late winter before the first shoots appear. Tulips are good container plants in a soil-based compost (soil mix); however, they may not flower as well after the first year, so remove and replant.

Propagation Separate offsets of species and cultivars after lifting in summer and grow on. Seed sown from the species takes 4–7 years to produce flowers. Sow seed in autumn in containers in a cold frame or cold greenhouse.

Pests and diseases Slugs, stem and bulb eelworms, tulip fire, bulb rots and viruses.

Single Early Group
(Division 1)

These have single, cup-shaped flowers in early to mid-spring. They are suitable for borders and containers. All are hardy/Z3–8.

Tulipa 'Oranje Nassau'

Tulipa 'Apricot Beauty'

This Single Early is one of the best of all tulips for its soft apricot, tangerine-flushed colouring. Flowering in mid-spring, it looks excellent planted with pink-cupped daffodils, such as *Narcissus* 'Rainbow' or 'Salome', carpeted with *Tanacetum parthenium* 'Aureum' (golden feverfew) and backed by the vivid light green colouring of *Philadelphus coronarius* 'Aureus'. It is also stunning in a container with simple white pansies. H 45cm (18in). Hardy/Z3–8.

Tulipa 'Yokohama'

Bred in 1961, this has stood the test of time and proved to be a very good tulip with its cheerful bright yellow colouring. It resists all kinds of bad weather and lasts for a long time. It is an unusual Single Early tulip in that it has tapered flowers. H 30cm (12in). Hardy/Z3–8.

Double Early Group
(Division 2)

These tulips have double, bowl-shaped flowers in mid-spring, often margined or flecked with an additional colour. They are suitable for borders and containers. All are hardy/Z3–8.

Tulipa 'Abba'

This short, sturdy tulip bears large red flowers with a deep scarlet flame. It flowers in mid-spring. Plant in a border with violas and *Bellis* (daisy). It is striking when planted in a

container with *Muscari* (grape hyacinth). H 25cm (10in). Hardy/Z3–8.

Tulipa 'Kareol'

This short, sturdy tulip bears large yellow flowers. It blooms from early to mid-spring. Plant in a border with blue violas and red or white *Bellis* (daisy). It is also lovely planted with *Muscari* (grape hyacinth). H 25cm (10in). Hardy/Z3–8.

Tulipa 'Monte Carlo'

This short, sturdy tulip bears wonderful yellow flowers from early to mid-spring. Plant in a border with violas and *Bellis* (daisy). It associates beautifully with *Muscari* (grape hyacinth). H 30cm (12in). Hardy/Z3–8.

Tulipa 'Oranje Nassau'

This short, sturdy tulip bears large orange flowers from early to mid-spring. Plant in a border with violas, hyacinths and blue *Muscari* (grape hyacinth). It is excellent in containers. H 25cm (10in). Hardy/Z3–8.

Tulipa 'Peach Blossom'

This short, sturdy tulip bears large rose-pink flowers from early to mid-spring. Plant in a border with blue violas, pink *Bellis* (daisy) and blue *Muscari* (grape hyacinth). Excellent for containers and baskets. H 25cm (10in). Hardy/Z3–8.

Tulipa 'Peach Blossom'

Tulipa 'Attila'

Tulipa 'Negrita'

Triumph Group (Division 3)

The single cup-shaped flowers are produced from mid- to late spring. They are suitable for borders and containers. All are hardy/Z 3–8.

Tulipa 'Attila'

This Triumph tulip bears light purple flowers. Flowering in mid-spring, it looks good among pale dwarf wallflowers in a border or in a large container. H 50cm (20in). Hardy/Z 3–8.

Tulipa 'Golden Melody'

One of the Triumph hybrids, this has large golden-yellow flowers, which hold their petals for a long time. In borders they might be planted beside grey-leaved plants such as *Senecio cineraria*. It flowers in mid-spring and will survive well if left in the soil all year round. H 55cm (22in). Hardy/Z 3–8.

Tulipa 'Lustige Witwe' (syn. *T.* 'Merry Widow')

This Triumph hybrid bears large, single, cherry-pink flowers, edged in white. It is a late-spring-flowering tulip, which lasts a long time in flower. It can be planted to good effect with *Lunaria annua* (honesty), a flowering rosemary bush or other grey-leaved plants. H 35cm (14in). Hardy/Z 3–8.

Tulipa 'Negrita'

This Triumph hybrid flowers from mid- to late spring. The large beetroot purple flowers retain their poise for two weeks or more. It mixes well with the red or yellow Apeldoorn tulips or with purple-leaved *Heuchera*. It will survive well left in border soil and multiply to form good clumps. Alternatively, plant in containers with pale blue pansies. H 55cm (22in). Hardy/Z 3–8.

Tulipa 'New Design'

The variegated-leaved hybrid, which has a white edge to the leaves, looks stylish. The light pink petals deepen to a rosy pink around the edge. Plant in a group where you can enjoy them with the sun behind them: they look glorious backlit. They flower in mid-spring and are good partners for other silver-leaved foliage plants, while a carpet of snow white *Bellis* (daisy) would be the perfect accompaniment in a container. H 30cm (12in). Hardy/Z 3–8.

Tulipa 'Prinses Irene'

This Triumph hybrid has unusual orange flowers that are streaked with purple. It flowers in mid-spring and looks especially effective planted among dwarf, orange wallflowers in beds and borders. It also associates well with black violas or pansies. H 35cm (14in). Hardy/Z 3–8.

Tulipa 'Shirley'

The flowers of this Triumph hybrid are a combination of white with a mauve-purple edge, which becomes more defined with age. It flowers from mid- to late spring and is excellent planted with tall *Fritillaria persica* or *T.* 'Queen of Night', with which it shares a similar colouring on the edges of the petals. H 50cm (20in). Hardy/Z 3–8.

Tulipa 'Striped Bellona'

This Triumph hybrid, which flowers in mid-spring, has utterly stunning striped red and yellow flowers. It looks showy in the border and is just as good in a medium or large container. H 50cm (20in). Hardy/Z 3–8.

Darwin Hybrid Group (Division 4)

The large, single, oval flowers are carried at the top of tall, sturdy, erect stems, making them excellent for cutting. Among this group are some of the very best and most reliable of all border tulips. All are hardy/Z 3–8.

Tulipa 'Apeldoorn'

This Darwin hybrid flowers from mid- to late spring, and the large scarlet flowers retain their petals for a long period. This tulip looks beautiful with lime-green foliage. It will survive well left in border soil and multiply to form good clumps. Alternatively, plant in large containers. H 55cm (22in). Hardy/Z 3–8.

Tulipa 'Apeldoorn's Elite'

A Darwin hybrid, this flowers from mid- to late spring. The large scarlet flowers are edged with yellow. It will survive well left in border soil and multiply to form good clumps. It is also suitable for large containers. H 55cm (22in). Hardy/Z 3–8.

Tulipa 'Golden Melody'

Tulipa 'Prinses Irene'

Tulipa 'Apeldoorn'

Tulipa 'Beauty of Apeldoorn'
This Darwin hybrid flowers from mid- to late spring. The large yellow flowers are flushed with orange, and this tulip looks beautiful associated with yellows, lime-green and blues. It will survive well left in border soil and multiply to form good clumps. It is also suitable for containers. H 55cm (22in). Hardy/Z3–8.

Tulipa 'Gordon Cooper'
This Darwin hybrid is strong growing and bears pink flowers. It associates well with rose-coloured wallflowers and blue polyanthus. It flowers in mid-spring and will survive well if left in the soil all year round. H 60cm (24in). Hardy/Z3–8.

Tulipa 'Yellow Apeldoorn'
This Darwin hybrid flowers from mid- to late spring. The large golden-yellow flowers make an excellent show and are reliable, like other 'Apeldoorn' relations. This tulip looks beautiful with purple-leaved *Heuchera*. It will survive well left in border soil and multiply to form good clumps. Alternatively, plant in large containers. H 55cm (22in). Hardy/Z3–8.

Single Late Group (Division 5)
The flowers, which are cupped or goblet-shaped, are borne in late spring. Sometimes several to the stem, the flowers may be white to yellow, pink, red or almost black. Darwin and Cottage tulips belong in this group. All are hardy/Z3–8.

Tulipa 'Beauty of Apeldoorn'

Tulipa 'Esther'
This is one of the prettiest of the all-pink Single Late tulips. It flowers in late spring and is excellent planted with blue forget-me-nots or blue pansies; alternatively, plant it with the slightly later flowering *T*. 'Queen of Night'. H 50cm (20in). Hardy/Z3–8.

Tulipa 'Ile de France'
This is an impressive rich cardinal red tulip, which was introduced in 1968. It is very robust by nature and stands up well to windy and inclement weather. It looks equally good planted in containers, borders and beds. H 50cm (20in). Hardy/Z3–8.

Tulipa 'Paul Scherer'
This is a luscious, almost black tulip with a velvety maroon-black colouring just like blackberries. It is a good choice for borders, where it is especially impressive as it catches the sun, as well as for containers. Plant close to dark blue or black bicolour pansies. H 50cm (20in). Hardy/Z3–8.

Tulipa 'Yellow Apeldoorn'

Tulipa 'Esther'

Tulipa 'Paul Scherer'

Tulipa 'Queen of Night'

Tulipa 'Mona Lisa'

Tulipa 'West Point'

Tulipa 'Queen of Night'
This is a stunning dark purple tulip that flowers in late spring and looks beautiful beneath an arch of yellow laburnum flowers or against a backdrop of pale blue wisteria. Blue, pink or white forget-me-nots make an ideal partner in a border display or in a container. H 60cm (24in). Hardy/Z3–8.

Tulipa 'Swan Wings'
This is a tall tulip with elegant white flowers. The petals are delicately fringed. It flowers from mid- to late spring and is ideal for a border display or in a large container. Plant with black pansies or *Tanacetum parthenium* 'Aureum' (golden feverfew). H 55cm (22in). Hardy/Z3–8.

Lily-flowered Group (Division 6)
The petals of the slender flowers are often pointed and curve backwards. These tulips are late flowering and can be susceptible to wind damage. All are hardy/Z3–8.

Tulipa 'Ballerina'
A Lily-flowered hybrid, this is one of the most arresting of all tulips, with its scented, vibrant orange flowers. Flowering in mid-spring, it is excellent planted with other orange flowers or plants with bronze foliage. In containers combine it with deep blue pansies. H 55cm (22in). Hardy/Z3–8.

Tulipa 'Mona Lisa'
In mid- to late spring this large Lily-flowered hybrid bears yellow flowers that are streaked with a reddish raspberry-pink. This is a dramatic tulip for a sheltered spot. It is perfect beside bronze-coloured foliage or underplanted with yellow wallflowers or pansies. H 55cm (22in). Hardy/Z3–8.

Tulipa 'Pieter de Leur'
This is a cardinal-red tulip with blood-red shading at the tips and an ivory white base. It is a striking choice for containers, borders and beds, where it associates well with lime-green foliage or yellow bedding plants. H 25cm (10in). Hardy/Z3–8.

Tulipa 'West Point'
This late-spring-flowering Lily-flowered hybrid has distinctive primrose-yellow flowers, which look especially charming near blue forget-me-nots or purple wallflowers. H 50cm (20in). Hardy/Z3–8.

Tulipa 'White Triumphator'
This elegant late-spring-flowering Lily-flowered hybrid has distinctive pure white flowers, which look especially charming in borders underplanted with blue or white forget-me-nots or in association with white *Syringa* (lilac). H 60cm (24in). Hardy/Z3–8.

Fringed Group (Division 7)
The petals of the cup-shaped flowers are fringed at the edges, and sometimes a different colour may appear. The flowers are borne in late spring. All are hardy/Z3–8.

Tulipa 'Blue Heron'
This Fringed tulip bears large, violet-purple flowers with lilac-fringed petals. It is a strong-growing tulip, flowering in late spring. In borders it can be underplanted with grey-leaved plants or, for a more exciting combination, place it close to *Tanacetum parthenium* 'Aureum' (golden feverfew), which will really make it come alive. It is also an excellent bulb for planting in containers. H 60cm (24in). Hardy/Z3–8.

Tulipa 'Hamilton'
This tulip bears large yellow flowers, which are dramatically fringed. It is a strong-growing tulip that flowers in late spring. Grow it in a border or in a container and enjoy a great show of colour at the end of the tulip season. H 60cm (24in). Hardy/Z3–8.

Tulipa 'Pieter de Leur'

Tulipa 'Hamilton'

Viridiflora Group (Division 8)
The flowers are touched with various amounts of green, a feature that makes these tulips highly desirable. The flowers appear in late spring. All are hardy/Z3–8.

Tulipa 'Spring Green'
The flowers of this Viridiflora hybrid are an unusual creamy white with broad green stripes on the petals. Flowering in late spring, it looks delightful against bright green or green-grey foliage in the border or in a container with pansies. H 40cm (16in). Hardy/Z3–8.

Rembrandt Group (Division 9)
The cup-shaped flowers, which appear in late spring, are white, yellow or red with black, brown, bronze, purple, red or pink stripes or feathers. These tulips are good cut flowers. This type of tulip is depicted in paintings by Dutch Old Masters. Because the markings are actually caused by a virus, few are produced commercially nowadays. All are hardy/Z3–8.

Parrot Group (Division 10)
The cup-shaped flowers have twisted petals that are irregularly cut and banded with colours. Even in tight bud these tulips look amazing, then, as the petals unfurl, the full glorious shape and colours are revealed. As a result they are extremely flamboyant and a good choice if you want drama in your garden. The flowers appear in late spring. All are hardy/Z3–8.

Tulipa 'Spring Green'

Tulipa 'Apricot Parrot'
This is one of the most beautiful tulips, with its large pale apricot flowers feathered with tangerine and orange. Flowering in late spring, they are suitable planting partners for Tanacetum parthenium 'Aureum' (golden feverfew) or purple Heuchera. It also makes a great container plant grown with orange or purple wallflowers. H 45cm (18in). Hardy/Z3–8.

Tulipa 'Black Parrot'
Flowering in late spring, this handsome tulip is typical of the Parrot group. It has large black flowers, which open wide, but it is stunning even in bud, when the crinkled edges of the petals make fascinating patterns. Suitable partners include Tanacetum parthenium 'Aureum' (golden feverfew) and purple Heuchera. It also makes a great container planting combined with white and black pansies. H 45cm (18in). Hardy/Z3–8.

Tulipa 'Blue Parrot'

Tulipa 'Blue Parrot'
This tulip has single, large lilac-blue flowers, and irregular crimping along the edge of the petals. It flowers in late spring. In borders it can be planted with pink or blue forget-me-nots, and in containers pink, lavender or violet-blue pansies are perfect companions. H 60cm (24in). Hardy/Z3–8.

Tulipa 'Fantasy'
A Parrot group hybrid, flowering in late spring, this tulip has large pink flowers, crested with green, with irregular crimping along the edges of the petals. It is sensuous in bud, especially when the petals start to unfurl. Plant behind dark-leaved Heuchera. H 55cm (22in). Hardy/Z3–8.

Double Late Group (Division 11)
These tulips bear fully double, bowl-shaped flowers in late spring. The petals are often margined or flamed with an additional colour. They are suitable for borders and containers. All are hardy/Z3–8.

Tulipa 'Angélique'
This Double Late tulip, which flowers from mid- to late spring, bears large rose-pink flowers. It is a star performer and one of the most popular of all tulips. It looks beautiful planted in borders with pansies, pink forget-me-nots, arabis or aubrieta. In a container it is a good companion for lavender-blue pansies. H 45cm (18in). Hardy/Z3–8.

Tulipa 'Apricot Parrot'

Tulipa 'Fantasy'

Tulipa 'Angélique'

Tulipa 'Montreux'

Tulipa 'Chopin'

Tulipa 'Montreux'
This is a Double Late tulip, flowering from mid- to late spring, that bears fragrant, primrose-yellow flowers. It looks striking planted in borders with blue or white forget-me-nots, arabis or aubrieta. In a container it is a good companion for lavender-blue pansies. H 45cm (18in). Hardy/Z 3–8.

Tulipa 'Peaches and Cream'
This Double Late tulip bears fragrant, creamy white flowers with a pink flush from mid- to late spring. It looks striking planted in borders with forget-me-nots, arabis or aubrieta, and in a container underplanted with pastel-coloured pansies. H 45cm (18in). Hardy/Z 3–8.

Tulipa 'Tacoma'
This Double Late tulip bears large, fragrant, white flowers from mid- to late spring. It looks striking planted in borders with forget-me-nots, arabis or aubrieta, and in a container it would look stylish underplanted with black and white pansies. H 45cm (18in). Hardy/Z 3–8.

Tulipa 'Wirosa'
This Double Late tulip bears large, fragrant, red and white flowers from mid- to late spring. It looks striking planted in borders with white or blue forget-me-nots, and in a container it would make an eye-catching partnership with black or white pansies. H 35cm (14in). Hardy/Z 3–8.

Kaufmanniana Group (Division 12)
The group includes the species *T. kaufmanniana*, which is native to Central Asia, and its hybrids. These are small, sturdy tulips, which usually flower early in spring or in mid-spring. They often have bicoloured flowers, which open flat in sunshine, and are sometimes spotted bronze, red or purple on the foliage. They are suitable for borders and containers. All are hardy/Z 3–8.

Tulipa 'Chopin'
In early spring the large, single, yellow flowers are streaked with red, while the leaves have attractive mottled markings. This tulip looks beautiful associated with primroses and dwarf daffodils. The bulbs will continue to flower well in future seasons. They are also perfect for containers, underplanted with rich blue violas. H 25cm (10in). Hardy/Z 3–8.

Tulipa 'Heart's Delight'
Like many of the Kaufmanniana hybrids, this has irregularly striped leaves. It is a small tulip, and the white edges of the dark pink petals create a pretty feathering effect. It is excellent planted beside blue primulas, violas or dwarf daffodils, or plant it near the deep wine-red foliage of *Ajuga reptans* 'Burgundy Glow'. It flowers in early spring and will survive well if left in the ground all year round. H 25cm (10in). Hardy/Z 3–8.

Tulipa 'Tacoma'

Tulipa 'Heart's Delight'

Tulipa 'Shakespeare'

Tulipa 'Shakespeare'
This small, elegant and early-flowering tulip has comparatively long flowers, which are salmon-pink, flushed with orange and yellow. In a border they can be planted beside primroses and dwarf daffodils; in a container *Muscari* (grape hyacinths) or *Anemone blanda* would be perfect partners. H 25cm (10in). Hardy/Z3–8.

Tulipa 'Stresa'
This small but showy early-spring-flowering tulip has red flowers with broad yellow edges to the petals. It creates a stunning display in borders, where it associates well with primroses and dwarf daffodils. The bulbs can be left in the ground all year and will

continue to flower well in future seasons. H 25cm (10in). Hardy/Z3–8.

Fosteriana Group (Division 13)
This group includes the species *T. fosteriana* and its hybrids, which include crosses with those of this species and *T. kaufmanniana* and *T. greigii*. They have many similarities to Kaufmanniana and Greigii tulips, but the flowers of Fosteriana tulips are taller and larger. The leaves are sometimes marked with red or purple. They are suitable for borders and containers. All are hardy/Z3–8.

Tulipa 'Concerto'
The white flowers open in mid-spring and as a small group make an attractive and refreshing display alongside other whites, creams or soft yellows. H 20cm (8in). Hardy/Z3–8.

Tulipa 'Madame Lefeber' (syn. T. 'Red Emperor')
This is a popular cultivar with showy red flowers, which open in the sun to reveal a yellow base. The flowers are borne in mid-spring and are perfect beside black, blue or yellow pansies or violas. Left in the border it will naturalize well. H 40cm (16in). Hardy/Z3–8.

Tulipa 'Orange Emperor'
This is a popular cultivar of *T. fosteriana*, a species that is native to Central Asia. The orange

Tulipa 'Concerto'

flowers are showy, opening in the sun to reveal a yellow base. The flowers appear in mid-spring and are perfect beside bronze-coloured foliage or yellow wallflowers or pansies. Left in the border it will naturalize well. H 40cm (16in). Hardy/Z3–8.

Greigii Group (Division 14)
This group includes the species *T. greigii* and its hybrids, which include crosses with those of this species and *T. kaufmanniana*. They have single, bowl-shaped flowers in early to mid-spring. They are usually yellow to red, sometimes flamed. The blue-grey leaves have wavy margins and are sometimes marked with maroon. They are suitable for borders and containers. All are hardy/Z3–8.

Tulipa 'Cape Cod'
This is a sturdy tulip with large, orange-edged, yellow flowers and interesting purple-striped foliage. The flowers appear in mid-spring. H 30cm (12in). Hardy/Z3–8.

Tulipa 'Pinocchio'
This cultivar has leaves with purple markings. It flowers in mid-spring, having red flowers edged with white. It is good for naturalizing in borders. H 25cm (10in). Hardy/Z3–8.

Tulipa 'Plaisir'
This is a carmine-red tulip with lemon-yellow feathering at the edge of the petals. The leaves are heavily mottled. It is a good choice for containers and borders. H 25cm (10in). Hardy/Z3–8.

Tulipa 'Madame Lefeber'

Tulipa 'Plaisir'

Tulipa 'Quebec'

This tulip provides an outstanding show in mid-spring, when its multiflowering heads sometimes carry 3–5 blooms on each stem. The scarlet-edged flowers are pale chartreuse. The leaves are less obviously striped than those of other tulips in this group. Plant alongside polyanthus or violas. It is excellent for a tub or patio planter. H 35cm (14in). Hardy/Z3–8.

Tulipa 'Red Riding Hood'

This Greigii hybrid is one of the best-known tulips, with large scarlet flowers and outstanding purple-striped foliage. Flowering in mid-spring, it is a good partner for violas and dwarf daffodils. It is also excellent for a medium container. H 30cm (12in). Hardy/Z3–8.

Tulipa 'Toronto'

This popular Greigii hybrid produces several pretty pink flowers on each stem and characteristic purple-striped foliage. Flowering in mid-spring, it is a good partner for primroses and dwarf daffodils, and a carpet of black violas would provide the perfect contrast in a container. H 35cm (14in). Hardy/Z3–8.

Miscellaneous Group (Division 15)

The group includes species tulips and selected forms and hybrids that are not in the other divisions. All are hardy/Z3–8.

Tulipa clusiana

This species tulip originates in an area extending from Iran to the western Himalayas. It flowers from early to mid-spring. The slim, white flowers have a distinctive dark pink stripe on the outside, with purple markings inside and purple stamens. Plant near the front of a border with aubrieta or arabis for partners where the bulbs will flower happily for years if left undisturbed. H 30cm (12in). Hardy/Z3–8.

Tulipa clusiana 'Lady Jane'

This is a delightful dwarf cultivar. The outer petals are a combination of rose-pink and white, and the inner ones are purely white. It flowers in mid-spring and is the perfect companion for pink or white Bellis (daisy). It is also ideal for hanging baskets and other small to medium containers. H 15cm (6in). Hardy/Z3–8.

Tulipa 'Honky Tonk'

This is a little jewel, with soft yellow flowers delicately flushed with pink. It flowers from mid- to late spring and is excellent planted with little violas in a rock garden or in a small container. H 15cm (6in). Hardy/Z3–8.

Tulipa humilis Violacea Group

The species from which the cultivars developed is native to Turkey and Iran. Although it is one of the shortest tulips, the

Tulipa kolpakowskiana

violet-pink flowers, with blue-black basal markings, make a strong statement, particularly near the front of a border with aubrieta or violas. The flowers appear in early spring, and plants will survive well if left in the soil all year round. H 8cm (3in). Hardy/Z3–8.

Tulipa kolpakowskiana

This species, which originates in Central Asia, has small, elegant yellow flowers, which fade to pale orange, flushed violet-grey on the outside. The flowers, which appear in late spring, are held on curved stems. This is an easy tulip to grow at the front of a border or in a small container. Creamy little violas would make suitable planting partners. H 20cm (8in). Hardy/Z3–8.

Tulipa linifolia

This is a popular species, which is native to Central Asia. It flowers

in late spring, producing bright red flowers and narrow leaves. Little violas would make a suitable planting partner in a rock garden or in a small container. H 15cm (6in). Hardy/Z3–8.

Tulipa linifolia Batalinii Group 'Bright Gem'

A short, late-flowering cultivar, closely related to the species tulip (see above), it flowers in late spring and has bronze-yellow flowers. It is ideal for small baskets, wall pots or any other small container. H 15cm (6in). Hardy/Z3–8.

Tulipa 'Little Princess'

The orange-red flowers open wide to reveal black centres. This little tulip, which flowers from mid- to late spring, looks striking in a painted wire basket or other small container, underplanted with black violas. H 10cm (4in). Hardy/Z3–8.

Tulipa linifolia

Bulbs that are good as cut flowers

Agapanthus (many)	Gladiolus (many)
Allium cristophii	Hippeastrum (many)
Allium giganteum	Iris xiphium (many)
Allium 'Purple Sensation'	Lilium (many)
Anemone coronaria	Muscari (many)
Eucomis (many)	Narcissus (many)
Dahlia (many)	Nerine (many)
Freesia (many)	Tulipa (many)
Fritillaria imperialis	Triteleia laxa 'Koningin Fabiola'

Tulipa tarda planted with T. urumiensis

Tulipa saxatilis

Tulipa saxatilis

This species tulip from Crete flowers in mid-spring. The delicate lilac-pink petals have a strongly contrasting yellow centre. Its glossy leaves appear in late winter. Choose a sunny spot and plant close to pastel-coloured or dark purple plants. H 15cm (6in). Hardy/Z3–8.

Tulipa saxatilis Bakeri Group 'Lilac Wonder'

Closely related to the species *T. saxatilis* this small Bakeri Group cultivar is slightly darker. It is excellent planted around the edge of small containers where it will soften the rim. Plant with *Millium effusum* 'Aureum' (Bowles' golden grass) or *Tanacetum parthenium* 'Aureum' (golden feverfew). H 15cm (6in). Hardy/Z3–8.

Tulipa sylvestris

This short species tulip is native to open woodlands of Italy, Sicily and Sardinia but has become naturalized further north in Europe, including in the Netherlands and Britain. The delicate yellow flowers appear in mid-spring. Try planting it in borders or grass in light shade. H 25cm (10in). Hardy/Z3–8.

Tulipa tarda

This is a short species tulip, originally from Central Asia, which flowers from mid- to late spring. The rather floppy flowers are white and yellow, and each bulb might produce more than one flowering stem. It is ideal for planting at the front of hanging baskets or other small to medium containers. H 10cm (4in). Hardy/Z3–8.

Tulipa 'Tinka'

This short cultivar flowers from mid- to late spring. It has red flowers edged in yellow, the whole effect being delicate rather than strident. It is ideal for a hanging basket or other small to medium container. H 10cm (4in). Hardy/Z3–8.

Tulipa turkestanica

This short species tulip is native to Central Asia, and it is one of the first tulips to flower, appearing in late winter or early spring. Its white petals are distinctly pointed, and each has a yellow base. Choose a sheltered, sunny site and plant at the front of a border or in a medium container. H 25–30cm (10–12in). Hardy/Z3–8.

Tulipa urumiensis

This dwarf species tulip, which probably originated in western Iran, flowers from mid- to late spring. It bears several small yellow flowers, which are green-bronze on the outside, and is worth being seen at close quarters at the front of a border or raised bed. Like *T. tarda*, it is ideal for the front of a hanging basket or other small to medium container. The two can be combined for subtle but interesting results. H 10cm (4in). Hardy/Z3–8.

Tulipa saxatilis 'Lilac Wonder'

Tulipa turkestanica

VELTHEIMIA

Named after a German patron of botany, August Ferdinand Graf von Veltheim (1741–1801), this is a genus of only two species of perennial bulbs, which are found growing on rocky and grassy hillsides in South Africa. They are cultivated for their beautiful spring flowers and make excellent houseplants.

Cultivation Plant in autumn with the neck of the bulb just above the soil surface. In frost-prone areas treat as a houseplant and plant in a small pot using a soil-based compost (soil mix) with added sharp sand. Place in a sunny position and begin to water as soon as growth begins, giving a fortnightly low-nitrogen liquid feed. Keep just moist once the leaves have faded and the bulb is dormant.

Propagation Sow seed at 19–24°C (66–75°F) in autumn. Remove offsets in late summer.

Pests and diseases None.

Veltheimia bracteata
(syn. *V. viridifolia*)

This is a robust perennial bulb, native to South Africa, which flowers in spring. It bears thick, wavy, dark green leaves and dense racemes of up to 60 pendent, tubular, pinkish-purple flowers on stout, erect, yellow-spotted purple stems. Sometimes the flowers are red or yellowish-red. It makes a spectacular display indoors, which can be repeated year after year. H 45cm (16in) S 30cm (12in). Tender/Z10.

VERATRUM

This is a genus of about 45 species of large, vigorous perennials growing from poisonous black rhizomes, which give rise to its Latin name, from *vere* (truly) and *ater* (black). It grows in damp meadows and open woodland of the northern hemisphere. Its pleated, heavily veined, mid- to dark green leaves are particularly distinctive.

Cultivation Grow in a moist, shady site in a mixed border or in a woodland or wild garden. Provide shelter from drying winds. All parts are highly toxic if ingested.

Propagation Sow seed in a cold frame as soon as it is ripe, or in spring. Divide in autumn or early spring.

Pests and diseases Slugs and snails may be a problem.

Veratrum album
False hellebore, white hellebore

Native to Europe, North Africa and north Asia, this species has pleated basal leaves to 30cm (12in) long and a few stem leaves. It flowers in early and midsummer, bearing numerous star-shaped, greenish-white to white flowers on erect, freely branched panicles to 60cm (24in) long. H 1.8m (6ft) S 60cm (24in). Hardy/Z7–9.

Veratrum nigrum

This species, which is native to Europe and Russia, China and Korea, has long, pleated, basal leaves, to 35cm (14in) long. It flowers in mid- and late summer, bearing numerous star-shaped, almost black flowers on erect, freely branched panicles to 45cm (18in) long. They have an unpleasant scent. H 60–120cm (2–4ft) S 60cm (24in). Hardy/Z7–9.

WATSONIA
Bugle lily

The genus is named in honour of Sir William Watson (1715–87), an English apothecary, physician and naturalist who is known for his research into electricity. It is a genus of about 60 species of corms, usually found on grassy slopes and plateaux of South Africa and Madagascar, and the plants are not dissimilar to gladioli.

Cultivation Grow in light, sandy soil, in a sheltered position in full sun. In autumn or spring plant the corms 15cm (6in) deep in a sheltered sunny border; plants need the protection of a winter mulch. They enjoy the same conditions as autumn-flowering nerines and, like them, are best left undisturbed to form good clumps. Alternatively, plant the bulbs in soil-based compost (soil mix) in a large, deep container standing on a sunny, sheltered patio; or plunge the pot in the open border in summer. Overwinter in a frost-free environment.

Propagation Sow seed at 13–18°C (55–64°F) in autumn. Separate corms when dormant, and pot them up in a sandy compost. Keep them dry during the winter and start watering the young plants in the spring.

Pests and diseases None.

Watsonia angusta

This evergreen species is native to South Africa, blooming in late spring or early summer. The long flower spikes bear up to 20 graceful, pale orange flowers, each about 4cm (1½in) long. H 60–90cm (24–36in) S 10cm (4in). Half-hardy/Z9–10.

Watsonia angusta

Watsonia marginata

This clump-forming species is native to Western Cape in South Africa. The narrow leaves, to 45cm (18in) long, are arranged in a fan-like formation. In late spring to early summer the flower spikes are covered with fragrant pink flowers, each to 5cm (2in) long. H 1–1.5m (3–5ft) S 15cm (6in). Tender/Z10.

Watsonia 'Tresco Dwarf Pink'

This is a pretty cultivar producing spikes of shell-pink flowers in late spring or early summer. It was bred in southwest Scotland. H 30cm (12in). Tender/Z10.

Veltheimia bracteata

Veratrum album

Watsonia 'Tresco Dwarf Pink'

ZANTEDESCHIA
Arum lily, calla lily

This genus, which is named in honour of Giovanni Zantedeschi (1773–1846), an Italian botanist and physician, includes about 6 species of rhizomatous plants, usually found in moist soil around lakes or swamps in southern and eastern Africa. They are evergreen in warmer climates but deciduous in cooler areas. The flowers are good for cutting.
Cultivation Grow in consistently damp soil in a sheltered site in full sun. It prefers acidic to mildly acidic soil. In spring plant the rhizomes 15cm (6in) deep in soil-based compost (soil mix) in deep containers, 30–45cm (12–18in) apart, or in a sunny, sheltered border where the protection of a winter mulch is important. Alternatively, plant one tuber to a pot and plunge the container into an open border or beside water for the summer months. It is vital that the tubers are kept moist during the growing period. Bring containers under shelter in winter and repot in spring. *Z. aethiopia* 'Crowborough' can be grown as an aquatic plant in a planting basket, 25–30cm (10–12in) across, in heavy loam soil and placed in water to 30cm (12in) deep. Retrieve for winter months and keep sheltered and frost-free.
Propagation Divide in spring.
Pests and diseases Fungi and aphids.

Zantedeschia aethiopica 'Crowborough'

The species from which this cultivar originates is widely naturalized in tropical and temperate regions of South Africa. Large, white, funnel-shaped spathes are carried above the glossy leaves. It flowers from early to midsummer. H 90cm (36in) S 60cm (24in). Borderline hardy/Z8–10.

Zantedeschia aethiopica 'Green Goddess'

A succession of green spathes, with a central white area splashed with green, appear in summer above deep green, arrow-shaped leaves. This is a curious plant, which will appeal to anyone with a keen eye for design or flower arranging. It is a little more susceptible to frost than *Z. aethiopica* 'Crowborough'. H 75cm (30in) S 60cm (24in). Borderline hardy/Z9–10.

Zantedeschia 'Anneke'

This cultivar, which is partly derived from *Z. elliottiana*, produces large, claret-red, funnel-shaped spathes. The leaves are mottled. It makes a striking contribution in the midsummer garden in borders, as a marginal aquatic or in a container. H 50cm (24in) S 10cm (4in). Tender/Z9–10.

Zantedeschia 'Black Magic'

This cultivar, partly derived from *Z. elliottiana*, produces large, funnel-shaped spathes, which are a rich yellow with a black mark at the throat. The leaves are mottled. Try planting in black containers for the midsummer garden. H 60–90cm (24–36in) S 10cm (4in). Tender/Z9–10.

Zantedeschia 'Cameo'

This cultivar, partly derived from *Z. elliottiana*, produces large, salmon-pink, funnel-shaped spathes, which have a contrasting black mark at the throat. The leaves are mottled. It makes an attractive choice for the midsummer garden, in borders, as a marginal aquatic or in a container. H 50cm (24in) S 10cm (4in). Tender/Z9–10.

Zantedeschia 'Flame'

Although the colouring may vary, this cultivar generally produces funnel-shaped spathes which open yellow with a red edge, maturing through shades of orange to a glowing red flame. The leaves are dark green with white spots. H 40–65cm (16–26in) S 60cm (24in). Tender/Z9–10.

Zantedeschia 'Pink Mist'

A succession of funnel-shaped spathes, which are white with a blush of pink, makes this a really attractive plant, flowering in summer above deep green, arrow-shaped leaves. H 75cm (30in) S 60cm (24in). Borderline hardy/Z9–10.

Zantedeschia 'Picasso'

A succession of sensational funnel-shaped spathes, which are dark purple with white rims, make this a striking plant. It flowers in summer above dark green, arrow-shaped leaves, which have lighter flecks. H 75cm (30in) S 60cm (24in). Borderline hardy/Z9–10.

Zantedeschia 'Pink Persuasion'

This cultivar, partly derived from *Z. elliottiana*, produces large pink, funnel-shaped spathes. The leaves are mottled. This makes a pretty plant in the midsummer garden in a border, as a marginal aquatic or in a container. H 50cm (24in) S 10cm (4in). Tender/Z9–10.

Zantedeschia rehmannii
Pink arum

This eye-catching species is native to eastern South Africa and Swaziland. The leaves are spotted light green or white, and in summer the flower stem carries a yellow spadix surrounded by a reddish-pink spathe, to 8cm (3in) long. The pink becomes more intense if the soil is acidic. Treat as a houseplant or as a container plant on the patio. H 40cm (16in) S 25cm (10in). Tender/Z9–10.

Zantedeschia 'Flame'

Zantedeschia 'Schwarzwalder'

A succession of funnel-shaped, almost black spathes makes this a really striking plant. It flowers in summer above deep green, arrow-shaped leaves, which have lighter flecks. H 75cm (30in) S 60cm (24in). Borderline hardy/Z9–10.

Zantedeschia 'Solfatare'

This cultivar, partly derived from *Z. elliottiana*, produces large, funnel-shaped spathes, which are a rich yellow with a black blush. The leaves are heavily mottled. It makes an impressive container plant. H 60–90cm (24–36in) S 10cm (4in). Tender/Z9–10.

Zantedeschia aethiopica 'Crowborough'

Glossary

Annual A plant that grows from seed, flowers, sets seed again and dies in one year.

Aquatic A plant that lives in water: it can be completely submerged, floating or live with its roots in the water and shoots in the air.

Bare-root A plant that is sold with no soil or compost around the roots. They are dug up from the nursery field and are ready for planting during the dormant season.

Bedding plant A plant that is raised for use in a temporary garden display; spring, summer and winter types are available.

Biennial A plant that grows from seed to form a small plant in the first year and flowers and sets seed in the following year.

Biological control The use of a pest's natural enemies to control its numbers in the garden or greenhouse.

Bog garden An area of ground that remains permanently wet and is used to grow bog plants that thrive in such conditions.

Capillary matting An absorbent material that holds a lot of water on which containers are placed and from which they can draw all the moisture they need via capillary action.

Certified stock Plants that have been inspected and declared free of specific pests and diseases. They can be used as stock plants for propagation material.

Chit A technique used to encourage a potato tuber to begin to sprout before planting.

Cloche A small structure made from glass, clear plastic or polythene that can be moved around easily in order to warm small areas of soil or protect vulnerable plants.

Compost (soil mix) A mixture that is used for growing plants in containers. It can be loam-based or peat-based. Peat-free versions are now available based on coir, composted bark or other organic waste material.

Compost, garden A material that has been produced from the decomposition of organic waste material in a compost bin or heap. Useful as a soil improver or planting mixture.

Cordon A trained form of tree or bush with a main stem, vertical or at an angle, and with sideshoots shortened to form fruiting spurs.

Crop covers Various porous materials used to protect plants or crops. Horticultural fleece is a woven fabric that can be used to protect plants from frost and flying insect pests; insect-proof mesh is a well-ventilated fabric, ideal for keeping out insects throughout the summer, but offers no frost protection.

Damping down Wetting surfaces in a greenhouse in order to raise overall air humidity and to help to keep temperatures under control.

Deadhead To remove spent flowers to tidy the display, prevent the formation of seeds and improve future flowering performance.

Earth up To draw up soil around a plant forming a mound. Potatoes are earthed up to protect new shoots from frost and to prevent tubers from being exposed to light, which turns them green.

Espalier A trained form of tree or bush where the main stem is vertical and pairs of sideshoots are at a set spacing and trained out horizontally.

Fan A trained form of tree or bush where the main stem is vertical and pairs of sideshoots are pruned at set spacing and trained out either side to form a fan shape.

Grafted plant An ornamental plant that has been attached on to the rootstock of another, more vigorous, variety.

Ground cover plants These are densely growing, mat-forming plants that can be used to cover the ground with foliage to prevent weeds germinating.

Hardening-off A method of gradually weaning off a plant from the conditions inside to those outside without causing a check to growth.

Hardiness The amount of cold a type of plant is able to withstand. Hardy plants can tolerate frost; half-hardy and tender plants cannot.

Herbaceous plants Plants that produce sappy, green, non-woody growth. Herbaceous perennials die down in winter, but re-grow from basal shoots the following spring.

Horticultural fleece *see* crop covers.

Humus The organic residue of decayed organic matter found in soil. It improves soil fertility.

Insect-proof mesh *see* crop covers.

Leafmould A material that has been produced from the decomposition of leaves in a leaf bin or heap. Useful as a soil improver or planting mixture.

Manure A bulky organic animal waste that is rotted down and used to improve soil structure and fertility.

Mulch A material that is laid on the surface of the soil to prevent moisture loss through evaporation and suppress weed growth. Can be loose and organic, such as composted bark or garden compost, loose and inorganic, such as gravel, or a fabric, such as mulch matting or landscape fabric.

Perennial A plant that lives for more than two years. Usually applied to a hardy non-woody plant (*see* herbaceous plants). A tender perennial is a non-woody plant that cannot tolerate frost.

Pricking out The spacing of seedlings while still small so that they have room to grow on.

Rootball A mass of roots and compost that holds together when a plant is removed from its container.

Runner A horizontal shoot that spreads out from the plant, roots and forms another plant.

Slow-release fertilizer A specially coated inorganic fertilizer that releases its nutrients slowly.

Sucker A shoot that arises from the roots underground. The term is usually applied to shoots from the rootstock of a grafted plant that has different characteristics to the ornamental variety.

Transplanting The transfer of seedlings or young plants from a nursery bed where they were sown to their final growing position.

Windbreak A hedge, fence, wall or fabric that is used to filter the wind and reduce the damage it may cause.

Sidalcea 'Elsie Heugh'

Acknowledgements

Unless listed below, photographs are © Anness Publishing Ltd t=top;
b=bottom, c=centre; r=right; l=left
RICHARD BIRD PLANT PICTURES: 45b; 48b; 78t (& on 354 bl); 86tl
(& on 366 tc); 86tr (& on 372tc); 259br; 261tr; 262tc; 263tl; 263tr;
264br; 268tl; 278br; 279b; 290tl; 290tc; 290bl; 290bc; 294bl; 295tc;
295bl; 299bl; 299br; 304tr; 305b; 307t; 308tr; 314tr; 319bl; 323cb;
326tr; 329bc; 334tc; 334tr; 334bl; 334bcl; 334br; 335tl; 335bl;
335br; 336tr; 336br; 33/bcl; 33/bcr; 338bl; 338br; 339tcl; 339tr;
339bcl; 340; 342tl; 342tr; 342bcl; 342br; 343tl; 343tr; 343bcl;
344tcl; 344tcr; 344tr; 344bl; 345tl; 345tr; 346tl; 346tcr; 346bcl;
347t; 347bcl; 348tr; 348br; 349tc; 349tr; 349bl; 349bcl; 349br;
350bl; 351bcl; 352tl; 353tl; 353tc; 353bl; 354tl; 354bl; 354br; 355tl;
355tcl; 355tr; 355bl; 355bcl; 355br; 356tl; 356tr; 356bl; 357tl;
357tr; 357br; 358tl; 358bl; 359br; 360tl; 360bl; 361 tl; 362tl; 363tl;
202tc; 363bc; 363bl; 364tl; 364br; 365tr; 365br; 366br; 367tl;
367tc; 367tr; 367bl; 367bc; 368tc; 368br; 369br; 370; 371bl; 371bc;

Malva moschata alba

372tr; 372bl; 372bcl; 372bcr; 373tr; 373 bcl; 373bcr; 373br; 374tl; 374tcr; 375tcl; 376bc; 377tl; 377bl; 377br; 378tcl; 378tr; 378br; 379tl;
379br; 380bcr; 381tc; 381br; 382tl; 362tc; 382bl; 382bc; 382br; 383tcr; 383tr; 384tc; 384tr; 384bl; 385tr; 385br; 386tcl; 386bl; 386br;
387tl; 388br; 389tcr; 389 bl; 389bc; 389br; 390tcl; 390tr; 390bl; 390bc; 390br; 391bl; 392tcr; 392bc; 394tc; 394tr; 394br; 395; 395br;
396tc; 396bl; 397tl; 397tc; 397tr; 397br; 398tc; 398tr; 398bl; 398br; 399tr; 399bl; 341tl; 341tc; 341tr; 341bcl; 341bcr; 341br; 342tl; 342bc;
343bl; 344tl; 344tr; 344bl; 344bcl; 344bcr; 345tr; 345br; 346tcl; 346tcr; 347tl; 347bl; 348tl; 348tr; 348bl; 348br; 349tl; 349tr; 350tr;
350bc; 351tc; 352tl; 352bl; 352br; 353bc; 353bc. **RAY COX:** 352 bl. **MARY EVANS PICTURE LIBRARY:** 105t, 106t, 107t; Garden Picture
Library: 426tl (John Glover), 426tc (Howard Rice), 426br (Mark Bolton), 427tl (J S Sira), 429tc (Chris Burrows), 439tr (Brian Carter),
439br (Geoff Dann), 453tr (Densey Clyne); 453br (Clive Nichols), 453tl (Howard Rice), 453bl (John Glover), 453br (J. S. Sira), 457tr
(Howard Rice), 459tl (Juliette Wade), 459tc (David England), 461tl (James Guilliam), 461tc (Chris Burrows), 461bl (Philippe Bonduel),
479br (Philippe Bonduel), 482tr (Sunniva Harte), 482br (John Glover), 483tl (Neil Holmes), 483bl (Chris Burrows), 485br (Sunniva
Harte), 486tl (Philippe Bonduel), 487tl (Chris Burrows), 487br (John Glover), 488tl (Sunniva Harte), 488tc (Howard Rice), 488bl
(Dennis Davis), 499tr (John Glover). **GARDEN PICTURE LIBRARY:** All pictures Garden Picture Library/photographer: 258tl /Eric Crichton;
260bl /David Cavagnaro; 262tl /John Glover; 262tr /JS Sira; 262bl /Chris Burrows; 270tl /Eric Crichton; 270bl /Bjorn Forsberg; 270tr /Brian
Carter; 270br /David Askham; 275tr /Mel Watson; 277bl /Kim Blaxland; 281tl /Howard Rice; 281tr /David Cavagnaro; 282br /Howard Rice;
283tl /Philippe Bonduel; 283tr /Chris Burrows; 283br /Chris Burrows; 284br /Chris Burrows; 289tr /Chris Burrows; 291t /Sunniva Harte; 293t
/Howard Rice; 294tc /Eric Crichton; 295tr /Howard Rice; 296b /John Glover; 298tl /Howard Rice; 298bl /David Cavagnaro; 301tr /Jerry Pavia;
306b /Brian Carter; 309br /Howard Rice; 312tl /JS Sira; 313b /Marijke Heuff; 317tl /Sunniva Harte; 320tr /Jerry Pavia; 320bl /Chris Burrows;
322tr /John Glover; 322br /Brian Carter; 161tr /John Glover; 161bl /Mark Bolton; 161br /Juliette Wade; 324tr /Howard Rice; 324b /Friedrich
Strauss; 325t /Marie O'Hara; 325b /Didier Willery; 327br /Howard Rice; 330br /Howard Rice; 351br /John Glover. 426tl (John Glover), 426tc
(Howard Rice), 426br (Mark Bolton), 427tl (J S Sira), 429tc (Chris Burrows), 439tr (Brian Carter), 439br (Geoff Dann), 453tr (Densey
Clyne); 453br (Clive Nichols), 453tl (Howard Rice), 453bl (John Glover), 453br (J. S. Sira), 457tr (Howard Rice), 459tl (Juliette Wade),
459tc (David England), 461tl (James Guilliam), 461tc (Chris Burrows), 461bl (Philippe Bonduel), 479br (Philippe Bonduel), 482tr
(Sunniva Harte), 482br (John Glover), 483tl (Neil Holmes), 483bl (Chris Burrows), 485br (Sunniva Harte), 486tl (Philippe Bonduel),
487tl (Chris Burrows), 487br (John Glover), 488tl (Sunniva Harte), 488tc (Howard Rice), 488bl (Dennis Davis), 499tr (John Glover);
GARDENWORLD IMAGES: 285bl: D. Gould/GWI; 287bl: C. Fairweather/GWI; 288b: GardenWorld Images; 291b: GardenWorld Images; 305tr:
GardenWorld Images. **HOLT STUDIOS:** 140bl, 141tl, 143bl, 143br, 144tl, 144tc; **PETER MCHOY:** 84b; 260tr; 261tl; 261br; 264bl; 265t;
265b; 266tr; 266br; 270bc; 273tr; 274tl; 275tr; 276tl; 278tl; 280tl; 281cl; 281cr; 281bl; 281bc; 283br; 285tl; 287t; 288t; 289tl; 292br;
294br; 295br; 297tl; 298tr; 300br; 301br; 302t; 303t; 303b; 304tl; 306tl; 306tc; 306tr; 307b; 308tr; 312b; 314tl; 314bl; 316br; 317tl; 318tr;
318b; 320tl; 322br; 323tl; 328tr; 328bl; 328br; 330tr; 331tl; 343br; 351bcr; 352tr; 364bl; 365tl; 349bl. 425tl, 425b, 429tl, 430br, 431tr,
431bl, 431br, 435tl, 435tr, 437tc, 437bc, 438tr, 460br, 470bl, 475bl,
477bl, 478bl, 479tr, 479bl, 480br, 482tl, 482bc, 498bl; **SCIENCE
PHOTO LIBRARY:** 104bl, 104tr, 140tr, 140bc, 141br, 142tl, 143tl,
144br, 157bl, 187tc, 187br.

The publishers would also like to thank:
Peter Anderson and Ray Cox for their work on the photography and
Unwins for giving access to their grounds for photography, as well as the
following gardens, which are photographed in this book: Beth Chatto
Gardens, Chenies Manor, The Coppice, East Lambrook, Great Dixter, Kew
Gardens, Lamport Hall, RHS Rosemoor, RHS Wisley, The Savill Garden,
Upper Mill Cottage.

Salvia sclarea

Crocus tommasinianus

Index

Felicia amelloides

Dahlia 'Decorative'

Cosmos bipinnatus 'Sonata Pink'

Gazania hybrids

Matthiola incana 'Legacy Mixed'

Coreopsis verticillata 'Zagreb'

Osteospermum 'White Pim'

Iris 'Purple Sensation'

Ipomoea lobata

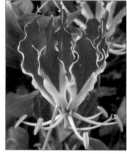

Centaurea macrocephala

Agapanthus 'Ben Hope'

Allium unifolium

Salpiglossis sinuata 'Ice Maiden'

Chionodoxa sardensis

Canna 'Durban'

Colchicum 'Violet Queen'

Crocus 'Blue Pearl'

Caltha palustris 'Alba'

Dahlia 'David Howard'

U V W

Allium sphaerocephalon

Amaryllis belladonna

Plant hardiness zones

Plant entries for annuals and perennials in this book have been given zone numbers, and these zones relate to their hardiness. The zonal system used, shown below, was developed by the Agricultural Research Service of the U.S. Dept of Agriculture. According to this system, there are 11 zones in total, based on the average annual minimum temperature in a particular geographical zone. When a range of zones is given for a plant, the smaller number indicates the northernmost zone in which a plant can survive the winter, and the higher number gives the most southerly area in which it will perform consistently.

This is not a hard and fast system, but simply a rough indicator, as many factors other than temperature also play an important part where hardiness is concerned. These factors include altitude, wind exposure, proximity to water, soil type, the presence of snow or shade, night temperature, and the amount of water received by a plant. This kind of factor can easily alter a plant's hardiness by as much as two zones.

Zone 1	Above 4°C (40°F)	
Zone 2	-1 to 4°C (30 to 40°F)	
Zone 3	-7 to -1°C (20 to 30°F)	
Zone 4	-12 to -7°C (10 to 20°F)	
Zone 5	-18 to -12°C (0 to 10°F)	
Zone 6	-23 to -18°C (-10 to 0°F)	
Zone 7	-29 to -23°C (-20 to -10°F)	
Zone 8	-34 to -29°C (-30 to -20°F)	
Zone 9	-40 to -34°C (-40 to -30°F)	
Zone 10	-45 to -40°C (-50 to -40°F)	
Zone 11	Below -45°C (-50°F)